THE OBSERVER'S

MILITARY VEHICLES
DIRECTORY FROM 1945

RESEARCH AND EDITING BY
BART H. VANDERVEEN
OLYSLAGER ORGANISATION NV

FREDERICK WARNE & CO LTD   London
FREDERICK WARNE & CO INC.   New York

CONTENTS

FOREWORD	3	HUNGARY	223
ACKNOWLEDGEMENTS	3	INDIA	227
KEY TO TECHNICAL DATA	4	ISRAEL	232
ABBREVIATIONS	5	ITALY	233
		JAPAN	245
AUSTRALIA	6	NETHERLANDS	262
AUSTRIA	14	POLAND	281
BELGIUM	25	PORTUGAL	284
BRAZIL	38	RUMANIA	285
CANADA	41	SOUTH AFRICA	287
CHINA (People's Republic)	50	SPAIN	288
CZECHOSLOVAKIA	51	SWEDEN	294
DENMARK	65	SWITZERLAND	308
EGYPT	69	USA	319
FINLAND	70	USSR	386
FRANCE	74	OTHER COUNTRIES	411
GERMAN DEMOCRATIC REPUBLIC	114		
GERMAN FEDERAL REPUBLIC	123	INDEX	421
GREAT BRITAIN	159		

Published by FREDERICK WARNE & CO. LTD LONDON ENGLAND 1972
© OLYSLAGER ORGANISATION NV and B. H. VANDERVEEN 1972
Printed by WM CLOWES & SONS LTD ENGLAND 1999.272

LIBRARY OF CONGRESS CATALOG CARD
No. 72–81142
SBN 7232 1435 2

FOREWORD

"Victory is the beautiful bright-coloured flower; transport is the stem, without which it could never have blossomed".

These words were spoken by the late Sir Winston Churchill, K.G., O.M., C.H.

The widespread enthusiasm with which *The Observer's Fighting Vehicles Directory—World War II* was received clearly showed how great was the need for a reference work covering the multiplicity of transport and other vehicles of that period.

This new volume, *The Observer's Military Vehicles Directory*, gives similar treatment to vehicles produced since 1945 for military service throughout the world, again with the emphasis on 'soft-skin' types. Its purpose is to provide a historical record and a handy reference work for military historians, hobbyists, scale modellers, dealers and others who are interested in cross-country, amphibious and other unusual vehicles. In addition to tactical trucks, it deals with 'administrative' types, as well as motorcycles, cars, buses, ambulances and many special vehicles such as crash/fire tenders, wreckers, truck-mounted cranes, earthmovers, tank transporters, armoured cars and carriers, etc. Many experimental models and prototypes are included also, not because they are likely to be actually encountered but because they are part of automotive history and hardly recorded anywhere else.

Most western countries which possess an automotive industry have developed their own tactical transport vehicles. This is obviously of great importance for their local industries, but certainly not the least expensive and most logical way of running a military transport fleet. There are exceptions: the US Army and the Canadian forces both have a fleet of tactical transport vehicles in the $\frac{1}{4}$- to 5-ton load class which to a large extent are virtually identical. There are also certain types of 'pseudo-military' vehicles which are used in several different countries, such as the British Land-Rover, the German Mercedes-Benz 'Unimog' S-type and the US Jeep, but this is usually not for the sake of standardization. Efforts to produce, for example, one standard vehicle of any given class for use by all NATO countries have so far failed although work on a common $\frac{1}{2}$-ton 4×4 multi-purpose vehicle is still in progress. Eastern European countries have more international standardization, although there, too, some nations have developed and put into service their own designs in addition to Soviet-built or -designed vehicles.

Altogether the multiplicity of vehicles is both enormous and complex.

I believe that this comprehensive catalogue fills another gap which existed in the world's automotive and military literature.

Piet Olyslager, MSIA, MSAE, KIVI

ACKNOWLEDGEMENTS

The Editor would like to sincerely thank the many individuals, manufacturers, government agencies and other organizations who have assisted him in building up the private collection of material on which this book is based. Special thanks are extended to a number of friends who have kindly answered specific requests for additional information and illustrations, notably:

George Avramidis, Noël Ayliffe-Jones, Brian S. Baxter, Sven Bengtson, Günter Buchwald, John Church, J. M. van Hest, Col. Robert J. Icks, Aimé van Ingelom, Jean-Gabriel Jeudy, William F. Murray, Yasuo Ohtsuka, Jens-Jórgen Pedersen, Malcolm J. R. Smith, Walter J. Spielberger, Norman Weeding and Laurie A. Wright.

Note: Inasmuch as the value of a work of this kind is determined by the degree of accuracy of its contents, the editor would like to ask readers and users to call to his attention any errors and omissions they may detect. Constructive criticism and supplementary material, factual and/or pictorial, will always be welcomed. [Editorial Productions Division, Olyslager Organisation NV, Book House, Vincent Lane, Dorking, Surrey RH4 3HW, England.]

KEY TO TECHNICAL DATA

Abbreviations: See page 5.

Vehicle Nomenclature: A uniform system has been used, wherever practicable, throughout the book, regardless of vehicle's country of origin. Example: Truck, 5-ton, 6 × 6, Cargo, w/Winch = 6-wheeled, 6-wheel drive cargo truck with rated payload capacity of five tons and equipped with power-driven winch. '4 × 2' indicates a *four*-wheeled vehicle with *two*-wheel drive, etc. For this purpose dual tyres count as single wheels. The vehicle type is followed by the make and model designation in parentheses.

Year(s) of manufacture: The year given indicates the year when the vehicle was first produced or, when used in other(s) than the country of origin, the year when it entered military service there. Therefore a single year does not necessarily mean that the vehicle was in production during that year only. 'From 19. .' is used when additional variants were produced during subsequent years. In some cases the dates are estimated.

Engine: Engine make is usually the same as the vehicle make, unless stated otherwise. Fuel is petrol (gasoline) unless stated otherwise. Power output is the highest known, e.g. where DIN and SAE figures were available the latter is quoted. Cubic capacity is stated in cubic inches or cubic centimetres, according to use in country of origin. Letter combinations in 'Technical Data' indicate engine type, e.g. I-I-A-F = cylinders in-line, valves in head (OHV), air-cooled, front-mounted; V-L-W-C = cylinders in-Vee, side valves (L-head), water-cooled, centrally-mounted, etc.

Transmission: Number of gears forward and reverse and number of ratios in transfer or auxiliary gearbox. Example: 4F1R × 2 = four-speed main gearbox and two-speed transfer, providing total of eight forward and two reverse ratios.

Wheelbase: Distance between centres of front and rear wheels, or, in the case of tandem axles the centre of the bogie. '(BC)' indicates the wheelbase of the tandem bogie. Thus, wheelbase 160 (BC 50) in indicates a distance of 160 in between centre of front wheel and centre of rear bogie and 50 in between centres of rear wheels. This wheelbase dimension could alternatively be indicated as 135 + 50 in.

Dimensions: Overall length, width and height are given, where available, in the units generally used in the country of origin. Where only two dimensions are given they refer to length and width. Figures in parentheses are the minimum (reducible) dimensions, e.g. after folding the vehicle's superstructure for air transport purposes or for reducing the vehicle's silhouette in combat.

Weights: Vehicle weights are approximate net kerb weights (unladen) unless stated otherwise.

Conversions

Length
1 inch (1″ or 1 in) = 25.40 mm
1 foot (1′ or 1 ft) = 12 in = 304.8 mm = 0.30 m
1 mile = 1760 yards = 1609 m
1 millimetre (mm) = 0.039 in
1 centimetre (cm) = 10 mm = 0.39 in
1 metre (m) = 1000 mm = 39.37 in = 3.28 ft
1 kilometre (km) = 1000 m = 0.62 mile

Weights
1 pound (1 lb) = 0.45 kg
1 quarter = 28 lb = 12.70 kg
1 cwt = 4 qtr = 112 lb = 50.80 kg
1 long ton = 20 cwt = 1.12 short tons = 1016 kg
1 short ton = 2000 lb = 0.89 long ton = 907.2 kg
1 kilogram (kg) = 2.2 lb
1 metric ton = 1000 kg = 0.98 long ton = 1.1 short tons

Capacities
1 cubic inch (1 cu. in) = 16.39 cc
1 Imperial gallon = 1.2 US gallons = 4.55 litres
1 US gallon = 0.833 Imp. gal = 3.79 litres
1 cubic centimetre (1 cc or cm³) = 0.061 cu. in
1 litre (1 ltr) = 1000 cc = 61.025 cu. in

ABBREVIATIONS

A	Austria
AA	Anti-Aircraft
A/C	Armoured Car
ACV	Armoured Command Vehicle
AFV	Armoured Fighting Vehicle
AOP	Armoured Observation Post
APC	Armoured Personnel Carrier
APG	Aberdeen Proving Ground (US)
ARV	Armoured Recovery Vehicle
AT	Anti-Tank
AUS	Australia
auto.	automatic
aux.	auxiliary
BAOR	British Army of the Rhine
BC	bogie centres
bhp	brake horsepower
BxS	bore and stroke
c.	*circa* (approximate date)
cap.	capacity
cc	cubic centimetre(s)
CDN	Canada
CID	cubic inches displacement
CKD	completely knocked down
COE	cab over engine
comm.	commercial
CR	compression ratio
CS	Czechoslovakia
cu. in	cubic inch(es)
D	West Germany
DBP	drawbar pull
DDR	East Germany
DED	diesel engine driven (US)
diff(s)	differential(s)
Dim.	dimensions
D/S	dropside (body)
DT	dual tyres
exp.	experimental(ly)
F	France
FC	forward control
FFR, W	fitted for radio, wireless
F/R	front/rear

FVRDE	Fighting Vehicles Research and Development Establishment (GB; now MVEE)
GB	Great Britain
GED	gasoline engine driven (US)
GPM, gpm	gallons per minute
GS	general service
GCW	gross combination weight
GTW	gross train weight
GVW	gross vehicle weight
HO	horizontally-opposed
How.	howitzer
hyd.	hydraulic
I	Italy
IFS	independent front suspension
IRS	independent rear suspension
J	Japan
LAA	Light Anti-Aircraft
LHD	left-hand drive
Lkw	Lastkraftwagen (D; truck)
LVT	Landing Vehicle, Tracked
LWB	long wheelbase
MAP	Military Assistance Program (US)
MEXE	Military Engineering Experimental Establishment (GB; now MVEE)
m/f	multi-fuel
mfr(s)	manufacturer(s)
MG	machine gun
MOD	Ministry of Defence (GB)
mod(s)	modification(s)
MOS	Ministry of Supply (GB)
MVEE	Military Vehicles and Engineering Establishment (GB)
NATO	North Atlantic Treaty Organisation
NC	normal control
NL	Netherlands
NSW	normal service weight

OD	overdrive
OHC	overhead camshaft
OHV	overhead valves
PAB	power-assisted brakes
PAS	power-assisted steering
pass.	passenger
Pkw	Personenkraftwagen (D; car)
POL	Poland
psi	pounds per sq. in (lb/sq. in)
PTO	power take-off
qv	*quod vide* (which see)
RAF	Royal Air Force (GB)
RCT	Royal Corps of Transport (GB)
RHD	right-hand drive
RN	Royal Navy (GB)
rpm	rev(olutions) per minute
S	Sweden
SAE	Soc. of Automotive Engineers (US)
SAS	Special Air Services (GB)
SC	sidecar
SP	self-propelled
S-T	semi-trailer
std	standard
SV	side valves
SWB	short wheelbase
TAF	Tactical Air Force (GB)
TC	torque converter
trans.	transmission
UN	United Nations
US(A)	United States (of America)
USSR	Union of Soviet Socialist Republics
w/	with
wb, WB	wheelbase
wh.	wheel
w/o	without
Wt	weight
WWII	World War II

AUSTRALIA

Post-war 'base type' (administrative) vehicles of the Australian Army, Air Force and Navy, have been almost exclusively Australian-built or -assembled standard conventional or modified conventional commercial types, notably Holden sedans, station sedans (station wagons), coupé utilities (car-style pickups), Ford sedans, coupé utilities, ambulances, cargo and dump trucks, International station wagons, pickups, vans and trucks of various types, Dodge station wagons, ambulances and trucks, Volkswagen 'Transporters' and US Bedford buses. Of other types only small batches have sometimes been used.

Post-war tactical vehicles in the $\frac{1}{4}$- to $\frac{3}{4}$-ton class have been mainly British Land-Rovers, assembled and modified in Australia. $2\frac{1}{2}$- and 5-ton tactical types are from a family of 4 × 4 and 6 × 6 COE trucks developed jointly by the Army and International Harvester. They are employed with a variety of body styles. About 1960 the Australian Army made efforts towards a greater compatibility with US equipment. One result was that the once-standard 3-ton load classification was changed to $2\frac{1}{2}$-ton for that class of vehicle.

In addition to the 'soft-skin' 'B' vehicles shown and/or listed in the following pages the Australian Forces have used a large number of special purpose vehicles (mobile cranes, motorized scrapers, dozers, loaders, excavators, etc., known as 'C' vehicles) and AFVs (armoured fighting vehicles, or 'A' vehicles) including British 'Ferret' scout cars, 'Saracen' APCs, 'Saladin' armoured cars, 'Centurion' tanks (incl. ARV and bridge-laying variants) and US M113 full-track APC variations. Some of the latter were fitted with 'Saladin' turrets for use in Vietnam.

Standard Army vehicle colour is now olive-drab, found to be the most suitable camouflage for the areas in which Australian troops are involved. From 1953 to 1967 the standard colour was deep bronze green and prior to this it was khaki green. RAAF vehicles are a dark smoky blue, generally with white roof, and RAN vehicles are battleship grey.

Who's Who in the Australian Automotive Industry

BLMC	British Leyland Motor Corp. of Australia Ltd, Waterloo, NSW and West Footscray, Vic. (handles Austin, Morris, Land-Rover, Leyland, etc).
Chrysler (Dodge)	Chrysler Australia Ltd, Finsbury (truck plant).
Ford	Ford Motor Co. of Australia Pty Ltd, Melbourne, Vic.
Holden	General Motors-Holden's Pty Ltd, Fisherman's Bend, Port Melbourne, Vic. (several mfg plants; also handles imported GM products).
International	International Harvester Co. of Australia Pty Ltd, Melbourne, Vic. (truck plant: Dandenong).
Volkswagen	Volkswagen Australasia Ltd, Melbourne, Vic.
Willys, Jeep	Kaiser Jeep of Australia Pty Ltd, Salisbury North, Brisbane, Queensland.

Typical Australian Army 'C' vehicles.

CARS, FIELD CARS, LIGHT TRUCKS and MOTORCYCLES

Makes and Models: *Cars: Sedans:* Chevrolet, Chrysler, Holden (various types, from 1952), Ford ('Customline' and 'Fairlane', from 1953), Humber ('Super Snipe', GB), etc.; *Station wagons:* Holden (station sedans), Dodge and International ('Suburban' vans or 'Carryalls'), Toyota (J), etc.
Field Cars: Austin FV1801 'Champ' ($\frac{1}{4}$-ton, 4 × 4, c. 1960, GB). BLMC 'Moke' ($\frac{1}{4}$-ton, 4 × 2, 1966). International 'Scout' 80 ($\frac{1}{2}$-ton, 4 × 4, 1966, US). Land-Rover Series I, II, IIA ($\frac{1}{4}$-ton, 4 × 4, from c. 1957, GB). Toyota 'Land-Cruiser' ($\frac{1}{4}$-ton, 4 × 4, 1971, J). Willys/Kaiser Jeep CJ3B, CJ5, M38A1 ($\frac{1}{4}$-ton, 4 × 4, from 1959, US).
Light Trucks and Ambulances: Dodge, various models ($\frac{3}{4}$- and 1-ton, 4 × 2 and 4 × 4, from c. 1958). Dodge 'Power Wagon' (1-ton, 4 × 4, c. 1955, US). Ford 'Falcon' Utility/Pickups ($\frac{1}{2}$-ton, 4 × 2, from 1966); 'Mainline' Ambulances (4 × 2, from 1954), etc. Holden Utility/Pickups ($\frac{1}{2}$-ton, 4 × 2, from c. 1952). Humber FV1601 (1-ton, 4 × 4, c. 1960, GB). International, various models (12- and 15-cwt, $\frac{1}{2}$-, $\frac{3}{4}$- and 1-ton, 4 × 2 and 4 × 4, from c. 1952). Land-Rover Series IIA ($\frac{3}{4}$-ton, 4 × 4, c. 1964, GB). Steyr-Puch 700AP 'Haflinger' ($\frac{1}{4}$-ton, 4 × 4, 1966, A). Toyota (1-ton, 4 × 2, c. 1971, J). Volkswagen 'Transporter' ($\frac{3}{4}$- and 1-ton, 4 × 2, from 1961, D). Willys/Kaiser Jeep CJ6 ($\frac{1}{2}$-ton, 4 × 4, 1958, US); L6-226, FC170 and 'Overlander' ($\frac{3}{4}$-ton, 4 × 4, from c. 1960).
Motorcycles: BSA B40 (Solo, c. 1966, GB).

General Data: Practically all 4 × 2 models listed above were produced in Australia. Others, like Volkswagens and Land-Rovers, were assembled.
　　In 1968 the Army's Design Establishment at Maribynong, Victoria, produced an experimental 1-ton 4 × 4 GS truck as a possible replacement for the $\frac{3}{4}$-ton Land-Rover. Ford and IHC were awarded contracts for its further development. Both firms had a prototype on trial in 1971.

Vehicle shown (typical): Truck, 1-ton, 4 × 2, Cargo and Personnel (International C1200)
Technical Data:
Engine: International 6-282 6-cylinder, I-I-W-F, 282 cu. in (4621 cc), 117 bhp @ 3300 rpm.
Transmission: 4F1R.
Brakes: hydraulic (hydrovac).
Tyres: 7.50–16.
Wheelbase: 114 in.
Overall l × w × h: 197 × 80 × 95 in.
Weight: 4650 lb.
Note: Preceding Model AB 120 (prior to 1968) had different grille, dual headlights. Similar trucks produced by Chrysler (Dodge). From about 1952 International Harvester supplied numerous light trucks for all three services (Series AL, AR, AS, AB, C1100, etc.)

Truck, ½-ton, 4 × 2, Utility/Pickup (Holden EJ) 6-cyl., 75 bhp, 3F1R, wb 105 in, 177 × 68 × 58 in, 2500 lb. 1963. Known as: Car, CL, Light Utility. One of many military Holdens. Used either as shown or with canvas cover over steel superstructure. Folding seat in rear body. Similar: Ford 'Falcon' (from 1966).

Truck, 1-ton, 4 × 2, Ambulance (Dodge 114) 6-cyl., 121 bhp, 4F1R, wb 114 in, GVW 6000 lb. Basically 1966 Aust. commercial model. Front end similar (but not identical) to that of Aust. Internationals. Other ambulances incl. earlier type Dodge (15-cwt with 'Surburban' body), Ford, Humber (car chassis), etc.

Truck, ¾-ton, 4 × 4, Fire Fighting (Land-Rover 109, Series IIA) 4-cyl., 67 bhp, 4F1R × 2, wb 109 in, GVW 5905 lb. Std. tactical type, 1968. Note modified front wings which were feature of Australian-assembled military Land-Rovers. GS types had radiator brush guard. Also ambulance, workshop, hardtop, etc.

Truck, ¼-ton, 4 × 4, Recoilless Rifle (Land-Rover 88, Series IIA) 4-cyl., 67 bhp, 4F1R × 2, wb 88 in, GVW 4453 lb. Specially-modified air-transportable SP mount for US 106-mm Recoilless Rifle, M40. Note .50 cal. spotting rifle mounted on main weapon. Known as: Truck, Utility, ¼-ton, GS, Land-Rover, fitted for Rifle 106 mm.

TRUCKS, MEDIUM and HEAVY 4 × 2 and BUSES

Makes and Models: Austin FGK40 (15- to 20-seater bus, 1963, GB). Bedford SB, etc. (24/36-seater buses, from *c.* 1952, GB); VAM (ambulance/bus, 1967, GB). Dodge AT4/329 (1½-ton, cargo, 1964); 460 (2½-ton, cargo/personnel, 1968); W2-26, 6-71, A3-59D, A6-71C (3-ton, cargo, platform, van, from 1958); 6-71 (10-ton tractor, 1959), etc. Ford F500 (3-ton (later 2½-ton), cargo/personnel, platform, dump, 1953/54); D400 (2½-ton, cargo/personnel, 1969), 'Transit' (12-seater bus), R1015 (R192) (40-seater bus, 1971), etc.
    International Series AL, AR, AS, AA, AB, C (1¼- to 5-ton, cargo/personnel, platform, dump, tractor, wrecker, etc., from *c.* 1952); AACO (tractors, from *c.* 1965), etc. LeTourneau-Westinghouse 30 'Haulpak' (30-ton, dump, *c.* 1965). Leyland 'Comet' 90 (10-ton tractor, 1954, GB), etc. Shelvoke & Drewry W (fire appliance, 1952, GB).

General Data: All post-war trucks in the medium 4 × 2 category have been conventional or modified conventional commercial models. Main supplier has been International Harvester with various models of virtually all post-war series being used by one or another of the three Armed Services. Ford supplied some F500 3-ton trucks (cargo and dump) in 1953/54, then none until securing an \$A2,000,000 contract in 1969 for 2½-ton cargo trucks based on their D400 model COE chassis.
    The LeTourneau-Westinghouse 30 'Haulpak' was a heavy rear dump truck, a number of which were acquired by the RAAF for airfield construction and similar duties. They were powered by 335-bhp Cummins diesel engines, had 18.00–25 (2DT) tyres and a GVW of 106,350 lb.
    Standard bus (coach) for all Services was the British Bedford chassis with Australian bodywork. Some had large equipment doors fitted to the rear. The RAAF acquired a number of air-conditioned bus-ambulances on Bedford VAM chassis with 114-bhp engine. These had a capacity of 18 stretcher cases or 36 seated patients, or a combination of both, accommodation for two attendants, and double rear doors.

Vehicle shown (typical): Truck, 5-ton, 4 × 2, Tractor (International AACO-172)

Technical Data:
Engine: International AGD-282 6-cylinder, I-I-W-F, 282 cu. in (4621 cc), 148 bhp (gross) @ 3800 rpm.
Transmission: 5F1R.
Brakes: vacuum hydraulic.
Tyres: 9.00–20.
Wheelbase: 118 in.
Overall l × w × h: not available.
Weight: GVW 27,250 lb. GCW 51,000 lb.
Note: Basically similar to AB-184 but with heavier front axle and military pattern forward control cab. Used mainly to haul cargo semi-trailers. Official designation: Truck, Tractor, 5-Ton, CL, IHC.

Truck, 2½-ton, 4 × 2, Cargo and Personnel (International AS 162) 6-cyl., 118 bhp, 4F1R, wb 153 in. Standard pattern Australian Army GS truck, used from about 1952 until superseded by 'C' Series about 1968. Steel body with fixed sides and folding troop seats. Also in this class: Ford F500 (cargo and dump versions).

Truck, 2½-ton, 4 × 2, Cargo and Personnel (International C1510) 6-cyl., 142 bhp, 4F1R, wb 171 in, 282 × 94 × 114 (85½) in. Military version of commercial truck. Superseded the earlier style (shown on left). Body had lower floor, dropsides and folding troop seats. Cab similar to Australian Dodge. Similar body on Ford D400 (COE).

Truck, 2½-ton, 4 × 2, Cargo and Personnel (Dodge 460) 6-cyl., 158 bhp, 4F1R, wb 160 in, GVW 12,500 lb. Tyres 7.00–17. Long steel cargo body with folding troop seats. Used by RAAF (Air Force) from late 1960s. Also with platform ('tabletop') and dump body. Note exhaust below front bumper.

Bus, 24/36-passenger, 4 × 2 (Bedford SB) 6-cyl., 114 bhp, 5F1R, wb 216 in, GVW 20,160 lb. Chassis weight 5750 lb. British chassis, supplied through GM-Holden's and fitted with Australian bodywork. 1969 model shown. Used by all services. Australian nomenclature: Coach, CL, 24/36-seater, 4 × 2, Bedford.

TRUCKS,
MEDIUM and HEAVY
4 × 4, 6 × 4 and 6 × 6

Makes and Models: AEC 'Militant' (10-ton, 6 × 6, Coles crane, *c.* 1960, GB). Autocar (White) DC7564 (6 × 4, tractor, 1964, US); DC7366 (12-ton, 6 × 6, dump, 1970, US). Diamond Reo (White) C11464DB (6 × 4, tractor, 1969, US). International 'A' and 'C' Series (2½- and 3-ton, 4 × 4, from 1958); R-190 (5-ton, 4 × 4, 1961); Mk I, II, III, IV (2½-ton, 4 × 4, cargo, tanker, etc., from 1959); Mk V (5-ton, 6 × 6, cargo, dump, platform, tanker, from 1966); ACCOF-1840 (6 × 4, 2500-gal. refueller, 1969); RF-190 (10-ton and tractor, 6 × 6, from 1959); RF-205A (20-ton tractor, 6 × 6, 1956); etc. International M543 (5-ton, 6 × 6, wrecker, *c.* 1960, US). LeTourneau-Westinghouse LARC V (5-ton, 4 × 4, amphibian, *c.* 1969, US). Leyland 19H 'Hippo' (6 × 4, refueller, 1953, GB). Reo/Studebaker M35 (2½-ton, 6 × 6, cargo, 1956, US). Thornycroft 'Nubian' (4 × 4, fire-fighter, 1952, GB); TFA/B81 'Nubian' (6 × 6, fire-fighter, 1959, GB).

General Data: During the late 1950s a number of new Studebaker US6 trucks were assembled from WWII CKD kits and put into service, replacing worn-out GMC and other WWII trucks. In March 1953 a meeting between the Dept. of Supply, the Army Design Establishment and International Harvester Co. of Australia, discussed the production possibilities of a new tactical GS truck with an Australian content as high as possible. After strenuous prototype tests during 1955–59 the first 100 were delivered to the Army on 17 April 1959. These were subjected to user trials throughout Australia and in Antarctica. In 1962 IHC was awarded a contract for 600 and on delivery of the first 20 in 1963 another 610 units were ordered. These had an Australian content of over 90%. More orders followed and by 1966 over 1500 were in service. Meanwhile, in 1958 IHC had started design of a 6 × 6 variant. Two pilot models were delivered in 1960, followed by two cargo and dump prototypes in 1964. In 1966 series production commenced with an initial order for 390. The first of these was delivered on 15 November 1966. A modified version of the military cab was used on certain commercial models. The Dept. of Supply used Scammell 'Constructor' and 'Contractor' tractors with tank transporter trailers.

Vehicle shown (typical): Truck, 2½-ton, 4 × 4, Cargo and Personnel, w/Winch (International No 1, Mk III)

Technical Data:
Engine: International AGD-282 6-cylinder, I-I-W-F, 282 cu. in (4621 cc), 148 bhp @ 3800 rpm (gross; net: 123 @ 3300).
Transmission: 5F1R × 2.
Brakes: air-hydraulic.
Tyres: 12.00–20.
Wheelbase: 145 in. *Track:* 74 in.
Overall l × w × h: 244½ × 96 × 99 in.
Weight: 11,326 lb. *GVW:* 17,707 lb.
Note: Standard Australian Army GS truck. 1963 model shown. Olding-Garwood winch fitted amidships. Dropside steel body. Steel cab with fibre glass wings. Mk IV had revised cab front and steel wings. Mk IV type cab also used for rebuilt Mk III trucks.

12

Truck, 2½-ton, 4 × 4, Cargo and Personnel (International Mk I) 6-cyl., 120 bhp (net), 5F1R × 2, wb 145 in, 248 × 96 × 100 in, 10,110 lb. First Australian designed 4 × 4 GS truck, officially designated: Truck, Cargo, 2½-ton, Aust., No 1, Mk I. Mk II was similar but equipped with winch. Both appeared in 1959.

Truck, 2½-ton, 4 × 4, Dump (International AA-160) 6-cyl., 142 bhp, 4F1R × 2, wb 153 in, chassis/cab: 254 × 86 in, 6468 lb. GVW 17,500 lb. Produced in 1958/59, with hyd. rear dump body. Tubular tilt supports, when not in use, carried under body. Similar bodywork on AB160 and C1600 chassis (w/Winch).

Truck, 5-ton, 6 × 6, Dump, w/Winch (International Mk V) 6-cyl., 150 bhp, 5F1R × 2, wb 148½ in, 252 × 98 × 130(99) in approx. Design of this model began in 1958. Shown is a prototype (1964) with dual rear tyres. Production model (1966) had different body (4 cu. yd; aluminium). GVW on/off road: 30,000/25,000 lb.

Truck, 5-ton, 6 × 6, Cargo, w/Winch (International Mk V) 6-cyl., 150 bhp, 5F1R × 2, wb 148½ in, 270 × 96 × 99 in. Shown with sides, bows, tilt and troop seats removed. A special container-carrying version was also produced. All Mk V 6 × 6 models had twin carburettors for increased engine power.

Truck, 10-ton, 6 × 4, Refueller, 2500-Gallon (International ACCOF-1840) V-8-cyl., 177 bhp, 5F1R × 3, wb 148 (BC 50) in, chassis/cab: 294 × 93 × 94 in, GVW 40,250 lb. Commercial chassis with overhead-boom fueller equipment for RAAF. Various power unit and transmission options, incl. Perkins diesel engine. 1970.

Truck, 20-ton, 6 × 4, Tractor (Diamond Reo C11464 DB) Cummins NTC-335 6-cyl. diesel, 270 bhp, Allison (GM) auto. trans., wb 140 in. Assembled in Australia, derived from US model C114. Rockwell SLHD rear bogie. 'Royalex' bonnet and wings. PAS. 30 ordered in 1968 by Army, with 38 Fruehauf S-Ts. WWII Diamond T and Federal 6 × 4 tractors were used also.

Truck, 25-ton, 6 × 4, Tractor, w/Winch (Autocar DC7564) Detroit (GM) 6/71E 6-cyl. diesel, 220 bhp, Allison (GM) auto. trans., wb 160 in. Tyres 10.00-20. Axle ratings F/R 16,000/ 38,000 lb. GCW 100,000 lb. 7-litre (426 cu. in) engine. Air brakes. Olding-Garwood winch. Ten supplied to RAAF, 1964.

Truck, 12-ton, 6 × 6, Dump (Autocar DC7366) Basically as DC7564 but with transfer case and driven front axle. Wb 207 in. Operated by RAAF with trailer which had same body, wheels, tyres (11.00–20), and brakes. Min. height 106 in, for air-transport (items above cab top level easily removable).

AUSTRIA

When the Austrian Federal Army (*Österreichische Bundesheer*) was formed in 1955, many of the vehicles with which it was equipped were of American origin and produced during World War II. This automotive equipment comprised Willys and Ford ¼-ton 4 × 4s (used for various purposes including mounting of 106-mm recoilless gun, M40A1), Dodge ¾-ton 4 × 4 Command Cars and Weapons Carriers (some of which were fitted with house-type van and ambulance bodywork, others mounting a 20-mm AA gun, M58), GMC 2½-ton 6 × 6 trucks of various types (swb CCKW-352 and lwb CCKW-353 with open and closed cabs, some equipped with winch, fitted with cargo or specialist type bodywork), Mack and Corbitt/White 6-ton 6 × 6 prime movers for 155-mm howitzer, M1, Pacific M26 (armoured) tank recovery tractors with tank transporter semi-trailers, M15, International 13-ton High Speed tractors, M5 (and M5A4) for 155-mm howitzer, M1, Allis Chalmers 18-ton High Speed tractors, M4, for 155-mm field gun, M2, and Caterpillar D7 crawler tractors. Some post-war US 'M-Series' trucks were also acquired, albeit in small numbers, namely the ,Dodge ¾-ton 4 × 4 and the Reo 2½-ton 6 × 6. Some of the latter had a house-type van body.

Other imported post-war military vehicles included the Praga 6 × 6 V3S (13-cm rocket launcher) from Czechoslovakia, the Alvis 'Stalwart' 6 × 6 amphibious load carrier from Great Britain, the Berliet 6 × 6 GBC 5-tonner from France and various types from Germany, notably Volkswagen. Since about 1959 strenuous efforts have been made to replace as much of this multitude of models as possible by Austrian products. Principal examples are the 'Haflinger', the 'Husar', the Steyr 680M range and various heavy types by Gräf & Stift.

Armoured fighting vehicles acquired since 1954 included the American WWII 'Greyhound' armoured car, M8, various types of half-tracks including the APC, M3, and mortar carrier, M4, the 'Chaffee' light tank, M24, and the SP 105-mm, M7B2 (on 'Sherman' medium tank chassis).

Post-war American AFVs acquired by the Austrian Army were the 'Walker Bulldog' light tank, M41, and its SP AA gun derivation, M42, the medium tanks, M47 'Patton' and M60A1,

and the ARV (armoured recovery vehicle), M88 (on M48A2 medium tank chassis). From France the AMX-13 light tank and AMX-55 ARV were purchased. The Austrian Saurer factory produced various types of full-track APCs (*Schützenpanzer*, 4K series) and of these there were several variants, including a tank (*Panzerjäger 'K'*) with 105-mm AT gun.

Who's Who in the Austrian Automotive Industry

Gräf & Stift	Gräf & Stift Automobilfabrik AG, Dobling, Wien (now merged with ÖAF, *qv*).
ÖAF	Österreichische Automobilfabrik ÖAF-Gräf & Stift AG, Wien (controlled by Steyr, *qv*).
Puch	(see Steyr).
Saurer	Österreichische Saurerwerke AG, Wien (now *Werke Wien* of Steyr, *qv*).
Steyr, Steyr-Puch	Steyr-Daimler-Puch AG, Wien, Graz, Steyr.

Wartime US GMC in post-war Austrian Army.

14

CARS, FIELD CARS
and MOTORCYCLES

Makes and Models: *Cars:* Various (comm.), incl. Volkswagen (D).
Field Cars: Steyr-Puch 700 AP 'Haflinger' (0.4-ton, 4 × 4, 1959). Steyr-Puch 710M, K 'Pinzgauer' (1-ton, 4 × 4, 1965).
WWII types: Ford GPW and Willys MB (¼-ton, 4 × 4, US), Dodge T214-WC56/57 (¾-ton, 4 × 4, US).
Motorcycles: BMW (D). Puch MCH175 (1958).

General Data: From about 1959 various types of Austrian vehicles were introduced to gradually replace the ageing American types. The 'Haflinger', developed and produced by Steyr-Daimler-Puch at Graz, was a light multi-purpose cross-country vehicle and exists in many forms, notably as personnel/cargo and weapons-carrier. It is air-transportable and has an air-cooled horizontally-opposed twin-cylinder engine mounted at the rear. The chassis is of the central tubular backbone type and the wheels are independently sprung on 'swing' axles incorporating step-down final drive gear cases providing ample ground clearance.

Optional equipment included extra low (crawler) gear (until introduction of 5-speed gearbox), PTO (Model 700 APL), tropical equipment, etc.

It was named after a type of powerful horse, bred for work in mountainous areas, and the basic design was the work of Steyr-Daimler-Puch's Chief Designer Dipl. Ing. Erich Ledwinka, son of the famous designer Dr. techn. h.c. Hans Ledwinka (1878–1967) who was responsible for the interesting Tatra cars and trucks of the 1920s and 1930s (which were rather revolutionary in having tubular backbone chassis, independent suspension with swing axles, air-cooled engines, etc.). He himself had worked for Steyr during 1916–1920. The 'Haflinger' could be called a typical example of central European vehicle design. It was exported to many countries for civilian and military use, especially in Africa and the Far East (Australia, Indonesia). A wide range of accessories and implements was made available such as winches, snow ploughs, welding equipment, etc. A fire-fighting version with longer wheelbase was introduced in 1961.

Vehicle shown (typical): Truck, 0.4-ton, 4 × 4, Command, Personnel and Cargo (Steyr-Puch 700 AP 'Haflinger') (*gl Lkw, B; Kdo- und Truppfahrzeug sowie Lastentrager*)

Technical Data:
Engine: Steyr-Puch 2-cylinder, H-I-A-R, 643 cc, 24 bhp @ 4500 rpm (from 1967: 27 bhp (30 SAE) @ 4800 rpm).
Transmission: 4F1R (from 1966: 5F1R).
Brakes: hydraulic.
Tyres: 145 × 12, 165 × 12 or 5.20–12.
Wheelbase: 1.50 m.
Overall l × w × h: 2.83 × 1.35 × 1.74 (1.36) m.
Weight: 650 kg approx. GVW 1150 kg.
Note: Ind. susp. with coil/rubber springs. Gradability up to 60%.

Motorcycle, Solo (Puch MCH 175) 1-cyl., 10 bhp, 4F, wb 1.26 m, 1.92 × 0.68 × 0.92 m, 120 kg. Austrian nomenclature: *gl Kraftrad 175*. 172 cc 2-stroke double-piston engine. Speed 80 km/h. Ground clearance 190 mm. Gradability 45%. Carrying capacity 150 kg. 1958–59.

Truck, 0.4-ton, 4 × 4 (Steyr-Puch 700 AP 'Haflinger') 2-cyl., 24 bhp, 4F1R. wb 1.50 m, 2.83 × 1.35 × 1.74 (1.36) m, 600 kg. Minimum height (1.36 m) to top of steering wheel. Rear seats are collapsible and fold into floor wells. 1959/60 model engine output was 22 bhp. Lockable front and rear differentials.

Motorcycle, Solo (BMW) and Car, 4 × 2, Command/ Patrol (Volkswagen 1500 'Variant') Two military versions of commercial vehicles imported from W. Germany and employed by the *Militär-Streife* (military police patrol) for patrol and general police duties. 'KdO' (on VW) = *Kommando*.

Truck, 0.9-ton, 4 × 2, Personnel Carrier (Volkswagen 1500 'Transporter') 4-cyl., 44 bhp, 4F1R, wb 2.40 m, 4.28 × 1.75 × 1.92 (roof) m, 1200 kg approx. Basically commercial *'Kombi'* version of German Volkswagen 'Transporter', modified to meet military requirements. Aerials on roof and at rear.

Truck, 0.4-ton, 4×4, Radio (Steyr-Puch 700 AP 'Haflinger') 2-cyl., 24 bhp, 4F1R, wb 1.50 m, 2.83×1.35×1.74 (roof) m. Basically the standard 'Haflinger' but fitted with radio equipment (*Ausführung mit Funkanlage*) and shown with doors fitted and top erected. Fording depth (all models): 400 mm.

Truck, 0.4-ton, 4×4, Anti-Tank Gun (Steyr-Puch 700 AP 'Haflinger') 2-cyl., 27 bhp, 5F1R, wb 1.50 m. Basic 'Haflinger' modified for mounting of Swedish *'Bofors'-Pak* recoilless anti-tank gun (*rPAK, 90-mm*). Note spotting rifle, modified front end and gun clamp. 1968.

Truck, 0.4-ton, 4×4, 'Bantam' Rocket Launcher (Steyr-Puch 700 AP 'Haflinger') Mobile launcher for Swedish wire-guided anti-tank missile system. 'Bantam' = Bofors anti-tank missile. Could fire six missiles forward, eight rearward. Used by Swedish and Swiss armed forces.

Truck, 0.4-ton, 4×4, 'Mosquito' Rocket Launcher (Steyr-Puch 700 AP 'Haflinger') Equipped for firing of four Swiss 'Mosquito' anti-tank missiles. Rear side panels swung open to expose four missiles, mounted on launching frames. Four further rockets carried on back of vehicle.

Truck, 0.4-ton, 4×4, Cargo (Steyr-Puch 700 AP 'Haflinger') 2-cyl., 27 bhp, 5F1R, wb 1.50 m, 2.83 × 1.35 × 1.74 (1.36) m, 600 kg approx. The 'Haflinger' was exported for military and other uses. This RHD unit with trailer was operated by the Australian Armed Forces. Note bumper overriders.

Truck, 0.4-ton, 4×4, Cargo and Personnel (Steyr-Puch 700 AP 'Haflinger' LWB) 2-cyl., 27 bhp, 5F1R, wb 1.80 m, 3.15 × 1.35 × 1.74 m, 700 kg approx. Long-wheelbase model with optional fibre-glass cab and four rear seats, introduced in 1962/63 (LWB fire-fighting version from 1961).

Truck, 1-ton, 4×4, Cargo and Personnel (Steyr-Puch 'Pinzgauer') 4-cyl., 74 bhp, 4F1R, wb 2.20 m, 4.10 × 1.70 × 2.05 m, 1300 kg approx. Track 1.43 m. Air-cooled engine. Prototype introduced in 1965. Speed 90 km/h. Crew 10. Series production from 1971 (with 87- or 92-bhp engine).

Truck, 1-ton, 4×4, Cargo and Personnel (Steyr-Puch 710M 'Pinzgauer') 4-cyl., 87 (or 92) bhp, 5F1R × 2, wb 2.20 m, 4.20 × 1.76 × 2.05 m, 1600 kg approx. Coilspring IFS/IRS. Variants: 710K *Kommandowagen* and 6×6 (*qv*). 1968 pilot model illustrated.

TRUCKS
4×2 and 4×4

Makes and Models: Dodge T245 M37 (¾-ton, 4×4, c. 1960, US). Gräf & Stift LAVT-9F (6-ton, 4×4, 1959). Mercedes-Benz 'Unimog' S404 (1½-ton, 4×4, c. 1960, D). ÖAF HA-2-90 'Husar' (1½-ton, 4×4, 1966). Saurer 6GAVFR-L and -Z (6-ton, 4×4, 1958). Saurer 8GA3H-Z (10-ton, 4×4, 1958). Steyr 480 (4-ton, 4×2, 1955), 580g and 586g (3-ton, 4×4, 1959), 680M (2½-ton, 4×4, 1965), etc. Steyr-Puch 700AP 'Haflinger' (0.4-ton, 4×4, 1959) and 710M 'Pinzgauer' (1-ton, 4×4, 1965). Volkswagen 265B 'Transporter' (¾-ton, 4×2, D).
WWII types: Dodge T214-WC51 and 52 (¾-ton, 4×4, US), etc.

General Data: One of the first post-war Austrian 4×2 trucks was the Steyr Model 370 3-tonner, a development from the wartime Steyr 1500A/2000A series from which it inherited the front-end sheet metal and the air-cooled 3.5-litre V8 engine. It soon developed into the diesel-engined 380, 480 and 580 series which were produced for civilian and military purposes (4×2 and 4×4). Several versions are shown here. The forward control Steyr 680M (4×4) and its 6×6 derivation 680M3 appeared in 1965. The 'Husar' *Heereslastkraftwagen* was developed by ÖAF in conjunction with the *Amt für Wehrtechnik*, specially for military use, and first appeared in 1966. It went into series production in 1968. German Volkswagen 'Transporters' are used as personnel carrier (*Kombi*), small workshop (*Instandsetzungs-KW, B*), etc. During the mid-1960s a new light 4×4 cross-country truck was designed by Steyr. Named 'Pinzgauer' it went into series production for the Austrian and Swiss armed forces in 1971. A 6×6 variant was also developed. The general design of the 'Pinzgauer' 4×4 is much the same as that of the smaller 'Haflinger' (see page 15), featuring a tubular backbone chassis with swinging axles, lockable differentials, etc., but the engine is a 2.5-litre air-cooled four-cylinder in-line unit, located between the front seats. Both were named after once well-known Austrian workhorses of compact build, great stamina and particular ability for mountainous work.

Vehicle shown (typical): Truck, 1½-ton, 4×4, Cargo (ÖAF HA-2-90 'Husar') (*leichter geländegängiger Lastkraftwagen*)

Technical Data:
Engine: ÖAF diesel, 4-cylinder, I-I-W-F, 4700 cc, 90 bhp @ 2500 rpm.
Transmission: 5F1R × 2 (OD top).
Brakes: hydraulic, air-assisted.
Tyres: 9.00–20.
Wheelbase: 3.40 m.
Overall l × w × h: 5.40 × 2.06 × 2.76 m.
Weight: 3750 kg. GVW 6700 kg.
Note: Payload on roads 2500 kg. Speed range 3.5 to 92 km/h. 3½-ton winch optional. Also available for fire fighting and other special purposes. Introduced in 1966.

Truck, 4-ton, 4 × 2, Cargo (Steyr 480) 4-cyl. diesel, 95 bhp, 5F1R, wb 3.71 m, 6.80 × 2.40 × 2.30(cab) m, 4000 kg approx. Engine capacity 5322 cc. Speed 78 km/h. Typical general purpose truck, used for transport of personnel and general cargo.

Truck, 3-ton, 4 × 4, Cargo (Steyr 580g) 4-cyl. diesel, 95 bhp, 5F1R × 2, wb 3.71 m, 6.84 × 2.40 × 3.30 m, 5000 kg approx. Payload on roads 5 tons. Speed 69 km/h. Model 586g was similar but powered by a 120-bhp 6-cyl. 5975-cc engine.

Truck, 3-ton, 4 × 4, Cargo (Steyr 580g) 4-cyl. diesel, 95 bhp, 5F1R × 2, wb 3.71 m, 6.84 × 2.40 × 3.30 m, 5000 kg approx. Version with soft-top cab. All 480 and 580 models had seating accommodation for 20 (with centre bench: 32). Towed load 8½ tons. Also with closed double cab (driving instr. vehicles).

Truck, 2½-ton, 4 × 4, Cargo (Steyr 680M) 6-cyl. diesel, 120 bhp, 5F1R × 2, wb 3.70 m, 6.57 × 2.40 × 2.97 m, 5430 kg (w/Winch 5830 kg). Payload on roads 4½ tons. Seating for 20. Speed 80 km/h. Engine capacity 5975 cc. Also 6 × 6 version (Model 680 M3, *qv*).

Truck, 3-ton, 4 × 4, Fire Fighting and Rescue, w/Winch (Steyr 580g) 4-cyl. diesel, 95 bhp, 5F1R × 2, wb 3.71 m. Comprehensively equipped *Bergungs- und Brandschutzfahrzeug* on chassis *gl LKW, D, 3 t (Steyr 580g/Allrad)*. 5-ton winch. Portable pump unit powered by Volkswagen engine.

Truck, 3-ton, 4 × 4, Fire Fighting (Steyr 586g) 6-cyl. diesel, 120 bhp, 5F1R × 2. wb 3.71 m. Vehicle shown is *Schlauch-fahrzeug* and carried a total of 1800 m of pressure hose and other equipment including three field-telephone units. Chassis: *gl LKW, D, 3 t (Steyr 586g/Allrad)*.

Truck, 6-ton, 4 × 4, Shop Van (Saurer 6 GAVFR-L) 6-cyl. diesel, 140 bhp, 5F1R × 2, wb 4.30 m, 7.10 × 2.20 × 3.00 m approx. Engine capacity 7983 cc. Standardized chassis *(Einheitsfahrgestell)*. Speed 67 km/h. Fording depth 600 mm. Turning circle 9.2 m. Late type body shown.

Truck, ¾-ton, 4 × 4, Teleprinter (Dodge T214-WC51) 6-cyl., 76 bhp (DIN), 4F1R × 1, wb 2.49 m, 4.24 × 2.09 m. Ex-US Army weapons carrier with Austrian bodywork *(gl FMKW, B, ¾ t, o/m SW; Lohneraufbau)*. Also on this chassis: ambulance, self-propelled mount for Oerlikon AA gun, etc.

Truck, 6-ton, 4×4, Cargo (Gräf & Stift LAVT-9F) 6-cyl. diesel, 145 bhp, 5F1R×2, wb 3.86 m, 6.50×2.40×2.66 m, 7000 kg. Shown with trailer, carrying bridging equipment. Designated *m LKW(gl)*, in full: *mittlerer Lastkraftwagen (geländegängig)*, (medium cross-country truck).

Truck, 6-ton, 4×4, Cargo and Prime Mover (Gräf & Stift LAVT-9F/1) 6-cyl. diesel, 145 bhp, 5F1R×2, wb 3.86 m, 6.49×2.40×2.73 m, 7000 kg. Special version with extended cab. Speed 66 km/h. 11.00–20 tyres. 4½-ton winch. 1968. *Einheitsfahrgestell* (standardized chassis).

Truck, 6-ton, 4×4, Prime Mover (Saurer 6 GAVFR-Z) 6-cyl. diesel, 140 bhp, 5F1R×2, wb 3.60 m, 7.00×2.20×2.72 m. Used for towing radar equipment and Bofors 4-cm 55/57 AA gun. Seating for 10. Speed 67 km/h. Designated *gl ZKW 6 t*. Engine cubic capacity 8 litres.

Truck, 10-ton, 4×4, Cargo and Prime Mover (Saurer 8GA3H-Z) V-8-cyl. diesel, 200 bhp, 6F1R×2, wb 4.00 m, 7.35×2.40×2.68 m, 7800 kg. GVW 18,000 kg. Engine cubic capacity 11.6 litres. Speed 67 km/h. Designated *s LKW (gl)*. Tyres 11.00–20. Only one was used, mainly as tractor for loads of up to 75 tons.

TRUCKS and TRACTORS
6 × 6

Makes and Models: Alvis 'Stalwart' (5-ton, 1968, GB).
Berliet GBC 8 MT (5-ton, 1967, F). Gräf & Stift ZA-200/1
(8-ton), ZA-210/3 and ZAFD-210/36 (10-ton). Praga
V3S (3-ton, CS). Reo/Studebaker M35A1, M35A2,
M185A3 (2½-ton, 6 × 6, c. 1965, US). Steyr 680 M3
(2½-ton, 1965). Steyr-Puch 'Pinzgauer' (1½-ton, 1968).
WWII types: GMC CCKW-352 and 353 (2½-ton, 6 × 6,
US), Corbitt/White 666 (6-ton, 6 × 6, US), Mack NM
(6-ton, 6 × 6, US), Pacific TR-1 M26 (12-ton, 6 × 6, US),
etc.

General Data: The post-war Austrian Army, between
1955 and 1959, acquired many 6 × 6 trucks of American
origin, principally in the 2½- and 6-ton classes. In recent years their gradual replacement by modern vehicles of Austrian (Steyr) and French (Berliet) manufacture has
taken place. Heavy and specialist 6 × 6 vehicles have been produced by Gräf & Stift
since the mid-1950s. The American tank transporter M25 ('Dragon Wagon'),
incorporating the Pacific tractor M26, was used for haulage of tanks up to 50 tons.
Wartime American GMC 6 × 6 trucks were fitted with various types of specialist
bodies, in addition to the common cargo GS type.

In 1967 a total of 110 French Berliet Model GBC 8 MT 5-ton 6 × 6 trucks was
purchased through the firm of Gräf & Stift with which Berliet had entered into a
marketing agreement in 1966. Later they were supplied directly by Berliet. In 1968
a number of British Alvis 'Stalwart' 5-ton 6 × 6 amphibious trucks was acquired for
use by the Army Engineers and for civilian relief and rescue operations.

Vehicle shown (typical): Truck, 8-ton,
6 × 6, Cargo and Prime Mover (Gräf &
Stift ZA-200/1) (*schwerer geländegängiger Lastkraftwagen*)

Technical Data:
Engine: Gräf & Stift 6VT-200 diesel
(licence Daimler-Benz) 6-cylinder, I-I-
W-F, 10,809 cc, 200 bhp @ 2200 rpm.
Transmission: 6F1R × 2 (OD top).
Brakes: air plus exhaust brake.
Tyres: 11.00–20.
Wheelbase: 4.32 m, BC 1.40 m.
Overall l × w × h: 8.35 × 2.40 × 2.90 m.
Weight: 8200 kg.
Note: Extended cab, seating five. Em-
ployed mainly for transport of Engineers'
equipment (*Pioniergerät*). Also supplied
with single cab and longer cargo body.
Speed 70 km/h. 4½-ton winch.

Truck, 1½-ton, 6×6, Cargo (Steyr-Puch 'Pinzgauer') 4-cyl. air-cooled engine. Experimental prototype, developed from the 'Pinzgauer' 4×4, announced in 1968. Like the 'Haflinger' this vehicle had high ground clearance due to swing axle design with 'step down' final drive gear cases. Series production (92-bhp engine) from 1971. (See also page 19).

Truck, 2½-ton, 6×6, Cargo (Steyr 680 M3) 6-cyl. diesel, 150 bhp, 5F1R × 2, wb 3.80 (BC 1.20) m, 6.57 × 2.40 × 2.97 m, 6500 kg (w/Winch 6900 kg). Crew 2+18. 6×6 modification of Steyr 680M. Payload on roads and towed load both 4½ tons. Speed 80 km/h. Steyr WD 609 engine.

Truck, 10-ton, 6×6, Crane Mounted (Gräf & Stift ZAFD-210/36) 6-cyl. diesel, 210 bhp, 6F1R × 2, wb 4.32 (BC 1.40) m, chassis/cab: 7.73 × 2.40 × 2.90 m, 8530 kg. 15-ton Kässbohrer KS-45M fully revolving crane for use by Army Engineers.

Truck, 10-ton, 6×6, Prime Mover (Gräf & Stift ZA-210/3) 6-cyl. diesel, 210 bhp, 6F1R × 2, wb 4.32 (BC 1.40) m, 8.55 × 2.40 × 2.74 m, 10,650 kg. Tractive unit for low-bed 50-ton HET (Heavy Equipment Transporter) trailer. Chassis/cab also used for aircraft refueller.

BELGIUM

At the end of the Second World War the Belgian armed forces were re-equipped with a vast array of Allied wartime production vehicles. From 1948 new vehicles were gradually taken into service, mainly military versions of American and British commercial types assembled in Belgium using a maximum content of Belgian-manufactured parts and bodywork. In 1946 the British allocated a part of their occupation zone of Germany to the re-established Belgian 1st Army Corps. These forces acquired relatively large quantities of new German-made cars and trucks. From May 1955 the Allied contingents in Western Germany were no longer occupation forces but stayed on as NATO defence forces. Many German-made vehicles, particularly Ford and Magirus-Deutz, were also used by the Belgian Army and para-military *Gendarmerie* (police forces) at home. By the mid-1960s the Belgian Army possessed just over 25,000 vehicles, including over 11,000 trucks in the 2.5- to 3-ton payload class. About 80% of these had been acquired during the period 1952–54 and many of the remainder dated from WWII.

Tracked AFVs have for a long time been almost exclusively of American origin. The Belgians used the light tanks M24 'Chaffee' and M41 'Walker Bulldog', and the medium M4 'Sherman', M26 'Pershing' and M47 'Patton'. The latter have now been superseded by the German 'Leopard'. In addition there were other tracked vehicles like the M75 APC, and SP guns, including the M7 'Priest', M44, M55, M108 and M109. A. B. L. Famileureaux produced (under licence) the French AMX-VTT/VTP armoured personnel carrier. Armoured cars have included the American Chevrolet 'Staghound', Ford M8 'Greyhound' and White M3A1 scout car, the Canadian GM C15TA and the British AEC, Humber and Morris, all of WWII vintage. Also in use were American M4 and M5 high-speed artillery tractors, British Bren Carriers and various types of US half-tracks. As in other countries, most of the older types of vehicles have been phased out in recent years and currently a much less-varied vehicle inventory is kept.

In 1971 it was announced that British Leyland had received an order for 130 Alvis 'Scorpion' tracked AFVs and that this was the first of a series of contracts with Belgium involving some 700 vehicles. Assembly and part-manufacture would take place in a new Belgian government factory.

Who's Who in the Belgian Automotive Industry

Brossel	Brossel Frères Bovy et Pipe SA, Bruxelles.
Chrysler	Chrysler Benelux SA, Anvers (assembly of Dodge, etc.).
FN	Fabrique Nationale Herstal SA (formerly: Fabrique Nationale d'Armes de Guerre SA), Herstal.
Ford	Ford Motor Co. (Belgium) SA, Anvers (assembly of Ford).
Gillet	Gillet SA, Herstal.*
General Motors	General Motors Continental SA, Anvers (assembly of Bedford, Chevrolet, Opel, etc.).
Miesse	Auto Miesse SA, Bruxelles.
Minerva	Sté Nlle Minerva SA, Bruxelles & Mortsel, Anvers.*
Renault	Renault (RNUR), Vilvoorde (assembly of Renault).
Sarolea	SA Sarolea, Herstal.

*Now defunct

German Ford G798BA and US Willys CJ3A.

CARS, MOTORCYCLES
and THREE-WHEELERS

Makes and Models: *Cars:* Various commercial types: Chevrolet (US), Ford 'Taunus' 15M (D), Hillman (GB), Mercedes-Benz (D), Opel 'Olympia', 'Rekord' and 'Kapitän' (D), Volkswagen 1200 (D), etc.
WWII types: British Austin, Hillman and Morris 10 HP (Light Utility) and Ford WOA2 and Humber 4 × 4 (Heavy Utility).
Motorcycles: FN 450-cc XIII M (1950). Gillet 400-cc and 500-cc 'Lateral' (1951). Harley-Davidson 1213-cc 67 FL 'Electra Glide' (1967, US) (*Gendarmerie*). Sarolea 350-cc AS, 400-cc 51A4 (1951).
WWII types: American Harley-Davidson and Indian; British Ariel, BSA, Matchless, Royal Enfield and Triumph 350-cc, and Norton 500-cc. Also American Cushman 53 airborne motor scooters.
Three-Wheelers: FN AS 24 (3 × 2, 1959).

General Data: The most unusual vehicle in this section is certainly the FN AS 24 *Véhicule Aeroporte*. It was designed by the late Nicholas Straussler in London and one prototype was produced by WMD Waggon- und Maschinenbau GmbH of Donauworth, Germany, in 1958/59. The wide low-pressure 'Lypsoid' 22″ × 12″ tyres, also a Straussler invention, were produced by Metzeler Gummiwerke AG of Munich. These had a load capacity of 280 kg at a pressure of 1.3 kg/cm² (18 lb/sq. in) and a maximum speed of 65 km/h. Dimensions of these 4-ply tyres were 570 mm (diameter) by 320 mm (max. width) and for maximum off-road performance the pressure could be reduced to about 0.5 kg/cm² (7 lb/sq. in). The prototype was powered by a 15-bhp British Anzani 322-cc twin-cylinder two-stroke engine with Albion 3F1R gearbox. Quantity production was taken up in 1959 by the well-known Belgian armaments firm of FN (Fabrique Nationale d'Armes de Guerre SA) who slightly modified it and fitted their own engine/transmission unit. It is used for a variety of purposes and can carry four soldiers or one with a 250 kg load. It can also be used as a fire fighting vehicle, a field ambulance with two stretchers or as a guided missile launcher. The two frame members are telescopic and the seat is collapsible. This enables the vehicle to be reduced in size for transport, parachuting and storage.

Vehicle shown (typical): Vehicle, Lightweight, 3 × 2, Air-transportable (FN AS 24) (*Véhicule Aeroporte* or *Tricar Parachutable*)

Technical Data:
Engine: FN 24 twin-cylinder, I-T-A-R, 243.5 cc, 15 bhp (SAE) @ 5300 rpm.
Transmission: 4F. No reverse.
Brakes: mech. on rear wheels.
Tyres: 'Lypsoid' 22–12.
Wheelbase: 1.27 m. Track, rear: 1.33 m.
Overall l × w × h: 1.84 × 1.64 × 0.90 m.
Weight: 220 kg. GVW: 550 kg.
Note: Built under Straussler licence. Rear wheel drive with differential. **Max.** speed 57 km/h. Magneto ignition (**no** other electrical equipment). Also **with** fire-fighting and other special equipment. About 500 were produced.

Vehicle, Lightweight, 3 × 2 (FN AS 24) 2-cyl., 15 bhp, 4F, wb 1.27 m, 1.84 × 1.64 × 0.90 m.   Capable of carrying four armed men. In this photograph it is shown with a machine gun, on a special mount, fixed to the front cross member.

Vehicle, Lightweight, 3 × 2 (FN AS 24) *Tricar Parachutable* after airdrop, tied to special platform with ammunition and other supplies. When 'folded' the vehicle measures 1.04 × 1.64 × 0.77 m. It takes only one minute to get the vehicle operational.

Vehicle, Lightweight, Fire Fighting (FN AS 24) Equipped with ten powder extinguishers.   Alternatively two 50-litre water containers could be carried, each with a compressed air bottle and jet pipes. Used for combating aircraft, vehicle and other fires.

Vehicle, Lightweight, Half-Track (FN AS 24) 2-cyl., 15 bhp. 4F, wb 1.27 m, 1.90 × 1.64 × 0.90 m.   Experimental half-track conversion, featuring additional idler wheels with overall chains. Note steering brake levers. A special two-wheeled Lypsoid-tyred trailer was also developed.

Motorcycle, Solo (FN XIII M) 1-cyl., 11.5 bhp, 4F, 2.20 × 0.83 × 1.03 m, 160 kg. Military version of civilian machine with rubber front suspension. 450-cc (84.5 × 80 mm) side-valve engine. Tyres 3.50–26. Lucas or Miller mag-dyno. Maximum speed 102.5 km/h. Gradability 40%.

Motorcycle, Solo (Gillet 500 'Lateral') 1-cyl., 16 bhp, 4F, 2.05 × 0.72 × 1.08 m approx., 150 kg, 500-cc (75 × 105 mm) side-valve engine. Tyres 3.00–25. Telescopic front fork and rear susp. struts. Supplied to Belgian Army in 1950/51. 400-cc 14-bhp model also produced.

Motorcycle, Solo (Sarolea AS 350) 1-cyl., 10 bhp, 4F, wb 1.40 m, 2.12 × 0.70 × 1.10 m, 130 kg, 350-cc (75 × 79 mm) side-valve engine. Tyres 3.50–26. Sarolea also produced a 400-cc model (51A4) for the Belgian Army. Both had telescopic front and rear suspension.

Field Car, 4-seater, 4 × 2 (Ford 'Taunus' G73A) 4-cyl., 34 bhp, 3F1R, wb 3.39 m, GVW 1250 kg. Military pattern bodywork with canvas top and rear locker on 1949 'Taunus' car/van chassis, used by Belgian forces in Germany. 1172-cc SV engine. Transveral leaf springs front and rear.

TRUCKS, ¼-TON
4 × 4

Makes and Models: Land-Rover Series I (GB) (*Gendarmerie*). Minerva C20 (1954), M20 (1955), C22 (1955). Minerva/Land-Rover (1952/53, B/GB). Willys CJ3A (1951, US).
World War II types: Ford GPW and Willys MB (US), 6- and 12-volt versions.

General Data: To supplement and later replace the war-time 'Jeep', the Belgian forces first acquired quantities of the post-war civilian Willys 'Universal Jeep' CJ3A which was modified in several respects to meet their requirements. About 1951 the now-defunct Société Nouvelle Minerva SA commenced production of a slightly modified version of the British Land-Rover in their Antwerp/Mortsel plant. These vehicles were supplied for military, police and civilian use, differing from the British parent design by having restyled front wings and radiator grille. Originally this was the '80-inch' (wb) model but later the '86-inch' was offered. 63% of each vehicle was claimed to be of Belgian manufacture, produced under licence. The remainder was imported and assembled. Minerva soon started designing their own *Tout-Terrain* vehicle and the first prototypes appeared in 1954. It had an integral body/chassis with a subframe for the engine/transmission/front axle assembly. This complete unit could be easily removed by unbolting and lifting the front end of the body clear from it. The original model was designated C20 and had a 2.03-m (80-in) wheelbase but this was soon replaced by a slightly longer version (C22) with 2.18-m (86-in) wheelbase. The military model (M20) had the short wheelbase. It would appear that very few were actually produced and sold although some were exported to Australia as late as 1957. The British-built Land-Rover was used only by the *Gendarmerie*.

Vehicle shown (typical): Truck, ¼-ton, 4 × 4, Ambulance (Minerva/Land-Rover 'Tout-Terrain')

Technical Data:
Engine: Rover 4-cylinder, I-F-W-F, 1997 cc, 52 bhp @ 4000 rpm.
Transmission: 4F1R × 2.
Brakes: hydraulic.
Tyres: 6.00–16.
Wheelbase: 2.03 m.
Overall l × w × h: 3.58 × 1.55 × 1.87 (1.42) m (std vehicle).
Weight: 1370 kg. GVW 1820 kg.
Note: Belgian version of British Land-Rover, 1952–53. Also offered with 2.18-m wb. Shown in field ambulance role (two stretchers, rear extension).

Truck, ¼-ton, 4 × 4 (Minerva M20) Continental F4162 (2.6-litre) 4-cyl., 69 bhp, 4F1R × 2, wb 2.05 m, 3.65 × 1.54 × 1.82 (1.40) m, 1150 kg. Civilian version designated C20. Unitary body-cum-chassis but complete power unit and front axle on easily removable subframe. Detachable side screens and half-doors.

Truck, ¼-ton, 4 × 4 (Minerva C22) Continental F4140 (2.3-litre) 4-cyl., 59 bhp (optional: F4162 as M20, or Jenbach JW35 2-cyl. 2-stroke 40-bhp diesel). 4F1R × 2, wb 2.20 m, 3.86 × 1.65 × 1.82 (1.40) m, 1250 kg. Lengthwise rear seats and automatic diff. locks optional. Replaced C20 in 1955.

Truck, ¼-ton, 4 × 4 (Willys CJ3A) 4-cyl., 60 bhp, 3F1R × 2, wb 2.03 m, 3.35 × 1.36 × 1.75 (1.38) m, 1350 kg. Military version of 'Universal' Jeep, used for various purposes incl. Radio (shown), A/T missiles (Entac), snow plough, etc. Differed from war-time 'Jeep' in having larger headlights, one-piece windscreen and other details.

Truck, ¼-ton, 4 × 4, Para-Commando (Minerva/Land-Rover) Rover 4-cyl., 52 bhp, 4F1R × 2, wb 2.03 m. Special Paratroop and Commando conversion, armed with three FN MAG 7.62-mm machine guns. Replaced similarly modified wartime US ¼-ton 4 × 4 which had twin .50 cal. machine guns.

TRUCKS, ¾- to 2-TON
4 × 2, 4 × 4 and 6 × 6

Makes and Models: Dodge and Fargo 'Power-Wagon' (¾-ton, 4 × 4, 1951, US). FN 4RM/62(F) 'Ardennes' (1- and 1½-ton, 4 × 4, from 1957). Ford F3 (1-ton, 4 × 2, 1948, US) (*Gendarmerie*), F4 (Ambulance, 4 × 2, 1948, US). Ford/Marmon-Herrington F3 COE (1½-ton, 4 × 4, 1950, US/B). Mercedes-Benz L406 (Ambulance, 4 × 2, 1969, D). 'Unimog' S (1½-ton, 4 × 4, 1966, D). Renault 'Armée Belge' 3302 (Ambulance, 4 × 2), 3304 (Ambulance, 4 × 4, 1958, F), 3403 (1.4-ton, 4 × 2), 3406 (¾-ton, 4 × 4, 1958, F). Tempo 'Matador' (1.2-ton, 4 × 2, 1955, D). Volkswagen 'Transporter' (0.8-ton, 4 × 2, from 1953, D) (various body types, incl. Ambulance). Willys 475-4WD (¾-ton, 4 × 4, *c*. 1955, US).

WW II types: American ¾-ton, 4 × 4 (Dodge, incl. ambulances), 1½-ton, 4 × 2 (Ford), 4 × 4 (Chevrolet, Dodge), 6 × 6 (Dodge); British ¾-ton, 4 × 2 (Bedford, Fordson, Morris-Commercial), 1½-ton, 4 × 4 (Fordson) and Ambulances, 4 × 2 (Austin), 4 × 4 (Humber); Canadian ¾-ton, 4 × 2 (Dodge, Ford), 4 × 4 (Chevrolet, Ford), etc.

General Data: As replacements for the original variety of World-War II types, the Belgian Forces acquired relatively large numbers of, at first, American and French trucks in the ¾- to 1½-ton payload class. These were mainly of Ford and Renault manufacture, assembled in Belgium. The first prototypes of the Belgian FN 'Ardennes' appeared about 1953 but series production of this type did not start until about 1957 when a number were ordered by the Belgian Air Force for use as fire fighters (*Véhicule Incendie*). In January 1966 the Belgian Army ordered 625 'Unimog' S trucks from Daimler-Benz following extensive trials at the Army's experimental establishment (CEM/EtE) at Brasschaat during 1965. Competitors had included Chrysler (US), Daimler-Benz (D), FN (B), Lancia and OM (I), Rover (GB), and Simca (F). The 'Unimogs', like the earlier Renaults, were issued with both cargo GS and ambulance bodywork. The Ford/Marmon-Herrington 4 × 4 COE as used by the Belgian Army was rather a unique vehicle. It had the chassis and front end of the American Ford 'Parcel Delivery' van which was introduced in the US on the F3 chassis in 1950. Cab doors, roof (steel or canvas), rear panel and bodywork, however, were Belgian. The transfer case and front drive were from Marmon-Herrington and the vehicles were assembled (like several other Ford/M.-H. types) by Ford's Antwerp plant.

Vehicle shown (typical): Truck, 1½-ton, 4 × 4, Cargo and Prime Mover (FN 4RM/62 'Ardennes') (*Tracteur-Porteur*)

Technical Data:
Engine: FN 652 6-cylinder, I-I-W-F, 4750 cc, 130 bhp @ 3500 rpm.
Transmission: 4F1R × 2.
Brakes: hydraulic.
Tyres: 9.00–20.
Wheelbase: 2.35 m.
Overall l × w × h: 4.33 × 2.13 × 2.25 (2.09) m.
Weight: 3300 kg.
Note: Front axle drive through divided prop shaft from 2-speed aux. gearbox/transfer in rear axle/diff. Banjo-type axles with diff. locks. Winch optional. Speed 105 km/h. 1963. Also with special bodywork, incl. Air Force Fire Fighter.

Truck, 1-ton, 4 × 4, Cargo (FN 4RM/62F 'Ardennes')
6-cyl., 106 bhp, 4F1R × 2, wb 2.35 m, 4.30 × 2.13 × 2.25
(2.09) m, 3160 kg. Tyres 9.00–16. FN 64PR 4275-cc engine.
Early model (1957). Later many detail differences were introduced (bodysides, front wings, wheels, headlight position, etc).

**Truck, 1½-ton, 4 × 4, Personnel Carrier (FN 4RM
'Ardennes')** 6-cyl., 130 bhp, 4F1R × 2, wb 2.35 m. Supplied
to *Gendarmerie* in 1963. Coachbuilt body on 'Ardennes'
chassis with revised military pattern front end which was also
used on a later version of the cargo truck (1965). Two circular
roof hatches.

Truck, 1½-ton, 4 × 4, Cargo (Ford/Marmon-Herrington)
6-cyl., 95 bhp, 4F1R × 2, wb 2.64 m. M.-H. four-wheel drive
conversion of 1951/52 American Ford F3 COE chassis/cowl,
assembled in Belgium. Also with earlier type radiator grille
(1950), canvas cab roof and integral full-length bodywork.

**Truck, ¾-ton, 4 × 4, Command (Dodge B3PW126 'Power
Wagon')** 6-cyl., 95 bhp, 4F1R × 2, wb 3.20 m, 5.35 × 2.10 ×
2.40 m, 2840 kg. Modified front wings and Belgian bodywork
on 1951/52 chassis. Used by Artillery and Infantry as staff
car. Belgian UNO Forces used ambulances based on similar
Fargo 'Power-Wagon' chassis.

TRUCKS, 2½- to 10-TON
4 × 2, 4 × 4, 6 × 4 and 6 × 6

Makes and Models: Bedford SLC (3-ton, 4 × 2, 1954, GB), SA (7-ton, tractor, 4 × 2, 1954, GB), SB (bus, 32-pass., 4 × 2, 1954, GB), and RLC (3-ton, 4 × 4, 1954, GB). Berliet TBU 15CLD (6-ton, wrecker, 6 × 6, 1969, F). Chevrolet 6400 (3-ton and 33-pass. bus, 4 × 2, 1948, US). Faun F60S (5-ton, tractor, 4 × 2, 1955, D). FN 62C 6-cyl. (3-ton, 4 × 2, 1948). FN/Brossel/Miesse 4RM/62C (4½-ton, 4 × 4, 1954). FN 4RM/64C-652 (1954) and 4RM/652-3M (3½-ton, 4 × 4, 1959). Ford 'Rhein' (3-ton, 4 × 2, c. 1950, D), and G398 TA, G398TS-S2 and G798 BA (COE) (3-ton, 4 × 4, from 1952, D). Ford F5 (3-ton, 4 × 2, 1948, US). Ford/Marmon-Herrington F6 COE (3-ton, 4 × 4, 1950–52, US). Fordson ET6 'Thames-Sussex' (3-ton, 6 × 4, c. 1958, GB). GMC HDCW (10-ton, 6 × 4, c. 1951, US). Hanomag (prime mover for 8-ton trailer, 4 × 2, 1948, D). International M40, M61, M62 and M139D (5-ton, 6 × 6, c. 1960, US). Leyland 19H 'Hippo' (10-ton, 6 × 4, c. 1958, GB). Magirus-Deutz 'Jupiter' (6½-ton, 4 × 2 and 4 × 4, 1953–54, D), 'Uranus' (tractor, 6 × 6, 1960, D). MAN 630L2AE-B (5-ton, 4 × 4, 1965, D). Reo/Studebaker G742 'M-Series' (2½-ton, 6 × 6, c. 1960, US). Thornycroft 'Nubian' (3-ton, 4 × 4, c. 1953, GB).
WWII types: British Austin, Bedford, Commer, Crossley, Dennis, Foden, Fordson, Karrier, Leyland, Scammell, Thornycroft; Canadian Chevrolet, Dodge, Ford; US Autocar, Diamond T, Federal, FWD, GMC, Mack, Pacific, Studebaker, Ward LaFrance, White, etc.

General Data: To supplement and later replace the multiplicity of WWII surplus cargo, tractor, wrecker and other types of the above makes, the Belgian forces bought locally assembled as well as national products, both 'administrative' and military 4 × 4 types (FN, Ford, General Motors). In 1964 trials were held for a new tactical medium truck with m/f engine. Of Berliet, International, Magirus, MAN, Mercedes-Benz and Volvo contestants the MAN was selected and 2000 were ordered in January 1965, for local assembly. Heavier types were imported.

Vehicle shown (typical): Truck, 3½-ton, 4 × 4, Cargo, w/Winch (FN 4RM/652-3M) (*Tracteur-Porteur*)

Technical Data:
Engine: FN 652 6-cylinder, I-I-W-F, 4750 cc, 130 bhp @ 3500 rpm.
Transmission: 4F1R × 2.
Brakes: air.
Tyres: 11.00–20.
Wheelbase: 3.00 m.
Overall l × w × h: 5.92 × 2.24 × 2.83 (2.07) m.
Weight: 4450 kg.
Note: Introduced in 1959. Designed to conform with NATO specifications. Speed 90 km/h. Cross-country payload 3 tons. Air-transportable. '4RM' in FN model designations indicates *4 Roues Mortrices* (4-wheel drive).

Truck, 4½-ton, 4 × 4, Cargo, w/Winch (FN/Brossel/ Miesse 4RM/62C) 6-cyl., 92 bhp, 4F1R × 2, wb 2.85 m, chassis/cab: 5.68 × 2.15 m, 3515 kg. Some had rad. grille with vertical bars. 4275-cc (90 × 112 mm) SV engine with 6.5:1 CR. Banjo-type rear axle. Split-type front axle with Rzeppa CV joints. Also tipper *(Benne)* version. 3750 built.

Truck, 3-ton, 4 × 4, Cargo, w/Winch (Bedford RLC) 6-cyl., 111 bhp, 4F1R × 2, wb 3.96 m, chassis/cab: 6.25 × 2.27 × 2.50 m, 3135 kg. GVW 8165 kg (off road: 7485 kg). Shown with container-type radio body. Also with special bodywork, including tanker. LHD version of British RLC, assembled by GM in Antwerp, 1954–55.

Truck, 3-ton, 4 × 4, Cargo, w/Winch (Ford/Marmon-Herrington F6 COE) 6-cyl., 95 bhp, 4F1R × 2, wb 3.40 m, 5.80 × 2.15 × 2.60 (cab) m. Tyres 8.25–20. Basically civilian truck, 1952, assembled by Ford in Antwerp with M.-H. front axle drive. Also special bodywork (workshop, ambulance, stores, etc.). 1948–50 style visible behind.

Truck, 5-ton, 4 × 4, Tipper (MAN 630 L2AE-B) 6-cyl. m/f, 130 bhp, 6F1R × 2, wb 4.10 m, 7.89 × 2.50 × 3.41 m, 8200 kg approx. Also cargo version (wb 4.60 m). Assembled in Belgium by Ets. Hocké at Grand-Bigard near Brussels. *Benne* (tipper) version used by Army Engineers. Model D.1246MV3A multi-fuel engine.

Truck, 7-ton, 4 × 2, Tractor (Bedford SA2) 6-cyl., 111 bhp, 4F1R, wb 2.18 m, 4.20 × 2.25 × 2.30 m, 3000 kg. Tyres 7.50–20. British commercial type, assembled by GM in Antwerp, *c.* 1955. 4927-cc engine (as Model RLC). Also used by *Gendarmerie*. Coupled to 7-ton 2-wh. Wood Body semi-trailer.

Truck, 3-ton, 4 × 4, Ambulance (Ford G39TA-K) V-8-cyl., 100 bhp, 4F1R × 2, wb 3.37 m, 5.73 × 2.32 × 2.90 m, 3430 kg. German coachbuilt bodywork on Ford-Köln ('Rhein') chassis, *c.* 1955. Similar model used by British RAF in Germany. Belgians also used 4.01-m wb G398TA, with petrol tank body.

Truck, 5–6-ton, 4 × 4, Aircraft Refueller (FWD SU-COE) Waukesha SRKR 6-cyl., 126 bhp, 5F1R × 1, wb 3.66 m. Post-war tanker with twin overhead booms on WWII American chassis, used by the Belgian Air Force. Permanent four-wheel drive (chain-drive transfer case with lockable diff.). Also artillery tractor version.

Truck, 7½-ton, 6 × 6, Cargo and Prime Mover (Mack NO) 6-cyl., 159 bhp, 5F1R × 2, wb 3.96 (BC 1.47) m, 7.54 × 2.62 × 3.15 m. This American WWII artillery tractor was used with its original soft-top cab and with coachbuilt closed cab. It towed the American 155-mm gun and 203-mm howitzer.

MISCELLANEOUS VEHICLES

The Ford/Marmon-Herrington 4 × 4 models shown in this section are only a few examples of such vehicles supplied by Ford's Antwerp plant for military and other uses. Other Ford/ M.-H. models included cargo trucks for the Luxembourg Army, civilian dump trucks and a variety of special vehicles for Belgian Government departments, incl. fire fighters, radio vehicles, etc., also on 1953/54 chassis. The Air Force had, amongst others, several types of British Thornycrofts, incl. (by 1954): 'Nubian' mobile power stations and crash tenders, 'Lewin-Thornycroft' sweeper/collectors, and 'Trusty' mobile cranes. In 1966 the Army ordered 44 American wheeled amphibious bridging units (Space Corp.).

Tractor, 4 × 4, Artillery (Ford/Marmon-Herrington F6 COE) 95-bhp 6-cyl. or 100-bhp V8, 4F1R × 2, wb 3.40 m. About 1949 tests were held with an American F6 chassis/cab and this F6 with full-length body, for gun towing. With modified body this tractor was subsequently produced in quantity. Front end shown: 1948–50.

Truck, 3-ton, 4 × 4, Wrecker (Ford/Marmon-Herrington F6 COE) 6-cyl., 95 bhp, 4F1R × 2, wb 4.02 m, 7.70 × 2.20 × 3.00 m. 1952 model with 4-door crew cab, 3-ton swinging-boom crane and front winch. Krupp/Ardelt diesel-electric mobile crane (4 × 4, 90-bhp diesel) with 6½-ton capacity was also used.

Tractor, 4 × 4, Artillery (Ford/Marmon-Herrington F6 COE) 6-cyl., 95 bhp, 4F1R × 2, wb 3.40 m, 5.80 × 2.25 × 2.58 m, 4830 kg. Production model of 1951. Also on 1950 chassis. Fitted with winch. 3.6-litre SV engine. Tyres 8.25–20. Towed British 25-pdr and US 105-mm gun and carried crew and ammunition.

Truck, 6½-ton, 4×4, Riot Control (Magirus-Deutz 'Jupiter' A6508) Deutz V-8-cyl. diesel, 170 bhp, 6F1R × 2. Twin water cannon on extended cab, used by *Gendarmerie*. Several types with SWB and LWB (1953–54) were used by Belgian Army with various body types (tractor, truck, house-type van, crane).

Car, Armoured, 4×4 (Les Forges de Zeebrugge) Produced by N. V. Les Forges de Zeebrugge of Herstal, near Liege, in the early 1950s. Only one prototype was completed for the Belgian Ministry of Defence. Based on a Ford/Marmon-Herrington 4×4 truck chassis. Note single rear wheels.

Car, Armoured, 4×4, 90 mm Gun (FN 4RM/62FAB) 6-cyl. 130 bhp, 4F1R × 2, 4.47 × 2.20 × 2.36 m, 7420 kg. Prototype (1964) on 'Ardennes' chassis. Also with different turret with mortar and two MGs. 61 of these vehicles (both versions) were ordered for the *Gendarmerie*. Production models differed in detail.

Carrier, Armoured, Full-Track, Tank Destroyer Gun (CATI) Ford V-8-cyl., 85 bhp, 4F1R, 4.15 × 2.06 × 1.57 m, 4500 kg. 90-mm 'Mecar' recoilless gun on modified WWII British 'Loyd' carrier. CATI = *Canon Anti-Tank d'Infanterie*. Crew 3. Speed 48 km/h. Used only by Belgian Army, mainly in Germany.

BRAZIL

During World War II the Brazilian Army used mainly US military vehicles, including Willys, Dodge and GMC. In recent years these have been supplemented or replaced by vehicles produced by Brazilian industry.

During the 1950s several firms started vehicle assembly and later production, including Ford, General Motors, Daimler-Benz, Volkswagen, Toyota, etc. Amongst the commercial cross-country vehicles produced (under licence) are American Jeeps (assembled during 1952–56) and the Japanese Toyota, both in several versions. The Auto Union 'Munga' was also marketed. The firm of Engesa converts 4×2 trucks into 4×4 and 6×6 tactical vehicles, and has designed 6×6, 8×4 and 8×8 military trucks, amphibious troop carriers and armoured amphibious reconnaissance vehicles.

Truck, $\frac{1}{4}$-ton, 4×4, Utility (Toyota OJ 40L 'Bandeirante') Daimler-Benz OM 324 diesel 4-cyl., 78 bhp, 4F1R×1, wb 2.28 m, 3.79 × 1.66 × 2.00 m, 1500 kg. Produced by Toyota do Brasil SA. Also Hard-top (OJ 40 LV) and LWB Pickup (OJ 45 LP-B) and Hard-top (OJ 40 LV-B) versions. 1969.

Truck, $\frac{3}{4}$-ton, 6×6, Cargo (Chevrolet C-1504/Engesa) 6-cyl., 151 bhp, 4F1R×1. Brazilian Chevrolet C-15 Series Pickup, converted by Engesa (Engenheiros Especializados SA) into 6×6 'Total Traction' (Heavy Duty Model, code TT-6M1). Similar conversions on Dodge D-100 and Ford F-100 Series. 1969.

Truck, $2\frac{1}{2}$-ton, 4×4, Cargo, w/Winch (Chevrolet C-65/ Engesa) 6-cyl., 151 bhp, 4F1R×2 (5F1R×2 optional). Engesa 'Total Traction' 4×4 conversion, code TT-4F. Applied to Chevrolet C- and D-60 Series, Ford F-600 and Dodge D-700 Series, petrol or diesel. Max. gradability 74% (85% with 5-speed trans.).

Truck, 2½-ton, 6×6, Cargo (Chevrolet C-65/Engesa) 6-cyl., 151 bhp, 5F1R × 2. 'Total Traction' 6×6 conversion (code T-66 IIB) by Engesa. Same conversion available on similar Dodge, Ford and other medium trucks. Payload on roads 5–7 tons. Max. gradability 85% (overall gear ratio 118:1).

Truck, 2½-ton, 6×6, Cargo (Chevrolet C-65/Engesa) 6-cyl., 151 bhp, 5F1R × 2. Similar to vehicle shown on left but single wheels with same track width front and rear for improved performance on sand (beaches, etc.). US type steel cargo body with folding troop seats.

Truck, 5-ton, 6×6, Cargo, w/Winch (Chevrolet C-65/ Engesa) 6-cyl., 151 bhp, 5F1R × 2. LWB model with Fruehauf rear bogie with double inverted semi-elliptic leaf springs (Engesa code TT-6C). Diff. in transfer case. Payload on roads 14 tons. Engesa-converted military trucks are also used in other South American countries.

Truck, 2½-ton, 6×6, Cargo, w/Winch (GMC CCKW-353/ Engesa) 6-cyl., 104 bhp, 5F1R × 2. Wartime GMC 2½-ton truck, rebuilt and converted by Engesa. 'Boomerang' type rear bogie, allowing up to one metre vertical movement for each pair of rear wheels. Tyres 11.00–20. Max. gradability 85%. Maximum payload 5 tons.

Truck, 2½-ton, 6×6, Cargo, w/Winch (Dodge D700/ Engesa) V-8-cyl., 198 bhp, 5F1R × 2, wb 4.43 m, 7.12 × 2.40 × 2.31 m, 6565 kg. Tyres 11.00–20. GVW on/off roads: 11,565/9,065 kg. 7½-ton twin-drum winch with 100 m of cable to front and 100 to rear. 1970.

Truck, 2½-ton, 6×6, Cargo/Prime Mover, w/Winch (Mercedes-Benz L1113/Engesa) 6-cyl. diesel, 130 bhp, 5F1R × 2, wb 3.81 m, 6.55 × 2.34 × 2.59 m, 7430 kg. GVW on/off roads: 12,306/9,831 kg. Engesa conversion with walking-beam rear bogie. 1970.

Carrier, Armoured, 6×6, Amphibious, CTR-A (Engesa EE-11 'Urutu') Saab-Scania 210-bhp (or Perkins 120-bhp) diesel or Chrysler 170-bhp V-8-cyl. engine. 5.90 × 2.45 × 2.00 m, 10 tons. Available as APC (crew 15, 7.62 MAG MG), Recce (crew 10, turret-mounted twin 20-mm MGs), A/C (crew 3, turreted, up to 90-mm gun). Speed land/water (props): 110/15 km/h.

Car, Armoured, 6×6, CRR (Engesa EE-9 'Cascavel') Light reconnaissance and combat vehicle, armed with up to 90-mm gun. Basically as CTR-A but not amphibious. 'Boomerang' rear bogie. IFS. Puncture-proof 11.00–20 tyres. High-alloy armour plate hull. Max. speed 100 km/h. Developed, produced and marketed by Engesa. 1971.

CANADA

During WWII the Canadian automotive industry produced three types of military trucks: conventional, modified conventional and military pattern. The first two categories comprised US type commercial trucks, more or less modified to meet military requirements. The latter group comprised tactical vehicles designed in accordance with British WD specifications and could be called a North American interpretation of British military 'B' vehicle requirements. Not long after 1945 a major change was made in Canadian defence policy, namely a change-over from British to US type equipment. The reasoning behind this was that in case of war the two neighbouring countries, which already had so much in common, could fight together, using the same equipment and the same supply lines. In consequence large requirements against US production developed and Canadian production facilities were required to manufacture to US designs and specifications. These common objectives were set out in a directive of the US Department of Defense dated 27 November, 1951, entitled 'Joint Industrial Military Co-operation with Canada'. In automotive terms, this meant that the Canadian armed forces were re-equipped with US type tactical trucks, mainly in the $\frac{1}{4}$-ton, $\frac{3}{4}$-ton and $2\frac{1}{2}$-ton categories. The main difference with US standardization was that the Canadians standardized the 'deuce-and-a-half' ($2\frac{1}{2}$-ton, 6×6) as produced by GMC whereas the US forces concentrated on the type developed by Reo (originally known as the 'Eager Beaver'). The subsequent story of Canadian standard military trucks is therefore not significantly different from that of the US, with the notable exception of certain tracked carriers which in Canada were developed to a high degree, in various configurations, particularly by Robin-Nodwell. These Nodwell carriers were also supplied for special purpose uses by the US Army and Navy in the Alaskan, New-foundland and Antarctic areas. Another interesting Canadian development was the articulated four-track Canadair 'Dynatrac'. Several of these tracked vehicles were supplied to the US armed forces also.

Armoured fighting vehicles used by the Canadian forces were mainly of British and US origin and include the British 'Ferret' FV 701 Scout car and 'Centurion' tank, and the US armoured car, M706 'Commando', light tank, M41, medium tank, M48, and APC, M113. The US tracked cargo carrier, 6-ton, M548 was also used. In February 1968 the Canadian armed forces—Army, Navy and Air Force—were unified. Canada is a member of NATO and has part of her forces stationed in Europe. These forces employed a variety of German cars, trucks, buses, etc.

Canadian Army vehicle registration numbers are prefixed by two figures indicating the year of acquisition (e.g. '54' for 1954). Vehicles of the Canadian Defence Staff in Britain have British military type registration numbers consisting of the letters ZZ between two double numerals, e.g. 00ZZ50.

Who's Who in the Canadian Automotive Industry

Bombardier	Bombardier Snowmobile Ltd, Valcourt, Quebec.
Canadair	Canadair Ltd, Montreal, Quebec.
Chevrolet	(see GMC).
Dodge	Chrysler Canada Ltd, Windsor, Ontario.
Ford	Ford Motor Co. of Canada, Ltd, Oakville, Ontario.
FWD	FWD Corp. Ltd, Kitchener, Ontario.
GMC	General Motors of Canada Ltd, Oshawa, Ontario.
International	International Harvester Co. of Canada, Ltd, Hamilton, Ontario.
Jeep	American Motors (Canada) Ltd, Brampton, Ontario. (prior to 1970: Kaiser Jeep of Canada Ltd, Windsor, Ontario).
Nodwell, Flextrac Nodwell	Robin-Nodwell Mfg Ltd, Calgary, Alberta (later Flextrac-Nodwell Div. of Canadair).
Sicard	Sicard Inc., Montreal, Quebec.

CARS, UTILITY TRUCKS and MOTORCYCLES

Makes and Models: *Cars:* Various (commercial, 4 × 2, Chevrolet, etc.).
Utility Trucks: Ford GPW (¼-ton, 4 × 4, WWII, US). Willys MB (¼-ton, 4 × 4, WWII, US). Willys MC M38CDN (¼-ton, 4 × 4, 1950, US/CDN). Willys MD M38A1CDN (¼-ton, 4 × 4, 1953, US/CDN).
Motorcycles: Triumph TRW 500cc Mk I (solo, *c.* 1952, GB).

General Data: Canadian military passenger cars (sedans and station wagons) are not standardized and are of various makes, models and years. They are, as in other countries, replaced by new, current, models as and when they need to be replaced. Certain German cars, e.g. Ford 'Taunus', were used by the Canadian Forces in Germany. Utility trucks are all US-type Jeeps. Standardized were the M38 and M38A1 most of which were assembled by the Ford Motor Company of Canada Ltd. These Canadian-built models were, in fact, designated M38CDN and M38A1CDN respectively. They supplemented and later replaced the wartime Willys model. Both the M38CDN and M38A1CDN appeared fitted with modification kits, including ambulance, electric welding and wireless (No. 19 set). The recoilless rifle mounted version was also used. The ambulance and wireless modification kits were supplied by Leyland Motors (Canada) Ltd. The M38A1CDN was supplied with and without winch. In December 1962, the US Department of the Army issued a Technical Bulletin (TB 34-9-133) which read, in part: 'The Armies of the United States and Canada have approved an interchangeability agreement to enable the major vehicle assemblies and components of the Truck, Utility, ¼-Ton, 4 × 4, M38A1, manufactured by one country, to be used in the vehicles of the other'. The same applied to various other types of trucks and trailers.

The Trailer, ¼-ton, Cargo, M100 was also produced in Canada and was identical to its US counterpart.

Vehicle shown (typical): Truck, ¼-ton, 4 × 4, Utility, M38CDN (Willys MC)

Technical Data:
Engine: Willys MC 4-cylinder, I-L-W-F, 134.2 cu. in, 60 bhp @ 4000 rpm.
Transmission: 3F1R × 2.
Brakes: hydraulic.
Tyres: 7.00–16.
Wheelbase: 80 in. Track: 49¼ in.
Overall l × w × h: 133 × 62 × 67¼ (54) in.
Weight: 2625 lb.
Note: Canadian version, assembled by Ford, 1952. Semi-floating rear axle and drum-type parking brake, otherwise mechanically very similar to wartime model.

Truck, ¼-ton, 4×4, Utility/Wireless, M38CDN (Willys MC) 4-cyl., 60 bhp, 3F1R×2, wb 80 in. Basically M38CDN but equipped with Wireless kit (No. 19 set). Note hinged tailgate and spare wheel on side. M38(CDN) was military version of CJ3A Jeep 'Universal', introduced in the US in 1950.

Truck, ¼-ton, 4×4, Utility/Welding, M38CDN (Willys MC) 4-cyl., 60 bhp, 3F1R×2, wb 80 in. Basically Ford-assembled M38CDN, equipped with self-contained electric welding kit. Note jerrycan holder on tailgate. Tyres 7.00–16. Side-mounted spare wheel, as on CJ3A Jeep 'Universal'.

Truck, ¼-ton, 4×4, Utility, M38A1CDN (Willys MD) 4-cyl., 72 bhp, 3F1R×2, wb 81 in, 138⅝×61×73¾ (56½) in, 2665 lb. Assembled by Ford Canada, 1967; later in the US. Identical to US M38A1. F-head (inlet-over-exhaust) engine. Full weather protection installed. Military version of CJ5 Jeep 'Universal'.

Truck, ¼-ton, 4×4, Utility/Ambulance, M38A1CDN (Willys MD) 4-cyl., 72 bhp, 3F1R×2, wb 81 in. Basically standard utility truck, with two-stretcher ambulance modification kit (Leyland). A single-stretcher rack kit was also used (passenger seat tilted forward). Mfr's name changed to Kaiser Jeep, in 1963.

TRUCKS, ½- to 5-TON
4×2 and 4×4

Makes and Models: Bickle-Seagrave 400-B (fire fighting, 5-ton, 4×2, 1953, US). Chevrolet (various comm. 4×2 types). Dodge (various comm. 4×2 types). Dodge T245 M37CDN, M37B1CDN (cargo, ¾-ton, 4×4, US/CDN), T245 M43CDN (ambulance, ¾-ton, 4×4, US/CDN), T245 M53CDN, M56CDN (chassis, ¾-ton, 4×4, US/CDN), T245 M152CDN (panel utility, ¾-ton, 4×4, US/CDN). Dodge Ram I (cargo, amphibious, 1¼-ton, 4×4, 1966). Ford (various comm. 4×2 types). FWD AU (snow remover, high speed, 4×4, 1952, US). GMC (various comm. 4×2 types). International (various comm. 4×2 types). Oshkosh W1700/Elcombe 66 DLO (dump, 5-ton, 4×4, 1951, US/CDN). Oshkosh MB-1 (fire fighting, 4×4, 1971, US). Sicard (snow fighters, 4×4). Volkswagen 'Transporter' (1-ton, 4×2, D). Walter (fire fighting, 4×4, US). *WWII types:* conventional, modified conventional and military pattern, Chevrolet, Dodge, Ford, GMC, Maple Leaf, etc.

General Data: The Canadian armed forces use a large number of 'administrative' commercial trucks of different makes, models and years. As these become non-servicable they are replaced by newer models. They include ½-, ¾-, 1-, 2- and 3-ton types with panel, cargo and other body styles. Most light tactical trucks are based on the Dodge T245 ¾-ton 4×4 chassis. These were produced by Chrysler's Canadian plant in Windsor, Ontario, and were almost identical to the US parent vehicles. They superseded the wartime US Dodge 'Beep' Weapons Carrier, the Canadian version of which was the T236 D¾APT (Airportable). Most of Canada's surplus wartime automotive equipment was taken over by the newly established armies of several countries in Europe, the Middle East, etc. Some were 'demobilised' and made available to civilian operators in various countries, including (via UNRRA) Czechoslovakia and Yugoslavia. The Volkswagen 'Transporter' was used by the Canadian Forces in Germany with various bodystyles, incl. a fire fighting version. Special equipment and special purpose 4×2 and 4×4 vehicles include fire trucks, snow fighters, etc., produced by such firms as FWD, Sicard and Walter. The Dodge Ram I was produced by Chrysler as a test rig and as a possible replacement for the Dodge T245 range.

Vehicle shown (typical): Truck, ¾-ton, 4×4, Panel, Utility, M152CDN (Dodge T245)

Technical Data:
Engine: Dodge T245 6-cylinder, I-L-W-F, 230.2 cu. in, 94 bhp @ 3400 rpm.
Transmission: 4F1R × 2.
Brakes: hydraulic.
Tyres: 9.00–16.
Wheelbase: 126 in.
Overall l × w × h: 200 × 73½ × 92 in.
Weight: approx. 7000 lb. GVW 8550 lb.
Note: basically same bodyshell as ambulance (M43) but wire mesh-protected side windows and single door in centre of rear panel. Also special arcticized version.

Truck, ¾-ton, 4×4, Cargo/Cable Laying, M37CDN (Dodge T245) 6-cyl., 94 bhp, 4F1R×2, wb 112 in, 185×73½×93 in, 5687 lb (w/o equipment). Cargo truck, equipped with cable laying kit. Winch-equipped models were five inches longer. Hard-top cab (standard on Canadian models).

Truck, 4×4, Snow Fighter (Sicard 'Snowmaster') One of various types produced by Sicard. Shown is a Model BL with 102×72 in cutting width and height. Allis-Chalmers 340-bhp diesel blower engine. Hundreds of these snow blowers were supplied to Canadian and US forces. Weight approx. 27,500 lb.

Truck, 3-ton, 4×2, Cargo (International R 160) 6-cyl., 108 bhp, 4F1R, wb 154 in. Typical 'administrative' vehicle. Many 'R'-line Internationals (introduced in 1953) were used by the Canadian forces at home and abroad. This RHD unit was operated by the RCAF in Great Britain.

Truck, 5-ton, 4×2, Fire (Bickle-Seagrave 400-B/G11) V-12-cyl. engine, with dual ignition (24 spark plugs), 5F1R, GVW 23,000 lb. These US-built fire trucks were produced in 1953 and used by the Royal Canadian Air Force in Germany. Units shown were 'demobilised' and bought by a Dutch dealer in 1970.

TRUCKS
6 × 4 and 6 × 6

Makes and Models: Alvis 'Salamander' (fire fighting, 6 × 6, GB). FWD (cargo, 10-ton, 6 × 6, 1964). FWD DF5-5177, RSC07-5184 (fuel tankers, 6 × 4, 1965–67). GMC M135CDN (cargo and tractor, 2½-ton, 6 × 6, US/CDN), M211CDN (cargo, 2½-ton, 6 × 6, US/CDN), M216CDN (dump, 2½-ton, 6 × 6, US/CDN), M220CDN (shop van, 2½-ton, 6 × 6, US/CDN), M222CDN (water tank, 2½-ton, 6 × 6, US/CDN). International G744 M41 (cargo, 5-ton, 6 × 6, US), M51 (dump, 5-ton, 6 × 6, US), M52 (tractor, 5-ton, 6 × 6, US), M54 (cargo, 5-ton, 6 × 6, US), M62 (wrecker, 5-ton, 6 × 6, US), M328 (bridging, 5-ton, 6 × 6, US). Sicard (fire fighting, 6 × 6).

WWII types: various US 6 × 6 trucks, including GMC 2½-ton, Diamond T 4-ton, Mack 6-ton and Pacific 12-ton (tractor, M26A1 (C1A1), for tank-transporter S-T).

General Data: The most common vehicle in this category is the 2½-ton ('deuce-and-a-half') 6 × 6 GMC. The chassis were assembled by General Motors' Canadian plant at Oshawa, Ontario, and fitted with a variety of bodies, incl. cargo, dump, shop van, etc. They were virtually identical to the US GMCs introduced in 1950, with the exception of the M135CDN tractor and the M216CDN dump truck which had single rear tyres (the US Army counterparts were the M221 and M215 respectively, with dual rear tyres). All these GMCs featured 'Hydramatic' Model 302M dual-range automatic transmission. The Canadian models had a hard-top cab. In addition to the models listed above, the Canadians also used the M135CDN as a launching vehicle for the Canadair CL89 (AN/USD 501) reconnaissance drone. The drone was launched by a booster rocket which was jettisoned, and powered in flight by a turbojet sustainer engine providing a speed of nearly Mach 1. This sophisticated equipment was designed in collaboration with Britain and Germany to be used for photo-reconnaissance, etc. The 5-ton 6 × 6 range of vehicles is listed above as International but some of them may have been produced by other US manufacturers, to the same basic (military) design (see US section also). The Alvis, FWD and Sicard were special vehicles, used mainly by the RCAF. US military pattern 2-wheel trailers produced in Canada included ¾-ton and 1½-ton models (chassis, cargo, water).

Vehicle shown (typical): Truck, 2½-ton, 6 × 6, Cargo, M135CDN (GMC)

Technical Data:
Engine: GMC 302M 6-cylinder, I-I-W-F, 301.6 cu. in, 130 bhp @ 3200 rpm.
Transmission: 'Hydramatic' 4F1R × 2 × 1.
Brakes: hydraulic, air-assisted.
Tyres: 11.00–20.
Wheelbase: 156 in, BC 48 in.
Overall l × w × h: 255 × 88 × 105 (80) in.
Weight: 12,330 lb (w/winch 12,740 lb).
Note: Automatic transmission with high and low ranges. Also tractor truck for semi-trailers (US tractor equivalent, M221, had dual rear tyres). Max. speed 58 mph (governed).

Truck, 2½-ton, 6×6, Cargo, w/Winch, M211CDN (GMC)
6-cyl., 130 bhp, auto. 4F1R×2×1, wb 156 (BC 48) in,
269×96×112 (78) in, 13,580 lb (w/o winch 13,170 lb).
Similar to M135 but dual rear tyres (9.00–20) and flatbed body.
Note bumper (inverted on winch-trucks) and vertical exhaust.

**Truck, 2½-ton, 6×6, Shop Van, Signals, M220CDN
(GMC)** 6-cyl., 130 bhp, auto. 4F1R×2×1, wb 156 (BC 48) in,
266×96×131 in, 15,100 lb approx. Standard shop van body,
modified for signals role. Banjo type axles with torque rods.
Rear springs were double inverted semi-elliptic (top one fixed
to frame).

Truck, 2½-ton, 6×6, Dump, M216CDN (GMC) 6-cyl.,
130 bhp, auto. 4F1R×2×1, wb 144 (BC 48) in, 240×92×
110 in, 14,200 lb. In the US Army this model was used only
with 9.00–20 tyres, dual rear, designated M215. Canadian
version had 11.00–20 tyres as shown. Removable cab protector.

Truck, Fueller, 4000-Gallon, 6×4 (FWD DF5-5177) There
were two models made, the first (shown) in 1965/66, the second
(Model RSC07-5184) in 1967. Both were similar in appearance
and air-transportable. Fruehauf bodywork with 4000-gal.
(Imp.) stainless steel tank. Similar cab was used on an exp.
6×6 'bulk load carrier' in 1964.

TRACKED VEHICLES

The Canadian industry, notably Bombardier Snowmobile and Nodwell, produced some interesting types of civilian and military full-track carriers, designed for traversing mud, snow and other weak surfaces. Much development took place after the war, especially with twin-unit models which steer by articulation. Canadair Ltd of Montreal (a subsidiary of General Dynamics), following a new policy of diversification from aircraft production, collaborated with the Canadian Army Directorate of Vehicle Development in developing the 'bellyless' articulated 'RAT' and later developed the 'Dynatrac'. A tracked 'snow scooter' (Ski-do) with two-stroke engine appeared about 1966. Among the tracked AFVs were the US APC M113A1 and a special C&R version of it, named 'Lynx' (1968). In turn, the US forces used some of the Canadian tracked carriers.

Carrier, Utility, Articulated, 'RAT' (Canadair) Volkswagen 4-cyl., 30 bhp, 4F1R, 157 × 48 × 61 (36) in, 1500 lb. GVW 2500 lb. Steering by articulation (radius 11 ft). Pneumatic tyres. Tracks extended over almost full width of vehicle. Original design by Canadian Army (1955/56).

Carrier, Utility, Articulated, XM571 (Canadair 'Dynatrac' CL-91) Chevrolet HD 164 'Corvair' 6-cyl., 70 bhp, 4F1R × 2, 228 × 64 × 85 (72) in, 5300 lb. GVW 7500 lb. Shown with arctic/tropical enclosure installation. First prototype delivered to US Army in Nov. 1962. Trailing arm torsion bar suspension. Track width 18 in.

Carrier, Utility, Articulated, XM571 (Canadair 'Dynatrac' CL-91) Later version (1968) with various modifications. The 'Dynatrac' featured a hydraulic system for articulated steering and a clutch-brake system for solo use of the front unit. The use of a third unit was possible (total payload then 3500 lb).

Carrier, Full-Track, Personnel, w/Winch (Nodwell RN75) Ford 223 CID 6-cyl., 107 bhp, 4F1R, 193 × 109 × 106 in, 9930 lb (basic). GVW 17,430 lb. Track width 40 in. Tyres 7.50–20. Three axles. Crew 10. Used by US Navy in Alaska. Also with truck body and as crash rescue vehicle (RCAF).

Carrier, Full-Track, Personnel, w/Winch (Nodwell RN 110) Ford 292 CID V-8-cyl., 167 bhp, 4F1R, 228 × 109 × 106 in, 11,450 lb (basic). GVW 22,450 lb. Tracks and tyres as RN75 but four axles. 1964. Various body options, incl. amphibian (known as RN 110 Floater). Handled in US by FMC Corp.

Carrier, Full-Track, Cargo and Personnel, w/Winch (Nodwell RN110B) Basically similar to RN 110. 5-ton payload. Also with stake rack cargo body. Largest model (not shown) was 12-ton articulated logistic transporter, consisting of four-axle tractor with ditto semi-trailer (four tracks, each pair driven by a GM diesel engine).

Carrier, Full-Track, Armoured, Personnel, ATC1 'Bobcat' Front-mounted 180-bhp engine, rear-mounted transmission. Tracks consisted of two rubber bands with steel cross bars. Cupolas for driver (LHD) and machine-gunner (rotating). Three prototypes built for tests in 1958. No quantity production.

CHINA (People's Republic)

The People's Republic of China was proclaimed on 1 October 1949. The Chinese Communist Army first used a variety of ex-WWII vehicles, mainly of US and Japanese origin. Later they imported new vehicles from other communist countries, for example Soviet GAZ, MAZ and ZIS/ZIL trucks, East German IFA S-4000 trucks, Hungarian Csepel K-800 tracked prime movers, etc. Several types of West European vehicles are also used. Their own motor industry commenced in October 1956 when the Soviet-built Tse-Fan factory at Changchun (later renamed No. 1 Automobile Plant) began production of the 'Liberation' truck. Later other cars and trucks were launched by the Shanghai Automobile Plant. Other plants at Peking, Nanking, Tsinan, etc. followed with various other types.

Civilian vehicle production, mostly trucks, is very much decentralized, almost every province making vehicles of some kind. They range from 3-wheelers to 40-ton dump trucks but most are in the 2½- to 5-ton class.

Field Car, 4-door, 4- to 5-seater, 4 × 4 (Shangai) 4-cyl., 70-bhp twin-carb. light-alloy engine. Max. speed 60 mph. Payload 0.8 ton. From 1966. Other field cars (mil. and civ.) have included British Austin 'Gipsy' and Land-Rover, Soviet GAZ-67 and -69 and US Willys and Ford WWII models.

Truck, 4-ton, 4 × 2, Cargo (Jay-Fong CA1OZ) 6-cyl., 95 bhp, 4F1R, wb 4.00 m, 6.60 × 2.46 × 2.20 m, 3800 kg. Air brakes. Tyres 9.00–20. Introduced in 1956, named 'Liberation' (licence-built Soviet ZIL-164). Soviet GAZ-63A (2-ton, 4 × 4, NS230) was also produced.

Truck, 6-ton, 6 × 6, Cargo and Prime Mover (Berliet GCH) Variant of Berliet's Model GBU (different engine, etc.). 800 ordered in 1970, as well as 2200 of the lighter Model GBC 8MT. Other imported all-wheel drive trucks included Soviet GAZ-63 (4 × 4) and ZIS/ZIL-151 (6 × 6).

CZECHOSLOVAKIA

Before World War II the Czechoslovak motor industry produced a variety of civilian and military cross-country vehicles of sophisticated designs which were in high esteem both at home and abroad. These were the products of old-established firms like Praga, Skoda and Tatra. The German *Wehrmacht* took over and used most if not all of the Czech military vehicles, including tanks, when they 'annexed' the country and several types remained in production for them. After liberation in 1945 by the Russians and Americans the Czech motor industry soon recovered from war damage and by 1948 the pre-war production volume was greatly exceeded. Nationalization of the industry in 1948 meant the beginning of production concentration and centralization. Car production was concentrated in two enterprises, namely Skoda in Mladá Boleslav and Tatra in Kopřivnice, specializing on the '1101' and 'Tatraplan' respectively. The Aero 'Minor' (made by Motlet) and the Tatra T57 and T87 were gradually phased out of production.

Post-war commercial vehicle production was concentrated in three enterprises. Praga produced the Skoda-designed 1½-ton A 150, and continued their own 3-ton models RN and RND and the 7-ton ND. The Avia Aircraft Factory in Letňany began, in 1946, to produce the Skoda 706 R heavy trucks and 706 RO buses. Tatra continued the 10-ton 6 × 6 T111 Series and introduced the T114 and T115 3-tonners. Trucks and buses reached production volumes of nearly 7200 and 1112 respectively in 1948. In 1952 the manufacture of trucks and buses was transferred from Avia to the Rýnovice and Mnichovo Hradiště works, the latter two constituting the establishment of the new LIAZ (Liberec) motor works at Jablonec nad Nisou, while Avia was engaged in its original activity: aircraft production. Manufacture of the Skoda 706 RO buses was taken over by Karosa at Vysoké Mýto. Not long afterwards it was decided to turn Avia at Letňany into a modern motor vehicle manufacturing plant. At first the Tatra T805 1½-ton 4 × 4 trucks were assembled there and later Avia took over the production of Praga's 5-ton S5T 4 × 2 and V3S 6 × 6 trucks. Praga then concentrated on manufacture of transmissions and other special components.

Launching production of Renault-Saviem 1½- and 3-ton trucks in 1968 (under French licence), resulted in further expansion of Avia's Letňany works, which now had virtually discontinued production of aircraft and related components. Licence agreements for the production of Skoda 706 vehicles were arranged with Poland (Jelcz motor works) and more recently with Rumania. Tatra redesigned their famous 6 × 6 range and introduced the T138 series in 1956/57. Production of trailers and semi-trailers was carried out by some specialist firms, notably Brandýs, Orličom Choceň and Transporta. Motorcycles were produced by CZ and Jawa and achieved a high international reputation.

In 1965 an association was formed to integrate the interests of 26 manufacturers of motor vehicles, trailers, components, etc. This organization has its own research and development facilities and represents 91% of the Czech automotive industry.

Who's Who in the Czechoslovak Automotive Industry

Avia/Saviem	Avia Závody NP, Letňany (formerly Automobilové Závody Letňany).
LIAZ	Liberecké Automobilové Závody NP, Jablonec nad Nisou (near Liberec).
Praga (trucks)	(see Avia).
Skoda (cars, vans)	Skoda Automobilové Závody NP, Mladá Boleslav.
Skoda (trucks)	(see LIAZ).
Skoda (buses)	Karosa, Národní Podnik, Vysoké Mýto.
Tatra	Tatra, Národní Podnik, Kopřivnice.

CARS, FIELD CARS and MOTORCYCLES

Makes and Models: *Cars:* various (4 × 2, commercial, incl. Skoda, Tatra).
Field Cars: GAZ-69A (later UAZ-69A) (4 × 4, SU). Skoda 1101 VO (4 × 2, 1947–50), 1101 4 × 4 (4 × 4, 1949), 973P (4 × 4, 1952), 9972 (4 × 4, 1964). Tatra 57K (4 × 2, 1947), T800, T801, T802 (4 × 4, 1950–51), T803, T804 (4 × 4, 1951–52).
Motorcycles: Jawa 350 (2 × 1).

General Data: After 1945 the Czech forces employed various types of vehicles which during the War had been used by the Germans, including the Tatra 57K *'Kübel'*, which continued in production. In addition, a similar type *'Kübelwagen'* was produced by Skoda, designated 1101 VO. This model was based on the contemporary Skoda 1101 car. In 1949 a 4 × 4 version of the 1101 VO was designed (same engine but 4F1R × 2 transmission, 5.50–18 tyres, ground clearance 250 mm, track F/R 1.26/1.32 m, 4.07 × 1.62 × 1.64 m). Production was confined to two prototypes. It was followed by the Skoda 973P in 1952, but large-scale production of all these models was suspended in favour of the Russian GAZ-69 and -69A which were standardized for all services and which, together with the similar Rumanian-built M-461, also became available for non-military purposes. The Skoda 997Z 'Universal' was not unlike the Austrian 'Haflinger' (albeit somewhat larger) but again it was only produced in small numbers (mainly for agricultural purposes). The technically interesting Tatra T800–T804 range of 1950–52 also remained in the experimental stage but the design culminated in the T805 truck (*qv*). American 'Jeeps' (including the Willys MA) were also used in Czechoslovakia after the war and several of these still survive, owned by civilians.

The Jawa 350-cc motorcycle was a standardized universal machine and also appeared specially equipped for air-dropping (IL-14). The standard model weighed 139 kg and its 18-bhp (@ 5000 rpm) two-stroke engine provided a top speed of 120 km/h. It was also used in conjunction with a light trailer.

Vehicle shown (typical): Field Car, 4-seater, 4 × 2 (Skoda 1100 VO)

Technical Data:
Engine: Skoda 1100 4-cylinder, I-I-W-F, 1089 cc, 32 bhp @ 4200 rpm.
Transmission: 4F1R.
Brakes: hydraulic.
Tyres: 5.75–16.
Wheelbase: 2.48 m.
Overall l × w × h: 3.93 × 1.50 × 1.58 m.
Weight: 960 kg. Payload 400 kg.
Note: Ind. suspension with transversal leaf springs, front and rear. Speed 90 km/h. Gradability 28%. Ground clearance 190 mm. Track F/R 1.20/1.25 m. Also 4 × 4 version (exp.).

Carrier, Personnel, 4 × 4 (Skoda 973P) 4-cyl., 35 bhp, 4F1R × 2, wb 2.50 m, 3.96 × 1.69 × 1.87 m. Tyres 7.50–16. Hub reduction gears. Torsion bar IFS/IRS. Track 1.35 m. Ground clearance 360 mm. Limited production, 1952. Skoda 1221-cc OHV car engine.

Carrier, Cargo and Personnel, 4 × 4 (Skoda 997Z 'Universal') 4-cyl., 47.5 bhp. 4F1R × 2, wb 2.00 m, 3.54 × 1.68 × 1.85 (top of windscreen) m, 930 kg. Skoda 1202 (1221-cc) engine. Speed 80 km/h. Lockable diffs. Off-road payload 800 kg. Canvas doors and tilt. 1964.

Car, 5-seater, Command, 4 × 4 (Tatra T802) T902 V-8-cyl., 120 bhp, 4880 cc. Tubular backbone chassis with swing axles. Power unit above rear diff. and transfer case, which were in chassis tube. T800 (4-cyl., 2438 cc, 55 bhp) and T801 (6-cyl., 3650 cc, 90 bhp) were amphibious. Pilot models only.

Car, 4-seater, Command, 4 × 4 (Tatra T803) T903 V-8-cyl., 80 bhp, 3F1R × 2, wb 2.73 m, 1730 kg. 2545-cc air-cooled engine. Hub reduction gears. Torsion bar IFS/IRS (swing axles). Speed 109 km/h. T804 was special airborne version (1600 kg) and was tested with fluid coupling transmission.

TRUCKS, 1½- to 8½-TON 4 × 2

Makes and Models: Praga A150 (1½-ton, 1947), RN, RND (3-ton, 1946), S5T Series (5-ton, from 1953). Skoda 706R Series (7½-ton, from 1946), 706RT Series (8½-ton, from 1957). Tatra T114 (3-ton, 1945), T115 (3-ton, 1948).

General Data: Most of these 4 × 2 trucks were used for civilian and military purposes. The Praga A150 was a Skoda design, produced under licence by Praga from 1947 until 1952. Basically a commercial truck it was 'militarised' by the fitting of higher bodysides, two spare wheels, roof hatch in cab and lengthwise troop seats in rear body. It was superseded by the Tatra T805 (4 × 4).

From the early 1960s Praga trucks were produced by a division of the Avia aircraft factory (formerly Letňany Automobile Works). The Praga S5T was a 4 × 2 version of the V3S 6 × 6 and both were supplied for civilian and military service in several countries.

The S5T and V3S had a modified version of the cab used on the forward-control Tatra T805, hence the peculiar door sills. The S5T-2, introduced in 1964, had a revised frontal appearance and a more powerful engine than the original model. The latest version was the S5T-3 which was fitted with a new engine (T912-3). All were available with various types of bodywork including cargo GS, tipper (end and three-way), house type van and tractor for semi-trailers. The S5T2-TN was a forward control tractor-truck.

The Skoda 706 was in production for many years and appeared first as the 706R Series (normal control cargo and dump trucks), later as the 706RT Series (forward control cargo, tipper and tractor chassis). Other specialized bodies included tankers, buses, etc. The civilian 806R and 906R models were similar in appearance to the early 706R. Produced by LIAZ. The Tatra T114 and T115 were direct developments from the T27 range, the main difference being the fitting of an air-cooled engine.

The Praga RN and RND (diesel) were in production until 1953, with periodic modifications, from 1931 and 1933 resp. A total of 36,071 were made, about one third of which were diesels.

Vehicle shown (typical): Truck, 3-ton, 4 × 2, Van (Praga RN, RND)

Technical Data:

Engine: Praga 6-cylinder, I-I-W-F, 3468 cc, 73 bhp @ 3000 rpm (Model RND: 4-cyl. 4.5-litre 60-bhp diesel).

Transmission: 4F1R.

Brakes: hydraulic.

Tyres: 7.50–20.

Wheelbase: 4.20 m.

Overall l × w × h: 6.78 × 2.20 × 2.64 (2.27) m (cargo truck).

Weight: 2790 kg (cargo truck).

Note: Shown with house-type van body, used as ambulance or dental surgery. Speed 80 km/h. Gradability 21% (both for cargo truck; visible alongside). Produced 1946–53.

Truck, 1½-ton, 4×2, Cargo (Praga A150) 4-cyl., 55 bhp, 4F1R, wb 2.90 m, 5.35×1.93×2.05 (cab) m, 1800 kg. 6.00–18 tyres. IFS with two transversal leaf springs. Speed 85 km/h. Track F/R 1.50/1.42 m. Produced 1947–52, under Skoda licence.

Truck, 3-ton, 4×2, Cargo (Tatra T115) 4-cyl. diesel, 65 bhp, 4F1R, wb 4.00 m, 6.78×2.20×2.26 m, 3800 kg approx. Tyres 9.75–20. Speed 60 km/h. Track F/R 1.74/1.70 m. Model T114 basically similar but 7.25–20 tyres, dual rear. Design Ledwinka. Air-cooled engine.

Truck, 5-ton, 4×2, Cargo (Praga S5T-3) 6-cyl. diesel, 110 bhp, 4F1R, wb 4.09 m, 6.55×2.33×2.35 (cab) m, 4650 kg. Towed load 3100 kg. Air brakes. Tyres 9.00–20. Various body options. Also with 4.50-m wheelbase. Air-cooled Model T91?-3 engine.

Truck, 8½-ton, 4×2, Cargo (Skoda 706RT) 6-cyl. diesel, 160 bhp, 5F1R, wb 4.00 m, 7.60×2.35×2.50 (cab) m, 6100 kg. GVW 15 tons. Towed load 8 tons. Air brakes. Tyres 11.00–20. Also as tipper (706RTS), tractor-truck (706RTTN), etc. Bus version designated 706RO.

TRUCKS, $\frac{1}{2}$- to $7\frac{1}{4}$-TON 4 × 4

Makes and Models: GAZ-69 (later UAZ-69) ($\frac{1}{2}$-ton, SU). Skoda 4S (4-ton, 1946). Tatra T128, T128N (3-ton, 1951), T137 ($7\frac{1}{4}$-ton, 1956), T138, T138NT ($7\frac{1}{4}$-ton, 1959), T805 ($1\frac{1}{2}$-ton, 1953), 4-813 T2 (prime mover, 1968). UAZ-450 (0.8-ton, SU).

General Data: The Tatra T805 was a general purpose $1\frac{1}{2}$-ton 4 × 4 truck, introduced in 1953 to replace the $1\frac{1}{2}$-ton 4 × 2 Praga A150. It was a typical Tatra design with air-cooled V-8 (petrol) engine, tubular backbone chassis enclosing the propeller shafts and independent front and rear suspension with swing axles incorporating 'step-down' reduction gear cases at the wheel hubs, resulting in ample ground clearance. It had exceptional off-road characteristics and proved particularly suited for transportation in mountainous terrain. It was widely used by the Czech forces as a cargo and personnel carrier and for various specialist purposes when fitted with steel-panelled house-type van body. It was also available for non-military use and for export, and was produced at several different plants.

The Tatra T128 was widely used as a cargo truck and artillery tractor and with house-type van body also for special roles. It had much in common with the T111 6 × 6 trucks.

The Tatra T137 and T138-4 × 4 were derived from the T138-6 × 6. They have V-8 engines with separate air-cooled cylinders and torsion bar independent front suspension. They were also available with non-driving front axle (4 × 2).

A derivation from the Tatra T813 'Kolos' (8 × 8, qv) was the model 4-813T2 4 × 4, introduced in 1968. It was essentially envisaged as a heavy road tractor and shared most mechanical components with the bigger versions 4-183 T3 6 × 6 and T813 8 × 8. Some types of Soviet 4 × 4 trucks were also employed, notably the light GAZ-69 (truck version of GAZ-69A).

Vehicle shown (typical): Truck, $1\frac{1}{2}$-ton, 4 × 4, Cargo (Tatra T805)

Technical Data:
Engine: Tatra 603A 8-cylinder, V-I-A-F, 2545 cc, 75 bhp @ 4200 rpm.
Transmission: 4F1R × 2.
Brakes: hydraulic.
Tyres: 10.50–16.
Wheelbase: 2.70 m. Track: 1.60 m.
Overall l × w × h: 4.72 × 2.19 × 2.60 (2.36) m.
Weight: 2750 kg. Payload on road: $2\frac{1}{4}$ tons.
Note: Tubular backbone chassis with swing axles and hub reduction gears. Ground clearance 400 mm. Diff. lock. Torsion bar suspension. Speed 70 km/h. Also with house-type van body.

Truck, 1½-ton, 4 × 4, Van (Tatra T805) V-8-cyl., 75 bhp, 4F1R × 2, wb 2.70 m. Special bodywork, integral with cab. Air-cooled engine was down-rated version of that fitted in the Tatra T603 (rear-engined) car, with twin Solex carburettors and two belt-driven axial cooling fans.

Truck, 3-ton, 4 × 4, Cargo (Tatra T128) V-8-cyl. diesel (T108), 130 bhp, 5F1R × 2, wb 3.95 m, 6.54 × 2.27 × 2.58 (with tilt 2.91) m, 6020 kg. Tyres 12.00–20. Payload on roads 5½ tons. IFS and IRS. Air brakes. Also with house-type van body. T128N had winch.

Truck, 4-ton, 4 × 4, Cargo and Prime Mover (Skoda 4S) 6-cyl., 125 bhp, 6F1R, wb 3.75 m, 6850 kg. Tyres 12.00–20. 5-ton winch. Towed load 8 tons. Supplied to Norway in 1946 as artillery tractor. Speed 80 km/h. IFS and IRS with transversal leaf springs. 8.27-litre petrol engine.

Truck, 7¼-ton, 4 × 4, Tractor (Tatra T138 NT 4 × 4) V-8-cyl. diesel (T928-12), 180 bhp, 5F1R × 2, wb 3.875 m, 5.53 × 2.44 × 2.50 m, 6500 kg. Tyres 11.00–20. Air brakes. Civilian version shown. Military version (with roof hatch, etc.) was used mainly with heavy 4-wh. (4 DT) cargo S-Ts.

TRUCKS, 2½- to 10-TON
6 × 6 and 8 × 8

Makes and Models: Avia S-430 (3-ton, 6 × 6, 1969). Praga (Avia) V3S (3-ton, 6 × 6, 1953). Tatra T111 Series (10-ton, 6 × 6, 1946), T130 (5-ton, 6 × 6, 1952), T138, T138VN (8-ton, 6 × 6, 1957), T148VN (8-ton, 6 × 6, 1969), T813 'Kolos' (8-ton, 8 × 8, 1966), etc., 4-813T3 6 × 6 (prime mover, 6 × 6, 1968). ZIL-157 (2½-ton, 6 × 6, SU), ZIL-135 (10-ton, 8 × 8, SU).

General Data: Czech vehicles in this class are powered by air-cooled diesel engines and are renowned for their excellent cross-country performance. The Praga V3S was first introduced in 1953 and had much in common with the American WWII 2½-ton 6 × 6 GMC (of which there were a fair number in Czechoslovakia) the main differences being an air-cooled diesel engine and elevated axles with step-down final drives (incorporating 2.14:1 gear ratio). From about 1964 this truck was produced by Avia, an old-established aircraft firm, in their Letňany Automobile Works. The Tatra T111 dated right back to Hans Ledwinka's days at Kopřivnice and had all the classical Tatra features. It was produced in several variants including a heavy drawbar tractor (see next section) and was gradually superseded by the T138 series which appeared in even more variants (incl. 4 × 2, 4 × 4, and 6 × 4 versions), from about 1957. Tatra's masterpiece, however, made its debut in 1966, designated T813 and popularly known as the 'Kolos'. This huge 8 × 8 vehicle is of very sophisticated design in the finest Tatra tradition and entered series production in 1968. Its backbone chassis is formed by the four axle differentials and auxiliary gearbox, connected together by tubular sections. This makes possible the assembly of vehicles of different drive configurations (8 × 8, 4 × 4, 6 × 6). All wheels are independently sprung with swinging half axles and there is planetary hub reduction gearing. Tyre pressure is adjustable from the driver's seat. There are seven locking differentials and many other refinements. This truck was also exported to several countries. incl. East Germany.

Vehicle shown (typical): Truck, 3-ton, 6 × 6, Cargo (Praga V3S)

Technical Data:

Engine: Praga T912 diesel 6-cylinder (Tatra licence), I-I-A-F, 7412 cc, 95 bhp @ 2100 rpm (or T912-2, 110 bhp).

Transmission: 4F1R × 2.

Brakes: air.

Tyres: 8.25–20.

Wheelbase: 4.14 m, BC 1.12 m.

Overall dimensions: 6.91 × 2.32 × 2.92 (2.49) m.

Weight: 5350 kg (w/winch 5470 kg). GVW: 10,900 kg.

Note: Payload on roads 5¼ tons; towed load 6 tons. 3½-ton winch optional. Diff. locks in both rear axles. Elevated-type axles (height 400 mm). Series production by Avia.

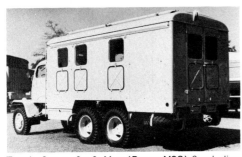

Truck, 3-ton, 6 × 6, Van (Praga V3S) 6-cyl. diesel, 95 bhp, 4F1R × 2, wb 4.14 (BC 1.12) m, 7.06 × 2.32 × 3.10 m, 6400 kg. 24-cu. yd house-type body, intended for various roles including comprehensively-equipped workshop. Hardwood frame construction with steel panelling.

Truck, 3-ton, 6 × 6, Cargo (Avia S-430) 6-cyl. diesel. Developed by Avia as possible replacement for the Praga V3S, featuring the same cab as used on a new Praga COE 4 × 2 truck, also developed by Avia. Prototypes designed and produced during 1968/69. Note large air-cleaner behind cab.

Truck, 3-ton, 6 × 6, Tanker (Praga V3S) 6-cyl. diesel, 95 bhp, 4F1R × 2, wb 4.14 (BC 1.12) m, 6.90 × 2.30 × 2.49 m. Tank capacity 3000 litres. Used for haulage of liquids (fuel, etc.) on and off roads. Other variants in the Praga V3S series include dump truck, wrecker, etc.

Truck, 5-ton, 6 × 6, Cargo (Tatra T130) V-8-cyl. diesel (T108), 130 bhp, 5F1R × 2. Track 1.80 m. 6 × 6 version of model T128 (4 × 4) but only produced in prototype form. Air-cooled 9883-cc engine (B × S 100 × 130 mm). Speed 80 km/h. Gradability 58%. 1952.

Truck, 10-ton, 6 × 6, Cargo and Prime Mover (Tatra T111 VN) V-12-cyl. diesel (T111A), 180 bhp, 4F1R × 2, wb 4.78 (BC 1.22) m, 8.30 × 2.50 × 3.00 (2.68) m, 9150 kg. 11.00–20 tyres. 6-ton winch. Air brakes. Lockable rear diffs. Various body options. Independent front and rear suspension with swing axles.

Truck, 10-ton, 6 × 6, Fuel Tank (Tatra T111C) V-12-cyl. diesel (T111A), 180 bhp, 4F1R × 2, wb 4.78 (BC 1.22) m, 8.25 × 2.50 × 2.56 m, 11,100 kg. 7000-litre oval tank with three compartments. Used for transport of fuel and as aircraft fueller. Specially modified T111 chassis. Air-cooled 14,825-cc engine.

Truck, 8-ton, 6 × 6, Airfield Lighting (Tatra T138 VN) V-8-cyl. diesel (T928-12), 180 bhp, 5F1R × 2, wb 4.92 (BC 1.32) m, 8.50 × 2.44 × 3.40 m. Air-cooled 11,762-cc engine. 11.00–20 tyres. 6-ton winch. Air brakes. Lockable rear diffs. Cargo truck modified for airfield lighting role.

Truck, 8-ton, 6 × 6, Tractor (Tatra T138 NT) V-8-cyl. diesel, 180 bhp, 4F1R × 2, wb 4.35 (BC 1.32) m, 6.66 × 2.45 × 2.48 m, 8000 kg. Max. load on fifth wheel 10 tons. Shown with N14V 14-ton cargo semi-trailer (8.16 × 2.36 × 3.24 (2.40) m, 4315 kg). Also used with other types.

Truck, 10-ton, 6 × 6, Crane Mounted (Tatra T111/K-32)
V-12-cyl. diesel (T111A), 180 bhp, 4F1R × 2, wb 4.78 (BC
1.22) m. Russian-made revolving crane, produced until 1954.
Driven by truck's engine. Superseded by HSC4 and HSC5
cranes on same chassis, later by AJ6 and AV8 on T138 chassis.

Truck, 8-ton, 6 × 6, Crane Mounted (Tatra T138/AJ6)
Hyd.-operated jib. Lifting capacity 6 tons at radii not exceeding
3 m, 5 tons between 3 and 4.8 m, 2½ tons at 8.5 m (max.).
AV8 had similar crane but mounted at forward end of platform
(behind cab).

Truck, 6 × 6, Heavy Tractor (Tatra T141) V-12-cyl. diesel
(T111A5), 185 bhp, 4F1R × 2, wb 4.11 (BC 1.22) m, 7.45 ×
2.58 × 2.80 m, 12,140 kg. 11.00–20 tyres. Planetary hub
reduction gearing (2.5:1). Towed up to 100 tons. Speed
range 2.5–38 km/h. 8-ton winch. Used with various types of
trailers. 4-door cab. Crew 8.

**Truck, 8-ton, 8 × 8, Cargo and Prime Mover (Tatra T813
'Kolos')** V-12-cyl. diesel (T930-3), 250 bhp, 5F1R × 2 × 2,
wb 1.65 + 2.20 + 1.45 m, 8.75 × 2.50 × 3.18 (2.78) m, 13,800
kg. Tyres 15.00–21. Speed 80 km/h. 22-ton winch. Also with
revolving crane (AD 350.1), etc. Towed load (on roads) up to
100 tons.

MISCELLANEOUS VEHICLES

After World War II the Czech forces took into use a relatively large number of ex-*Wehrmacht* semi-track vehicles of many types and sizes. Some types, including the sWS (*Schwerer Wehrmachtsschlepper*) had been produced by Czech industry during the German occupation and of these the *Sd. Kfz. 251* was continued in production (with certain modifications) as OT 810. OT stands for *Obrĕný Transportér* (APC). Another German WWII vehicle which was used in the post-war Czech Army was the 'Panther' ARV (*Bergepanzer, Sd. Kfz. 179*). Other ARVs were based on Soviet T34 and JS tank chassis. Some armoured vehicles were developed based on existing truck chassis. Czech tanks are of Soviet origin and there is a special bridge-laying version on the T34 chassis. The OT-62 is a Czech version of the Soviet BTR-50(P) full-track APC.

Trailer, 40-ton, 24-wheeled, Transporter (P32) Wb 4.96 (BC 1.10) m, 9.47 × 3.10 × 1.42 m, 10,600 kg. Tyres 8.25–20. Resembled WWII US Army 'Rogers' trailer. Also heavier 40-wheeled 63-ton version (P50) with tandem bogie at front and three rows of wheels at rear. Towed by Tatra T141 or T813.

Truck, Bulldozer-Mounted, 8 × 8, BZ-T-813 (Tatra T813) V-12-cyl. diesel, 250 bhp, 5F1R × 2 × 2, wb 1.65 + 2.20 + 1.45 m. Hyd.-actuated dozer blade (2.50 × 0.85 m). Replaced full-track types, except on very soft ground (better road performance; higher speeds, especially when reversing). 1967. Shown with bridging pontoon body.

Vehicle, Universal, Engineers, 4 × 4 (DOK) Tatra T930-42 diesel engine at rear, driving generator which in turn powers electric motor in each of the four wheel hubs. Multi-purpose vehicle, equipped with dozer blade, shovel, hyd. lift, winch, etc. Enclosed cab at front. Steering by articulation.

Car, Armoured, 4×4 (Tatra T805) V-8-cyl., 75 bhp, 4F1R×2, wb 2.70 m. Pilot model on T805 truck chassis, produced *c.* 1960. Crew 2. Speed 90 km/h. Duplicate driving controls at rear (but steering only on front wheels). Air-cooled T603A 2545-cc petrol engine.

Carrier, Armoured, Personnel, 6×6 (Praga V3S) 6-cyl. diesel, 98 bhp, 4F1R×2, wb 4.14 (BC 1.12) m. Pilot model on V3S truck chassis, produced 1958. Track, front 1.87 m, rear 1.75 m. Tyres 8.25–20. Air brakes. Air-cooled in-line 7412-cc T912 engine (Tatra licence).

Carriage, Motor, AA Gun, 6×6, M53/59 (Praga V3S) 6-cyl. diesel (T912-2), 110 bhp, 4F1R×2, wb 4.14 (BC 1.12) m, 6.98×2.38×2.50 m, 9500 kg. Armoured bodywork and twin 30-mm AA guns on V3S chassis. Speed 55 km/h. Introduced 1959. Also on V3S chassis (unarmoured): 130-mm 32-round rocket launcher.

Carrier, Armoured, Personnel, 8×8, OT-64 (Tatra) V-8-cyl. diesel (T928), 192 bhp, 20F4R (semi-automatic), 7.45×2.50×2.30 m, 12,500 kg. Developed jointly with Poland. Known as SKOT (medium wheeled amphibious transporter). Engine behind driver's compartment. Amphibious (water propulsion by propellers).

Carrier, Personnel, Armoured, Semi-Track, OT-810 (Tatra) V-8-cyl. diesel (T928-3), 120 bhp, 4F1R × 2, wb (to centre of track) 2.89 m, 5.71 × 2.10 × 1.88 m, 7500 kg. Crew 12. Speed 55 km/h. Gradability 70%. Similar to German WWII *Sd. Kfz.* 251 except 11,752-cc air-cooled engine and detail mods. 1958.

Tractor, 8-ton, Semi-Track, Crane (Krauss-Maffei) Maybach 6-cyl., 140 bhp, 4F1R × 2. Ex-*Wehrmacht Sd.Kfz.7* type semi-track, with 6-ton manual revolving crane, used by Czech Air Force. Probably ex-*Sd.Kfz.7/1* (*Flak*) chassis. Crane similar to that of *Sd.Kfz.9/1.*

Tractor, 8-ton, Semi-Track, Cargo and Prime Mover (Tatra T809) V-8-cyl. diesel, 140 bhp, 4F1R × 2, 6.70 × 2.50 × 2.80 m, 10,450 kg. Produced 1955–57. Prototype (1953) was modified (V-12 engined) Tatra-built *sWS* (German *schwerer Wehrmachtsschlepper*). Track ground pressure 0.6 kg/cm². Speed 45 km/h.

Carrier, 3-ton, Full-Track, Amphibious (Tatra T807) Soviet V2 V-12-cyl. diesel, 340 bhp, wb (outer bogie wheels) 3.95 m, payload 3 tons or 24 men. Experimental transporter, produced about 1955. 38.9-litre tank engine. Speed on land 65 km/h, in water 11 km/h. Gradability 37°.

DENMARK

The Danish armed forces after 1945 re-equipped themselves with a large variety of WWII vehicles of American, British and Canadian origin. In addition some 1939 US Ford cars and trucks were used, as well as Swedish Volvo trucks which had initially been issued to Free Danish troops in Sweden, during the war. These Volvos were brought back after Denmark's liberation in 1945 and employed by the infantry until about 1960. Some of the other wartime vehicles were used until the 1960s when they were gradually phased out of service and replaced by more modern European trucks. Some were still in use, however, by 1971 (Bedford MW, Diamond T, etc.).

Since the demise of the Triangel, Denmark's automotive industry has been confined to some assembly plants (Ford, General Motors). Other truck chassis are imported and fitted with Danish military bodywork, a good example being the Dodge 'Power Wagon'. The Danish Nimbus motorcycle was in production until 1955 and had a four-cylinder in-line engine. Many were used for military service, as solo machines or with sidecar. AFVs (armoured fighting vehicles) have also been of various origins and have included American Chevrolet 'Staghound' armoured cars, M24 'Chaffee' and M42 'Walker Bulldog' light tanks, M4 Series 'Sherman' and M47 medium tanks, M10 tank destroyers, M109 155-mm howitzer SPs, M113 APCs (some modified and equipped with 'Green Archer' radar), M106 mortar carriers (purchased less original mortar and fitted with 81-mm type), British Humber scout cars (Mk I, II) and armoured cars (Mk IV), Centurion tanks (up-gunned to 105-mm in 1963) and ARVs, etc. Other armoured vehicles included US International and White half-tracks and M578 full-track recovery vehicles, British Universal carriers and Canadian GM C15TA armoured trucks. Dummy tanks (for training purposes) were based on light truck chassis and Universal carriers.

In June, 1972, GM International in Copenhagen commenced assembly of 250 Bedford M-type 4-ton 4 × 4 trucks, supplied in CKD form by Vauxhall Motors Ltd. They differed from the British parent vehicle (*qv*) in having a load-sensing device (for overloads), and a two-line air and trailer braking system, etc.

Improvised armoured car on Ford AA truck chassis, used by Danish Resistance Movement in 1945.

Wartime US half-track M3 APC with Danish Army detail modifications.

65

CARS, MOTORCYCLES and LIGHT TRUCKS

Makes and Models: *Cars:* Ford (American 'Fairlane', 'Mainline', etc; British 'Pilot' and 'Zephyr', from 1947). Humber 'Hawk', 'Super Snipe' (from 1949, GB). Mercury 79M (1947, US). Volvo 144, 164 (1969, S). Volkswagen 1200, 1300 (from 1954, D), etc.
Motorcycles: BSA (*c.* 1965, GB). Nimbus 4-cyl. (1937–55) (solo and w/SC).
Light Trucks (up to 1-ton): Bedford K (1-ton, 4 × 2, 1951–53, GB), A2 (1954), J2 (1958, 1-ton, 4 × 2, GB). Dodge 'Power Wagon' (1-ton, 4 × 4, *c.* 1960, US). Ford M151 ($\frac{1}{4}$-ton, 4 × 4, *c.* 1967, US). Land Rover 109 Series IIA ($\frac{3}{4}$-ton, 4 × 4, *c.* 1969, GB). Steyr-Puch 'Haflinger' (0.4-ton, 4 × 4, *c.* 1969, A). Volkswagen 'Transporter' (1-ton, 4 × 2, from *c.* 1956, D). Willys M38, CJ3B, M38A1 ($\frac{1}{4}$-ton, 4 × 4, from *c.* 1950, US).
World War II types: American Dodge T214, Ford GPW, Willys MB, etc.; British Austin 10HP Light Utility, Bedford MW Series, Fordson WOT2E, Guy Quad Ant, Morris-Commercial C8, etc.; Canadian Chevrolet C8A and C15, GM C15TA (armoured), etc.

General Data: The cars listed above were basically civilian types. Ford and Volkswagen were prominent. The Nimbus motorcycles were national products. Rugged and reliable, they were produced with only minor alterations from 1937 to 1955.

British Bedford 4 × 2 1-tonners of the K, A, and J Series were common as administrative vehicles. Of the A Series (A2) there was also an ambulance version.

The US Dodge 'Power Wagon' chassis was acquired with open and closed cab. The former were mainly of the cargo/personnel type whereas the closed cab chassis were used with house-type ambulance bodywork and as radio trucks.

British Land-Rovers were employed with general purpose and station wagon bodywork. The Volkswagen appeared with various bodystyles, incl. van, pickup, minibus (Combi), etc. The VW 181 is believed to be in use also. Steyr-Puch 'Haflingers' were taken into service by the Air Force in the Faroe Islands.

Some other vehicles which have been in military service, albeit in very small quantities, include 1939 Ford sedan (US), 1951 Opel Olympia 'Car-A-Van', Borgward $\frac{3}{4}$-ton 4 × 4, and Mercedes-Benz 'Unimog' S.

Vehicle shown (typical): Truck, 1-ton, 4 × 4, Cargo and Personnel, w/Winch (Dodge W300M 'Power Wagon')

Technical Data:
Engine: Dodge T137 6-cylinder, I-L-W-F, 3330 cc, 94 bhp @ 3200 rpm.
Transmission: 4F1R × 2.
Brakes: hydraulic.
Tyres: 9.00–16.
Wheelbase: 3.20 m. Track: 1.64 m.
Overall l × w × h: 5.30 × 2.05 × 2.10 m approx.
Weight: GVW 3946 kg.
Note: Military version US Dodge 'Power Wagon' chassis/cowl/windshield with Danish bodywork. Also with closed cab and house-type body (ambulance, radio). PTO-driven front-mounted winch of 7500 lb capacity.

TRUCKS, over 1-TON and TRACTORS

Makes and Models: Bedford OLB, A5, J5 (3-ton, 4 × 2, from 1951, GB), OSS, TK (tractors for S-T, 4 × 2, from 1953, GB), RLC, RLW (3-ton, 4 × 4, 1962, GB). Ford 'Thames Trader' (3-ton, 4 × 2, 1958, GB). Ford/Marmon-Herrington (tractor, 4 × 4, 1958, US). Fordson 'Thames' (3-ton, 4 × 2, c. 1952, GB). International 'M-Series' (5-ton, 6 × 6, c. 1960, US). Magirus-Deutz 178D15AL (7-ton, 6 × 6, c. 1968, D). Mercedes-Benz LA328/LA911 (3-ton, 4 × 4, 1962, D), 1413 (10-ton, 4 × 2, c. 1967, D), etc. Reo/Studebaker 'M-Series' (2½-ton, 6 × 6, c. 1960, US).

WWII types: American Diamond T 968/969, and 980, FWD SU-COE, GMC CCKW-352/353, Kenworth and Ward LaFrance M1 and M1A1 wreckers, White/Corbitt 666, etc.; British Bedford QL Series, Fordson WOT6, Guy 'Quad Ant' art. tractor, Karrier K6, Morris-Commercial C8 art. tractor, Scammell Breakdown and Tank Transporter, etc.; Canadian Chevrolet C60S, GM C60X, etc.; Swedish Volvo 2-ton 4 × 2.

General Data: In addition to WWII vehicles from Allied surplus stocks, quantities of British 'administrative' 4 × 2 trucks were acquired (Bedford, Fordson). The Bedford A5 and J5 were obtained with petrol and diesel engines. Bedford buses were also used. All had Danish bodywork. About 1962 replacement of wartime tactical vehicles commenced and new 4 × 4 and 6 × 6 trucks were acquired. These included Bedfords (4 × 4), Magirus-Deutz (6 × 6) and Mercedes-Benz (4 × 4), all fitted with a variety of body types. The Magirus-Deutz, for example, appeared as cargo truck, artillery tractor (with loading crane) and wrecker, the Mercedes-Benz as cargo and tractor truck.

American 'M-Series' trucks were used in conjunction with certain weapons systems (2½-ton 6 × 6 for 'Hawk', 5-ton 6 × 6 for 'Honest John' batteries). The Ford/M.-H. 4 × 4 tractor towed a teleprinter semi-trailer. The Navy used various commercial type trucks (Mercedes-Benz 1413 4 × 2, Dodge 4 × 2, etc.) and buses (Ford 'Transit' 15-str, Mercedes-Benz, etc.).

Vehicle shown (typical): Truck, 3-ton, 4 × 4, Cargo and Personnel (Bedford RLC5)

Technical Data:
Engine: Bedford 300 CID 6-cylinder, I-I-W-F, 4927 cc, 130 bhp @ 3200 rpm.
Transmission: 4F1R × 2.
Brakes: hydraulic, air-assisted.
Tyres: 11.00–20.
Wheelbase: 3.96 m. Track: 1.85 m.
Overall l × w × h: 6.50 × 2.40 × 3.00 m approx.
Weight: 4500 kg approx. GVW 8164 kg.
Note: Standard Danish military load carrier in NATO 3-ton class. US-pattern cargo body. British LHD chassis, supplied through GM International A/S, Copenhagen. Superseded by Bedford M-type (see page 65).

Truck, 3-ton, 4×4, Cargo and Personnel, w/Winch (Bedford RLW3) 6-cyl., 130 bhp, 4F1R×2. Basically as RLC5 but fitted with power-driven winch under rear body (fair leads front and rear). Danish steel cargo body, consisting of three sections. Note machine gun ring mount above cab roof hatch.

Truck, 3-ton, 4×4, Shop Van (Bedford RLC5) 6-cyl., 130 bhp, 4F1R×2, wb 3.96 m, 6.35×2.45×3.15 m approx. GVW 8164 kg. Used for workshop and similar roles, replacing wartime US GMC 6×6 shop vans. Danish bodywork. Cab top with forward-sloping windscreen (double, opening) was Danish modification.

Truck, 3-ton, 4×4, Cargo (Mercedes-Benz LA 328 (LA911B/42)) 6-cyl. diesel, 110 bhp, 5F1R×2, wb 4.20 m, 6.75×2.35×2.60 m approx. Tyres 8.25–20 (2DT). German chassis with dropside GS body. Used by Mobile Columns of *Civilforsvaret* (civil defence forces). Similar trucks used by Danish Army.

Truck, 7-ton, 6×6, Cargo, w/Winch (Magirus-Deutz M178D15AL) Deutz V-8-cyl. diesel (F8L 714), 178 bhp, 6F1R×2, wb 4.80 (BC 1.28) m, 8.05×2.50×2.80 m approx. GVW 15,150 kg. Fitted with Rotzler winch. Basically similar to German Army version but detail modifications (lighting equipment, etc.).

EGYPT

Until the late 1950s Egypt used mainly American, British and Canadian war-surplus vehicles, supplemented by new American and British 'pseudo-military' types. The latter included US Dodge/Fargo 'Power Wagons', FWD Model LD cargo trucks, Willys 'Universal Jeeps' (CJ3A, 3B). Britain supplied Ford 'Thames Trader' 4 × 4, Scammell 'Explorer' recovery vehicles, and Thornycroft 'Mighty Antar' tractors. From about 1960 most new vehicles have come from Communist countries, notably the USSR. Among these were the light GAZ-69 and UAZ-450 and various types of GAZ, ZIL and KRAZ 4 × 2, 4 × 4 and 6 × 6 cargo trucks, as well as Czech Praga and Tatra 6 × 6. There are also Soviet APCs (BTR-40, -152, etc.), tracked prime movers, and tracked AFVs.

German Magirus-Deutz and MB 'Unimog' trucks are used in Egypt also.

Truck, 2½-ton, 4 × 4, Chassis (FWD LD) Hercules QXLD 6-cyl., 97 bhp, 5F1R × 2, wb 116 in, 6560 lb (with 12-ft mil. cargo and personnel body 8660 lb). Tyres 10.00–20. Earlier models had different wings with built-in headlights. Many of these were used by the Egyptian Army during the 1950s.

Tractor, Medium Artillery, 4 × 4 (FWD) Egyptian bodywork on American FWD chassis. Patterned on wartime British 'Quad' artillery tractors. A similar chassis with completely open cab was used as an SP mount for light anti-aircraft gun. Note large single tyres all round.

Carrier, Armoured, Personnel, 4 × 4 (Walid) Deutz air-cooled diesel engine. Patterned on Soviet BTR-40 (which was also used). Egyptian-made hull. Also supplied to Algeria. Example shown in use by Israeli border police, fitted with armoured 'pathfinder seat' in front.

FINLAND

Finland (Suomen Tasavalta) is one of Europe's neutral countries and its armed forces have used vehicles of Western as well as Eastern origin, especially German and Soviet. Many if not most of their current military trucks, however, are products of the Finnish motor industry, notably Sisu and Vanaja. After 1945 many types of pre-1945 vehicles remained in service, including Russian trucks, armoured cars and tanks, German semi-tracks and AFVs, British tanks ('Charioteer', 'Comet'), etc. War-surplus US half-tracks with most of the armour plating removed, were employed as artillery tractors. Post-war AFVs were mainly of Soviet origin and included the medium tank, T54, the amphibious tank, PT 76, and the amphibious APC, BTR-50P. British Daimler 'Ferret' scout cars saw service with the Finnish UN forces. Sisu trucks have been produced since 1931 and the present range of models is very comprehensive. Vanaja truck production commenced in 1943. During the war these two firms jointly formed another company, Ytheissisu, for the production of military trucks for the Finnish Army. Of the original order of 2000 units, only about half were delivered but many of these were captured and used by the Russians. Most of the post-war Sisu and Vanaja trucks and buses were powered by British diesel engines (Leyland and AEC resp.).

Military vehicles carry registration plates with a number of up to four digits, prefixed by the letters SA.

Who's Who in the Finnish Automotive Industry
Sisu   Oy Suomen Autoteollisuus AB, Helsinki.
Valmet Valmet Oy, Tampere.
Vanaja Vanajan Autotehdas Oy, Hämeenlinna.

Modified US half-tracks serving as artillery prime movers in Finnish Army.

Modern Finnish articulated-steer tractor.

CARS, TRUCKS and TRACTORS

Makes and Models: *Cars and Field Cars:* Various, commercial, 4 × 2, and GAZ-69A 4 × 4 (SU) and Land-Rover 4 × 4 (various types, GB).
Trucks: Fordson ET6 'Thames' (3-ton, 4 × 2, *c.* 1952, GB). GAZ-69 (½-ton, 4 × 4, SU). Magirus-Deutz 'Mercur' (5-ton, 4 × 4, D). Mercedes-Benz 'Unimog' (1-ton, 4 × 4, D), 'Unimog' S404 (1½-ton, 4 × 4, D). Sisu KB-48 (1½-ton, 4 × 4, 1959), KB-45 (3-ton, 4 × 4, 1965), KB-46 (4-ton, 6 × 6, 1969), K-137 (7-ton, 4 × 4, 1962). Vanaja A2-47/4300 (7-ton, 4 × 2, 1962), N2-47/4300 (7-ton, 4 × 4, 1962). ZIL-157K (2½-ton, 6 × 6, SU).
Tractors: AT-S (full-track, SU). Bolinder-Munktell (Volvo) BV202 (four-track, articulated, S). Valmet 70 HP (4 × 2 with 2-ton powered-axle trailer). Valmet Terra 865 BM (4 × 4, articulated, 1969) (early models: 4-363D). White M2/M3 (modified) (half-track, WWII, US).

General Data: In addition to the above vehicles, many types from World War II and earlier were in use for many years. Among them were German and Soviet trucks, half-tracks and tractors. The Sisu 3-ton 4 × 4 Model KB-45 tactical military truck was introduced in 1965 and a 4-ton 6 × 6, Model KB-46, followed in 1968/69. An interesting feature of these trucks is that they may be equipped with a hydraulic system to drive the wheels of trailers and guns coupled behind them. This hydromechanical transmission system, employing an engine-driven pump and hydraulic hub motors in the trailer wheels was developed to a high degree of sophistication and is also used for agricultural, forestry and industrial applications. Valmet, in addition to their articulated-steer 'Valmet Terra', developed power-driven trailers for use in conjunction with their agricultural and industrial tractors. The drive to the trailer axle is transmitted through a flexible shaft. In the Finnish Army such 6 × 6 combinations served to carry ammunition and tow light artillery, heavy mortars, etc.

Vehicle shown (typical): Truck, 3-ton, 4 × 4, Cargo and Personnel, w/Winch (Sisu KB-45)

Technical Data:
Engine: Leyland 0.400 diesel 6-cylinder, I-I-W-C, 6540 cc, 135 bhp @ 2400 rpm (with optional turbocharger: 160 bhp).
Transmission: 5F1R × 2 (OD top).
Brakes: air/hydraulic.
Tyres: 14.50–20.
Wheelbase: 3.40 m. Track: 1.85 m.
Overall l × w × h: 5.70 × 2.30 × 2.44 (1.75) m.
Weight: 5200 kg. GVW: 8600 kg.
Note: Engine behind cab. 6½-ton horizontal-spindle drum winch on RH side of chassis. Planetary reduction gears in wheel hubs. Removable cab top. Hinged windscreen and door windows. Height with tilt 2.80 m.

Truck, 3-ton, 4 × 4, Cargo and Personnel, w/Winch (Sisu KB-45) Sisu 'two-in-one' combination, consisting of KB-45 truck and howitzer with hydro-mechanical drive. Hydraulic hub motors have cam rings attached to wheel and radially-operating pistons on axle.

Truck, 3-ton, 4 × 4, Fire Fighting (Sisu KB-45) Fully-enclosed bodywork on slightly modified KB-45 chassis/cab. Produced in 1968. There was also a smaller airfield fire crash tender, the Halle-Sisu, on the lighter KB-48 4 × 4 chassis.

Truck, 7-ton, 4 × 2, Cargo (Vanaja A2-47/4300) AEC AVU-470 6-cyl. diesel, 144 bhp, 5F1R, wb 4.30 m, chassis/cab: 6.67 × 2.40 × 2.43 m, 4690 kg. GVW 12½ tons. Tyres 10.00–20. Shown during Finnish Army tests. From 1955, most Vanaja trucks and buses were fitted with British AEC diesel engines.

Truck, 7-ton, 4 × 4, Cargo (Kontio-Sisu K-137) Cummins V6-140/BD V-6-cyl. diesel, 140 bhp, 5F1R × 2, wb 4.30 m, chassis/cab: 6.65 × 2.30 × 2.65 m, 4900 kg. GVW 14 tons. Tyres 10.00–20. Planetary gears in front wheel hubs. ZF power steering. Commercial version shown (1965). Derived from 4 × 2 model K-138.

Truck, 4-ton, 6 × 6, Prime Mover (Sisu KB-46) Leyland 6-cyl. diesel, 165 bhp, 5F1R × 2. Weight 8650 kg. Towing capacity 5 to 7 tons (10 tons if equipped with hydromechanical trailer power transmission). All-enclosed tilt-cab. Fixed crew cab. Introduced in 1969.

Truck, 4-ton, 6 × 6, Prime Mover (Sisu KB-46) The KB-46 tactical truck, employed as an artillery tractor and shown here with a heavy 122-mm field gun, m/60 (Tampella). The Soviet AT-S full-track was also used to tow this gun.

Tractor/Carrier, 3-ton, 4 × 4, Articulated, w/Winch (Valmet 4-363D) Amphibious cross-country vehicle, steered by articulation. No road springs. Used to carry personnel and supplies and tow artillery pieces over difficult terrain and snow. Load 3 tons and 8 men or 22 men. Early model.

Tractor/Carrier, 3-ton, 4 × 4, Articulated, w/Winch (Valmet Terra 865BM) 4-cyl. diesel, 90 bhp, 8F2R, wb 3.27 m, 7.06 × 2.37 × 2.55 m, 6250 kg. Tyres 18.40–26. Road speed 32 km/h. Gradability 60%. Turning circle 10.6 m. Power steering. Disc air brakes. 6-ton winch. 4180-cc engine. Rear diff. lock.

FRANCE

The French forces at the end of World War II employed a wide variety of motor vehicles of very diverse types and origins. There were French vehicles of pre-war and wartime manufacture and Allied vehicles of American, British and Canadian origin. Many of the latter had originally been supplied to the Free French Forces. Some Japanese types, found in Indo-China, were also used. After the French motor industry re-started in 1945, relatively small quantities of new commercial vehicles were acquired and added to these were many new German vehicles for the French occupation forces in Germany (FFA).

It was soon decided to standardize on American equipment, and large numbers of 'Jeeps', Dodges, GMCs, Macks, Whites and other tactical types were taken into service. These vehicles remained in use for many years and new French developments were often based on the same basic specifications.

The war in Indo-China (1946), the Algerian conflict (1954), the availability of US equipment under the US Military Aid Program (Marshall Plan) and other causes delayed many of the new developments and it was not until the 1960s that large-scale replacement by French vehicles took place. This new generation of vehicles was designed in accordance with standard NATO requirements. There were, in addition, many other interesting vehicle types, designed for overseas use, export and special purposes. The French Air Force, in particular, operated several types of unusual and unique vehicles. Among outstanding examples of French ingenuity were the AML and EBR armoured cars and the AMX-13 and -30 tanks.

Several French manufacturers produced cross-country vehicles for possible military use, such as the George Irat VDB, designed by Emile Petit (with Dyna-Panhard engine) which appeared in several versions (1951–53) and more recently the 'Bison' designed by M. Bouffort. There were also some commercial field cars such as the Cournil (with Indenor diesel engine), the Hotchkiss-Willys JH101/102, the Renault 'Savane' *Tous*

Terrains, etc. In 1966 it was decided to develop a new military $\frac{1}{2}$-ton 4×4 (often referred to as 'NATO-Jeep'), jointly with Germany and Italy, and two international consortiums were formed (Saviem-MAN/Glas-Fiat and Hotchkiss-Büssing-Lancia), for its design and development.

In recent years when export of specialized vehicles became more important, much of the secrecy surrounding military vehicles was lifted and this was exemplified in 1967 and later years by impressive exhibitions of all kinds of military equipment at Satory, organised by the DTAT (*Direction Technique des Armaments Terrestres*).

Of the vehicles shown and/or listed in the following pages, not all saw service with the French forces; several were built as prototypes only or exported to other countries.

Who's Who in the French Automotive Industry

Note: many mergers have taken place between French manufacturers, especially during the 1950s and 1960s and several makes have now disappeared.

ALM (Atlantic)	Ateliers de Construction Mécanique de l'Atlantique, Saint-Nazaire (formerly Ateliers Legueu Meaux (ALM), Meaux).
Berliet	Automobiles M. Berliet, Courbevoie (also in Bourg, Lyon, Venissieux).
Chausson	S.A. des Usines Chausson, Asnières (later part of Saviem, *qv*).
Citroën	S.A. André Citroën, Paris.
Continental	Richard Continental, Villeurbanne.
Delahaye	Sté des Automobiles Delahaye, Paris (later Sté Hotchkiss-Delahaye, Saint-Denis; now discontinued).
Ford	S.A. Ford Française (S.A.F.), Poissy (later Poissy Division of Simca).
Griffet	Ets M. Griffet, Marseille.

FRANCE

Hotchkiss (-Willys)	Compagnie Française Thomson Houston-Hotchkiss Brandt, Departement Automobiles (formerly Sté Hotchkiss-Delahaye), Saint-Denis.
Isobloc	Sté Isobloc (SACA), Annonay, Ardeche (later part of Saviem, *qv*).
Labourier	Ets Labourier, Mouchard, Jura.
Latil	Compagnie des Automobiles Industrielles Latil, Suresnes (later part of Saviem, *qv*).
Marmon-Bocquet	S.A. Marmon-Bocquet, Villiers-le-Bel.
Marmon-Herrington	Marmon-Herrington S.A.F., Villiers-le-Bel (later Marmon-Bocquet, *qv*).
Matenin	Ets Matenin, Paris.
Panhard	Sté de Constructions Mécaniques Panhard & Levassor, Paris.
Peugeot	S.A. des Automobiles Peugeot, Paris.
Renault	cars, light vans: RNU Renault, Boulogne; trucks: (see Saviem).
Saurer	Automobiles Industriels Saurer, Suresnes (until 1954).
Saviem	SAVIEM (S.A. de Véhicules Industriels et d'Équipements Mécaniques), Suresnes. (Note: formed in 1955 by merging Somua, Latil and truck and bus division of Renault (LRS); joined by Floirat and Isobloc in 1956 and Chausson in 1960).
SFAC	Sté des Forges et Ateliers du Creusot, Paris.
Simca (-Marmon)	(see Unic).
Sinpar	Appareils Sinpar S.A., Colombes.
Unic	FFSA, Division Camions Unic, Suresnes (Note: after absorbing Saurer in 1955, Unic became part of Simca Industries in 1960).
Willème	Camions Willème S.A., Nanterre.

Berliet GBO 15P was used for military and civilian purposes.

Poissy-built Ford/M.-H. truck in Indo-China, *c.* 1946.

Line-up of typical French Army vehicles in the late 1960s.

CARS, FIELD CARS and MOTORCYCLES

Makes and Models: *Cars:* Various comm., 4 × 2, incl. Citroën (2CV, ID, DS), Mercedes-Benz, Opel, Peugeot, (203, 204, 403), Renault (R4), etc.
WWII types: Austin 8HP/AP (GB), Ford 1GA-73B (US), Plymouth P11 (US), etc.
Field Cars: Auto Union 'Munga' (4 × 4, 1956, D). Citroën 2CV 'Sahara' (4 × 4, 1958). Creusot-Loire VB100 'Bison' (4 × 4, 1967). Delahaye VLR1 (4 × 4, 1950), VLR, VLR-C12 (4 × 4, 1952). Georges Irat VDB (*Voiture du Bled*) (4 × 2, 1951). Hotchkiss/Willys M201 (4 × 4, 1953). Latil M17T1 (4 × 4, 1952). Peugeot 203R (4 × 4, 1950), 203RA (4 × 4, 1951), 403RB (4 × 4, 1955). Renault R2087 (4 × 4, 1953). Renault/Sinpar R4 (4 × 4, 1964).
WWII types: Dodge T214-WC53, 56, 57, 58 (4 × 4, US), Ford/Willys 'Jeep' (4 × 4, US).
Motorcycles and Scooters: Various comm., 2 × 1, incl. ACMA (Vespa TAP), BMW (R25, R27, R51, D), Gnome et Rhone (LX200), Peugeot (176 RC4), Terrot (HCT, RGST), etc.
WWII types: BSA M20 (GB), Cushman 53 (US), Harley-Davidson WLA, WLC (US), Indian 741 B, C (US), Norton 16H, 633 (3 × 2) (GB), Royal Enfield WD/CO (GB).

General Data: After the end of the war the French forces used a multitude of cars and motorcycles of various origins and including many pre-war types. The American 'Jeep' and Dodge Command vehicles became standard in their class and featured prominently. In fact, after a relatively brief production span the more sophisticated Delahaye VLR was dropped again in favour of the standard US 'Jeep', some 40,000 of which were then produced under Willys licence by Hotchkiss (1953 to 1969) with practically all parts interchangeable with the wartime original. The Hotchkiss version was also exported to several African nations. Like the British 'Champ', the Delahaye VLR was rather complex in design for a general purpose vehicle. The Peugeot 203 R(A), a private venture, seemed a much better proposition, especially from the economic point of view, but although it was offered to the Army, the Delahaye was accepted for series production. Several French companies produced cross-country vehicles for possible military use, such as the George Irat VDB (see page 74).

Vehicle shown (typical): Field Car, 4-seater, 4 × 4 (Delahaye VLR or VLRD) (*Véhicule Léger, Rapide* or *Voiture Légère de Reconnaissance* or *Voiture de Liaison et de Reconnaissance, Delahaye*.

Technical Data:
Engine: Delahaye 4-cylinder, I-I-W-F, 1992 cc, 63 bhp @ 3600–3800 rpm.
Transmission: 4F1R × 2.
Brakes: hydraulic.
Tyres: 7.00–16.
Wheelbase: 2.15 m.
Overall l × w × h: 3.46 × 1.57 × 1.85 (1.46) m.
Weight: 1400 kg.   Payload: 450–500 kg.
Notes: 'Dry sump' engine lubrication system with separate 9-litre oil reservoir. Early model shown (1951/52). 24-volt electrics.

Field Car, 4-seater, 4 × 4 (Delahaye VLR 1950) 4-cyl., 63 bhp, 4F1R × 2. Pilot model (1949/50) for French replacement for the US 'Jeep'. Independent suspension with torsion bars and trailing arms (similar to VW). Single-piece windscreen. Rear-hinged bonnet. (Photo ECA.)

Field Car, 4-seater, 4 × 4 (Delahaye VLR-C12) 4-cyl., 63 bhp, 4F1R × 2, wb 2.15 m, 3.46 × 1.57 × 1.86 (1.40) m, 1350 kg. Late model (1953–55) with exposed headlights. 12-volt electrics (Model VLR: 24-volt). Shown with non-original front towing attachments. Front-hinged bonnet.

Field Car, 4-seater, 4 × 4 (Peugeot 203RA 8CV) 4-cyl., 64 bhp, 4F1R × 2, wb 2.05 m, 3.40 × 1.62 × 1.75 m, 1136 kg. Tyres 7.00–16. Two produced in 1951. Model 203R (7CV), of which two were built in 1950, was similar except: 48.5-bhp engine, 6.00–16 tyres, weight 1014 kg.

Field Car, 4-seater, 4 × 4 (Peugeot VSP 403RB 8CV) 4-cyl., 64 bhp, 4F1R × 2, wb 2.10 m, 3.45 × 1.64 × 1.75 m, 1136 kg. Tyres 7.00–16. Twelve produced in 1955. Model 403-8 1468-cc (80 × 73 mm) engine. Rigid axles with semi-elliptic leaf springs. OD gearbox. Known as 'VSP' (*Véhicule Spéciale Peugeot*).

Field Car, 4-seater, 4×4 (Hotchkiss M201 VLTT) 4-cyl., 60 bhp, 3F1R × 2, wb 2.03 m, 3.36 × 1.58 × 1.77 (1.30) m, 1120 kg. Resembled WWII Willys MB except minor details (electrics, carburettor, wheels, etc.). Also with reinforced suspension and desert equipment. VLTT = *Véhicule de Liaison Tout Terrain*. Produced under Willys licence, 1953–69.

Field Car, Guided Missile Launcher, 4×4 (Hotchkiss M201/ENTAC) Standard M201 'Jeep' (Hotchkiss/Willys) as anti-tank missile launcher (four in firing position, three in reserve). Hotchkiss also produced Willys CJ3B but with SV engine or diesel (JH-101 1955–60, JH-102 from 1961, and HWL LWB version).

Field Car, Weapon Carrier, 4×4 (Hotchkiss M201/DTAT) Standard M201, modified for mounting 20-mm gun, M621. Gunner may be on vehicle or beside it, permitting various types of missions (close defence, ambush, AA). Gun elevation −5° to +50°. M201 also appeared with recoilless rifle.

Field Car, 4-seater, 4×4 (Renault/Sinpar R4 4×4) 4-cyl., 26 bhp, 4F1R, wb L/R 2.44/2.40 m, 3.66 × 1.48 × 1.55 m, 650 kg approx. PTO for rear wheel drive at front of (front-mounted) gearbox. Gradability 45%. Speed 110 km/h. Conversion of R4 Van, used by Air Force and Constabulary. Also 4-door *Berline*.

Field Car, 4-seater, 4 × 4 (Citroën 2CV 4 × 4 'Sahara')
Two twin-cyl. 14-bhp engines, 2 × 4F1R, wb 2.40 m, 3.78 ×
1.48 × 1.60 m, 735 kg.   Developed from normal 2CV car,
especially for desert use.   Could be used with either or both
engines driving. Power units not inter-connected. 155 × 400X
tyres. Gradability 45%. Road speed 100 km/h.

**Scooter, Motor, 2-wheel, Airborne (ACMA/Vespa TAP
56, 59)** Single-cyl., 5.5 bhp, 3F, wb 1.20 m, 1.70 × 0.70 × 1.05
m, 90 kg (dim. and weight for basic model). Fitted with recoilless
rifle, used by paratroops. 146.6-cc two-stroke engine at right-
hand side adjacent to rear wheel. Tyres 3.50–8. From 1957.

**Field Car, Airborne, 7-seater, 4 × 4 (Creusot-Loire VB 100
'Bison')** Chabay 90-bhp engine, 4.09 × 1.79 × 1.40 m, 2240 kg.
Speed 90 km/h. Amphibious *Véhicule de Servitude*, designed by
M. Bouffort. Prototypes by Batignolles-Chatillon (*c.* 1964),
later by SFAC (1967). Roles: command car, tractor, ambulance,
guided missile launcher, etc.

Field Car, 4 × 4, Command (Renault R2087) 4-cyl., 54 bhp,
4F1R × 2, wb 2.31 m, 4.80 × 1.95 × 2.45 m approx. Prototype
with special soft-top command car bodywork on standard ¾-ton
4 × 4 chassis. 9.00–16 tyres. 2141-cc (88 × 88 mm) OHV engine
at front, large locker at rear. Also tested by Netherlands Army.

AMBULANCES
4 × 2 and 4 × 4

War-surplus ambulances used by the French forces included the British Austin K2 and large numbers of the US Dodge T214-WC54/64. In Germany various types of Opels were used (based on 'Rekord Car-A-Van' and 'Blitz' 4 × 2 truck chassis). The majority of French military ambulances, however, were of Renault and later Saviem manufacture, notably the 4 × 2 Renault 206E1 (1945), R2065 'Voltigeur' (1957), R2066 (1956), R2086 'Goélette' (1956), and the four-wheel drive models R2067, R2069 (1956), R2087 (1958), SG2 (1966) and TP3 (1969). They could carry from two to six stretchers. In addition there were other 4 × 2 models such as the Citroën H (1966/67), ID (1967) and Peugeot 203 and 403 (two stretchers) and the bus-type Isobloc *Autocar Sanitaire* W843M (1945). The latter had a Ford V8 engine at rear and accommodated 30 patients.

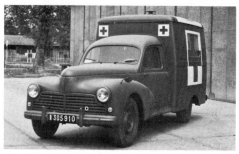

Ambulance, Light, 4 × 2 (Peugeot 203C8(S)-S3P) 4-cyl., 42 bhp, 4F1R, wb 2.78 m, 4.70 × 1.76 × 2.05 m, 1395 kg. GVW 1890 kg. Basically commercial type, with two stretchers, first introduced in 1949 as 203U8-S3. Discontinued in 1957. Tyre size 17 × 400. OD gearbox. Speed 90 km/h.

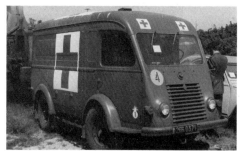

Ambulance, Medium, 4 × 2 (Renault R2065 'Voltigeur') 4-cyl., 54 bhp, 4F1R, wb 2.31 m, 4.56 × 1.93 × 2.35 m, 1850 kg approx. *'Véhicule Sanitaire Routier'* or *'Ambulance Moyenne'*. Also 4 × 4 versions (R2067, R2087). Normally carried four **stretchers**. Model 206E1 similar but headlamps not built-in.

Ambulance, Medium, 4 × 4 (Saviem/Renault TP3) 4-cyl., 78 bhp, 4F1R × 2, wb 2.64 m. Tyres 9.00–16. Six stretchers and two sitting cases or 12 sitting cases. 2.6-litre engine. Speed 95 km/h. Gradability 50%. SG2 basically similar but 65-bhp engine. Also control room version for *Gendarmerie*.

BUSES

Most buses and coaches used by the French armed forces were basically commercial models with slight modifications to meet military requirements. The Army used three categories, viz. *Autocars* with 7–19 seats, 20–39 seats and 40 and more seats. Some typical examples are shown. Small types included 10- to 15-pass. Citroën HY and 13-pass. Renault R2066 and R2086(S). Medium types were mainly Renault 'Galion' (23-pass. R2165 and R2168). Heavy types (40-pass. or more) included Berliet PHC 'Escapade' (1961), Chausson APE (1947) and AH521/522, Renault R2191, Saviem-Chausson APH and Saviem S45 (1966). In Germany use was made of Opel 'Blitz'-based 17-pass. models, rebodied GMC/Henschel CCKW-353 6 × 6 trucks, Volkswagen 'Transporters', Mercedes-Benz O3500, O4500, O321 H(U), etc.

Bus, 23-passenger, 4 × 2 (Renault 'Galion' R2168) 4-cyl., 56 bhp, wb 3.24 m. GVW 5500 kg. Special coachwork on commercial chassis with 2141-cc (88 × 88 mm) engine. 7.00–20 tyres on cast-steel spoke wheels with detachable rims. Also available with diesel engine. 1957.

Bus, 26-passenger, 6 × 6 (GMC CCKW-353, modified) Many wartime GMC 2½-ton 6 × 6 chassis were fitted with bus bodies, notably in Germany for the French and US forces. Some had modified front end, others partly (shown) or standard original pattern.

Bus, 45-passenger, 4 × 2 (Berliet PHC 'Escapade') 5-cyl. diesel, 150 bhp, 5F1R, wb 5.04 m, 9.68 × 2.50 × 2.95 m, 8100 kg. Three side doors. 7.9-litre (120 × 140 mm) *Magic* engine, mounted under floor. Single rear tyres. Power-assisted steering. Introduced in 1961.

TRUCKS, ¼- to 1¾-TON 4 × 2

Most vehicles in this class were and are commercial models with minor changes to meet military requirements and usually with special military bodywork (general or special purposes). Chassis/cabs or complete panel vans were supplied mainly by Citroën, Peugeot and Renault/Saviem. Principal models were the Citroën 2CV-AZU (van, from 1954) and forward-control H and 1000 Series (vans and pickups), Peugeot 203, 403 and 404 Series (various body types), Renault R2102 'Fourgonnette' (0.3-ton), R2130 'Estafette' (0.6-ton), R2065/2066/2086 ('Voltigeur', 'Goélette', 1- to 1.4-ton), Saviem/Renault SG2 (1¾-ton), etc. Foreign models have included British Bedford, Fordson and Morris-Commercial and Canadian Chevrolet, Dodge and Ford (all WWII ¾-ton types) and post-war Volkswagen and Opel 'Blitz' (FFA, Germany).

Truck, 1.4-ton, 4 × 2, Cargo (Renault R2086 'Goélette') 4-cyl., 56 bhp, 4F1R, wb 2.31 m, 4.73 × 1.98 × 2.48 m, 1765 kg. Shown as *Camionette 1400 kgs* with lengthwise bench seats for 10 in rear. Also supplied as steel-panelled van, 13-pass. bus and ambulance. 2141-cc engine. 7.50–16 tyres.

Truck, 1.4-ton, 4 × 2, Air Traffic Control 'Starter' (Renault R2086S 'Goélette') 4-cyl., 56 bhp, 4F1R, wb 2.31 m, 4.81 × 2.01 × 2.53 m. Also on 4 × 4 chassis (R2087). Body by Carrier. Painted black and yellow squares. Green plexiglass roof panels. Fitted with radio transmitter and other equipment. Air Force.

Truck, 1¾-ton, 4 × 2, Cargo (Saviem-Renault SG2) 4-cyl., 65 bhp, wb 2.68 m, chassis/cab 5.47 × 2.00 × 2.17 m. Military 'Super Goélette', 1967. Independent front suspension. GVW 3500 kg. Troop seats in rear. Speed 91 km/h. Used by Army and other military branches. Available in two lengths.

TRUCKS, ½- to 2-TON 4 × 4

Makes and Models: ALM/Atlantic TF4-10R, TF4-20-SM/SMT (2- to 2½-ton, from 1963). Citroën/Herwaythorn U23R (1¼-ton, 1956). Citroën/Sinpar U23R (1¼-ton, 1957). Dodge 'Power Wagon' (1-ton, *c.* 1950, US). Ford SAF/Marmon-Herrington (1½-ton, 1946). Hotchkiss (¾-ton, 1952). Hotchkiss/Herwaythorn PL25-HWT (1.4-ton, 1956). Latil M17T1 (1950), M18T2 (1¼-ton, 1956). Marmon-Herrington FF4 (¾-ton, 1952). Marmon-Herrington MH600B and BP (1½-ton, from 1957). Mercedes-Benz 'Unimog' 411 and S404 (1- and 1½-ton, D). Renault R2067, R2087 *Tous Terrains* (¾-ton, 1957). Renault/Herwaythorn R2060 (¾-ton), R2092/3 (½-ton, 1951). Renault/Sinpar R2167/2240 (1½-ton, 1958/59). Saviem-Renault SG2 *Tous Terrains* (1-ton, 1966), TP3L39 (1¼-ton, 1969). Saviem-Renault/Sinpar SG4 (1½-ton, 1968). Simca-Marmon (SUMB) MH600 BS (1½-ton, 1962). Sinpar 4 × 4 (Ford engine, 1962).

WWII types: American Dodge T214 (WC51, 52) ¾-ton, Chevrolet G7100 and Ford/MH 09W 1½-ton; Canadian Chevrolet C15A and C30, Ford F15A and F30 ¾-ton and 1½-ton.

General Data: For many years various models of the American Dodge ¾-ton 4 × 4 range were used. They were gradually superseded by 4 × 4 versions of contemporary forward-control Renault trucks and others. The Simca-Marmon MH600BS design was initiated by M. Bocquet, president of Marmon-Herrington SAF (which later became Marmon-Bocquet) who was also Simca-Vedette distributor at Saint-Ouen. It was eventually put into series production by the Unic division of Simca Industries after lengthy tests, and replaced various types including the wartime Dodge 1½-ton 6 × 6. Some of the types listed above were essentially commercial vehicles, sometimes modified in minor detail to meet French or foreign military requirements.

Vehicle shown (typical): Truck, 1½-ton, 4 × 4, Cargo (Simca-Unic-Marmon-Bocquet MH600BS) (*Camionette 4 × 4, 1.5 t*)

Technical Data:

Engine: Ford/Simca 324.04 type F7CWM 8-cylinder, V-L-W-F, 4184 cc, 100 bhp @ 3200 rpm.

Transmission: 4F1R × 2. Rear diff. lock.

Brakes: hydraulic, air-assisted.

Tyres: 10.00–20.

Wheelbase: 2.90 m.

Overall l × w × h: 5.10 × 2.10 × 2.84 (1.94) m.

Weight: 3550 kg. GVW: 5370 kg.

Notes: Series production from 1964 by FFSA-Camions Unic. Usually referred to as 'Simca-Marmon'. Elevated rigid axles with 18/34 final reduction. Coil spring suspension.

Truck, ¾-ton, 4 × 4, Cargo, w/Winch (Hotchkiss) Produced experimentally (one unit) in 1952/53 as a possible replacement for the American WWII Dodge Weapons Carrier (T214-WC52), which it resembled in general design. (Photo ECA).

Truck, 1¼-ton, 4 × 4, Cargo (Latil M18T2) Hotchkiss 6-cyl., 95 bhp, 4F1R × 2, wb 3.00 m, 4.96 × 2.00 m, 3500 kg. IFS and IRS with coil springs. Lockable diffs. Later known as Latil-Hotchkiss and Saviem-Latil. Limited production for Air Force (chassis for special purposes).

Truck, 1½-ton, 4 × 4, Cargo (Marmon-Herrington MH600B) Simca F6CW V-8-cyl., 85 bhp, 4F1R × 2, wb 2.90 m, 5.00 × 2.10 × 2.60 (1.95) m, 3500 kg. Exp. model, produced in 1957/58. Bodywork by Société Fernand Genève. 3923-cc engine (B × S 80.97 × 95.23 mm). Also civilian versions.

Truck, 1½-ton, 4 × 4, Cargo (Marmon-Herrington MH600BP) Panhard 4HDS 4-cyl., 90 bhp, 4F1R × 2, wb 2.90 m, 5.02 × 2.10 × 2.60 (1.94) m, 3090 kg. Similar to MH600BS but air-cooled HO 1996-cc (85 × 88 mm) engine. Tyres 10.00–20. Also available commercially. 1960–62.

Truck, 2-ton, 4×4, Cargo, VCOM/VLRA (ALM TF4-20-SM) Ford 589E 6-cyl., 125 bhp, 4F1R×2, wb 3.60 m, 5.96 × 2.07 × 2.60 (1.83) m, 4330 kg. Lockable diff. in transfer. Also w/Winch (TF4-20-SMT) and as missile launcher. Air-transportable (Nord Atlas 2501). TF4-10R was similar (for Chad *gendarmerie*).

Truck, ¾-ton, 4×4, Cargo/Radio (Renault R2087) 4-cyl., 54 bhp, 4F1R×2, wb 2.31 m, 4.81 × 1.99 × 2.40 m, 2300 kg. Signals container-type body under canvas tarpaulin. Winch, if fitted, below front bumper. Tyres 9.00–16. Developed from 'Goélette' R2086 4×2. Also supplied to Belgium.

Truck, 1½-ton, 4×4, Cargo (Renault/Sinpar R2167) 4-cyl., 56 bhp, 4F1R×2, wb 2.58 m, 5.18 × 1.98 × 2.60 m, 2200 kg (chassis/cab). GVW 5500 kg. *Special Brousse* conversion of Renault 'Galion' truck by Appareils Sinpar of Colombes. Available with tropical equipment, etc.

Truck, 1¼-ton, 4×4, Cargo (Saviem-Renault TP3L39) 4-cyl., 78 bhp, 4F1R×2, wb 2.64 m, 5.00 × 2.00 × 2.51 m, GVW 3900 kg. Tyres 9.00–16. Dropside 3-metre body with folding troop seats. Max. speed 90 km/h. Gradability 50%. Military version of commercial truck. 2/3-seater cab (*cabine torpédo*). 1971.

TRUCKS, 2- to 12-TON
4 × 2

Makes and Models: Berliet VDC22F (5-ton), GDR 28F (6-ton, 1945), GDR7D (7-ton, 1946), GLR8 A, B, R 'Saharien' (7-ton, 1956), GLC28 (7-ton, 1962), etc. Citroën T23 (2-ton, 1950), 45U (3½-ton, 1945), 55U (5-ton, 1955), 55E (5-ton, 1959), 60E (5-ton, 1964), 350 (3½-ton, 1971), etc. Ford 'Rhein' G398TS3, G618TS3 (3-ton, from 1943, D). Ford F798 WM (5-ton, 1947). Henschel HS140S (tractor, 12-ton, D). Mercedes-Benz L3500, L4500S, L5000, L325-46, etc. (from 3½-ton, D). Panhard K155 (5-ton, 1947). Renault AHS2 (2-ton, 1945), AHN2 (3½-ton, 1945), R2164, R2167, etc. Saviem-LRS-Renault R4153, R4154 DEFA (7½-ton, 1957) and R2185 DEFA (tractor, 10-ton, 1961). Saviem S6 (5-ton), S9 (9-ton, 1967), JL29 (10-ton 1965), JM200TEP (tractor, 12-ton, 1965), SM 170T (tractor, 12-ton, 1970), etc. Simca-Unic (formerly Ford) F569WML (5-ton, 1956). Unic ZU55ML (5½-ton, 1945). Willème L10 (12-ton, 1945), L10N (12-ton, 1950) and LD610N (10-ton, 1956).
WWII types: American International H542-11 (5-ton, tractor), British Bedford OY and Commer Q4; Canadian Dodge D60L (all 3-ton), etc.

General Data: For some time after 1945 the French Army used several types of trucks in this category which were produced before 1940, such as Citroëns (3½-ton 45U and S), Renaults (3½-ton ADR, 4½-ton AGR, 6-ton AGK), Panhards (5-ton K125), Rochet-Schneiders (5-ton S420VL) and Saurers (7-ton 3CTID). There also were some Fiat water tankers, probably ex-Italian Army. Most trucks in this class were basically commercial types with relatively small modifications to meet military requirements. Some were fitted with special bodywork or equipment. The Ford 'Rhein' G398TS3 was a wartime German truck which was continued in production after 1945 for civilian and military purposes. The French Ford plant at Poissy produced a similar model (originally for the German forces) and a small number of these saw service with the French Navy.

Vehicle shown (typical): Truck, 7-ton, 4 × 2, Cargo (Saviem-LRS-Renault R4153 DEFA) (*Camion Renault Type R4153 Modèle DEFA*)

Technical Data:
Engine: Saviem 572 diesel, 6-cylinder, I-I-W-C, 6230 cc, 115 bhp @ 2300 rpm.
Transmission: 5F1R.
Brakes: hydraulic with air servo.
Tyres: 5.20–20.
Wheelbase: 3.64 m.
Overall l × w × h: 6.84 × 2.47 × 2.96 m.
Weight: 6000 kg. GVW: 13,000 kg.
Notes: Military version of commercial R4153 with horizontal underfloor engine, behind cab. Soft-top cab, seating three. Trailer air brake connections, front and rear. Produced in 1957. Also LWB version.

Truck, 3½-ton, 4×2, Signals (Citroën 45U/T45) 6-cyl., 73 bhp, 4F1R, wb 3.60 m, 5.75×2.27 m. GVW 7000 kg. Model P38 4580-cc (94×110 mm) OHV engine. Model 45 chassis were produced from the mid-1930s until 1954. Model shown, with special body, was still in use in 1969/70.

Truck, 5-ton, 4×2, Cargo (Citroën 55U) 6-cyl., 73 bhp, 4F1R, wb 4.70 m, 7.36×2.37×3.06 m, 4570 kg. 4.5-litre (94×110 mm) OHV engine. Military version of commercial truck. Superseded by similar Model 55E in 1959, 60E in 1964. Tyres 9.00–20 XY. GMC-type pintle hook.

Truck, 5-ton, 4×2, Cargo (Ford F798WM) V-8-cyl., 95 bhp, 4F1R, wb 4.01 m, 6.83×2.35×3.00 m, 3800 kg. 3923-cc (80.97×95.25 mm) SV engine. Tyres 9.00–20. Produced during 1947–50 by Ford SAF (later the Poissy Division of Simca). Also supplied as bus chassis to the Dutch Air Force (1950).

Truck, 5-ton, 4×2, Cargo (Ford, Simca F569WML) V-8-cyl., 85 bhp, 4F1R, wb 3.66 m, 6.80×2.28×2.90 (1.90) m, 4370 kg. Tyres 9.00–20. Introduced in 1956 and basically similar to model F798WM except military pattern soft-top cab. Same cab produced with hard-top, for commercial application (Simca 'Cargo').

Truck, 7-ton, 4 × 2, Fuel Tanker (Berliet GLR8R) 5-cyl. diesel, 125 bhp, 5F1R, wb 4.44 m, 7.73 × 2.50 m. 8000-litre tank body by Coder. Produced 1954–1959, also with other body types, incl. cargo, 4500-litre water tank, etc. Originally used in Algeria and Sahara.

Truck, 10-ton, 4 × 2, Tractor (Saviem-LRS-Renault R2185 DEFA) 6-cyl., 120 bhp, 5F1R, wb 3.00 m, 5.54 × 2.43 × 2.40 m, 5000 kg. GTW 21 tons. Derived from commercial R4182, 1961. 6230-cc (105 × 120 mm) engine under chassis. Air/hyd. brakes with dual circuits plus emergency air brake system.

Truck, 12-ton, 4 × 2, Cargo (Willème L10) 6-cyl. diesel, 170 bhp approx., 8F1R, wb 5.12 m, 8.34 × 2.49 × 3.40 (2.76) m. Willème P517 13,450-cc engine. Tyre size 44 × 10. Air brakes. Basically a commercial model, supplied to the Army during 1945–47 and 1950–55 (L10N).

Truck, 10-ton, 4 × 2, Cargo (Willème LD610N) 6-cyl. diesel, 175 bhp, 6F1R, wb 5.42 m, 8.60 × 2.60 × 3.23 m. Willème Model 518-6 engine with bore and stroke of 130 × 170 mm. Tyres F20 or F24. Air brakes. Towed load up to 26 tons. GVW 16,740 kg. Produced during 1956–59.

TRUCKS, 3- to 6-TON 4 × 4

Makes and Models: Berliet GBK8 (3-ton, 1960), GBC8 (4-ton, 1970), GLB (3-ton, 1956), GLC28 (5-ton, 1960), etc. Citroën 55, P46, T46 'Sahara' (3½-ton, 1956), PW (3-ton, 1961), FOM (3- and 5-ton, 1964). Famé T65/36VA (3-ton, 1961/62, D). Ford G798 BA (3-ton, 1952, D). Ford/M.-H. F294 WM (3-ton, 1954). Henschel HS115 (5-ton, 1955, D). Hotchkiss PL 70 (1967), PL90 MAV (3-ton, 1968). Latil H14TL10, H14A1TL10, M12TRP (tractors, from c. 1949). Magirus-Deutz A3500, A6500, etc. (from 3½-ton, c. 1955, D). Marmon-Bocquet MB800 (4-ton, amphibious, 1969). Mercedes-Benz LA3500, LA311, LA312, etc. (from 3½-ton, c. 1955, D).

Saurer 3CM (6-ton, 1954). Saviem-LRS-Renault R2152 (3½-ton, 1958), R2182 (tractor, 6-ton, 1958). Saviem R7521 (6-ton), R7571 (tractor. 6-ton, 1961), S7036 (3-ton, 1962), SM8 (4-ton, 1971). Simca-Unic (formerly Ford) WML, WMC (3-ton, 1956). Simca-Unic S1 (3-ton, 1961), VLRA (3-ton, 1971). Willème L6DAT (tractor, c. 1956).

WWII types: American Autocar U-7144T and U-8144T, Federal 94 × 93, FWD HAR, Mack NJU; British Ford WOT6; Canadian Chevrolet C60L and Ford F60L, T, etc.

General Data: Some of the above models were conversions of commercial trucks by Herwaythorn, who, in addition, provided similar (commercial) conversions for other chassis. The Latil tractors were used by the French Air Force and Navy, the Saurers by the Air Force. The Berliet GBC8KT was available as 4 × 4 or 6 × 6 (*qv*). The Marmon-Bocquet MB800 amphibian is illustrated under 'Miscellaneous Vehicles'. Shortly after WWII the Civilian Colonial Ministry ordered about 400 4 × 4 versions of the Poissy-built Ford 3-ton truck, for use by the Army in Indo-China. The FFA used many German 4 × 4 trucks, with various body types. In May 1961 Faun (D) and the Société des Forges et Chantiers de la Méditerranée formed a new company, headquartered in Paris, called Famé (Faun Méditerranée), for truck production in France. Under this name six prototype 4 × 4 3-tonners were submitted to the French Army but the venture was shortlived.

Vehicle shown (typical): Truck, 3-ton, 4 × 4, Office (Simca-Unic F594 WML)

Technical Data:

Engine: Simca F6 CWM 8-cylinder, V-L-W-F, 3923 cc, 100 bhp @ 3800 rpm (governed to 85 bhp @ 2900 rpm, 80 km/h).

Transmission: 4F1R × 2.

Brakes: hydraulic, vacuum-assisted.

Tyres: 9.00–20 or 10.00–20.

Wheelbase: 3.65 m.

Overall l × w × h: 6.78 × 2.28 × 2.55 (cab) m.

Weight: GVW: 7925 kg.

Note: Marmon-Herrington transfer case and front drive. Shown with container-type body. Other body types included cargo, workshop, compressor, etc. F594 WMC (*court*) was SWB model.

Truck, 3-ton, 4 × 4, Cargo (Ford/Marmon-Herrington F294WM) V-8-cyl., 85 bhp, 4F1R × 2, wb 3.65 m, 6.80 × 2.29 × 3.20 m. Tyres 9.00–20 or 230 × 20. Produced by Ford SAF at Poissy during 1954–56. Model F09W side-valve 3923-cc engine. Commercially available.

Truck, 3-ton, 4 × 4, Tipper (Simca-Unic F594WMC) V-8-cyl., 85 bhp, 4F1R × 2, wb 3.04 m, 5.17 × 2.28 m. Other body types on this short-wheelbase chassis included water tank and wrecker (*Camion de Dépannage, Lot 7*). Civilian version (Simca 'Cargo') optionally with Hercules diesel engine.

Truck, 3-ton, 4 × 4, Missile Launcher (Simca-Unic F594WMC) Based on standard Simca-Unic 4 × 4 chassis (which, in turn, was a modification of the 5-ton 4 × 2 Model F569WML). Extended hard-top cab. Launcher for SE4200 guided missile (ground-to-ground, radius of action 100 km at 900 km/h).

Truck, 3-ton, 4 × 4, Cargo (Simca-Unic S1) About 1960 the French Army issued a specification for an up-dated 3-ton NATO-class 4 × 4 tactical loadcarrier. Several manufacturers submitted prototypes (see following page also) but project was discontinued in 1963.

Truck, 3-ton, 4×4, Cargo (Berliet GBK8) 5-cyl. diesel, 125 bhp, 6F1R×2, wb 3.50 m, 6.43×2.40×3.23 m, 7000 kg. Tyres 12.00–20. PAS. Fording depth 1.20 m. Air-actuated rear diff. lock. 1960–64. Small number supplied to Moroccan Army in 1962.

Truck, 3-ton, 4×4, Cargo, w/Winch (Saviem S7036) 4-cyl. diesel, 105 bhp, 5F1R×2, wb 3.60 m, 6.52×2.34×3.33 (2.12) m, 5550 kg. Tyres 12.00–20. Air brakes. Centrally-mounted 4½-ton winch with 60-metre cable and fair leads front and rear.

Truck, 3-ton, 4×4, Cargo, w/Winch (Citroën PW) 6-cyl., 145 bhp, 5F1R×2, wb 3.68 m, 6.53×2.28×3.12 m, 6400 kg. GVW 9550 kg. Produced to NATO standards, 1961/62. 5.2-litre (100×110 mm) petrol engine, developing 145 bhp (SAE) @ 3250 rpm. Air-assisted hyd. brakes. Sinpar winch at front.

Truck, 3-ton, 4×4, Cargo, w/Winch (Famé F65/36VA) Deutz F6L 614 V-6-cyl. air-cooled diesel, 125 bhp, 5F1R×2, wb 3.60 m, 5.95×2.42×3.20 m, 6290 kg. Tyres 12.00–20 'Sahara'. GVW 11,400 kg. 4½-ton winch under body. Air-assisted hyd. brakes. Basically Faun (D) (see also 'General Data').

Truck, 3-ton, 4 × 4, Cargo (Hotchkiss PL70) 4-cyl., 115 bhp, 4F1R × 2, wb 2.62 or 3.12 m, chassis/cab: 2750 kg. GVW 6500 kg. Also available with diesel engine (DH70) and higher GVW (PL80, DH80; GVW 7400 kg). Single tyres, 8.25 or 9.00–20. Tilting cab. Introduced 1967. Produced by Hotchkiss-Brandt.

Truck, 3-ton, 4 × 4, Cargo (Hotchkiss PL90 MAV) 4 cyl., 115 bhp, 4F1R × 2, wb 3.15 m, 5.88 × 2.21 × 3.20 (2.66) m, 4560 kg. GVW 9600 kg (off road 7600 kg). 11.00–20 tyres. PAS. 3456-cc engine (115 bhp @ 3500, 130 @ 4000 rpm). Gradability 50%. Road speed 70 km/h. Tested in Spain.

Truck, 3-ton, 4 × 4, Cargo (S.U.M.B. VLRA) V-8-cyl., 100 bhp, 4F1R × 2, wb 2.90 m, 5.10 × 2.15 × 2.09 m approx. GVW 6800 kg. Basically as Simca-Marmon MH600BS (1½-ton) but up-rated for 2½- to 3-ton payloads by fitting reinforced axles, suspension, etc. Tyres 12.50–20. Winch optional. 1971.

Truck, 4-ton, 4 × 4, Cargo (Saviem/Renault SM8) 6-cyl. diesel, 135 bhp, 5F1R × 2, wb 3.50 m, 6.43 × 2.20 × 2.66 (cab) m, 4375 kg (chassis/cab). GVW 9100 kg. Tyres 12.00–20. Air brakes. Saviem 597 engine with MAN 'M'-type injection system. Cubic capacity 5270 cc. Speed 90 km/h. Tilt cab. 1971.

Truck, 5-ton, 4×4, Cargo, Air-transportable (Citroën FOM) 6-cyl., 140 bhp, 5F1R × 2, wb 4.60 m, 7.01 × 2.48 × 3.09 (2.77) m, GVW 11 tons approx. Tyres 11.00–20 (12.00–20, single rear, for 3-ton version). Servo-assisted brakes and steering. 1964–67. Used by French Overseas Forces (F.O.M.) and several African countries.

Truck, 3½-ton, 4×4, Cargo (Saviem-LRS-Renault R2152) 6-cyl., 120 bhp, 5F1R × 2, wb 3.64 m, 6.85 × 2.28 × 2.95 m, 7000 kg. Model 672 6230-cc (105 × 120 mm) petrol engine, horizontally mounted under the chassis. 11.00–20 tyres. Overdrive (top gear) gearbox. Air-assisted hydraulic brakes.

Truck, 6-ton, 4×4, Tractor (Saviem-LRS-Renault R2182) 6-cyl., 120 bhp, 5F1R × 2, wb 3.64 m, 6.22 × 2.43 × 2.70 m, 5700 kg. Tractor for semi-trailers, derived from model R2152. Payload on roads 12 tons. GTW 15,700 kg (on roads 21,700 kg). Note MG ring-mount and window in door.

Truck, 6-ton, 4×4, Cargo (Saviem R7521) 6-cyl. diesel, 150 bhp, 5F1R × 2, wb 3.64 m, 7.28 × 2.50 (cab) m, chassis/cab: 5470 kg. Military 4×4 version of model R4152 truck. Underfloor 6840-cc (110 × 120 mm) engine, designated 'Fulgar 6 Horizontal'. Also tractor version (R7571).

Truck, 6-ton, 4×4, Cargo (Berliet GLC 28) 6-cyl., 145 bhp, 5F1R×2, wb 3.70 m, 7.14×2.49×2.60 m, 6980 kg. Also with 4.71-m wb (overall length 8.09 m, wt 7380 kg). Tyres 11.00–20. Other body types: recovery and tanker. Used by Air Force. Basically a civilian truck. 1960.

Truck, 6-ton, 4×4, Cargo (Saurer 3CM) 6-cyl. diesel, 130 bhp, 5F1R×2, wb 3.40 m. Chassis weight (w/o cab) 5500 kg. Load capacity (incl. cab and body) 8500 kg. Tyres 11.00–20. Air brakes. Rear diff. lock. Speed 67 km/h. Truck and tractor versions used by Air Force. 1954–57.

Truck, Tractor, 4×4 (Willème L6DAT) 6-cyl. diesel, 175 bhp, 6F1R×2, wb 4.00 m, 7.08×2.43×3.15 m, 8900 kg. Military version of commercial tractor-truck for heavy semi-trailers. Towed loads up to 50 tons. OD gearbox (0.72:1 in top gear). Max. speed 65 km/h. Note large roof hatch for AA MG ringmount.

Truck, Tractor, 4×4 (Latil M12TRP) 6-cyl., 120 bhp, 4F1R×2, wb 3.00 m, 6.13×2.41×2.90 m, 6500 kg. Tractor for semi-trailers with payloads up to 25 tons, shown with aircraft refuelling type. Model TRP (*tracteur porteur*) differed from TR (*tracteur*) mainly in having non-steering rear axle.

TRUCKS, 1½- to 5-TON
6 × 4 and 6 × 6

Makes and Models: (6 × 6 unless stated otherwise)
Alvis-Berliet 'Aurochs' (5-ton, amphibious, 1964).
Berliet GBA MT (3-ton, 1969), GBC8KT (4-ton, 1961),
TBC8KT and TBC8KT CMD (4-ton, 1962), GBC8 MK
(5-ton, 1960), GBC8MT (5-ton, 1967). DAF YF-328
(3-ton, 1956, NL). International G744 'M-Series' (5-ton,
c. 1960, US). Marmon-Herrington FF6 (1½-ton, 1958).
Panhard VS-243 (3½-ton, 1959). Latil M16A1TZ (1955)
and H16A1TZ (1958). Saviem M16A1TZ21N (fire-
fighting chassis). Simca (3- and 3½-ton, 1952/53).
WWII types: American Diamond T 967–972 series, Dodge
T223 (WC62,63), GMC CCKW-352, -353, AFKWX-353,
DUKW-353 (amphibious); British Karrier CK6, etc.

General Data: The post-war French forces used large numbers of American 6 × 6
trucks, notably GMC (2½-ton) and Dodge (1½-ton). The former have now largely
been replaced by the Berliet GBC/TBC range and the latter by the Simca-Marmon
MH600BS (4 × 4). The Berliet 4-ton 6 × 6 tactical truck is used with a wide range of
body types including cargo, tipper (dump), wrecker, tractor, 'Hawk' guided missiles,
compressors, fuel tank (Coder body, 5000-litre capacity), etc. It is also exported to
other countries, including 110 to Austria in 1967 and 2200 to the People's Republic
of China in 1970/71 (Model GBC8MT, with 5-cyl. diesel engine).
   The Alvis-Berliet 'Aurochs' was, in fact, the British Alvis 'Stalwart' which was
planned for production in France, with the progressive integration of Berliet components. This was part of an agreement between Alvis and Berliet to market each
other's military vehicles, which was terminated when Alvis became part of the British
Leyland Motor Corporation. Only two were imported. Under this agreement Alvis,
in 1965, sold two Alvis-Berliet TBU15CLD wreckers to the British Army. The
American G744 'M-Series' models (M62, M139) were produced by Diamond T,
International, etc.

Vehicle shown (typical): Truck, 4-ton,
6 × 6, Cargo (Berliet GBC8KT)

Technical Data:
Engine: Berliet MK520 multi-fuel (*poly-
   carburant*) 5-cylinder, I-I-W-F, 7900 cc,
   125 bhp @ 2100 rpm.
Transmission: 6F1R × 2 (OD top).
Brakes: air (3 circuits) and exhaust retarder.
Tyres: 12.00–20.
Wheelbase: 3.95 m. BC 1.28 m.
Overall l × w × h: 7.28 × 2.40 × 3.20 (cab
   2.70) m.
Weight: 8600 kg. GVW: 12,800 kg.
Note: Also available with winch, with
   longer wheelbase (4.35 m), and as
   4 × 4. Diff. locks in rear axles. ZF gearbox, Herwaythorn transfer box. 150-bhp
   diesel engine optional. GVW 18,000 kg
   when fitted with reinforced rear suspension.

Truck, 5-ton, 6 × 6, Cargo (Berliet GBC8 MK 'Gazelle')
5-cyl. m/f, 125 bhp, 5F1R × 2, wb 3.09 (BC 1.28) m, 7.12 ×
2.43 × 2.68 (cab) m, 7120 kg. GVW 12,400 kg. Tyres 11.00–20.
Rear diff. locks.   Produced 1960–62.   Widely used in Algeria.
Also recovery version (gantry type).

Truck, 3½-ton, 6 × 6, Cargo (Berliet GBC8 'Gazelle') 5-cyl.
diesel, 125 to 150 bhp, 5F1R × 2, wb 3.62 (BC 1.28) m. Military
version of commercial GBC8 *Porteur Moyen à Adhérence Totale*
(medium all-wheel-drive load carrier). Similar open-cab model
also offered for oil fields work, 1959. Developed into GBC8KT.

Truck, 4-ton, 6 × 6, Cargo, w/Winch (Berliet GBC8KT)
5-cyl. (MDU 35 MK) m/f, 125 bhp, 6F1R × 2, wb 3.95 (BC 1.28)
m, 7.28 × 2.40 × 2.99 m, 8600 kg.   Early production model
(1961), derived from Model GBC8 MK 'Gazelle'.   Front end
sheet metal was later re-styled. 5- to 7-ton winch.

Truck, 4-ton, 6 × 6, Tractor (Berliet TBC8KT) 5-cyl. m/f,
125 bhp, 6F1R × 2, wb 3.95 (BC 1.28) m, 6.53 × 2.40 × 2.67 m,
7740 kg. Coder fifth wheel semi-trailer coupling. Load on fifth
wheel 6475 kg. GTW 19 tons (for highway convoy work 22
tons). Track (all models) 1.86 m.

Truck, 4-ton, 6 × 6, Tipper (Berliet GBC8KT) 5-cyl. m/f, 125 bhp, 6F1R × 2, wb 3.95 (BC 1.28) m, 7.17 × 2.40 × 2.90 m, 9000 kg. Angles of approach and departure (all models) 45°. Ground clearance (all models) 280 mm. Multi-fuel engine, using either petrol or diesel fuel.

Truck, 4-ton, 6 × 6, Wrecker (Berliet TBC8KT CMD) 5-cyl. m/f, 125 bhp, 6F1R × 2, wb 3.95 (BC 1.28) m, 7.69 × 2.40 × 3.20 m, 13,650 kg. Hyd.-operated Austin-Western telescopic crane, rotating 270°. Jib winch driven by hyd. gear motor. 5- to 7-ton rear winch. Max. lift (using crane legs) 6 tons.

Truck, 4-ton, 6 × 6, Light Recovery (Berliet GBC8KT) 5-cyl. m/f, 125 bhp, 6F1R × 2, wb 3.95 (BC 1.28) m, 8.25 × 2.49 × 3.57 m, 9600 kg. Special body with 2-ton hoist which may be fixed at rear end of overhead rail for lifting vehicles and equipment. Central 5- to 7-ton winch for use at front or rear.

Truck, 4-ton, 6 × 6, Compressor, Model F1 (Berliet GBC8KT) 5-cyl. m/f, 125 bhp, 6F1R × 2, wb 3.95 (BC 1.28) m. Spiros air-cooled two-stage compressor, driven by air-cooled Alsthom 5-cyl. diesel engine. 100 lb/sq. in air supply for pneumatic tools. Similar type (Codimos C250) produced by Richier Group.

Truck, 2½-ton, 6 × 6, Command (GMC AFKWX-353) 6-cyl., 104 bhp (or converted to diesel), 5F1R × 2, wb 4.16 m. German cab and expansible body on WWII American GMC COE chassis. About 100 were in service with the FFA in Germany as caravans for high-ranking officers, later also as mobile workshops.

Truck, 6 × 6, Fire Fighting Chassis (Latil M16A1 TZ) 6-cyl., 180 bhp, 4F1R × 2, wb 3.62 (BC 1.36) m, chassis: 6.53 × 2.30 m, 5415 kg. High-performance cross-country chassis with 8355-cc (108 × 152.4 mm) triple-carburettor engine. Tyres 12.00–20. Similar: Saviem-LRS-Latil H16A1TZ.

Truck, 1½-ton, 6 × 6, Cargo (Marmon-Herrington FF6) Simca F6CW V-8-cyl., 85 bhp, 4F1R × 2, wb 3.18 (BC 1.15) m, 5.65 × 2.10 × 1.90 (min.) m, 4280 kg. M.-H. gearbox, transfer case and axles. Also available commercially (optionally with Perkins P6 diesel engine). Tyres 9.00–20. Track 1.70 m.

Truck, 3½-ton, 6 × 6, Cargo and Prime Mover (Simca) 6-cyl., 115 bhp, wb 3.35 m, 5.96 × 2.28 m, 5900 kg. Ground clearance 360 mm. Towed load 3 tons. 4597-cc engine. Also LWB (4.32 m) version as 3-ton cargo truck (length 7.49 m). Diff. locks at rear. Speed 86 km/h. Prototypes only.

TRUCKS, over 5-TON
6 × 4 and 6 × 6
(see also Tank Transporters)

Makes and Models: (6 × 6 unless stated otherwise) Berliet T6, T6-15 (6-ton, 1955), GBU 15 (6-ton, 1961), TBU 15, TBU 15 CLD (6-ton, 1959), GBO 15P (tractor, 1957), GBO 15, TBO 15 (15-ton, 6 × 4, 1956), TBO 15 M3 (tractor, 6 × 4, 1969). Bernard (fuel tanker, 6 × 4). Kaelble KDV 631/680/832 SF (tractors, 1952-54, D). Latil M16TRPZ (wrecker, 1956). Rochet-Schneider T6 (6-ton, c. 1951). Willème R15 (15-ton, 6 × 4, 1945/46), W6DAT (tractor, c. 1956), W8DTA (tractor, 6 × 4, 1960), RDC 615 (26-ton dump, 6 × 4), RC 615 (tractor, 6 × 4), TE25 (tractor), etc.

WWII types: American Brockway B666, Corbitt 50SD6 and C666, Mack NM and White 666 6-ton 6 × 6 trucks, Mack NO 7½-ton 6 × 6 prime movers, Kenworth and Ward LaFrance M1 and M1A1 wreckers, etc.

General Data: Various American types in this category, especially in the 6-ton 6 × 6 class, have gradually been replaced by French vehicles, notably of Berliet manufacture. One heavy six-wheeler of pre-war origin which was used in the French Army after 1945 was the Willème DG12, a 12-ton 6 × 4 water-tank truck of 1935 vintage. The Berliet GBU/TBU range has an interesting transmission system with a single differential in the forward axle of the rear bogie driving the two right-hand and the two left-hand wheels; an air-actuated brake system on a second differential located in the rear axle prevents the wheels on either side from moving relative to each other.

This model was a development of the T6 6-ton 6 × 6, a truck designed by Rochet-Schneider, which company was absorbed by Berliet in the early 1950s. In 1955 it was redesigned by Berliet and fitted with a multi-fuel engine (licence MAN). The resulting model (T6-15) was accepted by the Army and went into series production in 1959 as Model GBU and TBU (tractor) 15.

Vehicle shown (typical): Truck, 6-ton, 6 × 6, Heavy Wrecker (Berliet TBU 15 CLD) (*CLD: Camion Lourd de Dépannage*)

Technical Data:
Engine: Berliet MK640 multi-fuel (*polycarburant*) 6-cylinder, I-I-W-F, 14,750 cc, 200 bhp @ 1800 rpm.
Transmission: 5F1R × 2.
Brakes: air (3 circuits).
Tyres: 14.00–20.
Wheelbase: 4.20 m. BC 1.45 m.
Overall l × w × h: 8.88 × 2.50 × 3.00 (cab 2.95) m.
Weight: 21,200 kg. Max. lifted load: 10 tons.
Note: Hyd. telescopic crane jib, slewing through 270°. Outrigger jacks and spade-type anchors. Winches front (7-ton) and rear (14-ton). Pilot model shown.

100

Truck, 6-ton, 6 × 6, Cargo and Prime Mover (Berliet T6)
6-cyl., 220 bhp, 5F1R × 2, wb 4.45 m, 7.30 × 2.50 m, 14,000 kg.
Tyres 14.00–20. 11,150-cc petrol engine. Also as tractor-truck.
Designed by Rochet-Schneider. Taken over by Berliet and
developed into T6-15, later GBU 15. Ten produced.

**Truck, 6-ton, 6 × 6, Cargo and Prime Mover (Berliet GBU
15)** 6-cyl. m/f, 200 bhp, 5F1R × 2, wb 4.20 (BC 1.45) m,
7.98 × 2.50 × 3.35 m, 15,800 kg. Tyres 14.00–20. 8-ton winch
at rear. PAS. Four-door four-seater soft-top cab. Pneumatic
locking of diff. of both rear axles (see also 'General Data').

Truck, 6-ton, 6 × 6, Tractor (Berliet TBU 15) 6-cyl. m/f,
200 bhp, 5F1R × 2, wb 4.20 (BC 1.45) m, 7.44 × 2.50 × 2.95 m,
14,500 kg. 10-ton winch behind cab. Fifth wheel coupling for
low-loader S-Ts for transport of engineers' equipment and light
tanks. GTW 36.5 or 46.5 tons.

Truck, 6-ton, 6 × 6, Heavy Wrecker (Berliet TBU 15 CLD)
6-cyl. m/f, 200 bhp, 5F1R × 2, wb 4.20 (BC 1.45) m, 8.88 ×
2.50 × 3.00 m, 21,200 kg. Production model, 1962. Gradability
60%. Fording depth 1 m. Also supplied to Belgium (150 units,
1969) and Britain ('Alvis-Berliet', 2 units, 1965).

Truck, 10-ton, 6 × 6, Heavy Wrecker (Latil M16TRPZ) 6-cyl., 180 bhp, 4F1R × 2, wb 3.70 m, chassis/cab: 7.00 × 2.46 × 2.91 m, 8000 kg. Swinging boom crane. General layout similar to American heavy wreckers, M1 and M1A1, but greater capacity. Also with straight (shorter) jib.

Truck, 12-ton, 6 × 6, Tractor (Willème W6DAT) 6-cyl. diesel, 175 bhp, 6F1R × 2, wb 4.95 (BC 1.45) m, 9.14 × 2.43 × 3.10 m, 10,750 kg. Military version of W6DT commercial tractor-truck for heavy semi-trailers. Towed loads up to 65 tons. OD gearbox. Winch behind cab. Speed 65 km/h.

Truck, 15-ton, 6 × 4, Water Tank (Berliet GBO 15) 6-cyl. diesel, 225 bhp, 5F1R × 2, wb 4.97 (BC 1.45) m, chassis/cab: 10.67 × 2.80 × 2.75 m, GVW 34,200 kg. Coder 12,500-litre tank. Also with dump and cargo body (16 sq. metres load platform). Note large air cleaner. Used in Algeria.

Truck, 12-ton, 6 × 6, Tractor, w/Winch (Kaelble KDV 631SF/54) 6-cyl. diesel, 150 bhp, 6F1R × 1, wb 4.21 (BC 1.42) m, 7.95 × 2.47 × 2.90 m, 9900 kg. GVW 21,300 kg. Also with 200-bhp V8 diesel and 6F1R × 2 trans. (KDV832SF). Produced for French Forces in Germany (**FFA**), 1952–54.

TANK and
HEAVY EQUIPMENT
TRANSPORTERS

Makes and Models: Berliet T6 (6 × 6, used with 25-ton S-T, 1956). Berliet TBU15 (6 × 6, used with 17-ton Coder GM2E-1750 S-T, 1966). Berliet TBO15 (6 × 4, used with 55-ton Maduraud SRSD2-50 S-T). Berliet TBO15 M3 (6 × 4, used with 45-ton Coder GSP-BMT 35/45 S-T, 1967, and with 45-ton Titan S-T, 1969). Berliet TBO15A (6 × 6, used with 50-ton Coder S-T, 1969). Berliet T12 (8 × 8, used with 50-ton Coder S-T, 1955, and with 45-ton Coder GSP-BMT 35/45 S-T, 1965). Diamond T 980, 981 M20 (6 × 4, used with 45-ton Rogers M9 full-trailer, WWII, US). Pacific TR-1 M26 and M26A1 (6 × 6, used with 40- and 45-ton Fruehauf M15 and M15A1 S-T, forming tank transporter M25, WWII, US). Willème (6 × 4, used with 50-ton Coder HGM 50500 S-T, 1946).
Full Trailers: Crane 209 (6-ton, 6-wheeled, WWII, GB), Rogers (20-ton, 6-wheeled (6DT), WWII, US), Rogers (45-ton, 12-wheeled (12DT), M9, WWII, US; also produced by Fruehauf and others), etc.

General Data: For many years the American M25 'Dragon Wagon' tank transporter (Pacific tractor-truck, M26 (A1), with 40-ton Fruehauf semi-trailer, M15 (A1)) was in service with the French Army. Some attempts were made in the late 1940s by Berliet and Willème to produce French tractor-trucks for this purpose. The Berliet, designated T12, was designed about 1947 and a prototype appeared in the mid-1950s. It was intended for transporting American tanks such as the 'Patton', but remained in the experimental stage. A few years later it was redesigned and offered as tractor-truck and artillery prime mover. However, only two were made. For haulage of the much lighter AMX13 tanks the Berliet TBU tractor was used (see previous section). The Berliet TBO15M3, basically a commercial 6 × 4 model, appeared during the late 1960s and was designed for road transport of medium tanks such as the AMX30, followed by the TBO15A which was a sophisticated 6 × 6 tractor unit intended for transporting 50-ton tanks on and off roads, all in conjunction with semi-trailers.

Vehicle shown (typical): Truck, 20-ton, 6 × 4, Tractor (Berliet TBO15M3 6 × 4 HC) with Semi-Trailer, 35/45-ton, 8-Wh. (8DT) (Coder GSP BMT 35/45)

Technical Data (tractor):
Engine: Berliet 6-cylinder diesel, I-I-W-F, 14,780 cc, 255 bhp (240 net) @ 1800 rpm.
Transmission: dual-range 5F1R.
Brakes: air, and exhaust retarder.
Tyres: 16.00–20.
Wheelbase: 4.50 m. BC 1.52 m.
Overall l × w × h: 8.23 × 3.07 × 2.95 m.
Weight: 17,000 kg. GTW: 78,000 kg.
Note: Double-drum winch, 2 × 15 ton. PAS. Interaxle diff. Double-reduction final drive. Speed range 3.7–47 km/h. Crew 3.

Truck, 12-ton, 6 × 4, Tractor (Willème) with Semi-Trailer 50-ton, 8-wh. (8 DT) (Coder) Produced in 1946 as 50-ton tank-transporter (*Ensemble Porte-Char de 50 tonnes*). Winch behind open cab. Semi-trailer with detachable goose neck. Shown carrying a German 'Panther' tank. Tractor wb 5.30 m. Overall l × w: 17.81 × 3.60 m. (In 1949 Willème produced a commercial 8 × 4 tractor which, with its multi-axle Scari trailer, weighed 205 tons. Payload of this outfit was 125 tons.)

Truck, 10-ton, 8 × 8, Tractor (Berliet T12) with Semi-Trailer, 50-ton, 6-wh. (6 DT) (Coder) Produced *c.* 1955. The front axle bogie had two propeller shafts driving each pair of wheels on one side (as on the rear of the GBU models). If two wheels on one side (which revolved at the same speed) lost traction a diff. lock could be engaged. The V-12 engine had four Zenith carbs and magneto ignition. Originally the T12 was classed as a 12-ton 8 × 8.

103

Truck, 6-ton, 6 × 6, Tractor (Berliet T6) with Semi-Trailer, 25-ton, 4-wh. (4 DT), Tank Transporter Tractor-truck was designed by Rochet-Schneider in Lyon about 1950, taken over by Berliet in 1953. Ancestor of Berliet TBU15. T6 had 220-bhp petrol engine.

Truck, 10-ton, 8 × 8, Tractor (Berliet T12) V-12-cyl. diesel (m/f optional), 550 bhp, torque conv., 4F1R × 2, wb 4.45 m (between outer axles), 9.30 × 2.90 m, 28,000 kg. GTW 90 tons. *Véhicule de Transport Très Lourd.* PAS. Two winches. Two built, one as cargo/prime mover truck, 1965.

Truck, 6-ton, 6 × 6, Tractor (Berliet TBU15) with Semi-Trailer, 17/19-ton, 4-wh. (4 DT), Tank Transporter (Coder GM2E 1750) One of several types of mil. S-Ts produced by Coder of Marseille. Designed for transporting tanks of the 13-ton AMX type and engineers' equipment such as bulldozers. Tyres 12.00–20. 1966.

Truck, 20-ton, 6 × 6, Tractor (Berliet TBO15A) with Semi-Trailer, 50-ton, 6-wh. (6 DT) (Coder) Tractor: 6-cyl. diesel, 360 bhp, torque conv., 5F1R × 2, final gear reduction in wheel hubs. GVW 45/50 tons. GTW 90/95 tons. PAS. Double winch (2 × 15 tons). Gradability 20%. Fording depth 1.20 m. 1970.

TRACTORS

Prime movers or drawbar tractors (for trailed loads) are used mainly by the Air Force for aircraft towing. In the Army such machines are employed chiefly by the Engineers (*Génie*) and usually equipped with special fitments for special roles. Some typical models are shown here. Aircraft tractors were supplied mainly by Saviem (developments of the old but efficient Latil four-wheel steer 4 × 4 tractors) and Sinpar (using Renault mechanical components). The Army used mainly Agrip, Continental and Labourier special purpose machines. The FFA (French forces in Germany) had various German tractors, incl. Lanz D9506, Mercedes-Benz 'Unimog' and the large Hanomag ST100 4 × 2 road tractor.

Tractor, 4 × 4, 4-wh. steer (Latil H14TL10) H14 4-cyl. diesel, 65 bhp (M14 TL10: M14 4-cyl. petrol, 85 bhp), 4F1R × 2, wb 2.40 m, 4.42 × 1.85 m, 3500 kg approx. Specially adapted for road work. Air Force S-T with collapsible gooseneck produced by Genève (Model 250). One of many variants of the basic TL10 tractor.

Tractor, Light, 4 × 4, Airfield (Renault/Sinpar R2167/ 255A) 4-cyl., 56 bhp, 4F1R × 2, wb 2.09 m, 4.25 × 2.00 × 2.37 (1.89) m, 3350 kg. Tyres 9.00–16. Heavy load platform with additional ballast underneath. Special rear towing hook for drawbar attachment on seven different heights. Shortened wheelbase.

Tractor, 4 × 4, Airfield (Renault/Sinpar R2167) 4-cyl., 56 bhp, 4F1R × 2, wb 2.58 m, 5.20 × 2.00 × 2.60 m approx. Slightly larger and heavier than model 255A. Double-floor loading platform, accommodating removable ballast weights. Note twin jerrican holder behind cab, and lowered front wings.

Tractor, Heavy, 4×4, 4-wh. steer (Saviem-LRS-Latil M14A1 TL 12 CH) 4-cyl., 110 bhp, 4F1R × 2, wb 2.40 m, 4.67 × 2.00 × 1.90 (min.) m, 3700 kg (chassis/cab). Drawbar pull, depending on terrain, up to 80 tons. Payload 2300 kg. Front and rear axle both equipped with lockable differential. Model M14 petrol engine.

Tractor, Heavy, 4×4, 4-wh. steer (Saviem M14A1 TL 12 CH) 4-cyl., 110 bhp, 4F1R × 2, wb 2.40, 4.67 × 2.00 × 1.90 (min.) m, 3700 kg (chassis/cab). *'Version Armée de l'Air'* of Latil model TL 12 tractor, known as Saviem from 1962. 'CH' indicates *Coupleur Hydraulic* (Ferodo hyd. coupling between engine and clutch). M14 engine.

Tractor, Heavy, 4×4, 4-wh. steer (Labourier CL5) Perkins P6 6-cyl. diesel, 83 bhp, 5F1R × 2, wb 2.50 m, 4.18 × 2.06 × 2.33 (min.) m, 3500 kg approx. Tyres 11.00–24. Speed range 3½ to 48 km/h. Lockable diff. in transfer case. Air brakes. 12-ton 2F1R winch with air brake. Army Engineers version of commercial tractor, 1963.

Tractor, Heavy, 4×4 (Labourier LDU) Perkins 6.354 D 6-cyl. diesel, 140 bhp, 5F1R × 2, 4.64 × 2.20 m, 5000 kg approx. Tyres 12.75–24. Labourier products included tractors and trucks (4×4, 6×6) and bore a strong resemblance to the American FWD trucks, including chain-drive transfer boxes with third diff.

MISCELLANEOUS VEHICLES WHEELED AND TRACKED

Of the multitude of special equipment and special purpose vehicles used by the French Army, Navy, Air Force and *Gendarmerie* a representative selection of typical models is shown here. Special purpose vehicles differ from special equipment types in that their chassis are specially designed for the vehicles' purposes. In addition to the French types shown, there were many of US origin, made mainly during World War II. These included Caterpillar and Galion graders, Caterpillar and International crawler tractors, Coleman/Quick-Way truck-mounted cranes, etc. For Gillois-EWK bridging vehicles see German Federal Republic. A number of tracked over-snow vehicles was imported from Canada, e.g. the Flextrac-Nodwell 22L (1970).

Truck, 1½-ton, 4 × 4, Fire/Crash Tender, Type VIR 1800 (Renault/Sinpar R2240/2551) 4-cyl., 65 bhp, 4F1R × 2, wb 2.44 m, 5.08 × 1.96 × 2.98 (2.54) m, 4150 kg. VIR means *Véhicule d'Intervention Rapide*. Chassis conversion by Sinpar; fire-fighting equipment by Sides. Also on R2167 4 × 4 chassis.

Truck, 3½-ton, 4 × 2, Fire Fighter (Citroën P45) 6-cyl., 73 bhp, 4F1R, wb 3.60 m. Guinard Air Force type appliance, over 150 of which were produced by Drouville in 1947. Vehicle had 1200-litre water tank and carried foam compound in cans. Pump capacity **1500–2000 l/min.**

Truck, 5-ton, 4 × 4, Fire/Crash Tender (Berliet GLC) 6-cyl., 145 bhp, 5F1R × 2, 7.56 × 2.50 × 3.40 m, 7830 kg. Tyres 11.00–20. Body/equipment: Sides VMA38. Produced during 1958–61. Pump capacity 2000 l/min. Vehicle carried **3400 litres** of water and 420 litres of foam.

Truck, 4-ton, 4 × 4, Amphibious (Marmon-Bocquet MB 800) Hispano-Suiza 150-bhp diesel, 5F1R × 2, wb 3.48 m, 6.78 × 2.41 m, 6100 kg. Tyres 14.00–20. Power transmission to wheels or to 12-in Dowty Hydrojet water propulsion unit, or to both simultaneously. Hyd. disc brakes. Coil spring independent suspension.

Carriers, Full-Track, Cargo (Hotchkiss TTC501 and HB40) 4-cyl. petrol engine (diesel optional), 4F1R × 2. Final drive at rear. Commercially available from 1966 (HB40). HB40 was amphibious and used for Polar expedition in 1967. TTC501 was military prototype (1970) with tilt cab and 1½-ton load capacity.

Tractor/Bulldozer, 4 × 4 (Continental CR8) Berliet 6-cyl. diesel, 150 bhp, 3F1R × 2, 4.90 × 2.40 × 2.28 m, 12,200 kg. 20-ton winch. Multi-purpose tractor with 21.00–25 low pressure tyres. Used for earthmoving and other purposes in forward areas. High standard of cross-country performance and manœuvrability. Road speed 55 km/h. 1960.

Tractor/Bulldozer, Full-Track (Richard Continental CD10) 300-bhp diesel engine with mechanical 4F4R transmission or 310-bhp diesel engine with 3F3R torque converter transmission. Maximum drawbar pull 28.3 and 46 tons respectively. Similar model also supplied by Saviem. Various US types were also used.

Excavator, Light, 4×4, Air-transportable (Matenin NX7)
MAN 6-cyl. m/f, 140 bhp, 'Power Shift' trans., 7.40 × 2.45 ×
3.60 m, 14,000 kg approx. Tyres 16.00–25. Digs trenches of
variable depth (max. 1.60 m) and constant predetermined width
(0.60 m) at high speed. Road speed 65 km/h. 1967.

**Excavator, Medium, 4×4, F1 (Matenin/Creusot-Loire
KX609)** Alsthom 8-cyl. diesel, air-cooled, 178 bhp, 7.70 (6.70)
× 2.50 × 3.50 m, 17,000 kg approx. Tyres 18.00–24. Max.
excavating depth 1.80 m at 0.60 or 0.90 m width (interchangeable bucket chains). Hydrokinetic type trans. to wheels and
digger. 1962.

**Shovel, Light, Truck-Mounted, 4×4, F1 (S.U.M.B./
Poclain CP120)** Hyd.-operated fully-slewing 150-litre bucket
on std MH600BS chassis. 5.11 × 2.10 × 2.58 m (travelling),
5400 kg. Medium type ('Yumbo', 300-litre bucket) was on
half-cab chassis (5.90 × 2.50 × 3.80 m) with Deutz engine.

**Shovel, Heavy, Truck-Mounted, 6×6 (Willème W6DA/
Richier 45CA)** 6-cyl. diesel (Willème 518), 178 bhp, 6F1R × 2,
10.45 × 2.50 × 3.77 m, 26,000 kg. Oleomat hyd. boom on
turntable, actuated from gearbox PTO. Optional **equipment:**
500-litre bucket or clamshell, 350-litre dragline **bucket, 9-ton
crane.** 1967.

Crane, Medium, Truck-Mounted, 4 × 4 (Griffet 745MS)
Berliet MDX45M 4-cyl. diesel, 120 bhp, 5F3R × 2, wb 3.65 m,
7.75 × 2.50 × 3.50 m, 16,800 kg.   Tyres 12.00–20.   Electric
crane operation. Pneumatic suspension locking system. Max.
lift (along centre line) : 10 tons at 2.50, 2.2 at 8.15 m. From 1962.

Crane, Medium, Truck-Mounted, 6 × 6 (Griffet G8)
Berliet M620Z 6-cyl. diesel, 160–180 bhp, 5F3R × 2, wb 4.55
(BC 1.70) m, 8.71 × 2.50 × 4.00 m, 23,600 kg. Tyres 16.00–24.
Electric crane operation. Max. lift 9 tons. Telescopic crane boom
providing lengths of 6, 8 and 10½ metres. From 1962.

Crane, Heavy, Truck-Mounted, 6 × 6, F1 (Griffet G15)
Berliet 6-cyl. diesel, 340 bhp, 'Power Shift' 4F3R trans.,
10.12 × 2.83 × 4.00 m, 37,130 kg. Tyres 18.00–25. Front and
centre axles steering. 10-ton winch. Electric crane operation;
generator in front of main engine. Max. lift 18 tons. 1969.

Crane, Aircraft, Truck-Mounted, 8 × 4 (Willème CG-8 × 4)
6-cyl., 220 bhp. 6F1R × 2, 11.90 × 3.58 (2.85) × 3.00 m, GVW
80,000 kg. Tyres, F/R 14.00–24/18.00–24 (outer rear wheels
carried on chassis brackets to reduce width for road use).
Applevage hyd. crane, max. capacity 18 tons.   Road speed
80 km/h. 1956.

ARMOURED VEHICLES
WHEELED and TRACKED

In addition to tanks (mainly the AMX 13 and 30 and their derivatives) the French forces use various types of wheeled and tracked AFVs incl. cargo and personnel carriers, ambulances, mortar carriers, etc. Hotchkiss developed various types of tracked carriers, many of which were exported. At one time the French employed large numbers of US wheeled, half- and full-tracked AFVs, as well as some types of British armoured cars (Humber, Coventry, Daimler 'Ferret'). The French Panhard AML (*Automitrailleuse Légère*) 4 × 4 and EBR (*Engin Blindé de Reconnaissance*) 8 × 8 armoured cars, were also sold to several other countries.

Car, Armoured, Guided Missiles, 4 × 4 (Panhard AML)
4-cyl., 90 bhp, 6F1R × 2, wb 2.50 m, 3.79 × 1.97 m, 4500 kg. Air-cooled HO engine at rear. Shown with NA2 turret for launching of Nord-Aviation SS11 or 12 missiles. Other turrets were available with various types of armament. From 1961.

Carrier, Armoured, Personnel, 4 × 4 (Panhard M3/VTT)
Front-engined derivative of the AML with two side and two rear doors. Carrying capacity 12 men or 1350 kg. Also command, ambulance and workshop versions. 95% of components inter-changeable with AML. GVW 5800 kg. Floatable. 1970/71.

Carrier, Armoured, Personnel, 4 × 4 (Berliet VXB) V-8-cyl. diesel, 170 bhp, 6F1R × 2, wb 3.10 m, 5.99 × 2.44 × 2.05 m (basic vehicle), GVW 11,500 kg. PAS. Tyres 14.00–20. Amphibious. Offered with various types of fittings and equipment. Developed from BL12 (prototypes, from 1967). **1971.**

Truck, Armoured, Personnel, 4 × 4 (Marmon-Bocquet MB 601) Simca V-8-cyl., 100 bhp, 4F1R × 2, wb 2.90 m. Prototype *Camion Blindé* produced in 1964 for police use. Based on Marmon-Bocquet MH600BS 1½-ton 4 × 4 truck chassis. Double rear doors. Machine gun ring mount.

Truck, Armoured, Personnel, 6 × 6 (Lorraine/Simca) *Camion Blindé* with accommodation for 12–15 men. Originally developed by Lorraine on Simca/Marmon-Herrington 6 × 6 truck chassis. Later prototypes on Berliet std 6 × 6 chassis (Model GBC KT with 5-cyl. m/f 125-bhp engine). No quantity production.

Car, Armoured, 8 × 8 (Panhard EBR) 12-cyl., 200 bhp, 4F1R × 4, 5.56 × 2.43 × 2.24 m, 12,600 kg. Produced during the 1950s with 75-mm gun, later 'up-gunned' to 90-mm. Centre wheels (all metal) retractable for road use (up to 100 km/h). Also produced as APC (ETT) with pneumatic tyres on all wheels. (Photo ECA).

Carrier, Armoured, 8 × 8 (Panhard M2) Experimental amphibious vehicle, unveiled in 1971, with 260-bhp engine, automatic transmission, hydro-pneumatic suspension, servo-controlled steering and braking. 6.14 × 2.50 × 1.72–2.05 (adjustable) m, GVW 12–14 tons. Fully amphibious. Road speed 92 km/h.

Carrier, Armoured, Full-Track, Low Silhouette (Hotchkiss VP90) First introduced in 1955 this vehicle was intended for escorting AT infantry units. It carried a crew of two (driver and gunner) in lying position (combat) or seated (road and approach). $3.46 \times 1.75 \times 0.93$ m, 1900 kg. Road speed 85 km/h. Gradability 75%.

Carrier, Armoured, Full-Track, Ambulance (Hotchkiss SP IV) 6-cyl., 164 bhp, 4F1R, $4.66 \times 2.28 \times 1.84$ m, 8 tons (combat wt). Road speed 58 km/h. Crew: driver and two medical attendants. Accommodation for two stretchers and one sitting case. Also ACV. AOP, APC, recce, etc. (*Véhicules Chenilles Légers*), from 1958.

Carrier, Armoured, Full-Track, Personnel, AMX10P (DTAT) Hispano-Suiza supercharged diesel, 280 bhp, semi-auto. 4F1R, $5.85 \times 2.78 \times 2.54$ m, 13,800 kg (combat wt). First of a new series of light AFVs. Amphibious (propulsion by Hydrojets). A wheeled (6×6) version was also built (AMX10R). 1971.

Vehicle, Armoured, Full-Track, Recovery, AMX55 (DTAT/SFAC) Sofam 8-cyl., 270 bhp, 5F1R, $5.60 \times 2.60 \times 2.80$ m, 15 tons (combat wt). Designed for front line vehicle recovery and as repair vehicle in repair base. 15-ton main and 1-ton aux. winch. Lifting capacity 5 tons. Typical derivation from the famous AMX13 tank.

GERMAN DEMOCRATIC REPUBLIC

On 30 June 1946 eleven motor vehicle factories in the Soviet-occupied zone of Germany, including those of Auto Union, BMW, Phänomen, etc., were confiscated by the Soviet SAG AWTOWELO and subsequently re-established as *Volkseigener Betriebe* (VEB, People's Enterprises). War-damaged plants were rebuilt and some re-commenced manufacture of vehicle types as produced previously. One major obstacle that had to be overcome was that in the Soviet zone there was no accessory and components industry for the supply of carburettors, electrical equipment, etc. In due course, however, these problems were solved and various German motorcycles, cars and trucks were revived such as the DKW F8 'Meisterklasse' and BMW 2-litre cars and the Phänomen trucks. For export some of these vehicles carried the IFA emblem. Later production got more rationalized and vehicles were redesignated because the nationalized factories were renamed, which added to the identification confusion. For example, the S4000-1 truck and its predecessor, the H3A, have been known variously as Horch, IFA and Sachsenring and towards the end of their production span had no marque name at all. The S4000-1 was produced by VEB Ernst Grube in Werdau, like the G-5 trucks which never carried a name either. The name Horch was used only occasionally but later dropped altogether. Although the old Horch factory of Auto Union was in Saxony, East Germany, the sole rights to the names Horch, Audi and Wanderer were held by Auto Union which is based in Düsseldorf, West Germany. As in most other countries many civilian type vehicles are used by the military and *vice versa*. East Germany, like Czechoslovakia, uses relatively few Soviet-made trucks. Both countries have an extensive automotive industry themselves and also export to various other satellite countries. AFVs, special purpose vehicles and heavy trucks, however, are imported mainly from the Soviet Union and Czechoslovakia, with only a few exceptions.

Who's Who in the East German Automotive Industry

Barkas	VEB Barkas-Werke, Hainichen, Sachsen (now Karl-Marx-Stadt) (from 1956; formerly Framo).
Combiquick	VEB Industriewerk Halle-Nord, Halle.
EMW	VEB Eisenacher Motoren Werke, Eisenach, Thüringen (1952–55; formerly BMW) (see also Wartburg).
Ernst Grube	VEB Kraftfahrzeugwerke Ernst Grube, Werdau, Sachsen (from 1953).
IFA (F9) *	VEB IFA, Zwickau, later Eisenach, Thüringen (1948–56; formerly Auto-Union).
IFA (W50) *	VEB Industriewerke Ludwigsfelde, VEB IFA Automobilwerke, 172 Ludwigsfelde (from 1965).
MZ	VEB Motorradwerk Zschopau, Zschopau, Sachsen (from 1949; formerly Auto-Union/DKW).
Phänomen	VEB Kraftfahrzeugwerk Phänomen, Zittau, Sachsen (formerly Phänomen-Werke Gustav Hiller) (see also Robur).
Robur	VEB Robur-Werke, Zittau, Sachsen (from 1950; formerly Phänomen).
Sachsenring	VEB Sachsenring Automobilwerke, Zwickau, Sachsen (1956–59; formerly Auto-Union/Horch).
Trabant	VEB Sachsenring Automobilwerke, Zwickau, Sachsen (from 1959; formerly VEB Automobilwerk Zwickau).
Wartburg	VEB Automobilwerk Eisenach, Eisenach, Thüringen (from 1956; formerly EMW, qv).

* From 1948–1965 IFA was a combine of nationalized automotive firms (Industrieverband Fahrzeugbau der DDR) and the name was used on various vehicles, mainly for export.

CARS, FIELD CARS
and MOTORCYCLES

Makes and Models: *Cars:* EMW 340 (4 × 2). Moskvich (4 × 2, SU). Sachsenring (4 × 2). Wartburg 311, 312, 353 (4 × 2). Wolga M21 (4 × 2, SU).
Field Cars: GAZ-69A, 69AM (later UAZ) (4 × 4, SU). IFA F9 (4 × 2). P2M (4 × 4). P2S (4 × 4, amphibious). P3 (4 × 4). Trabant P601/A (4 × 2) ('*Grenztrabant*'). Wartburg 311/4 (4 × 2).
Motorcycles: EMW R35 (2 × 1). MZ ES 250/2A (2 × 1, 3 × 1).

General Data: In addition to the Soviet GAZ-69A and UAZ-69A the East German forces used their own four-wheel drive field cars P2M and P3 and the amphibious P2S which to a certain extent resembled the war-time VW '*Schwimmwagen*'. The P2M was not very successful and in 1962 was replaced by the P3 which had an up-rated version of the same 6-cyl. engine. The P2M had transversal torsion bars as its suspension medium, resulting in different wheel base sizes, left and right, and had rather excessive front overhang. The P3 had longitudinal torsion bars. P3 cars produced later had a different engine bonnet, hinged at the rear. East Germany was the only East-bloc country to manufacture its own light 4 × 4 vehicles in quantity. They were produced in the Zwickau works. The Wartburg 311/4 was a '*Kübel*'-type police patrol car with four-doors and folding top on the civilian 311 car chassis (3-cyl. 2-stroke engine, front-wheel drive).

The MZ ES motorcycle was a standardized machine with single-cylinder 250-cc two-stroke engine and 4-speed gearbox. It weighed 156 kg and had a max. speed of 105 km/h. It also appeared with sidecar.

Vehicle shown (typical): Field Car, 7-seater, 4 × 4 (P3) (*Pkw-Kübelfahrzeug P3*)

Technical Data:
Engine: OM-6/35L 6-cylinder, I-I-W-F, 2407 cc, 75 bhp @ 3750 rpm. Torque 17 kgm @ 1500 rpm.
Transmission: 4F1R × 2 (OD top).
Brakes: hydraulic.
Tyres: 7.50–16.
Wheelbase: 2.40 m.
Overall l × w × h: 3.71 × 1.95 × 1.95 m.
Weight: 1860 kg. Payload 700 kg.
Note: Introduced in 1962, superseding P2M. Multipurpose vehicle. Max. speed 95 km/h. Gradability 65%. Torsion bar IFS/IRS. Diff. locks front and rear.

Field Car, 4-seater, 4 × 4, Command (P2M) 6-cyl., 65bhp, 4F1R × 2, wb L/R 2.285/2.215 m, 3.75 × 1.68 × 1.83 m, 1770 kg. Produced approx. 1955–62. Payload 400 kg. Speed 95 km/h. Independent suspension with torsion bars. Four-door *'Kübel'* bodywork. Tyres 6.50–16.

Field Car, 4-seater, 4 × 4, Amphibious (P2S) 6-cyl., 65 bhp, 4F1R × 2, 5.10 × 1.83 × 1.86 m, 1969 kg. *'Schwimmwagen'* based on P2M field car. Max. speed on roads 95 km/h, in water (with propeller) 9 km/h. Ground clearance 300 mm. 2.4-litre engine (as P3 but less powerful). Payload 450 kg.

Field Car, 4-seater, 4 × 2 (IFA F9) 3-cyl. 2-stroke, 30 bhp, 4F1R, wb 2.35 m, 4.20 × 1.65 × 1.50 m, 1000 kg approx. *'Kübel'* bodywork on front-drive chassis built by EMW in Eisenach, *c.* 1954. Tyres 5.50–16. Similar bodywork later on Wartburg 311/4 chassis. Used mainly by *Volkspolizei*.

Field Car, 4-seater, 4 × 2 (Trabant P601/A) 2-cyl. 2-stroke, 23 bhp, 4F1R, wb 2.02 m, 3.47 × 1.50 × 1.51 m, 645 kg. *'Kübel'* conversion of Trabant car, used by border police and known as *'Grenztrabant'*. 594.5-cc air-cooled engine driving front wheels. Speed 100 km/h. Two body styles.

TRUCKS, ½- to 6½-TON
4×2 and 4×4

Makes and Models: Barkas (formerly Framo) V901/2 (0.8-ton, 4×2). Barkas B1000 (1-ton, 4×2). GAZ-63 (2-ton, 4×4, SU). GAZ-69, 69M (later UAZ) (½-ton, 4×4, SU). H3A (Horch) (3½-ton, 4×2). H6, Z6 (Horch, E. Grube) (6½-ton, 4×2). Phänomen 'Granit' 27, 30 (2-ton, 4×2). Robur 'Garant' 30K, 32 (2-ton, 4×2), 30K (1-ton, 4×4), LO-2500 (2½-ton, 4×2), LO-1800A, AKF, AKF/GA, AKF/KR (1.8-ton, 4×4). S4000-1 (Horch/IFA/E. Grube) (4-ton, 4×2). W45 (IFA) (3½-ton, 4×4). W50L, LK, L/A, L/W (IFA) (5-ton, 4×2). W50LA/A (3-ton, 4×4).

General Data: One of the first trucks to go into production in the Soviet-occupied zone of Germany after 1945 was the Phänomen 'Granit'. It was produced in the original Phänomen factory in Zittau and was later renamed Robur 'Garant'. Production of both 4×2 and 4×4 vehicles ceased in 1961 in favour of the new Robur LO (petrol) and LD (diesel) COE range. The S4000-1 was a standard commercial truck, developed from the Horch H3A which had been introduced in 1953. It was produced in Werdau by the Ernst Grube works until its replacement by the new W50 series in 1965. A 4×4 version followed in 1969. The IFA-LKW W50 was designed and developed by the Ernst Grube works but series production started on 17 July 1965 in a newly built factory at Ludwigsfelde. On 26 January 1970 the 50,000th W50 truck came off the assembly line. Some Soviet 4×4 truck types are also used, mainly for special purposes.

Vehicle shown (typical): Truck, 1.8-ton, 4×4, Cargo (Robur LO-1800A)

Technical Data:
Engine: LO4 6-cylinder, I-I-A-F, 3345 cc, 70 bhp @ 2800 rpm. Torque 22 kgm @ 1900 rpm.
Transmission: 5F1R × 2.
Brakes: hydraulic.
Tyres: 10.00–20 (LO-1800 AKF/GA: 9.00–20).
Wheelbase: 3.025 m.
Overall l × w × h: 5.38 × 2.36 × 2.73 m.
Weight: 3200 kg. Payload 1800 kg.
Note: Allrad (4×4) version of Robur LO-2500. Standardized chassis, also with other bodystyles, e.g. ambulance, signals, workshop and water purification (WFS 3000) (house-type van bodies). From 1960. Later models had restyled radiator grille.

118

Truck, 1-ton, 4×4, Cargo (Robur 30K) 4-cyl., 60 bhp, 4F1R×2, wb 3.77 m, 5.75×2.00×2.56 (2.18) m, 2700 kg. Derived from wartime Phänomen 1500A. Also with closed cab and other bodystyles, incl. ambulance and 'Kübel'. Air-cooled 3-litre engine. Payload on roads 2 tons.

Truck, 4-ton, 4×2, Cargo (S4000-1) 4-cyl. diesel, 90 bhp, 5F1R, wb 3.55 m, 6.49×2.37×2.34(cab) m, 4100 kg. Developed from Horch H3A. Superseded by W50 series. Many optional bodystyles, incl. tipper, house-type vans, fire fighters, etc. Also supplied to China, North Vietnam, etc.

Truck, 5-ton, 4×2, Cargo (IFA W50L/A) 4-cyl. diesel, 125 bhp, 5F1R, wb 3.20 m, 6.53×2.50×3.20 (2.60) m, 5080 kg. Double rear axle (main carrier with separate parallel driving axle). Also with house-type workshop body (W50L/W), tipper (W50L/K), etc. Built at Ludwigsfelde, from 1965 (design E. Grube).

Truck, 3-ton, 4×4, Cargo, w/Winch (IFA W50LA/A) 4-cyl. diesel, 125 bhp, 5F1R×2, 9300 kg. Special 16.00–20 tyres. Central tyre pressure regulating system. Power steering. Differential locks, front and rear. 4½-ton winch under body with fairlead pulleys at front and rear. Introduced in 1969.

TRUCKS, 2½- to 10-TON 6 × 6 and 8 × 8

Makes and Models: G-5, G-5/2, G-5/3 (E. Grube) (3½-ton, 6 × 6), G-5/TLF 15 (E. Grube) (fire fighter, 6 × 6). KrAZ-214 (7-ton, 6 × 6, SU). MAZ-543 (10-ton, 8 × 8, SU). Tatra T141 (prime mover, 6 × 6, CS), T813 (8-ton, 8 × 8, CS). Ural-375D (5-ton, 6 × 6, SU). ZIL-135 (10-ton, 8 × 8, SU), ZIL-157 (2½-ton, 6 × 6, SU), ZIL-485 (BAV) (amphibious, 2½-ton, 6 × 6, SU).

General Data: The 'workhorse' of the East German armed forces was the G-5 6 × 6 truck, produced from 1957 by *VEB Kraftfahrzeugwerk Ernst Grube*. It was used with many different body types by all services and also served as a prime mover for trailers and artillery. The riot control vehicle SK-2 was also based on this chassis. Some G-5 trucks had a soft-top cab with folding windscreen but usually a conventional closed cab was fitted, often with a circular roof hatch. Late production models had an up-rated engine (150 vs 120 bhp). Bodies included: cargo, tipper (dump), house-type van, tanker, revolving cranes, decontamination equipment, etc.

A much-modernized vehicle, the G-5/3, was developed as a possible replacement. It featured larger low-pressure tyres, single allround, with central pressure regulating system, an air-cooled V-8 diesel developing 150 bhp and entirely new bodywork. The actual replacement vehicle, however, was the Russian Ural-375D which was also produced (or assembled) in East Germany. The Soviet ZIL-157 was used mainly for special purposes and as a tractive unit for semi-trailers. Several other, heavier, Soviet 6 × 6 vehicles were also employed. The MAZ-543 and ZIL-135 8 × 8 were used in conjunction with mobile rocket launching systems.

Vehicle shown (typical): Truck, 3½-ton, 6 × 6, Cargo (Ernst Grube G-5)

Technical Data:
Engine: EMb W6-20 diesel, 6-cylinder, I-I-W-F, 9840 cc, 120 bhp @ 2000 rpm. Torque 48 kgm @ 1000 rpm.
Transmission: 5F1R × 2.
Brakes: air.
Tyres: 8.25–20.
Wheelbase: 4.42 m. BC 1.25 m.
Overall l × w × h: 7.17 × 2.50 × 3.00 (2.60) m.
Weight: 7850 kg.
Note: Payload on roads 5 tons. Max. speed 60 km/h. Gradability 42.5%. Fording depth 1.05 m. Also with soft-top cab. Model G5/2 had 150-bhp engine.

Truck, 3½-ton, 6 × 6, Dump (G-5) 6-cyl. diesel, 120 bhp, 5F1R × 2, wb 4.42 (BC 1.25) m, 8500 kg approx. Hopper-type all-steel tipper (dump) body, hydraulically-operated. Also produced with hydraulic three-way tipper body. Turning radius 9.5 m.

Truck, 3½-ton, 6 × 6, Tanker STW 1550 (TG-5/2) 6-cyl. diesel, 150 bhp, 5F1R × 2. *Strassentankwagen 1550* with 4000-litre capacity used for haulage of fuel and lubricating oils, often in conjunction with trailer 1565 (shown) with 4500-litre capacity.

Truck, 3½-ton, 6 × 6, Wrecker (G-5/2) 6-cyl. diesel, 150 bhp, 5F1R × 2. 3-ton Bleichert crane. Two large lockers behind cab for recovery equipment and tools. Crane was manually operated and revolved through 360°. Replaced by ADK hydraulic type.

Truck, 3½-ton, 6 × 6, Fire Fighting (G-5/TLF15) 6-cyl. diesel, 120 bhp, 5F1R × 2. Long-wheelbase G-5 chassis with crew cab and comprehensive equipment. TLF means *Tanklöschfahrzeug*. Front-mounted pump, driven by vehicle's engine. Also as airfield crash tender with foam cannon.

MISCELLANEOUS VEHICLES

In addition to the various wheeled cars and trucks listed in the foregoing pages the East German armed forces also employ many special equipment and special purpose vehicles on wheeled and tracked chassis. Some of these are shown in this section. Soviet types used have included tracked prime movers (AT-S, AT-T), a tracked APC (BTR-50(P)), various wheeled APCs and armoured cars (BTR-40, 40A and 40 (P) (BRDM) 4 × 4, BTR-152 and 152V 6 × 6, and BTR-60 (P) 8 × 8), tanks (T34/85, T54, T55, PT76, etc.). Some of the tracked AFV chassis were also used as bases for special purpose machines such as bull-dozers, ARVs, etc.

Gun, 85-mm, Anti-Tank, SFK 85 (HA) This is a Russian *Pak* M-45, normally towed by a 6 × 6 prime mover but equipped with a 750-cc 22-bhp auxiliary petrol engine for self-propulsion under suitable conditions. Maximum road speed 27 km/h.

Armoured Car, 4 × 4, SK-1 (Robur 30 K) 4-cyl., 55 bhp, 4F1R × 2, wb 3.77 m, 4.00 × 2.00 × 2.80 m, 5400 kg. Produced in 1954/55 on Robur 'Garant' 30K chassis. Crew 5. Used by the 'People's Police'. Armour 8-mm. Armament one 7.92-mm MG34. Air-cooled engine. Speed 80 km/h.

Truck, 3½-ton, 6 × 6, Riot Control, SK-2 (G-5) 6-cyl. diesel, 120 bhp, 5F1R × 2, wb 5.55 m, 7.50 × 2.50 × 4.30 m, 9100 kg. Turret-mounted water cannon with max. range of 70 m. Lightly armoured front end and cab. Large tank at rear. Note detail differences between units shown.

Vehicle, Universal, Engineers, 4 × 4 (GMG 2-70 'Combiquick') 4-cyl. diesel, 70 bhp (or petrol, 70 bhp), 5F5R × 1, wb 1.80 m, 3.76 × 2.20 × 2.40 m, 3300 kg. Universal carrier for various types of equipment, incl. fork lift, loading bucket, crane (max. 1.7 tons), shovel, dozer blade, etc. 2½-ton winch. Mid-1960s.

Tractor, Wheeled, 4 × 2 (ZT 300) 4-cyl. diesel (4VD 14.5/12-1 SRW), 90 bhp, 9F6R, 4.76 × 2.02 × 2.60 m, 5100 kg. Towed load 22 tons. Max. speed 30 km/h. Tyres, front 7.50–20, rear 15.00–30. Track width adjustable. Turning circle 5.1 m. Twin-disc clutch. Basically industrial/agricultural type.

Tractor, Bulldozer, Full-Track (KT-50) 4-cyl. diesel (4F 175D5), 63 bhp, 3F1R, 4.45 × 1.95 × 2.45 m, 7900 kg. Towed load 9 tons. Speed 6.6 km/h. Hydraulically-actuated dozer blade. Dozer blade width and height 2.70 × 0.80 m. Used by Army Engineers for road building and similar purposes.

Vehicle, Tank Recovery, Full-Track (Chassis SU-76) Twin 150-bhp 6-cyl. diesels, 5.03 × 2.68 × 2.10 m. Modification of war-time Soviet Gun Motor Carriage (SP assault gun SU-76), used as heavy recovery and repair vehicle. East German diesel engines replaced the original 140-bhp petrol units.

GERMAN FEDERAL REPUBLIC

Wheeled vehicles produced in the Federal Republic of Germany after 1945 could broadly be divided into three main groups, namely commercial, military commercial, and military tactical. The first of these groups covers a multitude of cars, buses, trucks and tractors which if used by armed forces were not, or very little, different from vehicles produced for civilian purposes. For military use they were only painted a different colour and sometimes modified in minor details. Examples of such 'administrative' vehicles were Opel 'Kapitän' sedans used by the US Forces in Germany, Hanomag prime movers used by the French occupation forces, Ford 'Rhein' trucks used by the Belgians, Volkswagens used by BAOR (British Army of the Rhine), etc. Several of these 4×2 cars and trucks were later also acquired by the semi-military German Border Police (*BGS, Bundesgrenzschutz*) and by the Federal Army (*Bundeswehr*) for administrative use. The second group comprises a large number of commercial vehicles which were equipped with all-wheel drive, intended mainly for civilian use (notably off-road tippers) and for export. Most of the big German truck manufacturers introduced such *Allrad* types during the early 1950s. These trucks were relatively inexpensive (compared with tactical types) because, apart from the transfer case and driven front axle, they were virtually identical to the mass-produced conventional models. Consequently they were acquired in considerable quantities by military authorities in and outside Germany and used with general purpose (cargo) or special bodywork. When in 1956 the *Bundeswehr* was formed, most of its initial equipment was supplied by the USA, with the exception of 'soft skin' vehicles, practically all of which were acquired from the German industry which from about 1954 had produced a variety of prototypes for tactical vehicles, mostly derived from models belonging to the second group mentioned above. Notable exceptions were three $\frac{1}{4}$-ton 4×4 field cars, developed by Auto Union, Goliath and Porsche, which were entirely new except for the engines and transmission components. Applying the lessons learned in World War II it was decided to keep the number of basic types down to an absolute minimum, although at first this was not entirely possible because of numerical needs (about 100,000) in relation to the manufacturers' capabilities in terms of production output. Following NATO standardization requirements for vehicle classifications the following truck types were standardized in 1956/57 and put into quantity production:

NATO Class	STAN* designation	Drive	Manufacturer(s)
$\frac{1}{4}$-ton	Lkw 0,25 t gl	4×4	Auto Union
1-ton	Lkw 0,75 t gl	4×4	Borgward
	Lkw 1,5 t gl	4×4	Daimler-Benz
3-ton	Lkw 3 t gl	4×4	Ford
6-ton	Lkw 5 t gl	4×4	Daimler-Benz, MAN
	Lkw 7 t gl	6×6	Klöckner-Humboldt-Deutz
10-ton	Lkw 10 t gl	6×6	Faun
	Lkw 12 t gl	6×6	Faun
	Lkw 15 t gl	6×6	Faun

* **Stärke- und Ausrüstungsnachweisung.** Load in tons is cross-country payload rating.

Production of the $\frac{1}{4}$-ton 4×4 Auto Union 'Munga' was discontinued in 1968. Its replacement for the 1970s, a $\frac{1}{2}$-ton 4×4, was first decided on in 1964/65 and will also replace various similar vehicles in other NATO countries. For the design and development of the new vehicle two groups of manufacturers were formed, namely MAN/Glas-Saviem-Fiat and Büssing-Hotchkiss-Lancia. Glas (BMW) completed their first prototype in 1966: a forward-control amphibious six-seater with 80-bhp 2-litre BMW engine and $4F1R \times 2$ transmission. Other prototypes followed. From the point of standardization the Magirus (Klöckner-Humboldt-Deutz) and Faun ranges of trucks were interesting in that both used air-cooled Deutz diesel and multi-fuel engines of various configurations but with a high number of interchangeable parts.

GERMAN FEDERAL REPUBLIC

The same family of Deutz engines was also used for many special purpose vehicles. Some of the vehicles shown and/or listed in the following pages remained in the prototype/ experimental stage or were only sold to commercial operators or non-military government departments, or for military use by other Governments.

By 1970 the German armed forces had in their inventory over 125,000 wheeled vehicles of all types, many of which had become sub-standard. A new generation of wheeled armoured vehicles and trucks in the 2-ton and higher payload classes was initiated by the German Ministry of Defence in the mid-1950s. In 1964 the German motor industry was approached with definite proposals. The requirements were for tactical 4×4, 6×6 and 8×8 vehicles in the following categories: armoured amphibious vehicles, unarmoured amphibious trucks, and unarmoured non-amphibious trucks. A very high degree of standardization of parts and components was specified. In order to deal with the design and production of these vehicles five major manufacturers joined together to form a Joint Project Office (*Gemeinschaftsbüro*) namely Büssing, Klöckner-Humboldt-Deutz, Krupp, MAN, and Rheinstahl-Henschel. In addition, the Daimler-Benz AG decided to participate independently. It was estimated that over 50,000 vehicles of eight different types would eventually be ordered from either of these two organisations following stringent trials and evaluation. Several models reached prototype stage during 1967–70. However, in 1971, at the suggestion of the Federal German Defence Ministry, the *Gemeinschaftsbüro* and Daimler-Benz decided to co-operate on the development of the overall programme. The former consortium then concentrated on the development of the unarmoured vehicles (with air-cooled m/f engines) whilst Daimler-Benz assumed responsibility for the armoured vehicles (with water-cooled m/f engines).

Who's Who in the West German Automotive Industry

Auto Union	Auto Union GmbH, Düsseldorf & Ingolstadt.
BMW	Bayerische Motorenwerke AG, München.
Borgward	Carl F. W. Borgward GmbH, Bremen.*
Büssing	Büssing Automobilwerke AG, Braunschweig.
Daimler-Benz	(see Mercedes-Benz).
Deutz	Klöckner-Humboldt-Deutz AG, Köln.
DKW	(see Auto Union).
EWK	H. W. Gehlen KG Eisenwerke, Kaiserslautern.
Faun	Faun-Werke Karl Schmidt, Lauf/Pegnitz.
Ford	Ford-Werke AG, Köln-Niehl.
Goliath	Goliath-Werk GmbH, Bremen.*
Hanomag	Rheinstahl Hanomag AG, Hannover-Linden.
Henschel	Rheinstahl Henschel AG, Kassel.
Kaelble	Carl Kaelble GmbH, Backnang bei Stuttgart.
Kässbohrer	Karl Kässbohrer Fahrzeugwerke GmbH, Ulm/Donau.
Krupp	Fried. Krupp GmbH, Essen.
Maico	Maico Fahrzeugfabrik GmbH, Pfaffingen.
Magirus	Klöckner-Humboldt-Deutz AG, Werk Ulm, Ulm/Donau.
MAN	Maschinenfabrik Augsburg-Nürnberg AG, München-Karlsfeld.
Mercedes-Benz	Daimler-Benz AG, Stuttgart-Untertürkheim (also Gaggenau & Mannheim).
Opel	Adam Opel AG, Rüsselsheim/Main.
Porsche	Dr.-Ing h.c.F. Porsche KG, Stuttgart-Zuffenhausen.
Still	Hans Still GmbH, Hamburg.
Tempo	Herbert Vidal & Co., Hamburg-Harburg.*
Volkswagen	Volkswagenwerk AG, Wolfsburg.

* now defunct

CARS and MOTORCYCLES

The German military forces used relatively few types of passenger cars (Auto Union 1000S, Opel, Volkswagen, etc). Many more were supplied to the American, Belgian, British and French forces stationed in Germany. Other German cars were exported for military use in Austria, Belgium, Denmark, the Netherlands, etc. They were mainly the products of Daimler-Benz, Ford-Köln, Opel and Volkswagen. In most respects they were similar to their civilian counterparts. The motorcycle which was standardized for military service in Germany was the Maico M250/B (from 1961) but Ardie, DKW (RT250 series) and twin-cyl. BMW machines were also employed. In 1971, the Maico was superseded by a similar but more modern machine produced by Hercules.

Motorcycle, Solo (Maico M250/B) 1-cyl., 14.9 bhp, 4F, wb 1.33 m, 2.01 × 0.80 × 1.07 m, 165 kg. Tyres 3.25/3.50–18. *Melder-Krad* or *Krad, geländegängig* with 247-cc two-stroke engine, used by *Bundeswehr* and *Bundesgrenzschutz*. Military version of civilian machine. 10,000 produced, 1961–66.

Car, Light, 4-seater, 4 × 2, Convertible (Volkswagen 151) 4-cyl., 34 bhp, 4F1R, wb 2.40 m, 4.07 × 1.54 × 1.50 m, 800 kg. Many VWs were supplied for military use in several countries. Cabriolet shown (1962/3) was for *Bundesgrenzschutz* and differed from civilian model mainly in colour and equipment.

Car, Medium, 4- to 5-seater, 4 × 2, Sedan (Opel 'Kapitän') 6-cyl., 55 bhp, 3F1R, wb 2.69 m. 1949/50. Early post-war 'Kapitän' differed from 1939/40 model mainly in shape of headlights (round instead of almost square). Opels were used by most military forces in Germany.

FIELD CARS

Makes and Models: Auto Union 'Munga' F91/4 (3035) ($\frac{1}{4}$-ton, 4 × 4, 1955), 'Munga 4' F91/4/1000 (3038) and 'Munga 6' F91/6 (3036) ($\frac{1}{4}$-ton, 4 × 4, 1958), 'Munga 6' F91/6/1000 (3039) and 'Munga 8' F91/8/1000 (3039) ($\frac{1}{4}$-ton, 4 × 4, 1962). Borgward B2000A/0 ($\frac{3}{4}$-ton, 4 × 4, 1955; 1962–68: Büssing). Büssing ($\frac{1}{2}$-ton, 4 × 4, 1969/70). Fahr 'Farmobil' (multi-purpose carrier, 4 × 2, 1960). Faun/ZU 'Kraka' (multi-purpose carrier, 4 × 2, 1962), 'Kraka' 640 (1970). Glas/BMW ($\frac{1}{2}$-ton, 4 × 4, 1967/68). Goliath 31 ($\frac{1}{4}$-ton, 4 × 4, 1954/55) and 34/GM1100J ($\frac{1}{4}$-ton, 4 × 4, 1957). Hanomag *Allrad* (1$\frac{1}{2}$-ton, 4 × 4, 1963). Land-Rover Series II(A), SWB and LWB ($\frac{1}{4}$- and $\frac{3}{4}$-ton, 4 × 4, 1967, GB). MBB ($\frac{1}{2}$-ton, 4 × 4, 1971). Porsche 597 ($\frac{1}{4}$-ton, 4 × 4, from 1954). Tempo/Land-Rover ($\frac{1}{4}$-ton, 4 × 4, 1952) and 041 ($\frac{1}{4}$-ton, 4 × 4, 1954). Volkswagen VW181 (0.4-ton, 4 × 2, 1969). Zweirad Union (ZU) (see Faun).

General Data: In 1954/55 three manufacturers supplied prototypes for a $\frac{1}{4}$-ton 4 × 4 vehicle (*Lkw 0,25 t gl*) for the new German Army, namely Auto Union, Goliath and Porsche. After initial tests orders followed for 50 Goliaths, 50 Porsches and 5000 Auto Unions. The former two did not go into mass production although a few were sold for civilian purposes. The Auto Union 'Munga' was standardized and about 55,000 were produced up to 1968. Munga stands for *Mehrzweck Universal Geländewagen mit Allradantrieb* (multi-purpose universal field car with all-wheel drive). Civilian versions were introduced also and many were exported. Foreign armies using the 'Munga' included the British (mainly in West Berlin), Dutch, French and Indonesian. Developments of a replacement vehicle commenced during the 1960s by several manufacturers in Germany, France and Italy.

Vehicle shown (typical): Field Car, 4-seater, 4 × 4 (Auto Union 'Munga' F91/4/1000 3038) (*Lkw 0,25 t gl*)

Technical Data:
Engine: Auto Union AU1000 3-cylinder, I-T-W-F, 980 cc, 44 bhp @ 4250 rpm (1956–58: 897 cc, 40 bhp @ 4000 rpm).
Transmission: 4F1R × 2 (permanent all-wheel drive, except on 1955–56 models).
Brakes: hydraulic.
Tyres: 6.00–16.
Wheelbase: 2.00 m.
Overall l × w × h: 3.45 × 1.70 × 1.75 (1.33) m.
Weight: 1200 kg approx.
Notes: IFS/IRS with transversal leaf springs. Two-stroke engine ('3 = 6'). Also known as 'Munga 4' (4-seater).

Field Car, 8-seater, 4×4 (Auto Union 'Munga 8' F91/8/1000 3039) 3-cyl., 44 bhp, 4F1R×2, wb 2.00 m, 3.59×1.77 ×1.92 m, GVW 1810 kg. 'Munga 6' 6-seater (F91/6/1000) similar but 150 mm shorter at rear. Both had lengthwise seats in rear body and hinged tail gate. Produced Feb. 1962 to Dec. 1968. Payload 690 kg.

Field Car, 4-seater, 4×4 (Porsche 597) 4-cyl., 50 bhp, 5F1R, wb 2.05 m, 3.62×1.60×1.50 m, 990 kg. Air-cooled 1582-cc engine at rear. Unitary body construction with torsion-bar IFS/IRS. Prototype (1954) had flat body panels and 1488-cc engine. Final (1957–58) model had four doors.

Field Car, 4-seater, 4×4 (Goliath 31) 2-cyl., 40 bhp, 5F1R, wb 2.15 m, 3.57×1.56×1.60 (1.23) m, 1000 kg. Tyres 7.00–16. Two-stroke 887-cc fuel injection engine. Prototype, 1955. With many modifications it went into limited production in 1956 but was soon succeeded by the 4-cyl. 34/GM1100J.

Field Car, 4-seater, 4×4 (Goliath 34/GM1100J) 4-cyl., 50 bhp, 4F1R×2, wb 2.00 m, 3.58×1.58×1.68 (1.27) m, 1150 kg. Tyres 6.00–16. Horizontally-opposed four-stroke OHV 1093-cc engine. IFS. Rigid rear axle. Permanent all-wheel drive. Limited production, 1957–59.

Carrier, Multi-purpose, 4 × 2 (Faun/ZU 'Kraka') BMW 2-cyl., 26 bhp, 4F1R, wb 2.01 m, 2.76 × 1.42 × 1.35 m (folded: 1.75 × 1.42 × 0.95 m), 640 kg. Designed by Nicholas Straussler and first produced by Zweirad Union, 1962. Taken over by Faun. 22–12 'Lypsoid' tyres. Also produced in Italy (MV). *'Kraka'* stands for *Kraftkarren*. Payload 750–1000 kg.

Field Car, 6-seater, 4 × 4 (Tempo/Land-Rover) 4-cyl., 52 bhp, 4F1R × 2, wb 2.03 m, 3.35 × 1.55 × 1.92 (1.42) m, 1200 kg. approx. 1952/53 model shown. 1954 Model 041 had 2.18 m wb and spare wheel on bonnet. Some had capstan winch at front. Used by *Bundesgrenzschutz*. Built under Rover licence.

Field Car, 4-seater, 4 × 2 (Volkswagen 181) 4-cyl., 44 bhp, 4F1R, wb 2.40 m, 3.78 × 1.64 × 1.62 m, 955 kg. 1493-cc (1500) (1971: 1600) engine. Rear wheel hub reduction gears (as 'Transporter'). Tyres 165–15. Speed 110 km/h. GVW 1340 kg. 2000 supplied in 1969 to *Bundeswehr* (designation: *Pkw 0,4 t).*

Field Car, Amphibious, 6-seater, 4 × 4 (Glas/BMW 0,5 t) BMW 2000 4-cyl., 80 bhp, 4F1R × 2, wb 2.00 m, 3.51 × 1.70 × 1.83 (1.26) m, 1300 kg. Produced experimentally, also with air-cooled MAN 70-bhp, 4-cyl. m/f engine. Speed 110 (in water 9) km/h. Tyres 7.00–16.

Field Car, Amphibious, 6-seater, 4 × 4 (Büssing 0,5 t)
Prototype for amphibious ½-ton 4 × 4 cross-country vehicle, designed by Büssing-Hotchkiss-Lancia consortium. Like the Glas prototype this model was powered by a BMW engine. 1969/70.

Field Car, Amphibious, 6-seater, 4 × 4 (MBB 0,5 t)
BMW 4-cyl., 95 bhp, wb 2.25 m, 3.91 × 1.64 × 1.18 (min.) m, 1700 kg. Max. speed 105 km/h. Gradability 60% at 4 km/h. Fibreglass sandwich-type body. Tyres 7.00–16. GVW 2200 kg. Developed by Messerschmitt-Bölkow-Blohm GmbH, 1970/71.

Field Car, Heavy, 9-seater, 4 × 4 (Borgward B2000A/0, 0,75 t gl) 6-cyl., 82 bhp, 4F1R × 2, wb 3.20 m, 5.28 × 1.90 × 2.15 (1.85) m, 2470 kg. 'Kübel' bodywork on light truck chassis. Also with hardtop. Tyres 9.00–16. GVW 3500 kg. Speed 95 km/h. Large locker at rear. Introduced 1955. Later produced by Büssing (1962–68).

Field Car, Heavy, 9-seater, 4 × 4 (Hanomag Allrad) 4-cyl. diesel, 70 bhp, 4F1R × 2, wb 3.48 m, 5.40 × 2.00 × 2.37 m. GVW 4700 kg. 'Kübel' bodywork (personnel carrier) for *Bundesgrenzschutz*. Chassis also supplied with hard-top cab and open or closed special bodies. Rheinstahl Hanomag Model D28ALAS engine.

TRUCKS and BUSES
4 × 2

The majority of vehicles in this category were supplied to occupation forces stationed in Germany and for export to other countries. They were all basically contemporary civilian types, sometimes fitted with special bodywork. Suppliers included Auto Union (DKW), Borgward, Büssing, Faun, Ford, Hanomag, Henschel, Magirus-Deutz, Opel, Still, Tempo and Volkswagen. Buses were supplied mainly by Daimler-Benz (various rear-engined types), Büssing, Ford (early COE models, later 'Transit' (also ambulance version)) and Magirus-Deutz. The French and US forces in Germany at one time operated Henschel-modified diesel-engined GMC CCKW–353 buses.

Truck, 2-ton, 4 × 2, Cargo (Still) Twin 40-volt electric motors, one driving each rear wheel. 3F1R. Rear wheel brakes only. Radius of action about 75 km. Speed 25–30 km/h. Produced by Hans Still GmbH, Hamburg, for British Army in Germany (1950s).

Truck, 1-ton, 4 × 2, Fire Fighting (Volkswagen 'Transporter') Based on early VW pickup truck, used by Canadian Army. VW 'Transporters' of various types (pickup truck, van, *Kombi*, microbus, etc.), are used for military purposes by many countries incl. Australia, Austria, Belgium, Great Britain, the Netherlands, etc.

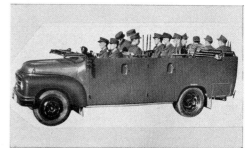

Truck, 1½-ton, 4 × 2, Personnel Carrier (Hanomag L28) 4-cyl. diesel truck chassis with 12-seater bodywork, equipped with folding windscreen, full-length folding-type canvas roof, equipment lockers, etc. Used by *Bundesgrenzschutz* as *Mannschaftstransportwagen*. Also with house-type radio body, *c.* 1957.

Truck, 1½-ton, 4 × 2, Radio (Hanomag L28) 4-cyl. diesel, 50 bhp, 4F1R, wb 4.00 m. GVW 4270 kg. *Funkwagen* (radio vehicle) of the German border police. Special house-type body on commercial chassis. Dutch Air Force used Hanomag 'Garant' forward-control 4 × 2 chassis with bus body.

Truck, 2½-ton, 4 × 2, End Dump (Ford G398 TS) V-8-cyl., 95 bhp, 4F1R, wb 4.01 m. Supplied to US Army in Germany, 1954–57. Also cargo (G398TH), shop van and diesel-engined models (G1Y8T, 1951). Ford-Köln COE bus chassis included G490B (British Army, 1954) and G199B (USAF, 1957).

Truck, 2½-ton, 4 × 2, Personnel Carrier (Borgward B2000) 4-cyl. diesel truck chassis, 1953, with soft-top bodywork. Borgward also supplied chassis of a later type (B1500, 1958, with built-in headlights) for ambulance (*Sanka*) bodywork of two types: house-type with separate cab and integral cab/body (Miesen).

Bus, 40-passenger, 4 × 2 (Mercedes-Benz O321H) 6-cyl. diesel, 110 bhp, 5F1R, wb 4.18 m, 9.22 × 2.50 × 2.95 m, GVW 10,150 kg. Model OM321 5.1-litre engine at rear. Unitary body/chassis construction. 1958–64. Used by *Bundeswehr*. Superseded in 1965 by Model O302KR. Büssing buses were used also.

TRUCKS, $\frac{3}{4}$- to $2\frac{1}{2}$-TON 4 × 4

Makes and Models: Borgward B2000A (2-ton, 1955), B2500A ($2\frac{1}{2}$-ton, 1956), B2000A/O Lkw 0,75 t gl ($\frac{3}{4}$-ton, 1955), Lkw 1,5 t gl ($1\frac{1}{2}$-ton, 1956). Ford G39TA, G39TH, G493SA-S1 ($2\frac{1}{2}$-ton, 1955). Hanomag AL28 ($1\frac{1}{2}$-ton, 1955), 70PS *Allrad* ($1\frac{1}{2}$-ton, 1965). Mercedes-Benz 'Unimog' (various types, 1-ton, from 1949), 'Unimog' S 404 ($1\frac{1}{2}$-ton, 1955). Opel 'Blitz' (1-ton, 1955).

General Data: When the *Bundeswehr* was organized in the mid-1950s, several manufacturers developed military all-wheel drive versions of their contemporary commercial trucks. Carl F. W. Borgward GmbH introduced two ranges of light 4 × 4 trucks, one with the then current civilian front end and cab and one of military pattern design. The former type was also supplied to the British forces in Germany and to civilian customers and government departments. Of the latter type there were three basic chassis versions viz. $\frac{3}{4}$-, $1\frac{1}{2}$- and $2\frac{1}{2}$-tonners, which differed mainly in tyre and brake equipment. Large quantities were produced until Borgward was closed down in 1961.

Hanomag introduced their 4 × 4 $1\frac{1}{2}$-tonner in 1955. It was, again, basically a commercial vehicle. Military customers for the Hanomag included the German *Bundesgrenzschutz* and the Dutch Air Force. By far the most widely used truck in this category, however, is the 'Unimog' of Daimler-Benz. The 'S' type $1\frac{1}{2}$-ton truck version is used by all the German military services and also by several foreign armies incl. the Austrian, Belgian, British (W. Berlin) and French. There was a variety of body types including various house-type vans (ambulance, radio, etc.). The 'Unimog' was first conceived in 1946 by Herr Friedrich of Daimler-Benz as a compact 4 × 4 multi-purpose vehicle for agricultural and industrial use and made its public debut in 1948. Daimler-Benz not having facilities for the production and marketing of agricultural machines, series production was taken up by Gebr. Boeringer in Goppingen, in 1949. During early 1951, however, production and further development of the 'Unimog' were transferred to the Gaggenau plant of Daimler-Benz. Many variations appeared, together with a multitude of accessories and special equipments. 'Unimog' stands for *Universal Motor Gerät* (universal power plant).

Vehicle shown (typical): Truck, $1\frac{1}{2}$-ton, 4 × 4, Cargo (Mercedes-Benz 'Unimog' S 404.114) (*Lkw 1,5 t gl*)

Technical Data:
Engine: Daimler-Benz M180 6-cylinder, I-I-W-F, 2195 cc, 80 bhp @ 4850 rpm.
Transmission: 6F2R.
Brakes: hydraulic.
Tyres: 10.00–20.
Wheelbase: 2.90 m.
Overall l × w × h: 4.93 × 2.15 × 2.60 (2.04) m.
Weight: 2900 kg. GVW: 4400 kg.
Note: Front and rear diff. locks. Speed range 1.5 to 95 km/h. Drop-side body. Elevated rigid axles. Coil spring suspension. Shown with special 5-seater cab. Optional equipment included closed cab, winch, etc.

Truck, 1-ton, 4×4, Prime Mover (Mercedes-Benz 'Unimog' U34/411) 4-cyl. diesel, 34 bhp, 6F2R, wb 1.72 m, 3.52×1.63×2.05 (1.60) m, 1700 kg approx. Basic version of the 'Unimog' range. 'Portal' axles with hub reduction gears. Coil spring suspension. Diff. locks. Four PTO points. Also with closed cab. Model 2010 similar.

Truck, 1½-ton, 4×4, Radio (Mercedes-Benz 'Unimog' S 404) 6-cyl., 80 bhp, 6F2R, wb 2.90 m. *Fernmelde* vehicle. Other house-type vans (*Kofferfahrzeuge*): *Sanka, Feuerleitstelle, Vermessung, Wartungstrupp*, etc. Note closed cab with roof hatch. Also basis for rotary snow plough units, produced by Beilhack of Rosenheim.

Truck, 1½-ton, 4×4, Cargo (Mercedes-Benz 'Unimog') 6-cyl., 80 bhp, 6F2R, wb 2.20 m, 4.12×2.10×2.16 m, GVW 3800 kg. Tyres 10.00–18. Prototype for 'Unimog' S type, produced in 1955. Similar to basic 'Unimog' but fitted with petrol engine (as in MB220 car). Gradability with full load 60%.

Truck, 1-ton, 4×4, Cargo (Opel 'Blitz') 6-cyl., 58 bhp, 4F1R×2, wb 3.30 m, 5.48×1.96×2.52 m, GVW 3600 kg. Prototype, 1955, also with house-type van body (height 2.70 m). Tyres 9.00–16. Speed 85 km/h. Derived from contemporary Opel 'Blitz' 2-ton 4×2 (many of which were used by the French Army in Germany (FFA)).

Truck, 2-ton, 4 × 4, Cargo (Borgward B2000A-Otto)
6-cyl., 82 bhp, 4F1R × 2, wb 3.40 m, 5.50 × 2.00 × 2.60 m, GVW 4100 kg. Military version of commercial truck. 6.50–20 tyres. Similar type used by British RAF, 1958, with GS body and water purification plant (tyres 7.50–20, air brakes instead of hyd.).

Truck, 2-ton, 4 × 4, Radio (Borgward B2000A-Diesel)
4-cyl. diesel, 60 bhp, 4F1R × 2, wb 3.40 m. Military 4 × 4 truck with house-type van body (*Koffer-Aufbau*) derived from commercial B2500A-Diesel. Truck also appeared with winch (at front), roof hatch, and different bodywork.

Truck, 1½-ton, 4 × 4, Personnel Carrier (Hanomag AL28)
4-cyl. diesel, 70 bhp, 4F1R × 2, wb 3.40 m, 5.48 × 2.13 × 2.28 m, GVW 4600 kg. Model D28ALA 2799-cc diesel engine with pre-combustion chamber and blower. Used by *Bundesgrenzschutz*. Transverse troop seats. Chassis/cab supplied to Dutch Air Force also.

Truck, 1½-ton, 4 × 4, Workshop (Hanomag AL28) 4-cyl. diesel, 65 bhp, 4F1R × 2, wb 3.40 m. GVW 4425 kg. House-type van body with side and rear doors, equipped for *Kraftfahrzeug-Instandsetzung* (motorvehicle repair). Used by *BGS*. Also with other body types, incl. ambulance, and with dual rear tyres.

Truck, ¾-ton, 4×4, Cargo (Borgward B2000A/O Lkw 0,75 t gl) 6-cyl., 82 bhp, 4F1R×2, wb 3.20 m, 5.32×1.98× 2.24 (1.80) m, 2470 kg. GVW 3500 kg. Body interchangeable with that of *'Kübelwagen'* version. Tyres 9.00–16. Speed range 3–95 km/h. Diff. locks and winch optional. Soft-top 3-seater cab.

Truck, 2½-ton, 4×4, Van (Borgward B2500A-Otto) 6-cyl., 82 bhp, 4F1R×2, wb 3.40 m, 5.46×2.18×2.26 m, 2430 kg. Commercial 4×4 chassis with military pattern front end and closed cab. 126 supplied in 1958 for civil defence (*Luftschutz Mannschaftskraftwagen*). Tyres 6.50–20 (2 DT).

Truck, 1½-ton, 4×4, Cargo, w/Winch (Borgward Lkw 1,5 t gl) 6-cyl., 82 bhp, 4F1R×2, wb 3.40, 5.91×2.15×2.79 (1.94) m, 2750 kg. Basically similar to ¾-ton model but fitted with 10.00–20 tyres, air-assisted brakes and trailer brake connections. GVW 4200 kg. Shown with optional front-mounted winch. Used by *Bundeswehr*.

Truck, 2½-ton, 4×4, Workshop (Ford G493 SA-S1) 6-cyl. diesel, 90 bhp, 4F1R×2, wb 4.01 m, 7.06×2.30×3.31 m. Also with cargo body and 100-bhp V-8 petrol engine. Front end was exclusive to these types. Model G39TA was G398TA (see next section) with 125-bhp V-8-engine. All 2½-tonners had 11.00–20 tyres, single rear.

TRUCKS, 3- to 4-TON 4 × 4

Makes and Models: Ford G398TA (3-ton, 1952), G398TS-S2 (3-ton, 1955), G798BA (3-ton, 1952), G398SAM, G398SAM-S3 (3-ton, 1956), FK3500A (3½-ton, 1956). Magirus-Deutz A3500 (3½-ton, 1954), 'Mercur' 132 AL (3-ton, 1960), 112D9AL (3½-ton, 1968), etc. MAN 400L1AE (3-ton, 1957), 415L1AR (4-ton, 1958), 415L1FAE (3-ton, 1958), 620 LA (4-ton, 1957), 640 FAEV (4-ton, 1965), etc. Mercedes-Benz LA3500, LG3500 (3½-ton, 1953), LA312, LG312, LGK312, (3-ton, 1957), LG321 (3-ton, 1958), LA 322 (3-ton, 1961; from 1963: LA1113), LA328 (3-ton, 1961; from 1963: LA911), LG499 (4-ton, 1969), etc.

General Data: Of the above vehicles, most were developed from commercial trucks. The Ford-Köln 4 × 4 models of 1950–1955 were produced mainly for occupation forces, either as chassis/cab or chassis/cowl. About 1955 Ford produced several prototypes by modifying these chassis (fitting of larger single tyres, etc.) and the final result of these developments was the 'Ford Sam' (G398SAM), 6800 of which were produced during 1956–1961 for the *Bundeswehr*. During this period the German Ford range of commercial vehicles was changed drastically (new cab and front end, 4- and 6-cyl. diesels), but by the early 1960s their production was transferred to Great Britain ('Thames' K series, new grille, British Ford engines) and Ford of Cologne only continued the light 'Transit' models.

The Magirus-Deutz A3500 and 'Mercur' were used extensively by the British RAF in Germany as load carriers and also formed the basis for snow-fighting vehicles. These trucks differed from the wartime Klöckner A3000 mainly in having an air-cooled Deutz F4L 514 engine. Daimler-Benz produced several Mercedes-Benz commercial four-wheel drive truck models and some of these were sold for military use after certain alterations to meet military requirements. Others, like the LA3500, were used by various military authorities in virtually standard form.

MAN military 4 × 4 trucks were produced with normal and forward control. One model, the normal control 415L1AR, was also produced in India.

Vehicle shown (typical): Truck, 3-ton, 4 × 4, Cargo (Ford G398SAM) (*Lkw 3 t gl*)

Technical Data:

Engine: Ford G29T 8-cylinder, V-L-W-F, 3924 cc, 92 bhp @ 3500 rpm (SAE: 100 @ 3700).

Transmission: 4F1R × 2.

Brakes: hydraulic, air-assisted.

Tyres: 11.00–20.

Wheelbase: 4.01 m.

Overall l × w × h: 7.25 × 2.55 × 3.18 (2.13) m.

Weight: 3970 kg (w/Winch 4270 kg). GVW 7480 kg.

Note: Produced 1956–1961. Also with hard-top cab. Model G398SAM-S3 chassis was supplied for special body-work. Later also used by Israeli Army.

Truck, 3-ton, 4 × 4, Chassis/Cab (Ford G398TA) V-8-cyl., 106 bhp (diesel optional), 4F1R × 2, wb 4.01 m, 5.73 × 2.19 × 2.25 m, 2435 kg. 1952–56. From 1955 different badge on bonnet (FK). Used by Belgian Army, Dutch Air Force, etc. Also with integral ambulance body (G39TA-K).

Truck, 3-ton, 4 × 4, Chassis/Cab (Ford G798BA) V-8-cyl., 106 bhp, 4F1R × 2. Produced during 1952–57 for various occupation forces and NATO members (Belgium, France, Great Britain). Used with house-type van body (signals, workshop, etc.). Some had different cab styling. Modified bus chassis.

Truck, 3-ton, 4 × 4, Workshop (Ford G398SAM-S3) V-8-cyl., 92 bhp, 4F1R × 2, wb 4.01 m, 6.85 × 2.55 × 2.98 m, GVW 7480 kg. Chassis/cab as G398SAM but with trailer coupling and adapted for shop van bodies (workshop, ambulance, etc.). Interior 4.00 × 2.25 × 2.81 m. Ambulance had **double rear doors.**

Truck, 3-ton, 4 × 4, Cargo (MAN 400L1AE) 6-cyl. diesel, 100 bhp, 5F1R × 2, wb 4.20 m, length 7.16 m, 4480 kg. 5880-cc engine. Tyres 8.25–20. Superseded by 4-ton Model 415L1AR which had dual rear tyres (also produced in India, *qv*). NATO class: 3-ton.

Truck, 4-ton, 4 × 4, Cargo (MAN 640 FAEV) 6-cyl. diesel, 140 bhp, 5F1R × 2, wb 3.80 m, length 6.42 m, 6225 kg. Developed from Model 415L1F, which, in turn, was *Frontlenker* (forward control) version of 415L1. 12.00–20 single tyres. Prototype was 415L1FAE (1958). Note MG ringmount.

Truck, 3½-ton, 4 × 4, Cargo (Magirus-Deutz A3500) Deutz F4L 414 4-cyl. diesel, 90 bhp, 5F1R × 2, wb 3.70 m, GVW 5100 kg. Air-cooled 5322-cc engine. OD gearbox. Tyres 8.25–25 (2 DT). Widely used by British and other military forces in Germany. Also used by Indonesian Army (with 6-cyl. engine).

Truck, 3-ton, 4 × 4, Cargo (Magirus-Deutz 'Mercur' 132 AL) Deutz F4L 514 4-cyl. diesel, 95 bhp, 5F1R × 2, wb 4.60 m. Basically a commercial truck but modified in many respects to meet military requirements. Also produced with 6-cyl. engine (all air-cooled) and 4.25-m wheelbase.

Truck, 3-ton, 4 × 4, Cargo (Magirus-Deutz 'Mercur') Deutz F6L 614 6-cyl. diesel, 112 bhp, 5F1R × 2, wb 4.20 m, GVW 8500 kg. Military version of commercial truck, supplied to German *BGS*, British RAF (for use in Germany), etc. Slightly different model (112 D9AL) supplied to Egypt. Drop-side cargo/platform body.

Truck, 3-ton, 4×4, Cargo (Mercedes-Benz LG3500)
6-cyl. diesel, 100 bhp, 5F1R × 2, wb 3.60 m, 6.33 × 2.50 × 2.58 m, 3300 kg.   Tyres 11.00–20.   Military version of LA3500 (which had 8.25–20 (2 DT) tyres). LA3500 (later LA312) was one of Germany's first post-war 4 × 4 trucks.

Truck, 3-ton, 4×4, Cargo (Mercedes-Benz LG312)
6-cyl. diesel, 100 bhp, 5F1R × 2, wb 3.60 m, 6.33 × 2.50 × 2.58 m, 3500 kg.   Tyres 11.00–20.   Military version of all-wheel drive LA312, 1959.   Model LA312 was also produced for Indian Army (*qv*).

Truck, 3-ton, 4×4, Cargo (Mercedes-Benz) 6-cyl. diesel, 110 bhp, 5F1R × 2, wb 3.60 m, 6.11 × 2.48 × 2.55 m, GVW 8100 kg. Tyres 11.00–20. 5-ton winch. Prototype COE version of LG3500, *c.* 1955. Also with house-type van body (workshop) and 110-bhp petrol engine. No quantity production.

Truck, 3-ton, 4×4, Cargo (Mercedes-Benz LA328/LA 911) 6-cyl. diesel, 110 bhp, 5F1R × 2, wb 3.60 m, 6.05 × 2.35 × 2.60 m, 3300 kg. Tyres 11.00–20. Actual payload on/off roads 5200/3400 kg.   NATO class 3-ton.   Redesignated LA911 in 1963.   Variants were used by the *BGS* (LA328/42) and Denmark (*qv*).

TRUCKS, 4½- to 10-TON 4 × 4

Makes and Models: Borgward B4500A (4½-ton, 1953; from 1959: B555A). Büssing 6000A (6-ton, 1952), LU 11AW (6-ton, 1955). Faun F60F (6-ton, 1956), GT6/15 and GT8/15 (10-ton, 1959). Ford FK4500A (4½-ton, 1956). Henschel HS100A (5-ton, 1953), HS115 (5-ton, 1953), HS 11 HAL (5-ton, 1962), etc. Krupp AL6Dr3 'Drache' (6-ton, 1955/56; earlier named Süd-werke). Magirus-Deutz A4500 'Mercur' (4½-ton, 1956), A6500 'Jupiter' (6½- to 7-ton, 1953), A7500 'Jupiter' (7-ton, 1958), etc. MAN MK25A (5-ton, 1955), 630L2A, 630L2AE (5-ton, 1956), 670L3AE (5-ton, 1959), etc. Mercedes-Benz LA4500 (4½-ton, 1953), LA6600, LG6600 (5-ton, 1953), LG315/46 (5-ton, 1957), LA315 (8- to 10-ton, 1954), LG326/46 (5-ton, 1959), etc.

General Data: Most German truck manufacturers introduced 4 × 4 versions of their medium range models in about 1952/53, usually for tipper use but also with an eye on possible military applications. Not all of the above models did actually see military service. The Borgward B4500A was first introduced in 1953 and bore a certain resemblance to the wartime B3000A. It was used by various government branches, including *Bundeswehr, Bundesgrenzschutz, Bereitschaftspolizei* and *Technisches Hilfswerk*. It appeared with a variety of body styles and also with single rear wheels. The Faun F60F, Henschel HS115 and Krupp AL6 Dr3 'Drache' were all forward-control trucks with single rear tyres (*Einzelbereifung*). Standardized for service in the *Bundeswehr* were the MAN 630 L2A/L2AE and Mercedes-Benz LG315. The Magirus-Deutz 'Jupiter' was employed in smaller numbers and, like the MAN, was also used by the Belgian Army. In 1959 Daimler-Benz and MAN produced proto-types for new trucks which were introduced to eventually supersede their 630L2A(E) and LG315 models resp. After only a few had been produced these projects (Models 670L3AE and LG326 resp.) were shelved in favour of a completely new generation of 4 × 4, 6 × 6 and 8 × 8 tactical vehicles which will be introduced gradually during the 1970s (see Introduction). About 1966 the German Navy (*Bundesmarine*) acquired 260 American LARC-5 and -15 4 × 4 amphibians to replace wartime GMC DUKWs.

Vehicle shown (typical): Truck, 5-ton, 4 × 4, Cargo, w/Winch (MAN 630 L2AE) (*Lkw 5 t gl*)

Technical Data:
Engine: MAN D1246MVA 6-cylinder multi-fuel, I-I-W-F, 8276 cc, 130 bhp @ 2000 rpm.
Transmission: 6F1R × 2.
Brakes: air, and exhaust brake.
Tyres: 14.00–20 (11.00–20 dual rear on Model 630 L2A).
Wheelbase: 4.60 m.
Overall l × w × h: 8.27 × 2.50 × 2.84 (2.20) m.
Weight: 7700 kg. GVW 13,000 kg.
Note: Standard truck of German *Bundes-wehr* (630 L2AE-BW). Also used by Belgian Army (630 L2AE-B). Available with shorter wb (4.10 m) as tractor and tipper.

Truck, 5-ton, 4×4, Cargo and Personnel (MAN MK25A)
6-cyl. diesel, 120 bhp, 5F1R × 2, wb 4.60 m, 7.49 × 2.40 × 2.97 m, GVW 12,050 kg. Tyres 11.00–20. 7980-cc engine. Air brakes. Experimental model, developed from commercial truck in 1955. One metre high double drop sides.

Truck, 5-ton, 4×4, Three-way Tipper (MAN 630L2A)
6-cyl. m/f, 130 bhp, 6F1R × 2, wb 4.10 m. Tyres 11.00–20. Same chassis also with fifth wheel as *Sattelschlepper* (tractor-truck). Tipper version of 630L2AE had 14.00–20 tyres, single rear.

Truck, 5-ton, 4×4, Field Kitchen (MAN 630L2A) 6-cyl. m/f, 130 bhp, 6F1R × 2, wb 4.60 m, 7.84 × 2.50 × 2.98 m. Tyres 11.00–20 (2DT). Standard *Kofferaufbau* (house-type van) produced by Peter Bauer. Also Ambulance and other versions. Speed 67.5 km/h. Gradability 50%. 1959.

Truck, 5-ton, 4×4, Cargo, w/Winch (MAN 670L3AE)
6-cyl. diesel, 175 bhp, 6F1R × 2, wb 4.60 m, overall length 8.12 m, 8200 kg. GVW 13,200 kg. Detachable winch unit Also with hard-top cab and different bumper. Tyres 14.00–20. 9660-cc engine. Few produced, 1959/60.

142

**Truck, 4½-ton, 4 × 4, Field Kitchen (Mercedes-Benz
LA4500)** 6-cyl. diesel, 90 bhp, 5F1R × 2, wb 4.20 m, 6.20 ×
2.30 m, GVW 8100 kg. Tyres 8.25–20. Commercial 4 × 4
chassis, also with other special bodywork incl. NATO Air Force
Fire/Crash Tender. Similar to LA3500 but higher payload,
lower speed. 1956.

Truck, 5-ton, 4 × 4, Cargo (Mercedes-Benz LG315/46)
6-cyl. m/f, 145 bhp, 6F1R × 2, wb 4.60 m, 8.12 × 2.50 × 3.00
(2.12) m, 7600 kg. Standard *Bundeswehr* truck, developed
from LG6600. Also with closed cab and conventional front
wings. 8276-cc engine. Tyres 14.00–20. Produced at D-B
Gaggenau plant.

Truck, 5-ton, 4 × 4, Wrecker (Mercedes-Benz LG315/46)
6-cyl. m/f, 145 bhp, 6F1R × 2, wb 4.60 m, 9.30 × 2.50 × 3.00 m,
GVW 12,825 kg. Billstein *Drehkran* (revolving crane) employed for vehicle recovery, heavy lifting at field workshops,
etc. Chassis also used for hyd. telescopic *Beobachtungsmast*
(Observation tower). 1959.

Truck, 5-ton, 4 × 4, Cargo (Mercedes-Benz LG326/46)
6-cyl. diesel, 172 bhp, 6F1R × 2, wb 4.60 m, 7.68 × 2.50 × 3.27
m, 7700 kg (w/winch). GVW 13,400 kg. Model OM326V
engine. Tyres 14.00–20. Air brakes. PAS. Cab with removable
hard-top. Four produced, 1959/60 (see General Data).
Speed range 4.5–75 km/h.

Truck, 6-ton, 4×4, Cargo (Büssing 6000A) 6-cyl. diesel, 120 bhp, 5F1R × 2, wb 4.80 m, 8.21 × 2.40 × 2.91 m, GVW 12,600 kg. Tyres 11.00−20. Military version of commercial truck, 1952, supplied to Turkish Army. British RAF in Germany used tractor version for refueller S-Ts (AVTUR).

Truck, 6-ton, 4×4, Cargo (Büssing LU11AW) 6-cyl. diesel, 175 bhp, 5F1R × 2, wb 4.50 m. Horizontal 11-litre 'underfloor' engine, mounted centrally. No quantity production. In 1966/67 Büssing produced an exp. amphibious 4-ton 4 × 4 truck (200 bhp, wb 3.50 m, 8.00 × 2.95 × 2.20 m, tyres 16.00−20).

Truck, 4½-ton, 4×4, Personnel (Borgward B4500A) 6-cyl. diesel, 95 bhp, 5F1R × 2, wb 4.20 m, GVW 8500 kg. Borgward D6M5 4962-cc engine. Tyres 8.25−20. Special bodywork for *Bundesgrenzschutz* with full-length folding canvas top. Also other types of bodywork, incl. workshop.

Truck, 4½-ton, 4×4, Cargo, w/Winch (Borgward B4500A) 6-cyl. diesel, 95 bhp, 5F1R × 2, wb 4.20 m, 7.00 × 2.40 × 2.35 m approx. GVW 8405 kg. Tyres 8.25−20. Also produced as 3½-tonner, with 11.00−20 tyres, single rear (GVW 7700 kg). Winch optional. Mid 1950s.

Truck, 5-ton, 4 × 4, Cargo, w/Winch (Henschel HS100A)
6-cyl. diesel, 105 bhp, 5F1R × 2, wb 3.85 m, 6.80 (w/o winch) × 2.35 × 2.51 (cab) m, 4700 kg. Military version of commercial truck with dropside body. Sold to various NATO forces. Model HS 11 HAL of 1962 was similar in appearance but had 4.48-m wheelbase.

Truck, 5-ton, 4 × 4, Cargo (Henschel HS115) 6-cyl. diesel, 125 bhp (petrol engine optional), 5F1R × 2, wb 3.85 (or 4.20) m, 6.87 (or 7.40) × 2.50 × 2.60 m, 6300 kg. GVW 11,500 kg. Tyres 12.00–20. Used mainly by French forces in Germany (FFA), also with recovery crane. NATO 6-ton class.

Truck, 6-ton, 4 × 4, Cargo (Faun F60F) Prototype for NATO 6-ton class, produced about 1956. F60S and F68/36S were 4 × 2 tractor-trucks with normal control and were supplied to several NATO members incl. Belgium and US forces in Germany. All had Deutz air-cooled diesel engines.

Truck, 6-ton, 4 × 4, Cargo (Krupp AL6Dr3 'Drache') 3-cyl. diesel, 120 bhp, 8F1R × 1, wb 3.90 m, 6.85 × 2.50 × 2.70 (cab) m, 5700 kg. GVW 12,000 kg. Tyres 12.00–22. Krupp D344.8 two-stroke 4362-cc engine. All-synchromesh gearbox with OD top. Air brakes. Used by British Army.

Truck, 6½-ton, 4×4, Cargo (Magirus-Deutz A6508 'Jupiter') Deutz F8L 614 V-8-cyl. diesel, 175 bhp, 6F1R × 2, wb 4.41 or 4.82 m, GVW 12,400 kg. Lockable diff. in transfer case. Used by several military forces with various types of bodywork. Speed range 3.8–73 km/h. Gradability 55%. 1953.

Truck, 5-ton, 4×4, Cargo/Dump, w/Winch (Magirus-Deutz 'Jupiter') Deutz F8L 714 V-8-cyl. diesel, 175 bhp, 6F1R × 2, wb 4.41 m, 7.52 × 2.50 × 2.50 (min.) m, GVW 13,000 kg. Air brakes. Tyres 11.00–20. 1957. The British Army in Germany used a fleet of a later type, with cargo bodies, as 10-tonners.

Truck, 7-ton, 4×4, Workshop (Magirus-Deutz A6508 'Jupiter') Deutz F8L 614 V-8-cyl. diesel, 175 bhp, 6F1R × 2, wb 4.82 m. Tyres 11.00–20. 1954 pattern front end. Also with cargo body, soft-top cab, 5-ton crane (SWB Recovery), Wilhag rev. crane (BGS), Beilhack rotary snow plough (USAF), etc.

Truck, 7-ton, 4×4, Tractor (Magirus-Deutz A7500 'Jupiter') Deutz F8L 714A V-8-cyl. m/f, 178 bhp, 6F1R × 2, wb 4.41 m, 7.16 × 2.50 × 2.60 (2.17) m, 7200 kg. Used by *Luftwaffe* with long two-axle 12½-ton S-T for transport of aircraft ('Starfighter'), missiles, etc. Tyres 11.00–20. Air brakes.

TRUCKS, 4- to 20-TON
6 × 6 and 8 × 8

Makes and Models (6 × 6 unless stated otherwise):
Alvis 'Stalwart' (5-ton, amphibious, 1966, GB). Faun
L908/ATW (12-ton, 1967; airfield tanker), L908/ATW
(15-ton, 1967; tanker), L908/SAT, L908/SA (10-ton,
1958; tractor-truck), L908/21 Bo (10-ton, 1961; pontoon carrier)*, L908/54 VA (10-ton, 1960; truck),
L908/425 A (10-ton, 1958; truck), LK908/A (10-ton,
1958; wrecker), LK908/45 A (10-ton, 1958; crane
carrier), L912/SA (15-ton, 1957; tractor-truck),
L912/VSA (20-ton, 1960; tractor-truck), L912/21 (12-
ton, 1958; transporter)*, L912/21 HOH (10-ton, 1960;
bridging truck)*, Z912/21-203 (10-ton, 1964 and 1969;
prime-mover)*, L912/21-Mun (10-ton, 1960; ammunition truck)*, L912/45 A
(15-ton, 1958; truck), L912/5050 A(K) (10-ton, 1959; sliding tipper), L1212/45
VSA (20-ton, 1960; tractor-truck), LK1212/485 (12-ton, 1960; crane carrier),
LK1212/485 II (10-ton, 1961; crane carrier), LK1221/400 (12-ton, 1961; crane
carrier)*, LK12111/485 (12-ton, 1961; crane carrier), etc. Hanomag-Henschel
H151 AK (7-ton, 1969). Henschel HS3-14 HA, HS22 HA (7-ton, 1964), HS3-160 A
(18-ton, 1963). International G744 'M-Series' (5-ton, c. 1955, US). Kaelble
KDV832 (15-ton, 1956). Magirus-Deutz 'Jupiter' (7-ton, 1962), M178D15AL, AK
(7-ton, 1964), M180D15AL (7-ton, 1971), 'Uranus', 250D25A (12-ton, 1956), etc.
Mercedes-Benz (4-ton, 1955), LG498 (7-ton, 1969), LG497 (10-ton, 8 × 8, 1969).
Reo G742 'M-Series' (2½-ton, c. 1955, US).

General Data: Most vehicles in the heavy payload class were produced by Faun.
Faun also supplied 4 × 4 and 8 × 8 models to the *Bundeswehr* and several 4- and
6-wheeled types to the American and British occupation forces, e.g. Model F603V
(12,000-litre 6 × 6 tanker, 1955) for the RAF and Model L908/45 A (6 × 6 truck and
tipper, 1956) for the US Army. The Henschel HS22 HA was supplied to Switzerland
as HS22 HA-CH. The *Bundeswehr* and *Bundesmarine* also used some American
6 × 6 vehicles, notably the Reo 2½-ton M35, the amphibious GMC DUKW-353 and
the International 5-ton M139C.

* steering tandem axles at front, single axle at rear.

Vehicle shown (typical): Truck, 15-ton,
6 × 6, Tractor (Faun L912/SA) (*Lkw
15 t gl*)

Technical Data:
Engine: Deutz F12L 714A multi-fuel
12-cylinder, V-I-A-F, 15,966 cc, 265
bhp @ 2300 rpm.
Transmission: 6F1R × 2.
Brakes: air, with exhaust retarder.
Tyres: 12.00–24.
Wheelbase: 4.50 (BC 1.46) m.
Overall l × w × h: 7.61 × 2.50 × 2.80 m.
Weight: 12,500 kg. GVW 27,000 kg.
Note: 10-ton winch. Introduced 1957.
Also with cargo body as heavy prime
mover (L912/45 A) and with 5.05-m wb
as *Gleitkipper* (L912/5050 A; see sec-
tion 'Miscellaneous Vehicles').

Truck, 10-ton, 6 × 6, Cargo (Faun L908/54 VA) Deutz F8L 714A m/f V-8-cyl., 178 bhp, 6F1R × 2, wb 5.40 (BC 1.40) m, 9.65 × 2.50 × 2.78 (2.55) m, 11,500 kg. Tyres 14.00–20. Loading platform 6.70 × 2.35 m. Most mechanical components same as on L908/425A. Also with 1-ton loading crane.

Truck, 12-ton, 6 × 6, Crane (Faun LK1212/485) Deutz F12L 714A m/f V-12-cyl., 265 bhp, 6F1R × 2, wb 4.85 (BC 1.70) m, 9.14 × 2.50 × 3.00 m. 13-ton revolving crane by Orenstein & Koppel (shown) or Wilhag. Model LK 12111/485 basically similar except steering foremost rear axle and Krupp-Ardelt crane.

Truck, 12-ton, 6 × 6, Transporter/Tractor (Faun L912/21) Deutz F12L 714A m/f V-12-cyl., 265 bhp, 6F1R × 2, wb 3.50 (front BC 1.78) m, 9.00 × 2.50 × 2.83 (2.42) m, 16,500 kg. Equipped with 1-ton hyd. lift, 10-ton winch and dozer blade. 8-seater cab. Tyres 16.00–24. Power-assisted two-axle steering.

Truck, 10-ton, 6 × 6, Artillery Tractor (Faun Z912/21-203) Deutz F12L 714A m/f V-12-cyl., 265 bhp, 6F1R × 2, wb 4.00 (front BC 1.78) m, 8.05 × 2.50 × 2.80 m, 16,400 kg. GVW 26,400 kg. 10-ton winch. Tyres 16.00–25. Similar chassis/cab equipped with 11-ton Wilhag hyd. crane (LK 1221/400).

Truck, 12-ton, 6 × 6, Aircraft Tanker (Faun L908/ATW)
Deutz F8L 714A m/f V-8-cyl., 178 bhp, 6F1R × 2, wb 5.65
(BC 1.32) m, 9.13 × 2.50 × 2.94 m, 13,050 kg. Tyres 11.00–20.
GVW 25,400 kg. Capacity 12,000 litres. Also supplied as road-
going tanker with 15,000-litre capacity.

**Truck, 10-ton, 6 × 6, Transporter, Slide Loading (Hen-
schel HS3-160A)** 6-cyl. diesel, 180 bhp, 6F1R × 2, wb
5.20 (BC 1.31) m, chassis/cab: 9.02 × 2.50 × 2.87 m, GVW
32,400 kg. Used for recovery and transporting tracked APCs
(HS30 shown). Loading and unloading with tipping/sliding
platform took about 30 sec.

Truck, 4-ton, 6 × 6, Cargo (Mercedes-Benz) 6-cyl.,
110 bhp, 5F1R × 2, wb 3.50 m, 6.27 × 2.50 × 2.55 m, chassis
3450 kg. GVW 9500 kg. Tyres 11.00–20. Air-assisted hyd.
brakes. 4580-cc petrol engine. 5-ton winch. Developed about
1955 from LG3500 4 × 4 (qv) but not produced in quantity.

**Truck, 6-7-ton, 6 × 6, Cargo, Amphibious (Mercedes-
Benz LG498)** 10-cyl. m/f (turbocharged), 390 bhp, planetary
(ZF 8F8R) or s/m trans., wb 4.57 (BC 1.40) m, 8.10 × 2.50 ×
2.75 m, GVW 17 tons. Also 2- and 4-axle and non-amphibious
versions. PAS. Air-hyd. brakes. Tyres 14.00–20. Experimental,
1969.

Truck, 7-ton, 6 × 6, Cargo (Magirus-Deutz M178D15AL 6 × 6) Deutz F8L 714A m/f V-8-cyl., 178 bhp, 6F1R × 2, wb 4.80 (BC 1.28) m, 8.05 × 2.50 × 2.80 m, 7450 kg. GVW 15,150 kg. Rotzler winch optional. Tyres 11.00–20. Later equipped with 180-bhp F8L 413 engine (M180D15AL).

Truck, 7-ton, 6 × 6, Tipper, w/Winch (Magirus-Deutz M178D15AK 6 × 6) Deutz F8L 714A m/f V-8-cyl., 178 bhp, 6F1R × 2, wb 4.40 (BC 1.28) m. Other specialist bodywork on this chassis included: Wilhag 4-ton revolving crane, aircraft refueller, shop van, fifth wheel for S-T, etc. From 1962 to 1964 known as 'Jupiter'.

Truck, 7-ton, 6 × 6, Fire, Crash (Magirus-Deutz M178 D15AL 6 × 6) Deutz F8L 714 diesel V-8-cyl., 178 bhp, 6F1R × 2, wb 4.80 (BC 1.28) m. Bachert bodywork, 1961. 3800-litre tank. High-pressure fog foam cannon. Also used in Austria (FKFZ 3800/400). These chassis were developed from the 'Uranus' 170A of 1957.

Truck, 7-ton, 6 × 6, Rocket Launcher, LARS (Magirus-Deutz M178D15AL 6 × 6) Deutz F8L 714A m/f V-8-cyl., 178 bhp, 6F1R × 2, wb 4.80 (BC 1.28) m, 7.50 × 2.50 m, combat weight 15 tons approx. One of two types. Twin 18-rocket barrel clusters. All rockets could be fired in 18 secs. Maximum traverse 100°.

Truck, 17-ton, 6×4, Aircraft Fueller (Faun F603V)
Deutz F6L 514 6-cyl. diesel, air-cooled, 125 bhp. 12,000-litre
AVTAG overhead-boom aircraft fueller, one of a series produced
for the British RAF (TAF) in Germany. British nomenclature:
Truck, 17-ton, Tanker, Aircraft, 2500-gallon, 6 × 4.

Truck, 10-ton, 6×6, Cargo (Faun L908/55A) Deutz F8L
614 V-8-cyl. diesel, air-cooled, 175 bhp, 6F1R × 2. 10,000 kg.
GVW 22,000 kg. Tyres 14.00–20. Produced in 1956 for
British RAF (TAF) in Germany. GS cargo body with double
dropsides. ZF transmission.

Truck, 10-ton, 6×4, Dump (Faun F603K) Deutz F6L
514 6-cyl. diesel, air-cooled, 125 bhp, 5F1R. GVW 22 tons.
Hyd.-actuated (twin-ram) end tipper, supplied to US Army,
Corps of Engineers, in Germany, during the early 1950s.
Note mounting brackets for snow plough at front.

**Truck, 10-ton, 6×6, Recovery (Magirus-Deutz M250
D25A 'Uranus')** Deutz F12L 614 V-12-cyl. diesel, air-cooled,
250 bhp, 6F1R × 2, wb 4.44 (BC 1.38) m. One of several
types of heavy recovery vehicles supplied to British forces in
Germany. Bilstein revolving crane. Others had hydraulic crane
on similar chassis.

TRACTORS, WHEELED (PRIME MOVERS)

Shown in this section are some wheeled prime movers, which were designed specifically to tow heavy full-trailers, artillery, etc. Such vehicles often have a relatively small rear body for carrying ballast in order to improve wheel adhesion. Prime movers which are also cargo carriers are covered in the preceding sections, as are tractor-trucks with 'fifth wheel' for semi-trailers, except for types designed as HETs (heavy equipment transporters, tank transporters; see following section). Hanomag supplied some types of 4 × 2 tractors for full-trailers to the Belgian and French forces in Germany. The latter, Model ST100, was very similar to the pre-war Hanomag SS100 and had a four-door cab extending to above the rear axle.

Prime Mover, Medium, 4 × 4 (Faun L8/475 VA) 6-cyl. diesel, 175 bhp, 5F1R × 2. Tyres 12.00–20. Air brakes. Winch between crew cab and ballast body. Produced about 1954 for use by British RAF (TAF) in Germany. Water-cooled engine.

Prime Mover, Heavy, 4 × 4 (Faun Z12/31 A) Deutz F12L 614 V-12-cyl. diesel (at rear), 250 bhp, 6F1R × 2, wb 3.10 m, 6.79 × 2.50 × 2.85 m, 14,500 kg (incl. ballast). Towed loads up to 80 tons. Tyres 16.00–24. Winch at front. 8-seater cab. 1958.

Prime Mover, Heavy, 6 × 6 (Magirus-Deutz 250AE-L 'Uranus') Deutz F12L 614 V-12-cyl. diesel, 250 bhp, 6F1R × 2, wb 4.44 (BC 1.38) m, 7.69 × 2.50 × 2.92 m, 25,000 kg approx. Epicyclic hub reduction gears. Towed loads 60 tons. Used in Belgium, Germany, Switzerland, Middle East, etc. From 1956. Supplied with single and double cab, LHD and RHD.

TANK and HEAVY EQUIPMENT TRANSPORTERS

Makes and Models: Faun L912/SA (6 × 6, used with semi-trailers), L912/VSA (6 × 6, used with semi-trailers), L912/5050 A (K) (6 × 6, *Gleitkipper*, sliding tipper), L1212/45 VSA (6 × 6, used with semi-trailers), L1212/50 VS (8 × 8, for semi-trailers or full-trailers), LH70/420 (8 × 8, with Krupp SH70/8EL 4-axle semi-trailer, forming SLT-70). Henschel HS3-160A (6 × 6, *Gleitkipper*).

General Data: The Faun L1212/50 VS 8 × 8 was first introduced in 1965 as a prototype for evaluation by NATO. It was not accepted by the *Bundeswehr* because the bilateral construction of the new SLT-70 by Chrysler in the USA (as HET-70) and Faun and Krupp in Germany had already begun. SLT stands for *Schwerlast-Transporter*. It was originally intended for the US/German MBT-70 main battle tank. The first prototypes appeared in 1968. Faun also developed an 8 × 8 ballast tractor, model L1412/45 V, for special (commercial) purposes. This tractor, which weighed about 42 tons, was powered by two 400-bhp diesel engines, one driving the two front and one the two rear axles. With a power to weight ratio of about 22.5 bhp per ton, this 10.5-metre long vehicle could reach 100 km/h in only 61 seconds. Its gradability was 52%. Faun are among Germany's best known specialist vehicle builders and produce various types of ultra heavy six- and eight-wheeled chassis. The Faun L1212/45 VSA, introduced in 1964, was the standard *Bundeswehr* tank transporter tractor and was also tested by the Swedish Army (together with the British Thornycroft 'Mighty Antar'). Magirus-Deutz supplied their heavy 'Uranus' prime movers (Models 250 AE-L and 250D25A) as tractors for tank transporter trailers and as a tractor-truck for certain commercial applications. Various wb and tyre sizes were available. Engines were Deutz air-cooled V-8 or V-12 diesels.

Vehicle shown (typical): Truck, 25-ton, 6 × 6, Tractor (Faun L1212/45 VSA)

Technical Data:
Engine: Deutz BF12L 714 diesel, V-I-A-F, 19,000 cc, 340 bhp @ 2300 rpm.
Transmission: 6F1R × 2.
Brakes: air.
Tyres: 14.00–24.
Wheelbase: 4.50 m. BC 1.50 m.
Overall l × w × h: 7.84 × 2.90 × 3.04 m.
Weight: 18,100 kg.
Note: GCW 90 tons. Shown with 50-ton S-T carrying American M47 tank. Two 20-ton winches. Superseded earlier Model L912/VSA.

Truck, 20-ton, 6×6, Tractor (Faun L912/VSA) Deutz
BF12L 614 V-12-cyl., diesel, 300 bhp, 6F1R×2, wb 4.50 m,
7.74 × 2.90 × 3.05 m, 14,000 kg. Tyres 14.00–24. Max. load
on fifth wheel 25 tons. Air-cooled engine with dry-sump
lubrication system. Introduced in 1958. Crew 6+2.

Truck, 25-ton, 8×8, Tractor (Faun L1212/50 VS) Daimler-
Benz MB837 Ea 500 V-8-cyl. diesel, 640 bhp, ZF-Hydromedia
trans. Air brakes and hyd. trans. brake. Tyres 24.00–24.
Two 20-ton winches. Towed load up to 200 tons. Max. load
on fifth wheel 38 tons. Ballast body optional.

**Heavy Equipment Transporter (SLT-
70). Tractor: Faun LH70/420-8×8:**
Daimler-Benz MB837 Ea-500 V-8-cyl.
diesel, 730 bhp (DIN), 29,920 cc, ZF
'hot-shift' 4F2R×2, wb 1.50+2.70+
1.50 m, 22,680 kg. PAS. Two 17-ton
winches.
Semi-Trailer: Krupp SH70/8EL: 13.10
× 3.15 × 3.28 m, 16,160 kg. Length of
platform 8.00 m. All axles steering.
Combination: length 18.97 m. Payload
47,700 kg. GCW 86,540 kg. Air brakes.
Tyres 18.00–22.5. Speed range 2.5–70
km/h.

MISCELLANEOUS VEHICLES WHEELED and TRACKED

When the *Bundeswehr* was first established it was equipped with American half- and full-track vehicles (incl. half-track AA, M16, tanks, M41, M47 (1200) and M48, SPs, M7B2, M44 and M52, carrier, T16, high-speed tractor, M4, etc.). In due course several German and French AFVs made their appearance, notably products of Henschel, Krauss-Maffei ('Leopard'), Rheinstahl-Hanomag and Hotchkiss (F). The *Bundesgrenzschutz* employed US M8 'Greyhound' and British Alvis 'Saladin' armoured cars. For the 1970s a new generation of wheeled AFVs was developed. Also shown here are some examples of unarmoured special purpose vehicles.

Snow Plough, High Capacity, 4 × 4 (Mercedes-Benz 'Unimog' S404/Beilhack HS230) Twin rotors, propelled by separate 110-bhp engine mounted on rear of chassis. Ploughing width 2.30 m. Snow is thrown sideways over distance of 10–40 m. One of several types built by Beilhack.

Vehicle, Amphibious, 4 × 4, Bridging/Ferrying, M2 (EWK/KHD 'Alligator' MCL 60) Twin Deutz F8L 714A V-8-cyl. m/f, 2 × 178 bhp, 6F1R × 2, wb 5.35 m, 11.30 × 3.00 × 3.58 m, 22,000 kg. Independent adjustable suspension. Tyres 16.00–20. Twin propellers. Introduced in 1967 (prototypes from 1963).

Vehicle, Amphibious, 4 × 4, Bridging/Ferrying (Gillois-EWK) Invented by Gillois, a French Army Officer, this German-produced equipment is used by several NATO countries. Ramp on top can be turned 90° and vehicle floats by means of inflated rubber 'blisters' on sides. Bridge or ferry is formed by linking several units.

Loader, 4×4, Fork-Lift (Hatra SL 125) Deutz F6L 714A 6-cyl. m/f, 125 bhp, with TC and 4-speed trans., wb 2.60 m, 7.44×2.50×3.01 m, 13,636 kg. All-wheel steer. Known as *Feldumschlaggerät* or *Feldarbeitsgerät* (*FAG*). Also with other implements, incl. digging bucket. Similar type supplied by MFL (Wilhag).

Loader, 4×4, Swinging Bucket (Ahlmann A50) Deutz F4L 912 4-cyl. diesel, 65 bhp, approx. 6.80×2.35×2.90 m, GVW 8800 kg. Known as *Schwenkschaufler* or *Schwenklader*. Used by Engineers (*Pioniertruppe*), also with other implements. Produced by Ahlmann-Carlshütte KG, Rendsburg, 1959–63. Rear-wheel steer.

Carrier, 10-ton, 4×4, Artillery (Faun GT 8/15) Deutz F8L 714A V-8-cyl. m/f, 178 bhp, 6F1R×2, wb 3.40 m, 6.60×2.80×2.50 (min.) m, 13,500 kg. Hyd. lifting equipment for 105-mm howitzer. 1959. Dozer blade at front. GT6/15 had 6-cyl. engine. GK 8/15 had 13-ton revolving crane (O & K). Tyres 16.00–25.

Gun, 90-mm, Anti-Tank, Self-Propelled (Rheinmetall) Normally towed by 5-ton (or heavier) truck but fitted with Porsche 4-cyl. 1500-cc auxiliary engine driving hyd. system and main wheels. Steering by twin tail wheels (steering wheel) or driven wheels (steering lever). Prototypes, 1965/66. Length 7.30 m.

Carrier, Armoured, 4×4, Personnel (Daimler-Benz/ Rheinstahl U-R 416) Daimler-Benz OM 352 6-cyl. diesel, 100 bhp, 6F2R, wb 2.90 m, 4.86 × 2.25 × 2.13 (roof) m, 5 tons. One of several AFVs based on the 'Unimog'. Speed 80 km/h. Range 700 km. Crew: 1 + 9. Tyres 12.50–20 or special combat type. 1969.

Carrier, Armoured, 4×4, Multipurpose (Henschel HW R 07) 6-cyl. diesel, 132 bhp, 5F1R×2, wb 2.72 m, 5.89 × 2.50 × 2.51 m, 9 tons. Prototype (1960). Various applications incl. APC, Recce with 2-cm gun (shown) and/or MG in turret, rocket or water projector, etc. Four-wheel steer. Tyres 11.00–20.

Carrier, Armoured, 4×4, Personnel (Henschel BGS-SWI) Prototype (MR 8-01) produced by Mowag in Switzerland in 1960. Series production in Germany by Henschel from 1962. Used by *Bundesgrenzschutz* from 1963. Dim. 5.31 × 2.20 × 1.89 m. Model MR 8-09 similar but armed with 2-cm gun in turret.

Car, Armoured, 8×8, Reconnaissance, Amphibious (Mercedes-Benz LG494) 10-cyl. m/f, 390 bhp, semi-auto. trans., wb 3.76 (BC 1.40) m, 7.34 × 2.98 × 2.50 m approx., combat wt 19 tons. Exp., 1970/71. Also 4 × 4 (LG496), 6 × 6 (LG493) and 8 × 8 (LG495) APCs, and trucks (LG497/8/9) with many components in common.

Tractor, Full-Track, Bulldozer (Deutz 60, Frisch) Deutz 4-cyl. diesel, 60 bhp, air-cooled, 4.83 × 2.46 × 2.45 m, 9355 kg. Designation: *Planierraupe 60 PS*. Winch at rear. Speed 7.5 km/h. Transported on *Gleitkipper* (Faun L912/ 5050A, shown) or low-loader trailer.

Tractor, Full-Track, Angledozer (Kaelble PR660) 6-cyl. diesel, 160 bhp, 5.97 × 4.10 (tractor 2.56) × 2.92 m, 18,650 kg. Designation: *Planierraupe 160 PS, Schwenkschild*. Dozer blade may be turned 25° to either side. Water-cooled 14,330-cc engine. Multi-shank ripper or winch at rear.

Carrier, Armoured, Full-Track, Cargo, CC-2 (Hotchkiss SP10) 6-cyl., 145 bhp, 3.70 × 2.30 × 1.50 m, 5500 kg. One of many models developed by Hotchkiss (F). This supply carrier was specially designed to meet *Bundeswehr* requirements (*Deutscher Nachschubpanzer, Ausf.* 1959). Engine located to right of driver.

Carrier, Armoured, Full-Track, Personnel (Henschel HS 30) One of the early models in this series, originally conceived by Hispano-Suiza (HS 30 AA tank, 1955). Subsequent production of various versions by Hanomag, Henschel and British Leyland. Engines (229 bhp) supplied by Rolls-Royce. US APCs M113 were also used.

GREAT BRITAIN

After 1945 the British Government sold its surplus wartime military vehicles to other countries to re-equip their armed forces and to civilian operators. Ample quantities were kept for Britain's own Army, Navy and Air Force and some of these vehicles remained in service for another 25 years. Plans for a new generation of tactical wheeled vehicles had commenced before the war came to an end and some of these projects were carried on after 1945. Others, inevitably, had to be shelved. By the end of the 1940s, however, the Army had defined a new family of wheeled combat vehicles. These were to have standardized Rolls-Royce B-Series engines, but not all of them reached the production stage. By 1951 it was found impracticable to build up a wheeled vehicle fleet independent of the commercial market and therefore a compromise was made by including 16 per cent combat vehicles (designated CT types), 34 per cent general service vehicles (GS types) and the remaining 50 per cent standard commercial chassis (CL types) with standard or special bodywork.

The CT type vehicles were designed for full cross-country operation and incorporated many standardized parts and components. They were given FV (fighting vehicle) serial numbers with four numerals, e.g. FV1801 was a Truck, $\frac{1}{4}$-ton, 4×4, CT, Cargo (Austin-built, Rolls-Royce B40 4-cyl. engine, successor to the wartime US 'Jeep'). FV1802 was a Utility variant, the last two figures always indicating the body type. The GS type trucks were modified commercial types, incorporating all-wheel drive, special tyre equipment, etc. These had an FV number with five numerals, the third of which indicated the manufacturer. Of the last group (CL types) only certain models were given FV numbers and these were in the same category as the GS types.

The following basic types were planned and most of these went into quantity production.

Combat (CT) vehicles: FV1100 Series: 10-ton, 6×6, Leyland. FV1200 Series: 30-ton, 6×6, Leyland (pilots only). FV1300 Series: 3-ton, 6×6, Vauxhall (pilots only). FV1600 Series: 1-ton, 4×4, Humber. FV1800 Series: $\frac{1}{4}$-ton, 4×4, Austin.

General Service (GS) vehicles: FV11000 Series: 10-ton, AEC (11000), Albion (11100), Leyland (11200), Scammell (11300), Thornycroft (11400), Douglas (11500). FV12000 Series: over 10-ton, Thornycroft (12000), Scammell (12100), AEC (12200 and 12300). FV13000 Series: 3-ton, Austin (13000 and 13700), Bedford (13100 and 13800), Commer (13200 and 13900), Ford (13300), Thornycroft (13400). FV16000 Series: 1-ton, Austin (16000), Morris-Commercial (16100). FV18000 Series: $\frac{1}{4}$- and $\frac{3}{4}$-ton, Rover (18000), Austin (18700). AFVs, motorcycles and trailers had their own FV serial number systems. As time went on, the proportion of CL and GS vehicles in relation to CT types increased considerably and most CT types were 'reclassified' to become GS types. The FV1100 and 1800 designs were released for commercial marketing also.

The RN and RAF looked after their own transport fleets until 1965 when the Defence Minister decided that the Army was to assume the supply and repair of vehicles for all services, claiming that this integration would save at least £500,000 annually. By this time the majority of GS vehicles of all services consisted of Rovers ($\frac{1}{4}$- and $\frac{3}{4}$-ton), Austins (1-ton), Bedfords (3-ton) and AECs (10-ton). In 1968 the 3-ton class was uprated to 4-ton. All British military vehicles are sub-divided into three main groups, viz 'A' vehicles (AFVs), 'B' vehicles (transport) and 'C' vehicles (special purpose vehicles e.g. mobile cranes, crawler tractors, etc.). The British forces have also used quantities of foreign vehicles, notably American, German (BAOR, W. Berlin, TAF) and Swedish. In turn, some of the vehicles shown and/or listed in this section were used only by foreign Governments.

By 1971 plans were ready for a new Army fleet of logistic vehicles for the 1970s and 1980s. The new rationalized range was planned with the need of cost effectiveness in mind more than ever before. Three grades were envisaged, viz. straight 'off-the-shelf' models for static administrative units (low mobility), military versions of commercial trucks (medium mobility) and tactical and GS vehicles built from well proven commercial components for use in fighting units and by supporting units in the Corps area (high mobility). Payload classes: $\frac{1}{2}$- to $\frac{3}{4}$-ton, 1- to $2\frac{1}{2}$-ton, 4-ton, 8-ton and 16- to 20-ton (all metric tons). In addition a new tank transporter was planned (for 'Chieftain').

Registration Numbers: Military vehicles have a black number plate, usually with two white letters between two white two-digit numbers. The two numbers, when joined, form the actual serial number. The Royal Navy, in addition to the above, also uses (and re-uses) four-figure numbers with the letters RN before or after them. The Air Force has the former system and the first of the two letters is always an A. The Army also has the former system, which commenced in the early 1950s with the letters BA (00BA01, etc.) for new vehicles and letters from the end of the alphabet for re-numbered WWII vehicles, except ZZ which was used by the Canadian Defence staff in London.

Army 'workhorses': Bedford RL (right) and MK 4-tonners of the 1960s and 1970s resp.

Who's Who in the British Automotive Industry

Note: in view of the many mergers and other changes which have taken place in postwar years only those makes are included which were in production in 1970.

AEC	AEC Ltd (British Leyland), Southall, Middx.
Albion	Albion Motors Ltd (BLMC), Scotstoun, Glasgow.
Allis-Chalmers	Allis-Chalmers GB Ltd, Essendine, Stamford, Lincs.
Alvis	Alvis Ltd (BLMC), Coventry.
Austin	cars: Austin Morris Division, BLMC, Longbridge, Birmingham. vans: Commercial Vehicle Division, BLMC, Longbridge, Birmingham.
Bedford	(see Vauxhall)
Bray	Bray Construction Equipment Ltd, Feltham, Middx.
BSA	BSA Motor Cycles Ltd, Small Heath, Birmingham.
Caterpillar	Caterpillar Tractor Co. Ltd, Glasgow.
Coles	Coles Cranes Ltd, Sunderland, Co. Durham.
Commer	Chrysler UK Ltd, Commer Karrier Division, Dunstable, Beds.
Daimler	The Daimler Co. Ltd (BLMC), Coventry.
David Brown	David Brown Tractors Ltd, Huddersfield.
Dennis	Dennis Bros. Ltd, Guildford, Surrey.
Douglas	F. L. Douglas (Equipment) Ltd, Arle, Cheltenham, Glos.
Ferguson	(see Massey Ferguson)
Foden	Fodens Ltd, Sandbach, Cheshire.
Ford	Ford Motor Co. Ltd, Brentwood, Essex (plants: Dagenham, Basildon, etc.).
Fordson	(see Ford)
Fowler	John Fowler & Co. Ltd, Hunslet, Leeds.
Hillman	Chrysler UK Ltd, Car Division, Ryton-on-Dunsmore, nr. Coventry.
Humber	(see Hillman)
Jaguar	Jaguar Cars Ltd (BLMC), Coventry.
Karrier	(see Commer)
Land-Rover	(see Rover)
Leyland	Leyland Motors Ltd (BLMC), Leyland, Lancs.
Massey Ferguson	Massey Ferguson (GB) Ltd, Coventry.
Michigan	Clark Equipment Ltd, Camberley, Surrey.
Morris	(see Austin)
Rover	The Rover Co. Ltd (BLMC), Solihull, War.
Scammell	Scammell Lorries Ltd (BLMC), Watford, Herts.
Thornycroft	Transport Equipment (Thornycroft) Ltd (BLMC), Basingstoke, Hants.
Triumph	Triumph Motor Co. Ltd (BLMC), Coventry.
Vauxhall	Vauxhall Motors Ltd (GM), Luton and Dunstable, Beds.

MOTORCYCLES

In 1945 the British had over a quarter of a million military motorcycles and many of these (Ariel, BSA, Harley-Davidson, Matchless, Norton, Royal Enfield, Triumph, Velocette) remained in service. They were, however, gradually phased out and replaced by more modern machines. Various makes and models were employed, varying from 98-cc lightweights to 500-cc twins (2-cyl.). The lightweights (98- and 147-cc) were supplied by James, the heavier models mainly by BSA and Triumph.

Douglas/Vespa 125- and 150-cc and Triumph 'Tina' scooters were used by the Royal Navy. In addition to the British armed forces, the governments of several other countries purchased British motorcycles for military service. The Dutch Army, for example, purchased 1100 Triumph 350-cc machines during the 1960s.

Motorcycle, Solo (James J10 'Comet') Single-cyl., 2.8 bhp, 2F, wb 4'1", 6'7" × 2'1½" × 2'9½" (w/o windscreen), 150 lb. Used by RAF/Air Ministry for messenger service. Villiers Mk 1F 98-cc two-stroke engine. 1948–52. Models J11 and L1 had Villiers Mk 4F engine. Max speed 42 mph.

Motorcycle, Solo, FV2001 (Triumph TRW Mk 1) Twin-cyl., 16.8 bhp, 4F, wb 4'5", 6'10½" × 2'4½" × 3'5", 370 lb. 499-cc (63 × 80 mm) side-valve engine. Tyres, front 3.25–19, rear 4.00–19. Model TRW Mk 2 similar but cast-iron cylinder head. Rigid frame. Speed 65 mph. Used by Canadian forces also.

Motorcycle, Solo, FV2003 (BSA 'Star' B40 Mk I) Single-cyl., 18 bhp, 4F, wb 4'5½", 6'9" × 2'5½" × 3'7", 358 lb. Standardized in late 1960s. 343-cc OHV engine. Machine behind is similar but equipped with police escort duties conversion. Speed on/off road 55/25 mph. Tyres, front/rear 3.25–18/4.00–18.

CARS, SALOON
and UTILITY, 4 × 2

In addition to certain wartime staff cars (chiefly Humber) the British forces have used a wide variety of civilian type cars (saloons) and estate cars (utilities), including Armstrong-Siddeley (346 'Sapphire'), Austin (16 HP, A40, A70, 1800 Mk I and II, A135 and Princess Vanden Plas), BMC/BLMC 'Mini', Daimler, Ford (100E and 1100 'Escort' Estates, 'Zephyr' Mk I, III and IV, 'Executive'), Hillman ('Husky' Estate), Humber ('Hawk', 'Super Snipe', 'Pullman'), Jaguar (Mk VIII and IX, 420G), Morris ('Mini', '1000'), Rover (3.5-Litre and 4 × 2 version of Land-Rover (Car, Utility, Light, CL, 4 × 2, Rover, 88-in wb)), Standard ('Vanguard' and 'Ensign', various types), Vauxhall ('Velox', 'Victor', 'Ventora'), etc. German cars used in BAOR and Berlin included Mercedes-Benz 300SE, Opel 'Olympia' and 'Kapitän' and Volkswagen (from 1946).

Car, 4-seater, 4 × 2, Saloon (Morris M/A2S6 'Mini' 850 Mk II) 4-cyl., 34 bhp, 4F1R, wb 6'8", 10'0¼" × 4'7½" × 4'5", 1400 lb. Known also as 'Staff Car, Grade 5, Morris Mini'. Transversally mounted 848-cc BMC Series A engine. Front-wheel drive. Speed 74 mph. From 1967. Make became Mini in 1969.

Car, 4- to 6-seater, 4 × 2, Saloon (Humber 'Hawk' Series III) 4-cyl., 75 bhp, 4F1R, wb 9'2", 15'4¾" × 5'9½" × 5'1", 3180 lb. Used by Army (shown) and RAF (Humber Hawk, 4 × 2, 1963 Model (RHD), Grade 3, AOC Car). One of many Humber models used by these two services. Humber 'Super Snipe' also with LHD.

Car, 4- to 6-seater, 4 × 2, Saloon (Ford 211E 'Zephyr 4' Mk III) 4-cyl., 68 bhp, 4F1R, wb 8'11", 15'0¼" × 5'9" × 4'9½", 2600 lb. Factory-fitted options included fog lamp, rad. blind, heater, wing mirrors, seat belts. Used by Army as 'Saloon, Grade 4' (shown) and RAF. Also supplied with LHD for use in Germany.

Car, 4- to 6-seater, 4 × 2, Saloon (Austin 1800 Mk II)
4-cyl., 90 bhp, 4F1R, 13'10" × 5'7" × 4'8", 2600 lb. Transversally-mounted 1798-cc engine. Mk I version (1964–68) was also used. Mk II was introduced in 1968. Front-wheel drive. 'Hydrolastic' IFS/IRS. Max. speed 94 mph.

Car, 4- to 6-seater, 4 × 2, Saloon (Vauxhall 'Victor 3300')
6-cyl., 140 bhp, 4F1R, wb 8'6", 14'8¾" × 5'7" × 4'4½", 2600 lb. 3.3-litre engine. LHD. Issued to RMP (Royal Military Police) 'redcaps' in Germany, in 1969, followed by estate cars in 1971. Speed over 100 mph. Std 'Victor' saloons and estates were used by the RN.

Car, 6-seater, 4 × 2, Saloon (Jaguar 420G) 6-cyl., 255 bhp, 4F1R, wb 10'0", 16'4" × 6'4¼" × 4'6½", 4000 lb. Grade 1 staff car. Introduced 1966. 4235-cc twin-OHC engine. RHD or LHD. Earlier Jaguars used by Army and RAF were Mk VIIIB and IX. Speed 120 mph.

Car, 6- to 8-seater, 4 × 2, Limousine (Daimler 4.2 Litre) 6-cyl., 245 bhp, auto. 3F1R, wb 11'9", 18'10" × 6'5½" × 5'3¾", 4800 lb. Grade 1 staff car, 1970. Coachwork by Vanden Plas. Jaguar 4235-cc engine and IFS/IRS units with coil springs. Power-assisted steering and disc brakes. Speed 110 mph.

Car, Utility, Light, 4 × 2 (Hillman 'Husky' Series III)
4-cyl., 43.5 bhp, 4F1R, wb 7'2", 12'5½" × 5'0½" × 5'1", 2025 lb.
More than 2500 of these dual-purpose cars had been acquired
(since 1959) when a final order for 406 was placed in Oct. 1964.
Supplied with RHD and LHD, the latter for BAOR.

Car, Utility, Light, 4 × 2 (Morris 'Minor 1000 Traveller')
4-cyl., 35 bhp, 4F1R, wb 7'2", 12'5" × 5'1" × 5'0½", 1830 lb.
Replaced the Hillman 'Husky' when it was discontinued in
1966. Produced 1963–1970. Also used by RAF/AM. Superseded, in turn, by Ford 'Escort' 1100 in 1971.

**Car, Utility, 4 × 2 (Austin 16 HP 'Countryman' Series
BW1)** 4-cyl., 58 bhp, 4F1R, wb 8'8½", 14'3" × 5'7" × 6'0"
approx. Estate car version of Series BS1 Sixteen saloon.
Introduced in May 1947. Vehicle shown was used by Royal
Navy (Royal Naval Air Station, Lee-on-Solent). 2199-cc
OHV engine.

Car, Utility, 4 × 2 (Standard 'Ensign' DeLuxe) 4-cyl.,
68 bhp, 4F1R (some fitted with OD), wb 8'6", 14'4" × 5'8" ×
5'2", 2970 lb. Standards ('Vanguard' and 'Ensign') were used
in large numbers by the RAF, with various body styles. Model
shown was designated 'Standard, 4 × 2, Passenger Car'.
2138-cc OHV engine.

CARS, UTILITY, 4×4

The wartime Humber 4×4 Heavy Utility cars were used for many years after 1945. A Utility version of the Austin 'Champ' was developed but not taken into service. Standardized post-war 4×4 Utility cars were military versions of the Land-Rover Series I, II and IIA station wagons.

Although commercial designs, these met the military requirements with little modification. The Land-Rover LWB station wagon was similar to the LWB basic model but had a different superstructure, extra seats and side doors, etc. The Army also had the Regular SWB Land-Rover with station wagon bodywork; this model did not have the extra side doors. The military Range Rover was a private venture introduced by Rover at the 1970 CV Motor Show in London. It was equipped with H/F radio equipment, roof-mounted aerial, map reading table, rearranged rear seating, roof rack to carry spare wheel, camouflage netting and tent, water and fuel cans, etc.

Car, Utility, Heavy, 4×4, Rover Mk 4, FV18004 (Land-Rover Series I '107') 4-cyl., 52 bhp, 4F1R × 2, wb 8′11″, 14′10″ × 5′3″ × 6′6″, 3696 lb. Tyres 7.00–16. Max. speed 55 mph. Normally carried five men and a No. 19 wireless set. Two extra men could be carried. Five doors. c. 1954.

Car, Utility, Heavy, 4×4, Rover Mk 7, FV18000 Series (Land-Rover Series II and IIA '109') 4-cyl., 77 bhp, 4F1R × 2, wb 9′1″, 14′10″ × 5′6″ × 6′9″, 3925 lb. Tyres 7.50–16. Military version of commercial LWB station wagon. Used by Army and Navy. Series II production: 1958–61, IIA: from 1961.

Car, Command, 4×4 (Rover 'Range Rover') V-8-cyl., 156 bhp, 4F1R × 2, wb 8′4″, basic vehicle: 14′8″ × 5′10″ × 5′10″, 3800 lb. GVW 5300 lb. Commercial model, military version as private venture by Rover, 1970. Fitted with H/F radio and other equipment. Permanent four-wheel drive with lockable third diff. Max. speed 95 mph.

VANS, 4 × 2

For administrative use all services have employed a variety of vans, ranging from the small Austin/Morris 'Minivan' to large boxvans on truck chassis. Shown here are a few typical examples.

Vans used by the Army included the Bedford/Hawson 'Easy Access' and larger types on the TJ Series chassis (J3LC2, J3C2), Commer 'Cob' (van version of Hillman 'Husky'), Morris 'Mini', J- and Y-types (small postal vans), Morris-Commercial LD4 (police van), Trojan, etc. The RAF used panel van ('rigid body') versions of the Standard 'Vanguard', the Morris J2 (also as mini-bus), etc. The RN operated many types of Bedfords, varying from the small CA to truck-based 'Luton vans'. A few types of light pickups were in RN service, including air-transportable Citroën 2 CV-AZP and BMC 'Mini'. The RAF in Germany at one time used crew-cab Tempo 'Matador' pickups.

Van, ¼-ton, 4 × 2 (Austin A/AV7 'Mini-Van') 4-cyl., 34 bhp, 4F1R, wb 7'0", 10'10" × 4'7½" × 4'6½", 1290 lb. GVW 2044 lb. Tyres 5.20–10. Used by all Services. RAF and RN also used pickup version, as 'Truck, Lightweight, Air-transportable'. Van shown served with RN & RM Careers Office.

Van, 15-cwt, 4 × 2 (Morris J2M16) 4-cyl., 42 bhp, 4F1R, wb 7'6", 14'2" × 6'2" × 7'0", 2980 lb. 'Minibus' version shown; standard van had no rear side windows. Introduced as J2 (comm.) in 1956, became J2M16 in 1962. Model 250 JU and heavier LD types (from 1-ton) were also used.

Van, 35-cwt, 4 × 2 (Bedford/Hawson J1 'Easy Access') 6-cyl., 100 bhp (4-cyl. 64-bhp diesel optional), 4F1R, wb 9'11", 18'2" × 6'8½" × 8'6", 4710 lb. Commercial model. 350-cu. ft body by Hawson on modified (semi-FC) Bedford TJ series chassis. Tyres 7.50–16. Introduced in 1964.

AMBULANCES, 4 × 2

To replace various wartime ambulances, principally the well-known Austin K2 (some of which were fitted with cab doors), various types of commercial models were acquired. Bodywork was supplied by several firms, including Lomas, Spurling and Wadhams. Field ambulances are based on 4 × 4 chassis and are dealt with in the appropriate chassis sections. Principal 4 × 2 models used by the Army included Bedford CA-, TA- and TJ-range types and the Morris-Commercial NVS 12/3 and LC5. The Air Force had Bedfords (A2Z and convertible buses, e.g. the Model SB with 31-seater/16-stretcher coach/ambulance body), Morris-Commercial (CV 11/30), etc. The Navy had Bedfords (incl. TA and TJ), Ford 'Thames' 15-cwt, Morris-Commercial CV11/30, etc. The RAF also had large ambulances on the 3-ton 6 × 4 Fordson 'Thames-Sussex' chassis. In W. Berlin Mercedes-Benz L319 type ambulances were used.

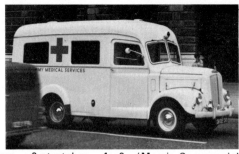

Ambulance, 2-stretcher, 4 × 2 (Morris-Commercial LC5/Lomas) 4-cyl., 46 bhp, 4F1R, wb 10'1", 17'9" × 6'9" × 8'2", 5490 lb. Commercial 1½-ton truck chassis with 2.2-litre OHV engine, produced 1953–60 (also as Austin 301, 1956–60). Used by Army Medical Corps. Bodywork by Herbert Lomas Ltd.

Ambulance, 2- to 3-stretcher, 4 × 2 (Bedford A2Z/Lomas) 6-cyl., 75 bhp, 4F1R, wb 9'11", 18'8" × 7'1" × 8'11", 6275 lb. Tyres 9.00–16. Road ambulance body shown (accommodation for two stretcher and three sitting cases, or 3 stretchers); clinic ambulance had sliding door next to LH cab door. *c.* 1956.

Ambulance, 2- to 3-stretcher, 4 × 2 (Bedford J1Z/Spurling) 6-cyl., 100 bhp, 4F1R, wb 11'2", 19'0" × 7'1" × 7'10", 6000 lb approx. Tyres 8.25–16. Based on standard TJ Bedford-Spurling van of the 1960s. Similar bodywork also on earlier A2Z (TA-range) chassis. Both had Baico wheelbase extension.

COACHES

Coaches, or buses, as used by the Services, were usually civilian types with certain minor modifications. In recent years practically all models have been built on Bedford chassis (models TD, TJ, SB3, SBG, VAS, VAM). Earlier there were 26-, 28- and 32-seaters on Bedford OB and OWB chassis, 36-seaters on AEC 'Regal', Bedford, Dennis and Leyland chassis, 41-seaters on Commer CD510, etc. Commer 'Commando' 20-seaters with lower and upper decks were used by the RAF, from about 1946. In addition there were military 'mini-buses' based on Bedford CA and Morris J2 type vans and 10- and 14-seater Bedford aircrew and service coaches (RAF). The US forces in Britain also employed British buses (Bedford, Ford). Ford-Köln buses were at one time in service with the British forces in Germany. The RN used the Bedford VAL (6 × 2) chassis with Mass Radiography bodywork.

Coach, Aircrew, 10-seater, 4 × 2 (Bedford A3LZ) 6-cyl., 75 bhp, 4F1R, wb 11'11", 21'4" × 7'6" × 9'10", 6860 lb. Tyres 6.50–20 (2DT). Transported aircraft crews dressed in ventilated flying suits. Towed air-conditioning trailer, connected to coach, to supply ventilating air to occupants' clothing. c. 1956.

Coach, Service, 14-seater, 4 × 2 (Bedford J1Z2) 6-cyl., 100 bhp, 4F1R, wb 9'11", 18'4" × 6'8" × 7'10", 4930 lb. General-purpose RAF personnel carrier, seating 14, incl. driver, all facing forward. Body mounted on commercial Bedford TJ-range 35-cwt chassis, early 1960s.

Coach, Air Passenger, 20-seater, 4 × 2 (Commer Q4 'Commando' Mk II) 6-cyl., 90 bhp, 4F1R, wb 15'9", 26'1½" × 7'6" × 10'10½", 10,640 lb. Observation body with lower and upper compartment. 180-cu. ft luggage compartment, accessible by two rear doors. Mk III had LHD. Also used by BOAC.

Coach, Passenger, 32-seater, 4×2 (Bedford OB) 6-cyl., 72 bhp, 4F1R, wb 14'6", chassis: 24'1" × 7'4¼". Laden weight 7 tons. Tyres, front 7.50–20, rear 8.25–20. Produced mid-1940s. Similar bodywork on wartime Model OWB (Utility) chassis, which had different rear axle gear ratio.

Coach, Service, 31-seater, 4×2 (Bedford SB3) 6-cyl., 110 bhp, 4F1R, wb 18'0", 29'9½" × 8'0" × 9'7", 9745 lb. Tyres 8.25–20. LHD or RHD. RHD version had quick-detachable seats which could be removed when vehicle was required for ambulance duties. Used by RAF and RN.

Coach/Ambulance, 39-seater/16-stretcher, 4×2, FV13198 (A) (Bedford SB3) 6-cyl., 130 bhp, 4F1R, wb 18'0", 30'4¾" × 8'0" × 9'7", 11,228 lb. Bodywork by Strachans, convertible to temporary ambulance role in emergency. LHD version shown. Used by Army and RAF. Similar bodywork on SWB chassis.

Coach, Passenger, 44-seater, 4×2 (Bedford VAM) One of a fleet of Marshall-bodied buses operated since 1969 by 62 (Berlin) Squadron RCT. Purchased for RCT by W. German Gov't (as part of cost of maintaining British forces in Berlin). Used as school buses, route buses, troop carriers and for coach tours.

LIGHT CROSS-COUNTRY VEHICLES
4 × 2 and 4 × 4

(For Trucks, ¼-Ton, 4 × 4, see following section)

Makes and Models: Austin/Morris 'Moke' and 'Mini-Moke' (various versions, 4 × 2, from 1960). Austin 'Twini-Moke' (4 × 4, 1963), 'Ant' (4 × 4, 1966). Chrysler/Rootes 'Farmobil' (4 × 2, 1965). Hunting-Percival 'Harrier' (4 × 2, 1957). Steyr-Puch 'Haflinger' (4 × 4, c. 1965, A). Triumph 'Pony' (4 × 4, 1965).

General Data: The 'Mini-Moke' was a direct development from the Austin/Morris 'Mini' car and first appeared in 1960 as an experimental lightweight air-transportable military vehicle. Only a few were delivered to the armed forces and in 1964 the vehicle was made available to civilian purchasers, after many detail modifications had been incorporated. A twin-engined conversion (4 × 4) was developed in 1963 and both were also tested by the US Army. In 1969 production of the 4 × 2 standard model was transferred to British Leyland in Australia, where it was modified in various respects (incl. larger wheels). The Austin 'Ant' was a 4 × 4 development of the BMC 1100, with a 'Midi-Moke' type body structure. The rear wheels were driven by a propeller shaft from the transfer box which was integral with the engine/transmission unit. Normal drive was to the front wheels. Rear wheel drive and low range could be engaged independently. The 'Farmobil' was designed by Fahr in Gottmadingen, Germany. Quantity production was by Farco in Greece, a company taken over by Chrysler Corp. in 1963. In Germany the Farmobil was marketed by BMW. The Imp-engined version shown here was purely experimental. The 'Harrier' was a design of a Mr. J. Dolphin of Marlow, Bucks. (Patent No. 687794, 1953) and four prototypes were produced by Hunting Percival Aircraft Ltd. of Luton, Beds. Transported as a coffin-like box it could be lifted by its crew of four, unfolded and running in about one minute.

The Triumph 'Pony' was designed by Standard-Triumph around the Triumph 1300 engine (front-wheel drive; addition of rear-wheel drive). Series production was taken up by Autocars in Haifa, Israel ('Dragoon').

Vehicle shown (typical): Truck, ¼-ton, 4 × 2, Cargo (Austin 'Mini-Moke')

Technical Data:
Engine: BMC Series 'A' 4-cylinder, I-I-W-F, 948 cc, 34 bhp @ 5000 rpm.
Transmission: 4F1R. Front-wheel drive.
Brakes: hydraulic.
Tyres: 5.20–10.
Wheelbase: 6'0½".
Overall l × w × h: 9'2" × 4'6" × 4'9" (3'4").
Weight: 1180 lb. GVW 1867 lb.
Note: 1962 version shown. Earlier prototypes ('Moke', 1960/61) and civilian production models (from 1964) had longer wheelbase and different bodywork. Developed from BMC ADO 15 'Mini'.

Truck, ¼-ton, 4×4, Twin-Engined (BMC 'Twini-Moke')
2×4-cyl., 2×55 bhp, 2×4F1R, wb 6'8". Experimental vehicle with two 1100-cc engines, one at front and one at rear, each driving the adjacent wheels separately. This and an 850-cc 4×2 model were tested by the US Army in 1964.

Truck, Lightweight, Air-transportable, 4×4 (Austin 'Ant') 4-cyl., 50 bhp, 4F1R×2, wb 6'5½", 9'3"×4'6"×4'11", 1598 lb. Experimental vehicle, using various components of BMC 1100 cars. Torsion bar IFS/IRS. Transversal engine/gearbox/transfer unit. Tyres 5.60–12. Track 3'11½". 1966. A pickup truck version appeared also.

Car, Folding, 4-seater, 4×2 (Hunting Percival 'Harrier')
BSA A10 650-cc twin-cyl., 30 bhp, 4F, wb 7'10", 8'9"× 4'0"×2'10¾" (top of engine), 700 lb. Speed 60 mph. Vehicle could be folded into a box-shaped unit measuring 10'4"×1'9" ×3'0" for ease of transport. Four built for air drop trials, 1957.

Truck, Lightweight, 4×2 (Chrysler/Rootes 'Farmobil')
Hillman Imp 4-cyl., 39 bhp, 4F1R, wb 5'8½", 11'0"×5'3"× 3'7". Original model had BMW twin-cyl. air-cooled engine. Vehicle shown was exp. fitted with British water-cooled engine; hence addition of radiator at front (see also General Data).

TRUCKS, ¼- and ½-TON 4×4

Makes and Models: Austin FV1800 Series 'Champ' WN1 ¼-ton: FV1801(A) Cargo, FV1801A(1) Cargo FFW, FV1802(A) Utility (from 1952). Austin 'Champ' WN2 ¼-ton (A90 engine, 1953) and WN3 ¼-ton (civilian version, A90 engine, 1952). Austin 'Gipsy' ¼-ton: Series I (1957), Series II (G2M10, 1960), Series IV (GM4M10, 1962). Auto Union 'Munga' ¼-ton (various types, from c. 1960). Nuffield Light Car, 5-cwt, 4×4, 'Gutty' (1946/47). Nuffield (Wolseley) FV1800 Light Car, 5-cwt, 4×4 (1949/50). Rover FV18000 Series 'Land-Rover' ¼-ton: Mk 1 and 2 (80-in wb), Mk 3 (86-in wb), Mk 5 and 6 (88-in wb), Rover 8 and 10 (88-in wb) (Note: Mk 4, Rover 7, 9 and 11 were LWB models) (from 1949); Lightweight Rover Mk 1 ¼-ton (1966). Rover GS Truck, ½-ton, Mk 1 (1968).

General Data: The wartime US 'Jeep' was used extensively by the British forces, but supplies ceased with the end of Lend-Lease. Towards the end of the war design work had already started on a British edition of the 'Car, 5-cwt, 4×4' by the Nuffield Organization, under the direction of Mr (later Sir) Alec Issigonis, for the Ministry of Supply. The original design featured a horizontally opposed four-cyl. engine, not unlike that which was designed for the 'Mosquito' car (the later Morris 'Minor'). The first prototypes, produced shortly after the war, had this engine but the Army decided to use a standardized Rolls-Royce B-Series power unit. In 1950 the prototype FV1800 Series '5-cwt 4×4 combat car' appeared. Like the earlier 'Gutty', the new model (sometimes referred to as 'Mudlark') had torsion bar IFS/IRS and a stressed-skin integral body/chassis. After further development this became the Austin-built 'Champ' which was in service from 1952 to 1966. Meanwhile, the Rover Co. had modified a US 'Jeep', fitted with certain Rover units and developed this until it was unveiled in 1948 as the 100% Rover-built 'Land-Rover'. From 1949 large numbers were supplied for military service. A few were fitted with RR B40 engine, others with non-driven front axle. Improved Series II and III models were introduced in 1958 and 1971 respectively.

Vehicle shown (typical): Truck, ¼-ton, 4×4, Cargo, Austin, Mk 1, FV1801 (A) (Austin WN1 'Champ')

Technical Data:
Engine: Rolls-Royce B40, No 1, Mk 2A/4 or 5A, 4-cylinder, I-F-W-F, 2838 cc, 69 bhp @ 3750 rpm (gross: 80 @ 3750).
Transmission: 5F5R.
Brakes: hydraulic.
Tyres: 7.50–16 (6.50–16 optional).
Wheelbase: 7'0". Track: 4'1".
Overall l×w×h: 12'0½"×5'1⅜"×6'2" (4'7").
Weight: 3668 lb. GVW: 4480 lb.
Note: 5-speed all-s/m gearbox, forward/reverse and front axle declutch in transfer box which was integral with rear diff. Torsion-bar IFS/IRS. Cargo FFW version had 2-speed generator.

Car, 5-cwt, 4 × 4 (Nuffield Mechanizations 'Gutty')
One of the prototypes for the FV1800 Series, built in 1947. Another (3 were built) had horizontal rad. grille cut-outs and no separate wings. Nuffield water-cooled horizontally-opposed 4-cyl. L-head engine, with 4F1R × 2 trans/final drive.

Car, 5-cwt, 4 × 4 (Nuffield/Wolseley 'Mudlark') Rolls-Royce-engined pre-production model of FV1800 vehicle, produced in 1949/50. Main difference with final design was in wings and other body panels. Shown equipped with hard-top, which also appeared on the later 'Champ'.

Truck, ¼-ton, 4 × 4, Utility, FV1802(A) (Austin WN1 'Champ') RR B40 4-cyl., 80 bhp, 5F5R, wb 7'0", 12'0" × 5'5" × 6'0" (4'7"), 3752 lb. Modification of standard 'Champ', featuring wider body with detachable side doors and tailboard loading. Max. load capacity 10 cwt. Prototype(s) only. 1954.

Truck, ¼-ton, 4 × 4 (Austin WN3 'Champ') Civilian version of FV1801, fitted with Austin A90 4-cyl. 75-bhp 2660-cc engine. No electrical suppression or waterproof equipment. Introduced July 1952 (military WN1: Nov. 1952). In Feb. 1953 a military version with A90 engine (WN2) was introduced. Few of these were made.

Truck, ¼-ton, 4 × 4 (Austin 'Gipsy' Series I) 4-cyl., 62 bhp, 4F1R × 2, wb 7'6", 11'7" × 5'6¾" × 6'1½" (4'8½"), 2915 lb. Introduced in 1958 this vehicle had 'Flexitor' rubber IFS/IRS, developed by Spencer, Moulton & Co. It was sold to several countries, incl. Tunisia (shown).

Truck, ¼-ton, 4 × 4, Cargo, FV18701 (Austin G4M10 'Gipsy' Series IV) 4-cyl., 70 bhp, 4F1R × 2, wb 7'6", 12'2¾" × 5'6½" × 6'5" (4'10"), 3448 lb. Late model with leaf spring suspension, rigid axles. 1966. Many mods. in order to meet military requirements. 'Gipsy' production ceased in mid-1968.

Truck, ¼-ton, 4 × 4, Cargo, Rover, Mk 1, FV18001 (Land Rover Series I '80') 4-cyl., 55 bhp, 4F1R × 2, wb 6'8", 11'0" × 5'1" × 5'10" (4'8"), 2610 lb. First production type (1948–51). Headlights behind radiator grille. Front-wheel drive with over-run freewheel. 1595-cc Rover '60' engine. In military service from 1949.

Truck, ¼-ton, 4 × 4, Cargo, Rover, Mk 2, FV18001 (Land-Rover Series I '80') 4-cyl., 52 bhp, 4F1R × 2, wb 6'8", 11'8" × 5'2" × 6'4" (4'8"), 2864 lb. Mk 2 (from 1951) had 2-litre (1997½-cc) engine and selective front-drive engagement by dog clutch. Late production had exposed headlights, as shown.

Truck, ¼-ton, 4 × 4, SAS, Rover, Mk 3, FV18006 (Land-Rover Series I '86') 4-cyl., 52 bhp, 4F1R × 2, wb 7'2", 13'4" × 5'6" × 4'9", 4704 lb (laden). Special Air Services (SAS) version of 1953–56 86-in wb (Mk 3) model, with reinforced suspension to carry extra load. Mk 5 had 88-in wb. Mk 6 had restyled bodywork (Series II, 1958).

Truck, ¼-ton, 4 × 4, FFR, Rover 8, FV18031 (Land-Rover Series IIA '88') 4-cyl., 77 bhp, 4F1R × 2, wb 7'4", 12'5" × 5'6½" × 6'5", 3748 lb (w/o radio equipment). Wheelbase of regular models was increased to 88 in from 1956 (Series I). Restyled front end in 1969 (Benelux 1968). Rover 10 had negative earth electrics.

Truck, ¼-ton, 4 × 4, Lightweight, Rover Mk 1 (Land-Rover Series IIA '88', modified) 4-cyl., 77 bhp, 4F1R × 2, wb 7'4", 11'11" × 5'0" × 4'10", 3100 lb. Experimental stripped-down air-transportable, helicopter liftable version of new design military Land-Rover, 1966. Shown with 8.20–15 special desert tyres.

Truck, ½-ton, 4 × 4, GS, FFR, Rover I (Land-Rover) 4-cyl., 77 bhp, 4F1R × 2, wb 7'4", 12'0" × 5'0" × 6'5" (4'10"), 3300 lb. New body design for the 1970s. 24-volt electrics. Mechanically similar to Rover 10. 1969/70 models had head-lights in different position (as shown on left).

TRUCKS, $\frac{3}{4}$-TON, 4×4

Most vehicles in this class were military versions of the long-wheelbase Land-Rover, which was first introduced in 1953 (107-in wb 'Long'). Of these, the Army used the station wagon (heavy utility) version (Mk 4). At the time they were classed as $\frac{1}{4}$-ton vehicles. The RAF used the pick-up truck modified as a crash rescue vehicle and an ambulance. Of the later Series II and IIA models large numbers were acquired by all services. The military designations for these were Rover 7 and 9. The Rover 9 (and short-wheelbase 8) had strengthened front and rear diffs. and rear axle shafts. The 9/1 (and 8/1) did not have the strengthened front diff. On the 9/2 (and 8/2) neither diffs. nor axle shafts had been strengthened. Rover 11 was military version of Land-Rover 1969/70 model with headlights in wings. There were numerous derivatives from the basic models. The Austin 'Gipsy' made only a brief appearance as a British military vehicle.

Truck, $\frac{1}{4}$-ton, 4×4, Ambulance, Special, Rover Mk 4, FV18005 (Land-Rover Series I '107') 4-cyl., 52 bhp, 4F1R×2, wb 8'11", 15'4½"×6'3"×7'5", 3808 lb. 2-litre engine. c. 1954. Later Mk 4 models (1956) had 9'1" wb ('109'). 2-stretcher bodywork by Bonallack, for Mountain Rescue purposes (RAF).

Truck, $\frac{3}{4}$-ton, 4×4, FFR, Rover 9, FV18053 (Land-Rover Series IIA '109') 4-cyl., 77 bhp, 4F1R×2, wb 9'1", 15'3"× 5'5½"×6'6", 4060 lb. 24-volt 40-amp. rectified AC electrical system with provision for charging radio batteries. Fully equipped for radio role, otherwise as FV 18052 (cargo).

Truck, $\frac{3}{4}$-ton, 4×4, FFR, Rover 11, FV18062 (Land-Rover Series IIA '109') 4-cyl., 81 bhp, 4F1R×2, wb 9'1", 15'3"× 5'5½"×6'6". From late 1968 the military split-rim wheels were replaced by a new well-base rim type, which was also standardized for civ. models. 1969 style front end.

Truck, ¾-ton, 4 × 4, Ambulance, Rover 7, FV18044 (Land-Rover Series IIA '109') 4-cyl., 77 bhp, 4F1R × 2, wb 9'1", 15'10" × 6'3" × 7'0½", 4144 lb. Used by Army and RAF. RAF version had rad. guard (as on Rover 7 FV18047 Airfield Crash Rescue truck). Two stretchers (or one and three sitting cases).

Truck, ¾-ton, 4 × 4, Cargo, Rover 9 (Land-Rover Series IIA '109') One of many variants of the basic LWB Land-Rover. This armed version with oversize (9.00–16) desert tyres was comprehensively equipped for patrol work. Others were used as mounts for AT weapons such as 'Wombat', 'Vigilant' and 'Swingfire'.

Truck, ¾-ton, 4 × 4, Cargo, for Power Trailers (Land-Rover) 6-cyl., 110 bhp, 4F1R × 2, wb 9'2", 14'3" × 6'0" × 6'8", 3300 lb. 3-litre (3L7) engine. ENV gearbox. Lightweight style body. 9.00–16 tyres. Coupled to Rubery Owen 1-ton trailer with driven axle. Similar trailers mfd by Scottorn/RB. 1966.

Truck, ¾-ton, 4 × 4, FFR (Austin G4M15 'Gipsy' Series IV) 4-cyl., 70 bhp, 4F1R × 2, wb 9'3", 13'11¾" × 5'6½" × 6'5½", 3990 lb (w/o radio sets). Radio version of FV18711 cargo truck, tested for possible Army use. Equipped with 24-volt 90-amp. rectified AC electrical system, aerial brackets, operators seats, etc.

TRUCKS, 1-TON
4 × 2 and 4 × 4

Makes and Models: Austin 'Loadstar' (4 × 2, c. 1948), K9WD FV16000 Series, Mk 1, Mk 2, Series 3 (4 × 4, from 1952). Bedford KO (4 × 2, c. 1950), TA (A2C, 4 × 2, c. 1955), RL, modified (4 × 4, c. 1953). Commer Q2 (4 × 2, 1951). Humber FV1600 Series (4 × 4, 1952). Morris-Commercial CV9/40, PV (4 × 2, from c. 1947), MRA1 FV16100 Series (4 × 4, 1952). Rover, Land-Rover FV18500 and 18600 Series (4 × 4, 1962), Forward Control '110' (4 × 4, 1966), '101' (4 × 4, 1970), etc.

General Data: Some types of wartime 15-cwt trucks remained in use after 1945 (principally Bedford and Morris-Commercial) and were uprated to 1-tonners. They were superseded by post-war designs of three categories: CL (commercial, with detail modifications), GS (general service, commercial 4 × 4 designs) and CT (combat trucks, military high-mobility designs).

All could be fitted with various body types, incl. cargo and house-type vans. The CT trucks, designated the FV1600 Series, were produced by Rootes in Maidstone and supplied under the Humber name. They had RR B60 engines and independent suspension. There were soft-skin and armoured versions. They were later reclassified as GS types.

Vehicles in the FV16000 Series (GS types) were furnished by Austin and Morris-Commercial. Both were fitted with various body types incl. water tankers ('bowsers'). The Austin eventually appeared with a 5.1-litre multi-fuel engine (early 1960s), wider rear track, heavy duty suspension, wider spaced rear springs and reinforced chassis frame, but few of these were made. Both the Austin and the Morris-Commercial were modifications of contemporary 4 × 2 commercial trucks. Modifications included front-wheel drive, larger tyres (single rear), etc.

In addition there were several CL types which were slightly modified commercial 4 × 2 trucks, usually with military bodywork (Austin, Bedford, Commer, Morris-Commercial). A modified Bedford RL, with shortened chassis and 9.00-20 tyres, was also experimented with.

Rover produced a variety of experimental 1-ton 4 × 4s. A six-wheeler was also designed.

Vehicle shown (typical): Truck, 1-ton, 4 × 4, Cargo, w/Winch, Humber, FV1601 (A) (Rootes)

Technical Data:

Engine: Rolls-Royce B60, No 1, Mk 2A or 5 6-cylinder, I-F-W-F, 4250 cc, 98 bhp @ 3750 rpm (gross: 110 @ 3750).

Transmission: 5F1R × 1 (transfer: single speed and PTO).

Brakes: hydraulic.

Tyres: 9.00–20.

Wheelbase: 9'0". Track: 5'8".

Overall l × w × h: 16'7" × 6'10" × 7'9" (6'4").

Weight: 7468 lb. GVW: 11,480 lb.

Note: Torsion-bar IFS/IRS. 2-ton single-drum winch. Variants: FV1602(A): FFW; FV1604(A): Wireless; FV1621: missile supply; FV1622: missile test. For armoured versions see **relevant** section.

Truck, 1-ton, 4 × 4, Cargo, Humber (Rootes, prototype) RR 6-cyl., 98 bhp, 5F1R × 1. Prototype for FV1800 range, produced in 1950 in conjunction with Design Dept. of MoS. Suspension could be released (at points 'A') to lower overall height for air transport. Production cab was double-skin closed type.

Truck, 1-ton, 4 × 4, Wireless, Humber, FV1604(A) (Rootes) RR 6-cyl., 98 bhp, 5F1R × 1, wb 9'0", 17'4" × 7'5" × 9'1", 8764 lb. Basically as FV1601(A) but 2-speed generator and no winch. House-type body with two compartments and rear door. Waterproof tent for fitting at either side. Speed 55 mph.

Truck, 1-ton, 4 × 2, Cargo (Bedford KC) 6-cyl., 72–76 bhp, 4F1R, wb 10'0", 16'3" × 6'2" × 6'8" (cab), 4620 lb approx. Basically commercial 30-cwt Bedford K Series chassis/cab with military cargo body, hoops and tilt (not shown). Tyre size 7.00–20 (other sizes optional). RAF used KC with signals body.

Truck, 1-ton, 4 × 2, Wireless (Commer Q2) 6-cyl., 80 bhp, 4F1R, wb 10'2", 17'2" × 6'9" × 8'2", 6552 lb. Military version of Model S2 2/3-ton 'Superpoise', supplied with wireless van (shown) and cargo bodywork. Single 6.00–16 divided wheels with 9.00–16 tyres. Originally classed as 15-cwt (1951).

Truck, 1-ton, 4×4, Cargo, FV16001 (Austin K9WD) 6-cyl., 90 bhp, 4F1R×2, wb 11'5¼", 17'2"×7'3"×8'8" (7'10¾"), 6300 lb. Military version of 4×2 'Loadstar'. Tyres 9.00–20. Variants: FV16002 (FFW), FV16003 (wireless), FV16004 (radio repair), FV16009 (water), etc. Was commercially available as 1½-tonner (1953–55).

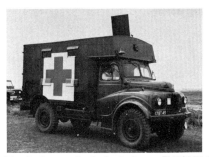

Truck, 1-ton, 4×4, Ambulance FV16005 (Austin K9WD) 6-cyl., 90 bhp, 4F1R×2, wb 11'5¼", 18'0"×7'1"×10'2½", 9000 lb. Originally developed as RAF crash rescue vehicle. Carried four or two stretchers and comprehensive crash/emergency equipment. Chassis as FV16001 but special 'soft' rear suspension.

Truck, 1-ton, 4×4, Cargo, FV16101 (Morris-Commercial MRA1) 6-cyl., 72 bhp, 4F1R×2, wb 10'3", 17'7½"×6'10"× 8'8½" (7'7"), 7140 lb. Military version of civilian truck, also available commercially (1½-ton, 4×4). Variants: FV16102 (water), FV16103 (dry air charging), FV16104 (welding), etc. 9.00–20 tyres on divided or three-piece wheels.

Truck, 1-ton, 4×4, Water, FV16102 (Morris-Commercial MRA1) 6-cyl., 72 bhp, 4F1R×2, wb 10'3", 17'0"×6'10"× 7'7", 7840 lb. As FV16101 but fitted with 200-gallon water tank. Provided with superstructure and canvas canopy (as shown). Both Austin and Morris also supplied with cab roof hatch.

Truck, 1-ton, 4 × 4, Cargo, FV16012 (Austin) 6-cyl. m/f, 90 bhp, 4F1R × 2, wb 11′9″, 19′8″ × 7′6″ × 10′4″, 8288 lb. Latest version of Austin 1-ton 4 × 4 (also referred to as 30-cwt), with BMC 5103-cc engine and dropside body. Also ambulance (FV16013) and container truck (FV16018). Few produced.

Truck, 1-ton, 4 × 4, Cargo (Land-Rover FC '110') 4-cyl. 77 bhp, 4F1R × 2, wb 9′2″, 16′7½″ × 5′10¾″ × 8′6″ (cab 7′4½″), 4480 lb. Commercial forward-control Land-Rover, fitted with heavy duty ENV axles. Track 4′9½″. Tyres 9.00–16. Tested by FVRDE for possible military use. 1966.

Truck, 1-ton, 4 × 4, Cargo (Land-Rover) 6-cyl., 110 bhp, 4F1R × 2, wb 8′5″, 14′1″ × 6′0″ × 7′2″, 4910 lb. Experimental light forward-control cargo truck with Rover 3-litre car engine. Shown working in conjunction with powered-axle 1-ton trailer (axle driven from truck transmission PTO). 1970.

Truck, 1-ton, 4 × 4, Cargo (Land-Rover) V-8-cyl., 162 bhp, 4F1R × 2, wb 8′5″, 14′0½″ × 6′0½″ × 7′2″, 4093 lb. Multi-purpose GS truck with removable superstructure and down-rated Rover 3.5-litre car engine. Positive lock on inter-axle diff. (as on 'Range Rover'). 1971.

Truck, 1-ton, 4×4, Cargo (Land-Rover) with Trailer, 1-ton, Powered Axle, Cargo (Rubery Owen) Prototype 2-wh. trailer, measuring 11′3″×5′1″×4′0″. Weight 1540 lb. laden 3780 lb. Tyres 9.00–16 (truck and trailer). 5.57:1 (hypoid) fully-floating axle.

Truck, 1-ton, 4×4, Amphibious (Land-Rover) 6-cyl., 83 bhp, 4F1R×2, wb 8′1″, 14′6¾″×5′9¾″×6′10½″, 3950 lb. GVW 6350 lb. Tyres 9.00–16. 2.6-litre engine. Prototype only. built in 1965 at request of Australian Army, using many parts of standard Land-Rover.

Truck, 1-ton, 4×4, Airportable, GP, Scheme A, FV18501 (Land-Rover) 4-cyl., 77 bhp, 4F1R×2, wb 9′1″, 13′9″× 5′11″×7′0″, 4088 lb. No doors. Shown with flotation kit consisting of four air bags, inflated by truck's exhaust (as such: 21′10″×11′2″, 4255 lb). Propeller on rear prop shaft.

Truck, 1-ton, 4×4, Airportable, GP, Scheme B, FV18601 (Land-Rover) 4-cyl., 77 bhp, 4F1R×1, wb 8′1″, 14′0″× 6′0″×7′0″, 3499 lb. Body of exoskeletal form to provide inherent flotation. Mock-up only. 1962. Of contemporary FV18501 (Scheme A) a small number was produced and issued.

TRUCKS, 1½-TON
4 × 2 and 4 × 4

Few types of 1½-ton (30-cwt) 4 × 2 and 4 × 4 trucks were used by the British armed forces after World War II. Some wartime types remained in use, supplemented by new vehicles, mainly Bedford 4 × 2. In 1966 new BMC (Austin), Vauxhall (Bedford), Rootes (Commer) and Rover (Land-Rover) 4 × 4 models appeared. These were tested by the FVRDE. The Land-Rover had a (Perkins) diesel, the others multi-fuel engines. They were designed to meet a requirement for a GS 30-cwt/1½-ton load carrier. Bedfords were also converted to the 4 × 4 configuration by AWD/Vickers (1962) and Reynolds Boughton ('Packhorse', 1969) for civilian use. Mercedes-Benz 'Unimog' S 1½-ton 4 × 4 trucks saw service with the British Army in W. Berlin, Borgward B2000A 4 × 4 2-tonners with the RAF in W. Germany.

Truck, 30-cwt, 4 × 2, Signals (Type E Body) (Bedford KC) 6-cyl., 76 bhp, 4F1R, wb 10'0". Tyres 9.00–16. RAF signals shell body with wheel-arch floor. Mk 3 body of similar type but 'tropicalized' and with flat floor was mounted on Austin K9 1-ton 4 × 4. Double rear door.

Truck, 30-cwt, 4 × 2, Cargo (Bedford J1) 6-cyl., 100 bhp, 4F1R, wb 9'11", 16'9½" × 6'11" × 8'10", 5400 lb. Commercial chassis/cab. Flat-floor steel body with fixed sides and hinged tailboard. Light-alloy hard-top with canvas flaps at rear. Tyres 7.50–16. Used by RAF (as 1-tonner).

Truck, 1½-ton, 4 × 4, Cargo (Turner) 3-cyl., blown 2-stroke m/f 60-bhp diesel engine, originally of Austrian design. Developed to British Army specification, mid-1950s. Fibreglass front end. Integral body/chassis built up from rolled steel sections. No volume production.

Truck, 1½-ton, 4×4, Cargo (Bedford J 4×4) 6-cyl., 133 bhp (or 107-bhp diesel), 4F1R×2, wb 10'0", 17'2"× 6'0"×7'1½", 5820 lb. Derived from J5S (4×2), in conjunction with Vickers Armstrongs (Onions) Ltd, 1964. R-type transfer. Mil. version (exp., 1966) had 102-bhp m/f engine. GVW 9000 lb.

Truck, 1½-ton, 4×4, Cargo (Commer 'Superpoise') Perkins Q6.354 6-cyl. m/f, 105 bhp, 4F1R×2, wb 10'2", 17'4"×8'0"×7'3", 8568 lb. Prototype, 1966. Fitted with positive differential lock, air-hyd. brakes, 11.00–16 tyres (on 3-piece wheels), radiator guard. 5.8-litre engine.

Truck, 1½-ton, 4×4, Cargo (Austin) BMC 6-cyl. m/f, 105 bhp, 4F1R×2, wb 9'2", 15'11"×7'8"×7'5", 6888 lb. Two types of cabs with minor styling differences. 5.7-litre (5655-cc) engine, using petrol or diesel fuel. 11.00–16 tyres. Air-hyd. brakes (dual air system) and trailer air brakes. Prototypes only, 1966.

Truck, 1½-ton, 4×4, Cargo (Land-Rover) Perkins 6.354 6-cyl. diesel, 5F1R×2, wb 9'4", 15'6½"×7'3¼"×8'8½", 7460 lb. 5.8-litre engine. Air-assisted hyd. brakes. Positive diff. locks. Hub reduction gearing. 24-volt electrics. Air brake system for trailers. Experimental vehicle, 1966.

TRUCKS, 2- to 5-TON
4 × 2

From about 1950 wartime trucks in this category were supplemented and replaced by new vehicles, all of which were basically commercial trucks, fitted with bodywork to military specifications. Some wartime types, mainly on Bedford OY chassis, were still in service in the mid-1960s. Post-war 3-ton types included Austins ('Loadstar'), Bedfords (various types, normal and forward control), Commers (BF, QX5), Fordsons (Thames ET6, 500E, 564E, etc.), Morris-Commercials (FV 12/5, NVS 13/5), etc. Many types of bodies were fitted on these chassis, including van, cargo, horsebox, fuel tanker, water tanker, office, tipper, etc. Shown in this section are only a few typical examples of these 4 × 2 applications.

Truck, 2-ton, 4 × 2, Airfield Control (Karrier 'Bantam' Mk V) 4-cyl., 53 bhp, 4F1R, wb 8'2". Mk III similar but 48-bhp SV engine and 'crash'-type gearbox. Mk IV (1954–55) had synchro-mesh. Mk V (from 1955) had OHV engine. Body variants included cargo, platform, hydrant fueller and refuse collecting. RAF.

Truck, 3-ton, 4 × 2, Cargo (Austin K4DE Series II 'Loadstar') 6-cyl., 68 bhp, 4F1R, wb 13'1¾", 21'9" × 7'3" × 7'1", 6272 lb. Commercial 5-ton truck with General Service cargo body of composite steel and wooden construction with canvas tilt on tubular frame. Used by Army and Air Force. Produced 1949–55.

Truck, 3-ton, 4 × 2, Tipper (Bedford OSBC) 6-cyl., 72 bhp, 4F1R, wb 9'3", 16'0" × 7'2" × 7'0", 5936 lb. Commercial 5-ton tipper chassis/cab with all-steel dump body. Other body types on OS and OL chassis included cargo trucks, tractors (for S-T), water tankers, etc. OL series had 13'1" wb.

Truck, 3- to 5-ton, 4×2, Servicing Platform (Bedford SLC3) 6-cyl., 94 bhp, 4F1R, wb 13'0", 26'0"×7'2"×12'0", 12,180 lb. Used by RAF and Army for aircraft servicing. Simon hyd. platform; height 2'9" up to 36'0". RN had similar equipment on Morris-Commercial 5K Series III chassis.

Truck, 4-ton, 4×2, Cargo (Bedford KCC) Dropside body on TK Series chassis (RAF). All services used Bedfords of the O, S, TA, TJ and TK Series with numerous body types, incl. tippers, tractors for S-T, boxvans, fuel tankers, aircraft servicing vehicles, etc.

Truck, 3-ton, 4×2, Cargo (Fordson ET6 'Thames') V-8-cyl., 85 bhp, 4F1R, wb 13'1", 21'0"×7'4"×10'0" (7'4"), 6720 lb. Commercial 4-tonner with military GS body (Army). Similar types used by RAF and RN (some with 4D diesel engine). Also SWB tractor for refuelling S-T and boxvan.

Truck, 3-ton, 4×2, Office (Morris-Commercial FV12/5) 4-cyl., 80 bhp, 4F1R, wb 12'6", 21'9"×8'0"×10'0", 8000 lb approx. Also as caravan (similar bodywork). Commercial 5-ton chassis, produced 1948 to 1953. Also in Army service was NC version (Model NVS 13/5R, 70 bhp, 6-cyl., wb 13'9").

TRUCKS, 3- to 4½-TON 4×4

Makes and Models: Austin FF, FV13000 Series (3- to 5-ton, from 1956), FJ, FV13700 Series (4½-ton, 1966). Bedford RL and RS, FV13100 Series (RLB, RLC, RLD, RLE, RLF, RLG, RLW, RSC, etc.; 3- to 4-ton, from 1952), R Mk 2 (3- to 5-ton, 1956), RK/R2LC15, FV13800 Series (4½-ton, 1966), MK, FV13800 Series (4-ton, 1970). Commer Q4, FV13200 Series (3-ton, 1952), CB, FV13900 Series (4½-ton, from 1956). Ford 'Thames', FV13300 Series (E2, E3, E4; 3-ton. 1951). Ford-Köln, Kaelble, Magirus-Deutz, Mercedes-Benz, etc. (see General Data). Leyland 'Laird' (4½-ton, 1971). Thornycroft TF/B80, B81 'Nubian', FV13400 Series, etc. (3-ton, from c. 1950).

General Data: Some types of wartime 3-ton 4×4 trucks, particularly the Bedford QL, remained in service for many years. The Thornycroft 'Nubian' was reintroduced after the war as cargo truck and 10-ton tractor, now with Rolls-Royce engine. Between 1950 and 1952 three new 3-tonners were developed by Ford, Rootes (Commer) and Vauxhall (Bedford). Of all three considerable quantities were acquired and they were also available for export, but the Bedford RL, which remained in production until 1969 (73,135 were made for military and civilian purposes), was the most common and was used by the Army, Air Force and Navy with numerous body types. One- and five-ton (6×6) versions were also envisaged but remained in the experimental stage.

By 1968 the RL's payload capacity was uprated to 4-ton. Meanwhile several other firms produced 4×4 trucks in the 3- to 5-ton payload class. Some were conversions of existing commercial trucks (Albion/Scammell, Austin/Harper, Bedford/RB, Commer/AWD, Dodge/AWD, Ford/AWD, Ford/Harper, Leyland/AWD, etc.). These were basically civilian types but some were sold to foreign Governments for military service.

Following extensive trials during the 1960s with new types submitted by BMC, Rootes and Vauxhall, the Bedford MK of the last manufacturer was selected as the new 4-ton 4×4 truck for the British Army. The British forces in Germany employed a variety of German 4×4 trucks with 3-ton and higher payload ratings, including Büssing, Ford, Kaelble, Magirus-Deutz and Mercedes-Benz.

Vehicle shown (typical): Truck, 3-ton, 4×4, Cargo, w/Winch, FV13105 (Bedford RLF)

Technical Data:

Engine: Bedford 300 CID 6-cylinder, I-I-W-F, 4927 cc, 110 bhp @ 3200 rpm (later models 130 @ 3200).

Transmission: 4F1R × 2.

Brakes: hyd. with air assistance (vacuum servo on certain models, incl. RAF vehicles).

Tyres: 11.00–20.

Wheelbase: 13'0".

Overall l × w × h: 21'7½" × 8'0" × 10'4½" (8'6½").

Weight: 11,225 lb.

Note: Early model with Vauxhall body (RLW had FV body). Based on FV13101 but fitted with 5-ton winch under body. Developed from 7-ton 4×2 Model SLC.

Truck, 4-ton, 4 × 4, Bulk Fuel Tanker (Bedford RLC)
6-cyl., 130 bhp, 4F1R × 2, wb 13′0″, 21′6″ × 7′6″ × 8′6″,
10,300 lb approx. Late type chassis/cab with Thompson
bodywork. 600-gallon tank. 50-gpm discharge pump. Four
reels, each with 60 ft of hose and trigger nozzles. 1969.

**Truck, 3-ton, 4 × 4, Tipper, w/Winch, FV13111 (Bedford
RSW)** 6-cyl., 130 bhp, 4F1R × 2, wb 11′0″, 18′3″ × 7′4½″ ×
9′11″, 11,004 lb. Short-wheelbase chassis/cab with Edbro
4½-cu. yd hydraulic dump body with canvas tilt. 5-ton winch.
Tyres 9.00–20 (2DT). Used by RAF. RAF had many RL trucks,
also with various body types.

Truck, 3-ton, 4 × 4, Wrecker (Bedford RSC) 6-cyl.,
130 bhp, 4F1R × 2, wb 11′0″, 19′1″ × 7′6″ × 9′0″. Commercial
twin-boom wrecker with two power winches and two manual
winches, produced by Reynolds Boughton on RS chassis.
Some were supplied to Royal Navy in 1966 (shown). Navy
also used RL models.

**Truck, 3-ton, 4 × 4, Wrecker, w/Winch, FV13115 (Bedford
RLC)** 6-cyl., 130 bhp, 4F1R × 2, wb 13′0″, 26′2″ × 7′7½″ ×
8′10½″, 17,920 lb (laden). Designated 'Recovery Vehicle
Wheeled, Light'. 3-ton (max.) capacity swinging jib. Bodywork by Marshall. Similar type by Reynolds Boughton.
7-ton main winch.

Truck, 4-ton, 4 × 4, Bridging, w/Winch (Bedford RLW) 6-cyl., 130 bhp, 4F1R, wb 13′0″, 20′10″ × 7′9″. Carried pontoons and other parts for light floating bridge and towed special 2-wh. trailer for same purpose. Note raised front bumper and headlight guards.

Truck, 3-ton, 4 × 4, Water Tanker, 600-gal. (Bedford RLC3Z) Tropical version of RL chassis with mild steel open cab (known as mine cab or armoured half cab) affording protection against mine blast. Several hundred produced, from 1966, by Wharton. Used in Aden, also with GS cargo body.

Truck, 3-ton, 4 × 4, Helicopter Support Tender (Bedford RLC) Special bodywork by Marshall, fire fighting equipment by Merryweather. Three produced, in 1968, for the Queen's Flight for use during all helicopter flights. 4-ft chassis extension at rear. Comprehensively equipped. Colour grey.

Truck, 4-ton, 4 × 4, Cargo, w/Winch (Bedford MKP2BMO) 6-cyl. m/f, 108 bhp, 4F1R × 2, wb 13′0″, 21′9″ × 8′2″ × 11′2″ (cab 9′3″), 10,700 lb approx. Tyres 12.00–20. Air/hyd. brakes, 3-line with trailer connection. 5420-cc (330 CID) engine, 98 net bhp. Turner 5-ton winch under body. Marshall D/S body.

Truck, 4-ton, 4×4, Container (Bedford MKP2BMO) Development of the M- or MK-Series commenced in the early 1960s. First known as RK it was derived from the Bedford TK (4×2). Body was produced by Marshall of Cambridge, who had supplied over 30,000 cargo bodies for the RL, as well as specialist bodywork.

Truck, 3- to 5-ton, 4×4, Cargo (Austin FF) BMC 6-cyl. m/f, 118 bhp, 5F1R×2, wb 12′5″, 20′5″×8′0″×8′5″ (cab), 9250 lb. Exp. 4×4 adaptation of FF K140 (7-ton 4×2) truck. Turbocharged 5.1-litre engine. Also with 5.7-litre normally aspirated m/f engine. 1962. Earlier prototype had different cab (Series III type).

Truck, 4½-ton, 4×4, Cargo, FV13701 (Austin FJ) BMC 6-cyl. m/f, 105 bhp, 5F1R×2, wb 11′9″, 20′2¾″×8′0″× 11′6″, 12,740 lb. One of several prototypes of the mid-1960s. Marshall aluminium dropside body. 5.7-litre multi-fuel engine. Tyres 12.00–20. Dual air/hyd. brake system.

Truck, 4½-ton, 4×4, Cargo (Leyland 'Laird') 6-cyl. diesel (5.7-litre Underfloor), 105 bhp, 5F1R×2, wb 11′9″, 20′6″×7′11″×8′9″ (cab), 8146 lb approx. Prototype for 4½- to 5-ton cargo truck available commercially, introduced in 1971. Twin-line air-hyd. brakes. Tyres 12.00–20.

Truck, 3-ton, 4×4, Tipper, w/Winch, FV13219 (Commer Q4) 6-cyl., 95 bhp, 4F1R×2, wb 13'11", 20'5"×7'5½"×8'1", 11,680 lb. Tyres 11.00–20. As FV13201 (cargo truck) but Edbro 3.11-cu. yd hyd. end-tipping body, 5-ton winch underneath and cab protector. 1952. Mk 2 (FV13225) generally similar.

Truck, 3-ton, 4×4, Radar Repair, FV13209 (Commer Q4) 6-cyl., 95 bhp, 4F1R×2, wb 13'11", 22'10½"×7'7"×11'6", 14,056 lb. Insulated house type body, equipped for radar equipment repair. Similar bodies for other roles (FV13203–10 and 16). FV13218 was Recovery truck (Mann Egerton body).

Truck, 3-ton, 4×4, Cargo (Commer/AWD BAS4.669) Perkins 6.354 6-cyl. diesel, 108 bhp, 4F1R×2, wb 14'1¼", chassis/cab: 22'3"×7'2"×7'10", GVW 18,000 lb. Typical example of commercial 4×4 truck of the 1960s, supplied to armies of Iraq, Somalia, etc. 1962. Dodge/AWD W205 looked similar.

Truck, 4½-ton, 4×4, Cargo, FV13901 (Commer CB) Rootes TS3A 2-stroke horizontally-opposed m/f, 117 bhp, 5F1R×2, wb 13'6", 21'1½"×7'11¾"×11'3½", 11,872 lb. Concurrently with Austin and Vauxhall, Rootes produced 3- to 5-ton 4×4 prototypes and submitted these for tests during the 1960s. 1966 edition shown.

Truck, 3-ton, 4 × 4, LAA Tractor, w/Winch, FV13303 (Ford 'Thames' E4) V-8-cyl., 87 bhp, 4F1R × 2, wb 12'6", 21'2" × 7'11½" × 10'10½" (7'11½"), 11,452 lb. Known as 'Commer cab' model since it had the same BLSP cab as contemporary Commer FC trucks. Turner 5-ton winch below body. 1952.

Truck, 3-ton, 4 × 4, Ambulance, FV13304 (Ford 'Thames' E3) V-8-cyl., 87 bhp, 4F1R × 2, wb 12'6", 21'10" × 7'4" × 10'7½", 11,312 lb. Converted FV13301 (Model E2 Container Store, Binned). Purpose-built ambulances were the FV13302 (Spurling body) and FV13305 (Mulliner). They differed in detail but all had four stretchers.

Truck, 3-ton, 4 × 4, Light Mobile Digger, Airportable (Thornycroft 'Nubian') RR B81 8-cyl., 210 bhp, 4F1R × 2, wb 11'8", 22'9" × 7'8" × 8'6", 20,496 lb. Hyd.-drive trench digger. Secondary hyd. trans. for creep speeds. Developed by MEXE, Christchurch. Excavated 4'6" × 2'0" pits and trenches at 12 ft/min. 1963.

Truck, 3-ton, 4 × 4, Missile Handling, Airportable (Thornycroft/Bedford) Rocket lifting equipment on special 'Nubian' chassis with Bedford RL running gear (engine, transmission, axles). Removable cab top. Used by School of Artillery. 1965. 'Nubian' chassis were widely used for specialist vehicles, notably fire tenders.

TRUCKS, $2\frac{1}{2}$- to 5-TON
6 × 4 and 6 × 6

Makes and Models: Albion FT103N 'Clansman', FV13581 (3-ton, 6 × 4, 1949), WD66N, FV14000 Series (5-ton, 6 × 6, 1955), FV1300 Series (3-ton, 6 × 6, 1951). Alvis 'Stalwart' FV600 Series (5-ton, 6 × 6, from 1959). Bedford/Douglas RL, modified (5-ton, 6 × 6, c. 1953). Fordson ET6 'Thames Sussex' (3-ton, 6 × 4, c. 1950). GMC DUKW-353 'Duck' ($2\frac{1}{2}$-ton, 6 × 6, amphibious, US, WWII). International/Diamond T G744 'M-Series' (5-ton, 6 × 6, c. 1960). Reo/Studebaker G742 'M-Series' ($2\frac{1}{2}$-ton, 6 × 6, c. 1960). Thornycroft TFA/B80, B81 'Nubian', FV14100 Series, etc. (5-ton, 6 × 6, from c. 1954). Vauxhall FV1300 Series (3-ton, 6 × 6, c. 1950).

General Data: The only new 3-ton 6 × 4 vehicles which were taken into service after 1945 were the Albion FT103N (Army) and the Fordson 'Thames-Sussex' (Air Force). They supplemented left-over stocks of WWII origin such as the Fordson WOT1, Leyland 'Retriever' and Thornycroft 'Tartar'. Immediately after the war the Army had a requirement for a 3-ton 6 × 6 range of vehicles and after preliminary design studies discussions were held with Vauxhall Motors in June 1947 as a result of which a contract was placed with that firm for detailed design, development and manufacture of prototypes. In due course several prototypes, with short and long wheelbase, single and double cab, were produced. In 1951 the vehicle's 'parentage' was changed to Albion Motors. In all, eight were produced. The requirement was cancelled in 1953 on grounds of high cost. More conventional 6 × 6 trucks were subsequently acquired from Albion and Thornycroft. The latter chassis became very popular for fire fighting vehicles (qv). In 1959 Alvis produced a high-mobility load carrier (as a private venture) on the 'Salamander' crash/rescue vehicle chassis. Named 'Stalwart' it was followed in 1961 by an amphibious version (PV2) which was thoroughly tested by the Army. Shortly afterwards it went into volume production for the British Army and it was also exported to some other countries. An improved version (Mk 2) was introduced in 1966 and produced until April 1971. Wartime US GMC 'Duck' (DUKW-353) amphibians were in service with the RASC/RCT until the 1970s. Post-war US $2\frac{1}{2}$- and 5-ton 6 × 6 trucks were used in conjunction with certain weapons systems.

Vehicle shown (typical): Truck, 5-ton, 6 × 6, Cargo, Amphibious, FV622 (Alvis 'Stalwart' Mk 2) (High Mobility Load Carrier)

Technical Data:

Engine: Rolls-Royce B81 Mk 8B, 8-cylinder, I-I-W-R, 6522 cc, 220 bhp @ 3750 rpm.

Transmission: 5F5R.

Brakes: Air-hyd., discs.

Tyres: 14.00–20.

Wheelbase: 10'0" (5'+5'). Track: 6'8".

Overall l × w × h: 20'10" × 8'7" × 8'4".

Weight: 19,600 lb. GVW: 31,890 lb.

Note: Similar to Mk 1 but better visibility (larger windows), self-recovery winch, increased water speed ($6\frac{1}{4}$ mph), etc. Road speed 30 mph. Also with HIAB crane.

Truck, 5-ton, 6 × 6, Cargo, High Mobility (Alvis PV1 'Stalwart') Rolls-Royce B81 8-cyl., 220 bhp, 5F5R, wb 10'0", 20'5" × 8'4" × 8'0" approx. Prototype cross-country load carrier produced by Alvis in 1959 on FV601 'Salamander' fire crash truck chassis. Not amphibious. Tested by British Army (Reg. No. 15BT16). IFS/IRS with torsion bars.

Truck, 5-ton, 6 × 6, Cargo, Amphibious, FV620 (Alvis PV2 'Stalwart') Rolls-Royce B81 8-cyl., 220 bhp, 5F5R, wb 10'0", 21'1" × 8'4" × 7'11½", 17,760 lb. Second prototype, 1961. Built-in propulsion units gave speed in still water of approx. 4.5 knots. With detail modifications became 'Stalwart' Mk 1, later Mk 2 (1966). PAS on front and centre wheels.

Truck, 3-ton, 6 × 4, Machinery No. 10 Mk 4, FV13581 (Albion FT103N 'Clansman') 4-cyl. diesel, 75 bhp, 5F1R, wb 11'9½" (BC 4'3"), 20'10" × 7'6" × 11'0", 16,150 lb. Used by Army with various specialist bodies (REME). Basically a 1949–51 commercial chassis, modified by fitting single rear wheels and 9.00–20 tyres.

Truck, 3-ton, 6 × 4, Signals (Fordson ET6 'Thames Sussex') V-8-cyl., 85 bhp, 4F1R or 4F1R × 2, wb 13'1". Commercial chassis, used by RAF to supplement wartime Fordson WOT1 chassis for mounting specialist bodies, incl. ambulances. Shown: Signals Container Body Mk 3. Also used by Belgian Air Force.

Truck, 3-ton, 6 × 6, Field Art. Tractor, FV1313 (Vauxhall, Albion) RR B80 8-cyl., 60 bhp, 6F2R, wb 12'0", 20'0" × 7'10" × 8'6" approx. IFS, IRS. Two produced, c. 1951. In all eight FV1300 series prototypes were made, incl. five with single cab and 14'0" wb. Various bodies were planned, incl. wrecker, tipper, cargo, ambulance.

Truck, 5-ton, 6 × 6, Cargo, FV14001 (Albion WD66N) RR B80 8-cyl., 160 bhp, 5F1R × 2, wb 12'6", 23'6" × 8'0" × 10'9", 15,900 lb. Nine produced, May 1955–May 1956, with cargo (shown) and artillery tractor bodies, and a recovery chassis. Chassis constructed from commercial components. Body by Strachans.

Truck, 5-ton, 6 × 6, Field Art. Tractor, FV14103 (Thornycroft TF/B80 'Nubian') RR B80 8-cyl., 160 bhp, 5F1R × 2, wb 12'3", 20'9" × 8'0" × 10'0", 15,900 lb. Tyres 11.00–20. Early prototype (c. 1952), developed from 4 × 4 'Nubian'. Speed on/off road: 35/15 mph. Later models had different cab and body and 12.00–20 tyres. Diesel engine optional.

Truck, 5-ton, 6 × 6, Cargo, FV14101 (Thornycroft TFA/B80 'Nubian') RR B80 8-cyl., 160 bhp, 5F1R × 2, wb 12'0", 22'3" × 8'0" × 10'9", 15,900 lb. Commercial truck, modified to meet military requirements. 14-ft body by Strachans. Air-assisted hyd. brakes Chassis also used for aircraft fire fighter (FV14151) with 215-bhp B81 engine.

TRUCKS, 5- to 10-TON, 4×2 and TRACTORS for SEMI-TRAILERS, 3×2 and 4×2

Shown in this section are some examples of the heavier 4×2 trucks which served with the British armed forces, as well as some tractor trucks which, fitted with a 'fifth wheel' coupling, towed semi-trailers of various kinds. Most of these vehicles were of standard commercial design and used for domestic purposes in roles where off-road capabilities were not required, for example for road haulage of supplies and equipment, on airfields, etc. Of post-war 4×2 trucks and tractors AECs and Bedfords were the most common, especially in the RAF and RN. The British forces in Germany used several types of Mercedes-Benz 4×2 trucks and tractors, e.g. the LK 334 and LPS 337. In 1970 32 Tasker 20-ton semi-trailers, with AEC 'Mammoth Major' 6×4 tractors went into Army service in W. Germany.

Truck, 5-ton, 4×2, Mass Min. Radiography (Leyland 'Beaver') Some of these commercial chassis were equipped as Mobile radiography units for the Army Medical Services. A four-wheel trailer with generating set was towed. The Navy used AEC 'Regent' and Bedford VAL bus chassis for this purpose.

Truck, 10-ton, 4×2, Missile Transporter, FV11081 (AEC 'Mandator') 6-cyl. diesel, 179 bhp, 5F1R, wb 19'0", unladen: 30'6"×9'0"×12'6", 36,500 lb. Model AV690 11,310-cc diesel engine. Equipped for transporting and (un)loading 'Blue Steel' missile. Early 1960s. Navy used similar chassis for refuellers (Gloster Saro).

Truck, 10-ton, 4×2, Fuel Tanker, Aircraft Servicing, FV12381 (AEC 'Mercury' Mk 2) 6-cyl. diesel, 138 bhp, 5F1R, wb 17'3", 30'0"×8'1"×6'2", 14,000 lb. Transportable in Argosy aircraft. Equipment by Zwicky. 2200-gallon tank. Cab top and steering wheel removable. Fuel delivery rate max. 300 gpm. 1963.

Truck, 3-ton, 3 × 2, Tractor (Scammell MH3 'Mechanical Horse') Perkins 4.99 4-cyl. diesel, 4F1R, wb 8'10¾", 13'2" × 6'2" × 7'0", 2690 lb. Commercial 'motive unit', also available with 2090-cc petrol engine. Heavier MH6 (6-ton) was also in service. Some had ballast body and towed full-trailers.

Truck, 10-ton, 4 × 2, Tractor (Bedford SAG) 6-cyl., 113 bhp, 4F1R, wb 7'2", 13'6¾" × 7'5" × 7'7", 5265 lb. Eaton 2-speed rear axle. Shown with Tasker coupling and 'Queen Mary' 5-ton semi-trailer for carrying aircraft. SA8A (Leyland diesel) and TJ-Series (NC) tractors were also used.

Truck, 6-ton, 4 × 2, Tractor (Bedford KEA, KFA) 6-cyl., 86–133 bhp, 4F1R, wb 8'0", 14'4½" × 7'3" × 7'1", 5490 lb. Shown with Tasker Semi-Trailer, Cargo, 2-wh., 6-ton. Standard commercial TK-series tractor with certain optional equipment, incl. grille guard. *c.* 1967. Similar type used by Royal Navy (KGA).

Truck, 4 × 2, Tractor (Scammell) Meadows 60C630 6-cyl. 10.35-litre diesel, 130 bhp (or Gardner 6LW 6-cyl. 8.4-litre diesel, 102 bhp), 6F1R, wb 10'0". Used by Royal Navy with Scammell 'knock-out axle' 20-ton semi-trailer as machinery carrier. Heavy duty turntable coupling (Scammell). 1949.

TRUCKS, 10-TON
6 × 2, 6 × 4 and 6 × 6

Makes and Models: AEC 'Mammoth Major' and 'Marshal', various models (6 × 2, 6 × 4, from *c.* 1950), 0859 (6 × 4) and 0860 (6 × 6), 'Militant' Mk 1, FV11000 Series (from 1952), 0870 (RHD) and 0880 (LHD) (6 × 6), 'Militant' Mk 3, FV11000 Series (1966). Albion WD/HD/23N and 23S (6 × 4), FV11100 Series (1951). Faun L908/55A (6 × 6, 1956, D). Foden 6E6/22 (6 × 4, 1967). Leyland 'Martian' (6 × 6), FV1100 Series (from 1950), 19H/1, 19H/3, 19H/7, 'Hippo' Mk III, IV (6 × 4), FV11200 Series (from 1952), 'Bison' (24-ton GVW, 6 × 4, 1971). Magirus-Deutz 'Uranus' (recovery trucks, 6 × 6, D). Rotinoff 'Viscount' (6 × 6, *c.* 1955). Scammell 'Explorer' (6 × 6), FV11300 Series (1950), 'Constructor' (6 × 6, 1960). Thornycroft SM/GRN6 and 6/2 (6 × 4) 'Big Ben' FV11400 Series (1953). Volvo FB 88/EKA (recovery truck, 6 × 4, 1970, S).

General Data: The Leyland 'Hippo' 10-ton 6 × 4 chassis which had been put into production in 1944, remained in service with the British Army and Air Force with several body types for many years and developed into the 19H range which the RAF used for various roles. From the early 1950s the Army acquired relatively large quantities of AEC 'Militant' 10-tonners of both the 6 × 4 and 6 × 6 configuration. Although during the 1950s 10-ton 6-wheelers were also furnished by Albion and Thornycroft, AEC remained a regular supplier for this type of vehicle. The 'Militant' was used with numerous body types, including revolving cranes (qv). For heavy recovery tractors the military authorities turned to Scammells who had developed a 6 × 6 version of the famous 6 × 4 'Pioneer'. This all-wheel drive model became the standard 10-ton 6 × 6 GS Recovery Tractor and had a Scammell/Meadows petrol engine. Designated 'Explorer' it was also exported for civil and military duties. Some were delivered to the armies of New Zealand and Egypt. The RAF also employed it as a heavy drawbar tractor with ballast body. In the Army it was eventually superseded by a unit based on the AEC 'Militant' Mk 3. A Volvo FB88 with EKA recovery equipment was acquired in 1970 (see 'Sweden').

Vehicle shown (typical): Truck, 10-ton, 6 × 4, Artillery Tractor, w/Winch, FV11001 (AEC 0859 'Militant' Mk I)

Technical Data:

Engine: AEC A223 diesel, 6-cylinder, I-I-W-F, 11,300 cc, 150 bhp *ω* 1800 rpm.

Transmission: 5F1R × 2.

Brakes: air (2-line).

Tyres: 14.00–20.

Wheelbase: 12'10½". BC 4'6".

Overall l × w × h: 24'2" × 8'0" × 10'0".

Weight: 22,716 lb.

Note: Tractor for medium artillery and heavy AA guns. FV11002 (AEC 0860) was 6 × 6 version. 5-ton winch. Other 6 × 4 variants: Tipping (FV11005), Cargo, 14 ft (007) and 18 ft (008), Fuel Tanker (009), Crane (013), High-Pressure Refueller (RAF).

Truck, 10-ton, 6 × 6, Cargo, w/Winch, FV11018 (AEC 0860 'Militant' Mk 1) 6-cyl. diesel, 152 bhp, 5F1R × 2, wb 16'0" (BC 4'6"), 30'0" × 8'2" × 11'10", 24,640 lb. Superseded by Mk 3 (only a prototype of Mk 2, FV11041 M/H AA Tractor, appeared in 1962). Dropside body. 7-ton winch. 1952.

Truck, 10-ton, 6 × 6, Recovery, Medium, FV11044 (AEC 0870 'Militant' Mk 3) 6-cyl. diesel, 226 bhp, 6F1R × 2, wb 12'10½" (BC 4'6"), 25'0" × 8'2½" × 10'4", NSW 46,340 lb. Model AV760 12,473-cc engine. Recovery equipment by Thornycroft. Hyd. telescopic crane. Replacement for FV11301. Also cargo body (FV11047) and ACV (FV11061). 1966.

Truck, 10-ton, 6 × 2, Cargo, Platform (AEC 'Mammoth Major') 6-cyl. diesel, 125 bhp, 5F1R. Tyres 9.00–20. Used by Army Ordnance Depots for transport of cargo, wheeled AFVs, etc. The RAF and RN used 'Mammoth Majors' equipped as aircraft fuellers, water bowsers, cargo trucks, etc., with double drive bogie (6 × 4).

Truck, 10-ton, 6 × 4, Oxygen Plant (AEC 'Marshal') 6-cyl. diesel. Insulated van type body with access doors on right hand side and at rear. Similar to wartime AEC 0854. Purpose: separation of oxygen and nitrogen gas from air induced into the plant and compression of gas into storage cylinders.

Truck, 10-ton, 6 × 4, Aircraft Fueller, 3000 Gallon (AEC TG6RB 'Mammoth Major') 'Ergomatic' tilt cab. Bodywork by Gloster Saro (Hawker Siddeley). Supplied to RAF and Imperial Iranian Air Force, from 1968. Fuelling rate up to 500 gpm. Air-transportable (in Hercules C130, Galaxy C5A, Belfast). Also with 4500-gal. tank trailer.

Truck, 10-ton, 6 × 4, Machinery RE, FV11102 (Albion WD/HD/23N) 6-cyl., 160 bhp, 5F1R × 2, wb 16'0" (BC 4'6"), 27'2" × 8'0" × 10'11½", 34,720 lb. EN257C 10,454-cc petrol engine. 14.00–20 tyres. Air brakes. Insulated van body, equipped as mobile workshop. Also on same LWB chassis: FV11101 Cargo (18 ft body) and FV11103 Crane (KL 66).

Truck, 10-ton, 6 × 4, Tipper, 3-Way, FV11105 (Albion WD/HD/23S) 6-cyl., 160 bhp, 5F1R × 2, wb 13'3" (BC 4'6"), 22'6" × 8'0" × 9'9½", 22,624 lb. 7-cu. yd. Edbro hydraulically operated all-steel body, tipping to angle of 50°. Also on this SWB chassis: FV11108 Cargo (14-ft body). FV11100 series production period: 1951–54.

Truck, 10-ton, 6 × 4, Cargo (Foden 6E6/22) 6-cyl. diesel, 180 bhp. 18.00–22.5 'Super Single' rear tyres. In 1966/67 the Army carried out tests to ascertain the suitability of commercial 6 × 4 trucks as logistical cargo carriers. Contestants included AEC ('Marshal' and 'Mammoth Major'), Foden (shown) and Leyland ('Hippo').

Truck, 10-ton, 6×4, Signals, FV11211 (Leyland 19H/1 'Hippo' Mk 3) 6-cyl. diesel, 133 bhp, 5F1R × 2, wb 15'6" (BC 4'7"), 27'7" × 8'1" × 13'0", 25,600 lb. approx. Chassis used for various body types incl. glider winch and radar head (cab top could be folded forward to permit rotation of aerial). 19H/7 similar appearance but fixed cab top. O600 engine.

Truck, 10-ton, 6×4, Cargo (Leyland 'Bison') 6-cyl. diesel, 170 bhp (Leyland 500; optional: Model 510 turbocharged 220-bhp diesel), 6F1R (or 10F2R). Inter-axle diff. lock. Epicyclic hub reduction. PAS. Air brakes. Designed for up to 24 tons GVW. Tilt cab. 1971.

Truck, 10-ton, 6×6, Artillery Tractor, w/Winch, FV1103(A) (Leyland 'Martian') RR B81 No. 1 Mk 5H 8-cyl., 215 bhp, 4F1R × 3, wb 14'6" (BC 4'7"), 26'10$\frac{1}{4}$" × 8'6" × 10'1", 31,556 lb. Medium art. tractor for 5.5-inch and other howitzers. Crew 12. 10-ton winch (vertical spindle). Also 17'9" wb cargo (FV1110A) and other variants.

Truck, 10-ton, 6×6, Recovery, Heavy, FV1119 (Leyland 'Martian') RR B81 Mk 5K 8-cyl., 195 bhp, 4F1R × 3, wb 14'6" (BC 4'7"), 29'2" × 8'6" × 10'2", 47,628 lb. Hyd. power-operated rev. crane (cap. 15 ton with jib stays, 1.5 tons at max. radius w/o stays). Hyd. winch. Hyd.-operated spade (for rear pulls of up to 40 tons).

Truck, 10-ton, 6 × 6, Recovery Tractor, FV11301 (Scammell 'Explorer') Meadows 6-cyl., 181 bhp, 6F1R, wb 11'6" (BC 4'3¾"), 20'7½" × 8'6" × 10'4½", 26,180 lb. 15-ton main winch. Power-operated jib winch, capacity 4.5 tons with two-fall reeving. Speed on/off road 29/12 mph. 'Walking beam' rear suspension. 14.00–20 tyres.

Truck, 10-ton, 6 × 6, High-Speed Road Surfacing (Scammell 'Constructor') Rolls-Royce C6NFL 6-cyl. diesel, 185 bhp, 6F1R × 2, 32'5½" × 8'7½" × 9'9½", 20 tons (laden). Built by MEXE for British and US Army. Carried 11 tons of grit and 700 gal. of high-viscosity tar for road laying at speeds from 4–15 mph. Fully laden weight 33 tons. 1960/61.

Truck, 10-ton, 6 × 4, Cargo, FV11402 (Thornycroft SM/GRN6/2 'Big Ben') 6-cyl., 180 bhp, 4F1R × 2, wb 16'9" (BC 4'6"), 28'4" × 8'2" × 9'9", 25,960 lb. Marshall 18-ft body with fixed sides. No seats in rear. Tyres 14.00–20. Two-line air pressure brakes. Road speed 26 mph. Was commercially available, also with diesel engine.

Truck, 10-ton, 6 × 4, Tractor, FV11401 (Thornycroft SM/GRN6 'Big Ben') 6-cyl., 180 bhp, 4F1R × 2, wb 13'6" (BC 4'6"), 21'7" × 8'0" × 9'9", 21,042 lb. Designed for towing FV2700 range of 10-ton semi-trailers (house type, as shown, and missile transporter). Similar type supplied to India. Overall length with semi-trailer 44'2". GTW 61,600 lb.

TRACTORS, HEAVY
6×4 and 6×6 and
TANK TRANSPORTERS

Makes and Models: Diamond T 980/981 (RR diesel) (tractor, 50-ton, 6×4, WWII, US). Leyland FV1201(A) (HAT, 30-ton, 6×4, 1954). Lomount (earlier Rotinoff) GR7 'Atlantic' and 'Super Atlantic' (tractors, 6×4, from c. 1955). Mack NO Series (HAT, 20-ton, 6×6, WWII, US). Scammell 'Constructor' FV12100 Series (tractors, 20-ton, 6×6, from 1953), 'Super Constructor' (tractor, 30-ton, 6×6, 1965), 'Contractor' (tractors, 30-ton, 6×4, etc.). Thornycroft 'Antar' Mk 1–3, FV12000 Series (tractors, 30- to 60-ton, 6×4, from 1952).

General Data: Artillery and recovery tractors which were based on truck chassis are dealt with in the sections covering the basic truck, e.g. the Leyland FV1103 medium artillery tractor will be found in the section on Trucks, 10-ton, 6×6. Shown here are various types of heavy tractors for full- and semi-trailers. With the exception of the ultra-heavy Leyland FV1200 Series tractor, which was a specially-designed combat (CT) type, all these vehicles were basically commercial vehicles, modified to meet military requirements. The Scammell 'Constructor' and Thornycroft 'Antar' were the most common. The latter was a military version of the civilian 'Mighty Antar' (which had originally been designed for oil pipe transport in Middle East to a specification laid down by Geo. Wimpey & Co. Ltd). Until the 1960s the wartime American Diamond T 980/981 M20 remained in service as prime mover for tank transporter trailers. A number of these were reworked and fitted with Rolls-Royce diesel engines. Gradually they were all superseded by 'Antars', both with full- and semi-trailers. The 'Antar' also appeared with a heavy derrick, erected at the rear of the chassis. Among British tractors which were not adopted by the British Army for use as tank transporter prime movers were the 'Atlantic' and 'Super Atlantic' of Lomount (Rotinoff) and the 'Constructor' and 'Super Constructor' of Scammell. These were, however, purchased by several foreign countries. Thornycroft 'Antar' tractors were also exported, mainly for military service, to the Netherlands, India, Pakistan, etc. The 'Antar' was also used by the RAF, as a ballast tractor. The US Mack 7½-ton 6×6 was used until the early 1970s as a 20-ton tractor (for 8-in Howitzer).

Vehicle shown (typical): Tractor, 20-ton, 6×6, for Full-Trailer, w/Winch, FV12101 (Scammell 'Constructor')

Technical Data:
Engine: Scammell/Meadows 6PC630, 6-cylinder, I-I-W-F, 10,350 cc, 181 bhp @ 2400 rpm.
Transmission: 6F1R×2 (OD top).
Brakes: air (2-line).
Tyres: 12.00–20.
Wheelbase: 15'9". BC 4'8".
Overall l×w×h: 24'10"×8'8"×9'9".
Weight: 31,472 lb.
Note: Used chiefly for towing 20-ton low-loaders (RE; FV3621) giving a gross towed load of 31 tons. Partitioned ballast body to carry tools, equipment and ballast. Small hand davit for handling heavy items. Provision for mounting AAAA weapon (All Arms Anti-Aircraft).

Tractor, 20-ton, 6 × 6, for 30-ton Semi-Trailer, w/Winch, FV12102 (Scammell 'Constructor') Rolls-Royce C6NFL-140 6-cyl. diesel, 184 bhp, 6F1R × 2, wb 15'9" (BC 4'8"), 24'6" × 9'4" × 10'2", 32,370 lb. Used for RE plant semi-trailer. Various type front mudguards where used, incl. 'cycle wing'.

Tractor, 20-ton, 6 × 6, for 30-ton Full-Trailer, w/Winch, FV12105 (Scammell 'Constructor') Rolls-Royce C6NFL-142A 6-cyl. diesel, 184 bhp, 6F1R × 2, wb 15'9" (BC 4'8"), 37,527 lb. Used by RAF for towing trailers and carrying cargo and engineering equipment. 15-ton winch. 20 supplied in 1960. Tyres 14.00–20.

Tractor, 30-ton, 6 × 6, Heavy Artillery, FV1201(A) (Leyland) Rover Meteorite 80 No. 2 Mk 1 V-8-cyl. w/petrol injection, 510 bhp, 5F1R × 3 (2-pedal control), wb 16'0", 27'7" × 11'0" × 11'0", 54,880 lb. Tyres 18.00–24. Three-point susp. 12" wheel articulation (unsprung 'walking beams' at rear). PAS. 15-ton winch. Crew 12. Prototypes only.

Truck-Trailer, 50/60-ton, Tank Transporter (Scammell/Dyson) Consisting of 'Super Constructor' 6 × 6 tractor (RR C6SFL 250-bhp turbo-charged diesel, 8-speed semi-auto. trans., Darlington 40-ton winch, wb 17'2½") with Dyson 8-wh. (8DT) S-T with unsprung 'walking-beam' bogie suspension. Export model, 1965.

Tractor, 50-ton, 6×4, for Trailer (Diamond T 980) RR C6N 6-cyl. diesel, 184 bhp (British Army modification) or Hercules DFXE 6-cyl. diesel, 201 bhp (original equipment), 4F1R×3. Shown with FV3601(A) (Crane, Dyson) 50-ton trailer, alongside 'Antar' Mk 1 with FV3001(A) (Sankey) 60-ton semi-trailer.

Tractor, 50-ton, 6×4, for Trailer, FV12001 (Thornycroft R8 'Antar' Mk 1) Rover Meteorite Mk 204 V-8-cyl., 285 bhp, 4F1R×3, wb 15'6" (BC 5'2"), 27'6"×10'6"×10'0", 44,800 lb. First of 'Antar' range, with permanent steel ballast body. 20-ton winch. 14.00–24 tyres. PAS. 2-line air brakes. 18-litre engine. Bonallack cab.

Tractor, 60-ton, 6×4, for Semi-Trailer, FV12002 (Thornycroft 'Antar' Mk 2) Basically similar to Mk 1. Of both Marks there were tractors for full- and for semi-trailers. FV12002 shown was used with 50- or 60-ton S-T, for which it had a Davies Magnet fifth wheel hitch, and measured 26'9"×10'3"×10'4½". Weight, solo, 43,204 lb.

Tractor, 50-ton, 6×4, for Trailer, FV12003 (Thornycroft 'Antar' Mk 1B) Basically an FV12002 but fitted with wooden ballast body which could be removed to facilitate easy conversion to tractor for S-T. Normally about 14 tons of ballast were carried but this could be increased up to 27 tons for maximum tractive effort.

Tractor, 60-ton, 6×4, for Semi-Trailer (Thornycroft 'Antar') AEC 6-cyl. diesel, 360 bhp. Shortly after Thornycroft was taken over by the ACV Group, an 'Antar' was equipped with a turbocharged AEC AV1100 17,750-cc engine (as fitted in AEC 'Dumptruk'). It was tested and used from 1963 (Reg. No. 02SP27), sold in 1971.

Tractor, 50/60-ton, 6×4, for Trailer, FV12006 (Thornycroft 'Antar' Mk 3A) RR C8SFL-843 8-cyl. diesel, 333 bhp, 4F1R×3, wb 16'0" (BC 5'2"), 28'6½"×10'6"×10'4", 51,632 lb. Temporary ballast body. 16,200-cc turbocharged engine. Towed 50-ton trailer (FV3601A) but could be used as FV12004 (tractor for S-T). From 1958–59.

Trailer, 50-ton, Transporter, FV3601 (Cranes, Dyson) Used primarily for haulage of tracked AFVs. Loading platform completely decked to permit carrying other types of loads. 16 dual wheels with 36×8 tyres. 29'9" (33'6" incl. towbar) ×10'6"×7'3", 41,100 lb. Unsprung 'walking beam' suspension.

Semi-Trailer, 50-ton, Tank Transporter, FV3011 (GKN, Sankey, Taskers) Eight dual wheels with 12.00–20 tyres. 39'1½"×11'0"×10'1½", 36,064 lb. 'Walking beam' suspension. A 60-ton type was also used (FV3001; Sankey). It measured 41'9½"×12'0"×9'10", weighed 41,720 lb, had 13.00–20 tyres and carried one spare wheel, horizontally.

TRACTORS, WHEELED
MISCELLANEOUS TYPES

Wheeled tractors were used by all services. Some were straight-forward agricultural and industrial types for base and depot use (principally Ferguson and Fordson), others were designed and produced specifically for specialist roles like aircraft towing (on airfields and on aircraft carriers). Some specimens are shown here. In addition there were tractors for semi- and full-trailers and artillery tractors, derived from or based on truck chassis. Some of these are illustrated elsewhere, as are the full-track crawler types. British-built wheeled tractors were also exported to other countries for military use. The Dutch Air Force (*Kon. Luchtmacht*), for example, had Fordson 'Major' agricultural types, and David Brown 'Taskmasters' for aircraft towing. About 1970 the RAF acquired the 20-ton Dennis Mercury aircraft tractor with a DBP of 300,000 lb.

Tractor, Wheeled, Industrial (Ferguson) Ferguson industrial tractors were based on agricultural types (same engine, trans., etc.). Model shown has industrial pattern wings, front bumper, horn, front and rear lights for use on public highways, special brakes and tyres, etc.

Tractor, Wheeled, Aircraft Towing (David Brown 'Taskmaster') 4-cyl. diesel, 36 bhp, dry twin-plate clutch and torque conv., 4F1R (Mk 1, 2) or 6F1R (Mk 3), wb 7'3", 10'11" × 5'9½" × 5'5", 7400 lb. Towed aircraft of up to 60,000 lb. One of various types supplied to RAF and other air forces. Note ballast weights.

Tractor, Wheeled, Aircraft, Heavy (Sentinel 4 × 4) RR B80 No. 1 Mk 5 8-cyl., 160 bhp, semi-auto. 4F1R × 2, wb 9'2", 21'4" × 8'0" × 7'2½" (st. wh.), 27,580 lb. Air brakes. PAS. 7.6-ton winch. Generating set to maintain aircraft electrical services. Improved production version of Douglas 'Tugmaster'. 1961.

CRANES and EXCAVATORS, TRUCK-MOUNTED
6 × 4 and 6 × 6

During the second World War most British truck-mounted cranes were of Coles manufacture, mounted on AEC, Austin, Crossley, Leyland and Thornycroft chassis. Some US types were also employed. Many of these remained in service for a number of years. More modern vehicles, gradually replaced them. All Wheel Drive Ltd of Camberley was a major supplier of crane and excavator carrier chassis. They used a high content of AEC 'Militant' components, as did Coles/Steels, who supplied many types to both the Air Force and the Army. A few examples of 6 × 4 and 6 × 6 types are shown here. There was also an 8-wheeled model (Jones KL15-30) for aircraft handling and several unusual types saw service with the RN, incl. Thornycroft and Mack/Northwest.

Crane, 6-ton, Fully-Slewing, 6 × 4 (AWD/AEC/Jones KL66) General purpose crane with lifting capacity of 6 tons at 10' radius when equipped with 30' jib (40' and 50' jibs could also be fitted). Modified FV11000 series chassis ('walking-beam' rear susp., etc.) Early models were on Albion chassis (FV11103). Tyres 15.00–20.

Crane, 7-ton, Fully-Slewing, Bridging, 6 × 6, FV11003 (AEC/Coles L96404–7) AEC 6-cyl. diesel, 150 bhp, 5F1R × 2, wb 14'9" (BC 4'6"), 38'8½" × 8'0" × 13'9", NSW 53,350 lb. 30' jib, capable of lifting 7 tons at 9'6" radius, 1¼ tons at 30'. Diesel/electric crane operation (Coles Variable Voltage System). Also as 4 × 4 SP. c. 1954.

Crane, 6/10-ton, Fully-Slewing, 6 × 6 (AWD/AEC/Jones KL10-6) Developed from Jones KL66. Blocked capacity 10 tons and 6 tons 'free-on-wheels', both at 10' radius. Chassis by All Wheel Drive Ltd, 1960/61, using mostly AEC components, incl. 11.3-litre diesel engine. Turntable engine was Perkins 4.192 diesel.

208

Crane, 7/10-ton, Fully-Slewing, 6×6 (AEC/Coles L96404-5) AEC A187K 6-cyl. diesel, 95 bhp, 4F1R×2, wb 12′9″ (BC 4′6″), 39′0″×8′2″×13′8″, 53,984 lb. Perkins P4 diesel engine in turntable (diesel-electric crane operation). L96404–1 similar but 14′9″ wb, AEC petrol engine (some converted to diesel) and Ford V8 in turntable.

Crane, 7/10-ton, Fully-Slewing, Bridging, 6×6 (AEC/Coles Mk 5 L96404-11) AEC AV760 6-cyl. diesel, 215 bhp, 5F1R×2, wb 14′9″, 28′8½″×8′2″×13′7″, 26 tons gross. Perkins diesel turntable engine, driving generator. 1968–70. Capacity max. 7 tons at 9 ft radius (mobile) or 10 tons (with outriggers) at 10 ft decreasing to 1¼ and 2½ tons resp. at 30′.

Excavator, Truck-Mounted, ½-cu. yd, 6×4 (Dennis G7 'Jubilant'/Blaw Knox BK50 Mk 1 and 2) 6-cyl. diesel, 108 bhp, 5F1R×2 (OD top), wb 13′6″, 28′0″×8′0″×12′6″, 43,120 lb. Excavator had Perkins P6 diesel engine, mounted in operator's cab. Rear bogie with three differentials and inverted semi-elliptical leaf springs. 1956.

Excavator, Truck-Mounted, ½-cu. yd, 6×6 (AWD/AEC/Blaw Knox BK50 Mk 3) AEC 6-cyl. diesel, 150 bhp, 5F1R×2, wb 12′10½″ (BC 4′6″), 44′2″ (max.)×8′0″×13′6″, 47,000 lb. AWD Model ECA 64/171 chassis. Superstructure could also be adapted for crane, drag line, shovel and pile driving operations. Mid-1950s.

FIRE FIGHTERS

Shown in this section are some of the fire fighters and crash/rescue vehicles, as used by the Air Force, Army and Navy. The Alvis 'Salamander' belonged to the same family as the 'Saracen' and 'Saladin' armoured vehicles (*qv*), and had a very good cross-country performance. The Thornycroft 'Nubian' was made in 4 × 4 and 6 × 6 form. In 1964 Thornycroft launched its heavy duty 'Nubian Major' TMA/300 fire/crash tender chassis for 18–20 tons GVW. It had a Cummins V8 diesel engine with semi-auto. transmission and shared axles and transfer box with the AEC 'Militant' Mk 3. Alvis and Thornycroft fire fighters are in service with many governments, principally at airports, all over the world. In Germany the RAF used a number of Mercedes-Benz 4 × 4 fire fighters. The RAF also used Land-Rover LWB airfield crash rescue vehicles (FV18047).

Truck, 1-ton, 4 × 4, Fire Appliance (Land-Rover/Carmichael; FT/6 'Redwing') 4-cyl., 77 bhp, 4F1R × 2, wb 9'1", basic vehicle: 16'3" × 5'4" × 7'4", 4557 lb approx. Forward control conversion and light alloy bodywork by Carmichaels of Worcester. Fibreglass roof with ladder stowage. First aid water tank. PTO-driven hose reel pump.

Truck, 3-ton, 4 × 4, Fire Pump (Bedford RLHZ) 'Special Appliances' version of Bedford RL series chassis, fitted with 1000-gpm PTO-driven Sigmund pump at rear. Produced to Home Office specification. Used mainly by Civil Defence Corps and Aux. Fire Service (also 4 × 2 version). Some were issued to the Army Fire Service. *c.* 1956.

Truck, 3-ton, 4 × 4, Fire Tender, Dual Purpose, FV13403 (Thornycroft TF(B)/B80 'Nubian'/Foamite). RR B80 8-cyl., 140 bhp, 4F1R × 2, wb 12'0", 20'5" × 7'7" × 9'11", NSW 22,930 lb. Used by RAF as supplementary vehicle to FV651 (see next page) but also equipped for domestic fire fighting. 700-gal. water tank. 500-gpm pump. 1956.

Truck, 6×6, Fire Crash Foam Mk 6 GP, FV651(A) (Alvis 'Salamander') RR B81 8-cyl., 240 bhp, semi-auto. 5F5R, wb 10'0", 18'0"×8'3"×10'0", NSW 30,240 lb. Based on FV600 series. Equipment by Pyrene (shown) or Foamite. Could produce 9000 gallons of foam in two minutes. Used by RAF (shown) and Army (1). FV652 was Alvis Mk 6A.

Truck, 5-ton, 6×6, Fire Crash Foam, FV14161 (Thornycroft TFA/B81 'Nubian'/Sun) RR B81 8-cyl., 215 bhp, 4F1R×2, wb 12'3", 22'5"×7'6"×10'5", NSW 27,016 lb. Developed for Admiralty for use on RN Air Stations. 1000-gallon water tank, 50-gallon foam tank. Pump driven by separate RR B60 engine. Road speed 60 mph. *c.* 1958.

Truck, 5-ton, 6×6, Fire Crash Foam (Thornycroft TFA/B81 'Nubian' Mk VII/Pyrene) RR B81 Mk 70K 8-cyl., 235 bhp, 5F1R×2, wb 12'3", 23'10½"×8'0"×10'4", NSW 31,360 lb. Foam monitor can produce 5000-gpm for 1.8 minutes with a throw of 95'. Road speed 65 mph. 700/110-gal. **water/foam tanks.** *c.* 1962.

Truck, 5-ton, 6×6, Fire Crash Foam (Thornycroft TFA/B81 'Nubian'/Gloster Saro) RR B81 8-cyl. Dual-purpose fire/crash tender with 1000/50-gal. water/foam tanks and Coventry Climax UFP Mk 6 pump supplying Trinity TMU 2500 monitor (throw 170', output 440 gpm water), branchlines and first aid hose reel. Air-transportable (C130, etc). 1970.

SNOW FIGHTERS

These vehicles are used for dispersal of deep snow from runways and other flat surfaces and for dispersing deep snow which has been windrowed by scraper type ploughs. In certain cases the direction of dispersal could be controlled to either side of the vehicle or the snow could be loaded into trucks. Wartime models which remained in service for many years were the Ford/Marmon-Herrington 4 × 4 and FWD SU 4 × 4 with Snogo rotary snow plough and the Diamond T 6 × 6 and FWD HAR-1 4 × 4 with Bros equipment. The latter equipment was also used on a few post-war British chassis (Douglas, Steels). In Germany the RAF successfully used modified Magirus-Deutz 4 × 4 chassis with Rolba equipment. A standard British chassis not being available for the Rolba type plough, All Wheel Drive Ltd designed a special prime mover with twin front axles. These were produced during 1958–63.

Snow Removal Unit, SP, 5-ton, Rotary (All Wheel Drive S4) Perkins P6 6-cyl. diesel, 83 bhp, 4F1R × 2 (+ 2-speed creeper gearbox). PAS on both front axles. 12-cyl. 210-bhp plough driving engine, mounted in rear body. BLSP cab (as used by Commer, Dodge, etc.) with Kent 'Clearvu' rotating disc in windscreen.

Snow Removal Unit, SP, Rotary, Type 35500 (Douglas/Bros M9A-270/360P 'Snow-Flyr') Rolls-Royce B80 Mk 2K 8-cyl., 160 bhp, 5F1R × 2, wb 14′6″, 33′10″ × 9′2″ × 11′0″. Rotary plough, driven by two Meadows 6PJ630 180-bhp 6-cyl. petrol engines. Plough unit on push frame, hinged to truck frame.

Snow Removal Unit, SP, Rotary, Type 35200 (Steels/Bros M9A-270/360P 'Snow-Flyr') Meadows 6PC630 6-cyl., 180 bhp, 4F1R × 2, wb 14′6″, 33′8″ × 9′2″ × 11′0″, 17½ tons (with plough unit raised). American plough, supplied by British Rotary Snow Plough Co, and plough engines as on Douglas-built unit. Early 1950s.

HANDLING EQUIPMENT and TRACTORS, EARTHMOVING, WHEELED

Like commercial enterprises, modern armies have been equipping themselves with increasing numbers of sophisticated mechanical devices to facilitate handling of cargo, stores and equipment as well as earth, building materials, etc. At one time this was largely carried out with commercial (industrial) mobile cranes, fork lift trucks and attachments fitted on conventional tractors, but in recent years many ingenious special machines have been designed and developed. Good examples of these are the multi-purpose rubber-tyred tractors with various attachments as supplied by Clark (Michigan) and others, and the 'rough terrain' type fork lift trucks and cranes. Air Force and Navy also use many different models incl. special types for use on aircraft carriers.

Tractor, Wheeled, Fork Lift, 4000-lb, Rough Terrain, Light (ROF 'Eager Beaver') Perkins 4/236 4-cyl. diesel, 78 bhp, 4F1R × 2, wb 8′4″, 17′10¾″ × 6′1″ × 7′10″ (5′9″), 6100 lb. 4 × 4, dual steer. Produced by Royal Ordnance Factory, using Bedford RL gearbox and axle components, Thornycroft transfer, etc. Road speed 40 mph. 1969.

Tractor, Wheeled, Fork Lift, 4000-lb, Waterproofed (Bray 455M) Leyland 6-cyl. diesel, 96 bhp. 4 × 4, dual steer. Tyres 14.00–24. Waterproofed for ship-to-shore cargo carrying. Could also be fitted with loading shovel or crane hook. Max. speed, forward and reverse, 25 mph. Mid-1960s.

Tractor, Wheeled, Fork Lift, 8000-lb, Rough Terrain, Heavy (Michigan 175 DS) Leyland 6-cyl. diesel, 160 bhp. Dual steer, 4 × 4. Max. speed in either direction 25 mph. Developed from Model 175A tractor shovel. Could wade in seawater to depths of 6′6″. Tyres 18.00–25. Could be fitted with loading shovel or crane hook. Mid-1960s.

Truck, Side-Loader, 4 × 2, Mk 1 and 1A (Lancer 5/6TD 11 TTCW) Ford 592E 4-cyl. diesel, 62 bhp, semi-auto. 2F1R (Mk 1A: 3F1R), wb 9′0″. Basically self-(side-)loading fork lift truck, but fork could be removed from lifting mast and replaced by attachment as shown, for lifting missiles. Mid-1960s.

Crane, 4-ton, Fast Mobile, 4 × 2 (British Hoist & Crane Co. 4FM 'Iron Fairy') Ford 592E 4-cyl. diesel, 62 bhp, 4F1R, wb 7′0″, 17′2″ × 7′9″ × 8′5″, 21,028 lb. Hyd. crane operation incl. powerjib telescoping, derricking and 360° continuous duo-directional superstructure rotation. Rear-wheel steer. Early 1960s.

Crane, 3-ton, Semi-Slewing, 4 × 4 (Taylor/Br. Crane & Excavator Corp. Series 42 'Jumbo') Ford 590E 4-cyl. diesel, 86 bhp, 5F1R × 2, wb 8′6″, 18′10″ (jib retracted) × 8′0″ × 9′10½″, 26,096 lb. Tyres 15.00–20. Max. road speed 43 mph. Slewing arc 180°. Hydraulic crane operation. Used for handling 'Thunderbird' missiles.

Crane, 10-ton, Fully-Slewing, Rough Terrain, 4 × 4 (Smith) RR C8NFL 8-cyl. diesel, 250 bhp, torque conv., 4F4R × 1. Tyres 24.00–29 with central pressure control. Disc brakes. Hyd. telescopic boom with 10-ton max. lift. Could work in water up to 6′6″. Two- or four-wheel steer, or crab steer. Road speed 35 mph. 1970.

Tractor, Wheeled, Earthmoving, Light (Michigan 75 DS) In 1961 Michigan (GB) Ltd (later Clark Equipment Ltd) supplied 127 dual steer tractors to the Army, all powered by Leyland UE350 diesel engines. More deliveries of improved models followed (Mk 2 and 2/1 light, Mk 2/2 and 2/3 medium). They were used with various attachments.

Tractor, Wheeled, Earthmoving, Medium (Marshall 'Gainsborough') Leyland 6-cyl. diesel, 145 bhp, 5F5R (semi-auto.), wb 7'3", 21'9" × 9'6" × 9'10" approx, 15 tons. Tyres 18.00–25. Drawbar pull in first gear 20,000 lb. 4-wh. steer, 4 × 4. Fitted with hyd. shovel, recovery winch, double-drum cable control unit. Early 1950s.

Tractor, Wheeled, Earthmoving, Medium (Allis-Chalmers 645) AEC AV505 6-cyl. diesel, 142 bhp, 4F2R (power shift), wb 9'8", 24'4" × 8'10" × 10'10", 27,530 lb. Tyres 20.50–25. 4 × 4. Steering by articulation. 2½-cu. yd bucket. Turning radius 17' with bucket at 'carry'. Boughton winch. 1968.

Tractor, Wheeled, Earthmoving, Heavy (Michigan 285) RR 300-bhp or Cummins 310-bhp 6-cyl. turbocharged diesel (Mk I and I/I resp.), 4F4R (semi-auto.), wb 12'8", 32'1" × 11'9" × 11'7½", 60,500 lb. Tyres 29.50–25. Articulated steering. 4 × 4. Boughton hyd. winch at rear. 5-cu. yd bucket. Vickers cable control unit. Late 1960s.

ARMOURED VEHICLES, WHEELED

The first post-war British wheeled armoured vehicles were the 4 × 4 'Ferret' Mk 1 and 2. They succeeded the wartime Daimler scout car and went into service in 1951. About the same time the 6 × 6 'Saracen' APC appeared, followed by the 'Saladin' armoured car and other variants on the same basic chassis. These two families of armoured vehicles (4 × 4 FV700 series and 6 × 6 FV600 series) were produced by Daimler and Alvis respectively and were used in many parts of the world by the British and a number of other governments. During the late 1960s a new family of vehicles, known as CVR (Combat Vehicle Reconnaissance) was introduced, including wheeled and tracked types. Less sophisticated armoured vehicles for police and other purposes had meanwhile been produced on various types of truck chassis.

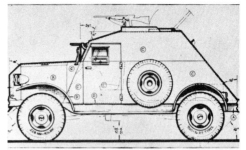

Car, Scout, 4 × 4 (Dodge/Glover, Webb & Liversidge)
'Econamour' range of para-military vehicles (scout car, APC, ambulance) was designed by Glover, Webb & Liversidge, Ltd, London, on American Dodge 'Power Wagon' 1-ton 4 × 4 chassis at request of Crown Agents for use overseas. *c.* 1966. No quantity production.

Car, Armoured, Patrol, 4 × 4 (Land-Rover Series I '109')
In a number of instances (e.g. in Northern Ireland) standard Land-Rovers were fitted with armour plates for crew protection. Example shown was used in the Far East. Later the Shorland armoured patrol car was designed to cater for these requirements.

Car, Armoured, Patrol, 4 × 4 (Rover/Short Bros & Harland 'Shorland') Rover 2¼-litre 4-cyl., 77 bhp (Mk 3: 2.6-litre 6-cyl., 95 bhp); 4F1R × 2, wb 9'1", 15'1" × 5'10" × 7'6", 6450 lb. Suitable for border patrol, internal security, riot control and similar duties. Based on std '109' Land-Rover. Commercially available. Early model (1965) shown.

Truck, 1-ton, 4×4, Armoured, FV1611 (Humber) RR B60 Mk 5A 6-cyl., 120 bhp, 5F1R × 1, wb 9′0″, 16′2″ × 6′8½″ × 6′11½″, 10,528 lb. Based on FV1600 series 1-ton truck. No winch. Bodies by Sankey and ROF. Variants: FFR (FV1612), ambulance (FV1613), air-transportable launcher (FV1620 'Malkara'), etc. Generally known as 'Pig'.

Truck, 3-ton, 4×4, Armoured (Bedford RL) Armoured hull on reinforced RL chassis with stronger suspension and 12.00–20 tyres. Produced in Singapore Base Workshops in relatively small quantities. Used for APC and similar roles, first in Malaya, later also elsewhere.

Car, Scout, 4×4, Reconnaissance, 'Ferret' Mk 2 FV701 (Daimler) RR B60 6-cyl., 130 bhp, semi-auto. 5F5R, wb 7′6″, 12′7″ × 6′3″ × 6′2″, 9688 lb (laden). Crew: 2. Mk 1 (shown on right) similar but no turret. Many variants. Superseded by 'Bigwheel' Mks 3, 4 and 5 which had 11.00–20 (vs 9.00–16) tyres and amphibious capabilities.

Combat Vehicle, Reconnaissance, Wheeled, 'Fox' (Daimler) Jaguar 6-cyl., 195 bhp, semi-auto. 5F5R, wb 8′1″, 13′4″ × 7′0″ × 7′0″, 12,550 lb (laden). Developed from 'Ferret' but built largely of aluminium. Military version of Jaguar 4.2-litre engine. PAS, PAB (discs). Tyres 11.00–20. Prototype shown (1969).

Car, Armoured, 6 × 6, 'Saladin', FV601 (Alvis) RR B80
Mk 6A or 6D 8-cyl., 160 bhp, semi-auto. 5F5R, wb 10′0″,
16′2″ (gun front 17′4″) × 8′4″ × 7′5″, 25,536 lb (laden).
Tyres 12.00–20. 76-mm QF (quick-firing) gun. Crew: 3.
Rear engine. Speed 45 mph. Hyd. disc brakes. From 1958
(prototype: Crossley, 1954).

**Carrier, Armoured, Personnel, 6 × 6, 'Saracen', FV603
(Alvis)** RR B80 Mk 3A 8-cyl., 160 bhp, semi-auto. 5F5R, wb
10′10″, 15′11″ × 8′3″ × 8′0″, 22,400 lb (laden). Mechanically
similar to 'Saracen' except engine at front. Crew: 12. From
1952 (prototype: 1950). FV604 was ACV version.

**Carrier, Armoured, Command, GPO/CPO, 6 × 6, FV610
(Alvis)** RR B80 Mk 6A 8-cyl., 170 bhp, semi-auto. 5F5R,
wb 10′0″, 15′11″ × 8′3″ × 7′9″, 23,520 lb (laden). Regi-
mental/Brigade/Division command vehicle, based on 'Saracen'
but with wider and higher hull. Reverse-flow cooling system.
1971.

**Vehicle, Armoured, Command, Heavy, 6 × 6, FV11061
(AEC)** 6-cyl. diesel, 226 bhp, 6F1R × 2, wb 12′6″, 25′0″ ×
8′2½″ × 10′8″, 33,200 lb. Produced by Royal Ordnance
Factory (Leeds) on SWB 'Militant' Mk 3 chassis, 1966.
Designed for staff and signals use. Equipped with air-condition-
ing. Left-hand drive.

TRACTORS, FULL-TRACK

Full-track (or crawler) tractors, together with earthmoving equipment (excavators, graders, scrapers, etc.), dumpers, SP cranes, and similar engineers' equipment, are known as 'C' vehicles. There were four classes of crawler tractors, namely Size 1 (Super Heavy). Size 2 (Heavy), Size 3 (Medium) and Size 4 (Medium Light). The following makes and models were among those used by the Army: Size 1: Caterpillar D8(H) and Vickers 'Vigor'; Size 2: Fowler 'Challenger 3' and International TD18; Size 3: Caterpillar D6C and International TD 14; Size 4: Caterpillar D4 and International BTD6 and TD9.

These machines were used with or without various types of ancillaries such as winches, bulldozers, angledozers and rippers. Some of the tractors were built in the USA (Caterpillar, International), others, like the Fowler and Vickers were British made.

Tractor, Full-Tracked, Medium (Caterpillar D6C) 6-cyl. diesel, 125 flywheel-hp, 'Power-Shift' or direct-drive trans., 16'3" × 10'0" (blade) × 6'11" (min.), 29,000 lb approx. Shown with cabin and angling dozer blade (adjustable 25° to either side or straight).

Tractor, Full-Tracked, Heavy (Fowler 'Challenger' 3M3) Leyland 680 6-cyl. diesel, 125 bhp, 6F4R, bare tractor: 14'6" × 7'8" × 8'9½", 28,000 lb. One of several basically commercial type crawler tractors supplied by the Marshall Organisation. They were used with various attachments and for towing.

Tractor, Full-Tracked, Super Heavy (Vickers 'Vigor') Rolls-Royce C6SFL supercharged 6-cyl. diesel, 180 bhp, 6F3R (or RR torque converter with 3-speed gearbox), bare tractor: 14'8½" × 8'6" × 9'11", 36,000 lb approx. Commercial type, manufactured by Vickers-Armstrong (Tractors) Ltd during 1958–59. Note large wheels.

CARRIERS, FULL-TRACK

During WWII the British 'Universal Carrier' had proved a most useful general purpose vehicle, and an improved version, the CT20 'Oxford', made its appearance in 1945. Relatively few of this and a later model, the 'Cambridge', were made, however. It was not until the early 1960s that a new family of tracked carriers appeared, known originally as 'Trojan' (FV430). Several variants were developed, varying from an APC-based ambulance to an SP gun carriage ('Abbot'). By 1971 the Alvis-built CVR(T) family of tracked combat vehicles appeared; these were based on the FV101 'Scorpion' light tank. Heavier tracked AFVs comprised tanks and tank-based special vehicles such as ARVs and bridge-layers. The Atkinson 'Alligator' was supplied to the MoS for recovery of 'Blue Streak' missile heads at a testing range.

Carrier, Full-Track, Cargo and Personnel (Atkinson 'Alligator') Ford V-8-cyl. (at rear), 100 bhp, 4F1R × 1 (2.3:1 red.), 12′0″ × 6′0″ × 4′3″ (min.), 7280 lb. Payload 1 ton. Controlled-diff tiller steering. Front drive. 20-in. 'Atkitraks'; ground pressure (unladen) 2.5 lb/sq. in.

Carrier, Full-Track, Amphibious (Atkinson 'Alligator') Basically as std version but with ballast tanks and shrouded propeller. Overall length 14′0″. Long semi-elliptical leafsprings with main beams and two 4-wh. bogies per side. Only a few produced, by Atkinson of Clitheroe Ltd, late 1940s.

Carrier, Full-Track, Articulated (Volvo/BM BV202E 'Snowcat') During 1968–70 the Army acquired about 150 of these Swedish amphibious over-snow vehicles, mainly for NATO use in Norway. The command version shown (with hard-top rear unit) was one of several variants (see 'Sweden').

Carrier, Full-Track, Armoured, CT20, 'Oxford' Mk 1
Cadillac V-8-cyl., 140 bhp, 'Hydramatic' 8F1R, 14'9" × 7'6½" × 6'8" (5'7"), 14,336 lb. Cletrac controlled diff. for normal steering, Girling brakes for skid steering. Used for nine different carrying and towing roles. 12-in tracks.

Carrier, Full-Track, Armoured, FV401, 'Cambridge'
RR B80 8-cyl., 160 bhp, rear-mounted. 15'4" × 8'5" × 5'7", 20,700 lb approx. Projected successor for 'Oxford', featuring torsion bar suspension (replacing Horstmann type). Collapsible flotation screen. Pilot models only. 1950.

Carrier, Full-Track, Armoured, FV103, 'Spartan' (Alvis)
APC variant of Combat Vehicle, Reconnaissance (Tracked) (CVR(T)) family for 1970s. 16'0" × 7'3" × 7'4", combat wt 18,016 lb. Jaguar 4.2 engine. Also: 'Samaritan' (ambulance), 'Sultan' (ACV), 'Samson' (ARV), 'Striker' (AT), etc.

Carrier, Full-Track, Armoured, FV432 (GKN Sankey)
RR K60 m/f 6-cyl., 240 bhp, GM Allison auto., 6F1R, 16'9" × 9'3" × 6'2", 30,300 lb approx. APC, convertible for other roles, incl. ambulance (shown). 13.5-in tracks; ground pressure 11.3 lb/sq. in. From mid-1960s.

MISCELLANEOUS VEHICLES

Shown in this section are some examples of unconventional vehicles. They are grouped together because they do not fit into any of the previous sections and because they present an interesting array of vehicle types, using wheels, tracks, trackways and air cushions. The air cushion vehicle (ACV) or hovercraft has great possibilities for cross-country travel and is amphibious, but it is unlikely to ever replace wheeled or tracked vehicles. ACVs, however, are already in service with the British and US armed forces for missions which no other vehicle type can accomplish. The question 'wheels or tracks' for cross-country vehicles, which has caused fierce arguments since the beginning of this century, still has not been answered and it does not look as if it ever will be, possibly because both systems have been perfected to an extent where their earlier inherent shortcomings, namely the difference in on- and off-road performance, have been almost eliminated.

Test Vehicle, 6 × 6, Skid-Steering, TV1000 (FVRDE 'Rhino') Meteorite V-8-cyl., 535 bhp, Merritt Brown trans., 20'0" × 10'6", 21 tons approx. Tyres 18.00–24 with central pressure control. Produced in late 1950s as test rig for experimental AFV transmission systems. Controlled differential steering. Chain drive.

Truck, Tanker, 5000-Gallon, 8 × 4 (AEC 'Mammoth Major') AEC AV760 6-cyl. diesel, 204 bhp, 6F1R (OD top). Tyres 10.00–20. Air brakes. PAS. LHD. Limited off-road capability. Designed for bulk transportation of fuel. Supplied to BAOR in late 1960s. Eight-wheelers were rare in British Army.

Truck, 3-ton, 4 × 4, with Trackway, Class 30 (Bedford RL/Cammell Laird) Portable roadway, developed by the MoD, launched from truck-mounted carriage assembly and after use recovered on to the truck (over the rear). Standard type trackway measured 150'9" × 11'0". Suitable for all wheeled and some tracked vehicles.

Truck, Half-Track, REME Fitters, w/Winch, w/Jib (International M14, modified) Obsolete as APCs, a number of WWII US M5, M9 and M14 half-tracks were converted by REME workshops into armoured repair vehicles. 18-ft crane jib could be folded, as shown. Welding and other equipment was carried.

Truck, Four-Track, Cargo (Land-Rover Series II/Cuthbertson) Undercarriage with four tracked bogies, driven by sprockets replacing the standard wheels. PAS. Unit shown had 27½-in ground clearance and max. speed of 30 mph. Military application was mainly for bomb disposal work (88″ and 109″ wb, c. 1962).

Vehicle, Air Cushion (Land-Rover Series II '109' modified) Experimental application of air cushion principle to LWB Land-Rover. The skirt was made of rubber and the air cushion was produced by a 30-in fan, driven by a Ford 'Classic' engine. It was dubbed 'Hover Rover' and appeared in the early 1960s.

Vehicle, Air Cushion (Br. Hovercraft Corp. SRN6) RR 900-shp 'Marine Gnome' gas turbine. 48′5″ × 23′0″ × 15′0″ approx. Normal gross wt 10.7 tons. Military variant of 'Winchester' class hovercraft. Typical mil. loads: 30 armed troops, 150-mm howitzer with crew, etc. Cruising speed over 45 knots. Used by Army and Navy.

HUNGARY

Like most of the Warsaw Pact countries, Hungary employs large numbers of Soviet-built vehicles for its armed forces. Most of the wheeled vehicles, however, are now of domestic manufacture, supplemented by models imported from Czechoslovakia, the DDR (East Germany) and Poland. During the late 1940s and the 1950s a number of wartime vehicles was used, varying from US Dodge Weapons Carriers (a replica of which was later produced by Csepel) to German semi-track tractors. AFVs were mainly of Soviet origin and included the BTR40P (BRDM) armoured car, the PT76 amphibious tank and the T34(85), T54 and T55 medium and heavy tanks. A Hungarian development was the FUG(-65) amphibious scout car, which was also supplied to Czechoslovakia, where it was designated OT-65, and Poland. This 4×4 vehicle had a 100-bhp Csepel Model D414.44 4-cylinder diesel engine, a wheelbase of 3.20 m, and 12.00–18 tyres. Overall dimensions and weight were approx. 5.79 × 2.36 × 1.90 m and 6100 kg resp. It was patterned on the Soviet BTR40P(BRDM) but had the engine at the rear and twin hydrojet water propulsion units. Series production was by the Rába works at Györ. A turreted version with 23-mm gun and 7.62-mm MG also appeared. The Csepel full-track artillery prime mover was an improved version of the Soviet light artillery tractor, M2, and was also exported to other countries, notably Communist China and Yugoslavia. Cab and front end were basically the same as used on contemporary Csepel trucks.

Csepel 526/Ikarus 4 × 4 fire fighter.

FUG-65 4 × 4 amphibious scout car.

223

TRUCKS and TRACTORS

Makes and Models: *Trucks:* Csepel 130 (1-ton, 4 × 4, 1953), D344, D445 (3-ton, 4 × 4, 1963), D350, D350B, D352, D352B (3½-ton, 4 × 2), D400, D420, D420B (4½-ton, 4 × 2), D450, D450B, D450N, D455, D455B (5-ton, 4 × 2), D462, D464 (7-ton, 4 × 2, 1969), D700 Series (7- to 8-ton, 4 × 2), K300 (3-ton, 6 × 6), D566 (5-ton, 6 × 6), D588 (8-ton, 8 × 8), D717.01 (10-ton, 6 × 6). GAZ-69, 69M (later UAZ) (½-ton, 4 × 4, SU), GAZ-63 (1½-ton, 4 × 4, SU), GAZ-66 (2-ton, 4 × 4, SU). Robur 30K (1-ton, 4 × 4, DDR), LO-1800A (1.8-ton, 4 × 4, DDR). Ural-375 D (5-ton, 6 × 6, SU). ZIL-151, -157 (2½-ton, 6 × 6, SU). *Tractors:* Csepel K800, GJ800 (full-track, from 1955). Various Soviet types.

General Data: Most of the trucks used by the Hungarian armed forces were military versions of commercial models, produced by the Csepel factory near Budapest. This firm's products are exported, for civilian purposes, through the state-operated export-import organization Mogürt (Hungarian Trading Company for Motor Vehicles) in Budapest. In addition to Csepel there are two other Hungarian motor vehicle manufacturers, namely Ikarus and Rába. Ikarus in Budapest produces buses and special equipment vehicles, e.g. fire fighters. Rába produces trucks, engines, axles and other components, in their Railway Carriage and Machine Works at Györ on the river Rába.

Csepel all-wheel drive trucks featured twin front axle propeller shafts, which enabled the engine to be set lower than on conventional 4 × 4 trucks. Csepel cooperates with Steyr in Austria, Rába with MAN in Germany (licence agreements, supply of components, etc.). Csepel also developed 6 × 6 and 8 × 8 truck chassis with independent suspension and Rába-MAN diesel engines. These made their public debut in 1971 as D566 and D588 respectively.

Vehicle shown (typical): Truck, 3-ton, 4 × 4, Cargo, w/Winch (Csepel D344)

Technical Data:
Engine: Csepel D414h diesel 4-cylinder, I-I-W-F, 5517 cc, 100 bhp @ 2300 rpm.
Transmission: 5F1R × 2.
Brakes: air.
Tyres: 9.00–20.
Wheelbase: 3.75 m.
Overall l × w × h: 6.77 × 2.31 × 2.77 (cab 2.28) m.
Weight: 5440 kg. GVW: 10,100 kg.
Note: 4-ton 4-way mid-chassis winch. Twin front axle drive shafts from differential in transfer case. Max. road speed 82 km/h. Max. payload (on roads) 3½ tons. Trailer load 2 tons. D445 was dump truck version.

Truck, 1-ton, 4 × 4, Cargo and Personnel (Csepel 130)
4-cyl. diesel, 85 bhp, 5F1 R × 1, wb 3.00 m, 4.84 × 2.15 × 2.20 m, 2200 kg. Tyres 9.00–20. Patterned on US WWII Dodge Weapons Carrier ('Beep'). GVW 3500 kg. Max. payload 1300 kg.

Truck, 1-ton, 4 × 4, Cargo and Personnel (Csepel 130)
Three-quarter rear view of truck shown on left. Introduced in 1953. Engine was a 5322-cc (110 × 140 mm) four-cylinder diesel, developing 85 bhp @ 2200 rpm. Max. speed 78 km/h, gradability 58%. 3½-ton winch optional.

Truck, 1-ton, 4 × 4, Personnel Carrier (Csepel 130)
Personnel-carrying version with closed cab and house-type body with double rear doors. All models: track, front 1.70 m, rear 1.67 m, axle ground clearance 0.31 m, turning radius 7.35 m, **fuel tank capacity 112 litres.**

Truck, 3½-ton, 4 × 4, Tanker (Csepel D350) 4-cyl. diesel (D413) 85 bhp, 5F1R, wb 3.71 m, approx 6.20 × 2.20 × 2.13 m. Also cargo, shop van and dump truck (D350B) versions. Built under Austrian Steyr licence. 5322-cc engine. One of the first post-war Hungarian trucks.

Truck, 4½-ton, 4×2, Cargo (Csepel D420) 4-cyl. diesel (D413), 85 bhp, 5F1R, wb 3.71 m, 6.72 × 2.31 × 2.28 m, 3800 kg. GVW 8300 kg. Superseded D350 in 1955. Also tanker, shop van (signals, ambulance, workshop) and 4 × 4 versions (D344, D445). Tyres 8.25 or 8.50–20.

Truck, 5-ton, 4×2, Cargo (Csepel D450) 4-cyl. diesel (D414c), 100 bhp, 5F1R, wb 3.71 m, 6.73 × 2.30 × 2.74 (cab 2.20) m, 4100 kg. GVW 9360 kg. Tyres 8.25–20. Air brakes. 5517-cc (112 × 140 mm) engine. Also SWB and COE versions. Various body options.

Truck, 3-ton, 6×6, Shop Van (Csepel K300) 6-cyl. diesel, 125 bhp, 5F1R × 2, wb 4.50 m, 7.00 × 2.45 × 2.75 m, 5445 kg. Tyres 9.00–20. Derived from Model D350, fitted with more powerful engine. Also with single cab and cargo body. Replaced by Soviet ZIL-157 (K).

Tractor, Full-Track, Artillery (Csepel K-800, GJ-800) 6-cyl. diesel (D613), 125 bhp, 5F1R, 5.04 × 2.72 × 2.47 m, 6980 kg. Track width 317 mm. Payload 2 tons plus crew of eight. Max. trailer weight 8 tons. 7980-cc engine. Speed 32 km/h. Torsion bar susp. Gradability 30° (laden 18°). 1955.

INDIA

Before and during the second World War production of motor vehicles in India was confined to assembly of imported CKD units (General Motors, from 1928, Ford Motor Company, from 1931, etc.). Output was relatively low. Other vehicles were imported. During WWII serious attempts were made to create an Indian automotive industry and the first manufacturers to be established were Hindustan Motors Ltd in Calcutta (1942) and Premier Automobiles Ltd in Bombay (1944). These firms commenced, after the war, with the assembly of foreign vehicles but manufactured an increasing number of components. The amount of imported parts, in turn, decreased gradually. In 1949 the first all-Indian motor vehicle came off the assembly line. By this time General Motors had discontinued manufacture in India as they considered it unprofitable. Ford India (a subsidiary of Ford Canada) closed down during the 1950s. In 1958 the Ministry of Defence of the Indian Government commenced production of military tactical vehicles under licence agreements with various manufacturers, namely MAN of West Germany (trucks, from 1958), Nissan of Japan (trucks, from 1961) and Vickers of Great Britain (tanks). Other military vehicles were imported directly by the Government or acquired from commercial assembly plants. In case of war, a large proportion of the Indian automotive industry can be switched over to manufacture army vehicles and many civilian-operated trucks can be requisitioned for military purposes. Soviet military trucks came into service in 1971. AFVs include British 'Centurion', British/Indian Vickers 'Vijayata' (Victory), and French AMX-13 tanks, supplemented by Czech OT-64 ('Skot') amphibious 8 × 8 APCs, etc.

The Vickers 'Vijayata' medium battle tank is produced by Vickers in England and at the Avadi Ordnance Factory in Madras. It features many of the automotive components of the British 'Chieftain' tank.

Who's Who in the Indian Automotive Industry

Ashok Leyland	Ashok Leyland Ltd, Ennore, Madras 57 (1948–55: Ashok Motors Ltd).
Dodge, Fargo	The Premier Automobiles Ltd, Kurla, Bombay 70.
Hindustan	Hindustan Motors Ltd, Uttarpara, Calcutta.
Jeep	Mahindra & Mahindra Ltd, Bombay 67NB.
Standard	Standard Motor Products of India Ltd, Madras.
Tata/Mercedes-Benz	Tata Engineering & Locomotive Co. Ltd, Bombay 1 (plant at Jamshedpur).

Military parade in Delhi, 1961.

TRUCKS and TRACTORS
4 × 2, 4 × 4, 6 × 4 and 6 × 6

Makes and Models: Ashok Leyland 'Comet' AL-CO-3/2 Special (5-ton, 4 × 4, 1968) and AL-CO-3/4 Special (tractor, 4 × 4, 1968), 'Hippo' AL-H-1/4 (tractor, 6 × 4, 1965). Commer R541 (5-ton, 4 × 2, c. 1950, GB). Dodge/Fargo PWC-95, PNWC-95 (1-ton, 4 × 4), K-ZW-6 Special (3-ton, 4 × 4), PWT-190 (3-ton, 4 × 4), etc. GAZ/UAZ-69M (0.8-ton, 4 × 4, SU). Jeep CJ3A, CJ3B, CJ4, FC160, etc. ($\frac{1}{4}$- to $\frac{3}{4}$-ton, 4 × 2 and 4 × 4, from 1949). Magirus-Deutz 'Jupiter' (7-ton, 6 × 6, D). Mercedes-Benz 'Unimog' S (1$\frac{1}{2}$-ton, 4 × 4, D). Nissan 'Patrol' ($\frac{1}{4}$-ton, 4 × 4) and D4W73 'Carrier' ($\frac{3}{4}$-ton, 4 × 4, 1961). Shaktiman/MAN 415L1AR (5-ton, 4 × 4, 1958). Tata/Mercedes-Benz LA312 (3-ton, 4 × 4, c. 1960), etc. Thornycroft 'Big Ben' (10-ton, 6 × 4), 'Mighty Antar' (tractor, 6 × 4), TFA/B81 'Nubian' (crash tender, 6 × 6), etc.

General Data: Most of the vehicles listed above were manufactured in India under licence agreements, others were assembled from imported components or part-manufactured. Some special types, like the Thornycroft 'Mighty Antar' tank transporters and 'Nubian' crash tenders were imported as complete vehicles. The Shaktiman (MAN) and Nissan trucks were produced, under licence, in the Defence Unit (Ordnance Factory) at Jabalpur. This factory also produced a $\frac{1}{4}$-ton 4 × 4 field car, called 'Jonga'. British Land-Rovers were supplied to the fire services and the Bengal Police. Hindustan Motors Ltd has a plant at Uttarpara near Calcutta and until 1958 produced American Studebaker trucks and British Morris cars. From 1958 this company concentrated on the production of Hindustan Bedford trucks and (from 1964) 'Ambassador' Mk II cars, the latter resembling the British Morris 'Oxford' Series III of 1956–59. The company is also involved in the manufacture of cranes and earthmoving equipment. From 1971 various types of Soviet tactical trucks entered service with the Indian armed forces.

Vehicle shown (typical): Truck, $\frac{3}{4}$-ton, 4 × 4, Cargo, w/Winch (Nissan D4W73 'Carrier')

Technical Data:
Engine: Nissan 242 CID 6-cylinder, I-I-W-F, 3956 cc, 125 bhp @ 3800 rpm.
Transmission: 4F1R × 2.
Brakes: hydraulic.
Tyres: 7.50–20.
Wheelbase: 110$\frac{1}{4}$ in. Track: 63 in.
Overall l × w × h: 195 × 80$\frac{1}{2}$ × 93 (max.) in.
Weight: 6000 lb approx.
Note: Japanese truck, produced under licence by Indian Government. Folding troop seats in rear body. GVW 9230 lb.

Truck, ½-ton, 4 × 4, Utility (Jeep 'Universal' CJ4) 4-cyl., 71 bhp, 3F1R × 2, wb 91 in, 141 × 69 × 66 in, 2500 lb. Length-ened CJ3B, introduced in 1967. Available as 4 × 2 also. Other Indian-built Jeep vehicles included the CJ3B, FC160 ¾-ton trucks, ambulances and station wagons.

Truck, 5-ton, 4 × 2, Chassis (Commer R541) 6-cyl., 109 bhp, 4F1R, wb 141 in. Underfloor engine. Part of an order of 250 units, assembled by Simpson & Co. Ltd, Rootes Group distributors in Madras, for Indian Army, about 1950.

Truck, 1-ton, 4 × 4, Chassis (Dodge PNWC-95) 6-cyl., 110 bhp, 4F1R × 2, wb 132½ in, overall length 212½ in, height 83¼ in. GVW 9500 lb. Tyres 9.00–16. Supplied only as chassis with cowl and windscreen. American pattern front end. Model PA-6 engine.

Truck, 3-ton, 4 × 4, Cargo, w/Winch (Dodge K-ZW-6) 6-cyl., 107 bhp, 4F1R × 2, wb 170 in, 269 (w/o winch 256) × 84 × 84¼ (cab) in, 8990 lb. GVW 18,900 lb. Tyres 12.00–20. Chrysler Model 250.6 engine. Timken transfer case. Shown as used by Indian UN forces in Congo.

Truck, 1-ton, 4 × 4, Cargo (Dodge PWC-95) 6-cyl., 110 bhp, 4F1R × 2, wb 132½ in, overall length 216¼ in, height 90 in. GVW 9500 lb. Tyres 9.00–16. Model PA-6 engine (110 bhp @ 3600 rpm). British pattern front end (Dodge Kew).

Truck, 3-ton, 4 × 4, Chassis (Dodge PWT-190) Perkins P6/354 6-cyl. diesel, 120 bhp, 5F1R × 2, wb 165 in, overall length 261½, height 93¼ in, 7409 lb. GVW 19,000 lb. Tyres 8.25–20. Supplied with cowl and windscreen, also under the Fargo trade name.

Truck, 5-ton, 4 × 4, Tractor (Ashok Leyland 'Comet' AL-CO-3/4 Special) 6-cyl. diesel, 110 bhp, 6F1R × 1 (OD top), wb 119 in, 212¼ × 89 in, 9240 lb. Tyres 11.00–20 (or 9.00–20, twin rear). AL370 'Power Plus' engine. Air brakes. Similar chassis also with Coles revolving crane.

Truck, 5-ton, 4 × 4, Cargo/APBV (Ashok Leyland 'Comet' AL-CO-3/2 Special) 6-cyl. diesel, 110 bhp, 6F1R × 1 (OD top), wb 164 in, 270¼ × 89 in, 9526 lb. GVW 22,880 lb. Tyres 9.00–20. 'Hippo' AL-H-1/4 mil. tractor had same engine but 4F1R trans., 150-in wb, 11.00–20 tyres and measured 265 × 96 × 106 in. The 'Hippo' had a tandem-drive rear bogie (6 × 4).

Truck, 3-ton, 4 × 4, Cargo (Tata/Mercedes-Benz LA312)
German 'pseudo-military' diesel truck, produced under licence
by Tata Eng. & Locomotive Co. Ltd. Some had a soft-top cab.
Company was founded in 1945, started truck production in
1954. Other models included L4500 (L312) and L1210.

Truck, 5-ton, 4 × 4, Cargo (Shaktiman/MAN 415 L1AR)
German tactical military truck with multi-fuel engine, produced
under licence in Jabalpur, India. Between 1958 and 1963
5000 units were built, initial production being mainly from
imported components.

**Truck, 10-ton, 6 × 4, Tractor, w/Winch (Thornycroft
SM/GRN6 'Big Ben')** British tractor unit with van-bodied
semi-trailer. Note winch behind cab. S-T convertible to full-
trailer by using dolly which in picture is towed behind. Thornycroft also supplied 'Mighty Antar' and 'Nubian' vehicles.

**Truck, 7-ton, 6 × 6, Cargo and Prime Mover, w/Winch
(Magirus-Deutz 'Jupiter')** German tactical military truck
with air-cooled Deutz V-8-cyl. diesel engine in service with
Indian Army. Front-mounted power winch. Shown here towing
American 8-in heavy howitzer, M115.

CARS, TRUCKS,
TRACTORS, AFVs

Makes and Models: *Cars:* Autocars Sabra 'Carmel', 'Ducas' and 'Sussita' (station wagon), Citroën 2CV (F), Dodge 'Dart' 1970, etc.
Field Cars ($\frac{1}{4}$- to $\frac{1}{2}$-ton, 4 × 4): Ford M151 (US). GAZ/ UAZ-69A(M) (SU). Jeep M38A1, CJ5, etc. (US). Land-Rover '88' (GB).
Trucks, 4 × 2: Autocars 'Sussita' (lt. pickup). Dodge, various models ($\frac{3}{4}$- to 4-ton). Ford, various models (1- to 5-ton, US). Leyland, various models incl. 'Beaver' (3- to 4-ton).
Trucks, 4 × 4: Autocars 'Dragoon' ($\frac{1}{2}$-ton). Dodge T214 ($\frac{3}{4}$-ton, WWII, US) and 'Power Wagon' (1-ton, US). Ford, various models (US). Ford-Köln G398 SAM (3-ton, D). GAZ-63A ($1\frac{1}{2}$-ton), GAZ-69 ($\frac{1}{2}$-ton), etc. (SU). Jeep (incl. Kaiser and Willys) CJ6, 'Wagoneer', M715, etc. ($\frac{1}{2}$- to $1\frac{1}{4}$-ton, US). Land-Rover '109' ($\frac{3}{4}$-ton, GB). UAZ-450/452 (0.8-ton, SU).
Trucks, 6 × 6: Dodge T223 ($1\frac{1}{2}$-ton, WWII, US). GMC CCKW-352/353 ($2\frac{1}{2}$-ton, WWII, US). Praga V3S (3-ton, CS). Reo G742 'M-Series' ($2\frac{1}{2}$-ton, US). Tatra T138 (8-ton, CS). ZIL-157 ($2\frac{1}{2}$-ton, 6 × 6, SU).
Tractors: Diamond T 980 (6 × 4, WWII, US). Leyland/Scammell 'Contractor' (6 × 4).
AFVs (except full-track): BTR-40 (4 × 4) and -152 (6 × 6) APCs (SU). Walid (4 × 4) scout car/APC (Egypt). White M3A1 (4 × 4) scout car/APC (WWII, US). White, IHC, etc. (half-track) ambulance, APC, ARV, command, SP, etc. (WWII, modified, US).

General Data: Of the above vehicles, those which are of East European and Egyptian origin were captured from neighbouring Arab countries in sufficient quantities to be standardized for use by the Israeli forces. During the 7-day war in June 1967 alone about 6000 Soviet trucks and 1000 APCs were captured. Jordanian booty included many US vehicles (Ford, Jeep) as well as British Land-Rovers, etc. Israeli automotive production and assembly includes Autocars Co. of Haifa (which took over Kaiser-Ilin), Leyland-Ashdod and Automotive Industries (Dodge, Ford). The Autocars Co. 'Dragoon' entered production in 1967 and is supplied mainly for export. It is a multi-purpose vehicle with various body and equipment options.

Vehicle shown (typical): Truck, $\frac{1}{2}$-ton, 4 × 4, Multi-purpose (Autocars 'Dragoon')

Technical Data:
Engine: Triumph 4-cylinder, I-I-W-F, 1498 cc, 56 bhp @ 4300 rpm.
Transmission: 4F1R × 2.
Brakes: hydraulic.
Tyres: 6.50–13.
Wheelbase: 2.01 m.
Overall l × w × h: 3.43 × 1.57 × 1.93 (max.) m.
Weight: 991 kg.   GVW on/off road: 1638/1435 kg.
Note: Normally front-wheel drive, engagement of rear wheel drive also engages low range. DeDion-type front axle. Semi-elliptic springs front and rear. Produced to British design (Triumph 'Pony').

ITALY

During most of the Second World War Italy ranked among the Axis powers but in 1943 a swing to the Allies took place. From that time, Italian armed units in the North took sides with the Allies whereas in the South the foundation was laid for a new post-war Italian Army. In 1949 the Italian Republic together with eleven other states signed the NATO pact. During those early post-war years the Italian armed forces equipped themselves with a great variety of motor transport including pre-war and wartime military vehicles. Many of Italy's wartime vehicles had been produced for or been taken over by the German forces and a few types remained in production for military and, in the case of load carriers, civilian purposes. Added to these were quantities of war-surplus American, British and Canadian vehicles and these remained in use for many years. From the early 1950s some types of new Italian-made tactical 4×4 vehicles made their appearance, notably field cars and light and medium trucks. In 1956 OM, a division of Fiat, commenced production of a truck which looked similar to the US Army 'M-Series' 5-ton 6×6 chassis, fitted with stake-type bridge transporting body. Power plant and drive train were of Italian design. Other special vehicles which have been produced in Italy to American design are the full-track armoured personnel carrier, M113(A1), the howitzer carriage, M109 and the medium tank, M60A1. These were built under licence by Oto Melara, an armaments manufacturer in La Spezia. A proportion of these vehicles was supplied to other NATO partners.

Italian Vehicle Nomenclature
The following designations are used for motor vehicles:

Motorcycle	*Motociclo*
Passenger Car	*Autovettura*
Ambulance	*Autoambulanza*
Utility Truck (Field Car)	*Autovettura da Ricognizione* (AR) (literally: reconnaissance car)
Light Truck	*Autocarro Leggero* (CL)
Medium Truck	*Autocarro Medio* (CM)
Heavy Truck	*Autocarro Pesante* (CP)
Light Tractor	*Trattore Leggero* (TL)
Medium Tractor	*Trattore Medio* (TM)
Heavy Tractor	*Trattore Pesante* (TP)
Wrecker Truck	*Autosoccorso* or *Autoricupero*
Semi-Track	*Semicingolato*
Armoured Car	*Autoblinda*
Scout Car	*Autocarro Protetto*
APC (tracked)	*Transporto Cingolato* or *Mezzo da Combattimento*
Tank, light, medium	*Carro Armato Leggero, Medio*
SP Gun (tracked)	*Cannone Semovente*
SP Howitzer (tracked)	*Obice Semovente*

The two numerals which appear after the letter code in truck and tractor designations indicate the year when the model was introduced. Example: CM52- *Carro Medio 1952:* medium truck, 1952 model.

Registration Numbers
White number plates with black numerals prefixed by a red letter code as follows: EI for Army (*Esercito Italiano*), AM for Air Force (*Aeronautica Militare*) and MM for Navy (*Marina Militare*).

Who's Who in the Italian Automotive Industry

Alfa Romeo	Alfa Romeo SpA, Milano.
Autobianchi, Bianchi	Autobianchi, Azienda della Fiat SpA, Milano.
Fiat	Fiat SpA, Torino (main plant).
Lancia	Lancia & C. Fabrica Automobili Torino SpA, Torino.
Moto Guzzi	SEIMM (Soc. Es. Ind. Motor Meccaniche) SpA, Mandello del Lario (Como).
MV Agusta	Meccanica Verghera, Gallarate.
OM	Fiat Azienda OM, Brescia.

CARS, MOTORCYCLES
and MOTORTRICYCLES

Cars in service with the Italian armed forces are conventional civilian models. Motorcycles were supplied by Moto Gilera and Moto Guzzi. The Moto Guzzi 'Mulo Meccanico' (mechanical mule) was an unusual three-wheeled 'power cart', designed for use in mountainous areas. It carried 500 kg in addition to the driver and could be quickly converted into a half-track vehicle. Several firms introduced civilian field cars (leisure vehicles) using mechanical components of various Fiat cars. Examples: CAP 'Scoiattola' (4×2 and 4×4), Delta 'Yeti 850' (4×4), FART 'Breack' (4×2), Ferves 'Ranger' (4×2 and 4×4), OSI 'Cross Country' (4×2), Savio 'Jungle' and 'Savana' (4×2), etc. MV Agusta built the German 'Kraka' under licence, as well as a closed version ('Diana').

Motorcycle, Solo (Moto Guzzi 'Superalce') 1-cyl., 18.5 bhp, 4F, wb 1.45 m, 2.22 × 0.79 × 1.06 m, 200 kg. Horizontal 500-cc engine. 'Sprung' frame. Tyres 3.50–19. Ground clearance 0.21 m. Speed 110 km/h. Official designation *Motociclo Militare*. 1946.

Motortricycle, 3×3 (Moto Guzzi 'Mulo Meccanico') V-2-cyl., 20 bhp, 6F1R, wb 2.05 m, 3.00 × 1.10–1.57 × 1.42 m, 1000 kg. Adjustable rear track width. Tyres 6.00–15. 754-cc air-cooled engine. Known as *Autoveicolo da Montagna Tre-per-Tre* (3×3). Introduced in 1959/60.

Motortricycle, 3×3, (Moto Guzzi 'Mulo Meccanico') Shown here with overall chains fitted over rear wheels and lowered rear idlers. Steering wheel actuated front wheel through reduction gearbox. Torque-dividing differential design (1/5 to front wheel, 4/5 to rear wheels).

TRUCKS, $\frac{1}{4}$- to 2-TON
4×2 and 4×4

Makes and Models: Alfa Romeo 1900R 'Folle' ($\frac{1}{4}$-ton, 4×4, 1950/51), AR52 'Matta' ($\frac{1}{4}$-ton, 4×4, 1952), 'Romeo 2°' (1-ton, 4×2, from c. 1955). Autobianchi CL51 (2-ton, 4×2, 1951). Fiat 1900 'Campagnola' ($\frac{1}{4}$-ton, 4×4, 1950), AR51, AR55, AR59 'Campagnola' ($\frac{1}{4}$-ton, 4×4, from 1951), 'Campagnola B' and 'C' (diesel; $\frac{1}{4}$-ton, 4×4, from 1953). Fiat/Spa TL37 (1-ton, 4×4, 1937–48). MV 55 (1.2-ton, 4×4, 1965). Lancia CL51 200.00 (Z20), 200.01 (Z20A) (1.8-ton, 4×4, 1952), CL51 200.02 (Z20AA), 200.03 (Z21AA) (special chassis, 4×4, 1952), TL51 201.00 (Z30) (1.8-ton, 4×4, 1952). OM 'Leoncino' NC (1$\frac{1}{2}$-ton, 4×4, 1961), CL65 20.110 'Leoncino' NC (1$\frac{1}{2}$-ton, 4×4, 1965), CL51, CL52 'Leoncino' (2-ton, 4×4, from 1951).

General Data: In 1950 Alfa Romeo and Fiat introduced prototypes for two new $\frac{1}{4}$-ton 4×4 vehicles. After certain alterations had been made, mainly to the bodywork, both went into quantity production for the Italian Forces and for civilian purposes. The Fiat 'Campagnola' (civilian designation) was also exported, notably to Latin America (Bolivia, Mexico, Venezuela) and Africa and was produced, under licence, in Yugoslavia. An optional diesel engine was introduced in 1953. Both the Alfa Romeo and the Fiat were available commercially with various types of bodywork and special equipment, including station wagon, fire truck, snow plough, wrecker, etc. Of the military versions there were fewer Alfa Romeos than Fiats. Of the latter there was also a weapons carrier version. The Alfa's production ceased in 1955. The Autobianchi, Lancia and OM CL51 (light truck, 1951) were built to a common general specification but differed in many details. Of the OM version a normal-control version was designed about 1960. This model subsequently appeared in several variants, with petrol or diesel engine and was also available for civilian operators. The Fiat/Spa TL37 was a pre-war design but continued in production for a few years after the war.

Vehicle shown (typical): Truck, $\frac{1}{4}$-ton, 4×4, Utility, AR59 (Fiat 'Campagnola A')

Technical Data:
Engine: Fiat 105B.017 4-cylinder, I-I-W-F, 1901 cc, 56 bhp @ 4000 rpm (later 63 @ 4000).
Transmission: 4F1R × 2.
Brakes: hydraulic.
Tyres: 6.40–16.
Wheelbase: 2.25 m.
Overall l × w × h: 3.60 × 1.57 × 1.75 (1.37) m.
Weight: 1430 kg. GVW: 1900 kg.
Note: Independent front suspension. Rigid rear axle with semi-elliptic leaf springs. Doors could be fixed in open position (as shown). 24-volt electrics. 'Campagnola B' and 'C' had diesel engine. NATO class $\frac{1}{2}$-ton.

Truck, ¼-ton, 4 × 4 (Fiat 1900 'Campagnola') 4-cyl., 53 bhp, 4F1R × 2. Prototype of Fiat's post-war field car, first unveiled in the summer of 1950. Power unit was long-stroke version of Fiat 1400 car of that period. IFS incorporated enclosed coil springs (as on 1100).

Truck, ¼-ton, 4 × 4, AR59 (Fiat 'Campagnola A') Shown here with full weather protection installed. Used as a general purpose personnel/cargo carrier, reconnaissance, command and communications vehicle. Normal seating accommodation was for two in front and four in rear.

Truck, ¼-ton, 4 × 4 (Alfa Romeo 1900 R) 4-cyl., 70 bhp, 4F1R × 2, wb 2.20 m, 3.52 × 1.48 × 1.82 m, 1300 kg. Twin-OHC 1884-cc engine. Dry-sump lubrication system. IFS with torsion bars. RHD. Produced in 1950/51 and dubbed 'Folle'. Predecessor of the 'Matta' (AR52).

Truck, ¼-ton, 4 × 4, AR52 (Alfa Romeo 1900 'Matta') 4-cyl., 70 bhp, 4F1R × 2, wb 2.20 m, 3.52 × 1.48 × 1.82 m, 1300 kg. Similar to 1900R 'Folle' but restyled bodywork. Produced for Italian Forces, 1952–55. Tyres 6.00–16. Speed 105 km/h. Engine was modified 1900 car unit.

Truck, ¼-ton, 4 × 4, AR59 (Fiat 'Campagnola A') The AR59 was adapted for several special duties such as SP mount for guided missiles and recoilless rifle as shown here in a military parade in Rome in 1965. There was also a 24-round 100-mm rocket launcher version.

Truck, 1½-ton, 4 × 4, Cargo and Personnel (OM 'Leoncino' NC) 4-cyl., 58 bhp, 5F1R × 2, wb 2.50 m, 4.42 × 2.00 × 2.10 m, 2500 kg approx. OM 20.010 2545-cc petrol engine. Tyres 9.00–16. 2½-ton winch optional (at rear). RHD. Introduced in 1961 as normal control version of 2-ton 'Leoncino' (*qv*).

Truck, 1½-ton, 4 × 4, Cargo and Personnel, CL65 (OM 20.110 'Leoncino' NC) 4-cyl. diesel, 85 bhp, 2860 kg approx. CO2D 4397-cc diesel engine, otherwise generally similar to petrol-engine version. NATO class 1-ton. Crew 12. Introduced in 1965. Also civ. version. Winch (front) optional.

Truck, 1½-ton, 4 × 4, Drone Control Centre, w/Winch (OM 12.401 'Leoncino' NC) 4-cyl. diesel, 85 bhp, 5F1R × 2, wb 2.50 m. Control vehicle for Italian Meteor 'Gufone' tactical surveillance drone system. Drone equipped for photography with normal and infra-red film, day and night; weight 330 lb, speed 400 knots. 1971.

238

Truck, 2-ton, 4 × 2, Cargo, CL51 (Autobianchi) 4-cyl.,
44 bhp, 4F1R, wb 2.50 m, 4.82 × 1.98 × 2.50 m, 2300 kg.
Bianchi 'Sforzesco' (licence Cattaneo) 1810-cc petrol engine.
Tyres 7.00–18. Track, front 1.56, rear 1.57 m. Produced from
1951 to 1953.

Truck, 1.8-ton, 4 × 4, Cargo, CL51 (Lancia Z20, Z20A)
4-cyl., 62.5 bhp, 5F1R × 2, wb 2.55 m, 4.48 × 2.00 × 2.67 (2.26)
m, 2830 kg. Coil spring IFS. Variants: TL51 (Z30) cargo/prime
mover w/Winch (similar in appearance) and CL51 *Autoveicoli
da Campo* (special long chassis). Produced 1952–70.

**Truck, 2-ton, 4 × 4, Cargo and Personnel, CL51 (OM
'Leoncino')** 4-cyl., 60 bhp, 5F1R × 2, wb 2.50 m, 4.65 × 2.00 ×
2.65 (2.25) m, 2800 kg approx. Tyres 8.25–20. OM 20.005
2545-cc engine. Early model (wooden body, no cab roof hatch).
Also with rocket launcher and integral ambulance bodywork.

**Truck, 2-ton, 4 × 4, Cargo and Personnel, CL52 (OM
'Leoncino')** 4-cyl. diesel, 54 bhp, 5F1R × 2, wb 2.50 m,
4.65 × 2.00 × 2.65 (2.25) m, 2900 kg approx. GVW 4900 kg.
NATO class 1-ton. Composite steel/wood body with steel sides
and troop seats. Model COD-A 3770-cc diesel. Also exported.

TRUCKS, 2½- to 10-TON
4 × 2, 4 × 4, 6 × 4 and 6 × 6

Makes and Models: Alfa Romeo 450 (3½-ton, 4 × 4, 1950), 800RE (6-ton, 4 × 2, 1940–50). Autobianchi 'Civis' and 'Miles' (3½-ton, 4 × 2, 1946), 'Audax' (3½-ton, 4 × 2, 1948), CM51, CM54 (3-ton, 4 × 4, from 1952). Fiat T40 (2½-ton, 4 × 4, 1941–48), TM48 (2½-ton, 4 × 4, 1948), 639N CM50 (3½-ton, 4 × 4, 1950), 639N2 and 6601 CM52 (4-ton, 4 × 4, from 1952), 6602 CP62 (5-ton, 4 × 4, 1962), DOV.35 (3-ton, 6 × 4, 1936–48), DOV.41 (5-ton, 6 × 6, 1943–48), DOV.50 (5-ton, 6 × 6, 1950), 6607 CP62 (6-ton, 6 × 6, 1962), A10000 (10-ton, 6 × 4, 1945). Fiat/OM 6600 CP56 (10-ton, 6 × 6, 1956). International G744 'M-Series' (5-ton, 6 × 6, US). Lancia 6 RO M CP48 (6-ton, 4 × 2, 1949), 506.00 and 506.12 (5-ton, 4 × 4, 1959). OM 25N2-4 × 4 (2½-ton, 4 × 4, 1958), CO1D/11 'Tigrotto M' (4½-ton, 4 × 2, 1961), etc.

General Data: After 1945 the Italian armed forces first employed wartime and pre-war trucks of domestic production, supplemented by American, British and Canadian war surplus vehicles. The Fiat Dovunque 50 (*Dovunque* means cross-country) 6 × 6 truck was produced during 1950–53 and was rather similar to the Dovunque 41 which went into production in 1943 and was continued until 1948. Several other WWII vehicles remained in production during the immediate post-war years. During the 1950s the first generation of post-war military vehicles was gradually taken into service. These included the Fiat 639N and the Lancia 506. In 1955/56 the OM division of Fiat launched a 6 × 6 truck which except for engine, drive train, wheels and tyres resembled the American 5-ton 6 × 6 bridging truck. This vehicle was supplied to various NATO countries, including the Netherlands, and also to Venezuela. The Lancia 506 and Fiat/OM 6600 chassis were also used for fire/crash tenders (Bergomi). The second generation of post-war tactical vehicles was put into production during the 1960s and included the Fiat 6602 (CP 62) and 6607 (CP 62). Artillery tractor variants of several of the above trucks are covered in the following section. The American M25 'Dragon Wagon' was used for haulage of tanks and heavy equipment.

Vehicle shown (typical): Truck, 6-ton, 4 × 4, Cargo, CP62 (Fiat 6602) (*Carro Pesante*, Heavy Truck, 1962)

Technical Data:
Engine: Fiat 219B petrol 6-cylinder, I-I-W-F, 7977 cc, 160–165 bhp @ 2700 rpm.
Transmission: 5F1R × 2.
Brakes: air.
Tyres: 11.00–20.
Wheelbase: 3.57 m.
Overall l × w × h: 6.56 × 2.46 × 2.98 (2.13) m.
Weight: 7173 kg. GVW: 12,200 kg.
Note: Introduced in 1962, NATO class 6-ton. Dropside body. Soft-top cab seating two. Power-assisted steering. 10-ton winch at rear.

Truck, 3½-ton, 4×4, Cargo, CM50 (Alfa Romeo 450) 4-cyl. diesel, 90 bhp, 4F1R×2. Weight 4800 kg. Produced from 1950 until 1952. Typical *Autocarro Militare* of the first post-war generation of Italian military vehicles. Basically a military version of a commercial chassis.

Truck, 6-ton, 4×2, Cargo, CP48 (Alfa Romeo 800RE) 6-cyl. diesel, 115 bhp, 4F1R×2, wb 3.80 m, 6.85×2.35×2.85 m, 5500 kg. GVW 12,000 kg. Tyres 10.50–20. Similar to wartime *Autocarro Unificato Pesante* (standard heavy truck), continued in production for military purposes until 1950.

Truck, 3-ton, 4×4, Cargo, CM54 (Autobianchi) 4-cyl. diesel, 80 bhp, 4F1R×2, wb 3.26 m, 5.95×2.29×2.89 m, 4800 kg. Tyres 11.00–20. MD11 5230-cc engine, 1954–57. CM51 (1952–54) similar but MD01 84-bhp engine. 'Civis' 46 (4×2) was produced as cargo truck and COE integral ambulance.

Truck, 3½-ton, 4×2, Cargo (Fiat 639) 6-cyl., 72 bhp, 5F1R, wb 3.27 m, 6.22×2.35×2.91 m, 4815 kg. GVW 8455 kg. Tyres 10.00–20. 6032-cc petrol engine. Speed 60 km/h. Air-assisted brakes. One of several military versions of Fiat commercial trucks. Produced during 1950–51.

Truck, 4-ton, 4 × 4, Cargo, CM52 (Fiat 639N2, 6601) 6-cyl. diesel, 89.5 bhp, 4F1R × 2, wb 3.27 m, 6.19 × 2.37 × 2.95 m, 5215 kg. Successor of CM50 Model 639N (which had petrol engine). Variants of CM50: wrecker, office, ambulance. Also exported (Mexico, Venezuela, Somalia, etc.).

Truck, 5-ton, 4 × 4, Cargo (Lancia 506.00) 6-cyl., 170 bhp, 4F1R × 2, wb 3.70 m, 6.35 × 2.50 × 3.09 (2.09) m, 7530 kg. Air brakes. Tyres 11.00–20. Produced for Italian Air Force, 1959–68. Prototypes (1958) had different windscreen design. The 6786-cc engine was inclined at an angle of 30°.

Truck, 6-ton, 4 × 2, Cargo, CP48 (Lancia 6 RO M) 6-cyl. diesel, 122 bhp, 4F1R × 2, wb 4.30 m, 7.76 × 2.42 × 3.03 m, 6300 kg. Tyres 270–20. Military version of commercial truck ('Esatau' Militare) with 8245-cc engine. Produced from 1949 to 1958 with cargo (shown) and fuel tanker bodywork.

Truck, 4½-ton, 4 × 2, Personnel Carrier (OM CO1D/11 'Tigrotto' M) 4-cyl. diesel, 77 bhp, 5F1R, wb 3.00 m, 5.30 × 2.18 × 2.70 m, 4700 kg approx. Commercial chassis with coachbuilt bodywork, used by para-military police force. Produced 1961–62. 'Tigrotto' was also supplied with four-wheel drive (CO1D/11 4 × 4).

Truck, 5-ton, 6 × 6, Cargo (Fiat Dovunque 50) 6-cyl. diesel, 110 bhp, 5F1R × 2, wb 3.22 m, 6.90 × 2.36 × 2.92 m, 8800 kg. Tyres 12.00–24. Model 368-Var. 18 10,170-cc engine. Speed 50 km/h. Produced 1950–53. Superseded Dovunque 41 (1943–48). Also wrecker and other derivatives.

Truck, 10-ton, 6 × 4, Cargo (Fiat/Spa A10000) 6-cyl. diesel, 108 bhp, 5F1R × 2, wb 4.85 (BC 1.36) m, 8.67 × 2.46 × 3.29 (cab 2.63) m, 8000 kg. Tyres 12.75–20. Model 366 9365-cc engine, 1945–47. 1948 model had 113-bhp engine, weighed 8100 kg and measured 8.84 × 2.50 m. Derived from Fiat 666N7.

Truck, 6-ton, 6 × 6, Cargo, CP62 (Fiat 6607) 6-cyl., 160–165 bhp, 5F1R × 2, wb 4.20 (BC 1.25) m, 7.82 × 2.40 × 2.70 (cab) (2.10) m, 8560 kg. Tyres 11.00–20. Used as cargo and missile carrier. Model 219B 7977-cc engine. Windscreen folded over against cab front panel. D/S body, 5.55 × 2.27 m.

Truck, 10-ton, 6 × 6, Bridging, CP56 (Fiat/OM 6600) 6-cyl., 196 bhp, 4F1R × 2 × 2, wb 5.46 (BC 1.42) m, 9.55 × 2.92 × 2.93 m, 12,775 kg. Tyres 14.00–20. Fiat 203B 10,676-cc engine (220 SAE-bhp). Built by OM from 1956 as *Autocarro da ponte* for NATO. Patterned on US Army 5-ton 6 × 6 bridge truck.

MISCELLANEOUS VEHICLES

Two wartime artillery tractors remained in production for a few years, namely the Fiat/Spa TL37 (light, 4 × 4, 1937–48) and TM40 (medium, 4 × 4, 1941–48). The latter was superseded by the TM48. Heavier types were the 6 × 6 Dovunque 50 and TP50, and the later TL65, TM65 and TM69. US high-speed full-track tractors were used for towing heavy artillery. AFVs were mainly of American origin, produced during and after the war and included the White scout car, M3A1, Ford armoured car, M8, various armoured half-tracks, light tanks, M5 and M41, medium tanks, M4, M26 and M47, and a variety of SP guns and howitzers. The American M113 (APC), M109 (SP) and M60A1 (tank) were produced under licence. The British Universal Carrier and the French AMX-VTT APC were also used. In 1970 Fiat developed a 4 × 4 armoured vehicle.

Tractor, Artillery, Medium, 4 × 4, TM48 (Fiat) 6-cyl. diesel, 110 bhp, 5F1R, wb 2.60 m, 4.83 × 2.10 × 2.62 m, 6500 kg. Tyres 12.00–24. 10,170-cc engine. IFS/IRS. Basically similar to TM40 but modified wings, larger amn. storage space, etc. 1948–52.

Tractor, Artillery, Heavy, 6 × 6 (Fiat Dovunque 50) 6-cyl. diesel, 110 bhp, 5F1R × 2, wb 3.90 m, 6.99 × 2.39 × 2.79 m, GVW 14,200 kg. Engine and tyres as TM48. Payload 4290 kg and 11 men. Speed 50 km/h. Derived from Dov. 50 truck. 2-speed gear set between clutch and gearbox. 1950–53.

Tractor, Artillery, Heavy, 6 × 6, TP50 (Fiat) 6-cyl. diesel, 140 bhp, 5R1R × 2, wb 3.90 m, 6.92 × 2.39 × 2.79 m. GVW 14,200 kg. Payload 4230 kg and 11 men. Air-assisted hyd. brakes. 24-volt electrics. Improved and more powerful version of Dovunque 50. Produced 1953–54.

Tractor, Artillery, Light, 6×6, TL65 (Fiat 6606) 6-cyl., 165 bhp, 5F1R × 2, wb 3.00 m, 6.02 × 2.40 × 2.86 (2.15) m, 7270 kg. Tyres 11.00–20 (12.00–20 optional). 5-ton winch at rear. Tractor for light artillery, introduced 1965. Crew 1 + 6. Payload 3240 kg. NATO class 3-ton.

Tractor, Artillery, Medium, 6×6, TM65 (Fiat/OM 6605) 6-cyl., 206 bhp, 4F1R × 2 × 2, wb 3.90 m, 7.31 × 2.50 × 2.89 m, 11,800 kg. Fiat 203B 10,676-cc engine. Speed 79 km/h. Crew 1 + 12. 10-ton winch. Tyres 14.00–20. NATO class 6-ton. 1965. TM69 (1969) had 216-bhp diesel engine.

Truck, 5-ton, 4×4, Hyd. Platform (Lancia 506.12) 6-cyl., 195 bhp, 4F1R × 2, wb 3.70 m, GVW 10,500 kg. Special chassis with up-rated engine, 14.00–20 tyres, different gear ratios and PAS, used for emergency (fire, rescue, etc.) vehicles. Shown: Air Force *Veicoli di soccorso per interventi di emergenza.*

Truck, 5-ton, 4×4, Fire Crash (Lancia 506.12/Bergomi) 6-cyl., 195 bhp, 4F1R × 2. Foam crash unit with 3000-litre water and 45-litre foam liquid tanks, 130-bhp pump engine (BPM Arctic), long-range foam monitor and other fire-fighting equipment. NSW 13,900 kg.

JAPAN

After large-scale destruction of the Japanese industry during the latter stages of World War II, reconstruction was soon commenced and progress was rapid. The automotive industry had suffered relatively minor damage from the war and the resumption of truck production was ordered by the occupation authorities during 1945, using materials then available. Such trucks were known as 'lost war models'. The initial ban on production of passenger cars was lifted in 1949 and their manufacture commenced during the same year. Thus, production was resumed by almost all the former motor vehicle manufacturers, supplemented by a few newcomers. The giant Mitsubishi concern, a Krupp-like banking, commercial and industrial group which had produced a large proportion of Japan's AFVs, Zero fighters and the battleships which nearly won the Battle of Midway, was dissolved by the MacArthur military government soon after VJ-Day and was reorganised in a number of smaller companies. Its motor vehicle production activities were part of a new company, then called Mitsubishi Nippon Heavy Industries, Reorganised, Ltd. The dramatic subsequent development of Japan's automotive industry compared with that before and during the War was due largely to the liberation of national trade and industry from the long-time government control which had war production as its main aim. By 1970, Japan had 14 thriving motor vehicle manufacturers; three of these only built trucks, two only two-wheelers, the other nine produced cars, trucks, buses and special vehicles. To give some idea of the production growth since 1945, here are some statistics of output in units:

A very large proportion of these were exported to many countries.

After VJ-Day in August 1945, Japan was prohibited from maintaining armed forces under her new constitution as a defeated nation. In 1950, however, due to improving relations with the USA, a National Police Reserve was created. About this time production of US-pattern all-wheel drive (4×4 and 6×6) vehicles was commenced on a small scale. Since 1954 there have been three carefully named 'Defence Forces'. These forces (Ground, Maritime, and Air) were controlled by a joint Staff Council under the Director General of the Japanese Self-Defence Agency, who is a cabinet minister. Their equipment was largely of American manufacture, supplied under the Japan-USA mutual defence assistance pact of 1954. For trucks, however, most of the Japanese military equipment is now of Japanese manufacture. Production of 4×4 and 6×6 trucks (incl. commercial types) rose from 8,565 in 1957 to 42,473 in 1969. Several Japanese AFV types have been in production from about 1960.

Who's Who in the Japanese Automotive Industry

(Head office locations of Military Vehicle Manufacturers)

Hino	Hino Motors, Ltd, Hino-shi, Tokyo.
Isuzu	Isuzu Motors Ltd, Shinagawa-ku, Tokyo.
Mitsubishi, Fuso	Mitsubishi Motors Corp., Minato-ku, Tokyo.
Nissan/Minsei*	Nissan Diesel Motor Co. Ltd, Kawaguchi-ken, Saitama-ken.
Nissan/Datsun†	Nissan Motor Co., Ltd, Chuo-ku, Tokyo.
Toyota	Toyota Motor Co., Ltd, Toyoda-shi, Aichi-ken.

*Minsei Diesel Industries Ltd until 1960.
†Datsun name used for certain models.

	Cars	Trucks	Buses
1945	—	1461	—
1950	1594	26,501	3502
1955	20,268	43,857	4807
1960	165,094	308,020	8437
1965	696,176	1,160,090	19,348
1970	3,178,708	2,063,883	46,566

JAPAN 246

TRUCKS, ¼-TON
4 × 4

Makes and Models: Mitsubishi 'Jeep' CJ3B-J3 (LHD), -J3 and -J3R (RHD), CJ3B-JC3 and -J55 (LHD), -J3RD and -J54 (RHD) (Diesel), CJ3B-J4 (12-V) (LHD), CJ3B-J4C (24-V) (LHD), CJ3B-J10 (Petrol and Diesel), J20 and J24 (RHD), J21 and J25 (LHD), J20D (RHD), J21D (LHD) (Diesel), J32 (RHD), J32D (RHD, Diesel), etc. Nissan 'Patrol' 4W60 (RHD), 4W66 (RHD or LHD), 60 and K60 (RHD), L60 and KL60 (LHD), G60 (RHD), LG60 (LHD), etc. Toyota BJ (RHD), 'Land Cruiser' FJ25 (RHD or LHD), FJ25L (LHD), 'Land Cruiser' FJ40 (RHD), FJ40L (LHD), 'Land Cruiser' FJ43 (RHD), FJ43L (LHD), etc.

General Data: The above list includes Japanese built ¼-ton 4 × 4 vehicles, available for commercial and military purposes. All three manufacturers also offer a wide range of variants based on the same chassis or long-wheelbase versions. These include station wagons, pickup trucks, ambulances, fire fighters, etc. Only the basic soft-top versions are listed. A few 4 × 2 field cars have also been produced, e.g. the Daiyo JLC/ORDX of 1948, and the Isuzu 'Unicab' KR80 and KR85 which were introduced in 1967. The first ¼-ton 4 × 4 trucks of Nissan and Toyota were clearly patterned on the American war-time 'Jeep' but both had a six-cylinder truck engine with four-speed gearbox and single-speed transfer case. When these two vehicles were restyled in the late 1950s they still had this transmission system but from the early 1960s they featured the more usual 3F1R × 2 configuration. The Toyota 'Land Cruiser' is also used for military purposes (Middle East, South America, Australia), and in Brazil it is produced under licence. In 1953 Mitsubishi entered into a licence agreement with Willys (later Kaiser Jeep) for the local manufacture of the Model CJ3B 'Jeep' and large numbers of the military version have since been produced for the armed forces of Japan, the USA (for use in the Far East) and several other countries, incl. South Vietnam and South Korea. Mitsubishi also offers a wide range of derivations, incl. diesel-engined models. In 1971 Suzuki introduced a little 4 × 4 field car, designated Model LJ10 (2-cyl., 27 bhp, 8F1R, wb 1.93 m, 586 kg).

Vehicle shown (typical): Truck, ¼-ton, 4 × 4, Utility (Mitsubishi/Willys 'Jeep' CJ3B-J4 and -J4C)

Technical Data:
Engine: Mitsubishi JM63148 4-cylinder, I-F-W-F, 2199 cc, 70 bhp @ 4000 rpm.
Transmission: 3F1R × 2.
Brakes: hydraulic.
Tyres: 6.00–16.
Wheelbase: 2.03 m.
Overall l × w × h: 3.35 × 1.45 × 1.85 (1.40) m.
Weight: 1240 kg (CJ3-J4C: 1230 kg).
Note: Produced under Willys/Kaiser Jeep licence. CJ3B-J4C differed from CJ3B-J4 mainly in having 24- instead of 12-volt electrical equipment. Also special version with recoilless rifle, and ambulance conversion kit.

Truck, ¼-ton, 4 × 4 (Mitsubishi 'Jeep' CJ3B-J3R) 4-cyl., 76 bhp, 3F1R × 2, wb 2.03 m, 3.39 × 1.46 × 1.89 (1.45) m, 1080 kg. JH4 'Hurricane' F-head engine (or Mitsubishi KE-31 2199-cc 61-bhp diesel (CJ3B-J3RD)). CJ3B-J10 had longer rear overhang. Dashboard/instrument panel differed from US CJ3B.

Truck, ¼-ton, 4 × 4 (Mitsubishi 'Jeep' J20) 4-cyl., 76 bhp, 3F1R × 2, wb 2.22 m, 3.68 × 1.67 × 1.94 m, 1285 kg. Differed from CJ3B-J3R in having longer wb, different front wings, windscreen, and bodywork with doors. Diesel engine optional (J20D). RHD models had steering column gear shift.

Truck, ¼-ton, 4 × 4 (Toyota BJ) 6-cyl., 82–85 bhp, 4F1R × 1, wb 2.40 m, 3.79 × 1.57 × 1.90 m, 1645 kg. Tyres 6.00–16. 3386-cc (84.1 × 101.6 mm) OHV engine, not unlike US Chevrolet. Steel half-doors optional. Also fire-fighter version. Introduced early 1950s, mainly for police use.

Truck, ¼-ton, 4 × 4 (Nissan 'Patrol' 4W60) 6-cyl., 85 bhp, 4F1R × 1, wb 2.20 m, 3.69 × 1.70 × 1.90 m, 1570 kg. Nissan NB 3670-cc (82.5 × 114.3 mm) L-head engine. Patterned on US 'Jeep'. Max. speed 106 km/h. Tyres 6.00–16. GVW 1790 kg. RHD. Available also as chassis/cowl. 1952.

Truck, ¼-ton, 4 × 4 (Nissan 'Patrol' 4W66) 6-cyl., 125 bhp, 4F1R × 1, wb 2.21 m, 3.54 × 1.70 × 1.94 m, 1550 kg. Six seats. 3956-cc OHV engine. Speed 117 km/h. Tyres 6.50–16. Outward opening rear doors. 1959/60. Preceding model (1958) had front wings like earlier 'Patrol' 4W60.

Truck, ¼-ton, 4 × 4 (Nissan 'Patrol' 60) 6-cyl., 125 (later 145) bhp, 3F1R × 2, wb 2.20 m, 3.83 × 1.70 × 1.97 m, 1540 kg. 3956-cc (85.7 × 114.3 mm) OHV engine. Speed 120 km/h. Tyres 6.50–16. RHD or LHD. G60 had 2.50-m wb. Also sold as Datsun. Several body styles, incl. Station Wagon, from 1961.

Truck, ¼-ton, 4 × 4 (Toyota 'Land Cruiser' FJ25 (L)) 6-cyl., 105 bhp, 4F1R × 1, wb 2.28 m, 3.84 × 1.66 × 1.85 m, 1450 kg. Toyota F 3878-cc (90 × 101.6 mm) OHV engine. Four or six seats. Outward opening double rear doors. Spare wheel on RH side. Canvas or steel doors and RHD optional. 1958.

Truck, ¼-ton, 4 × 4 (Toyota 'Land Cruiser' FJ40) 6-cyl., 125 bhp, 3F1R × 2, wb 2.28 m, 3.87 × 1.66 × 1.95 m, 1480 kg. Engine as FJ25 but higher output (SAE: 135 bhp). Also with steel doors or hard-top. Several other body options on LWB (2.43- and 2.65-m) chassis. Choice of 7.10 or 7.60–15 tyres. 1965.

TRUCKS, ¾- to 5½-TON
4 × 2 and 4 × 4

Makes and Models: Hino HB10, 11, 12, 13 (4- to 5-ton, 4 × 4, 1953), WB300 (4½-ton, 4 × 4, 1968), HC10 (6-ton tractor, 4 × 2, 1960), WA100 (8-ton, 4 × 4, 1968), TH13, TH15K (8000-litre tankers, 4 × 2, 1959), HA10.20 (16½-ton trailer truck), BK11 and RB (underfloor engine buses, 4 × 2), etc. Isuzu TS (5½-ton, 4 × 4, 1951), TS 540 (2½- to 5-ton, 4 × 4, 1959), TSD 40 (5½-ton, 4 × 4, 1963), etc. Mitsubishi 2W400 (Universal Tractor, 4 × 4, 1967). Nissan 'Carrier' 4W73, D4W73(U), etc. (¾-ton, 4 × 4, from 1959), 180 (2½-ton, 4 × 2, 1946), etc. Toyota FQ10 (¾-ton, 4 × 4, 1959), FQ15L (¾-ton, 4 × 4, 1963), 2FQ15L (¾-ton, 4 × 4, 1964), etc.

General Data: In addition to the above models the Japanese industry has produced several types of medium and heavy 4 × 4 trucks exclusively for commercial purposes. The 'Weapons Carrier' type trucks (Nissan and Toyota) were originally patterned on the wartime American Dodge T214 ¾-ton 4 × 4 Model WC52 for use by the Japanese armed forces. Later these trucks were further developed and used by the military forces of several other countries including those of South Korea and South Vietnam. The US Army in the Far East used many Toyota ¾-tonners, supplementing their own Dodge M37 trucks and ambulances. In South Vietnam the Toyota also appeared with armour shields along the bodysides and some were fitted with a pedestal-mounted machine gun in the rear body. The Nissan 'Carrier' was built under licence in India by the Ordnance Factory at Jabalpur.

The Hino HB 4–5-ton 4 × 4 tractor-truck was similar in design to the corresponding American wartime models produced by Autocar, White and Federal and was used to haul various types of 10-ton cargo and van-type semi-trailers. The Mitsubishi 2W400 was much like the SWB Daimler-Benz 'Unimog'. In 1967 an amphibious ambulance was produced on a 4 × 4 truck chassis for use by the Yokohama Municipal Fire Board. It had a cruising speed of five knots in water, 44 mph on land.

Vehicle shown (typical): Truck, ¾-ton, 4 × 4, Cargo (Toyota 2FQ15L)

Technical Data:

Engine: Toyota F 6-cylinder, I-I-W-F, 3878 cc, 105 bhp @ 3200 rpm.

Transmission: 4F1R × 1.

Brakes: hydraulic.

Tyres: 7.50–20.

Wheelbase: 3.00 m.

Overall l × w × h: 5.08 × 2.02 × 2.32 m.

Weight: 2800 kg. GVW on/off road: 3867/3640 kg.

Note: Same power unit as used in Toyota 'Land Cruiser' (¼-ton, 4 × 4). Speed 82 km/h. Used by several military forces, incl. US Army. Also with Ambulance Conversion Kit. FQ15L similar in appearance.

Truck, ¾-ton, 4×4, Cargo, w/Winch (Toyota 'Weapon Carrier' FQ10, FQ15) 6-cyl., 125 bhp, 4F1R×1, wb 3.00 m, 5.10×2.06×2.32 m, 2810 kg. Max. speed 85 km/h. Patterned on WWII Dodge Weapons Carrier but fitted with conventional wheels with 7.50–20 tyres. Right-hand drive.

Truck, ¾-ton, 4×4, Ambulance (Toyota 2FQ15L) 6-cyl., 105 bhp, 4F1R×1, wb 3.00 m, 5.09×2.02×2.32 m, 3280 kg. Steel-panelled ambulance body with accommodation for five patients plus attendant. Used by armed forces of USA, South Korea (shown), etc.

Truck, ¾-ton, 4×4, Cargo, w/Winch (Nissan 'Carrier') 6-cyl., 85 bhp, 4F1R×1. Early model (mid-1950s), like Toyota FQ10 patterned on US Dodge ¾-ton 4×4 Weapons Carrier. Powered by same side-valve (L-head) engine as early Nissan 'Patrol' ¼-ton 4×4. Used by Japanese Self-Defence Forces.

Truck, ¾-ton, 4×4, Cargo (Nissan 'Carrier' D4W73) 6-cyl., 125 (later 145) bhp, 4F1R×2, wb 2.80 m, 4.73×2.04×2.35 m. 2730 kg. Max. payload 1½ ton. Tyres 7.50–20. Speed 94 km/h. 3956-cc (85.7×114.3 mm) OHV engine. Also with integral ambulance bodywork and as fire fighter.

Truck, 2½-ton, 4 × 2, Cargo (Nissan 180, 380) 6-cyl., 85 bhp, 4F1R, wb 4.00 m, 6.85 × 2.18 × 2.21 m, 2970 kg. Post-war version of wartime Nissan 180 ('lost war model'). Model 380 had same cab but restyled front end, built-in headlights. 3670-cc SV engine. Used by Japanese Self-Defence Forces. Speed 78 km/h.

Truck, 2½-ton, 4 × 4, Cargo, w/Winch (Isuzu TS540) 6-cyl. diesel, 125 bhp, 4F1R × 2, wb 4.00 m, 7.06 × 2.34 × 2.46 m, 5155 kg. Max. payload on/off road 5/2½ tons. Speed 80 km/h. Tyres 8.25–20. 4-ton winch. Two-axle version of 6 × 6 model TW540. Model DA120 6126-cc engine.

Truck, 4½-ton, 4 × 4, Cargo, w/Winch (Hino WB300) 6-cyl. diesel (Hino DM100), 90 bhp, 5F1R × 2, wb 2.65 m, 5.27 × 2.08 × 2.51 m, 3330 kg. GVW on/off road 7800/6800 kg. 4-ton winch. Tyres 7.50–20. 4313-cc engine. Developed from 4 × 2 Model KM. Model WA was 8-ton 4 × 4 version of 4 × 2 TE.

Truck, 4–5-ton, 4 × 4, Tractor (Hino HB10) 6-cyl. diesel (Hino DS11), 110 bhp. Patterned on US WWII 4–5-ton 4 × 4 tractor. Similar models: HB11 with DS12 125-bhp engine, and HB12 and 13 with DS30 150-bhp engine. Production period of DS11 (7.01-litre) engine: 1950–55, DS12 (7.01-litre) and DS30 (7.69-litre): 1955–60.

TRUCKS, 2½-TON
6×6

Makes and Models: Isuzu TW (1953), TW340 (1957), TW540 (1959), TWD20 (1963), TWD20-D (1963), etc. Toyota FQS (1955), FW (1958), DW10 (1959), FW10 (1959), DW15L (1964), 2DW15 (1964), 2DW15L (1965), DW15L-W (1964), 2DW15L-W (1965), 2DW15L-D (1965), etc.

General Data: In 1953 the Isuzu Motor Co. Ltd of Tokyo announced Japan's first post-war 6×6 truck, the TW. Except for the (diesel) engine this was virtually a copy of the American wartime GMC 2½-ton 6×6. In 1957 the Isuzu TW passed rigid tests at the US Army Aberdeen Proving Ground, resulting in the subsequent acquisition of large quantities of these trucks for the Japanese Self-Defence Forces. In June 1957, a contract was signed with the US Army Procurement Agency, Japan, for the supply of 3678 model TW340 2½-ton 6×6 trucks from Isuzu under the Japan-USA Military Assistance Vehicle Exchange Program. About 1955 Toyota introduced a 2½-ton 6×6 model, also diesel-engined, and from the early 1960s relatively large quantities of these were obtained by the US forces for use in Japan and other Far East countries. They were also supplied to South Korea, South Vietnam, the Philippines and other overseas territories. The US Army used the Toyota models DW15L and 2DW15L series chassis with various types of bodywork, namely: DW15L and 2DW15L (w/o winch): cargo, 700-gal. water tank, shop van, and fire-fighting (pumper); 2DW15LD: dump; DW15L-W and 2DW15L-W (w/winch): cargo, repair shop and telephone construction. All these featured left-hand drive.

The South Vietnamese Army used the Toyota with cargo, dump, compressor and other types of bodywork, including a light wrecker conversion of the former. Pedestal-mounted AA machine guns were also fitted on South Vietnamese Toyota cargo trucks. The Japanese forces used the Isuzu range on a large scale, also with a variety of body types. Both Isuzu and Toyota models were commercially available with soft-top or closed cab.

Vehicle shown (typical): Truck, 2½-ton, 6×6, Cargo, w/Winch (Toyota 2DW15L-W)

Technical Data:
Engine: Toyota Diesel 6-cylinder, I-I-W-F, 5890 cc, 105 bhp @ 2600 rpm.
Transmission: 4F1R×2.
Brakes: hydraulic, vacuum-assisted.
Tyres: 7.50–20.
Wheelbase: 4.00 m. BC 1.12 m.
Overall l×w×h: 6.85×2.26×2.79 m.
Weight: 5235 kg (w/o Winch 5070 kg).
Note: Model 2DW15L had no winch. 'L' denoted LHD. Model DW15L differed in minor details (front towing hooks instead of shackles, smaller fuel tank capacity: 114 vs 144 litres, etc.) and was approx. 150 kg lighter.

Truck, 2½-ton, 6×6, Cargo (Toyota FQS, FW) 6-cyl. diesel, 110 bhp, 4F1R×2, wb 4.00 (BC 1.12) m, approx. 4980 kg. Tyres 7.50–20. RHD. Toyota's first 6×6 tactical truck, patterned on the American GMC CCKW-353. Payload on roads 5 tons. 1956.

Truck, 2½-ton, 6×6, Air Compressor (Toyota 2DW15L) 6-cyl. diesel, 105 bhp, 4F1R×2, wb 4.00 (BC 1.12) m. American LeRoi air compressor unit. Used by South Vietnamese Army Engineers as power supply unit for pneumatic tools. South Vietnamese also used other variants (cargo, dump, etc.).

Truck, 2½-ton, 6×6, Cargo, w/Winch (Isuzu TW) 6-cyl. diesel, 120 bhp, 4F1R×2, wb 4.00 (BC 1.16) m, 7.10×2.35×2.50 m approx. Similar to US 2½-ton 6×6. Used by Japanese Self-Defence Forces. US Army in Japan obtained similar trucks with different cabs, in 1957 (TW340).

Truck, 2½-ton, 6×6, Shop Van (Isuzu TW) 6-cyl. diesel, 120 bhp, 4F1R×2, wb 4.00 (BC 1.16) m. Similar chassis as cargo truck shown on left but closed cab and American type shop van body (as on GMC CCKW-353). Used for a variety of Ordnance repair and maintenance purposes. No winch.

Truck, 2½-ton, 6 × 6, Cargo (Isuzu TWD20) 6-cyl. diesel, 125 bhp, 4F1R × 2, wb 4.00 (BC 1.16) m, 7.29 × 2.36 × 2.44 m, 5525 kg. Isuzu DA120 6126-cc engine. Tyres 7.50–20. Max. payload 6 tons. Hydrovac brakes. Split-type axles. Commercially available as 6 × 6 and 4 × 4 (TSD40).

Truck, 2½-ton, 6 × 6, Cargo (Isuzu TW540/TWD20) 6-cyl. diesel, 125 bhp, 4F1R × 2, wb 4.00 (BC 1.16) m, 7.06 × 2.34 × 2.44 m, 5565 kg. Tyres 7.50–20 (4DT; also supplied with 8.25–20, single rear). 4-ton front-mounted winch optional. Used by Japanese Army (RHD).

Truck, 2½-ton, 6 × 6, Dump, w/Winch (Isuzu TWD20 SWB) 6-cyl. diesel, 125 bhp, 4F1R × 2. Short-wheelbase chassis with hyd.-actuated rear dump body. Japanese Army also had longer wb chassis with special long body (used by missile units). All resembled corresponding US Army models very closely.

Truck, 2½-ton, 6 × 6, Air Compressor (Isuzu TWD20) 6-cyl. diesel, 125 bhp, 4F1R × 2, wb 4.00 (BC 1.16) m, 7.30 × 2.35 m. Special body with self-contained diesel engine driving air compressor unit for Army Engineers. Reels at rear (both sides) for high-pressure air hose.

TRUCKS, 4- to 11-TON
6 × 6

Makes and Models: Hino 'ZC' Series, 4-ton, 6 × 6: ZC35, ZC46 (Cargo and Prime Mover), ZC35, ZC36 (Water Sprinkler), ZC35B (Wrecker), ZC36 (Coaltar Sprinkler), ZC37A (Dump), ZC46C, ZC47C (Hyd. Wrecker), ZC47D (Snow Plough). Mitsubishi Fuso 'W' and '6W' Series, 6-ton, 6 × 6: W11 and 6W100R (Tractor), W11 and 6W100W (Wrecker), W21 and 6W210R (Tractor), W22 and 6W202W (Wrecker), W22A and 6W202WH (Hyd. Wrecker), W23 and 6W203G (Cargo and Prime Mover), W24 and 6W204Y (Bridge Erection, Treadway), W24A and 6W205B (Bridge Equipment/Cargo). Mitsubishi 6W120 (10-ton, 6 × 6, Cargo, LWB), 6W150L (11-ton, 6 × 6, Cargo), etc.

General Data: Hino and Mitsubishi are the producers of heavy duty 6 × 6 trucks for the Japanese armed forces. Most of the military vehicles they designed were patterned on corresponding American models in the 5-ton (post-war) and 6-ton (WWII) classes. The basic chassis and in some cases the bodywork were also available to commercial operators. Early types produced for the Japanese armed forces usually had the American WWII style cab with canvas doors. Later production had the post-war American military pattern cabs with 'half doors' and crank-down windows. The Mitsubishi Fuso 'W' Series was superseded by the improved '6W' series in 1963/64. The latter had a restyled front end with flat-top wings, built-in headlights and other detail modifications. Mitsubishi also produced an ultra heavy 6 × 4 tractive unit, Model 4W220R, for hauling towed loads of up to 300 tons. Its maximum fifth wheel load capacity was 40 tons and its cab and front end were the same as that of the '6W' series. Hino Motors produced their first 6 × 6 'Ordnance trucks' in 1951. Some special equipment and special purpose 6 × 6 vehicles are shown in the section 'Miscellaneous Vehicles'.

Vehicle shown (typical): Truck, 4-ton, 6 × 6, Cargo and Prime Mover, w/Winch (Hino ZC 35)

Technical Data:

Engine: Hino DS12 diesel 6-cylinder, I-I-W-F, 7010 cc, 125 bhp @ 2400 rpm.

Transmission: 5F1R × 2 (OD top).

Brakes: air.

Tyres: 9.00–20.

Wheelbase: 4.37 m.

Overall l × w × h: (chassis w/o cab) 7.52 × 2.43 × 2.06 m.

Weight: (chassis w/o cab) 6400 kg. GVW 18,970 kg.

Note: Model ZC 46 had Hino DS30 7690-cc 150-bhp diesel engine. Early models had headlights on sides of radiator shell.

Truck, 4-ton, 6 × 6, Dump, w/Winch (Hino ZC37A) 6-cyl. diesel, 150 bhp, 5F1R × 2, wb 3.90 m. Chassis w/o cab: 7.52 × 2.43 × 2.06 m, 6400 kg. Hino DS30 7.69-litre (110 × 135 mm) engine. Produced 1955–1960. All-steel rear dump body, hydraulically actuated.

Truck, 4-ton, 6 × 6, Wrecker, w/Winch (Hino ZC46C and ZC47C) 6-cyl. diesel, 150 bhp, 5F1R × 2, wb 4.37 m. Austin-Western type revolving hydraulic telescopic crane, similar to that of US 5-ton 6 × 6 medium wrecker, M62. Soft-top cab. ZC35B wrecker had 125-bhp diesel engine (Hino DS12).

Truck, 4-ton, 6 × 6, Rocket Launcher (Hino ZC) 6-cyl. diesel, 150 bhp, 5F1R × 2, wb 4.37 m. RKT-30 rocket launcher (rocket length 4.50 m, diameter 30 cm, range 30 km). Introduced in 1957. Superstructure similar (but not identical) to US Army 'Honest John' launcher, M386.

Truck, 4-ton, 6 × 6, Rocket Transporter (Hino ZC) 6-cyl. diesel, 150 bhp, 5F1R × 2, wb 4.37 m. Carried rockets for RKT-30 launcher. Hydraulic jib crane behind cab for loading and unloading. Hino ZC series was only produced with RHD and was available commercially, with closed cab.

Truck, 4-ton, 6 × 6, Water Sprinkler, w/Winch (Hino ZC35 and ZC36) 6-cyl. diesel, 125 bhp, 5F1R × 2. Hino DS12 7.01-litre (105 × 135 mm) engine. Model ZC36 similar but 150-bhp DS30 7.69-litre engine (bore 5 mm larger). Both engines were in production during 1955–60. ZC36 chassis also used with tar sprinkler body.

Truck, 6-ton, 6 × 6, Wrecker (Mitsubishi Fuso W11) 6-cyl. diesel, 160 bhp, 4F1R × 2, wb 4.00 m, 8.47 × 2.42 × 3.02 m, 10,100 kg. Tyres 9.00–20. Swinging boom crane (as on US Army heavy wreckers, M1, M1A1) produced for Japanese Army about 1960. Also with closed cab and different wings (commercial).

Truck, 6-ton, 6 × 6, Cargo and Prime Mover (Mitsubishi Fuso W23) 6-cyl. diesel, 160 bhp, 5F1R × 2, wb 4.00 m, 7.42 × 2.43 × 3.00 m, 15,610 kg. Tyres 9.00–20. Resembled US Army wartime 6-ton 6 × 6 trucks as produced by Corbitt, White, etc. Winch with capstan pulley behind cab. RHD. Early 1960s.

Truck, 6-ton, 6 × 6, Tractor (Mitsubishi Fuso W21) 6-cyl. diesel, 160 bhp, 5F1R × 2, wb 4.00 m, 7.35 × 2.40 × 2.80 m approx., 9500 kg. Used by Japanese Army Engineers for towing semi-trailers and full-trailers. Canvas-top cab with folding windscreen. Air brakes. Max. road speed 56 km/h.

Truck, 6-ton, 6 × 6, Wrecker (Mitsubishi Fuso W22) 6-cyl. diesel, 200 bhp, 5F1R × 2, wb 4.70 m, 9.90 × 2.48 × 3.45 m, 13,435 kg (fully equipped 16,395 kg). Swinging boom crane. Lifting capacity 7¼ tons. 6-ton front winch, 15-ton rear winch. Model W22A had hyd. crane. Closed cab optional. Tyres 11.00–20.

Truck, 6-ton, 6 × 6, Bridge Erection (Mitsubishi Fuso W24) 6-cyl. diesel, 200 bhp, 5F1R × 2, 9.52 × 2.40 × 2.90 m, 18,860 kg. Used by Engineers for Transporting Treadway bridging equipment. Resembled corresponding US Army wartime model. Hydraulically-actuated loading/unloading device.

Truck, 6-ton, 6 × 6, Tractor (Mitsubishi Fuso 6W210R) 6-cyl. diesel, 200 bhp, 5F1R × 2, wb 4.70 m, 7.08 × 2.50 × 2.80 m, 9900 kg. Introduced about 1964, superseding Model W21. Tyres 11.00–20. Model DH21W 13,741-cc engine. Max. load on 'fifth wheel' 14½ tons.

Truck, 6-ton, 6 × 6, Wrecker (Mitsubishi Fuso 6W202WH) 6-cyl. diesel, 200 bhp, 5F1R × 2, wb 4.70 m, 9.32 × 2.48 × 3.01 m, 16,275 kg. Hydraulic crane (mechanical type optional). Generally similar to Model W22A but late type front end styling. Road speed 73 km/h. Lifting capacity 7200 kg at 3-m radius.

MISCELLANEOUS VEHICLES

Many of Japan's military special equipment and special purpose vehicles are very similar in general design and appearance to corresponding US models. This was because the Japanese Self-Defence Forces were originally supplied with large quantities of war-surplus American equipment and the supplementary and replacement vehicles made by the Japanese industry closely followed the same pattern.

Among the US AFVs supplied to Japan were various types and variants of armoured half-tracks, light tanks (M24 'Chaffee'), medium tanks (M4 'Sherman' and variants), SP guns and howitzers, etc. During the 1950s several Japanese AFVs were developed, culminating in a 35-ton tank (STA-4, Type 61), a twin-106-mm SP gun (SS-4, Type 60) and an APC (SU, Type 60). The Japanese also used the US M25 'Dragon Wagon' tank retriever/transporter, the post-war FWD 6 × 6 truck-mounted crane, and other US specialist vehicles.

Truck, 4-ton, 6 × 6, Snow Plough (Hino ZC47D) 6-cyl. diesel, 150 bhp, 5F1R × 2 (OD top), wb 4.37 m. Basically dump truck. Plough blades lifted hydraulically (via chain at front, cable and sheave at side). Front blade, when lowered, supported on caster wheels.

Truck, 10-ton, 6 × 4, Refueller (Hino TC30) 6-cyl. diesel, 200 bhp, 5F1R, wb 5.10 m, 9.00 × 2.50 × 2.70 m approx. Twin-steer chassis with 2000-gallon tank. Other Hino tankers included TC10 6 × 4 and the TH13 and TH15K 4 × 2, all with 150-bhp DS30 7.69-litre engine (1955–60).

Truck, Fire, Crash, 6 × 6 (Mitsubishi W32L) Patterned on US Air Force fire crash trucks. Superseded by Model 6W300LF which was similar in appearance. Mitsubishi DH58 6-cyl. 14.78-litre (140 × 160 mm) diesel engine with Roots blower, 280 bhp at 2000 rpm. Twin turret-type foam nozzles.

Truck, Fire, Crash, 4×4 (Nissan Diesel MF61/Tokyu MB-5) 6-cyl. diesel, 230 bhp, 5F1R×2, wb 4.00 m, 7.20 × 2.50 × 3.50 m, NSW 10,000 kg. Rotary vane type pump. Turret nozzle capacity 1000 l/min. approx. Carried 1900 litres of water, 120 litres of foam liquid.

Truck, Fire, Crash, 4×4 (Nissan Diesel/Tokyu AMB-10) 6-cyl. diesel, 230 bhp, 5F1R×2, wb 4.00 m, 8.22 × 2.50 × 3.50 m, NSW 14,500 kg. Tyres 11.00–20. Water/foam liquid tanks cap. 3700/450 litres. Pump cap. 2800 l/min. UD6 7412-cc 2-stroke engine (as MB-5). Speed 95 km/h.

Truck, Fire, Crash, 6×6 (Nissan Diesel MF81/Tokyu MB-1) V-8-cyl. diesel, 320 bhp, 5F1R×2, wb 4.40 m, 9.85 × 2.50 × 3.50 m, NSW 19,700 kg. Separate engine for driving rotary vane type main pump. Twin 1000 l/min. turret nozzles with remote control from within cab. Crew 6. UDV8 2-stroke engine.

Truck, Fire, Crash, 6×6 (Nissan Diesel MF82/Tokyu A-MB-1) V-8-cyl. diesel (UDV8), 320 bhp, 5F1R×2, wb 4.40 m, 9.85 × 2.50 m, NSW 18,000 kg. Single engine. Flywheel-driven PTO. Twin 750 l/min. turret nozzles. Additional nozzles at front (3) and underneath (2). Carried 3600 litres of water, 360 litres of foam liquid.

Crane, Truck-Mounted (Chassis: 10-ton, 6 × 6) 6-cyl. diesel. Separate engine in crane turntable. Chassis fitted with outriggers for stability. Patterned on US wartime models. Used by Engineers for crane, shovel, clamshell, and other purposes. Mfrs. of mobile cranes: Hino, Mitsubishi, Nissan Diesel.

Tractor, Crawler, Bulldozer (Mitsubishi BE10) 6-cyl. diesel, 210 bhp, 3F3R (torque converter transmission), 6.48 × 4.14 × 2.75 m, 24,500 kg. 21,200-cc engine. Speed 12 km/h. Dozer blade: angling, hydraulically controlled for height, 1.15 m high. One of several types.

Carrier, Armoured, Personnel, Full-Track (SU, Type 60) Mitsubishi V-8-cyl. diesel, 240 bhp, 4.85 × 2.40 × 1.70 m, 12,000 kg. Air-cooled Model 8HA21WT supercharged 10.8 litre engine. Max. speed 45 km/h. First conceived in 1958. Chassis patterned on US Armoured Utility Vehicle, M39. Crew 2+8.

Carrier, Armoured, Mortar, Full-Track (SX, Type 60) Mitsubishi V-8-cyl. diesel, 240 bhp, 4.85 × 2.40 × 1.70 m. Basically similar to APC SU but 4.2-in (106-mm) trench mortar in rear compartment. Similar: SV, Type 60, with 81 mm mortar. Engine located centrally on left. RHD. All three entered service in 1960.

THE NETHERLANDS

The armed forces of the Netherlands re-equipped themselves after 1945 with a vast array of vehicles, most of which were war-surplus Canadian and British. Large quantities of American wartime vehicles were added, as well as small numbers of new civilian cars and trucks for administrative purposes. About 1948 the Dutch firm of DAF at Eindhoven embarked on the production of trucks and among the first was a military version of the Model A30. Soon afterwards DAF commenced design of a new family of high-mobility military tactical vehicles, starting with the famed YA 318 and YA 126 both of which featured an American Hercules petrol engine driving a centrally-mounted transfer-cum-differential unit with side extensions from the ends of which individual worm drive propeller shafts drove the front and rear wheels by means of worm drive gear casings at each wheel hub. The YA 318, a 6×6, was soon superseded by the more powerful YA 328, and shortly afterwards these two basic types were supplemented by a 3-ton 4×4 (YA 314) and a 6-ton 6×6 (YA 616) of conventional COE design with 'rigid' axles. There were several variants of each basic model and the military range was supplemented by military versions of DAF commercial types employed for various purposes. DAF, as well as some other manufacturers (Groenewegen, Holland Nautic, Jongerius, Pennock, etc.) also produced a large diversity of military trailers and semi-trailers. DAF military tactical vehicle model designations consist of a letter and number combination, the explanation of which is as follows: first letter: Y = military vehicle; second letter: A = truck, B = wrecker, C = crash/fire, F = fuel/oil tanker, K = dump (tipper, *kipper*), P = armoured (*pantser*), T = tractor. These letters are followed by a number, usually of three digits: first digit: payload class (in tons); second digit: development number or 'mark'; third digit: number of wheels (incl. spare wheels if these are mounted on hubs to act as support wheels). Thus a YB616 is a military tactical vehicle (Y), designed for use as a wrecker (B), in the 6-ton load class (6), of the first design (1), with six (6) wheels.

Quantity production of DAF tactical vehicles was largely made possible by the American 'Marshall Plan', from which funds 175 million guilders were made available for this purpose in 1950. Within the framework of NATO, DAF, in 1952, also received orders for 200 refuelling semi-trailers and 80 aircraft oil servicing vehicles for use by several other NATO forces, including the USAFE (US Air Force, Europe). American financial aid made the phenomenal growth of the DAF company possible, and by 1959 a total of 14,000 trucks had been produced for the Dutch Army alone. Trailers, semi-trailers and vehicles for the Dutch Air Force and Navy accounted for many thousands more. By the mid-1960s most of the medium and heavy wartime tactical wheeled vehicles had been phased out and been replaced by DAFs. In the $\frac{1}{4}$-ton class the wartime 'Jeep' was supplemented and later superseded by various types of post-war Willys and Kaiser Jeep models and the German Auto Union 'Munga' and VW 181.

Registration numbers: Wartime production vehicles retained their original numbers until the 1950s when the remaining ones were allocated new numbers as first introduced for new vehicles in about 1948. These consist of two letters, followed by four numerals (in two pairs), all in black on yellow plates. The letters indicate the using arm, as follows:

KL, KN to KZ: Army (KL = *Koninklijke Landmacht*)*
KM: Navy and Marines (*Koninklijke Marine* and *Korps Mariniers*)
LM: Air Force (*Koninklijke Luchtmacht*)†
MC: Corps of Mobile Columns (aux. emergency forces).

*incl. the *Koninklijke Marechaussee* (para-mil. police forces).
†LSK (*Lucht Strijdkrachten*) before becoming *Koninklijk* (Royal) in 1953.

Who's Who in the Dutch Automotive Industry
DAF   Van Doorne's Automobielfabriek NV, Eindhoven.
Verheul   NV Auto-Industrie Verheul, Waddinxveen*.

*now British Leyland (Nederland) NV, Gouda.

Note: in addition there is the NV Ned. Ford Automobielfabriek with an assembly plant near Amsterdam, and Willys Jeeps used to be assembled by NEKAF (Ned. Kaiser-Frazer-fabrieken NV) in Rotterdam and by Van Twist in Dordrecht.

CARS, FIELD CARS and MOTORCYCLES

Makes and Models: *Cars:* various types, of Austin, Chevrolet, Citroën, DAF, Dodge, Ford (D, F, GB, US), Mercedes-Benz, Mercury, Oldsmobile, Opel, Peugeot, Pontiac, Renault, Simca, Vauxhall, Volkswagen, etc.
WWII types: British Austin (10 HP LU), Ford (WOA2 HU), Hillman (10 HP LU) Humber (4×4 HU and 'Pullman').
Field Cars: Auto Union F91/4/1000 (3038) 'Munga' ($\frac{1}{4}$-ton, 4×4, 1963, D). DAF YA 054 ($\frac{1}{4}$-ton, 4×4, 1952). Land-Rover 80, 86, 88 ($\frac{1}{4}$-ton, 4×4, from 1952, GB). Volkswagen 181 ($\frac{1}{4}$-ton, 4×2, 1970). Willys CJ3A and CJ3B 'Jeep' ($\frac{1}{4}$-ton, 4×4, from 1951, US).
Willys/NEKAF MD 'Jeep' M38A1, M38C1 ($\frac{1}{4}$-ton, 4×4, from 1955, US/NL).
WWII types: Ford GPA, GPW and Willys MB ($\frac{1}{4}$-ton, 4×4, US).
Motorcycles: BMW R27 (250 cc), R60 (600 cc) (from 1961, D). BSA B30, M20 (1947–53, GB). Harley-Davidson 56/KH (1956, US). Matchless G3L (S) (1949–61, GB). Triumph 200 cc and 350 cc (from *c.* 1963, GB), etc.
WWII types: British BSA, Matchless and Norton; US Harley-Davidson (WLA) and Indian (741), etc.

General Data: DAF, the Netherlands' principal supplier of military vehicles, designed a $\frac{1}{4}$-ton 4×4 vehicle in 1951 but after producing prototypes this project was cancelled. From about 1951 new Willys CJ3A 'Universal Jeeps' were acquired and militarized and on 28 May 1955 the first Willys M38A1 came off the assembly line of the NEKAF plant in Rotterdam. About 5500 were produced and a relatively high content of Dutch material and components from 25 suppliers was incorporated. Subsequently Kemper & Van Twist Diesel NV in Dordrecht assembled about 2000 units. In addition to the standard model there were variants with MG, 106-mm recoilless rifle, wireless set, a 2-stretcher ambulance, etc. A Jeep-based snow-fighter was used by the Air Force. In 1963 the lighter Auto Union 'Munga' made its appearance. 800 were supplied. The British Land-Rover was acquired by the Dutch Navy and Marines. In 1970 the KMA (Royal Military Academy) in Breda developed an experimental DAF-engined 4×4 light vehicle with Variomatic automatic transmission.

Vehicle shown (typical): Truck, $\frac{1}{4}$-ton, 4×4, Utility, M38A1 (Willys/NEKAF MD)

Technical Data:
Engine: Willys 'Hurricane' 4-cylinder, I-F-W-F, 2199 cc, 72 bhp @ 4000 rpm.
Transmission: 3F1R $\times$ 2.
Brakes: hydraulic.
Tyres: 6.00–16.
Wheelbase: 2.06 m.
Overall l $\times$ w $\times$ h: 3.50 $\times$ 1.50 $\times$ 1.85 m.
Weight: 1210 kg. GVW: 1700 kg.
Notes: Differed from US M38A1 in minor details, incl. white reflectors on front wings, turn indicators adjacent to blackout/parking lights, etc. Several variants, incl. ambulance, recoilless rifle mount, etc. Assembly also by Kemper & Van Twist Diesel NV.

Truck, ¼-ton, 4×4 (Ford GPW, Willys MB) 4-cyl., 54 bhp, 3F1R × 2, wb 2.03 m, 3.40 × 1.58 × 1.84 m, 1200 kg approx. Basically wartime 'Jeep', reworked by Army workshops. 12 volt electrical equipment. Raised passenger seat, covering batteries, necessitated extension to windscreen top for increased headroom.

Truck, ¼-ton, 4×4 (DAF YA 054) Hercules JX4C 4-cyl., 60 bhp, 3F1R × 2, wb 2.20 m, 3.55 × 1.57 × 1.75 m. 3.1-litre engine. 'H-drive' (central diff.). Rear-wheel drive could be disengaged. Torsion-bar IFS, coil-spring IRS, both with trailing arms. Tyres 7.00–16. Two prototypes, 1951/52.

Truck, ¼-ton, 4×4 (Willys CJ3B) 4-cyl., 72 bhp, 3F1R × 2, wb 2.03 m. 'Universal Jeep' with ambulance conversion kit. Dutch Air Force. Army and Air Force also used CJ3A, in standard form as well as various airfield fire-fighting and rescue variants (converted by Kronenburg and Pennock resp.).

Motorcycle, Solo (Triumph 3TA Special) Twin-cyl., 18.5 bhp, 4F, wb 1.36 m, 2.11 × 0.68 × 0.96 m, 350 kg approx. Military version of civilian machine. 1100 supplied to the Dutch Army. 349-cc OHV engine. Rear suspension with Girling coil spring/hyd. damper units. Tyres 3.50–18, front and rear.

TRUCKS, ½- to 2-TON
4×2 and 4×4

Makes and Models: Austin K8MB 'Welfarer' (Ambulance, 4×2, 1950, GB). Chevrolet 3104 (½-ton, 4×2, 1952, US). DAF 750 (van, 4×2, 1963). DAF 'Pony' (½-ton, 4×4, 1963/64, exp. for US), A10, D400B (1-ton, and Ambulance, 4×2, from 1953), YA 126 (1-ton, and Ambulance, 4×4, 1952). Dodge 'Power-Wagon' (¾-ton, 4×4, c. 1948, US). Dodge M37 (¾-ton, 4×4, 1954, US). Ford 'Transit' (Ambulance, 4×2, c. 1956 and 1969, D), F1 (Van, 1-ton, 4×2, 1949, US), F2 (Mk I, II, III, 1-ton, 4×2, 1950–53, US/NL). Ford/Marmon-Herrington (1½-ton, 4×4, 1947/48, US). Fordson 'Thames' (1- and 2-ton, 4×2, 1950–53, GB). Hanomag ALO 28 (1½-ton, and Ambulance, 4×4, 1960, D). Hanomag 'Garant' (bus, 4×2, 1961, D). International C1300 (1-ton, 4×2 and 4×4, 1964, US). Mercedes-Benz 'Unimog' S (1½-ton, 4×4, c. 1965, D), O309 (bus, 4×2, 1969, D). Peugeot D4B (1.4-ton van/bus, 4×2, c. 1962, F). Renault R2095 (¾-ton, 4×2, 1954, F). Studebaker M16 (1½-ton, 1948, US). Tempo 'Matador' (1-ton, and Ambulance, 4×2, 1951–52, D). Volkswagen 'Transporter' (¾- to 1-ton, and Ambulance, 4×2, from 1951, D).
WWII types: British Albion AM463 (Ambulance, 4×2), Austin K2 (Ambulance, 4×2), Commer Q2 (¾-ton, 4×2), Fordson WOT2 (¾-ton, 4×2) and WOT8 (1½-ton, 4×4) and Standard 12HP (Ambulance, 4×2); Candian Chevrolet C8A (HUP, HUW, 4×4), C15 (¾-ton, 4×2) and C15A (¾-ton, 4×4), Dodge D15 (¾-ton, 4×2), Ford F15 (¾-ton, 4×2) and F15A (¾-ton, 4×4); US Chevrolet G7100 (1½-ton, 4×4), Dodge T214 (¾-ton, 4×4, incl. Ambulances), Ford GTB (1½-ton, 4×4), International M-2-4 (1-ton, 4×4), etc.

General Data: Before the standardization of the DAF YA 126 1-ton 4×4 the Dutch Army used a variety of ex-WWII tactical vehicles. In addition, standard or modified civilian vehicles have been used for administrative purposes. The Dutch Air Force during the early 1960s acquired a relatively large number of German Hanomag 4×4 chassis for use with cargo, fire fighter and ambulance bodywork. The Tempo 'Matador' was also used by the Air Force, with van, mini-bus and ambulance bodywork.

Vehicle shown (typical): Truck, 1-ton, 4×4, Cargo, w/o or w/Winch (DAF YA 126)

Technical Data:
Engine: Hercules JXC 6-cylinder, I-L-W-F, 4620 cc, 102 bhp @ 3200 rpm.
Transmission: 4F1R × 2.
Brakes: hydraulic, vacuum-assisted.
Tyres: 9.00–16.
Wheelbase: 2.83 m. Track: 1.70 m.
Overall l × w × h: 4.55 × 2.10 × 2.18 m.
Weight: 3400 kg.
Note: 'H-drive' transmission system. IFS/IRS with torsion bars and trailing arms. 2½-ton rear-mounted winch optional. 24-volt electrics. Speed 90 km/h. Gradability 65%.

Truck, 1-ton, 4 × 4, Cargo (DAF YA 126) Hercules JXC 6-cyl., 102 bhp, 4F1R × 2, wb 2.65 m, 4.38 × 2.00 × 2.15 m. One of the pilot models, 1951/52. Note unprotected spare wheels which also served as support wheels (preventing 'bellying'). Also with one-piece windscreen.

Truck, 1-ton, 4 × 4, Workshop (DAF YA 126) Hercules JXC 6-cyl., 102 bhp, 4F1R × 2, wb 2.83 m. Increased body height. Similar: Command Post and Radio versions. Road wheels driven individually from central transfer/diff. unit; front drive could be disengaged. 1959.

Truck, 1-ton, 4 × 4, Field Ambulance (DAF YA 126) Hercules JXC 6-cyl., 102 bhp, 4F1R × 2, wb 2.83 m, 5.00 × 2.10 m. Accommodation for four stretchers. Replaced WWII Dodge T214-WC54 and 64. Bodywork rather similar to Dodge WC64 (KD), with three rear doors, but not collapsible.

Truck, ½-ton, 4 × 4, Platform Carrier (DAF 'Pony') Twin-cyl., 500 cc, air-cooled, with auto. trans. (single-belt 'Vario-matic'). 3.05(2.54) × 1.27 × 1.28 (0.96) m. 7.50–10 tyres. Permanent 4 × 4. Developed 1962–64 for US Army. Pedestrian handling controls at rear. Magneto ignition, no other electrics (pull-type recoil starter).

Truck, 1-ton, 4×2, Cargo/Driving Instr. Mk I (Ford F2-7HA) 6-cyl., 95 bhp, 4F1R, wb 3.10 m, 5.23 × 1.85 × 1.90 m, 1912 kg. Commercial chassis, 1950. Body and 2-door crewcab by den Oudsten. Similar bodywork by Domburg, on 1951 chassis. 3710-cc L-head engine. Tyres 6.50–16. GVW 2600 kg.

Truck, 1-ton, 4×2, Cargo/Driving Instr., Mk III (Ford F2-H2-ANX) 6-cyl., 95 bhp, 4F1R, wb 3.10 m, 5.40 × 1.88 × 2.15 m, 1732 kg. 1952 chassis with soft-top four-door cab. Used mainly for driving instruction. Tyres 7.00 or 7.50–16. 150 delivered, 1953. Bodywork by Werkspoor of Utrecht.

Truck, ¾-ton, 4×2, Driving Instruction (Renault R2095) 4-cyl., 48 bhp, 4F1R, wb 2.66 m, 4.41 × 1.82 × 1.85 m, 1640 kg. Tyres 7.00–16. Military R2093 'Savane' with dual controls (brake and clutch). Model 668W 1997-cc (85 × 88 mm) OHV engine. Non-synchromesh gearbox. 200 supplied in 1954.

Truck, 1-ton, 4×4, Fire Fighting (International C1300) V-8-cyl., 180 bhp, 3F1R × 2, wb 3.28 m, GVW 4500 kg. Used by Air Force to combat fires resulting from aeroplane crashes. Capacity 600 kg of chemical (powder) per minute. American commercial chassis with four-door 'Travelette' cab.

TRUCKS, 3- to 8½-TON
4 × 2
and BUSES

Makes and Models: Bedford MLC, and OSS tractor (3-ton, 1949, GB). Citroën (bus, *c.* 1970, F). DAF commercial 3- to 8½-ton 4 × 2 trucks and tractors: 1949: A30; 1950: A40 and D40; 1952: D50 and A60; 1956: A1100 and A1300; 1963: A1600; 1964: T1502 and A2400; 1966: A2000; 1967: A2200 and T2200; 1969: FA1600; 1970: FT1600DF; etc. DAF commercial bus chassis: 1950: B50; 1952: B52; 1956: B1300; 1959: B1500DL; 1967: B1600; 1970: SB1600; etc. DAF YT1500L and YT1527/L32 (tractors, 5-ton, from 1954). Ford F798WM (bus, 32-pass., 1950, F/NL), F5 (3-ton, and bus, 32-pass., 1949, US/NL), F6 COE (tractor, 3-ton, and bus, 31-pass., 1950–53, US/NL). Fordson 'Thames' (3-ton, 1950, GB). International B152 (3-ton, 1960, US). Kromhout V6HF (6-ton, *c.* 1958). Magirus-Deutz (various types, from 3-ton, D). Seddon/van Twist (5-ton, GB/NL). Thornycroft TF 'Nippy' (3-ton, 1953, GB). Verheul V6HF (6-ton, 1959).
WVII types: British Bedford OXC and OYC (3-ton) and Commer Q4 (3-ton); Canadian Chevrolet, Dodge (D60L, L/D), and Ford (3-ton), etc.

General Data: Most Dutch military vehicles in this class were of DAF manufacture and usually military versions of commercial types. A few of these (YT 1500 Series) had military pattern soft-top cabs. The DAF A30 (one of DAF's first trucks) and the Ford F5 were used for transport of personnel and general cargo for many years and were superseded by other DAFs and the International B152 in the early 1960s. Several types of Magirus-Deutz trucks were supplied to the '*Korps Mobiele Colonnes*', an auxiliary emergency force equipped with fire/rescue and other equipment. The Seddon/van Twist had a large van-type body and was used by the CADI (canteen services). The Thornycroft TF and Ford 'Thames' were used by the Air Force with runway/road sweeping equipment but the latter also with various other body types. During the late 1940s the Dutch armed forces in the Netherlands East Indies (now Indonesia) used quantities of new commercial-type Chevrolet, Ford and Studebaker trucks, imported from North America.

Vehicle shown (typical): Truck, 5-ton, 4 × 2, Tractor (DAF YT 1527/L32)

Technical Data:
Engine: Hercules JXLD 6-cylinder, I-L-W-F, 5550 cc, 131 bhp @ 3200 rpm.
Transmission: 5F1R × 2 (2-speed rear axle).
Brakes: air-hydraulic.
Tyres: 9.00–20.
Wheelbase: 3.10 m. Track: 1.80 m.
Overall l × w × h: 5.08 × 2.35 × 2.46 m.
Weight: 3700 kg.
Note: Same engine as YA 328. Originally introduced as YT1500L (1954) with 4621-cc JXC engine (as in YA 318). Shown with DAF YTT 1004 10-ton cargo S-T. 1955. Also used with 6-ton 2-wh. YAA602 and refueller YF 101.

Truck, 3-ton, 4 × 2, Personnel and Cargo (DAF A30)
Hercules JXE3 6-cyl., 91 bhp, 4F1R, wb 3.40 m, 5.93 × 2.19 ×
2.92 m, 3600 kg. Tyres 7.50–20. 560 produced, 1949–50.
DAF hard-top drop-side body with side curtains and removable
double bench type troop seats.

Truck, 5-ton, 4 × 2, Ammunition (DAF D50) Perkins P6
6-cyl. diesel, 80 bhp, 4F1R, wb 3.40 m. Tyres 9.00–20.
Extended cab, seating five. Special steel bodywork with wood
lining inside. Fire screen between cab and body. Vehicle shown
converted for use as mobile canteen (CADI).

Truck, 5-ton, 4 × 2, Tractor (DAF T1502) 6-cyl. diesel,
120 bhp, 5F1R, wb 2.65 m, 3470 kg. GCW 18–24 tons. DAF
DD-265 5750-cc engine. Used with various types of semi-
trailers, incl. 7-ton 'Queen Mary' aircraft transporter. Discontinued in 1967.

Truck, 6-ton, 4 × 2, Chassis (Verheul V6HF) Kromhout
6-cyl. diesel, 140 bhp, 6F1R (OD top), wb 6.07 m, 9.58 × 2.41 m,
5650 kg. GVW 13,000 kg. Double-reduction rear axle (two-
speed optional). Produced in 1959/60 for Matradi (*Marine
Transport Dienst*). Air brakes. 10.00–20 tyres.

Truck, 3-ton, 4 × 2, Personnel and Cargo (Ford F5-8H8T-80) 6-cyl., 95 bhp, 4F1R, wb 4.01 m, 6.70 × 2.20 × 3.01 m, 2890 kg. 1949 US chassis, assembled by Ford Amsterdam. Dutch body and cab with 'half doors'. Model 8H8T 3.7-litre L-head engine. 7.50–20 tyres. Widely used during 1950s.

Truck, 3-ton, 4 × 2, Personnel and Cargo (International B152) 6-cyl., 140 bhp, 4F1R, wb 3.89 m. 210 of these military US built trucks superseded the Army's Ford F5s in 1960–61 for general purpose use. Removable lengthwise back-to-back bench-type seats in centre of body. 3936-cc OHV engine.

Truck, 3-ton, 4 × 2, Airfield Runway Sweeper (Fordson 'Thames'/Geesink) V-8-cyl., 85 bhp, 4F1R, wb 3.26 m. Max. sweeping width six metres. Thornycroft 'Nippy' sweepers were also used. Later came the DAF/Streicher Sweeper/Snow Fighter with Deutz V-8 auxiliary engine.

Bus, 40-passenger, 4 × 2 (DAF B1500DL) DAF-Leyland 6-cyl. diesel, 105 bhp, 5F1R, wb 5.80 m, 10.50 × 2.34 × 3.40 m, 7760 kg. Body by Hartogs of Beesd. One of many types of DAF buses used by the Dutch forces. Other bus body builders included Den Oudsten, Hainje, Smit, and Trapman.

TRUCKS, 3- to 6-TON 4×4

Makes and Models: DAF A414 (4-ton, 1951), V1100, V1300, V1600 (3- to 4-ton, from 1956), YA314 (3-ton, 1954), YA324 (3-ton, 1963), YT514 (tractor, 5-ton, 1961), etc. Ford G398TA (tractor, 3-ton, 1954, D), 'Trader' (3-ton, 1959, GB). Ford/Marmon-Herrington F5, C620, C800, C900 (from 1948, US). FWD/Kronenburg BA217D (crash tender, 1969/70, US/NL). International 'Loadstar' (3-ton, 1969, US). Thornycroft 'Nubian' (crash tenders, 1952–53, GB).
WWII types: British AEC 'Matador' (wireless truck), Austin K4 (3-ton), Bedford QL (3-ton), Crossley (tractor), and Fordson (WOT6); Canadian Chevrolet C60S, C60L (3-ton), and Ford F60S, F60L (3-ton); US Autocar U-7144T (tractor, 4–5-ton) and U-8144T (tractor, 5–6-ton), Federal 94×93 B, C (tractors, 4–5-ton), FWD HAR (tractor, 3-ton) and SU-COE (various types), and White 444T (tractor, 4–5-ton).

General Data: The WWII models listed, especially the Canadian Chevrolets and Fords, were used for many years by all branches of the Dutch armed forces, with many different types of bodywork (GS Cargo, Wrecker, Tanker, Ambulance, Light AA Tractor, Derrick, etc.) From the 1950s they were gradually replaced in service by more modern vehicles, notably of DAF manufacture. The DAF YA 314 became the standard vehicle in the 3-ton 4×4 (NATO) class. The American 4–5-ton and 5–6-ton 4×4 tractor trucks were replaced by the DAF YT 514. The Dutch Air Force used modified wartime FWD SU-COE trucks (ex-van Gend & Loos) with extended crew cab and fifth wheel and, later, the German Ford (FK) G398TA 4×4 with Dutch coachbuilt cab, as tractors for 'Queen Mary' and aircraft refuelling semi-trailers.

Vehicle shown (typical): Truck, 3-ton, 4×4, Cargo and Personnel (DAF YA 314)

Technical Data:
Engine: Hercules JXC 6-cylinder, I-L-W-F, 4620 cc, 102 bhp @ 3200 rpm.
Transmission: 4F1R × 2.
Brakes: hydraulic, air-assisted.
Tyres: 11.00–20.
Wheelbase: 3.60 m. Track: 1.90 m.
Overall l × w × h: 6.09 × 2.43 × 2.79 m.
Weight: 4760 kg. GVW 7700 kg.
Note: Engine and gearbox as YA 126 but conventional drive train with banjo-type axles. Speed 80 km/h. Gradability 40%. 4-ton winch optional.

272

Truck, 3-ton, 4×4, Air Compressor (DAF YA 314)
Hercules JXC 6-cyl., 102 bhp, 4F1R × 2, wb 3.60 m. Based on standard YA 314 chassis. American LeRoi 210 compressor unit, driven by separate engine. Used by Engineers as power supply unit for pneumatic tools.

Truck, 3-ton, 4×4, Office (DAF YA 314) Hercules JXC 6-cyl., 102 bhp, 4F1R × 2, wb 3.60 m. Relatively rare house-type bodywork incorporating office equipment and sleeping accommodation. 1959. Another version, with expansible inner shell, was also produced.

Truck, 3-ton, 4×4, Tipper, w/Winch (DAF YA 314)
Hercules JXC 6-cyl., 102 bhp, 4F1R × 2, wb 3.60 m. BAVO drop-side hyd.-operated three-way tipper body. Other versions included a workshop and a bomb carrier with overhead gantry-type crane, both based on the std. cargo body.

Truck, 3-ton, 4×4, Shop Van (DAF YA 324) Hercules JXC 6-cyl., 102 bhp, 4F1R × 2, wb 3.60 m. Second production version of YA 314 chassis, shown with radio body but also employed as workshop truck. The Dutch also used the GMC CCKW-353 with similar bodywork.

Truck, 4-ton, 4×4, Cargo (DAF A414) Hercules JXE3 6-cyl., 91 bhp, 4F1R×2, wb 3.60 m, 6.55×2.20×3.12 m. Produced in 1953 for *Kon. Marine* (Royal Navy). Bodywork by Jongerius of Utrecht. Also with other types of bodywork, incl. tipper and exp. 6×6 (Trado) chassis.

Truck, 5-ton, 4×4, Tractor (DAF YT514) 6-cyl. diesel, 165 bhp, 5F1R×2, wb 3.58 m, 5.68×2.35×2.63 m. Military version of DS256 commercial truck. DS575 5750-cc super-charged engine. Used with YAF-1014 10,000-litre gasoline and other semi-trailers. GCW (on road) 36 tons.

Truck, 3-ton, 4×4, Tractor (Ford/Marmon-Herrington C800) V-8-cyl., 200 bhp, 4F1R×2. Modified commercial Ford (US) 'Big Job', 1956, with Strüver-Deutz aircraft fueller S-T. Overall length 9.90 m. Tank capacity 12,000 litres. Pump equipment (capacity 750 l/min.) behind cab. Tyres 10.00–20.

Truck, 3-ton, 4×4, Tractor (Ford FK3500/G398TA) V-8-cyl., 106 bhp, 4F1R×2. German Ford 4×4 truck with Dutch cab and fifth wheel. Used by Air Force in conjunction with fueller and aircraft transporter (shown) semi-trailers, from mid-1950s. 3.92-litre SV engine.

TRUCKS, 2½- to 20-TON
6 × 4 and 6 × 6

Makes and Models: AEC A196-0854 (10-ton, 6 × 4, 1952, GB). DAF YA 318, YF 318 (3-ton, 6 × 6, from 1950), YA 328, YC 328, YF 328 (3-ton, 6 × 6, from 1953). DAF YA 616, YB 616, YF 616, YK 616, YT 616 (6-ton, 6 × 6, from 1956). Duplex/Crane Shovel 20TA (20-ton, rev. crane, 6 × 6, 1952). Faun (tractor, 6 × 6, D). Fiat/OM 6600 (10-ton, 6 × 6, 1956, I). Fordson 'Thames-Sussex' (3-ton, 6 × 4, 1953, GB). FWD MC (20-ton, rev. crane, 6 × 6, c. 1960, USA). FWD/Kronenburg BA417, 0-11-D, 0-153-L, etc. (crash trucks, 6 × 6, from 1957, USA/NL). International G-744 'M-Series' (5-ton, 6 × 6, 1957, US). Reo G-742 'M-Series' (2½-ton, 6 × 6, 1952, US). Scammell 'Constructor' (winch truck, 6 × 6, 1954, GB). Thornycroft 'Amazon' (Coles crane, 6 × 4, 1949, GB), 'Mighty Antar' (tractor, 6 × 4, 1953, GB).

WWII types: British AEC 854 (tanker, 6 × 6), Austin K6 (3-ton, 6 × 4), Fordson WOT1 (3-ton, 6 × 4), and Scammell SV/2S (wrecker, 6 × 4); Canadian GM C60X (3-ton, 6 × 6); US Brockway/Corbitt/White 666 (6-ton, 6 × 6), Diamond T 968–975 (4-ton, 6 × 6), and 980/981 (12-ton, 6 × 4), Dodge WK-60 (3-ton, 6 × 4), GMC CCKW-352/353 (2½-ton, 6 × 6), and DUKW-353 (amphibian, 2½-ton, 6 × 6), International M-5H-6 (2½-ton, 6 × 6), Kenworth and Ward LaFrance M1, M1A1 (wreckers, 6-ton, 6 × 6), Mack NM (6-ton, 6 × 6) and NO (7½-ton, 6 × 6), Mack LM-SW (wrecker, 5-ton, 6 × 4), and various types of truck-mounted revolving cranes.

General Data: The DAF YA 318 was first conceived in 1950 and was a sophisticated vehicle with a high cross-country performance. In 1952 it was approved for quantity production but the following year it was fitted with a more powerful engine and a 5-speed OD gearbox (YA 328). The YA 616 series was heavier and had much in common with the American 5-ton 6 × 6 standardized 'M-Series', employing similar engine (Continental), gearbox (Spicer), and axles (Timken/Rockwell Standard). Tank-transporter trailers were hauled by WWII Diamond T tractors and later by Thornycroft 'Mighty Antars'. In 1971 a fleet of Dutch FTF tractors was ordered for this purpose.

Vehicle shown (typical): Truck, 3-ton, 6 × 6, Artillery Tractor, w/Winch (DAF YA 328)

Technical Data:
Engine: Hercules JXLD 6-cylinder, I-L-W-F, 5556 cc, 131 bhp @ 3200 rpm.
Transmission: 5F1R × 2 (OD top).
Brakes: hydraulic, air-assisted.
Tyres: 9.00–20.
Wheelbase: 3.40 m. BC 1.30 m. Track: 2.08 m.
Overall l × w × h: 6.13 × 2.40 × 2.65 (1.94) m.
Weight: 6200 kg. GVW: 9900 kg.
Note: Trailing arm IFS (torsion bars). Twin parallel walking beam rear suspension. 'H-drive' with central diff. 4½-ton winch with 'automatic' towing hook.

Truck, 3-ton, 6×6, Artillery Tractor (DAF YA 318)
Hercules JXC 6-cyl., 102 bhp, 4F1R × 2, wb 3.40 (BC 1.30) m, 6.15 × 2.40 × 2.65 m, 5780 kg. One of the prototypes, 1950/51. Originally classed as 2½-ton. Spare wheels (both sides) acted as support wheels to prevent 'bellying'.

Truck, 3-ton, 6×6, Cargo (DAF YA 328) Hercules JXLD 6-cyl., 131 bhp, 5F1R × 2, wb 3.40 (BC 1.30) m, 6.19 × 2.40 × 2.65 m, 6000 kg. Truck version had longer body than artillery tractor (4.20 vs 3.75 m, inside). Winch optional. Also with quadruple AA guns mounted in body. Note spare wheel removed.

Truck, 3-ton, 6×6, Fire, Crash (DAF YC 328) Based on YA 328 chassis but twin-carb. engine for improved acceleration. Produced to Navy requirements. Pump capacity: max. 2500 litres of water or 13,600 litres of foam per minute. Tanks for 2000 litres of water and 400 litres of foam compound.

Truck, 3-ton, 6×6, Oil Servicing (DAF YF 318 and 328) Based on YA 318 and (later) YA 328. Used to deliver lubricating oil to aircraft, also under extremely low ambient temperatures (down to −40°C). Heated 2800-litre tank. Used by USAFE and French Air Force. Pumping rate 100 litre/min.

Truck, 3-ton, 6 × 6, Fire Fighting (DAF YA 328) Based on YA 328 chassis but without the spare/support wheels. Relatively rare model, built about 1958/59. Some were produced with closed cab and fifth wheel for cargo and tanker semi-trailers in Dutch New Guinea.

Truck, 6-ton, 6 × 6, Cargo and Prime Mover, w/Winch (DAF YA 616) Continental R6602 6-cyl., 232 bhp, 5F1R × 2, wb 4.16 (BC 1.37) m, 7.16 × 2.45 × 2.95 m, 10,130 kg. Tyres 14.00–20. 9-ton winch behind cab. Timken bevel drive, top mounted, double-reduction, single-speed type axles. Introduced 1956.

Truck, 6-ton, 6 × 6, Tipper, w/Winch (DAF YK 616) Continental R6602 6-cyl., 232 bhp, 5F1R × 2, wb 4.16 (BC 1.37) m, 7.30 × 2.45 × 2.98 (cab) m, 12,000 kg. Tyres 11.00–20 (or 14.00–20 singles). BAVO hyd.-operated three-way tipper. Detachable cab protector. 9-ton winch. 1959.

Truck, 6-ton, 6 × 6, Cargo, w/Winch (DAF YA 616 VL) Basically as YA 616 but winch at front. 'VL' body (*Vlakke Laadvloer*, flat platform) for containers and palletized goods. Detachable side boards. All 616 models had Continental 'Red Seal' 9866-cc petrol engines, PAS, and 24-volt electrics.

Truck, 6-ton, 6 × 6, Tractor, w/Winch (DAF YT 616)
Continental R6602 6-cyl., 232 bhp, 5F1R × 2, wb 4.16 (BC 1.37) m, 7.30 × 2.46 × 2.84 (2.39) m, 10,150 kg. Tyres 11.00–20. Max. load on fifth wheel 10,700 kg. Used mainly for low-loader S-Ts (Engineers).

Truck, 6-ton, 6 × 6, Wrecker, w/Winch (DAF YB 616)
Continental R6602 6-cyl., 232 bhp, 5F1R × 2, wb 4.16 m, 8.85 × 2.49 × 3.00 m, 15,513 kg. Austin-Western crane (built under licence), operated by hyd. motors and cylinders. Approx. 300 supplied to Army and Air Force. Winches front and rear.

Truck, 6-ton, 6 × 6, Fuel Tanker, w/Winch (DAF YF 616)
Basically as YA 616 with 14.00–20 tyres, single rear. Tank capacity 7000 litres. Introduced in 1963. Note quadruple windscreen wipers, air horn, and pioneer tools rack above radiator brush guard. Max. speed approx. 70 km/h.

Truck, 4-ton, 6 × 6, Water Tanker (Diamond T 975A)
Hercules RXC 6-cyl., 106 bhp, 5F1R × 2, wb 5.10 (BC 1.32) m, 8.20 × 2.44 × 2.85 m. Re-bodied ex-Canadian Army WWII LWB chassis. Several types, incl. Fire Fighting (Foam). Also with original equipment e.g. Coles revolving crane.

MISCELLANEOUS VEHICLES

Ex-WWII AFVs included British scout cars (Humber), armoured cars (Daimler and Humber), and 'Universal' carriers; Canadian scout cars ('Lynx'), APCs (GM C15TA), recce cars ('Otter') and carriers ('Windsor'); US scout cars (White M3A1), A/Cs ('Staghound') and half-tracks (M3, M5, M9, M16, etc.). Tanks were of British, Canadian, French and US origin, e.g. AMX, 'Chaffee', 'Sherman', and 'Centurion'. To replace the latter the German 'Leopard' was selected. The US M113(A1) and French AMX-VTT full-track APCs were also used. Artillery tractors included Canadian 4 × 4 FATS and US high-speed full-tracks (M4, M5). Conventional tractors were mainly from David Brown and Ford, crawler tractors of Caterpillar (D4, D7) manufacture.

Crane, Mobile, Aircraft, 9-ton, 4 × 2 (Unicum 'Safe Power') GM 6004 6-cyl. diesel, 190 bhp, wb 6.50 m, max. 15.40 × 4.12 × 10.00 m (travelling: 12.00 × 2.95 × 3.04 m), 19,000 kg. 6.96-litre two-stroke engine. Hyd. collapsible crane. Built by Unicum, Weert, 1952. Tyres F/R: 18.00–25/27.00–33.

Semi-Trailer, Aircraft Fueller, 9500 litre (DAF YF 102) Wb (from kingpin) 5.46 m, 9.04 × 2.41 × 2.30 m. Used for under-wing fuelling of jet aircraft by Air Force and Navy, USAF (Europe), Pakistan, Portugal, etc. High-capacity diesel-powered pumping system. Over 350 produced (1952/53).

Semi-Trailer, Aircraft Fueller, 10,000 litre (DAF YF 101) Over-wing fueller, designed in 1949 in collaboration with Air Force and Shell Nederland. Capable of delivering 2300 litres of kerosene in three minutes. Tractors: FWD SU-COE (shown), Ford F6 COE, DAF YT 1500L, etc. Tyres 12.00–20.

Truck, ¼-ton, 4 × 4, Rescue, w/Winch (Willys CJ3A/Pennock) 4-cyl., 60 bhp, 3F1R × 2, wb 2.03 m, 3.73 × 1.78 × 2.00 m. Used by Air Force for emergency rescue work. Equipped with searchlights, fire extinguishers, ladder, spades, radio equipment, etc. 1953. Similar: foam tender (Kronenburg).

Truck, 3½-ton, 4 × 2, Fire Fighter (Magirus-Deutz) One of a large fleet of Deutz air-cooled engine fire appliances of the 'Mobile Columns'. Others had no crew cab and towed a 2500 l/min. Magirus pump on a trailer. Superseded by DAF-based appliance (forward control, BW150).

Truck, 4 × 4, Crash (FWD/Kronenburg BA-217-D) Continental R6602 6-cyl., 224 bhp, 6F1R × 1 (OD top), wb 3.80 m, 6.60 × 2.43 × 3.40 (2.90) m, NSW 12,000 kg. GM V-8-cyl. 206-bhp pump engine. Turret discharge capacity 300 gpm @ 200 psi. Also handlines and ground sweep nozzles.

Truck, 6 × 6, Crash (FWD/Kronenburg BA-417) Waukesha 145 G2B 6-cyl., 275 bhp, 5F1R × 2, wb 4.30 m, 8.08 × 2.65 × 3.53 m, NSW 14,670 kg. 51 produced, 1959–63. Continental 4-cyl. 110-bhp pump engine. Two monitors, two bumper nozzles and two handlines. Tyres 11.00–20.

Semi-trailer, 52-ton, Tank Transporter (DAF YTS 10060)
Wb (from kingpin) 12.00 m, 15.70 × 3.40 m, 25,790 kg. Used with Thornycroft 'Mighty Antar' for transport of 'Centurion' tanks, etc. Tyres 10.00–24. 1961. Also shorter type (YTS 10050) with payload of 54 tons and 11.00–20 tyres.

Car, Armoured, Reconnaissance, 4 × 4 (DAF YP 104)
Hercules JXLD 6-cyl., 131 bhp, 5F1R (with reversing gear for driving in opposite direction by second driver), 4.33 × 2.08 × 1.50 m. Crew 3. Prototypes, based on chassis components of the YA 126. Max. speed 100 km/h. 1959/60.

Carrier, Armoured, Personnel, 8 × 6 (DAF YP 408) Hercules JXLD 6-cyl., 133 bhp, 5F1R × 2, 6.10 × 2.40 × 1.80 m, 9000 kg. Prototype, designed in 1958 by Army and DAF, using components of YA 328 truck. Second pair of wheels steers but not driven. Speed range 2–90 km/h. Crew 1 + 11. Gradability 50%.

Carrier, Armoured, Personnel, 8 × 6 (DAF YP 408) DAF DS575 6-cyl. diesel, 165 bhp, 5F1R × 2, wb 3.42 m, 6.23 × 2.40 × 2.36 (1.80) m, 9900 kg. Combat wt. 11 tons. Air hyd. brakes on 6 driven wheels. PAS. About 750 produced, from 1964. Several variants, incl. mortar, ambulance, etc.

POLAND

The Polish armed forces employ both domestic and imported
vehicles. The latter are mainly of Soviet, Czech and East
German origin. Some Soviet types have been produced under
licence. The Polish industry, however, developed several trucks
of their own design, ranging from light forward control models
(Nysa, Zuk) to the Star 6 × 6 tactical trucks. The latter chassis,
with single or double cab, were used for the mounting of a
variety of body types and were also exported. Several civilian
models, notably the FSO Warszawa sedan and pickup and 4 × 2
Star trucks were widely used for military service. Armoured
vehicles were mainly of Soviet origin, the main exception being
the 'SKOT' 8 × 8 which was developed jointly with Czechoslovakia. During the first post-war years the Poles employed
many wartime vehicles, including US Dodge, Ford and GMC.

Truck, ¼-ton, 4 × 4, Utility (Borsuk) 4-cyl., wb 2.00 m,
3.00 × 1.60 × 1.65 m. Experimental six-seater general purpose
vehicle, probably with Skoda engine as joint venture with
Czechoslovakia. IFS/IRS with swing axles. Standard field cars
were the Soviet GAZ-67B and -69A.

Truck, 2-ton, 4 × 2, Cargo and Personnel (Lublin-51)
6-cyl., 70 bhp, 4F1R, wb 3.30 m, 5.55 × 2.20 × 2.15 m, 2710 kg.
Soviet GAZ-51, produced under licence during the 1950s.
Several Soviet vehicles were produced in Poland, ranging from
the Pobieda car (FSO Warszawa) to the BTR-152 APC.

Truck, 4-ton, 4 × 2, Cargo (Star 25) 6-cyl., 95 bhp (105 bhp
optional), 5F1R (OD top), wb 3.00 m, 5.90 × 2.97 × 2.80 (cab
2.20) m, 3600 kg. Developed from Star 20 (1948) and 21
(1958). Variants: 25L (wb 3.85 m), 3W25K (wb 2.50 m), C25
(tractor). Several body options and differences in cab styling.

Truck, 4-ton, 4 × 2, Cargo (Star 27) 6-cyl. diesel, 100 bhp, 5F1R (OD top), wb 3.00 m, 5.90 × 2.07 × 2.80 m, 4100 kg. Diesel-engined version of Star 25. Superseded by Star 28 and 29 resp. Introduced in 1962 by Poland's largest truck plant: FSC at Starachowice.

Truck, 8-ton, 4 × 2, Cargo (Zubr A80) 6-cyl. diesel, 155 bhp, 5F1R, wb 4.10 m, 7.35 × 2.50 × 3.10 m, 7000 kg. Tyres 12.00—22. GVW 15,300 kg. Air brakes. Produced by JZC at Jelcz k/Olawy. Also 4 × 4. Cab later restyled. Superseded by Jelcz 315. Czech Skoda 706R also used.

Truck, 2½-ton, 6 × 6, Cargo, w/Winch (Star 66) 6-cyl., 105 bhp, 5F1R × 2 (OD top), wb 3.46 (BC 1.20 m), 6.59 × 2.40 × 2.87 (cab 2.48) m, 5700 kg. Tyres 11.00—20. Model S-47 4680-cc OHV engine. Lockable rear diffs. 5.9-ton winch. Introduced in 1958 as A66. Max. payload 4 tons.

Truck, 2½-ton, 6 × 6, Cargo, w/Winch (Star 660 M1 and M2) 6-cyl., 105 bhp, 5F1R × 2 (OD top), wb 3.30 (BC 1.20) m, 6.53 × 2.40 × 2.87 m, 5800 kg. Tyres 12.00–18. 660M1 was developed from Star 66 in 1965. 660M2 (1968) had waterproof ignition. Also available: Model 660D with S530A1 100-bhp diesel engine.

Truck, 4-ton, 4 × 2, Workshop (Star 20) 6-cyl., 85 bhp, 4F1R, wb 3.00 m, 5.85 × 2.35 × 3.20 m approx. Body built by the Jelcz factory on the Star 20 and the improved Star 21 chassis/cab. Replaced by Type 574 (6 × 6). Shown is one of various cab designs used on Star 4 × 2 trucks.

Truck, 2½-ton, 6 × 6, Workshop T574, w/Winch (Star A660M2/Jelcz 574) 6.97 × 2.42 × 3.20 m, 9250 kg. Other variants: tanker, cranes (KS-251, ZSH-6), pontoon carrier, signals van, decontamination truck, carrier for SMT-1 truck-launched treadway bridge, etc. Some versions were used by North Vietnam.

Carrier, Armoured, Personnel, Amphibious, 8 × 8 (SKOT-2A) Tatra T928 V-8-cyl. diesel, 190 bhp, semi-automatic 5-speed trans., wb 1.30 + 2.15 + 1.38 m, 7.45 × 2.50 × 2.71 m, 12,800 kg. Tyres 13.00–18. Polish/Czech design. Shown with turret-mounted 14.5-mm gun. Speed 95 km/h. (8.9 in water).

Tractor, Full-Track, Artillery (Mazur 300) V-12-cyl. diesel, 300 bhp, 5.80 × 2.88 × 2.60 m, 13,600 kg. Earlier known as ACS. Powered by Soviet tank engine. Used in Poland and Czechoslovakia for towing 122-mm gun, 152-mm howitzer, and AA guns. Produced during early 1960s, patterned on Soviet design.

PORTUGAL

Like other NATO members the Portuguese were supplied with quantities of WWII and postwar US trucks, mainly of the ¼-, ¾-, 2½- and 5/6-ton classes. In addition, new trucks were acquired from Britain (Austin, Bedford, Land-Rover, Morris-Commercial), France (Berliet), Germany (Mercedes-Benz, 'Unimog' S), Spain (Barreiros), etc. Some Berliet types were assembled by MDF under the name Berliet-Tramagal. AFVs included American half-tracks (M3, M16, etc.) and tanks (M4, M41, M47, etc.), British Daimler 'Dingos' and Humber A/Cs, Canadian GM C15TA APCs, French AML and EBR75 A/Cs, etc.

Truck, ¼-ton, 4 × 4, Utility (Austin G4M10 'Gipsy') In 1965 the British Motor Corp. supplied 200 SWB (shown) and LWB units to the Portuguese Army, 40 of them for use as mobile radio transmitting/receiving units. Land-Rovers and US 'Jeeps' were also in service.

Truck, 4-ton, 4 × 4, Cargo (Berliet GBC8KT 4 × 4) Two-axle version of French Berliet GBC8KT 4-ton 6 × 6 (*qv*) to which it was otherwise generally similar. About 3000 supplied, as well as a small number of the 6 × 6 version. Winch optional. Rear diff. lock. GVW 11,000 kg. *c.* 1970.

Truck, 2½-ton, 6 × 6, Cargo, w/Winch (Berliet-Tramagal GBA MT) 4-cyl. diesel, 125 bhp, 5F1R × 2, wb 3.54 (BC 1.28) m, 6.88 × 2.23 × 2.99 m, 7500 kg. 4½-ton winch. Tyres 11.00–20. Axles and brakes as GBC8KT. Seating for 20 troops. Assembled by MDF. First two produced in France. *c.* 1970.

RUMANIA

Like most Warsaw Pact countries, Rumania uses large quantities of Soviet equipment. This includes APCs (BTR-40, BTR-152), tanks (T34/85, T54, T55), trucks (GAZ, ZIL, MAZ, KRAZ), etc. Czech Tatra and East-German Robur (LO-1800A) trucks were also operated. An increasing proportion of the current trucks, however, is of domestic production. One of the first Rumanian-built trucks was the SR-101, a copy of Soviet ZIL-150 4-ton 4 × 2. During the mid-1960s the 'Bucegi' and 'Carpati' medium-capacity trucks were introduced by the Brasov *Steagul Rosu* (Red Star) truck works. These were produced in various configurations, incl. 4 × 4 and COE. The Soviet GAZ/UAZ-69M is produced under licence and more recent Rumanian light trucks are the TV (COE, 4 × 2 and 4 × 4) and ARO (4 × 4), both with a variety of body styles. Rumania's export markets include China, Africa, South America and the Middle East.

Truck, ½-ton, 4 × 4, Cargo and Personnel (UMM M-461) 4-cyl., 70 bhp, 4F1R × 1, wb 2.33 m, 3.85 × 1.71 × 2.05 m, 1600 kg. Tyres 6.50–16. Similar to Soviet GAZ/UAZ-69 but 4F1R × 1 instead of 3F1R × 2 trans. Produced by M.I.C.M. Uzina Mecanica Muscel in Cimpulung, from 1964.

Field Car, 5-seater, 4 × 4 (ARO-244) Modern four-wheel drive station wagon, introduced in 1970 and available for export from 1972. Independent front suspension with coil springs. ARO-243 basically similar but two-door bodywork with hardtop or canvas tilt.

Truck, ½-ton, 4 × 4, Ambulance (TV-51S) 4-cyl., 70 bhp, 4F1R × 1, wb 2.45 m, 4.68 × 1.90 × 2.10 m, 2100 kg. Tyres 7.50–16. Two stretchers. 4 × 4 version of TV-41S. Body variants (4 × 2/4 × 4): cargo truck (41C/51C), van (41F/51F), microbus (41M/51M). M-207 2512-cc engine (as M-461).

Truck, 5-ton, 4 × 2, Cargo (Bucegi SR-113L) V-8-cyl., 140 bhp, 5F1R × 2, wb 4.80 m, 8.04 × 2.35 × 2.97 (2.20) m, GVW 9330 kg. Tyres 8.25–20. Model 211E 5.03-litre OHV engine. SR-113 and -113N had 4.00- and 4.40-m wb resp. SR-115 and -116 were 4.00-m wb tractor and tipper.

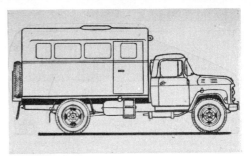

Truck, 5-ton, 4 × 2, Workshop (Bucegi SR-113) V-8-cyl., 140 bhp, 5F1R, wb 4.00 m, 6.90 × 2.44 × 2.97 m, 8500 kg. Type AM 113-2 shop van, produced by the Automecanica Works at Medias. Provision for A-frame type crane on front bumper. Comprehensively equipped with generating set, lathe, etc.

Truck, 2½-ton, 4 × 4, Cargo (Carpati SR-132) V-8-cyl., 140 bhp, 4F1R × 2, wb 3.40 m, 5.86 × 2.30 × 2.58 m, 3975 kg. Tyres 9.75–18 (single rear). Ground clearance 270 mm. Max. speed 95 km/h. Max. trailer weight 2 tons. Military version (SR-132M 2-tonner) differed only in small details. 1963.

Truck, 3½-ton, 4 × 4, Cargo (Bucegi SR-114M) V-8-cyl., 140 bhp, 5F1R × 2, wb 4.00 m, 6.57 × 2.54 × 2.85 (2.31) m, 4600 kg. Tyres 9.00–20. Model 211D engine. Speed 90 km/h. Body 4.50 × 2.35 m. Max. trailer weight 4½ tons. Commercial version (SR-114 4-tonner) differed in minor details. 1963.

SOUTH AFRICA

The defence forces of South Africa have, over the years, used mainly British and Canadian trucks, many of which were assembled and fitted with local bodywork. Light cross-country trucks/field cars have included the British Land-Rover and BMC 'Mini-Moke' and the US 'Jeep'. Cargo and special equipment trucks were mainly British Bedford (notably RL), Ford/AWD and Leyland, as well as Canadian Chevrolet and Ford and German Mercedes-Benz. Armoured cars included the British Alvis 'Saracen' (APC) and Daimler 'Ferret' and many South African-built French Panhard AML-245s. The Thornycroft 'Mighty Antar' was used as a prime mover for heavy transporters, carrying 'Centurion', 'Sherman' and 'Comet' tanks. In 1972 the Parts and Accessories Division of General Motors South African (Pty.) Ltd in Port Elizabeth became importers of the Brazilian Engesa four- and six-wheel drive truck conversion kits (*see* Brazil).

Truck, 3-ton, 4 × 4, Cargo (Ford Thames 'Trader' 75/AWD) 6-cyl., 112 bhp, 4F1R × 2 (5F1R × 2 optional). GVW on/off roads 23,600/18,000 lb. Commercial British truck, converted by All-Wheel Drive Ltd, and fitted with military type bodywork, etc. 1960. Similar trucks supplied to Egypt and Indonesia.

Car, Armoured, Light, 4 × 4 (Panhard AML-245) 4-cyl., 90 bhp, 6F1R × 2, wb 2.50 m, 3.79 × 1.97 × 1.89 m (w/o searchlight), 4800 kg. Produced under licence with H60 (shown) and H90 turret. Armed with mortar and MG. (H90: 90-mm gun). French design of late 1950s. Air-cooled HO engine.

Carriers, AA Missile System, 4 × 4 (Hotchkiss/Thomson-CSF/Engins Matra 'Crotale') French surface-to-air missile system (SAM) comprising highly-mobile target acquisition radar/data processing vehicle and up to three launching vehicles (shown in background). Also known as 'Cactus'. 1969.

SPAIN

During the Spanish Civil War (1936–1939) the number of Spanish vehicles, both civilian and military, was drastically cut due to large-scale destruction. During the ensuing World War, in which Spain remained neutral, acquisition of new military hardware was minimal and after 1945 quantities of war-surplus vehicles were acquired to supplement Spain's own vehicular equipment which consisted of ageing German, Italian, Russian and other military motorcycles, cars, trucks, tractors, etc. Many of these old vehicles, including German BMWs, Krupps, Phänomens, etc., remained in use until long after 1945. Agreements with the USA in 1953 brought in additional equipment, notably new and old 'Jeeps', Dodges, GMCs (incl. 'Ducks'), 'M-Series' 6 × 6, 2½- and 5-tonners, etc. Other material supplied by the USA from 1953 included half-track vehicles (M3 and variants), full-track artillery tractors (M4 and M5), scout cars (M3A1), armoured cars (M8), light (M24 and 41) and medium (M47 and 48) tanks, APCs (M113 and variants), ARVs (M74), SPs (M56 'Scorpion'), as well as aircraft, artillery and other equipment. In 1970 Germany agreed to supply 200 'Leopard' tanks to the Spanish Army.

After the Second World War the Spanish Government decided to encourage the establishment of a national motor industry by agreements between Spanish and foreign companies for the assembly and progressive local manufacture of vehicles. A National Institute of Industry was established and its first result in the automotive field was the forming, in 1946, of the Empresa Nacional de Autocamiones SA (ENASA). This company took over the old firm of Hispano Suiza and started producing trucks and buses under the name Pegaso. Later it entered into an agreement with Leyland of Britain for the manufacture of heavy trucks under licence, and with DAF of the Netherlands for military vehicles.

Another new manufacturer of motor vehicles was SEAT, which commenced in 1955 with the production under licence of certain Italian Fiat cars. The Barreiros Group of Companies was founded in 1954 by Eduardo Barreiros and three brothers and has produced a large variety of vehicles as well as engines and transmissions for other manufacturers. This group, consisting of about 20 companies, entered into agreements with AEC (GB), Chrysler (US), Hanomag (D), Rootes (GB), Star (PL) and others for assembly and part-manufacture of cars, trucks, buses, tractors and components. The biggest tie-up, eventually, was with Chrysler. This partnership became effective in 1965 with an investment of 40% on the part of Chrysler. In 1970 Barreiros was re-organised as Chrysler Espana SA. Both Barreiros and Pegaso are producers of military cross-country trucks for the Spanish Government and for export (mainly Portugal). In addition there are two producers of light cross-country vehicles, Metalurgica de Santa Ana SA and Vehiculos Industriales y Agricoles SA which, in 1958/59, began producing Spanish versions of the British Land-Rover and the American Jeep respectively. The proportion of Spanish-made components was increased progressively and several of their later models were Spanish exclusives. There are several other motor vehicle manufacturers in Spain but they produce only civilian models.

Military and Police vehicles carry white registration plates with the following letter codes preceding the actual serial number, both in black: ET—*Ejercito Terrano* (Army), EA—*Ejercito Aereano* (Air Force), EM—*Ejercito Marina* (Navy), GC—*Guardia Civil* (Civil Defence), PAT—*Policia Armado y Trafico* (Police).

Who's Who in the Spanish Automotive Industry

Barreiros	Chrysler Espana SA (formerly Barreiros Diesel SA), Villaverde-Madrid.
Ebro (Ford)	Motor Iberica SA, Barcelona (originally the pre-war Ford assembly plant).
Pegaso	Comercial Pegaso SA and Empresa Nacional de Autocamiones SA (ENASA), Madrid & Barcelona.
Santana (Land-Rover)	Metalurgica de Santa Ana SA, Linares (Jaen).
SEAT	Sociedad Espanola de Automoviles de Turismo SA (SEAT), Barcelona.
VIASA (Willys, Kaiser Jeep)	Construcciones y Auxiliar de Ferrocarriles SA, Division Viasa, Madrid (plant: Zaragoza).

CARS, MOTORCYCLES
and LIGHT TRUCKS

Makes and Models: *Cars:* Seat 1400 (Sedan, 4 × 2, 1958), etc.
Motorcycles: BMW R75 (w/sidecar, 3 × 2, WWII, D), etc.
Field Cars and Light Trucks: Barreiros KA-90 'Comando' (1½-ton, 4 × 4, 1963). Dodge T245 M37, M43, M43B1 (¾-ton, cargo and amb., 4 × 4, c. 1960, US). Jeep (Willys, Kaiser Jeep, VIASA) MC M38, MD M38A1, MB-CJ3B, MB-CJ6 'Largo', CJ3B, CJ6, FC170, etc. (¼- to ¾-ton, 4 × 4, from c. 1950, US/E). Land-Rover/Santana '88' and '109' Series II, '110' FC1300, etc. (¼- to 1¼-ton, 4 × 4, from c. 1957, GB/E). Willys M274 'Mechanical Mule' (½-ton, 4 × 4, 1960, US).
WWII types: Dodge T214 series (¾-ton, 4 × 4, US) and T223 (1½-ton, 6 × 6, US), Ford GPW and Willys MB (¼-ton, 4 × 4, US).

General Data: The majority of modern vehicles in the ¼- to ¾-ton class used by the Spanish forces are the products of Metalurgica de Santa Ana and VIASA who produce 'Land-Rovers' and 'Jeeps' respectively (various models, civilian and military). The name Willys for the 'Jeep' range of vehicles was discontinued in about 1969. The Barreiros 'Comando' was one of a family of three basic types of special military vehicles (see following section for 'Panter' 4 × 4 and 6 × 6). Their engines were interesting in that they could be converted from diesel to petrol by, it was claimed, one driver/mechanic in about one hour. This was done by changing the fuel in the tank, replacing the cylinder heads, replacing the fuel injection equipment by an ignition system (coil, distributor and petrol pump assembly) and fitting a carburettor on the inlet manifold. Converting back to diesel could be carried out just as easily. In addition to the models listed, the Spanish forces employed a number of commercial and military motor vehicles, including several German, Russian and US types of pre-1945 vintage, some even dating back to the Civil War period (1936–39). For example, 1938 1½-ton 4 × 2 American Chevrolet trucks were still in Army service in 1967.

Vehicle shown (typical): Truck, 1½-ton, 4 × 4, Cargo (Barreiros KA-90 'Comando')

Technical Data:
Engine: Barreiros A-90 (earlier A-26) diesel, 6-cylinder, I-I-W-F, 5010 cc, 90 bhp @ 2400 rpm.
Transmission: 5F1R × 2 (OD top).
Brakes: air.
Tyres: 9.00–20.
Wheelbase: 2.67 m.
Overall l × w × h: 4.78 × 2.25 × 2.42 (cab) m.
Weight: 4430 kg.
Note: Engine convertible for use with carburettor (see General Data). Payload on made roads 3 tons. Also made with different front end sheet metal.

Truck, ¼-ton, 4×4, with Recoilless Rifle (Land-Rover '88' Series I) 4-cyl., 52 bhp, 4F1R×2, wb 2.23 m, 3.58×1.59 m, 1400 kg approx. Regular 1957 model, mounting 106-mm (shown) or 105-mm 'Cetme' recoilless rifle. From 1958 Land-Rovers were produced in Spain for military, police and civilian use.

Truck, ½-ton, 4×4, Cargo and Personnel (Jeep/VIASA CJ6 'Largo') 4-cyl., 72 bhp, 3F1R×2, wb 2.57 m, 3.83×1.78×1.86 m, 1100 kg. F-head 'Hurricane' engine or diesel (Barreiros C-65, Perkins 192-E). Some had lengthwise troop seats in rear. Early models (MB-CJ6, 1960–63) used MB L-head engine.

Truck, ¾-ton, 4×4, Personnel Carrier (Land-Rover/Santana '109' Series II) 4-cyl., 77 bhp, 4F1R×2, wb 2.77 m, 4.63×1.63×2.00 (1.50) m, 1500 kg approx. Spanish Army soft-top version of '109' 12-seater station wagon. Conventional '88' Regular and '109' petrol and diesel trucks were also used by the Spanish forces.

Truck, 1¼-ton, 4×4, Cargo and Personnel (Land-Rover/Santana 1300) 6-cyl., 83 bhp, 4F1R×2, wb 2.79 m, 4.55×1.92×2.25 (1.75) m approx. Tyres 9.00–16. Special Spanish bodywork with two lengthwise seats for four men each in rear. Full-length tilt. Used for towing 2-wheeled multiple-rocket launcher, etc. Crew 1+9.

TRUCKS, 2½- to 18-TON
4×2, 4×4, 6×4 and 6×6

Makes and Models: Barreiros 'Super Saeta' (7½-ton) and 'Super Azor' (10-ton, 4×2). Barreiros TT-90.21 and TT-90.22 (2½-ton, 4×4, 1958), TMA-264 and -265 'Comando' (2½-ton, 4×4, 1961), PB-125 'Panter II' (2½-ton, 4×4, 1963) and 'Saeta TT' (2½-ton, 4×4, 1968). Barreiros PB-185 and 6618M 'Panter III' (5-ton, 6×6, 1963 and 1969 resp.). International/Diamond T, etc. G744 'M-Series' (M41, M62, M139, etc., 5-ton, 6×6, c. 1960, US). Pegaso 1100 (6-ton), 'Comet' 1090, 1090L and V (8-ton), 1065, 1065L (10-ton), 1061, 1061L (12- to 13-ton), 1063 (17- to 18-ton), 'Comet' 2030 (15-ton tractor), and 2011 (25-ton tractor) (all 4×2, mid-1960s). Pegaso 'Comet' 3020 and 3040 (4-ton, 4×4, 1964 and 1967 resp.). Pegaso/DAF 3020S (4-ton, 4×4, 1963), 3045 (5-ton, 4×4, 1970, E/NL). Reo/Studebaker, etc., G742 'M-Series' (M34, M35, M602, etc., 2½-ton, 6×6, c. 1960, US).
WWII types: GMC CCKW-353 (2½-ton, 6×6, US), GMC DUKW-353 (2½-ton amphibious 'El Pato', 6×6, US), White 666 (6-ton, 6×6, US), Ward LaFrance M1 (wrecker, 6×6, US), etc.

General Data: In addition to the makes and models listed above, the post-1945 Spanish Forces used quantities of British commercial 4×2 trucks (Austin, Bedford, Ford) and various 4×4 types of WWII origin, as well as a variety of ageing military trucks of Spanish, French, German and Russian manufacture. The development of modern Spanish logistical and tactical vehicles runs parallel to the development of Spain's post-war national motor industry, mainly that of Barreiros (now Chrysler Espana) and ENASA (Pegaso). These were supplemented by tactical 6×6 trucks of American origin, supply of which commenced during the mid-1950s. Main national producer of tactical trucks is Barreiros with its family of 4×4 and 6×6 'Comando' and 'Panter' models. Their power units may be used either as diesel or petrol engines, as described in the previous section. The 'Panter III' also appeared with a multi-barrel rocket launcher.

Vehicle shown (typical): Truck, 4-ton, 4×4, Cargo (Pegaso 'Comet' 3020-S)

Technical Data:
Engine: Pegaso-Comet 9026 diesel 6-cylinder, I-I-W-F, 6550 cc, 125 bhp @ 2400 rpm.
Transmission: 6F1R × 2 (OD top).
Brakes: air.
Tyres: 10.00–20.
Wheelbase: 3.70 m.
Overall l × w × h: 6.78 × 2.45 × 3.20 (2.21) m.
Weight: 5000 kg.   GVW on/off road: 12,000/9000 kg.
Note: Towed load 4 tons. Based on Dutch DAF YA-314. Model 3020 similar but with BB475V 130-bhp 6-cyl. 4769-cc petrol engine. Model 3040 (diesel) similar but closed cab.

292

Truck, 2½-ton, 4×4, Cargo, w/Winch (Barreiros 'Todo Terreno') 6-cyl. diesel (Barreiros EB-6), 90 bhp, 4F1R×2. Exp. *'Camion para todo terreno'* (truck for use on all terrains), produced in 1958. Developed into Models TT-90.21/22 COE trucks. Shown with conventional tyres but also tested with Straussler 'Lypsoid' tyres.

Truck, 2½-ton, 4×4, Cargo (Barreiros TT-90.22) 6-cyl. diesel, 83 bhp, 5F1R×2, wb 3.25 m, 6.00×2.40×2.40 (windscreen) m, 4600 kg. Payload on roads 6 tons. Tyres 10.00–20. Later redesignated: 'Comando' TMA-264. Gradability 42%. Speed 85 km/h. Also used by Portuguese Army.

Truck, 2½-ton, 4×4, Cargo (Barreiros 'Comando' TMA-265) 6-cyl. diesel, 90 bhp, 5F1R×2, wb 3.25. Similar to TMA-264 but hard-top cab and 'Lypsoid' tyres. Optional: 10.00–20 tyres (2 DT). Commercial closed-cab versions: 'Puma' TDA-26 (9.00–20 tyres, single rear) and TA-26 (dual rear), and 'Panter' TB-24 (115-bhp engine).

Truck, 2½-ton, 4×4, Cargo (Barreiros 'Panter II' PB-125) 4-cyl. diesel or petrol, 115 (later 125) bhp, 5F1R×2, wb 3.92 m, 6.14×2.25×2.64 (cab) m, 6960 kg. Tyres 11.00–20. B-24 6785-cc engine. Air brakes. Payload on roads 5 tons. Speed 75 km/h. Cab with removable hard-top.

Truck, 5-ton, 4 × 4, Cargo (Pegaso/DAF 3045) Prototype military truck. Series production commenced in 1970 by ENASA (Pegaso) in collaboration with DAF in the Netherlands (engines, electrical equipment, etc.) and DAF's Madrid subsidiary (DAF-S.A.E.; cabs and bodywork).

Truck, 5-ton, 6 × 6, Cargo (Barreiros 'Panter III') 6-cyl. diesel or petrol, 170 bhp, 5F1R × 2. Early model with cab similar to 'Comando' and 'Panter II' models except mounted in conventional position. Note double cab roof panelling, narrow engine compartment and large exterior air cleaner.

Truck, 5-ton, 6 × 6, Cargo, w/Winch (Barreiros 'Panter III' 6618M) 6-cyl. diesel or petrol, 170 bhp, 5F1R × 2, wb 4.06 (BC 1.37) m, 6.74 × 2.25 × 2.95 m, 8360 kg. Tyres 11.00 or 12.00–20. Payload on roads 10 tons. Patterned on American military 5-ton 6 × 6 truck (G744). Model PB-185 had no louvres in bonnet side panels.

Truck, 5-ton, 6 × 6, Chassis, w/Winch (Barreiros 'Panter III' COE) 6-cyl. diesel or petrol, 170 bhp, 5F1R × 2, wb 4.06 (BC 1.37) m, 6.74 × 2.25 × 2.60 (cab) m. COE version of 'Panter III' with same B26 10,179-cc (120 × 150 mm) diesel engine (convertible to petrol). Tyres 9.00–20. 7-ton (max.) power winch at rear of chassis.

SWEDEN

Like Switzerland, Sweden remained neutral during the Second World War and as both countries have a sizeable national automotive industry, the coverage of their military vehicles in this book starts from about 1940. Principal Swedish manufacturers of military transport vehicles have been, and are, Scania-Vabis (now Saab-Scania) and Volvo. Scania-Vabis was founded in 1911 when the firms of Scania of Malmö and Vabis of Södertälje (near Stockholm) merged. The new firm supplied many vehicles for the armed forces during World War I and in 1917 introduced a four-wheel steer 4 × 4 tractor truck. Subsequently military trucks of various types were produced, as well as engine units for aircraft, tanks, generating sets, etc. During WWII tanks (THN), armoured and other trucks were built for the services and in 1959 the company launched its impressive 6 × 6 'Myrsloken' prime mover truck. Volvo started car production in 1926/27, with the financial backing of SKF, the ball bearing concern (Volvo is Latin for 'I roll'). Volvo truck production commenced in 1930. Scania-Vabis ceased car production in 1924, concentrating on trucks and engines, and in 1969 merged with the famous aircraft and motor-car firm of SAAB to become the Saab-Scania Automotive Group. Both Saab-Scania and Volvo have subsidiaries manufacturing tractors, marine engines and other products. Two other important Swedish firms in the field of armaments are Bofors and Landsverk. Imported military vehicles used by the Swedish forces were mainly of American, British and German origin, although their proportion in relation to domestic products is decreasing.

Registration Numbers

Swedish military vehicles carry black number plates with five or six yellow numerals.

Military Vehicle Nomenclature

Motorcycle	*Motorcykel*
Passenger car	*Personbil*
Cross-country car	*Personterrängbil (tgpb)*
ditto, w/radio	*Radiopersonterrängbil (raptgb)*
Ambulance	*Sjuktransportbil*
Field ambulance	*Sjuktransportterrängbil*
Truck (cargo)	*Lastbil*

Prime mover	*Terrängdragbil (tgdb)*
Cross-country truck	*Lastterrängbil*
Wrecker	*Bärgningsterrängbil*
Wheeled tractor w/trailer	*Hjultraktor med traktorkärra*
ditto w/powered-axle trailer	*Hjultraktor med drivkärra*
Tracked vehicle	*Bandvagn (BV)*
Tracked APC	*Pansarbandvagn (PBV)*
SP gun	*Bandkanon* (variants: *Infanteriekannonvagn* (IKV) and *Pansarvärnskanonvagn* (PVKV))
Tank	*Stridsvagn* (STRV)

Who's Who in the Swedish Automotive Industry

Bolinder-Munktell	AB Bolinder-Munktell*, Eskilstuna.
Scania	Saab-Scania Automotive Group†, Södertälje.
Volvo	AB Volvo, Göteborg.

*member of the Volvo Group
†formerly: AB Scania-Vabis

Bandvagn BV202 afloat.

CARS, FIELD CARS and MOTORCYCLES

Makes and Models: *Cars:* Various commercial 4 × 2 types, incl. station wagons (Saab 95 V4, Volvo 210, PV445, PV833/834, Volkswagen 'micro-bus', etc.).
Field Cars: Dodge T214 (4 × 4, WWII, US). Dodge/Fargo 'Power Wagon' (4 × 4, *c.* 1950, US). Steyr-Puch 700 AP 'Haflinger' (4 × 4, *c.* 1965, A). Tempo G1200 (4 × 4, 1939, D). Volvo TPV m/43 (4 × 4, WWII), TP21 P2104 (4 × 4, 1956), P2104 Special (4 × 4, 1956), L2304 (4 × 4, 1959), L3304 (4 × 4, 1964), L3314 (HT) 'Laplander' (4 × 4, 1963), 4141 'Laplander' (4 × 4, 1969). Willys MB 'Jeep' (4 × 4, WWII, US), CJ2A, CJ3A 'Jeep' (4 × 4, from 1947, US).
Motorcycles: Various types, incl. Husqvarna and Monark m/42 (500 cc, WWII).

General Data: The Dodge and Fargo 'cars' were in fact American light truck chassis fitted with Swedish coachbuilt bodywork. In view of the prevailing ambient temperatures in Sweden the need for all-enclosed bodywork is obvious. During the war Volvo had produced a command car with four-wheel drive (m/43) and during the mid-1950s a new type was introduced (TP21 P2104) which became the standard model for command/radio car requirements. The Volvo P2104 'Special' had the same chassis as the TP21 and TL11 (light truck) but with station wagon-type bodywork. In 1959 the 'Laplander' was introduced, originally as Model L2304. This was a forward-control multi-purpose chassis and after extensive testing in various parts of the world it entered quantity production as Model L3314. In addition to several military versions (command car, ambulance, etc.), there are many civilian applications. The 'Laplander' is also used by the Norwegian armed forces. A more sophisticated development, the 4141, made its appearance in 1969 and was also tested in Great Britain. Of both 'Laplanders' experimental 6 × 6 models were produced. Until 1963 American Willys 'Jeeps' were imported and distributed in Sweden by Scania-Vabis (now Saab-Scania), who also import the German range of Volkswagen vehicles. Willys 'Jeeps' were in Sweden classed as ½-ton, Dodge T214 and 'Power Wagons' as 1½-ton. The WWII Willys MB 'Jeep' was officially designated 'tgb, ½-ton, 4 × 4, m/46'.

Motorcycles were of Swedish and Czech origin. Snow-scooters were also used.

Vehicle shown (typical): Car, 5-seater 4 × 4, Command/Radio (Volvo TP21 P2104) *(Radiopersonterrängbil 915)*

Technical Data:
Engine: Volvo ED 6-cylinder, I-L-W-F, 3650 cc, 90 bhp @ 3600 rpm.
Transmission: 4F1R × 2.
Brakes: hydraulic.
Tyres: 9.00–16.
Wheelbase: 2.68 m. Track F/R 1.55/1.60 m.
Overall l × w × h: 4.50 × 1.90 × 1.95 m.
Weight: 2880 kg. GVW 3200 kg.
Note: Light truck chassis with 5-seater (shown) or 7-seater ('Special') bodywork. Speed range 11 to 105 km/h. Rigid axles with Rzeppa CV joints at front. Diff locks front and rear. Empty weight 2600 kg. Known as *'Sugga'*.

Car, 5-seater, 4×4, Command/Radio, m/43 (Volvo TPV) 6-cyl., 86 bhp, 4F1R×2, wb 3.10 m, 4.67×1.80× 1.69 m, 2300 kg. Model EG 3.67-litre L-head engine. Tyres 7.00–16. Army designation: 'raptgb m/43' (radio car, 1943 model). Also w/o radio as 'tgpb m/43'. Superseded by TP21 (P2104).

Carrier, 4×4, 90-mm Recoilless Gun (Volvo L3304) 4-cyl., 68 bhp, 4F1R×2, wb 2.10 m, 4.00×1.65 m approx. Normal-control conversion of L3314, designated 'pvpjtgb 9031 MT', mounting AT gun (*9 cm Pansarvärnspjäs 1110*), used in armoured brigades. Note universal-jointed steering column.

Car, 8-seater, 4×4, Personnel (Volvo L3314 HT 'Laplander') 4-cyl., 68 bhp, 4F1R×2, wb 2.10 m, 3.99×1.66× 2.09 m, 1725 kg. B18A 1.78-litre engine. Also as Command/ Radio car (*Radiopersonterrängbil 9033*) and with canvas top (pltgb 903). Tyres 7.00 or 8.90–16. Ltd.-slip rear diff. Mil. designation: 'pltgb 903B'. Commercially available.

Car, 7-seater, 4×4, Personnel (Volvo 4141 'Laplander') 4-cyl., 94 bhp, 4F1R×2, wb 2.30 m, 4.26×1.81×2.07 m, 1900 kg. 1-ton truck ('tgb 11') chassis with B20B 1986-cc engine. Diff. locks. Also with 6-cyl. B30 engine and as 6×6 (1½-ton Model 4143, wb 2.30+1.00 m.). Prototype for new generation for the 1970s.

TRUCKS, ½- to 1½-TON
4 × 2, 4 × 4 and 6 × 6

Makes and Models: Dodge T214 (¾-ton *, 4 × 4, WWII, US), T223 (1½-ton, 6 × 6, WWII, US). Dodge/Fargo 'Power Wagon' (1-ton*, 4 × 4, c. 1950, US). Volkswagen 'Transporter' (1-ton, 4 × 2, D). Volvo TL11 P2104 (¾-ton, 4 × 4, 1956), L2304 (0.8-ton, 4 × 4, 1959), L3314 'Laplander' (0.8-ton, 4 × 4, 1963), 4141 'Laplander' (1-ton, 4 × 4, 1969) ('tgb 11', and 'tgb 12' 6 × 6 amphibian), TL21 (1½-ton, 6 × 6, 1955), TL22 L2204 (1½-ton, 6 × 6, 1956), 4143 'Laplander' (1½-ton, 6 × 6, 1969) ('tgb 13'). Willys CJ6 (½-ton, 4 × 4, c. 1960, US). Willys/Scania-Vabis COE 'Jeep' (¾-ton, 4 × 4, c. 1959, US/S).

*Swedish designation: 1½-ton.

General Data: In addition to several types of Volvo vehicles, which are prominent in this class, the Swedish Armed Forces have used ex-WWII and post-war American trucks, notably of Chrysler (Dodge, Fargo) manufacture. Many of these were fitted, in Sweden, with closed cabs. They were gradually replaced by Volvo products. The Volvo 'Laplander' became a standardized universal vehicle and there were several versions. At the time of its introduction in the late 1950s, Scania-Vabis produced two prototypes which were very similar to the 'Laplander'. They were based on the American Willys 'Jeep' forward-control chassis and submitted for tests by the Army. It was, however, dropped in favour of the all-Swedish Volvo. Lengthened 6 × 6 prototypes were developed by Volvo from both the L3314 and 4141 'Laplander' 4 × 4 versions. Of the latter an 8 × 8 version was also produced. The TL11 4 × 4 truck was based on the same P2104 chassis as the TP21 command/radio car. The TL22 L2204 6 × 6 was rather similar in design to the WWII Dodge T223. Except for a civilian-type closed cab it had the same front end as the TP21 and TL11. It was produced with several types of bodywork, including shop van and fire truck. The Dodge/Fargo 1-ton 4 × 4 'Power Wagon' was used with cargo (pickup), command, ambulance and air compressor bodywork and in the Swedish forces was classed as 1½-ton (this also applied to the WWII Dodge T214 range). American 1940 Chevrolet 1½-ton 4 × 2 cargo trucks with Swedish cab and gas producer were in service during WWII.

Vehicle shown (typical): Truck, 0.8-ton, 4 × 4, Personnel and Cargo (Volvo L3314 'Laplander')

Technical Data:
Engine: Volvo B18A 4-cylinder, I-I-W-F, 1778 cc, 68 bhp @ 4500 rpm.
Transmission: 4F1R × 2.
Brakes: hydraulic.
Tyres: 8.90–16.
Wheelbase: 2.10 m. Track 1.34 m.
Overall l × w × h: 3.99 × 1.66 × 2.05 m.
Weight: 1600 kg. GVW 2450 kg.
Note: Canvas-top 'pltgb 903' version shown (tested by British Army, with powered-axle trailer, 1969). Known in Sweden as *Valpen* ('puppy'). Variants: missile carrier ('pvrbtgb 9032'), radio ('rapltgb 9033'), ambulance, fire fighter (921), etc.

Truck, ¾-ton, 4 × 4, Personnel and Cargo (Willys/ Scania-Vabis) One of two prototypes produced by Scania-Vabis (then Sweden's Willys Jeep distributors). Based on Jeep FC-170 truck chassis with engine behind front axle. Bodywork similar to Volvo 'Laplander' with spare wheel on rear door. *c.* 1959.

Truck, ¾-ton, 4 × 4, Aircraft Starting (TL 11 P2104) 6-cyl., 90 bhp, 4F1R × 2, wb 2.68 m, 4.80 × 1.90 × 1.90 m approx., 2500 kg. Fitted with Penta equipment for starting jet plane engines. Chassis and front end sheet metal same as TP21 Command car (*qv*). Used by Swedish Air Force.

Truck, 1½-ton, 6 × 6, Personnel and Cargo, w/Winch (Volvo TL22 L2204) 6-cyl., 115 bhp, 4F1R × 2, wb 3.18 (BC 1.06) m, 5.86 × 1.90 × 2.56 m, 4200 kg. GVW on/off road: 6450/5700 kg. Tyres 11.00–16. 4.7-litre OHV engine. Vacuum-actuated differential locks, front and rear. Designation: *Lastterrängbil 912*. TL21 was prototype.

Truck, 1½-ton, 6 × 6, Shop Van, w/Winch (Volvo L2204) 6-cyl., 115 bhp, 4F1R × 2, wb 3.18 (BC 1.06) m, 5.90 × 1.90 m approx. House-type van bodywork (for signals or workshop role) on standard L2204 chassis. 4-ton winch mounted on right-hand side of frame, behind cab. Also fire-fighting version.

TRUCKS, 3- to 8-TON and BUSES 4 × 2 and 4 × 4

Makes and Models: Magirus/KHD A3000 (3-ton, 4 × 4, WWII, D). Scania LBA 110 (4½-ton, 4 × 4, 1971). Scania-Vabis (3-ton and COE signals van, 4 × 2, WWII), L36 (4-ton, 4 × 2, 1965), L55 (5-ton, 4 × 2, 1958), L75 (7-ton, 4 × 2, 1958), L76 (8-ton, 4 × 2, 1962), etc. Scania-Vabis F11 (3-ton, 4 × 4, WWII). Volvo LV120, LV140 and LV290 Series (3- to 5-ton, 4 × 2, from WWII), L4951 (COE) (6-ton, 4 × 2, 1959), F86 (bus, 4 × 2, 1970), etc. Volvo TLV131, 141 and 142 (3-ton, 4 × 4, from WWII), TL 388/L38545, TL 389/L38547 (4-ton, 4 × 4, 1954), L485/L48546 'Viking' (4½-ton, 4 × 4, 1963), etc.

General Data: Practically all vehicles in this class were products of Swedish industries. Some were commercial 4 × 2 types, used for administrative purposes and fitted with either GS cargo body or special purpose bodywork. Others were commercial four-wheel drive chassis, also with various types of bodywork. The Magirus/Klöckner-Humboldt-Deutz was similar to that used by the German armed forces during World War II. The Volvo L385 Series (which also appeared with flat-section front wings) was superseded by the L485 in 1963. Both appeared with various types of bodywork, including fire fighters. The Volvo F86 bus was one of several types used by the Swedish forces and was convertible for ambulance use. Since its merger with Saab, Scania-Vabis trucks are now marketed as Scanias. The Scania LBA 110 was a prototype for a new generation of tactical military trucks for the 1970s. Its 6 × 6 variant, the LBAT 110S is shown in the following section.

Vehicle shown (typical): Bus, 4 × 2 (Volvo F86/Hägglund)

Technical Data:
Engine: Volvo TD70A diesel 6-cylinder, I-I-W-F, 6700 cc, 170 bhp @ 2400 rpm (SAE: 195 @ 2400).
Transmission: 4F1R × 2.
Brakes: air.
Tyres: 10.00–20.
Wheelbase: 5.50 m.
Overall l × w × h: 10.05 × 2.50 × 3.23 m.
Weight: 8630 kg. GVW 13,200 kg.
Note: Convertible for use as ambulance or cargo carrier. Bodywork by AB Hägglund & Söner of Örnsköldsvik. Produced June 1970–Jan. 1971.

Truck, 3-ton, 4 × 2, Signals Van (Scania-Vabis) Produced during 1943–44 for the Swedish Army Signal Corps, these house type vans, based on a special short-wheelbase bus chassis, contained radio transmitting and receiving equipment. Note RHD and aerials stowed on roof.

Truck, 3-ton, 4 × 4, Shop Van, m/42VP (Volvo TLV141) 6-cyl., 105 bhp, 4F1R × 2, wb 3.80 m, 6.30 × 2.25 m approx. Four-wheel drive modification of commercial Model LV141. 5.65-litre (100 × 120 mm) OHV engine. Early production (TLV-131) had 90-bhp 4.4-litre engine.

Truck, 3-ton, 4 × 4, Cargo (Volvo TLV142) 6-cyl., 105 bhp, 4F1R × 2, wb 4.10 m, 6.50 × 2.25 m approx. Derived from LV142 4 × 2 5-tonner. Some had flat-section front wings. Used with various types of bodywork, incl. APC. Also exported (e.g. Argentina). Winch (side-mounted) was optional.

Truck, 4½-ton, 4 × 4, Cargo, w/Winch (Volvo L48546) 6-cyl. diesel, 125 bhp, 5F1R × 2, wb 4.40 m, 6.90 × 2.33 m approx., 6800 kg. Used extensively by Swedish forces, also with special bodywork and HIAB loading crane. L385 series was similar in appearance. Known as: *Lastterrängbil 939.*

Truck, 3-ton, 4 × 2, Crane (Scania-Vabis) Produced during World War II. Basically commercial truck, fitted with overhead gantry-type crane, used by Swedish Army Engineers. Shown with special low loader trailer for transporting crawler tractors and bulldozers. 4-cyl. 110-bhp engine.

Truck, 4-ton, 4 × 2, Shop Van (Scania-Vabis L36) 4-cyl. diesel, 102 bhp. 5F1R, wb 4.80 m, 5860 kg. GVW 10,500 kg. Over 800 supplied during 1965–67, with cargo body or as mobile workshop for ordnance maintenance and similar purposes. Known as: *Materielvardsbil 111*.

Truck, 7-ton, 4 × 2, Cargo (Scania-Vabis L75) 6-cyl. diesel, 165 bhp, 5F1R × 2. Commercial truck modified for use by Swedish Army Engineers. Equipped with HIAB hydraulic crane, front brackets for snowplough, auxiliary headlights, special towing hook for low-loader trailer for haulage of bulldozers, etc.

Truck, 8-ton, 4 × 2, Cargo (Scania-Vabis LS76A) 6-cyl. diesel, 195 bhp (255 bhp optional), 5F1R. Used by Swedish Air Force in conjunction with 4-wheel trailers for transport of British-made guided missiles 'Bloodhound II' launchers and ancillary equipment. Fitted with HIAB hydraulic 'Speed-loader'.

TRUCKS, 2½- to 10-TON and TRACTORS 6 × 4 and 6 × 6

Makes and Models: Alvis 'Stalwart' (5-ton, 6 × 6, 1965, GB). Brockway/Corbitt/White 666 (6-ton, 6 × 6, WWII, US). GMC CCKW-352/353 (2½-ton, 6 × 6, WWII, US). Kenworth/Ward LaFrance M1A1 (wreckers, 6 × 6, WWII, US). Scania LBAT 110S (6-ton, 6 × 6, 1971). Scania-Vabis LT110S (tractor, 6 × 4). Scania-Vabis LA82 'Myrsloken' (10-ton, 6 × 6, 1961). Volvo TVB (tractor, 6 × 4, 1940), TVC (tractor, 6 × 6, 1942). Volvo 88 (NB and FB) Series (6 × 4, from 1965), etc.

General Data: Some of the war-surplus American trucks in this class were modified for other roles. The Brockway 6-ton 6 × 6 (which was also produced by Corbitt and White) was fitted with a special crew cab for the Artillery and, for the Air Force, with a 10-ton HIAB crane. These vehicles, together with the M1A1 heavy wreckers, were gradually replaced by new models based on the Scania-Vabis LA82 *Myrsloken* ('Anteater') chassis which first entered service in the early 1960s. It was, at the time, claimed to be the largest truck ever built in Sweden. One variant was a tractor-truck used in conjunction with a Bofors 120-mm gun mounted on a semi-trailer. About 1939 Sweden had purchased a number of Czech Skoda 6V 6 × 6 heavy tractors to tow coastal artillery. In 1942 Volvo introduced its first 6 × 6, the TVC, to supplement and later replace the Skoda. The Volvo 88 Series, introduced in the mid-1960s as replacements for the L495 models, included both normal control (N) and COE (F) units with gross laden weights between 16 and 22 tons depending on the number of axles. The NB and FB had tandem axles at rear with single (6 × 2) or double (6 × 4) drive. They were powered by turbo-supercharged diesel engines and had final drives with double reduction or single reduction combined with hub reduction gears.

Vehicle shown (typical): Truck, 3-ton, 6 × 6, Cargo and Prime Mover, w/Winch (Volvo TL31 L3154) *(Lastterrängbil 934).*

Technical Data:
Engine: Volvo D96AS 6-cylinder diesel, I-I-W-F, 9586 cc, 150 bhp @ 2200 rpm.
Transmission: 5F1R × 2 (OD top).
Brakes: hydraulic, air-assisted.
Tyres: 11.00–20.
Wheelbase: 3.92 m. BC 1.25 m.
Overall l × w × h: 7.10 × 2.13 × 2.70 (cab) m.
Weight: 7320 kg.
Note: 8-ton winch, side-mounted. Shown with trailer with two powered axles and towing another 4-wheel trailer with test load. GCW 20.5 tons (off road: 11.5 tons).

Truck, 3-ton, 6×6, Cargo and Prime Mover, w/Winch (Volvo TL31) 6-cyl. diesel, 150 bhp, 5F1R×2, wb 3.92 (BC 1.25) m, 7.10×2.13×2.60 (cab) m, Chassis/cab weight 5590 kg. Prototype for L3154 truck with civilian-type cab, tested as artillery prime mover, about 1955. Note MG ring mount.

Truck, 3-ton, 6×6, Cargo and Prime Mover, w/Winch (Volvo TL31 L3154) 6-cyl. diesel, 150 bhp, 5F1R×2, wb 3.92 (BC 1.25) m, 7.10×2.13×2.70 (cab) m. Body had double dropsides, a side-hinged rear door and a tilt of which various sections could be individually strapped up in open position.

Truck, 3-ton, 6×6, Fire Crash and Rescue (Volvo TL31 L3154) 6-cyl. diesel, 150 bhp, 5F1R×2, wb 3.92 (BC 1.25) m, approx 7.10×2.15×2.90 m. One of several military fire fighters on Volvo 4×2 (e.g. Model L340) and 6×6 chassis. A twin swinging-boom wrecker (*Bärgningsterrängbil 965*) was also based on this 6×6 chassis.

Truck, 10-ton, 6×4, Wrecker (Volvo FB88) 260-bhp turbo-supercharged 6-cyl. diesel. Recovery equipment by EKA (Type D) comprising 20-ton hyd.-operated jib, lifting bar, 40-ton winch, hyd. stiff legs, radio remote control, etc. Supplied to British Army, 1970. Commercially available.

Truck, 20-ton, 6 × 4, Tractor (Scania-Vabis LT110S)
Tractive unit for Kalmar/DAF tank-transporter semi-trailer.
Known as *'Dragbil 981'*. Fitted with two 20-ton Hägglund
winches, powered independently by high-torque radial-piston
type hydraulic motors.

Truck, 6-ton, 6 × 6, Cargo, w/Winch (Scania LBAT 110S)
6-cyl. diesel, supercharged, 275 bhp (Model DS 11), hyd.-
actuated 4F1R × 2, GVW 14,800 kg. 4 × 4 version (LBA110)
similar except single rear axle and no supercharger (D11, 202
bhp). Prototypes, 1970. Quantity production expected in 1976.

Truck, 10-ton, 6 × 6, Tractor (Scania-Vabis LA82)
8-cyl. diesel, 200 bhp, 5F1R × 2, wb 4.06 (BC 1.32) m,
7.60 × 2.50 m approx. One of two prototypes (1958/59) of the
'Myrsloken' ('Anteater'; so called because of its steeply sloping
front end) which in modified form replaced a variety of older
vehicles.

**Truck, 10-ton, 6 × 6, Revolving Crane, w/Winch (Scania-
Vabis LA82)** 6-cyl. diesel, 220 bhp, 5F1R × 2, 19,850 kg.
20-ton crane. Known as *'Terrängkran 202'*. Other versions
included *'Lastterrängbil 957F'* (cargo truck) and *'Bärgningsterrängbil 970'* (wrecker with HIAB crane).

Tractor, 6 × 4, Artillery, m/40 (Volvo TVB) Designed before the war to supplement heavy Skoda 6 × 6 tractors for coastal artillery. Of both there were single- and double-cab versions and the TVB also appeared with frontal armour plating as an AA gun mount. Swing-type rear axles.

Tractor, 6 × 6, Artillery, m/42B (Volvo TVC 2) 6-cyl., 180 bhp, 5F1R × 2, wb 3.99 (BC 1.28) m, 7.29 × 2.75 × 2.62 m, 10,230 kg. Tyres 11.00–20. Model C6 10.6-litre twin-carb. engine. Coil spring IFS. Diff. locks. Early production (TVC tgdb m/42) had 135-bhp Model FB engine.

Tractor, 6 × 6, Tank Transporter, m/42C (Volvo TVC3) 6-cyl., 180 bhp, 4F1R × 2 (Wilson pre-selector type), wb 3.99 (BC 1.28) m, 7.29 × 2.80 × 2.62 m, 11,180 kg. Known as *Terrängdragbil* (tgdb). Winch under rear body. Used with 50-ton tank transporter trailer (in pairs; one vehicle pushing).

Tractor, 6 × 6, Artillery (Scania-Vabis LA82) 6-cyl. diesel, 220 bhp, 5F1R × 2, wb 4.06 (BC 1.32) m, 7.60 × 2.50 m approx. DS10 turbo-charged 10,261-cc (135 × 127 mm) engine (prototype had 8-cyl. engine). 10-ton winch. Air brakes. Payload 4800 kg. 1960s.

MISCELLANEOUS VEHICLES

Swedish AFVs included the well-known Scania-Vabis and Volvo armoured trucks, several tracked vehicles of Czech origin and a range of Swedish APCs, SPs, and tanks, the most unusual of which is the fixed-gun 'S'-tank. Another outstanding vehicle is the articulated-steering Bolinder-Munktell (Volvo) 'Bandvagn', which is also exported (Britain, Finland, Norway, etc.). Infantry brigades used Volvo, BM-Volvo, Ford and Massey-Ferguson agricultural-type tractors with semi-trailers ('Trupptransport-kärra 821'). For gun-towing these worked in conjunction with powered-axle 2-wheel trailers. Bolinder-Munktell produced a 4 × 4 articulated ammunition carrier ('Lasterrängtruck 611') derived from their civilian 'Skogs-Lisa'.

Tractor, Semi-Track, Light Artillery, m/43 (Volvo HBT)
At the beginning of WWII Sweden purchased some German Demag *Sd. Kfz.* 10 semi-tracks and a replica was subsequently produced, using Volvo engine and front end sheet metal, designated: *Artilleri Traktor, 2-ton, m/43, Volvo.*

Carrier, Full-Track, Articulated, Amphibious (Bolinder-Munktell BV202A) Volvo B18 4-cyl., 91 bhp, 4F1R × 2, 6.17 × 1.76 × 2.21 m, 3200 kg. Introduced in 1963/64 this over-snow *Bandvagn* steered by controlled articulation of the two units. Power transmission to all four rubber tracks. BV203 was radio version. Also exported.

Carrier, Full-Track, Cargo (Nordverk) Volvo ED 6-cyl., 90 bhp, 3F1R, 4.20 × 1.78 × 2.21 m, 1100 kg. Payload capacity 1200 kg. Tractive power 2¼ tons approx. Maximum speed 56 km/h. Tractor and cargo carrier, designed primarily for operation over snow but could be used on hard ground.

Truck, 4×4, Armoured, Personnel, m/42 (Scania-Vabis F11/SKPF) 4-cyl. 115 bhp, 4F1R×2, wb 4.10 m, 6.80×2.30×2.28 m, 8500 kg. Crew 2+13. Armoured hull on Scania-Vabis F11 4×4 truck chassis, introduced during WWII but used until long afterwards (e.g. by the Swedish UN Forces). Also 6×6 version.

Truck, 4×4, Armoured, Personnel, m/42 (Volvo TLV/VKPF) 6-cyl., 105 bhp, 4F1R×2, wb 4.10 m, 6.80×2.30×2.28 m approx. APC bodywork (5–10 mm armour thickness) on TLV truck chassis. Similar to Scania-Vabis SKPF. Vertical-spindle power winch on side. Ringmount in cab roof for two 8-mm MGs.

Carrier, Full-Track, Armoured, Personnel, Amphibious, Pbv 302 (Hägglunds) Volvo THD100B 6-cyl. diesel, 280 bhp, 8F2R, 5.35×2.86×2.50 m, combat wt 13½ tons. *Pansarbandvagn*, designed in 1962/63, operational from 1966. Crew 2+10. Speed 65 km/h (in water, with track propulsion, 7 km/h).

Vehicle, Full-Track, Armoured, Recovery, Bgbv 82 (Hägglunds) Volvo THD 100C 6-cyl. diesel, 310 bhp, torque converter with 8F2R, 6.75×3.21×2.40 m, combat wt 24½ tons. Derived from Pbv 302 APC. Max. crane lift capacity 5 tons. 20-ton winch. On similar chassis: Bridgelayer 'Brobv 941'.

SWITZERLAND

For many years the Swiss military forces employed civilian type motor vehicles almost exclusively. During the Second World War (in which Switzerland did not take part) it became clear that such vehicles were not suitable for modern warfare and after 1945 a large number of tactical type vehicles were acquired, mainly from American World War II surplus stocks. Added to these were new tactical vehicles such as the American Jeep. From the early 1950s quantities of 'pseudo-military' vehicles were purchased, including the British Land-Rover, the Austrian 'Haflinger' and several versions of the German 'Unimog'. Some very sophisticated cross-country vehicles had been introduced by Saurer in the late 1930s and these remained in use for many years, supplemented by new post-war national products such as the range of Mowag 4 × 4 trucks (based on Chrysler Corp. mechanical components) and several heavier 4 × 4 models produced to standard military specifications by Saurer, Berna and FBW.

Relatively large numbers of pre-war Berna, Saurer and other military versions of 4 × 2 trucks also remained. During the 1939–45 period many of these had been converted to run on producer gas. In 1939 a special subsidy scheme was instituted by the Government for commercial users of certain Swiss-made trucks (*Requisitionsfahrzeuge*) which, in case of war, were suitable for military use. In 1950 a second scheme was devised for selected imported commercial cross-country vehicles. In this case two-thirds of the import duty was refunded to the owners of eligible vehicles. Obviously there were strict regulations ensuring that all subsidy vehicles (which would constitute 70% of the Swiss military vehicular requirements in case of mobilization) were kept in first-class condition and the list of eligible types was regularly amended.

In 1970 it was decided to institute a new subsidy scheme, to be operative from 1 Jan. 1972. The new scheme applies to selected types of all-wheel drive vehicles, whether nationally produced or imported, and certain types of vans which are suitable for use as ambulances. Most medium and heavy Swiss military vehicles have right-hand drive, which has advantages for driving in the country's mountainous regions.

Registration Numbers
White figures on black plate, prefixed 'M'. Early plates had red shield with white cross and red 'M' above number on higher and narrower plate with 'cut' top corners. (For both shapes see illustrations on following pages).

Vehicle Classification
Until 1967 military trucks were classified by payload capacity as follows:

Class*		Payload
small:		up to 1 ton
light:		1 to $2\frac{1}{2}$ tons
medium:		$2\frac{1}{2}$ to 5 tons
heavy:		over 5 tons

From 1967 vehicles have been classified according to their GVW (gross vehicle weight) as follows:

Class*	GVW	Payload (approx.)
small:	up to 2 tons	up to 900 kg
light:	2 to $3\frac{1}{2}$ tons	$\frac{3}{4}$ to 1.8 tons
medium:	$3\frac{1}{2}$ to 10 tons	$1\frac{1}{2}$ to 5 tons
heavy:	10 to 15 tons	$4\frac{1}{2}$ to 8 tons
extra heavy:	over 15 tons	over 7 tons

*applying to 4 × 2 and all-wheel-drive vehicles.

Who's Who in the Swiss Automotive Industry

Berna	Motorwagenfabrik Berna AG, Olten, Bern.
Bührer	Fritz Bührer Traktorenfabrik, Hinwil, Zürich.
Condor	Condor SA, Courfaivre.
FBW	Franz Brozincevic & Cie AG, Wetzikon, Zürich (later: Motorwagenfabrik FBW, Wetzikon).
Hürlimann	Hans Hürlimann Traktorenwerke, Will, St. Gallen.
Motosacoche	Motosacoche SA, Genf.
Mowag	Mowag Motorwagenfabrik AG, Kreuzlingen.
Saurer	AG Adolph Saurer, Arbon.
Vevey	Ateliers de Constructions Mécaniques de Vevey SA, Vevey.

CARS, LIGHT TRUCKS
and MOTORCYCLES

Makes and Models: *Cars:* various, commercial, 4 × 2, incl. Chevrolet, Citroën, Ford, Mercedes Benz, Opel, Vauxhall, Volkswagen.
Field Cars and Light Trucks: Dodge T214-WC51/52/54/56/57/58 ($\frac{3}{4}$-ton, 4 × 4, WWII, US). Ford GPW ($\frac{1}{4}$-ton, 4 × 4, WWII, US). Jeep 'Wagoneer' (6-str, 4 × 4, *c.* 1969, US). Land-Rover 88 Series II, IIA ($\frac{1}{4}$-ton, 4 × 4, from 1960, GB), 109 Series IIA (10-str, 4 × 4, 1970, GB). Mercedes-Benz 'Unimog' 401 (25PS), 411 (34PS) (1-ton, 4 × 4, from 1950, D), 'Unimog' S 404 (1$\frac{1}{2}$-ton, 4 × 4, from 1961, D). Mowag *Gelände-Lkw* ($\frac{3}{4}$- to 1$\frac{1}{2}$-ton, 4 × 4, from 1950). Steyr-Puch 700 AP 'Haflinger' (0.4-ton, 4 × 4, 1962, A), 710K 'Pinzgauer' (1-ton, 4 × 4, 1971, A). Volkswagen 'Transporter' (up to 1-ton, 4 × 2, from *c.* 1951, D). Willys MB ($\frac{1}{4}$-ton, 4 × 4, WWII, US). Willys and Kaiser Jeep CJ2A/3A/3B/5 ($\frac{1}{4}$-ton, 4 × 4, from *c.* 1946, US), M38A1 ($\frac{1}{4}$-ton, 4 × 4, 1960, US), CJ6 ($\frac{1}{2}$-ton, 4 × 4, 1962, US).
Motorcycles: Condor (and other mfrs): A-250, A-580, A-680, A-750, A-1000 (solo; heavy types also with sidecar), and Vespa 125-cc scooters.

General Data: The only Swiss products in these categories are motorcycles and the Mowag range of cross-country trucks. Swiss military motorcycles were usually to special Army designs (*Armee-Motorräder*), and produced by more than one manufacturer. The early A-680 and A-1000 motorcycles were superseded by new standardized models, the A-580 (solo) and A-750 (w/sidecar). Both had twin-cylinder engines (580 and 750 cc resp.) and 8-speed gearboxes (4F × 2). The Condor A-250 replaced all previous types in 1965, after more than 100 specimens of the prototype (model C-250) had undergone troop-trials over a three-year period. The change-over to this much lighter machine was due to alterations in military requirements and the advent of light cross-country (4 × 4) vehicles. Mowag 4 × 4 trucks were used for a variety of military and other special purposes (police, fire-fighting, etc.) and featured Dodge (US) mechanical components. Mowag also supplied civilian type Dodge trucks, including the 4 × 4 'Power Wagon'. The 1-ton 'Unimog' (4-cyl., 25 bhp) was also used with snow-fighting equipment (powered by separate 90-bhp engine).

Vehicle shown (typical): Truck, $\frac{3}{4}$-ton, 4 × 4, Command (Mowag 0,75 t) *(0,75 t 4 × 4 Kommandowagen).*

Technical Data:
Engine: Dodge 6-cylinder, I-L-W-F, 3760 cc, 103 bhp @ 3200 rpm.
Transmission: 4F1R × 2.
Brakes: hydraulic.
Tyres: 11.00–16.
Wheelbase: 2.60 m.
Overall l × w × h: 4.74 × 2.25 × 2.65 m.
Weight: 3200 kg. GVW 3950 kg.
Note: Dodge mechanical components. Right-hand drive. Speed 70 km/h. Crew: 2 in cab, 6 in rear compartment. Produced in 1952. One of several body styles.

Motorcycle, Light, Solo (Condor A-250) Single-cylinder, 15 bhp, 4F, wb 1.35 m, 2.05 × 0.69 × 1.05 m, 165 kg. OHV 248-cc (68 × 68 mm) engine with 8.5:1 CR. Shaft-drive with 4.16:1 final drive. Speed 100 km/h. 14-litre fuel tank providing radius of action of about 375 km.

Motorcycle, Heavy, Solo (Condor A-580-1) Twin-cylinder, 19.8 bhp. 4F × 2, wb 1.41 m, 2.15 × 0.76 × 1.05 m, 195 kg. Standardized *Armee-Motorrad*, introduced in 1948. 577-cc horizontally-opposed side-valve engine with shaft-drive. Rear suspension with telescopic struts.

Field Car, 7-seater, 4 × 4 (Land-Rover Regular 88, Series II/IIA) 4-cyl., 78 bhp, 4F1R × 2, wb 2.23 m, 3.62 × 1.63 × 1.94 m, 1370 kg. Note black-out lamp with plug and socket wiring connection. First Swiss Army order was for 240 in 1960. By 1965 there were 2200. From 1970 also LWB Station Wagon.

Field Car, 4-seater, 4 × 4 (Kaiser Jeep CJ-5) 4-cyl., 75 bhp, 3F1R × 2, wb 2.06 m, 3.62 × 1.52 × 1.86 m, 1185 kg. 'Militarized' civilian model, 1964. 12- and 24-volt versions. Note wire mesh radiator shield and military type folding top. M38A1 (w/recoilless rifle) and LWB CJ6 also used.

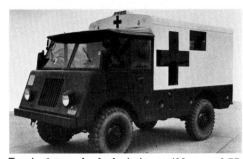

Truck, ¾-ton, 4×4, Ambulance (Mowag 0,75 t) Dodge 6-cyl., 103 (earlier 94) bhp, 4F1R×2, wb 2.60 m, 4.72× 2.00×2.64 m, 2800 kg. GVW 3500 kg. Capacity: 5 stretcher cases or 8 to 10 sitting patients. Tyres 9.00–16. Speed 89 km/h. 1952. Other ambulances: Dodge WC54, Ford, VW.

Truck, 1-ton, 4×4, Cargo, w/Winch (Mowag 1t) Dodge 6-cyl., 103 bhp, 4F1R×2, wb 2.60 m, 4.64×2.00× 2.38 m, 2600 kg. Max. payload 1500 kg. Lengthwise troop seats in back. First introduced in 1950 with 94-bhp engine. Also with other bodystyles, including several house-type vans.

Truck, 0.4-ton, 4×4, 'Moskito' AT Missile Launcher (Steyr-Puch 700 AP 'Haflinger') 2-cyl., 27 bhp, 5F1R, wb 1.50 m, 2.83×1.35×1.74 m, 680 kg (std vehicle). Launcher with motor-driven conveyor system developed by Contraves of Zürich. Five missiles were successively brought into firing position. Remote firing control possible.

Truck, 1-ton, 4×4, Command (Steyr-Puch 710K 'Pinz-gauer') 4-cyl., 74 bhp, 4F1R, wb 2.20 m, 4.00×1.68×2.00 m approx., 1600 kg. Prototype for Swiss Army, 1968. Independent suspension with coil springs and 'elevated' swing axles all round. Also other variants. In service from 1971 (with 87-bhp engine).

TRUCKS, 2- to 6-TON
4 × 2 and 4 × 4

Makes and Models: Berna 2UM (3½-ton, 4 × 4, 1950), 12 US (4-ton, 4 × 2, 1958), 2VM (4½-ton, 4 × 4, 1964), 4UM (5-ton, 4 × 4, 1952), etc. FBW AX35 (3½-ton, 4 × 4, c. 1958), AS46/HO-DD (5-ton, 4 × 2, 1942), AX40 (5-ton, 4 × 4, 1952), X50/70 V34 (5-ton, 4 × 4, 1960), L50/70/EDA (7-ton, 4 × 2, 1966), 50V-E3 (8-ton, 4 × 2, 1970), etc. Ford F60L (3-ton, 4 × 4, WWII, CDN). Magirus-Deutz A6500 (fire-fighter, 4 × 4, 1955, D). Saurer 4M, M4 (2-ton, 4 × 4, from 1938), CR1D (3-ton, 4 × 2, c. 1940), 2CM (3½-ton, 4 × 4, 1950), 2DM (4½-ton, 4 × 4, 1959), 4CT1D (5-ton, 4 × 2, c. 1940), 4CM (5-ton, 4 × 4, 1949), 5CM (6-ton, 4 × 4, 1950), 5DM (8½-ton, 4 × 4, 1960), etc. Steyr A680g (3-ton, 4 × 4, 1967, A).

General Data: Switzerland's own motor industry has a long-established and excellent reputation for trucks in the medium payload class. The best known manufacturers are Berna in Olten and Saurer in Arbon. In 1929 these two firms agreed between themselves to produce certain vehicles to a common specification. Berna and Saurer trucks in the 3½- to 6-ton, 4 × 4 class, which were identical except for their name plates, included the 2UM and 2CM, the 2VM and 2DM, the 4UM and 4CM and the 5UM and 5CM. Certain FBW 4 × 4 trucks are similar, but not identical, to corresponding Berna/Saurer models. In addition to the military trucks listed above there was a large number of 4 × 4 medium and heavy imported vehicles which were 'subsidized' (special taxation arrangement for civilian operators) and which would, in case of emergency, be requisitioned by the Army. These included certain 4 × 4 models of the following manufacturers: Bedford (GB), Berliet (F), DAF (NL), Daimler-Benz (D), Ford (GB), Henschel (D), International (US), Kramer (D), Krupp (D), Magirus-Deutz (D), MAN (D), ÖAF (A) and Steyr (A). For such vehicles a civilian owner was paid back 2/3 of the vehicle's import duty. Swiss military 4 × 2 trucks are modified commercial Bernas, FBWs and Saurers. Some pre-war 4 × 2 trucks were still in service by 1970. Buses included Bernas and Saurers (19- to 30-pass.), some dating back to 1938.

Vehicle shown (typical): Truck, 4½-ton, 4 × 4, Cargo, w/Winch (Saurer 2DM and Berna 2VM) *(Geländelastwagen 4,5 t 4 × 4 Saurer/Berna)*

Technical Data:
Engine: Saurer CT3D (Berna T3) diesel, 6-cylinder, I-I-W-F, 8100 cc, 135 bhp @ 2200 rpm.
Transmission: 8F2R × 2 (OD gearset built into main gearbox).
Brakes: air + exhaust retarder.
Tyres: 9.00–20.
Wheelbase: 4.20 m.
Overall l × w × h: 7.37 × 2.30 × 3.20 m.
Weight: 7100 kg. GVW 12,000 kg.
Note: 6-ton winch at rear of chassis. Seating capacity: 3 in cab, about 24 in rear body. Towed load 9 tons. Speed range 3.5 to 75 km/h. **Saurer** shown. Also tipper and tractor for **semi-trailers**.

Truck, 2-ton, 4 × 4, Cargo (Saurer 4M) 4-cyl. diesel, 50 bhp, 5F1R × 2, wb 2.50 m, 5.00 × 1.85 m, 2400 kg (chassis). Tyres 2.30 or 2.50 × 20. Payload on good roads 3300 kg. IFS and IRS with interconnected coil springs. Backbone chassis. Speed range 3.9–65 km/h. Pre-war design.

Truck, 3½-ton, 4 × 4, Cargo (Saurer 2CM/Berna 2UM) 4-cyl. diesel, 75 bhp, 5F1R × 2, wb 3.40 m, 5.90 × 2.21 × 3.14 m, 5500 kg. GVW 9000 kg. Tyres 7.00–20. Hyd. brakes with air assistance and exhaust retarder. CR2D 5.82-litre engine. Produced 1950–1957. Troop seat capacity: 24 approx.

Truck, 5-ton, 4 × 4, Cargo, w/Winch (Saurer 4CM/Berna 4UM) 6-cyl. diesel, 120 bhp, 5F1R × 2, wb 3.40 m, 6.45 × 2.20 × 3.15 m, 7000 kg. GVW 12,000 kg. Tyres 7.50–20. 6-ton winch. Saurer CT2D 8.72-litre engine. 8F2R × 2 trans. optional. Produced 1949–1957. Also tipper and bolster tractor versions.

Truck, 3-ton, 4 × 4, Signals (Steyr A680g) 6-cyl. diesel, 120 bhp, 5F1R × 2, wb 3.20 m, 6.22 × 2.30 × 3.20 m, 7720 kg. Special body on Austrian chassis. Also cargo version (wt. 5560 kg). Introduced in 1967/68 to fill gap between 1½-ton 'Unimog' S and 4½-ton Saurer 2DM/Berna 2VM and to replace Canadian Ford F60L.

Trucks, 5-ton, 4 × 2, Cargo (Saurer, FBW) Saurer (on left) : Model 4CT1D (1940s), 6-cyl. diesel, 100 bhp; FBW (on right) : Model AS46/HO-DD (1942–46), 6-cyl. diesel, 100 bhp, 4F1R, wb 4.60 m, 7.50 × 2.20 × 2.80 m, 6500 kg, GVW 12,000 kg, tyres 36 × 8, air-hyd. brakes.

Truck, 7-ton, 4 × 2, Fuel Tanker (FBW L50/70/EDA) 6-cyl. diesel, 220 bhp, 12F1R, wb 5.10 m, 9.02 × 2.30 × 2.68 m, 9180 kg, GVW 16,000 kg. Tyres 11.00–20. Air brakes. 11.02-litre engine. Produced 1966–68. Shown with four-wheeled tanker trailer of 3600 kg carrying capacity.

Truck, 5-ton, 4 × 4, Signals (FBW AX40) 6-cyl. diesel, 115 bhp, 4F1R × 2, wb 3.40 m, 7.20 × 2.35 × 3.40 m, 9850 kg. Laden wt. 10,050 kg. Tyres 10.00–20. Air-hyd. brakes. 8.55-litre engine. Official designation: *'FWB 5 t 4 × 4 Einsatzzentrale 58'*. Chassis produced from 1952. Also cargo version.

Truck, 8-ton, 4 × 2, Cargo (FBW 50V-E3) 6-cyl. diesel, 210 bhp, 12F1R (with electrically actuated planetary-type overdrive), wb 4.70 m, 8.50 × 2.30 × 3.45 m, 8000 kg. GVW 16,000 kg. Tyres 11.00–20. Air brakes. Produced 1970–72. Hydraulic loading lift (tail lift).

TRUCKS, 1½- to 10-TON and PRIME MOVERS 6×4, 6×6 and 8×8

Makes and Models: Diamond T 969 (wrecker, 6 × 6, WWII, US). Dodge T223-WC63 (1½-ton, 6 × 6, WWII, US). Faun LK1212/485 II (10-ton, 6 × 6, 15-ton Wilhag crane, 1967, D). GMC CCKW-353 (2½-ton, 6 × 6, WWII, US). Henschel HS22HA-CH, HS3-14HA-CH (7-ton, 6 × 6, from 1963, D). Lomount 'Super Atlantic' GR7 (prime mover, 6 × 4, 1958, GB). Magirus-Deutz 'Uranus' 250AE-L (prime mover, 6 × 6, 1956, D). Saurer 6M, M6 (2½-ton, 6 × 6, 1940), 8M, M8 (3½-ton, 8 × 8, 1943). Steyr 'Pinzgauer' (1½-ton, 6 × 6, 1971, A). Ward LaFrance/Kenworth M1A1 (wreckers, 6 × 6, WWII, US).

General Data: The Saurer models 6M and 8M (which later became known as M6 and M8 resp.) were first conceived in 1938 and belonged to the same family of high-mobility cross-country vehicles as the 4M (2-ton, 4 × 4, *qv*). They all featured a backbone chassis which carried the engine/gearbox assembly at the front end and contained the two, three or four final drive/differential units. All axles were of the 'elevated' swinging type with an ingenious suspension design incorporating coil springs which were interconnected across the chassis by means of bell-cranks and rods. Of the 4M model there was also a rear-engined version (see following section). Of the 6- and 8-wheeled versions a total of 166 had been delivered to the Army by mid-1944. An experimental 10-wheeler had also been designed and built (Model 2M, 1936). The American GMC 2½-ton 6 × 6 was used with various types of bodywork, including cargo, dump, mobile workshop and tanker. Other US 6 × 6 WWII vehicles included Diamond T medium and Ward LaFrance/Kenworth (M1A1) heavy wreckers. Heavy 6 × 6 trucks are imported mainly from Germany and tests were conducted with the Czech Tatra T813 8 × 8.

Vehicle shown (typical): Truck, 2½-ton, 6 × 6, Cargo and Prime Mover, w/Winch (Saurer 6M, M6)

Technical Data:
Engine: Saurer CTDM 6-cylinder diesel, I-I-W-F, 6750 cc, 85 bhp @ 1900 rpm.
Transmission: 5F1R × 2.
Brakes: hydraulic with air assistance.
Tyres: 9.00–20.
Wheelbase: 2.80 m. BC 1.10 m.
Overall l × w × h: 5.45 × 2.00 × 3.05 m.
Weight: 6100 kg. GVW 8600 kg.
Note: 5-ton winch. Towed load 10 tons. Used for towing medium artillery incl. AA guns, and by Engineers to tow trailers. Produced 1940–1948. Prototype (1938/ 39) had spare wheels mounted vertically.

Truck, 3½-ton, 8 × 8, Cargo and Prime Mover, w/Winch (Saurer 8M, M8) 6-cyl. diesel, 100 bhp, 5F1R × 2, wb 2.67 (front and rear BC 1.10) m, 5.88 × 2.00 × 3.05 m, 7400 kg. Similar to 6M but CT1DM 7.98-litre engine and extra (steering) front axle. Used for towing heavy artillery (10.5-cm How.). 1943–45.

Truck, 7-ton, 6 × 6, Cargo, w/Winch (Henschel HS22HA-CH and HS3-14HA-CH) 6-cyl. diesel, 192 bhp, 6F1R × 2, wb 4.36 (BC 1.31) m, 8.15 × 2.50 × 3.15 m, 9700 kg. Diff. locks and winch at rear. Towed load 10½ tons. Used mainly by Army Engineers, from 1963. Five versions, some with loading crane.

Truck, 20-ton, 6 × 6, Prime Mover (Magirus-Deutz 'Uranus' 250AE-L) Deutz F12L 614 V-12-cyl. diesel, 250 bhp, 6F1R × 2, wb 4.44 (BC 1.38) m, 7.65 × 2.50 × 3.22 m, 18,500 kg. Used with 16-ton full-trailer for transporting AMX and G13 AFVs and other heavy equipment. Also supplied with single cab and LHD.

Truck, 35-ton, 6 × 4, Prime Mover (Rotinoff/Lomount 'Atlantic' GR7) Rolls-Royce C6SFL 6-cyl. diesel, 253 bhp, 6F1R × 3, wb 5.21 (BC 1.73) m, 8.96 × 3.00 × 3.40 m, 21,000 kg. Tyres F/R 14.00-24/18.00-25. 'Super Atlantic' with 333-bhp RR C8SFL 8-cyl. diesel supplied also. Used with 50-ton 8-wh. (8DT) trailer. GCW 110 tons.

MISCELLANEOUS VEHICLES

The Mowag firm has produced a wide range of wheeled (4×4 and 6×6) and tracked AFVs. Saurer, in 1958/59, produced the 'Tartaruga', a Swiss version of the Austrian Saurer APC. The medium tanks *Panzer (Pz)* 58, 61 and 68 were also Swiss products. Other tracked AFVs came from Britain ('Centurion'), Czechoslovakia (G13), France (AMX), South Africa (used 'Centurions') and the US (SP M109, APC M113, etc.).

Wheeled and tracked Engineers equipment (crawler tractors, loaders, cranes, etc.) has been imported mainly from the US (Caterpillar, Hough, Michigan, etc.). The familiar American 6×6 truck-mounted crane is used in Switzerland with only two axles (Michigan T4 and S20, 4×4). Unarmoured tracked carriers included the Swiss Ratrac (1-ton) and US M548 (5-ton), both of 1968.

Tractor, Artillery, 6×6 (Saurer 6ML) 6-cyl. diesel, 85 bhp, 5F1R $\times$ 2, wb 2.80 (BC 1.10) m, $5.40 \times 2.00 \times 2.30$ m approx., 5500 kg. The Saurer 6ML was a modification of the Saurer 4MH rear-engined tractor (see below), using chassis components of the 6M truck.

Tractor, Artillery, 4×4 (Saurer M4, 4MH) 4-cyl. diesel, 75 bhp, 5F1R $\times$ 2, wb 2.90 m, $5.20 \times 2.00 \times 2.26$ m, 4250 kg. GVW 6500 kg. 9.00–20 tyres on Trilex light alloy rims. Saurer CR2DM 5.82-litre engine at rear. 2½-ton winch at front. Permanent four-wheel drive. 1952.

Tractor, Artillery, 4×4 (Saurer 4MH) 4-cyl. diesel, 70 bhp, 5F1R $\times$ 2, wb 2.90 m, $5.20 \times 1.95 \times 2.10$ m, 4200 kg. GVW 5700 kg. 5.32-litre engine. Max. speed 70 km/h. Used for towing light field howitzer. Open-sided bodywork. Eight seats. 1946.

Tractors, 4×2 (Bührer, Hürlimann, Vevey) Military versions of industrial type tractors. Shown on left: Hürlimann (4-cyl. diesel, 45 bhp, 2270 kg) with 2½-ton infantry trailer, on right: Bührer (4-cyl. diesel, 55 bhp, 2300 kg) with field sterilization trailer. Not shown: Vevey (6-cyl. diesel, 45 bhp, 3000 kg).

Car, Armoured, 4×4 (Mowag) Chrysler V-8-cyl., 168 bhp, 4F1R×2, wb 2.50 m, approx 4.45×2.01×2.03 m, 4000 kg. GVW 4700 kg. Prototype (1964) of one of a wide variety of armoured cars offered for military and police purposes. Speed 110 km/h. Gradability 80%. Crew 1+6.

Carrier, Universal, Full-Track (Ford T16) V-8-cyl., 100 bhp, 4F1R, 3.85×2.10 m approx., 4000 kg. Swiss modification of US-built WW II Universal Carrier, used by armoured units to accompany tanks in forward areas. Capacity 750 kg or crew of 9. Superstructure was of Swiss manufacture.

Carrier, Armoured, Personnel, Full-Track (Mowag 'Pirat' 12) Rolls-Royce 8-cyl., 250 bhp, 5.60×2.40×2.05 m, 12½ tons. Produced in 1958. About 1962 manufacturing was taken over by Henschel in Germany who offered it with 320-bhp engine as Henschel HMK12. First prototype was built by Mowag in 1957.

USA

The number of different types of vehicles produced since 1945 in the United States of America for military use, or designed and developed for possible military use, is higher than that of any other country and is probably at least doubled if the number of commercial-type vehicles is included. Not covered in this book are tanks and self-propelled artillery, but even without these complete coverage is impossible. The accent therefore is on soft-skin general purpose and special equipment vehicles. Of special purpose vehicles only typical examples are shown.

One factor contributing to the multitude of types of US military vehicles is the fact that various enterprising manufacturers have, over the years, designed and developed a relatively large number of vehicles as private ventures and offered them to the Government for evaluation. In some cases these efforts were influenced by the existence of certain military requirements. A good example is the 1¼-ton tactical truck known as 'Gama Goat'. The original concept was invented by Mr. R. Gamaunt in California. A prototype of his vehicle was produced by the Ling-Temco-Vought Aerospace Corp. of Dallas, Texas, in 1960. About this time the US Government decided to replace its ¾-ton 4 × 4 range (as produced by Dodge and developed from the war-time 'Beep') by a new 'Truck, Utility, High Mobility, Light Duty, XM561'. The new vehicle, with 1¼-ton payload rating, was originally planned to be a cab-forward 4 × 4 and industry was invited to submit suitable test vehicles. Several manufacturers entered, incl. Chrysler and GM. LTV entered the 'Gama Goat', a 6 × 6 articulated vehicle, which proved to have maximum potential to fulfil the Army's requirements. The vehicle was selected for further development and was eventually approved and standardized. When it came to series production, however, the contract was won by another manufacturer (Condec) who happened to be the lowest bidder in the US Government 'open-bid competition' system. The Army itself also designed and built numerous prototypes and pilot models, many of which remained in the experimental stage. In 1950 the US Army had introduced a new family of tactical trucks, commonly known as the 'M-Series', less frequently as the 'Korean war types' (as opposed to 'World War II types'). Generally these could be described as improved versions of the WWII tactical trucks, with higher degree of standardization and interchangeability of components and parts and embodying many of the lessons learned during WWII. The number of basic type ranges was reduced by more than half and consisted mainly of ¼-ton and ¾-ton 4 × 4 and 2½-, 5- and 10-ton 6 × 6 models. Logically, this also drastically reduced the number of spare parts required to be stocked. Over the years these vehicles were improved in various respects (e.g. introduction of multi-fuel power units). During the 1960s a four-category system of trucks for the Field Army emerged, namely (a) Military High-mobility Tactical, (b) Military Tactical, Standard, (c) Quasi Military, and (d) Commercial Administrative. The first (a) would be used for forward combat (or division) areas, providing maximum cross-country mobility as well as the ability to swim (example: M561 'Gama Goat' 1¼-ton 6 × 6 and M656 5-ton 8 × 8); the second (b) the current standard 'M-Series' Tactical Trucks (examples: M35 2½-ton 6 × 6 and M54 5-ton 6 × 6), for combat support and

1972 edition of ¼-ton 4 × 4 Utility Truck (M151A2)

other units requiring good off-road ability in rear Division and Corps areas; the third (c) to be de-militarized ('austere') versions of 'M-Series' trucks, to be used where only adequate or marginal mobility was acceptable, as well as for MAP (Military Assistance Program, i.e. aid to friendly nations) (included in this category are also commercial cross-country trucks which with relatively minor modifications are acceptable for military use, exemplified by the 1¼-ton 4 × 4 Jeep truck, M715) and finally (d) administrative trucks which are essentially straight commercial vehicles, for use in administrative fixed base units, etc. It was estimated that in the Army 20% of the truck fleet could be commercial types and in the other services (USAF, USMC, USN, etc.) as much as 75%. This would average 40% of the estimated total peace-time truck strength of half a million trucks, with obvious reductions in cost of upkeep, commercial trucks being less expensive to acquire and maintain. It may be of interest at this point to mention that especially during the 1950s the US occupation forces in Germany acquired many German-built commercial trucks, mainly for administrative purposes. These trucks carried a plate stating: 'Occupation Cost (DM) Procurement. Spare Parts can be Local Procured'. Likewise, US forces in Japan received considerable numbers of Japanese-built trucks.

By 1970 the Army's general-purpose fleet of tactical trucks consisted of four payload categories, namely ¼- and 1¼-ton (both 4 × 4), 2½-ton (6 × 6) and 5-ton (6 × 6 and 8 × 8). Of most types there was a military tactical version and an 'austere' version, available for international aid.

Design effort in new tactical and general purpose support vehicles is still aimed at higher off-road mobility to match combat vehicle (AFV) developments. By 1970 the Army Tank-Automotive Command (TACOM) was beginning experiments with a new light-weight infantry load carrier with better performance than the 'mechanical mule' (M274) and an articulated test rig with a 'walking' suspension system with the wheels mounted on articulated legs. A new ¾-ton concept under consideration was an 8 × 8 skid-steer vehicle which could also function as a tracked vehicle. A more conventional replacement for the old M37 ¾-ton 4 × 4 truck for use in areas behind brigade

rear was the XM705, designed with ease of maintenance in mind. This vehicle had many interesting features, including automatic trouble-spotting measurement points in engine and drive train.

Budget stringencies and the pressure of the Vietnam conflict in the late 1960s had the result that fewer new vehicles were obtained than originally planned. For 1971 about two-thirds of the budget for 1¼-ton trucks was allocated for the articulated 'Gama Goat' (M561), the rest for the 'quasi-military' M715 4 × 4 Jeep truck. 'Goer' vehicles were also planned for acquisition in the 1971 fiscal year.

Typical example of 2½-ton 6 × 6 'M-Series' truck after complete rebuild for civilian use in the Netherlands.

Who's Who in the US Automotive Industry
Note: some of the manufacturers who were no longer operational under their own name by 1970 or only supplied commercial-type vehicles or special equipment on other chassis have been omitted.

ACF-Brill	ACF-Brill Motor Co., Philadelphia, Pa.
Allis-Chalmers	Allis-Chalmers Mfg. Co., Milwaukee, Wisc.
AMC	American Motors Corp., Detroit, Mich. (and AM General Corp., Wayne, Mich.).

USA

American LaFrance	American LaFrance Div. of ATO Inc., Elmira, NY.	Harley-Davidson	Harley-Davidson Motor Co., Milwaukee, Wisc.
Autocar	Autocar Truck Div. of White Motor Corp., Exton, Pa.	Hendrickson	Hendrickson Mfg. Co., Lyons, Ill.
Bay City	Bay City Shovels, Inc., Bay City, Mich.	International	International Harvester Co., Chicago, Ill.
Brockway	Brockway Motor Truck Div. of Mack Trucks, Inc., Cortland, NY.	Jeep	Jeep Corporation, Subsidiary of AMC (qv). (Predecessors: Willys-Overland and Kaiser Jeep Corp., Toledo, Ohio).
Buick	Buick Motor Div. of GM Corp., Flint, Mich.	Kenworth	Kenworth Motor Truck Co., Seattle, Wash.
Cadillac	Cadillac Motor Car Div. of GM Corp., Detroit, Mich.	Lockheed	Lockheed Aircraft Services Co., Div. of Lockheed Aircraft Corp., Ontario, Cal.
Cadillac Gage	Cadillac Gage Co., Warren, Mich.	LTV	Ling-Temco-Vought, Inc., Dallas, Texas.
Caterpillar	Caterpillar Tractor Co., Peoria, Ill.	Mack	Mack Trucks, Inc., Allentown, Pa.
Checker	Checker Motors Corp., Kalamazoo, Mich.	Marmon-Herrington	Marmon-Herrington Automotive Div., Lebanon, Ind.
Chevrolet	Chevrolet Motor Div. of GM Corp., Detroit, Mich.	Oshkosh	Oshkosh Truck Corp., Oshkosh, Wisc.
Chrysler	Chrysler Motors Corp., Detroit, Mich.	PCF	Pacific Car & Foundry Co., Seattle, Wash.
Clark	Clark Equipment Co., Benton Harbor, Mich.	Pontiac	Pontiac Motor Div. of GM Corp., Pontiac, Mich.
Coleman	American Coleman Co., Littleton, Colo.	Reo	Diamond Reo Truck Div. of White Motor Corp., Lansing, Mich. (formerly Reo Motors Inc., Lansing, Mich.).
Condec, Consolidated	Consolidated Diesel Electric Div. of Condec Corp., Stamford, Conn.		
Corbitt	The Corbitt Co., Henderson, NC.		
Cushman	Cushman Motors Div. of Outboard Marine Corp., Lincoln, Neb.	Thew	Thew Lorain Div. of Koehring Co., Lorain, Ohio.
Diamond (T)	Diamond Reo Truck Div. of White Motor Corp., Lansing, Mich. (formerly Diamond T Motor Car Co., Chicago, Ill.).	Twin Coach	Highway Products, Inc., Kent, Ohio.
		WABCO	WABCO, Construction Equipment Div., an American-Standard Company, Peoria, Ill. (absorbed R. G. LeTourneau Inc. in 1953; equipment then known as LeTourneau-Westinghouse, later as WABCO).
Dodge	Dodge Div. of Chrysler Corp., Detroit, Mich.		
Duplex	Duplex Div. of Warner & Swasey Co., Lansing, Mich.		
Eimco	The Eimco Corp., Salt Lake City, Utah.	Walter	Walter Motor Truck Co., Voorheesville, NY.
Euclid	Euclid, Inc., Cleveland, Ohio.	Ward LaFrance	Ward LaFrance Truck Corp., Elmira Heights, NY.
FMC	Food Machinery Corp., Ordnance Div., San Jose, Cal.		
Ford	Ford Div. of Ford Motor Co., Dearborn, Mich.	Wayne	Wayne Works Div. of Divco-Wayne Corp., Richmond, Ind.
FWD	FWD Corp., Clintonville, Wisc.	White	White Truck Div. of White Motor Corp., Cleveland, Ohio.
GMC	GMC Truck & Coach Div. of GM Corp., Pontiac, Mich.	WNRE	Wilson, Nuttall, Raimond Engineers, Inc., Chestertown, Md.

HET-70—Heavy Equipment Transporter for the 1970s, developed jointly by the USA and W. Germany.

Undoubtedly the longest military vehicle ever built—the USATRECOM's 'Overland Train' built by R. G. LeTourneau, Inc. of Longview, Texas, in 1961/62.

MOTORCYCLES and MOTOR SCOOTERS

During WWII the two major US manufacturers of motorcycles, Harley-Davidson and Indian, supplied considerable numbers of military machines (mainly solo) to the US Government and its allies. After the war the US forces retained only relatively small quantities of these and few new ones were acquired. Main models used were the Harley-Davidson WL45 and WLA Series and the Indian 'extra light' Aerocycle Models 148 and 149M. Three-Wheelers included 'package delivery' motor scooters by Cushman and a heavy unit produced by Harley-Davidson (Model G, 1950). The former were frequently used on airfields. Experimental rough terrain 2- and 3-wheel motor scooters (XM713 and XM710 resp.) were developed during the 1960s.

Motorcycle, Solo, Extra Light (Indian 149M, T3) Single-cyl., 9 bhp, 4F, wb 53½ in, 86 × 29 × 38 in, 310 lb. Indian 149M 13.3-cu. in OHV engine. B × S 2¾ × 3 in. Tyre size 3.25–18. Speed 60 mph. Airborne machine, equipped with parachute attachment rings.

Motor Scooter, Package Delivery, 3-wheel (Cushman 67P) Single-cyl., 4.6 bhp, 2F, wb 62 in, 101 × 50 × 44 in, 486 lb. Other three-wheeled Cushmans used were the Model 39 'Package Car' and Model 32 side-car combination of WWII origin. USAF also had post-war forward-control model.

Motorcycle, Solo, 3-wheel (Harley-Davidson G) V-2-cyl., 23 bhp, 3F, wb 61½ in, 107 × 52 × 51¾ in, 500 lb. Tyres 5.00–16. 45-cu. in L-head engine. Purpose: to provide transportation for messenger service, convoy control, and police operations. GVW 1395 lb. Speed 45 mph. 1950.

CARS and
STATION WAGONS

Since 1945 the US armed forces have acquired considerable quantities of new civilian type cars (sedans) and station wagons of many model years. They are replaced by new current models as and when they become non-serviceable. Cars (officially: Automobile, Sedan) were supplied by American Motors (Ambassador, Rambler), Chrysler (Chrysler, Dodge, Plymouth), Ford (Ford, Lincoln, Mercury), General Motors (Buick, Cadillac, Chevrolet, Pontiac) and Packard. Station wagons (2- and 4-door, 2- and 3-seat models) were supplied by most of the above as well as Willys (4×2 and 4×4 models). In Germany the US forces employed numbers of cars obtained locally, e.g. Ford 'Taunus', Opel 'Rekord' and 'Kapitän', and Volkswagen and in France Renault 'Frégate', Simca 'Ariane'.

Car, Light Sedan, 5-passenger, 4×2 (Chevrolet GJ1553) 6-cyl., 83 bhp, 3F1R, wb 115 in, 197×74×65 in, 3220 lb. Tyres 6.70–15. 216.5 CID OHV engine. 1949 fast-back 'Fleetline Special' shown. Also used were GJ1503 'bustle back' 'Styleline Special' sedan and Chevrolets of many other model years.

Station Wagon, 3-seat, 4-door, 4×2 (Ford) Left (w/dual headlights): Model 71E 'Country Sedan' 1959, V-8-cyl., 200 bhp, auto. trans.; right (w/single headlights): Model 79 C 'Country Sedan' 1957, 6-cyl., 144 bhp, manual 3F1R trans. Used by USAF and Army. Vehicles shown were ex-USAF in UK.

Station Wagon, 3-seat, 4-door, 4×2 (Plymouth TP2-L 'Savoy') V-8-cyl., 230 bhp, 3F1R (or 'Torqueflite'), wb 116 in, 210×75×54 in. Tyres 7.00 or 7.50–16. IFS with torsion bars. 318 CID engine (6-cyl. and bigger V8s also available). 1963 model, used by USAF in UK (RHD).

CARRYALLS
4 × 2 and 4 × 4

Carryalls are basically commercial-type panel vans, modified by fitting additional side windows and seats in the rear compartment. They are operated by all services for conveyance of personnel and light cargo. Official nomenclature: Truck, Carryall, ½-ton, 4 × 2, etc., depending on basic type. Seating capacity varied from three to eight. Both conventional and forward control types were used. The Army used ½-ton 4 × 2 models supplied by Chevrolet, Dodge and International, ½-ton 4 × 4 models by Chevrolet, Dodge and Willys and 1-ton 4 × 4 models by Dodge. The latter were based on the 'Power Wagon' chassis.

Truck, ½-ton, 4 × 2, Carryall (International L112) 6-cyl., 100 bhp, 3F1R, wb 115 in, 192 × 79 × 81 in, 3945 lb. Seating capacity for eight. Based on 1949–52 L-line panel van. Model SD-220 engine ('Silver Diamond'). Loading space 90 × 60 × 54 in. R112 of 1954 was similar.

Truck, ½-ton, 4 × 2, Carryall (Dodge A100) 6-cyl., 101 bhp, 3F1R, wb 90 in. Commercial 'Tradesman Vision Van' carried aboard USS 'Providence' (USN) and used ashore when required. Available with several engine and transmission options, incl. V8 and auto. *c.* 1967.

Truck, 1-ton, 4 × 4, Carryall, XM678 (Kaiser Jeep FC170) Cerlist 3-cyl. diesel, 83 bhp, 3F1R × 2, wb 103½ in, 184 × 78 × 87 in, 4750 lb. 170 CID 2-stroke engine, developing 170 lb-ft of torque *(a* 1900 rpm. Four-door seven-seater with folding/removable rear seats. 1962.

AMBULANCES, 4×2

Most vehicles in this category were conversions of sedans, station wagons or panel vans. By the mid 1960s the following Army types were current: Automobile, Ambulance: 1-litter (stretcher): Dodge/Memphis (1956), Cadillac/Superior (1957), Pontiac/Sup. (1958); 4-litter: Cadillac/Sup., Cadillac/Meteor and Cadillac/Miller (1942–51), Packard/Henney (1942–51) and Pontiac/Sup. (1957–64). Superior Coach Corp. of Lima, Ohio, was the main supplier of bodywork for these vehicles.

Ambulances based on 4×2 light panel vans included 2- to 4-litter models on ½-ton Ford and GMC, and a 4-litter model on 1-ton International chassis. Commercial-type 4×4 ambulances were supplied by Dodge, International and Willys. The USAF acquired a GMC 6×4 ambulance with elevating body, about 1953, and used several 4×2 types, incl. Mercury and Pontiac. ACF-Brill, International and Twin Coach buses were also used as ambulances.

Ambulance, Metropolitan, ¾-ton, 4-litter (Cadillac/Superior 4986) V-8-cyl., 141 bhp, 3F1R, wb 163 in, 252 × 75 × 76 in, 5530 lb. 1949 Model 86 chassis with Superior body. Later renamed: Automobile, Ambulance, 4-litter, 3-door. Similar bodywork, as well as hearses, on earlier and later Cadillac (and other) chassis.

Truck, ½-ton, 4×2, Ambulance, 2-litter (GMC FC 101-22) 6-cyl., 100 bhp, 3F1R, wb 116 in, 197 × 75 × 81 in, 4006 lb. GVW 4600 lb. Derived from 'Suburban', 1951–53. Inside dimensions 92 × 62 × 50 in. Two rear doors. GMC 228 engine. Similar ambulance on 1955 Ford F100 chassis.

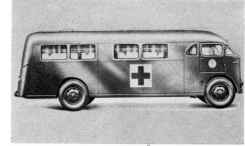

Truck, 1¼-ton, 4×2, Ambulance, 12-litter, Metropolitan, M423(Linn) Dodge T214 6-cyl., 94 bhp, 4F1R×1, wb 186 in, 300 × 88 × 105 in, 6500 lb. Front-wheel drive. Tyres 9.00-20 (single rear). Track, front 64¼ in, rear 73 in. Trailer-type rear axle. Later, converted integral-type buses were used as large capacity ambulances.

BUSES

Four basic types of buses have been used since 1945. The smallest were 11-passenger Checker 'Aerobus' models (from 1963). Medium-size normal control models for 17 and 20 passengers were produced by Superior Coach on Ford F5 (1950) and B500 (1963) and on Dodge chassis.

Larger types with normal control and school bus-type bodywork seating 29 to 37, were supplied by various firms (chassis: Chevrolet, Dodge, Ford, GMC, International, Reo; bodywork: Blue Bird, Carpenter, Hackney, Oneida, Superior, Thomas, Wayne, etc.). Finally there were the forward-control types, supplied by ACF-Brill, GMC, International, Madsen, Southern Coach, Twin Coach, Ward. These 'integral types' seated up to 53 and some were designed for ambulance and cargo carrier conversion. Some WWII types (incl. rebodied Dodge ¾-ton 4 × 4 and GMC 2½-ton 6 × 6) remained in use for several years and overseas foreign buses were employed (e.g. Bedford and Ford 'Trader' in Britain, Ford, Magirus-Deutz and Mercedes-Benz in Germany).

Bus, 20-passenger, 4 × 2 (Dodge D500) 6-cyl., 130 bhp, 4F1R, wb 129 in. Dodge D-series buses appeared in short (shown), medium and long wheelbase versions. Other chassis fitted with similar 'school bus' bodies included Chevrolet, Ford and GMC. Used by all services.

Bus, 11-passenger, 4 × 2 (Checker A12W8C 'Aerobus') Chrysler 318 V-8-cyl., 190 bhp, 3F1R, wb 189 in, 269¾ × 76 × 64 in, 4905 lb. Eight side doors. Tyres 7.60–15 (8.20–15 optional). Power-assisted steering and brakes. Commercially available (also 6-door 9-pass.).

Bus, Integral, 37-passenger, Utility Convertible (Twin Coach F32F) Fageol/Crofton Marine FTC210–21 6-cyl., 172 bhp, 4F1R, wb 222 in, 391 × 96 × 119 in, 15,620 lb. Removable seats for conversion to ambulance or cargo carrier. Horizontal, centrally mounted engine. Some had 2-speed rear axle. Early 1950s.

LIGHT TRUCKS
and PANEL VANS, 4 × 2

Light trucks are used with various types of bodywork, including Cargo, Pickup and Panel Van. Some formed the basis for ambulances and/or carryalls. Certain types were also supplied with four-wheel drive. Complete ½- and ¾-ton pickup trucks were supplied by Chevrolet, Dodge, Ford, GMC and International, panel vans by Chevrolet, Dodge and Ford. Some LWB pickups had a double cab, seating six. 1-ton 4 × 2 cargo and panel trucks were supplied by Chevrolet, Dodge and Ford, and 'Multistop Delivery' trucks with forward control and sliding-type doors by Chevrolet (1- and 1½-ton), Dodge and International (1-ton). Forward control panel vans were chiefly of Dodge and Ford ('Econoline') manufacture. Chassis/cabs (½- and ¾-ton) for special bodies (e.g. Telephone Maintenance) were acquired from Chevrolet, Dodge, Ford and International.

Truck, ½-ton, 4 × 2, Panel (Dodge B1-B108) 6-cyl., 82 bhp, 3F1R, wb 108 in, 190 × 63½ × 83 in, 3400 lb. Tyres 6.50–16. GVW 4850 lb. Model T142 218 CID L-head engine. 1948 model shown. B2–B108 of 1950 similar in appearance. Also ½- and ¾-ton pickup versions.

Truck, ½-ton, 4 × 2, Panel (Chevrolet Series 31 'Apache' 3105) 6-cyl., 135 bhp, 3F1R, wb 114 in. Tyres 6.70-15. 'Thriftmaster' 235.5 CID engine ('Trademaster' 283 CID V8 optional). Various transmission options, incl. 'Hydramatic', Also pickup body style. 1959.

Truck, ½-ton, 4 × 2, Panel (Ford 'Econoline') 6-cyl., 85 bhp, 3F1R, wb 90 in, 168½ × 76 × 78½ in, 2446 lb. Tyres 6.50–13. GVW 3375 lb (4177 with 7.00–13 tyres). Introduced in 1961 with Falcon 144.3 CID engine. Other body styles: pickup and 'station bus'. All were used by the military.

Truck, ½-ton, 4 × 2, Pickup (Chevrolet Series C10) 6-cyl., 140 bhp, 3F1R, wb 115 in, 186½ × 78¾ in, GVW 5000 lb. Tyres 6.70–15. RHD. 1963 model with right-hand drive, 'Stepside' body (full-width type was 'Fleetside') and metal enclosure. Used by USAF in Great Britain.

Truck, ½-ton, 4 × 2, Pickup (Ford F100) 6-cyl., 135 bhp, 3F1R, wb 114 in. 1961 model with 'Flareside' 6½-ft body. Max. GVW 5000 lb. 223 CID engine. Also available with 160-bhp V-8-cyl. engine, 122-in wheelbase and 8-ft body ('Flareside' or 'Styleside').

Truck, ¾-ton, 4 × 2, Pickup (Ford F250) 6-cyl., 139 bhp, 4F1R, wb 140 in. 1960 model with 'Flareside' body style (full-width type was 'Styleside') with metal enclosure. Double cab with six-person seating capacity. 223 CID engine (V8 292 CID optional).

Truck, ¾-ton, 4 × 2, Pickup (International C112) 6-cyl., 112 bhp, 3F1R (or 4F1R), wb 126 in, GVW 5800 lb. 'Travelette' six-seater four-door cab and six-foot 'Bonus-Load' (full-width) cargo box on 1961 C110 Series chassis. Used by USAF (4 × 4 version also).

TRUCKS, $\frac{1}{4}$-TON
4 × 2 and 4 × 4

Makes and Models: American Motors M422, M422A1 'Mighty Mite' (G843) (4 × 4, 1960), M151A2 (4 × 4, 1971). Crofton 'Bug' (4 × 2, 1960). Fletcher Flair 115 (4 × 4, 1953/54). Ford M107, M108, M151, M718, and variants (4 × 4, from 1960). International 'Scout' 80, 800 (4 × 2 and 4 × 4, from 1961). Kaiser Jeep CJ3A (RHD) (4 × 2, 1964), CJ3B and M606 (4 × 4, from 1963), MD M38A1, A1C, A1D, M606A2, A3 (G758) (4 × 4, from 1963), M151 (4 × 4, 1963). Kochler K622 'Fox' (4 × 4, 1961). Mitsubishi CJ3B-J4C (4 × 4, c. 1963, J). Mid-America Research Corp./USMC 'Mighty Mite' (4 × 4, 1950–53). Willys CJ2A, CJ3A, CJ3B (4 × 4, from c. 1947), MC M38 and variants (G740) (4 × 4, 1950), MD M38A1 and variants (G758) (4 × 4, 1952), MDA M170 (G758) (ambulance, 4 × 4, 1953), 'Bobcat' (4 × 4, 1953).

General Data: Until the early 1950s the war-time 'Jeep' remained in general use. When the Korean conflict started the US Army required an improved model with 24-volt electrics, better weather protection, deep water fording equipment, etc. As an interim solution, Willys developed a military version of the CJ3A 'Universal Jeep', designated M38, 60,345 of which were produced during 1950–52. In 1952 a new model made its debut, the M38A1. This model had a more powerful (F-head) engine and numerous other modifications, but it was still basically a commercial design. In 1951 the Army awarded a contract to the Ford Motor Co. for the design and development of an entirely new $\frac{1}{4}$-ton 4 × 4 vehicle. After extensive testing of prototypes (XM-151) and subsequent trials of pre-production models, this vehicle went into quantity production in 1960, standardized as M151.

US forces in Japan obtained the Mitsubishi Jeep which was the Willys CJ3B produced under licence. The M606 was a military version of the Kaiser Jeep CJ3B, supplied to several friendly nations. The M606A2 and A3 were military versions of CJ5s. Willys became Kaiser Jeep in 1963, and Jeep Corp. (Subsidiary of AMC) in 1970. In 1971 AMC formed a new company for military vehicle production, AM General Corp. 'JEEP' is the tradename for all vehicles produced by Jeep Corp.

Vehicle shown (typical): Truck, $\frac{1}{4}$-ton, 4 × 4, Utility, M151 (Ford, Kaiser Jeep)

Technical Data:
Engine: Continental M151 4-cylinder, I-I-W-F, 141.5 cu. in, 71 bhp @ 4000 rpm.
Transmission: 4F1R × 1.
Brakes: hydraulic.
Tyres: 7.00–16.
Wheelbase: 85 in. Track: 53 in.
Overall l × w × h: 132$\frac{3}{4}$ × 64 × 71 (52$\frac{1}{2}$) in.
Weight: 2350 lb (M151A1 : 2400 lb).
Note: Unitary body/chassis (by Fruehauf) with coil-spring IFS/IRS. Current nomenclature: 'Truck, Utility: $\frac{1}{4}$-ton. 4 × 4, M151'. 24-volt electrics. M151A1 (1964) and A2 (1970) were improved versions, the latter with redesigned IRS and other safety features.

Truck, ¼-ton, 4 × 4, Utility, XM151 (Ford) During 1951 Ford studied two basic designs for a new military utility tactical truck ('Mutt'). Design I had separate frame and body and rigid axles, II had unitary chassis/body, IFS/IRS. Design II was selected for further development. 1954 pilot model shown.

Truck, ¼-ton, 4 × 4, Weapons Carrier, M151A1C (RRAD) Modification of M151A1, for mounting 106-mm recoilless rifle, M40A1, on mount, M79. HD suspension. Another variant was the M718 front line ambulance. For the basic vehicle several modification kits were designed, incl. hard-top.

Truck, ¼-ton, 4 × 4, Utility, M38 (Willys MC) 4-cyl., 60 bhp, 3F1R × 2, wb 80 in, 133 × 62 × 74 (55) in, 2750 lb. Military version of CJ3A 'Universal Jeep', 1950–52. Basically as wartime MB but with many improvements. Fitted with snorkels for underwater-driving. Winch optional. Also made in Canada (*qv*).

Truck, ¼-ton, 4 × 4, Utility, M606 (Kaiser Jeep CJ3B, mod.) 4-cyl., 71 bhp, 3F1R × 2, wb 80 in, 130 × 69 × 68 in, 2418 lb. Military version of CJ3B 'Universal' for US military aid program (MAP). Basically as CJ3A but 'Hurricane' F4–134 F-head engine (hence higher hood and grille). Used in Philippines, Vietnam, etc.

Truck, ¼-ton, 4 × 4, Utility, M38A1 (Willys MD) 4-cyl., 72 bhp, 3F1R × 2, wb 81 in, 139½ × 61½ × 73 (55) in, 2665 lb. First introduced in 1952. Civilian version: CJ5. M38A1C (split windshield) was recoilless rifle carrier modification. 24-volt electrics. 7.00–16 tyres. Track 49 in.

Truck, ¼-ton, 4 × 4, Utility, Lightweight (Willys 'Bobcat') 4-cyl., 60 bhp, 3F1R × 2, wb 80 in, 100 × 60 × 65½ in, 1475 lb. Exp. 'Aero Jeep', 1953. MC L-head engine under MD-type hood. Aluminium body (81 lb) and magnesium wheels (41 lb). Speed 72 mph. Tested (Army, Marines) but no quantity production.

Truck, ¼-ton, 4 × 4, Utility, M606A2 (Kaiser Jeep CJ5M) 4-cyl., 72 bhp, 3F1R × 2, wb 81 in, 139 × 72 × 70 (52) in, 2564 lb. Military version of CJ5 'Universal' (not to be confused with M38A1) superseding M606, for MAP. M606A3 was radio version. GVW 3750 lb (M606: 3500 lb). CJ5-type canvas top, steps, etc.

Truck, ¼-ton, 4 × 4, Ambulance, Front Line, M170 (Willys MDA) 4-cyl., 72 bhp, 3F1R × 2, wb 101 m, 155 × 60½ × 80 in, 2963 lb. LWB variant of M38A1. Six sitting patients or three litters (stretchers) (or three and two resp.). Military version of CJ6. First made in 1952 (with different front end). Also used as communications vehicle (MK-87 FAC).

Truck, ¼-ton, 4 × 4, Utility, Lightweight (Mid-America Research Corp. 'Mighty Mite') Porsche 4-cyl., 44 bhp, 3F1R × 2, wb 64 in, 96 × 58 × 58 in, 1496 lb. Designed by Ben F. Gregory. One of several pilot models, 1953 (USMC 179846–54). Permanent all-wheel drive. Tyres 5.90–15. Cantilever leaf spring IFS/IRS.

Truck, ¼-ton, 4 × 4, Utility, Lightweight, M422 (American Motors) V-4-cyl., 55 bhp, 4F1R × 1, wb 65 in, 107 × 60½ × 59½ (43½) in, 1700 lb. Tyres 6.00–16. Model AV–108–4 107.8-cu. in air-cooled engine. Early model shown. M422A1 had 113-in overall length. 1250 built for USMC (2672 M422A1s), 1960–63. Known as 'Mighty Mite'.

Truck, ¼-ton, 4 × 4, Utility, Lightweight (Fletcher Flair 115) Porsche 4-cyl., 50 bhp, 4F1R. In 1953 the Fletcher Aviation Corp. in Pasadena, Calif., produced an exp. rear-engined (Porsche 1582 cc) semi-amphibious six-seater field car for possible mil. use. The four-seater shown was a further development (1954). No series production.

Truck, ¼-ton, 4 × 2, Utility (International 'Scout' 800) 4-cyl., 93 bhp, 3F1R, wb 100 in, 154 × 69 × 67 in, 2800 lb. Commercial vehicle, used by US Army, Navy and Marine Corps, mostly with all-wheel drive. Also 'cab-top' and 'travel-top' versions. Similar vehicles: Chevrolet 'Blazer, Ford 'Bronco', GMC 'Jimmy'.

TRUCKS, ½- to 1-TON
4 × 4, 6 × 6 and 8 × 8

Makes and Models: Note: cargo, 4 × 4, unless stated otherwise. Chevrolet 3654 (1-ton, 1958), 'Sidewinder' (¾-ton, 1964). Chrysler T53 (¾-ton, 1948). Dodge T245 Series (¾-ton, from 1950, G741); variants: M37, M42 (command), M43 (ambulance), M53 and M56 (chassis/cab), M152 (panel utility), M201 (V-41/GT Signals Corps maintenance), M283 (LWB cargo), XM708 (dump), XM711 (wrecker), etc. Dodge 'Power Wagon' Series (military type, 1-ton, from 1950); variants: B2PW126 and PW6 (closed cab), W300M, M601 (open cab), M615 (ambulance). Dodge 'Power Wagon' Series (comm. type, from 1959); variants: W100 (½-ton), W200 (1-ton, cargo and ambulance), W300 (1-ton); W200 also with LWB and 4-d. cab. Ford F250 (¾-ton, 1960). Ford/ATAC XM408 (¾-ton, 6 × 6, 1958), XM384 (1-ton, 8 × 8, 1958). International A120, C120 (1-ton, cargo and ambulances, from 1957). Kaiser Jeep FC170 (X)M676-679 (1-ton, cargo and ambulance, 1964). Toyota 2FQ15L (¾-ton, cargo and ambulance, 1964, J). Willys 4WD, 473-WD (1-ton, 1949–50), 475-4WD (½- and ¾-ton, 1955), 475-4WD, 6-226 (1-ton, ambulances, 1955–56). Willys (later: Baifield, Brunswick) M274 and variants, 'Mech. Mule' (½-ton, platform utility, from 1956). Willys XM 443(E1) (¾-ton, from 1958).

General Data: During the first years after 1945 the Dodge ¾-ton 4 × 4 'Beep' and its variants were still widely used. From 1950 these were supplemented and later gradually superseded by a new range of Dodge ¾-tonners.

In the Far East a similar type, produced by Toyota, was also employed. In addition there were many commercial types, principally products of Dodge and Willys. Dodge, immediately after the war, had introduced a civilian version of the war-time 'Beep', named 'Power Wagon'. This truck, of which there was a special military version with open cab and winch option, was used as a tactical military vehicle in many countries all over the world.

By the late 1960s the ¾-ton class was on the way out and the replacement for the Dodge T245 4 × 4 Series was a military Jeep truck, classed as a 1¼-tonner (see following section).

Vehicle shown (typical): Truck, ½-ton, 4 × 4, Platform, Utility, M274 (Willys 'Mechanical Mule')

Technical Data:
Engine: Willys AO53 4-cylinder, H-I-A-R, 53.5 cu. in, 15–17 bhp @ 3200 rpm.
Transmission: 3F1R × 2.
Brakes: mechanical.
Tyres: 7.50–10.
Wheelbase: 57 in. Track: 40½ in.
Overall l × w × h: 118¾ × 49¾ × 49 in.
Weight: 925 lb.
Note: Pilot models 1953–56. Production from 1956 by Willys, later by Baifield Industries (1965), Brunswick Corp. (1970). M274A2 to A5 had Continental Hercules AO42 2-cyl. 42.4-cu.in 12.5-bhp engine. Four-wheel steer and 'pedestrian control' possible.

Truck, ¾-ton, 4 × 4, Cargo and Personnel, XM443 (Willys) 4-cyl., 100 bhp, 3F1R × 2, wb 72 in, 131½ × 62 × 61½ in, 1500 lb. GVW 2440 lb. Speed 60 mph. Payload 1500 lb or 6 men (4 folding rear seats). Air-cooled aluminium engine (164 CID). Selective 2- or 4-wh. steering. 1958.

Truck, ¾-ton, 4 × 4, Cargo and Personnel, XM443E1 (Willys) 4-cyl., 100 bhp, 3F1R × 2, wb 80 in. Improved version of XM443. Five produced in 1959 for Army tests and evaluation. Exp. outgrowths of 'Mechanical Mule'. Central engine mounting. Some had single headlights.

Truck, ¾-ton, 4 × 4, Cargo, w/Winch, M37 (Dodge T245) 6-cyl., 94 bhp, 4F1R × 2, wb 112 in, 189 × 73½ × 89½ (63½) in, 5950 lb. M37B1 and M42 (command) similar in appearance. Shown with hard-top cab and snorkels (fording kit). More than 80,000 produced, from 1950, replacing wartime 'Beep'. Also produced in Canada (qv).

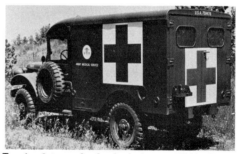

Truck, ¾-ton, 4 × 4, Ambulance, M43 (Dodge T245) 6-cyl., 94 bhp, 4F1R × 2, wb 126 in, 198 × 73½ × 92 in, 8550 lb. Tyres 9.00–16 (M43E2: 11.00–16). Steel bodywork (M43B1: aluminium) for 4 litters or 6–8 sitting patients. Swing-out spare wheel bracket. Door in cab rear wall. Adjustable spotlight on cab roof.

Truck, ¾-ton, 4 × 4, Cargo, w/Winch, T53 (Chrysler) Continental AO-402-1 6-cyl., 152 bhp, GM 2F1R (auto.) × 1, wb 114 in, 190½ × 83 × 89 (66) in, 6150 lb. Exp. cross country carrier with air-cooled 403.2 CID engine. Tyres 9.00–20. Three built in 1948, one converted to light-weight 2½-ton 6 × 6.

Truck, 1-ton, 4 × 4, Cargo, M601 (Dodge W300M) 6-cyl., 113 bhp, 4F1R × 2, wb 126 in, 199 × 79 × 85 in, 5000 lb. Tyres 9.00–16. Military version of 'Power Wagon', (Dodge, DeSoto, Fargo). Folding troop seats in back. Used by several countries, also with special bodywork (ambulance M615, etc.). Winch optional.

Truck, 1-ton, 4 × 4, Cargo, w/4-d. Cab (Dodge S6-W200) 6-cyl., 140 bhp, 4F1R × 2, wb 146 in. GVW 7000 lb. Commercial 'Power Wagon', 1962, with four-door cab. Used by all services. Also 4 × 2 and narrower 'Utiline' rear body (USAF 'Sweptline' shown). Similar type by IHC (Model C120–4 × 4).

Truck, 1-ton, 4 × 4, Cargo, w/4-d. Cab, XM677 (Kaiser Jeep FC170) Cerlist 3-cyl. 2-stroke diesel, 83 bhp, 3F1R × 2, wb 103½ in, 184 × 78 × 91 in, 4660 lb. GVW 7000 lb. Tyres 7.50–16. On same chassis: XM676 (single cab), XM678 (carryall) and XM679 (ambulance), all for US Navy, 1962. 'Powr-Lok' diffs. front and rear.

Truck, 1-ton, 3 × 3, Cargo, Pneumatic Roller Type (Dodge 'Power Wagon', modified) 6-cyl., 94 bhp, 4F1R × 2. Conversion of 1954. Goodyear 'Rolligon' tyres were driven by rollers (8 per wheel). Later versions had 3 chain-driven 'Terratires', and 4 'Terratires' on std. axles.

Truck, ¾-ton, 4 × 4, Cargo, Articulated (Chevrolet 'Sidewinder') V-8-cyl., 195 bhp, 2F1R (auto.), wb 132 in, 192 × 83 in, 4400 lb. GVW 6000 lb. Test-rig, developed in 1964 jointly with GM Defense Research Laboratories. Power-pack was in middle 'module'. Spinning tyres (14.00–20) allowed it to swim at over 2 mph.

Truck, ¾-ton, 6 × 6, Cargo and Personnel, XM408 (Ford) 4-cyl., 71 bhp, 4F1R × 1, 161¼ × 63 in, 2849 lb. Payload (cross-country) 1900 lb. Modification of M151 ¼-ton 4 × 4 by adding another M151 rear axle assembly, sprung by inverted semi-elliptic springs, and lengthening rear body. 1958.

Truck, 1-ton, 8 × 8, Cargo and Personnel, XM384 (US ATAC) This variant of the M151 was originally planned to be of the COE (cab-over-engine) configuration. Each wheel was independently suspended, with coil springs. Truck was wider than XM408 and weighed 3590 lb. Neither went into quantity production.

TRUCKS, 1¼- and 1½-TON
4 × 2, 4 × 4 and 6 × 6

Makes and Models: Chevrolet 4103, 4408, 6403, 6409, etc. (1½-ton, 4 × 2, from 1950). Chevrolet TASC (1¼-ton, 4 × 4, 1966). Condec M561 'Gama Goat' and variants (1¼-ton, 6 × 6, 1969). Dodge B1, B3, C1, C3, K6, L6, etc. (1½-ton, 4 × 2, from 1948). C1-QW6 (1½-ton, 4 × 4, 1954), W500 (1½-ton, 4 × 4, 1964). Dodge 'Ram' I (1¼-ton, 4 × 4, 1966). Ford F5, F500, F600, etc. (1½-ton, 4 × 2, from 1951). Ford-Köln G39TH (1½-ton, 4 × 4, 1955, D). Ford/Marmon-Herrington, various models (1½-ton, 4 × 4). General Motors XM705, XM737 (1¼-ton, 4 × 4, 1970). GMC 353-24, etc. (1½-ton, 4 × 2, from 1952). International KB5, KBS5, L152, 1600, etc. (1½-ton, 4 × 2, from 1947). Kaiser Jeep M715, M724, M725, M726, and variants (1¼-ton, 4 × 4, from 1967). Mercedes-Benz 'Unimog' S (1½-ton, 4 × 4, c. 1965, D). LTV/Chance Vought 'Gama Goat', XM561 (1¼-ton, 6 × 6, from 1960).

Vehicle shown (typical): Truck, 1¼-ton, 4 × 4, Ambulance, M725 (Kaiser Jeep)

General Data: Administrative 1½-ton 4 × 2 trucks are employed with cargo, stake, dump and other general purpose bodies. The 1¼-ton payload class was instituted to supersede the earlier ¾-ton 4 × 4 range. Throughout the 1960s experiments and testing took place with 4 × 4 and 6 × 6 vehicles, including an articulated 6 × 6 known as 'Gama Goat' and based on a design of Mr. Robert L. Gamaunt of Fawnskin, Calif. Ling-Temco-Vought Aerospace Corp. (LTV) of Dallas, Texas, produced the prototype, which was entered in the Army Mobility Evaluation in 1961. Of eight vehicles entered, this was the only one to negotiate the entire course. It consisted of two (detachable) units with a lockable jointed system between the two. The wheels exerted a uniform ground contact over most types of terrain. Improved prototypes were produced by LTV's Michigan Division and tested over some 232,500 miles in various countries. The vehicle was eventually approved and classified 'Standard A' (as M561) in June 1966. In 1968 LTV and Kaiser Jeep entered a joint bid for its quantity production but in the 'open-bid competition' system the contract for 1500 units, worth $132 million, went to the Consolidated Diesel Division of Condec Corp. at Schenectady, N.Y., where the first came off the line in the summer of 1969. An ambulance, M792, was developed also. Meanwhile, in 1966 Kaiser Jeep developed an interim 4 × 4 model, derived from their 'Gladiator' truck. Over 22,000 of these were produced.

Technical Data:

Engine: Kaiser Jeep OHC-6-230 6-cylinder, I-I-W-F, 230.5 cu. in, 132.5 bhp @ 4000 rpm (gross; net: 116 @ 4000).

Transmission: 4F1R × 2.

Brakes: hydraulic.

Tyres: 9.00–16.

Wheelbase: 126 in. Track: 67 in.

Overall l × w × h: 209¾ × 85 × 95 in.

Weight: 6400 lb. GVW: 8800 lb.

Note: 4-stretcher ambulance bodywork on chassis M724. Max. speed 60 mph, gradability 60%, both at gross weight. Superseded Dodge ambulance M43, from 1967.

Truck, 1¼-ton, 4×4, Cargo, M715 (Kaiser Jeep) 6-cyl., 132.5 bhp, 4F1R×2, wb 126 in, 209¾×85×95 (59) in, 5500 lb. 7500-lb capacity front-mounted winch optional. Interim successor to ¾-ton M37. Also: M724 (chassis/cab) and M726 (maintenance truck).

Truck, 1¼-ton, 4×4, Cargo, XM705 (GM) Chevrolet V-8-cyl., 140 bhp, 4F1R×2, wb 135 in, 200¾×83½×93 (72) in, 6900 lb. Utility truck, intended to replace the M37 and M715 used in that capacity, where M561's greater mobility is not required. Ambulance version: XM737. 1970.

Truck, 1¼-ton, 6×6, Cargo, Articulated (LTV 'Gama Goat') Chevrolet Corvair 6-cyl., 80 bhp, 4F1R×2, 202×82×58 in, 3640 lb. Articulated two-body design. Rear unit could roll to either side, and pitch. Steering not by articulation but front and rear wheels. Centre axle attached to front unit.

Truck, 1¼-ton, 6×6, Cargo, Articulated, XM561 'Gama Goat' (LTV) GM Detroit 3–53 3-cyl. diesel, 103 bhp, 4F1R×2, wb 80.7+84.8 in, 226×84×91 (65) in, 7000 lb. Tyres 11.00–18. Modified prototype of 1964. Quantity production from 1969 by Condec Corp. Modification kits for other roles, incl. ambulance. Some had winch.

Truck, 1¼-ton, 4×4, Cargo (Chevrolet TASC) V-8-cyl., 195 bhp, 2F1R (auto.) × 2, 202 × 85 in. TASC (tactical articulated swimmable carrier) was a development of the ¾-ton 'Sidewinder'. Chev. 283 CID engine and 'Powerglide' trans. were side by side in centre section. 1966.

Truck, 1¼-ton, 4×4, Cargo (Dodge 'Ram' I) V-8-cyl., 318 CID, auto. 3F1R × 2, wb 110 in, 175 × 86 × 97 (77) in, 5500 lb. Tyres 9.00–20. Prototype for high-mobility airdroppable and floatable truck. IFS, IRS, PAS, PAB (discs). Engine located centrally. 1966.

Truck, 1¼-ton, 4×4, Cargo (Jeep J200) 6-cyl., 145 bhp, 3F1R × 2, wb 120 in, 193½ × 79 × 94½ in, 3981 lb. GVW 7000 lb. Tyres 7.00–16. Pseudo-military cargo/personnel carrier version of J2700 Jeep 'Gladiator' (1965) from which M715 was derived in 1966–67.

Truck, 1½-ton, 4×4, Cargo, w/Winch (Dodge C1-QW6) 6-cyl., 97 bhp, 4F1R × 2, wb 170 in. Chassis/cab 7200 lb. GVW 18,000 lb. Tyres 8.25–20. Originally built for a foreign government but commercially available from 1954. Later all Chrysler-built comm. 4×4 and 6×6 trucks were named 'Power Wagon'.

TRUCKS, 2- to 7½-TON
4 × 2, 4 × 4 and 6 × 4

Makes and Models: Autocar C90T, etc. (5-ton, 4 × 2, from 1945). Chevrolet 6103, 6403, 8703, C50, etc. (2- to 5-ton, 4 × 2, from 1951). Clark XM520 'Goer' (5-ton, 4 × 4, 1959). Corbitt D800T35 (3-ton, 4 × 2, 1951). Diamond T 720 (5-ton, 4 × 2, c. 1952). Dodge VF31, C3, etc. (2½-ton. 4 × 2, from 1947), D500, D600, D700 (2½- to 5-ton, 4 × 2, from 1958), W500 (5-ton, 4 × 4, 1963). Faun F60S (5-ton, 4 × 2, 1955, D). Federal 25M2 (2½-ton, 4 × 2, 1949), 45 (5-ton, 4 × 2, from 1951). Ford F6, F500, F600, P500, etc. (2- to 5-ton, 4 × 2, from 1947). Ford-Köln G398 (2½-ton, 4 × 2, from 1954, D). FWD 181 (2½-ton, 4 × 4, 1957). GMC 414, 424, 451, 452, 453, 454, etc. (2½-ton, 4 × 2, from 1951), 632, 634, 652, 4009, etc. (5-ton, 4 × 2, from 1951). International A/B/L(C)/R(C) 160, 170, 180, 1600, etc. (2- and 2½-ton, 4 × 2 and 4 × 4, from 1950), L/R(D) 190, 200, 1700, 1800, etc. (5-ton, 4 × 2 and 4 × 4, from 1950), LF172 (2½-ton, 6 × 4, c. 1952), F1700 (5-ton, 6 × 4, 1964), etc. Marmon-Herrington MH630-4 (5-ton, 4 × 4, 1952). Oshkosh W703D (wrecker, 7½-ton, 4 × 4, 1949). White WC22PL, PLT (5-ton, 4 × 2, 1952).

General Data: With the main exception of two 'Goer'-type 5-ton 4 × 4 vehicles (Clark XM520 and USMC 'Scamp') virtually all these vehicles are straight commercial types (often with regular production options) with either general or special purpose bodywork. They are used overseas in Field Army service and COMMZ areas by transportation motor pools, service support units, and administrative units where off-road mobility is not required. They are also used in large numbers by administrative fixed base units in the USA where adequate commercial maintenance/supply facilities (for repairs and parts) make their use feasible. In this case the Army has no need to stock spare parts in its own supply system. The same applies to the other armed services. In certain overseas areas they are supplemented by locally produced trucks, for the same reasons. For example, the US forces in Germany at one time used relatively large numbers of Ford-Köln and Faun trucks.

Vehicle shown (typical): Truck, 2½-ton, 4 × 2, Gasoline Tank (GMC HC453)

Technical Data:
Engine: GMC 270 6-cylinder, I-I-W-F, 270 cu. in, 120 bhp @ 3600 rpm.
Transmission: 5F1R.
Brakes: hydraulic, vacuum-assisted.
Tyres: 8.50–20.
Wheelbase: 161 in.
Overall l × w × h: 273 × 93 × 84 in.
Weight: 9000 lb.
Note: 1200-gallon steel tank with 50-gpm power-operated pump. Two-speed rear axle. Also special aviation fuel version and 900-gal. water tanker. On similar GMC chassis: cargo, light wrecker, etc. c. 1951.

Truck, 5-ton, 4 × 2, Cargo (Chevrolet Series 50) Stake rack body, with tilt, on Chevrolet medium-duty chassis with '96-inch cab', which was new for 1967. Typical 'off-the-shelf' commercial truck, used for administrative purposes by US Army in Japan.

Truck, 3-ton, 4 × 2, Tractor (Corbitt D800T35) Cummins 6-cyl. diesel, 5F1R, wb 156 in, GVW 35,000 lb. Produced in the early 1950s. At this time Corbitt was also rebuilding ex-WWII 7½-ton 6 × 6 Mack artillery tractors, which were subsequently supplied to NATO countries, incl. GB.

Truck, 5-ton, 4 × 2, Tractor (Diamond T 720) Continental T6427 6-cyl., 148 bhp, 5F1R, wb 145 in. Two-speed rear axle. Air-hyd. brakes and trailer air brake connection. Used in conjunction with various types of semi-trailers incl. special Signal Corps TV camera van. Early 1950s.

Truck, 5-ton, 4 × 2, Tractor (Dodge D700) V-8-cyl., 194 bhp, 5F1R, wb 145 in. Two-speed axle. Air brakes. Shown with 12-ton 4-wheel stake (cargo) semi-trailer, M127(A1). Also LWB truck version with van body (USN). Similar tractors supplied by Ford (conv. and COE). Mid 1960s.

Truck, 5-ton, 4 × 2, Wrecker (Ford F600) Commercial 1961 Ford truck with Holmes twin-boom wrecker equipment, used by US Air Force in England. Many Ford trucks of various types and model years were acquired, fitted with general or special purpose bodywork.

Truck, 5-ton, 4 × 2, Dump (International 1800 'Loadstar') V-8-cyl., 193 bhp, 5F1R, wb 139 in. Two-speed rear axle. Air brakes. Heil SL11 hyd. dump body with removable cab protector, 6-cu. yd rated capacity. Tailgate top- or bottom-hinged. Body dimensions 108 × 84 × 31 in. Mid 1960s.

Truck, 2½-ton, 4 × 4, Crane, Bomb Service (International A160) 6-cyl., 153 bhp, 5F1R × 2, wb 153 in, GVW 15,000 lb. Tyres 9.00–20. Gar Wood HC4 4000-lb hyd. crane, revolving through 270°. Cantilever-type boom telescoped from 8 to 16 feet. Shown lifting Navy mine. Also on B184. (IHC 'A'-line: 1957–59; 'B'-line: 1959–61).

Truck, 5-ton, 4 × 4, Cargo, XM520 (Clark) Cummins 6-cyl. diesel, 110 bhp, wb 195 in, 303 × 102 × 108 in, 15,830 lb. Lightest of the exp. family of 'Goer' vehicles of the early 1960s. Derived from Model 75 Pulpwood Logger made by Clark Equipment Co. Tyres, F/R 15.00–24/18.00–26. Steering by articulation (45°).

TRUCKS, 2½-TON
6 × 6 and 8 × 8

Makes and Models: Chrysler T55, T55E3 (6 × 6, from 1948), XM410, XM410E1 (8 × 8, from 1958). DAF YF328 (6 × 6, 1953, NL). Detroit Arsenal XM521 (8 × 8, 1961). Dodge/Fargo WT500 (6 × 6, 1965/66). General Motors T51 (6 × 6, 1947/48). GMC G740, M133, M135, M207, M211, M215, M217, M220, M221, M222 and variants (6 × 6, from 1950). Studebaker (6 × 6, c. 1950). Toyota 2DW 15L, 2DW 15LD (6 × 6, 1964, J). USS XM761 (6 × 6, 1967).
'M-Series' (G742) (produced, from 1950, by Reo, Studebaker, Curtiss Wright, Kaiser Jeep, AM General Corp., White); principal models: Chassis/cab: M44, M45, M46, M57, M58, M209, M616, M617, M618, M619, and variants; Bolster trucks: M44, M45, M751, and variants; Cargo trucks: M34, M35, M36, M602, M621, and variants; Crane trucks: see Wrecker trucks; Dump trucks: M47, M59, M342, M608, M614, M624, and variants; Earth boring/pole setter trucks: V18A/MTQ (on M44 chassis), M764 (on M45A2); Shop van trucks: M109, XM112, M185, M292, XM472, XM512, XM567, M609, M613, M623, and variants; Tank trucks (gasoline): M49, M611, M622, and variants; (water): M50, M610, and variants; Telephone constr./maint. trucks: V17A/MTQ (on M44 chassis), M763 (on M45A2); Tractor trucks: M48, M275, M607, and variants; Wrecker trucks: M60, M108, and variants. Note: M44A2 series vehicles have m/f engine, M44 and M602 series vehicles have gasoline (petrol) engine, M45A2 and M46A2 have diesel engine.

General Data: From 1950–51 the wartime 2½-ton 6 × 6 range was gradually replaced by new models produced by Reo and GMC. They first saw combat service in Korea. The Reo ('Eager Beaver') was made by other firms also and with various modifications (diesel and m/f engines etc.) remained in production for over 20 years, carrying numerous body types (main types listed above). They were also supplied to friendly nations, through the MAP (mainly M602 'austere' models). Some high-mobility 8 × 8 designs were developed but not produced in quantity. For GMC 2½-ton 6 × 6 'M-Series' see also Canadian section.

Vehicle shown (typical): Truck, 2½-ton, 6 × 6, Shop Van, M109 (Reo)

Technical Data:
Engine: Reo OA-331 (or Continental COA-331) 6-cylinder, I-I-W-F, 331 cu. in, 147 bhp @ 3400 rpm (net: 127 @ 3400).
Transmission: 5F1R × 2.
Brakes: air-hydraulic.
Tyres: 9.00–20.
Wheelbase: 154 in. BC 48 in.
Overall l × w × h: 261¼ × 96 × 129 in.
Weight: 15,231 lb. GVW: 20,581 lb.
Note: 12-ft van body on M45 chassis. Models M109A1, M109C, M109D, etc. differed in detail. M220 similar to M109 but on GMC chassis (see Canadian section). Automatic front-wheel drive engagement (dual over-running clutch in transfer). Winch optional.

Truck, 2½-ton, 6 × 6, Cargo, M35A2 (Kaiser Jeep)
Continental LD465-1 m/f 6-cyl., 140 bhp, 5F1R × 2, wb 154
(BC 48) in, 264¼ × 96 × 115 (81) in, 13,050 lb.   M35 had
gasoline (petrol) engine. M35A1 had Continental LDS427-2
m/f engine. M34 had 11.00–20 tyres, single rear, with wheelhouses in cargo body.

**Truck, 2½-ton, 6 × 6, Telephone Construction and Main-
tenance, V17A/MTQ (Reo)** 6-cyl., 146 bhp, 5F1R × 2, wb
154 (BC 48) in, 276 × 94 × 120 in, 16,550 lb.   Rear winch in
front end of special body. Pole derrick, normally carried in LH
side of body, could be erected at rear. M44 chassis.

**Truck, 2½-ton, 6 × 6, Water Tank, w/Winch, M50A2
(Kaiser Jeep)** Continental LD465-1 m/f 6-cyl., 140 bhp,
5F1R × 2, wb 154 (BC 48) in, 277 × 93 × 97 (81) in, 14,580 lb.
1000-gal. tank on modified M45A2 chassis (full-torque PTO,
exhaust diverter, etc.).   GMC equivalent: M222. M49 (and
M217) were fuel tankers.

**Truck, 2½-ton, 6 × 6, Wrecker/Crane, w/Winch, M108
(Reo, Studebaker)** Reo OA-331 6-cyl., 5F1R × 2, wb 154
(BC 48) in, 302 × 96 × 99 (92) in, 19,785 lb. Austin Western
hyd. crane with 8000-lb max. lift (using outriggers), on M45
chassis. M60 was recovery vehicle (same crane). A twin-
boom type (XM60E1) existed also.

Truck, 2½-ton, 6 × 6, Dump, w/Winch, M215 (GMC)
6-cyl., 130 bhp (145 gross), auto. 4F1R × 2 × 1, wb 144 (BC 48) in, 240 × 96 × 108 (78) in, 14,870 lb. Soft-top cab. Reo equivalents: M47 (11.00–20 tyres), M59 (9.00–20, dual rear). For more GMCs see 'Canada'.

Truck, 2½-ton, 6 × 6, Cargo, w/Winch (Studebaker)
Produced concurrently with first Reo 'Eager Beaver' M34. Unlike the M34 it had no wheelhouses (note high body floor). Truck was not accepted and Studebaker co-produced the Reo design instead. Plant was later sold to Kaiser Jeep Corp.

Truck, 2½-ton, 6 × 6, Cargo, w/Winch (Dodge WT500 'Power Wagon') V-8-cyl., 165 bhp (202 gross), 5F1R × 2, wb 163 in, chassis length 270 in, GVW 25,000 lb. Tyres 8.25–20. Commercially available, mid-1960s. Perkins 6.354-2D diesel optional. Rockwell axles, Hendrickson rear bogie.

Truck, 2½-ton, 6 × 6, Cargo, w/Winch, XM761 (USS)
Continental LD465-3 m/f 6-cyl., 145 bhp, auto. 6F1R × 1, wb 129 (BC 46) in, 253 × 96 × 102 (73) in, 13,480 lb. Private venture by US Steel Corp., applying 'USS Family of Steels' concept. Tyres 16.00–20. IRS with coil springs.

Truck, 2½-ton, 6 × 6, Cargo, w/Winch, T51 (GM) Continental AO536-2 HO-8-cyl., 176 bhp (200 gross), auto. 3F1R × 1, wb 90½ + 66 in, 254 × 101 × 105 (85) in, 15,850 lb. Tyres 14.00–20. Ind. susp. with torsion bars. Two pilot models delivered, 1948. Air-cooled engine. Lockable diffs.

Truck, 2½-ton, 6 × 6, Cargo, T55E3 (Chrysler) Continental AO402-2 HO-6-cyl., 187 bhp (gross), auto. trans., 9000 lb. Aluminium body, axles, wheels, etc. Air-assisted hyd. disc brakes. Air-cooled engine with fuel injection. 1955. T55 (1948) was 6 × 6 mod. of T53 ¾-ton 4 × 4 (*qv*).

Truck, 2½-ton, 8 × 8, Cargo, XM521 (Detroit Arsenal) Continental HO-4-cyl., 94 bhp (105 gross), 4F1R × 2, 227 × 86 × 95 in, 4550 lb. Exp. truck with ability to swim, developed in 1961. Bonded body-frame structure of aluminium honeycomb, made by Whirlpool Corp. Twin propellers and rudders.

Truck, 2½-ton, 8 × 8, Cargo, w/Winch, XM410E1 (Chrysler) Continental LD465 6-cyl. m/f, 210 bhp, auto. 1F1R × 3 × 2, wb 160.4 in, 258 × 96 × 125 in, 11,250 lb. Aluminium body. Seven produced as continuation of XM410 development program, 1964. Six XM410s (from 1957) had 152-bhp Chrysler V8 engine. Tyres 14.00–18.

TRUCKS, 4- and 5-TON
6×6 and 8×8

Makes and Models: Note: 5-ton unless otherwise stated. Faun L908/45A (6×6, 1956, D). Ford XM453E2 (8×8, 1960; also 6×6 variant), M656, XM757, XM791, and variants (8×8, from 1964). FWD XM357 'Teracruzer' I (4-ton, 8×8, 1955). GMC XM453E1 (8×8, 1960; also 6×6 variant). Reo XM282 and variants (8×8, from 1955). White-Reo XM453E3 (8×8, 1960; also 6×6). *M-Series' (G744) (produced, from 1950, by Diamond T, International Harvester, Kaiser Jeep, AM General Corp., Mack);* principal models: Chassis/cab: M39, M40, M61, M63, M139, M809, M810, M811, M812, and variants; Bolster truck: M815; Bridge transport truck: M821; Cargo trucks: M41, M54, M55, M813, M814, and variants; Dump trucks: M51, M817, and variants; Shop van trucks: M64, M397, M820, and variants; Tractor trucks: M52, M818, and variants; Tractor/Wrecker trucks: M246, M819, and variants; Wrecker trucks: M62, M543, M816, and variants.

General Data: The M39 Series of 5-ton 6×6 trucks replaced the 4-, 6- and 7½-ton 6×6 types of the 1940s. The first of these new trucks, produced by Diamond T and International Harvester, appeared in 1950. Later they were also produced by others. There are many body types, most of which are listed above. In addition there are specialist bodies on the various basic chassis, including air compressor units, fire fighters, missile launchers, etc. In 1962 a diesel power-unit was introduced (Mack ENDT-673), followed by a multi-fuel engine (Continental and Hercules, military design) in 1963 (M39A2 Series). For MAP (Military Assistance Program) a Cummins diesel became available. Similar trucks were produced in Italy and Spain (*qv*).

In 1959/60 a new medium duty series truck programme was started by ATAC with Ford, GMC and Reo (i.e. the Lansing Div. of White) participating. Each contractor produced 3½-ton 6×6 (XM434) and 5-ton 8×8 (XM453) trucks, which were tested at APG but although each vehicle had certain attractive features the overall result caused termination of this phase of the programme. The 6×6 variants were dropped and a new 8×8 (XM656) was called for in 1961. Ford received a contract for design and development of this new 'Mover' (Motor Vehicle Requirements) vehicle. This truck was eventually type-classified 'Standard A' in April 1966, and the first series production contract was awarded to Ford in January 1968.

Vehicle shown (typical): Truck, 5-ton, 6×6, Dump, M51A2 (Kaiser Jeep)

Technical Data:
Engine: Continental or Hercules LDS465-1 multi-fuel 6-cylinder, turbocharged, I-I-W-F, 478 cu. in, 205–220 bhp @ 2800 rpm.
Transmission: 5F1R × 2.
Brakes: Air-hydraulic.
Tyres: 11.00–20.
Wheelbase: 167 in. BC 54 in.
Overall dimensions: 266 × 97 × 110 (87½) in.
Weight: 21,790 lb (w/Winch 22,473) lb.
Note: Earlier M51 model (produced by International) had 196-bhp Continental R6602 gasoline (petrol) engine. M817 is 'austere' model (MAP) with 250-bhp Cummins NHC250 diesel engine.

Truck, 5-ton, 6 × 6, Cargo, w/Winch, M54A2 (Kaiser Jeep) Continental LDS465-1 m/f 6-cyl., 210 bhp, 5F1R × 2, wb 179 (BC 54) in, 312½ × 98 × 117 (85) in, 20,400 lb. Std. body on M40A2 chassis of M39A2 series. 10-ton winch. Shown with fording equipment. Original model (M54) produced by International in early 1950s.

Truck, 5-ton, 6 × 6, Bridge Transport, w/Winch, M821 (AM General) Typical of M809 Series (1970), featuring commercial diesel engine and restyled grille. M821 measured 373 × 114 × 113 in, weighed 28,880 lb. Tyres 14.00–20. AM General was former General Products Div. of Jeep Corp., taken over by AMC.

Truck, 5-ton, 6 × 6, Wrecker, Medium, M543 (International) IHC 121500-R94 6-cyl., 224 bhp, 5F1R × 2, wb 179 (BC 54) in, 349 × 96 × 108 in, 33,675 lb. Also with Continental R6602 engine. M543A2 had m/f engine. Gar Wood hyd. crane. MAP equivalent: M816. M62 had Austin Western crane.

Truck, 5-ton, 6 × 6, Tractor Wrecker, M246A2 (Kaiser Jeep) Continental LDS465-1 m/f 6-cyl., 210 bhp, 5F1R × 2, wb 215 (BC 54) in, 352½ × 98 × 132 (89) in, 33,555 lb. M63A2 chassis with fifth wheel and Austin Western hyd. crane. Used for salvaging crashed aircraft, general towing, etc. MAP equivalent: M819 (Cummins diesel).

Truck, 5-ton, 6 × 6, Asphalt Distributor, M61 (International) Continental R6602 6-cyl., 196 bhp, 5F1R × 2, wb 167 (54) in, 318 × 97 × 110 in, 33,640 lb. Heats, transports and distributes bituminous materials for paving surfaces. Equipment by General Steel Tank Co. (Model SDC, 800-gal. cap., 1954). USAF.

Launcher, Rocket, 762-mm, Truck-Mounted, M289 'Honest John' rocket launcher on M139D (modified M139C) chassis. Later type, M386, had different launcher (w/o 'A'-frame at forward end). Missile servicing vehicles on similar chassis: M301 and M350 (air supply), M280 (servicing platform), M268 (propellant), etc.

Truck, 4-ton, 8 × 8, Cargo, XM357 (FWD 'Teracruzer' I) Continental HO-8-cyl., 340 bhp, GM Allison auto. 6F1R × 2, wb 148 in, 300 × 144 × 136 (112) in, 28,160 lb. Goodyear 'Rolligon' roller type 'tyres' (inventor: W. H. Albec) which, at 3–5 lb/sq. in (regulated by driver) also acted as springs, were driven by rollers, resting on top.

Truck, 5-ton, 8 × 8, Cargo, XM282 (Reo) 6-cyl., 170 bhp, 5F1R × 2, wb 140 in (between BCs), 262½ × 96 × 82¼ in, 15,550 lb. Tyres 11.00–20. Air-hyd. brakes. Reo 'Gold Comet' OM170 331-cu. in engine. Ross PAS. Payload on roads 7½ tons. Several produced, experimentally, from 1955.

Truck, 5-ton, 8 × 8, Cargo, XM453E1 (GMC) GM 6V-53
V-6-cyl. 2-stroke diesel, 190 bhp, 4F1R × 2. Produced in
1959/60 in 8 × 8 (shown) and 6 × 6 (3½-ton, XM434) configurations. Truck was floatable and could be equipped with
propeller drive and rudder kit. Welded aluminium cab and body.

Truck, 5-ton, 8 × 8, Cargo, XM453E2 (Ford) V-8-cyl.
diesel, 195 bhp, 6F1R × 1, wb 124 in (between BCs), 259 ×
96 × 121 in, 12,390 lb. Tyres 16–20 LPM. Prototype for XM453
'Mover' series for the 1960s. XM453E1 produced by GMC,
XM453E3 by White-Reo. Culminated in XM656, later M656.

Truck, 5-ton, 8 × 8, Cargo, XM656 (Ford) Continental
LDS465–2 m/f 6-cyl., 210 bhp, GM Allison auto. 6F1R × 2,
wb 148 (BC 58) in, 276 × 96 × 106 (81) in, 15,415 lb. Prototype, 1963/64. Turbo-charged engine. Floatable (air-inflated
weatherseals on cab and body doors) and air-droppable.

Truck, 5-ton, 8 × 8, Shop Van, XM791 (Ford) M656 truck
went into production in 1968 when Ford was awarded a contract for 500. Variants were used for the Pershing I–A missile
system, including BCC 'expando van' (battery control centre,
shown) and tractor truck (XM757) for erector/launcher S-T.

TRUCKS, 8- to 25-TON
4 × 4 and 6 × 2

Makes and Models: *'Goers':* Caterpillar XM520E1 (8-ton, cargo, 1961), XM559E1 (8-ton, 2500-gal. tanker, 1961), XM553 (10-ton, wrecker, 1961). LeTourneau-Westinghouse XM437 (15-ton, cargo, 1959), XM437E1 (16-ton, cargo, 1961), XM438 (15-ton, 5000-gal. tanker, 1959), XM554E1 (20-ton, wrecker, 1961).
Gun Lifters: Kenworth 10A M249 (25-ton, front truck, 1952), 10B M250 (25-ton, rear truck, 1952).

General Data: During the late 1950s the US Army investigated the possibilities of a new concept in military logistical vehicles, using components of vehicles which were used commercially for earthmoving and similar purposes, namely two-wheeled tractor units coupled to two-wheeled trailer units. The result led to the initiation of the 'Goer' programme, a family of highly mobile tactical support vehicles with a high payload-to-weight ratio. In 1957 tests were held with commercial Caterpillar, Euclid, International, and LeTourneau-Westinghouse 'off-the-shelf' machines, all featuring positive 'wagon steer' and large tyres which eliminated conventional suspension systems. By 1959 pilot models for military versions, which could also swim, were submitted by LeTourneau-Westinghouse (15-ton models), followed by Caterpillar in 1961 (8-ton models). A 5-tonner with articulated steering was built by Clark (see 5-ton 4 × 4 section). A contract for 23 'Goer' vehicles in the 8-ton class (13 cargo, 8 tanker and 2 wrecker trucks) was awarded to Caterpillar in May 1963. These were delivered in 1964 and sent to Germany for troop trials which lasted until early 1965. In 1966 the majority of these vehicles was transferred to Vietnam where they were used for cargo and fuel transportation, especially during the monsoon seasons. During two years of service (supporting the 4th US Infantry Division) these Caterpillar 'Goers' covered some 200,000 miles, hauling 15.5 thousand tons of cargo and 2 million gallons of fuel. Such was their performance that in 1970 the Army Material Command invited bids from the industry for production of 1300 'Goers' (812 8-ton cargo trucks, M520, 371 2500-gal. tankers, M559, and 117 10-ton wreckers, M553). The contract, worth $61.5 million, was awarded to Caterpillar in May 1971. Series production commenced in 1972.

Vehicle shown (typical): Truck, 8-ton, 4 × 4, Cargo, w/Winch, XM520E1 (Caterpillar)

Technical Data:
Engine: Caterpillar D333 multi-fuel, 6-cylinder, I-I-W-F, 525 cu. in, 213 bhp @ 2200 rpm.
Transmission: torque converter (Twin Disc) with auto. 6F1R 'Power Shift'.
Brakes: air.
Tyres: 18.00–33.
Wheelbase: 235 in.
Overall l × w × h: 381 × 108 × 101 (min.) in.
Weight: 26,645 lb (later models 23,950 lb).
Note: One of several prototypes for family of 'Goer' vehicles. Max. speed, loaded, 30 mph. Positive articulated steering. Rear-wheel drive possible only in first and second gears. Floatable. 5-ton winch.

Truck, 10-ton, 4 × 4, Wrecker, XM553 (Caterpillar)
6-cyl. m/f, 213 bhp, 6F1R (auto.), wb 235 in, 398 × 108 × 118 (min.) in, 39,150 lb. GVW 47,300 lb. Hyd. swinging crane version derived from XM520E1. Floatable. Freeboard (fully loaded), front unit 25 in, rear unit 16 in.

Truck, 8-ton, 4 × 4, Tank, 2500-gal., XM559E1 (Caterpillar) 6-cyl. m/f, 213 bhp, 6F1R (auto.), wb 235 in, 394 × 108 × 116 (min) in, 30,180 lb. Gradability (loaded), forward slope, 60%. Articulated steering allows 'Goers' to be 'duck-walked' (swung from side to side) over soft or wet terrain.

Truck, 15-ton, 4 × 4, Cargo, XM437 (LeTourneau-Westinghouse) GM Detroit 8V-71 diesel, V-8-cyl., 274 bhp, 5F1R × 2, wb 288 in, 434½ × 117 × 120 (106) in, 32,000 lb. GVW 62,000 lb. Tyres 29.50–25. Positive power 90° wagon steering. Air brakes. Prototype, 1959. In background: Mack M125 (10-ton, 6 × 6).

Truck, 15-ton, 4 × 4, Tank, 5000-gal., XM438 (LeTourneau-Westinghouse) GM Detroit 8V-71 diesel, V-8-cyl., 274 bhp, 5F1R × 2, wb 284 in, 427½ × 117 × 120 in, 34,700 lb. Logistical tanker, produced in 1959. Front-wheel drive (with electric assist motors in rear hubs for speeds up to 2½ mph, as on XM437).

Truck, 16-ton, 4 × 4, Cargo, w/Winch, XM437E1 (Le-Tourneau-Westinghouse) GM Detroit 8V-71 diesel, V-8-cyl., 336 bhp, 5F1R × 2, wb 315 in, 38,670 lb. Improved version of XM437. 10-ton winch at front and loading crane in rear body. Air and electric trailer brake connections. Note side door.

Truck, 16-ton, 6 × 2, Articulated, Container Transporter Dim. 40.7 × 9.5 ft. Weight 21.5 tons. Designed and built in 1966 by US Army and Barnes & Reinecke of Chicago, for transport, self-load and -unload of Army Containerized Express (CONEX). IHC 240-bhp diesel tractor unit. Handled three containers.

Trucks, 25-ton, 4 × 4, Gun Lifting, Front, M249, and Rear, M250, with Gun, 280-mm, M65, and Carriage, 280-mm Gun, M30 (T72) Introduced in 1952 as 'Transporter, Heavy Artillery, T10'. 100 ft long. Gun was lowered hydraulically and could fire atomic shells. Driver at front controls throttle and brakes of both units; steering was independent.

Truck, 25-ton, 4 × 4, Gun Lifting, Rear, M250 (Kenworth 10B) Continental A0895-4, 375 bhp, auto. 3F1R × 1, wb 120 in, 380¼ × 124 × 137½ in, 35,910 lb. Tyres 16.00−25. Air-cooled engine. Air brakes. M249 (Kenworth 10A, front unit) had same engine, trans., axles, etc. Interphone system between the two units. Trucks cost $77,318 each, gun $431,263.

TRUCKS, 6- to 30-TON
4 × 2 and 6 × 4

Makes and Models: Autocar C90 (10-ton, 4 × 2, 1951). Brockway 260 LQM (10-ton, 6 × 4, 1959), N260LFM (20-ton, 6 × 4, 1959). Corbitt D803 V46 (10-ton, 6 × 4, 1951). Diamond T 921N·36M-OH (10-ton, 6 × 4, 1954), 950S-42M (20-ton, 6 × 4, 1959). Dodge S8-D700 (6-ton, 4 × 2, 1964), S8-CT700 (6-ton, 6 × 4, 1964). Euclid 2FD, 4FD, 5FD, 27FDG, etc. (15- to 20-ton, 4 × 2, from c. 1950). Faun F603 (22-ton GVW tractor) and F603K (10-ton, dump, 6 × 4, c. 1955, D). Ford F700 (7½-ton, 6 × 4, 1967), CT-Series (10-ton, 6 × 4, 1962). GMC HC854, HC859 (10-ton, 4 × 2, 1951), HCWX853, W(X)504V(6), FMW-559, LWA 5513, etc. (10-ton, 6 × 4, from 1950), LWAX5513 (19-ton, 6 × 4, 1964), OFWX7110 (26- and 30-ton, 6 × 4, 1963), etc. International CG192 (6-ton, 4 × 2, 1963), 1890 (6-ton, 4 × 2, 1964), CO202 (7-ton, 4 × 2, 1959), DCO205H (7-ton, 4 × 2, 1964), F1700 'Loadstar' (7½-ton, 6 × 4, 1963), R190, R200, ACOF1854 (10-ton, 6 × 4, from 1952), etc. Leyland 'Hippo' (10-ton, 6 × 4, c. 1958, GB). Mack B61P (10-ton, 4 × 2, 1958), LR (15-ton, 4 × 2, 1953). Magirus-Deutz 6500 (6½-ton, 4 × 2, 1955, D). Reo C501B (6-ton, 4 × 2, 1960). White 4464TD (10-ton, 6 × 4, 1964).

General Data: The 4 × 2 chassis were employed mainly as tractor and dump trucks, 6 × 4 chassis as tractor trucks, fuellers, bulk liquid tankers, lifting platforms, wreckers, refuse collectors, etc. In most cases these chassis were obtained from the lowest bidder as and when the requirement arose and equipped with bodywork by another firm, e.g. Consolidated, Gar Wood, Heil, etc. In many cases these vehicles did the same jobs as the equivalent 'M-Series' tactical vehicle but at much lower cost and, of course, only where tactical requirements were not required to be met. For example, in Vietnam the cargo semi-trailers M127 (and variants) were hauled by the tractor-truck 5-ton 6 × 6 M52, whereas in Germany the 37th Transport Group used the same semi-trailers in conjunction with commercial type International DCO205H tilt-cab diesel 4 × 2 tractor units (the 37th Transport Group is the US Army trucking company for the whole of Western Europe and has over 2000 semi-trailers of various types).

Vehicle shown (typical): Truck, 15-ton, 4 × 2, Dump (Mack LR)

Technical Data:
Engine: Cummins NHB600 diesel, 6-cylinder, I-I-W-F, 743 cu. in, 200 bhp @ 2100 rpm.
Transmission: 10F2R.
Brakes: air.
Tyres: front 14.00–24, rear 16.00–24.
Wheelbase: 160 in.
Overall l × w × h: 300 × 129½ × 130 (122½) in.
Weight: 37,500 lb.
Note: Heil 10-cu. yd (144 × 100 × 31 in) body with cab protector. 'Plaindrive' rear axle with concentric cam and plunger type power divider differential and outboard planetary gears in wheel hubs. 1953. Used by Army and Air Force.

Truck, 10-ton, 6×4, Aircraft Fueller, Type R-5 (GMC 5500 Series) GM Detroit V-6-cyl. diesel (478 CID). Model 2191 bodywork by Consolidated Diesel Electric Co., 1966. $397\frac{3}{4} \times 102 \times 104\frac{1}{4}$ in, 21,000 lb (air-transportable in C124, C130, etc.). 5000-gal. capacity. Single-point and over-wing service, delivering 600 gpm.

Truck, 10-ton, 6×4, De-Mineralized Water, Type A-2 (International ACOF-1854) Body by Heil, 1959. Heil also supplied R-2 fuellers, which looked similar, on 1959 GMC FMW-559. These had platform on top of tank. In 1962 Consolidated supplied fuellers on Ford 'CT' 6×4. De-mineralized water is used for aircraft engine injection.

Truck, 7-ton, 4×2, Tractor (International DCO205H) Cummins NH220B 6-cyl. diesel, 220 bhp, 5F1R, wb 111 in, GVW 27,000 lb. 1200 ordered in 1964 for US Army in Germany for use by the 37th Transport Group in conjunction with various semi-trailers (shown: 7½-ton 2-wh. refrigerator van, M349A1).

Truck, 7½-ton, 6×4, Wrecker (International F1700) V-8-cyl., 193 bhp, 7F1R, wb 169 in. Holmes twin-boom wrecker with two drum type winches behind cab. 1963. Similar equipment on International F1800 9-ton 6×6 (1963), Ford F700 6×4 (c.1967) and GMC 6×6 chassis.

TRUCKS, over 5-TON
6 × 6 and 8 × 8

(*See also* Tank Transporters, *page 360*)

Makes and Models: Condec 2201 M123A1C (10-ton, 6 × 6, 1966). Corbitt T33, T33E1 (12-ton, 8 × 8, 1945). Detroit Arsenal T57 (10-ton, 8 × 8, 1951), T58 (15-ton, 8 × 8, 1951), XM194, XM194E2 (15-ton, 8 × 8, from 1952). FWD 8-320B, B2 MM-1 'Teracruzer' II (8-ton, 8 × 8, 1956). International F1800 (9-ton, 6 × 6, 1963), XM409 (10-ton, 8 × 8, 1957), XM523E2 (18-ton, 6 × 6, 1964). Kenworth XM194E4 (15-ton, 8 × 8, 1955), XM523, XM523E1 (25-ton, 6 × 6, from 1960). Mack M121, M123, M125 and variants, G792 (10-ton, 6 × 6, from 1953). Oshkosh WA1600 (10-ton, 6 × 6, *c.* 1965). Reo XM375 (25-ton 8 × 8, 1957). Sterling T26 and variants (12-ton, 8 × 8, from 1945), T29 (20-ton, 6 × 6, 1946), T46 (25-ton, 6 × 6, 1946), T35, T35E1 (25-ton, 6 × 6, 1947).

General Data: Many of the above vehicles were experimental and only produced as pilot models. The Sterling-built 6 × 6 and 8 × 8 trucks were originally conceived during WWII but pilot models (reduced in number when the war ended) were not delivered until 1946/47. Shortly afterwards the US Army's Detroit Arsenal (later ATAC) designed the T57 and T58 cab-forward trucks with air-cooled engines. The 'M-Series' 10-ton 6 × 6 was developed during 1950–55 and originally produced by Mack. Later Mack only supplied axles and transmissions and Consolidated Diesel Electric Co. undertook final assembly. These vehicles were similar in appearance to the 2½- and 5-ton 6 × 6 'M-Series', but considerably larger and heavier. The M-123 tractor version was the most common. The International F1800 and Oshkosh WA1600 were both commercial 6 × 6 chassis, fitted out as wreckers. The XM409 was another experimental vehicle, produced by International during the late 1950s and using many components of the 'M-Series' 5-ton 6 × 6. In appearance it was not unlike a scaled-up version of the XM410 2½-ton 8 × 8.

Vehicle shown (typical): Truck, 10-ton, 6 × 6, Tractor, w/Winch, M123 (Mack)

Technical Data:
Engine: LeRoi T-H844 V-8-cylinder, V-I-W-F, 844 cu. in, 286 bhp @ 2600 rpm.
Transmission: 5F1R × 2.
Brakes: air.
Tyres: 14.00–24.
Wheelbase: 181½ in. BC 60 in.
Overall l × w × h: 280 × 114 × 113 (91½) in.
Weight: 28,350 lb (later models 32,250 lb).
Note: dual winches mounted centrally, high-mounted fifth wheel (M123C single and low resp., M123D dual and low resp.). M123A1C, assembled by Consolidated (Model 2201), as M123C but 300-bhp V8 diesel engine.

Truck, 10-ton, 6 × 6, Cargo, w/Winch, M125 (Mack)
LeRoi T-H844 V-8-cyl., 286 bhp, 5F1R × 2, wb 181½ (BC 60)
in, 331½ × 114 × 129 (90) in, 30,000 lb.   Tyres 14.00–24.
Mack axles and rear bogie. Designed primarily for towing
155-mm gun and 8-in howitzer.   22½-ton winch.   Chassis
designation M121. Speed 43 mph.

Truck, 6-ton, 6 × 6, Cargo, w/Winch One of two types
tested by US Army in Japan. The other was generally similar
but had different grille, front wings and bumper, flat-top cab
doors, etc. Both had winch behind cab (w/gypsy head) and
looked like modernized versions of WWII 6-ton 6 × 6.

Truck, 25-ton, 6 × 6, Tractor, T35 (Sterling) Ford GAC
V-12-cyl., 695 bhp (770 gross), GM Allison auto. 6F3R × 1,
wb 190 (BC 74) in, 346 × 160½ (w/DT) × 135 (106) in,
62,000 lb.   Chain-drive bogie. Tyres 18.00–29. T35E1 had
Timken gear-drive bogie. T46 (T29E1) similar to T35 but
Ford GAA 525-bhp V8, 5F1R × 2 × 2.

Truck, 25-ton, 6 × 6, Tractor, XM523 (Kenworth)
Cummins NT380 6-cyl. diesel, 380 bhp, 5F1R × 3, wb 222 in.
Air brakes. 30-ton winch behind cab. XM523E1 was generally
similar but had 4F1R + OD × 1 trans. and shorter wb (192 in).
Both were used with various types of heavy semi-trailers, from
early 1960s.

Truck, 12-ton, 8 × 8, Cargo, T26E1 (Sterling) Ford GAA V-8-cyl., 525 bhp (gross). Developed from WWII exp. T26. Chain final drives. Hyd. platform steer. Variants: tractor, T26E1; wrecker, T26E2; cargo and tractor (w/extended cab), T26E3; cargo (w/Fuller torque conv. trans.), T26E4. Pilot models only, delivered 1947/48.

Truck, 8-ton, 8 × 8, Cargo, MM-1 (FWD 8-320B2 'Teracruzer' II) Continental PE200 HO-8-cyl., 250 bhp, Allison semi-auto. 4F1R × 1, wb 234 in, 373 × 108 × 114½ (101) in, 15,000 lb. USAF. Basic vehicle for TM61B ground support system. Goodyear 'Terra-tires', 42 × 40 × 10 in. Model 8-320B slightly different. Also w/S-T.

Truck, 15-ton, 8 × 8, Cargo, T58 (Detroit Arsenal) Ordnance AV1195, 545 bhp, semi-auto. trans. w/hyd. torque converter, wb 175 in, 42,000 lb. GVW on/off roads 43.5/35.3 tons, towed load on/off roads 40.8/16.3 tons. 19.58-litre engine behind cab. T57 was 10-ton 8 × 8 with same engine. c. 1951.

Truck, 15-ton, 8 × 8, Tractor, XM194E4 (Kenworth) Continental AVI-1790-8A V-8-cyl. diesel, 825 bhp (gross), auto. 3F1R × 1, wb 175 in, 352¾ × 124 × 121 (108) in, 52,200 lb. Tyres 16.00–25. Air brakes. Speed 45 mph. Air-cooled engine. XM194(E2) (Detroit Arsenal) was tractor version of T58.

TRANSPORTERS, TANK and HEAVY EQUIPMENT

During the immediate post-war period the US Army used the wartime 40-ton, M25 'Dragon Wagon'. This was the M26(A1) Pacific tractor with the M15(A1) semi-trailer. During the 1950s the Mack M123 10-ton 6 × 6 tractor was used with a modified M15 semi-trailer (M15A2), as an interim measure, while work on various new transporters was in progress. New exp. models included the XM194 series of tractors with M15A2 and XM160 S-Ts (50- and 60-ton resp.), the Reo XM375 with XM346 S-T (60-ton), the XM376/XM2/XM377 'Double Ender' (50-ton), and the Kenworth XM523(E1) with XM524(E1) S-T (also tried with XM528 load-divider dolly). None of these were satisfactory and a new approach was made in the 1960s with the 'Trackporter' S-T and a 5-axle 10 × 4 'Portall' truck. Meanwhile a commercial International was introduced as an interim prime mover (XM523E2) and Chrysler (concurrently with Faun and Krupp in Germany) developed the 60-ton 'HET-70'.

Truck, 10-ton, 6 × 6, M123 (Mack) with Semi-Trailer, 50-ton, 8-wh., M15A2 (Fruehauf) M123 tractor, designed for 25-ton S-T, was used temporarily to replace the 1945 Pacific M26A1. M15A2 was modified and reinforced M15A1 semi-trailer. Shown here with M48 tank, 1960.

Truck, 25-ton, 8 × 8, XM375 (Reo) with Semi-Trailer, 60-ton, 16-wh., XM346 (Dorsey) Developed by US Army Transportation Corps in 1957. Overall length 78 ft, weight 45 tons. Trailer had four axles but proved difficult to load/unload. Tests terminated in Nov. 1958.

Truck, 25-ton, 8 × 8, XM377 (Detroit Arsenal) Rear truck of 'Double Ender' tank transporter. Front truck (cab-forward type) was designated XM376, centre load carrying platform XM2. Similar, in principle, to WWII Mack T8 (two 4 × 4 lifting trucks). Payload 50 tons. 1957–59.

Truck, 15-ton, 6 × 6, Tractor (Kenworth 856) with Load-Dividing Dolly, 2-wh., and Semi-Trailer, Low-Bed, 4 wh. (Eidal) Hall Scott 400 6-cyl. engine. GVW (tractor) 57,000 lb, tyres (tractor) front 18.00–24, rear 14.00–20. Air brakes, PAS, dual ignition. Winch behind cab.

Truck, 25-ton, 6 × 6, Tractor, XM523E1 (Kenworth) with Semi-Trailer, Low-Bed, HET, 55-ton, XM524E1 (Fruehauf) Cummins NT380 diesel, 6-cyl., 380 bhp, 4F1R w/OD × 1, wb 192 in. Overall length 696 in, curb weight 38 tons. 30-ton winch. S-T had folding 'gooseneck'. Tank: M60.

Truck, 25-ton, 6 × 6, Tractor, M523E2 (International 8066) with Semi-Trailer, Low-Bed, HET, 55-ton, XM524E2 (Fruehauf) 6-cyl. diesel, 375 bhp, auto. 4F1R (Clark 'Power Shift'), wb 160 in, 286 × 120 × 132 in, 37,600 lb (tractor). Turbo-charged IHC DTI-817 engine. Hyd. 30-ton winch. Tyres 14.00–24. 1964.

Truck, 22½-ton, 8 × 8, Tractor, XM745 (Chrysler) with Semi-Trailer, Low-Bed, 52½-ton, XM747 (Transporter, Heavy Equipment, HET-70) V-12-cyl. m/f, 660 bhp, auto. 5F1R ('Power Shift'), 330 × 120 × 111 in (tractor). Overall dim. 723 × 138 × 111 in, wt 72,595 lb. GCW 177,595 lb. Tyres, tractor 18.00–22.5, S-T 15.00–19.5.

TRACTORS, WHEELED

The US Army, Air Force, Navy and Marine Corps use a wide variety of wheeled tractors for various purposes. Many of these are basically commercial types, others are designed specifically to meet military requirements. The latter applies particularly to aircraft towing tractors, used on airfields and aircraft carriers.

The most important USAF types were the Type A-2 (Euclid 2FPM, 1950/51), Type MB-2 (Euclid 7FPM, 1956; similar: Ward LaFrance, 1959, and Consolidated 2131, 1961) and Type MB-4 (Coleman). They are used to tow and push aircraft, trailer-mounted servicing equipment, etc.

The tall twin-cab models were produced by Coleman and Federal during 1949–53; there were three types, differing mainly in transmission details. Various types of tow tractors were also produced by Hough, LeTourneau, etc.

Tractor, Terminal, 4 × 4 (Walter HFGT) V-8-cyl., 250 bhp, auto. 4F2R ('Power Shift', w/TC), wb 100 in, 13,000 lb. Tyres 14.00–20. GVW 30,000 lb. 4- or 2-wh. steer. Designed to handle 30-ton S-Ts in ship 'Roll-on Roll-off' operations. Hyd. power lift fifth wheel. Similar: FWD 'Ro/Ro' (1970).

Tractor, Aircraft Towing, 4 × 4 (Federal F-55-AF) Buda LO-525 6-cyl., 125 bhp, Fuller 5A650 trans., wb 105 in, 255 × 91 × 113 in, 33,800 lb. Tyres 16.00–20. Air brakes. 4-wh. steer (PA). Coleman CF-55-AF (1950) and Federal TT-11 (1953) similar but with TC transmission. Twin GM cabs. 1949.

Tractor, Aircraft Towing, Type MB-2 (Euclid 7FPM, Ward LaFrance) GM Detroit 6-71 6-cyl. diesel, 200 bhp, GM Allison auto. trans. (w/TC), wb 134 in, 216 × 96 × 106 in, 32,000 lb. Tyres 16.00–25. 30-ton winch. Low-level crew cab on RH side. 1959. Similar tractor with Cummins diesel by Consolidated (1961). DBP 27,000 lb. 4-wh. steer.

CRANE CARRIERS

Crane carriers are special chassis for the mounting of revolving cranes. There were many types but basically similar in design: heavy chassis with forward-mounted one-man cab, three axles (usually 6 × 6, some 6 × 4), and heavy outriggers fore and aft of the rear bogie. Basic units came in five sizes: 10-, 12½-, 20-, 25- and 45-ton. Chassis manufacturers included Corbitt, Duplex, FWD and Hendrickson. Crane equipment was supplied by other firms, e.g. Browning, Crane Shovel, Gar Wood, Link-Belt and Unit. Others produced both crane and carrier (Bay City, Thew (Lorain), Wayne). Instead of a crane boom, other equipment could be fitted, e.g. backhoe, shovel, dragline, clamshell. During the 1950s some were acquired from Kaelble (with O & K crane) for the US Army in Germany. An air-transportable model was mounted on the standard 2½-ton 6 × 6 truck chassis.

Truck, Crane Carrier, 6 × 6 (Duplex 20TA) Waukesha 148DK 6-cyl., 200 bhp, 4F1R × 2, wb 178 in, 25,120 lb. Solid beam rear susp. Tyres 12.00–20. Lipe Rollway clutch, Fuller trans.. Timken transfer and axles. Bendix-Westinghouse air brakes, Ross steering. Supplied to Corps of Engineers, about 1956.

Truck, Crane Carrier, 6 × 6 (FWD MCU) Buda K248 or Waukesha 145 CKB 6-cyl., 5F1R × 2 × 2, wb 185 in, chassis: 305 × 96 in, 29,000 lb approx. Tyres 12.00–20. FWD axles, Hendrickson rear suspension. Designed for mounting 20-ton capacity cranes (Browning, Gar Wood, Link-Belt, etc.) 1952.

Truck, Crane-Shovel, 20-ton, 6 × 6 (Gar Wood M-20) Typical example of a complete truck-mounted crane. In travelling position (shown) the crane boom rests on a support bracket above the radiator. The crane is operated by a separate engine, mounted in the turntable.

FIRE FIGHTERS

Some military fire fighting vehicles are of the conventional civilian pattern but the majority are specials, equipped to perform emergency rescue work resulting from aircraft accidents. These usually have one or two turret type nozzles, discharging foam or carbon dioxide, in addition to handlines, and, sometimes, ground-sweep nozzles. Some typical examples are presented here. Not shown, but worth mentioning, is the USAF 'Truck, Airplane Crash, Fire and Forcible Entry Rescue, Type R-2'. This was a small unit, produced by ACF-Brill in 1954 on the Dodge ¾-ton 4 × 4 M56 chassis. It was designed to perform forcible entry into crashed aircraft, using a metal-cutting power saw, hand fire tools, and a three-pronged winch-operated grappling hook. A 230-volt generator supplied electrical power and bromochloro-methane (CB) was used to combat fires. Among the makers of US fire-fighters were Am. LaFrance-Foamite, Cardox, Darley, Howe, Minnesota, Oshkosh, and Ward LaFrance.

Truck, Fire, Powered Pumper, 4 × 4, 750 GPM (FWD S-750) Basically standard FWD chassis with 'sawn off' type cab, produced for US Navy in 1953. Pumping equipment was triple combination type with 750 gal. per minute capacity two-stage centrifugal pump.

Truck, Fire, Aircraft, Rescue, 4 × 4, Type MB-1 (Oshkosh) Caterpillar D334 6-cyl. diesel, 335 bhp, auto. 4F1R × 1 ('Power Shift'), wb 190 in, 307½ × 96 × 139 in, NSW 32,350 lb. Two foam pumps, driven by Perkins 4.236 diesels. Two main turrets, two handlines. Discharge capacity 6000+ gal. of expanded foam/min. 1970.

Truck, Fire, Aircraft, Rescue, 4 × 4, Type MB-5 (Oshkosh) Caterpillar 6-cyl. diesel, 273 bhp, auto. 4F1R × 1 ('Power Shift'), wb 140 in, 254 × 96 × 132 in, NSW 19,755 lb. Tyres 15.00–22.5. 60-mph, 400-gal. capacity. Delivered expanded foam over 100 ft at 3000 gpm. 1968. Earlier MB-5s were produced by American LaFrance.

Truck, Fire, Powered Pumper, Class 750A (Ward LaFrance CW-750) Continental R6602 6-cyl., 240 bhp, 5F1R, wb 166 in, 296 × 96 × 111 in, NSW 23,400 lb. Empty wt 16,400 lb. Tyres 11.00–20. Fire pump cap. 750 gpm @ 150 lb/sq. in (Waterous CA5 centrifugal pump, driven from main engine). Produced 1954–55.

Truck, Fire Fighting, Crash and Pumper, Class 1500 (Walter MF) 7-ton 4 × 4 186-in wb chassis with 6-man cab ahead of (gasoline) engine, 336 × 96 × 124 in, 25,570 lb. Hale ZHFW5 1500-gpm centrifugal pump, centrally mounted. Carried 950 gal. of water and 200 gal. of foam chemical. Front winch. *c.* 1960.

Truck, Fire, Powered Pumper, Class 530A (Reo, Studebaker) Standard mil. 2½-ton 6 × 6 chassis/cab, M44, equipped by Dakota or Howe. Centrifugal pump, capacity 530 gpm, driven by PTO from main engine. 294 × 94 × 98½ in, NSW 16,650 lb. Class 530B unit was equipped by Fire Master Corp. and had slab-sided bodywork.

Truck, Crash, Fire and Rescue, Type O-6 (Cardox) Continental R6602–99, 6-cyl., 240 bhp, 5F1R × 2, 300 × 98 × 127 in, NSW 19,545 lb. Spicer transmission, Timken-Detroit transfer and axles (as 2½-ton 6 × 6). Employed for emergency rescue work, using carbon dioxide as fire-extinguishing agent. Tyres 12.00–20. 1955.

Truck, Crash, Fire and Rescue, Type O-10 (American LaFrance-Foamite, and Marmon-Herrington) Continental R6602, 6-cyl., 240 bhp, 5F1R × 2, wb 165 (BC 49½) in, 321½ × 93 × 131 in, NSW 27,700 lb. Hale pump (300 gpm) driven by 4-cyl. Continental PE90. Used water/foam as primary, CB or CO₂ as secondary agent. 1951–52 (M-H: 1954).

Truck, Crash, Fire and Rescue, Type O-11(A) (American LaFrance-Foamite) Continental S6820 6-cyl. main engine, PE200–2 8-cyl. pump engine. 500-gpm Hale pump. Water/foam tank cap. 900/100 gal. (550/50 on Type O-10). Approx. 364½ × 99 × 137 in, NSW 42,520 lb. 1949–53. O-11A: 1953–54; two turret nozzles. O-12 was 8 × 8.

Truck, Fire, Aircraft, Rescue, 6 × 6, Type MB-1A (FWD) Continental 340-bhp rear-mounted engine to drive truck and pumps (low-pressure 6000-gpm main pump for twin turret nozzles, Waterous GP type aux. pump for handlines). Tank cap. **1000 gal.** water, 65 gal. foam solution. US Navy, 1962.

Truck, Crash, Fire and Rescue, Type P-2, 8 × 8 (FWD) Twin Continental 340-bhp engines. Acceleration 0 to 55 mph in 60 sec. One engine powered 1400-gpm pump, which delivered up to 22,500 gal. of foam a distance of 200 ft in under two minutes. 420 × 104 × 138½ in, NSW 65,000 lb. From 1962.

SNOW FIGHTERS

Many of the snow removal vehicles used by the US forces after 1945 were similar to those produced during WWII. Later more sophisticated designs were introduced. Major suppliers of trucks for rotary type snow ploughs (plows) were FWD and Oshkosh. These were equipped by the Klauer Mfg Co ('Snogo') of Dubuque in Iowa, and the Canadian firm of Sicard. Sicard also supplied complete units (over 400 to the USAF alone). Conventional snow ploughs (wings at front only, or front and sides) were fitted on various makes of chassis, incl. Duplex, FWD, Oshkosh and Walter. They were used mainly by the USAF for airfield snow removal and had a dump body at rear. Examples are the FWD A329 and Oshkosh WT2206. Roto-wing types were also employed. The USAF in Germany operated Beilhack Model HS14 rotary type snow ploughs on Magirus-Deutz A6500 chassis (1955).

Plough, Snow, Rotary, GED, Truck-Mounted (FWD/ Klauer) 'Snogo' Model TU-3 rotary snow remover, made by Klauer Mfg Co., mounted on 7½-ton 4 × 4 four-wheel steer FWD chassis. Similar equipment also on Oshkosh WT2206 chassis. Triple augers driven by separate engine. GED is 'Gasoline Engine Driven'.

Plough, Snow, Reversible, w/Dump Body, 4 × 4 (FWD C360) 128-in wb, 34,500-lb GVW chassis with Heil 5-cu. yd hyd. dump body, Wasau one-way reversible snow plough and underbody maintenance scraper blade. 32 supplied to USAF, 1961. Also 70 with 15-cu. yd snow hauling dump body.

Plough, Snow, Rotary, Deep Bank, GED, 4 × 4 (FWD CF9-4420) Special 4-wh. steer chassis with RHD and 92-in wide steel cab. Two rear-mounted engines (Roiline 330-bhp 884 CID) used separately to drive truck and plough. GVW 34,000 lb. Over 20 supplied to US Army for use in US and overseas, 1960/61.

AMPHIBIANS, WHEELED

For many years the wartime GMC Model DUKW ('Duck') remained the standard amphibious truck in the armies of the USA and many other countries. During the 1950s GMC developed the improved 'Superduck', which had a higher load capacity. The official designation of both was later changed to Landing Vehicle, Wheeled: 2½-ton, 6 × 6. An 8 × 8, the 'Drake', was also experimented with (1956). The first post-war amphibian produced in quantity, however, was the 4 × 4 LARC-V. The LARC was much larger than the 'Duck' and when used on the road suffered from 'pitching', but it hauled twice as much cargo twice as fast and was essentially a boat with wheels, rather than an amphibious truck. The even bigger LARC-XV had a bow ramp. Hydrofoil amphibians were developed chiefly for the USMC. These high-speed ship-to-shore cargo/personnel carriers were designed to 'fly' to the surf, cruise through it, and then drive inland, with a smooth uninterrupted transition.

Truck, ¾-ton, 4 × 4, Amphibious, XM531 (AMC 'Muskrat') Rambler 6-cyl., 129 bhp, 4F1R (Chrysler), wb 82 in, 148 × 82 in, 3900 lb. Tyres 7.50–20. Gradability 60%. Private venture by American Motors, 1961. Aluminium body/hull by Fruehauf. IFS/IRS. Self-locking diffs.

Truck, 2½–4-ton, 6 × 6, Amphibious, XM147 (GMC 'Superduck') 6-cyl., 145 bhp (gross), 4F1R × 2 × 1 (dual-range 'Hydramatic'), wb 164 in, 384 × 105 × 108½ (89) in, 18,000 lb. One of several prototypes, produced from 1953 (XM147-XM147E4). Tyres 12.50–20, with central pressure control (by driver). Air-hyd. brakes.

Truck, 8–10-ton, 8 × 8, Amphibious, XM157 (GMC 'Drake') Twin 6-cyl. 145 bhp each (gross), two 5F1R × 2 (Allison 'Powermatic'), wb 221 in, 504 × 120 × 130 in, 32,000 lb. No. 1 and 3 axles driven by port, No. 2 and 4 by starboard engine. Aluminium hull. Tyres 14.75–20. Air-bellow suspension. Air-hyd. brakes. PAS.

Truck, 5-ton, 6×6, Amphibious, XM148 (ACF-Brill 'Gull') Hall-Scott 6-cyl., 250 bhp, 5F1R × 2, wb 207½ (BC 61) in, 420 × 117 × 118½ in, 40,580 lb. Tyres 14.75–20. Trailing link type IFS/IRS with torsion bars. PAS. Fibreglass reinforced plastic hull. XM148E1 (1954) differed only in details.

Lighter, Amphibious, Resupply, Cargo, 5-ton, 4×4 (LARC-V) Cummins V-8-cyl. diesel, 300 bhp (early prod.: Ford V-8, 270 bhp), auto. trans., wb 192 in, 420 × 120 × 122 in, 30,600 lb. Developed by Ingersoll Kalamazoo (B-W), 1958/59. Quantity producers: LeTourneau-Westinghouse and Consolidated. Aluminium hull. 1961.

Lighter, Amphibious, Resupply, Cargo, 15-ton, 4×4 (LARC-XV) Twin Cummins V-8-cyl. diesel, 300 bhp each, (early prod.: twin 270-bhp Ford V-8s), auto. trans., 541½ × 176 × 184 in, 36,000 lb. Developed by Ingersoll Kalamazoo (B-W), 1959/60. Quantity production by Fruehauf. Aluminium hull. Loading ramp at front, driver at rear. 1963.

Lighter, Amphibious, Resupply, Cargo, 60-ton, 4×4 (LARC-LX) Four 6-cyl. 165-bhp diesels (one for each wheel) with 3F1R 'Torquematic' trans., 749 × 319 × 239 in, 97 tons. Developed by PCF (1951/52). Originally: Barge, Amphibious, Resupply, Cargo (BARC). Tyres 36.00–41, weighing 3300 lb each. Payload in emergencies 100 tons.

Landing Vehicle, Wheeled, 5-ton, 4 × 4, LVWX1 Lycoming TF2036 B1A gas turbine, 1500 shp, 2F2R (in water 1F1R), wb 204 in, 432 × 140 × 130 in, 16½ tons. Tyres 18.00–25. Max. land, speed (loaded) 35 mph. Steering: front wheels only, 4-wh. oblique, or 4-wh. radial. Designed by Ingersoll Kalamazoo (B-W), 1962.

Landing Vehicle, Wheeled, 5-ton, 4 × 4, LVWX1 Same vehicle as on left, shown in water, with wheels rotated 180°. Two 24-in 3-blade counter-rotating propellers provided speeds up to 30 knots. Steering by twin rudders. Testing and development was carried out by Chrysler's Defense Operations Division.

Landing Force Amphibious Support Vehicle, Hydrofoil, 5-ton, 4 × 4, LVHX2 Lycoming TF1460 gas turbine, 1000 shp. 444 × 126 in. Original vehicle (LVH) was produced by Lycoming Div. of Avco, LVHX2 by Ordnance Div. of FMC. In water the wheels retracted and vehicle could 'fly' (on its foils) at 35 knots or cruise at 12. Max. land speed 40 mph.

Mobile Floating Assault Bridge/Ferry, M88, 4 × 4, MOFAB/MAB 16-ton vehicle, mounted with either interior or end bay superstructure, to form a MOFAB unit. Produced by FMC, Chrysler, and Consolidated, from 1964. GM Detroit 335-bhp diesel. All-wheel steer. Superstructures turned 90° when in position for bridging, as shown. Army design.

MISCELLANEOUS MTVs and AMPHIBIOUS VEHICLES

During the 1960s several American companies designed and developed a variety of 'marginal terrain vehicles' (MTV). Some were developed at Government request, others were conceived as private ventures and offered to the Army and/or Navy for evaluation. Notable among these manufacturers were the Ingersoll Kalamazoo Div. of Borg-Warner Corp., the Lockheed Aircraft Service Co. (Div. of Lockheed Aircraft Corp.; under the direction of Robert W. and John P. Forsyth), and the LTV Aerospace Corp. (Subsidiary of Ling-Temco-Vought, Inc.). Several old (revived) and new propulsion systems were tried, varying from screw-like rotary pontoons (as first expounded by the Greek philosopher Archimedes in the second century B.C.) to tracks consisting of free-rolling 'Terra-Tires'. Some examples of experimental test rigs are shown here.

Carrier, ½-ton, 8 × 8, Multi-Purpose (LTV MACV) Wisconsin 4-cyl., 35 bhp, two hydrostatic transmissions, each driving four wheels on one side, 96 × 52 × 34 in, 1740 lb. Multi-purpose Airmobile Combat-support Vehicle (MACV), developed by LTV Aerospace Corp., 1967. Speed 20 (in water 3) mph.

Carrier, ½-ton, 12 × 12, Articulated, Multi-Purpose (Lockheed PacStar) Onan CCK, 21 bhp, hydrostatic transmission, 159¾ × 52¾ × 45¾ in, 1079 lb. Twelve 16 × 14.50–6 'Terra-Tires'. Tread 38½ in. Hyd. articulated steering. Speed 25 mph. Could 'swim' inland waterways. Prototypes (several variants) from 1964. Front unit also as solo vehicle.

Carrier, ½-ton, Marginal-Terrain Amphibian (Lockheed Terra Star II) 53 bhp engine, 4-speed trans. Four 'major wheels', each consisting of gear train and three 'minor wheels'. Operated either in minor wheel mode (roads) or major wheel ('paddling') mode (water, mud). 130¼ × 80 in, 2600 lb. Speed 35 (in water 6) mph.

Carrier, 1¼-ton, Amphibious (LTV PATA) Pneumatic All Terrain Amphibian (PATA) with Firestone air cell tracks, built experimentally by LTV Aerospace Corp., 1965. Max. pressure in cells 1½ lb/sq. in. In water the PATA was propelled by its tracks. Speed 35 (in water 10) mph.

Carrier, 1½-ton, Amphibious (Borg-Warner/USN 'Airoll') Chrysler V-8-engined 19,000-lb test vehicle, originally conceived by B-W (Ingersoll Kalamazoo Div.). 16 free-rolling Goodyear 'Terra-Tires' on each track. Intended for operation in deep mud, snow and watery swampland. 1962.

Carrier, 1½-ton, Cargo, Soft Tire, Tracked, XM759E1 (PCF) This version of the pneumatic track-type vehicle was tested and developed at Aberdeen Proving Ground. In 1966 Clark Equipment Co. introduced commercial PTVs, featuring regenerative hydrostatic differential steering system.

Carrier, ½-ton, Amphibious, Marsh Screw (Chrysler) 6-cyl. 225 CID engine. 164×100×57 in, 2330 lb. Two revolving screw-like pontoons propelled vehicle forwards, backwards, or sideways. 1962/63. Speed in muck 14, water 9½, snow 20 mph. 1969 development: Riverine Utility Craft (RUC).

MISCELLANEOUS AIR FORCE VEHICLES

Like civil airlines, military air forces employ many special purpose vehicles. In addition to aircraft towing tractors, fire fighters and snow fighters (qv), there are ground support vehicles, runway sweepers (SP and trailer-mounted types), warehouse cranes and tractors, forklift trucks, truck-mounted asphalt and water distributors, various types of construction equipment, etc. Shown here are some USAF ground support vehicles, designed for the multi-servicing requirements of jet and turbine driven aircraft and missiles. They could service an aircraft's electrical and pneumatic requirements simultaneously, tow it in position and provide starting power prior to take off. They were self-contained and could be driven off the road to reach isolated equipment. The USN used an open-cab model (Consolidated 2035) as Type NC-5B, which was otherwise not unlike the USAF MA-1.

Ground Support Unit, Multi-Purpose, SP, Type MA-1 (Consolidated 2000, 2001, 2002) Ford V-8-cyl., 332 CID, 5F1R (TC on Model 2002), wb 90 in, 148 × 63 × 94 in. 4 × 4 Marmon-Herrington chassis. 400-cycle AC and 28-volt DC outputs. 3500-lb/sq. in pneumatic source (Models 2001, 2).

Ground Support Unit, Multi-Purpose, SP, Type MA-2 (Consolidated 2015) Ford V-8-cyl., 332 CID, 5F1R (TC optional), wb 90 in, 166 × 73 × 94 in. Mobile source of AC and DC electric power and high-pressure and high-flow pneumatic power. Over 4500 lb drawbar pull. Tyres 7.50–16. M.-H. chassis.

Ground Support Unit, Multi-Purpose, SP, Type MA-3 (Beech Aircraft Corp.) FWD 4 × 4 4-wh. steer (PAS) chassis with reciprocating and gas turbine power plants, air conditioner, air compressor, generating systems for AC and DC electric power, etc. Drawbar pull 12,500 lb. Speed 45 mph. 1956.

MISCELLANEOUS HANDLING EQUIPMENT, WHEELED

Illustrated in this section are a few examples of the numerous types of self-propelled materials handling equipment used by the US armed forces. This equipment ranges from forklift trucks (commercial and rough terrain tactical types) to landing craft retrievers. Some types were standardized by one or more of the armed services, others remained in the experimental stage. By the mid-1950s the QMC materials handling equipment catalogue listed over 130 types, divided as follows (numbers of different models in brackets): Cranes, Truck, Warehouse (2 electric, 5 gasoline); Tractors Warehouse (8 electric, 15 gasoline); Tractors, Wheeled, Industrial, (5 gasoline); Trucks, Lift, Fork (24 electric, 67 gasoline); Trucks, Straddle, (6 gasoline).

Truck, Forklift, Pneumatic Tires, Rough Terrain, UL-42 'Sandpiper' 4000-lb capacity all-purpose forklift truck of US Army Material Command. Could be transported by fixed-wing and helicopter aircraft. Shown at Aberdeen Proving Ground, 1965.

Truck, Forklift, Pneumatic Tires, Rough Terrain (Chrysler) 6000-lb capacity general purpose cargo type. Deliveries of this 23,000-lb diesel-engined vehicle commenced in February 1967 by the Chrysler-operated Detroit Tank Plant. Speed range from 15 mph (fully loaded) up to 25 mph.

Crane, Wheel-Mounted, 5-ton, 4 × 4, Rough Terrain (Hanson) Hydraulic telescopic crane with reach of 25 ft and rotating 360° at 3½ rpm. Gross vehicle weight 36,700 lb. Produced by Hanson of Tiffin, Ohio. Engine at rear. Note bulldozer blade at front and folding stabilizers at the four corners.

Truck, Forklift/Crane, Pneumatic Tires, Rough Terrain (Clark) Missile-handling crane attachment on 'Ranger' forklift truck. Four-wheel steering. As a tractor it could pull 19,000 lb. As a forklift or crane its lifting capacity was five tons. Shown with Nike Hercules missile, 1959.

Crane, Truck-Mounted, Torpedo Handling (FWD 4-427 DN-ORD) FWD 6 × 4 40,000-lb GVW chassis. Swing-boom type crane with lift capacity of 4000 lb at 15½-ft radius. Crane assembly manufactured by Teale & Co. of Omaha, Nebraska. Platform body. 1960.

Truck, Aircraft Cargo Loading and Unloading, Type 25K (Condec 2205) Part of cargo handling equipment used with C130 Lockheed Hercules transport planes. Twin-steer front axles. Hyd. lift platform. Capacity up to 25,000 lb. Produced by Consolidated Diesel Electric Corp., from *c.* 1962.

Retriever, Landing Craft (LeTourneau) Designed by R. G. Le Tourneau, Inc., for US Army Transportation Corps to rescue immobilized vessels from surf and sand. Individual electric motors in each wheel operated under air pressure to keep water out. Tubeless tyres, 4 ft wide × 10 ft high. 1955.

EARTH MOVERS, WHEELED

Much progress has been made in recent years with regard to equipment intended for earth moving, road construction, etc. Equipment in this category is employed mainly by the US Corps of Engineers and the USAF and includes wheeled bulldozers, loaders, ditching machines, graders, and, more recently, universal engineer tractors which are used to perform a variety of jobs. In several cases wheeled equipment has partly replaced tracked vehicles. For example, wheeled multi-purpose tractors, equipped with dozer blades, have replaced crawler (full-track) types in many instances. These wheeled types are quieter in operation and much faster to move from one site to another, without the need to transport them on trailers. Crawler-types, however, have by no means been outmoded and are dealt with in a separate section.

Tractor, Articulated, Multi-Purpose, 4 × 4 (Caterpillar 830M) Cat D343 diesel 6-cyl., 335 bhp, 'Power Shift' trans., wb 140 in, 288 × 123½ × 136½ in, 52,220 lb. Centre-pivot PAS. Tyres 29.50–29. Designed for use as dozer and as tractor for scrapers, trailers, etc. Introduced in 1962.

Tractor, Earthmoving, Wheeled, w/Dozer Blade (Le-Tourneau-Westinghouse Super C 'Tournadozer') GM 210-bhp diesel engine, driving generator. Each wheel had electric motor with gear reduction unit. Tyres 21.00–25. Two electric power cable units at rear for hookup to other equipment. **1953.** Over 800 supplied.

Loader, Scoop Type (Clark 175A-M) Full nomenclature: 'Loader, Scoop Type: DED (diesel engine driven); 4 wheels; 2 single front wheels, driving, nonsteerable; 2 single rear wheels, driving, steerable; hyd. front loading, vertical lift, front dump; 2½ cu. yd; air-transportable'.

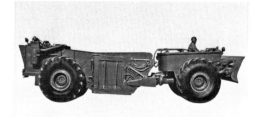

Tractor, Universal, Engineer (Hendrickson) 'Goer'-type Army Universal Engineer Tractor, produced by Hendrickson Mfg Co., Lyons, Illinois. The UET could perform the functions of tractor, scraper, bulldozer, and, with interchangeable centre sections, grader, cargo carrier, etc.

Grader, Road, Motorized, Model 12 (Caterpillar 112F) Cat D330 diesel 4-cyl., 100 bhp, 6F2R, wb 225 in, 300 × 98 × 89 in approx., GVW 26,595 lb. Tyres 13.00–24 (tubeless). Motor graders were also supplied by Austin-Western, Le-Tourneau-Westinghouse, Pettibone.

Ditching Machine, Wheel Mounted, Airborne (Gar Wood 831) Prototype, developed in 1957/58. Could dig trench 4 ft deep and 2 ft wide at 12 ft/min. Overall dim. 264 × 96 × 81 in, wt 16,900 lb. Followed by improved Model 832 (*c.* 1960). Air-droppable from C123 aircraft.

Ditching Machine, Wheel Mounted (Barber-Greene 750) International UD691 diesel engine, 5F1R trans., 324 × 149 × 96 in, 36,000 lb. Max. road speed 27 mph. 1960. Dug trenches 6 ft deep, 2 ft wide. Similar machine produced by Unit Rig and Equipment Co. of Tulsa, Oklahoma (model 4262).

MISCELLANEOUS WHEELED VEHICLES

In addition to the types dealt with in the foregoing sections, several other wheeled vehicles have made their appearance and some are shown here. Most of these were produced as 'one-off' jobs to perform special purposes, or in experimental/prototype form for evaluation by the armed forces. Several ultra-heavy vehicles were produced by the firm of R. G. LeTourneau Inc. of Longview, Texas. Most of these were of the electric drive type, i.e. driven by electric wheel motors which were powered by a generator, driven, in turn, by a diesel or petrol engine. These included crash cranes (USN), crash pushers (USAF), tow units (USAF, USN), missile transporters (USA, NATO), and the famous 'overland-train'. The latter, in its 1962 form, could carry a payload of 150 tons at 15–20 mph for a distance of up to 400 miles and was built for the US Army Transportation Research Command (USATRECOM).

Ground Pressure Testing Vehicle (LeTourneau) 'Tournapull' tractive unit (normally used with a scraper rear unit) linked to special trailer with centre wheel(s) which could be loaded to simulate aircraft wheel ground pressure on asphalt pavements, landing mats, etc.

Swamp Vehicle, 4 × 4 (Swamp Skipper, Model 5) This unusual vehicle was produced in 1948 and tested at Aberdeen Proving Ground. The large all-metal floating wheels were chain-driven and could each be fitted with two 'steppers'. It carried US reg. No. 7041764.

Cross-Country Vehicle, Articulated, 8 × 8 (Lockheed 'Twister') Exp. high-mobility vehicle, consisting of two 4-wheeled bodies linked by a pivoting yoke. Two engines. IFS. Walking-beam rear suspension. 1965. In 1972 a forward-control truck variant ('Dragon Wagon') with 225-bhp diesel engine was unveiled.

Traction Dynamometer Vehicle (Ordnance) Produced in 1947 this vehicle, which measured 50 × 11 × 12 ft and weighed about 50 tons, was designed to test tractive effort and rolling resistance of tanks and other heavy vehicles, by towing or being towed, at Aberdeen Proving Ground, Maryland.

Pusher, Crash, Type CP-1 (LeTourneau) Designed for removing crashed or disabled aircraft from runways these USAF Crash Pushers featured six 'electric wheels', delivering electro-mechanical power directly to the inside of each wheel. Dozer blades front and rear. Produced in 1955.

Erector, Guided Missile, Self-Propelled, M2 (Le-Tourneau) Designed in conjunction with Firestone Tire & Rubber Co, to pick up 'Corporal' guided missile and transport it to launching site. 'Electric wheels' with 24.00–33 tyres. Continental main engine, driving DC generator. Remote control possible. Introduced in 1957.

Carrier, Cargo, Logistical (LeTourneau) Experimental 'Overland Train', consisting of a control car, ten 15-ton cargo cars, and two power generating cars. Four Solar 10MC 1170-shp gas turbines drove the generators which powered the 54 'electric wheels'. Length 572 ft. Crew 6. 1962 version shown.

ARMOURED CARS

The only post-war US armoured car produced in quantity was the four-wheeled 'Commando', which was first introduced in 1961 as a private venture by the Cadillac Gage Company (not to be confused with the Cadillac Motor Car Division of General Motors). Unlike the sophisticated 'SWAT' and 'Twister', the 'Commando' was of a straight-forward 4 × 4 design with well-established mechanical components such as a Chrysler 361 engine (as used in the APC M113), a conventional 5-speed transmission, and Rockwell Standard axles similar to those of the standard 2½-ton 6 × 6 truck (M34, etc.; fitted with locking differentials). Series production commenced in 1964. Various versions were offered, incl. APC, convoy escort vehicle, police vehicle, etc. They were supplied to a number of countries and from about 1965 to the US Army and Air Force, mainly for use in Vietnam (from 1967).

Car, Armoured, 4 × 4, XM706 (Cadillac Gage V100) Chrysler 361 V-8-cyl., 210 bhp, 5F1R × 1, wb 105 in, 224 × 89 × 86½ in, 12,600 lb. Twin .30 cal. mgs shown; other armament available. M34 truck axles. 14.00–20 tyres. 5-ton hyd. winch. Amphibious. Speed 65 (in water 4) mph. 1964.

Car, Armoured, 8 × 8 (Chrysler SWAT) Special Warfare Armoured Transporter (SWAT), designed in 1966 by Chrysler Corp.'s Defense Operations Div., to perform several combat roles. Carried 12 fully equipped troops at up to 65 mph. Swimming capability by tyre spin. 240 × 96 × 96 in, 15,000 lb.

Vehicle, Combat, 8 × 8, XM808 (Lockheed) Based on Lockheed's 'Twister', featuring applique armour, armoured top structure (aluminium) and M27 cupola with M139 20-mm gun. Two Chrysler 440 CID engines, 582 bhp. Tyres 18–20, radial-ply. Speed 65 mph. Acceleration 0–45 mph in 13 sec. 1969.

TRACTORS, FULL-TRACK, LOW-SPEED

Many post-war crawler tractors were similar to those of World War II and were used either in their basic form for towing purposes or fitted with special attachments such as angledozers, bulldozers (hyd. and cable-operated), cranes, loaders and pipelayers. Among the most widely used crawler tractors were the Allis-Chalmers HD5, 7, 10, 14, 15 and 16, the Caterpillar D4, 6, 7 and 8, and the International Harvester TD9, 14, 15, 18, 20 and 24. Some were fitted with an armoured or soft-skin cab. Eimco supplied a rear-engined model. International Harvester developed a Universal Engineer Tractor (UET, Crawler) which could perform the tasks of bulldozer, grader, scraper, dump truck, cargo and troop carrier (see page 385).

Tractor, Full-Tracked, Low-Speed, DED, 12,000 to 17,000 DBP, with Hyd. Bulldozer, Air-transportable (Caterpillar D6) Oscillating tracks, minimum gauge 60 in. Dropped from an aeroplane, this tractor was ready to work as soon as it landed. For airdrops six parachutes were used.

Tractor, Full-Tracked, Low-Speed, DED, Medium DBP, with Hyd. Bulldozer (Caterpillar D7) 4-cyl. diesel, 199.5 bhp, 'Power Shift' trans. (w/TC), $176 \times 133\frac{1}{2} \times 96$ in, 31,870 lb. Used for general bulldozing, pan pushing, tree dozing, scraper towing and other types of construction work.

Tractor, Full-Tracked, Low-Speed, DED, Medium DBP, with Hyd. Bulldozer (Eimco 103MC/SH) GM Detroit 6V-71 6-cyl. diesel, 218 bhp, 'Power Shift' trans. (w/TC), $156 \times 104 \times 118(99)$ in, 34,600 lb (dim. and wt for basic tractor). Winch at rear to operate scraper bowl (Scraper, Earth Moving, Towed).

TRACTORS, FULL-TRACK, HIGH-SPEED

Towards the end of WWII development commenced of three new high-speed cargo tractors/prime movers. The 32,000-lb T43E1 (for 155-mm How.) was based on the light tank, M24, chassis and designed by IHC. The 48,000-lb T42 (for towed loads of 9–16 tons) was developed by Buick and later became the M8 (originally, in 1944–45, this was the T33, based on light tank, M24). Of the six pilots two were planned as basic vehicles for a fire fighting and a crash rescue vehicle. The basic tractor was developed into the M8E1 and M8E2. Finally there was the 92,000-lb T44 for towed loads of 20–32½ tons, powered by a 810-bhp air-cooled V-12 engine. T43E1 and T44 remained in the prototype stage. A 23-ton high-speed tractor (M85) was built about 1960. The WWII high-speed tractors, M4, M5, and M6, remained in use for many years. Of the 13-ton M5 several developments appeared.

Tractor, Full-Track, High-Speed, Cargo, T42 (Buick)
Continental R975D4 9-cyl., 475 bhp, 3F1R 'Torqmatic', 258½ × 117 × 114(84) in, 48,000 lb (combat loaded). Air-cooled radial engine. Designed early 1945, became M8 in Oct. 1945. Payload 5 tons. Speed 35 mph. 25-ton winch.

Tractor, Full-Track, High-Speed, Recovery, M8E1 (Allis-Chalmers) Wrecker equipment, T4, and bulldozer, T8E2, on basic cargo carrier, M8E1. Bulldozer blade enabled vehicle to assist in construction work, clear its way to damaged vehicles, etc. Hyd.-operated swinging booms.

Tractor, Full-Track, High-Speed, M8A1 (Allis-Chalmers)
Continental AOS895 6-cyl., 863 bhp, GM Allison cross-drive trans. Shown as prime mover for 75-mm AA gun (with bulldozer blade and rear-mounted hyd. hoist). Basic vehicle: 265 × 130½ × 120 in. M8A2 ('Mole') had fuel-inj. engine.

CARRIERS, FULL-TRACK, CARGO and PERSONNEL

Of the multitude of post-WWII US armoured and soft-skin full-track carriers and landing vehicles a few typical examples are shown here. The best known is the M113(A1) carrier vehicle family, the most used and accepted range of tracked vehicles in the Free World. The major models were the APC, M113(A1) and mortar carriers, M106(A1) and M125A1 (A1 suffixes indicate diesel engine). Other derivatives included a Command and Reconnaissance version (supplied to Canada and the Netherlands), the M474 guided missile ('Pershing') equipment carrier, and the M548 cargo carrier. The APC M113 replaced the APCs, M75 and M59 of the early 1950s and was also produced in Italy. Wilson, Nuttall, Raimond Engineers (WNRE) of Chestertown, Md., developed a number of high-mobility articulated and other carriers, some of which were used by the military (see also 'Canada').

Carrier, Full-Track, Cargo, Amphibious, M76 (T46E1) (Pontiac 'Otter') Continental AO268 HO-4-cyl., 127 bhp, cross-drive trans., 193(188) × 98 × 108 in, 12,162 lb. Vertically-mounted air-cooled engine at front. 30-in tracks. Aluminium hull. Hinged propeller. Ground pressure 2.1 psi. 1951.

Carrier, Full-Track, Cargo, Amphibious, M116 (PCF 'Husky') Chevrolet V-8-cyl., 160 bhp, 4F1R 'Hydramatic', 188 × 82 × 79(64) in, 7880 lb. Payload 1½ tons. 2½-ton winch. Removable soft- or hard-top. Speed 37 (in water 4) mph. Superseded 'Weasel' and 'Otter'. Air-transportable. 1958.

Carrier, Full-Track, Cargo, 6-ton, M548 (XM548E1) (FMC) GM Detroit 6V53 V-6-cyl. diesel, 210 bhp, GM Allison TX100 auto. trans., 226½ × 105¾ × 105½ in, 14,450 lb. Amphibious logistical support vehicle, based on M113A1. Basic vehicle for 'Chaparral' weapon system ('Sidewinder' missiles). 1966.

Carrier, Full-Track, Armored, Personnel, M113 (T113E2) (FMC) Chrysler 75M V-8-cyl., 215 bhp (M113A1: GM V-6-cyl. diesel, 210 bhp), GM Allison TX200 auto. trans., $191\frac{1}{2} \times 105\frac{3}{4} \times 98$ (79) in, 22,615 lb (combat wt). Crew 2 + 11. Amphibious air-droppable vehicle with many derivatives, widely used from late 1950s.

Carrier, Full-Track, Armored, Command and Reconnaissance, M114A1 (Cadillac) Chevrolet 283 CID V-8-cyl., 160 bhp, 'Hydramatic' auto. trans., $176 \times 92 \times 91$ in, 15,276 lb. Light-weight low-silhouette C&R vehicle. Armament: .50, M2, and 7.6-mm, M60 machine guns. Propulsion and steering (on land and in water) by tracks.

Landing Vehicle, Tracked, Personnel, Model 5 (LVTP5) (Armored Amphibian Assault Personnel and Cargo Carrier) (Borg-Warner) Continental V-12-cyl., 810 bhp, $356 \times 140 \times 103$ in, 87,780 lb (combat wt, land). Used for ship-to-shore operations, etc. Crew 3 + 34 (max.). Payload cap. 9 (in water 6) tons. 1954.

Landing Vehicle, Tracked, Personnel, Model X12 (LVTPX12) (Armored Amphibious Assault Personnel and Cargo Carrier) (FMC) Welded aluminium armour plate hull. Length 312 in. 400-bhp diesel engine. 38,500 lb (combat wt, land). Crew 3. Payload 25 troops or 5 tons. Speed 40 (in water 8) mph. 1966.

MISCELLANEOUS TRACKED VEHICLES

In addition to the types mentioned in the preceding pages there were many other tracked vehicles in service. Coverage of tanks and SP artillery is not within the scope of this book, but shown here are some examples of full-track vehicles other than tractors and carriers. Full-track recovery vehicles have included the heavy M51 (30-ton crane, 45-ton main winch), the medium M74 'Monster' (on medium tank M4A3 chassis), the medium M88 (25-ton crane, 45-ton main winch), and the light M578 (15-ton crane, 30-ton tow winch). Prototype tracked Universal Engineer Tractors (UET) by Caterpillar and International were tested from the mid-1960s. The Engineers' M728 combat engineer vehicle, a winch- and dozer-equipped M60 tank chassis with 165-mm demolition gun, proved highly effective in Vietnam and was dubbed 'bull of the woods'.

Tractor, Engineer, Universal (Crawler) (International) Highly mobile floatable armoured vehicle designed to transport troops and perform a variety of earthmoving and battlefield construction tasks. Hydro-pneumatic suspension ('lockable' for earthmoving operations). 1962/63 prototype (E1) shown.

Recovery Vehicle, Full-Track, Light, Armored, M578 (T120E1) GM Detroit 8V71T V-8-cyl. diesel, 425 bhp, GM Allison cross-drive trans., 250 × 124 × 130 in (travel position), 54,000 lb. Based on same chassis as SP heavy howitzer, 8-in, M110. Used for recovery of vehicles, as crane at workshops, etc.

Recovery Vehicle, Full-Track, Heavy, Armored, M51 Continental V-12-cyl. diesel, 1020 bhp, GM Allison cross-drive trans., 399 × 143 × 129 in (travel pos.), 120,000 lb. Spades front and rear. 30-ton hoist. 45-ton and 5-ton hyd. winches. Equipped for rescue and salvage operations in combat zones.

USSR

Before the second World War the Soviet motor industry was small in size and almost entirely confined to production of trucks and tractors. Most of these vehicles were patterned on American designs. During the war the USA supplied almost 500,000 vehicles of various sorts under 'Lend-Lease', an Allied programme of international aid and pooling of resources which commenced operation in 1941. Under this programme Britain and Canada also supplied large quantities of vehicles and other equipment. Logically, what remained of these supplies was retained in service for many years after VE Day. This also applied to many ageing Russian trucks of pre-war manufacture. The first post-war Soviet military trucks, developed during 1944–46, closely followed the design of some of the American WWII types, as will be seen in the following pages. A $\frac{1}{4}$-ton 4×4 vehicle had already been put into production during the war. This second generation of military vehicles was superseded during the late 1950s by improved models. Many of the older vehicles found their way to Russia's satellites, the 'Warsaw Pact countries', in addition to new vehicles supplied by the Soviet Union and the industries of Czechoslovakia, East Germany, etc. Later during the 1960s the third generation was gradually introduced. This group consisted of a range of sophisticated but sturdy high-mobility vehicles of the 4×4, 6×6 and 8×8 drive configuration. Many of these, as indeed most Soviet cross-country trucks, are available for civilian applications (usually in de-militarized form) in the Soviet Bloc and are also exported to other countries, e.g. Cuba, Egypt, Finland, etc.

Today the Soviet Union is among the largest truck-producing countries of the world, but passenger car production has also been stepped up considerably. There are about 25 plants producing cars, trucks, buses, tractors and/or components and equipment (bodies, cranes, etc.). The two most important plants are the Molotov Plant (GAZ, ZIM) in Gorkiy and the Likhachev Plant in Moscow (ZIL; formerly ZIS). These two factories produce cars, trucks, engines and components; the latter also for other factories. Total production of motor vehicles in 1950 was 362,900 (incl. 64,600 cars). By 1967 this had more than doubled (477,400 trucks and buses, 251,400 cars). In spite of increased output of national products, however, Russia commenced negotiations for new manufacturing facilities with several Western firms during the mid-1960s. By 1970 a Fiat car factory was in operation but no agreement had been reached regarding a truck and engine plant. Among the most impressive of current Soviet wheeled vehicles are the large 8×8 trucks produced by MAZ and ZIL. They are used principally as missile carriers/launchers. Except for these, most current Soviet military vehicles still show a strong American influence. A common feature of Soviet tactical wheeled vehicles is a central tyre pressure control system, enabling the driver to adjust the tyre pressures, from within the cab, to suit the prevailing soil conditions. This greatly enhances the vehicles' cross-country performance. Names and model designations of Soviet trucks usually consist of an abbreviation of the manufacturing plant, followed by a model number and, in many cases, a suffix letter indicating an improved development of the basic vehicle or a derivation. Example: GAZ-63D, in which 'GAZ' indicates the Gorkiy Automobile Plant (*Gorkovska Automobilova Zavod*), '63' the basic vehicle type ($1\frac{1}{2}$-ton, 4×4), and the suffix 'D' the tractor-truck variant. Transfer of production of certain vehicles from one plant to another has caused consequent changes in designations (GAZ/UAZ, JAAZ/KRAZ, etc.). The way in which designations are spelled is not internationally universal (e.g. JAAZ, JAAS, YaAZ, JaAZ, all applying to the same vehicle).

In the following pages the accent is on 'cargo trucks'. Many of these are multi-purpose types, being used not only to carry general cargo, personnel, etc., but also as prime movers for artillery and various types of trailers. Most chassis are also used for the mounting of specialized bodywork; many of these are listed and some typical examples are shown.

Who's Who in the Soviet Automotive Industry

Note: 'Automobile' in the plant names means 'motor vehicle' (passenger cars or trucks, or both)

BAZ	Bryansk Automobile Plant, Bryansk.
BELAZ (BelAZ)	Byelorussian Automobile Plant, Zhodino.
GAZ	Gor'kiy Automobile Plant Gor'kiy (also known as Molotov Plant/ZIM, *qv*).
GZA	Gor'kiy Bus Plant, Gor'kiy.
JAAZ (JaAZ)	Yaroslavl' Automobile Plant (now YaMZ), Yaroslavl'.
KAVZ	Kurgan Bus Plant, Kurgan.
KAZ	Kutaisi Automobile Plant, Kutaisi.
Kirovski	Kirovski (Red Star) Tractor Plant, Leningrad.*
KMZ	Kiyev Motorcycle Plant, Kiyev.
KRAZ (KrAZ)	Kremenchug Automobile Plant, Kremenchug.
LAZ	L'vov Bus Plant, L'vov.
LIAZ (LiAZ)	Likino Bus Plant, Likino.
MAZ	Minsk Automobile Plant, Minsk.
MOAZ (MoAZ)	Mogilev Lift and Hoist Plant, Mogilev (special purpose vehicles).
Moskvitch (MZMA)	Moscow Compact Car Plant, Moscow.
PAZ	Pavlovo Bus Plant, Pavlovo.
Pobieda (see GAZ)	
RAF	Riga Bus Plant, Riga.
SAZ	Saransk Automobile Plant, Saransk.
UAZ	Ul'yanovsk Automobile Plant, Ul'yanovsk.
URAL (Ural)	Ural Automobile Plant, Miass.
Volga (see GAZ)	
YaAZ (see JAAZ)	
YerAZ	Yerevan Automobile Plant, Yerevan.
Zaporozhets (see ZAZ)	
ZAZ	Kommunar Automobile Plant, Zaporozhe.

ZIL	Likhachev Automobile Plant, Moscow (produced buses also).
ZIM	Zavod Imeni Molotova (plant named after Molotov; alternative name for GAZ in Gor'kiy).

ZIS (pre-1957 name for ZIL)

Note: all vehicle exports are handled by V/O Avtoexport, Moscow 119902.

*Agricultural type crawler tractors are also produced in Kharkov, Gor'kiy, Kirov, Volgograd, etc.

8 × 8s in Moscow's Red Square.

CARS, FIELD CARS, LIGHT TRUCKS and MOTORCYCLES

Makes and Models: *Cars:* various commercial 4 × 2 sedans (GAZ, Pobieda (GAZ-M-20), Volga (GAZ-M-21), etc.).
Field Cars: GAZ-61 (5-seater sedan, 4 × 4, 1941–48). GAZ-67B (4-seater, 4 × 4, 1943–53). GAZ-69A (5-seater, 4 × 4, 1952). GAZ-46 (MAV) (5-seater amphibian, 4 × 4). GAZ-M-72 'Pobieda' (5-seater sedan, 4 × 4, 1955). Moskvitch-410, -410N (4-seater, sedans, 4 × 4, from 1956). UAZ-69A, -69AM (5-seater, 4 × 4, from 1956). UAZ-469 (7-seater, 4 × 4, from 1961).
Light Trucks: GAZ-69 (½-ton, 4 × 4, 1952). UAZ-69, -69M (½-ton, 4 × 4, from 1956). UAZ-451, -451D (0.8-ton, 4 × 2, from 1957). UAZ-450, -452, -455 (0.8-ton, 4 × 4, from 1957). ZAZ-969 (0.4-ton, 4 × 4, 1967).
Motorcycles: M-72, K-750 (Solo and w/Sidecar, from 1942).

General Data: In addition to the above the Soviet Army used various types of pre-1945 manufacture, including Willys 'Jeeps' (MA, MB) and other American vehicles which had been supplied under 'Lend-Lease' during WWII. From about 1947 most Russian passenger cars carried a marque name, rather than just a factory and type designation. For example, the GAZ-M-20 was named 'Pobieda' (Victory). Both the Pobieda and the smaller Moskvitch sedans also appeared in 4 × 4 form (M-72 and M-410 resp.). The wartime GAZ-61 and -67B remained in production for some time, until gradually superseded by the GAZ-M-72 and GAZ-69A resp. The latter was produced in the Molotov plant at Gorkiy from 1952 but its production (and that of the GAZ-69 truck version) was transferred to Ulyanovsk (UAZ) in 1956. Technically they then became the UAZ-69 series but both remained generally known as the GAZ-69(A). In 1961 UAZ introduced a replacement vehicle in prototype form (UAZ-469) using many part of a series of 0.8-ton COE trucks (UAZ-450, etc.), which had made its debut in 1957. The wartime motorcycle M-72 also continued in production. It was patterned on the German BMW R-71 and later became available commercially as K-750. They were used mainly with sidecars.

Vehicle shown (typical): Field Car, 5-seater, 4 × 4 (GAZ/UAZ-69AM)

Technical Data:
Engine: UAZ-69B 4-cylinder, I-I-W-F, 2430 cc (88 × 100 mm), 65 bhp @ 3800 rpm.
Transmission: 3F1R × 2.
Brakes: hydraulic.
Tyres: 6.50–16.
Wheelbase: 2.30 m. Track: 1.44 m.
Overall l × w × h: 3.85 × 1.75 × 1.95 m.
Weight: 1535 kg. GVW: 1960 kg.
Note: Performance: speed 95 km/h, gradability 30°, normal fuel consumption 14 l/100 km. Rigid axles with semi-elliptic leaf springs. Pre-1967 models (GAZ-69A and UAZ-69A) had 2120-cc (82 × 100 mm) 55-bhp engine.

Field Car, 4-seater Sedan, 4 × 4 (Moskvitch-410) 4-cyl., 35 bhp, 3F1R × 2, wb 2.38 m, 4.05 × 1.54 × 1.68 m, 1180 kg. Tyres 6.40–15. Model 402 1220-cc engine, 1956–58. From 1958 to 1960: 410 N with 407 1360-cc 45-bhp engine. Based on Moskvitch-402 4 × 2 sedan (1956–58).

Field Car, 5-seater Sedan, 4 × 4 (GAZ-M-72) 4-cyl., 52 bhp, 3F1R × 2, wb 2.71 m, 4.66 × 1.69 × 1.79 m, 1560 kg. Tyres 6.50–16. Produced from 1955 to 1958, derived from GAZ-M-20 'Pobieda' car. M-20 2450-cc (82 × 100 mm) L-head engine. Max. speed 90 km/h. Gradability 30°.

Field Car, 7-seater, 4 × 4 (UAZ-469) 4-cyl., 75 bhp, 4F1R × 2, wb 2.38 m, 4.04 × 1.77 × 2.02 m, 1600 kg. GVW 2350 kg. Track 1.44 m. Speed 100 km/h. Debut in 1961 (prototype) as eventual replacement for UAZ-69AM. Subsequently improved in detail. Tyres 8.40–15.

Motorcycle, w/Sidecar, 3 × 1 (M-72) 2-cyl., 22 bhp, 4F, wb 1.40 m, 2.38 × 1.59 × 1.00 m, 335 kg (solo: 2.15 × 0.82 × 1.00 m, 205 kg). Horizontally-opposed 746-cc (78 × 78 mm) L-head air-cooled engine. Shaft drive. Tyres 3.75–19. Speed 95 km/h. Produced from 1942.

Field Car, 4-seater, 4 × 4 (GAZ-67B) 4-cyl., 54 bhp, 4F1R × 1, wb 2.12 m, 3.35 × 1.00 × 1.70 m, 1320 kg. Tyres 7.00–16. GAZ-A 3280-cc L-head engine. First introduced in 1942 (as GAZ-67), continued until 1953. Widely used in Korean war (captured vehicle shown).

Amphibious Car, 5-seater, 4 × 4 (GAZ-46) 4-cyl., 55 bhp, 3F1R × 2, wb 2.30 m, 5.06 × 1.73 × 1.70 m, 1980 kg. Known as MAV (small amphibious truck). Copied from US WWII Ford GPA. Based on GAZ-69 chassis. Tyres 7.50–16. Speed 83 km/h (10 in water). Track 1.44 m.

Truck, ½-ton, 4 × 4, Cargo and Personnel (UAZ-69M) 4-cyl., 65 bhp, 3F1R × 2, wb 2.30 m, 3.85 × 1.85 × 2.03 m, 1525 kg. General purpose vehicle with lengthwise or transverse seats in back. Early models (GAZ-69, UAZ-69) had 55-bhp engine. Produced in Rumania with 4F1R × 1 trans. (M-461, *qv*).

Truck, ½-ton, 4 × 4, Missile Launcher (UAZ-69M) Modification of std UAZ-69M truck. Launching vehicle for wire-guided AT missiles, known as *'Shmel'* (bumble-bee). In the West it was known as *'Snapper'*. Firing control from passenger seat or remote. Used by various Warsaw Pact countries.

Truck, 0.4-ton, 4×4, Cargo and Personnel (ZAZ-968/969)
V-4-cyl., 27 bhp, 4F1R×1, wb 1.80 m, 3.20×1.60×1.80 m,
820 kg. Tyres 5.90–13. Prototype for light air-transportable
multi-purpose vehicle. Rear-wheel drive could be disengaged.
Torsion bar suspension. Derived from Zaporozhets (ZAZ-966)
car, 1965.

Truck, 0.4-ton, 4×4, Cargo and Personnel (ZAZ-969)
MeMZ V-4-cyl., 35 bhp, 5F1R×1, wb 1.80 m, 3.27×1.56×
1.77 m, 880 kg. 887-cc air-cooled engine. Carried four men
plus 100 kg or equivalent load. Also 4×2 and special low-
silhouette field ambulance. ZAZ-971 was 4-door forward-
control model.

Truck, 0.8-ton, 4×4, Cargo (UAZ-452D) 4-cyl., 70 bhp,
4F1R×2, wb 2.30 m, 4.46×2.04×2.04 m, 1660 kg. Tyres
8.40–15. Variants included van, ambulance and microbus, also
w/o front wheel drive (4×2). Shared many parts with UAZ-
69M and -469. First announced in 1957 (UAZ-450).

Truck, 0.8-ton, 4×4, Ambulance (UAZ-450A) 4-cyl.,
65 bhp, 3F1R×2, wb 2.30 m, 4.36×1.94×2.05 m, 1950 kg.
Two-stretcher ambulance, one of various body styles available.
Early type front end shown. 2430-cc engine (as UAZ-69M)
Superseded by UAZ-452A (70-bhp engine, 4-speed trans.).

TRUCKS, 2½- to 27-TON 4 × 2

Makes and Models: BelAZ-540, -548 (27-ton dump trucks, from 1965). GAZ-51, -51A, -51B, -51Zh (2½-ton, from 1946; variants: tractor truck (GAZ-51P), dump trucks (GAZ-93, -93A), etc.). GAZ-53, -53A, -53F (3½-ton, from 1961; variants: tractor truck (GAZ-53P), dump truck (GAZ-53B), etc.). KAZ-600B (3½-ton, from 1956; similar to ZIL-164). KAZ-606(A), -608 (9½-ton tractor trucks, from 1961). MAZ-200, -200G, -200P (7-ton, from 1947; variants: tractor trucks (MAZ-200B/M), dump truck (MAZ-205), etc.). MAZ-500, -512, -513 (7½-ton, COE, from 1965; variants: tractor truck (MAZ-504), dump truck (MAZ-503), etc.). MAZ-525 (25-ton dump truck, 1951–59; BelAZ-525 from 1959–65). URAL-355M (3½-ton, 1958). ZIL-150 (4-ton, 1946; variants: tractor truck (ZIL-120N), dump truck (ZIL-MMZ-385), crane (K-32), etc.). ZIL-156A, -166A (4-ton, from 1953). ZIL-164, -164A(R) (4-ton, from 1957; variants: tractor trucks (ZIL-164(A)N, dump truck (ZIL-MMZ-585), etc.). ZIL-130, -130A (6-ton, from 1964; variants: tractor truck (ZIL-130V), dump truck (ZIL-MMZ-554), etc.).

General Data: Practically all of the trucks listed above were used for both civilian and military purposes. In addition, many of the chassis were used for special purpose vehicles e.g. dump trucks, tankers (fuel, oil, water), cranes, fire fighters, etc. Several were produced with four-wheel drive also. The ZIL (ZIS until 'destalinization' in 1956/57) -150 and -130 formed the basis for 2½- and 3½-ton 6 × 6 trucks, namely the ZIL-151 and -131 respectively. The GAZ-51 truck was extensively used in most of the Warsaw Pact countries, with a variety of bodystyles, including ambulance, and was produced, under licence, in Poland as Lublin-51. It was supplemented in the early 1960s by the much modernized GAZ-53 which featured an OHV V-8 engine (the GAZ-53F was an interim model with a modified GAZ-51 engine; the prototypes were known as GAZ-52 and -52A).

Vehicle shown (typical): Truck, 2½-ton, 4 × 2, Cargo (GAZ-51A)

Technical Data:

Engine: GAZ-51 6-cylinder, I-L-W-F, 3480 cc, 70 bhp @ 2800 rpm.
Transmission: 4F1R.
Brakes: hydraulic.
Tyres: 7.50–20.
Wheelbase: 3.30 m.
Overall dimensions: 5.71 × 2.28 × 2.13 (cab) m.
Weight: 2710 kg. GVW: 5350 kg.
Note: Introduced in 1955 as improved version of GAZ-51 (1946–55). GAZ-51B was 3½-tonner with 80-bhp engine, stronger rear suspension and different final drive ratio.

Truck, 4-ton, 4 × 2, Crane-Mounted, K-32 (ZIL-150)
6-cyl., 90–95 bhp, 5F1R (OD top), wb 4.00 m, 9.00 × 2.26 × 3.41 m (travelling position), 7480 kg. Tyres 9.00–20. Max. lifting capacity 3 tons. Originally known as ZIS-150. Patterned on US International K-line trucks.

Truck, 4-ton, 4 × 2, Cargo (ZIL-164) 6-cyl., 100 bhp, 5F1R (OD top), wb 4.00 m, 6.70 × 2.47 × 2.18 (cab) m, 4100 kg. Superseded ZIL-150 in 1957. 5550-cc L-head engine. Air brakes. Also tractor and dump versions.

Truck, 6-ton, 4 × 2, Cargo (ZIL-130) V-8-cyl., 150 bhp, 5F1R, wb 3.80 m, 6.67 × 2.50 × 2.31 (cab) m, 4800 kg. Introduced by Moscow Likhachev Auto Plant in late 1964. Variants include SWB tractor and dump versions, LWB cargo truck (130 G), 6 × 6 (131), 6 × 4 (133), etc.

Truck, 7-ton, 4 × 2, Cargo (MAZ-200) JAAZ 4-cyl. 2-stroke diesel, 110 bhp, 5F1R (OD top), wb 4.52 m, 7.62 × 2.65 × 2.43 (cab) m, 6170 kg. Tyres 12.00–20. Air brakes. MAZ-200B was 4.52-m wb tractor for 16½-ton semi-trailers. Several other variants, incl. 4 × 4 (MAZ-502).

TRUCKS, 1- to 4½-TON 4 × 4

Makes and Models: GAZ-62 (1-ton, 1959; NC and FC). GAZ-63, -63A (1½-ton, from 1946; variants: tractor truck (GAZ-63D), ambulance, earth borer, rocket launcher, tanker, etc.). GAZ-66, -66A, -66E, -66EA (2-ton, from 1963; variants: tractor truck (GAZ-66P), shop van, etc.). MAZ-502, -502A (4-ton, from 1957; variants: tractor trucks (MAZ-501 (from 1955), -501V and -502V), shop van, etc.). MAZ-505 (4½-ton COE, 1962).

General Data: The most numerous trucks in this category were the GAZ-63(A) and MAZ-502(A). The former was developed in 1945, simultaneously with its 4 × 2 counterpart (GAZ-51) and the first prototypes had a cab and front end which were hardly distinguishable from those of the American Studebaker US6 of which the Soviet Union received over 100,000 under 'Lend-Lease' during WWII. Production models, however, had rounded front wings and other detail modifications. Large quantities were made until well into the 1960s when gradual replacement by the GAZ-66(A) commenced. Apart from the front axle drive the GAZ-63 differed from the basic 4 × 2 GAZ-51 mainly in having larger tyres (10.00–18 vs 7.50–20), single all round. The GAZ-63A had a front-mounted winch. Both vehicles were also used with special bodywork, ranging from ambulance to APC (armoured personnel carrier, BTR-40). The GAZ-66 was a COE truck with OHV V-8 engine. It was first announced in 1957 (with 85-bhp engine) and was commercially available, also for export. Of the closed-cab commercial basic model there are the following variants: GAZ-66-71 (with central tyre-pressure regulating system), GAZ-66-72 (with winch), GAZ-66-74 (with screened electrics) and GAZ-66-75 (combined features of -71 to -74). There were special tropical versions also. The military version with closed cab was designated GAZ-66-02. Of the special military model with soft-top cab there are the following variants: GAZ-66A (with winch and central tyre-pressure regulating system), GAZ-66E (with screened electrical equipment) and GAZ-66EA with all three features.

Vehicle shown (typical): Truck, 2-ton, 4 × 4, Cargo, w/Winch (GAZ-66-02)

Technical Data:

Engine: ZMZ GAZ-53 8-cyl., V-I-W-F, 4250 cc, 115 bhp @ 3200 rpm.

Transmission: 4F1R × 2.

Brakes: hydraulic, vacuum-assisted.

Tyres: 12.00–18.

Wheelbase: 3.30 m. Track, F/R: 1.80/1.75 m.

Overall dimensions: 5.65 × 2.34 × 2.44 m.

Weight: 3640 kg.

Note: Several variants (see General Data). Winch capacity 3½ tons. Hyd. power steering assistance. Max. speed 95 km/h. Gradability 38°.

Truck, 1-ton, 4 × 4, Cargo and Personnel (GAZ-62)
6-cyl., 80 bhp, 4F1R × 2, wb 2.70 m, 4.87 × 2.10 × 2.32 (1.70) m, 2600 kg. Scaled-down air-transportable version of GAZ-66A (prototypes looked like scaled-up normal control GAZ-69). Maximum trailer load 1200 kg. Max. road speed 80 km/h.

Truck, 1½-ton, 4 × 4, Cargo (GAZ-63) 6-cyl., 70 bhp, 4F1R × 2, wb 3.30 m, 5.52 × 2.20 × 2.81 (cab 2.24) m, 3020 kg. Tyres 10.00 or 9.75–18. 3480-cc (82 × 110 mm) L-head engine. Payload on roads 2000 kg. Max. trailer weight 2000 kg. 4 × 4 version of GAZ-51A. Early type cab shown.

Truck, 1½-ton, 4 × 4, Cargo, w/Winch (GAZ-63A)
6-cyl., 70 bhp, 4F1R × 2, wb 3.30 m, 5.80 × 2.20 × 2.81 (cab 2.24) m, 3440 kg. Tyres 10.00–18. 3½-ton front-mounted winch with 50-m steel cable, driven from gearbox PTO. Various body options. Gradability 28°.

Truck, 4-ton, 4 × 4, Cargo (MAZ-502) JAAZ M204B 4-cyl. 2-stroke diesel, 135 bhp, 5F1R × 2 (OD top), wb 4.52 m, 7.15 × 2.70 × 3.02 (cab 2.72) m, 7700 kg. Tyres 15.00–20. Introduced in 1957 as cargo version of MAZ-501 (4 × 4 timber tractor truck, introduced in 1955). MAZ-502A had winch.

TRUCKS, 2½- to 3½-TON 6 × 6

Makes and Models: ZIL-151 (2½-ton, 1947; variants: tractor trucks (ZIL-121D and -151D), shop van, crane truck, tanker, rocket launcher, etc.). ZIL-157, -157K (2½-ton, 1958; variants: tractor trucks (ZIL-157B, -157V and -157KV), shop van, crane truck, bridging truck, tanker, snow plough, fire fighter, etc.). ZIL-131 (3½-ton, from 1962; variants: tractor truck (ZIL-131V), dump truck (ZIL-131D), 8-ton, 6×4 cargo truck (ZIL-133), etc.). ZIS-151 (early designation for ZIL-151). ZIS/ZIL-485 (BAV), ZIL-485A (BAV-A) (2½-ton amphibians, from 1952).

General Data: For many years the ZIS/ZIL-151 and -157 series of 6×6 trucks have been the 'workhorses' of the Soviet and satellite armed forces. They were clearly patterned on the wartime American 'Lend-Lease' Studebakers, of which the Soviet Union possessed large quantities. The cab and front end of these ZIL 6×6 trucks were patterned on the American International K-line but over the years various minor styling changes took place. Similar in design, but with a 4×2 drive configuration were the ZIL-150 and -164. The ZIL-157 replaced the -151 in production in October 1958. Externally it differed from the ZIL-151 mainly in having larger-section tyres, single at rear, and a slightly restyled front end (which had first been introduced on late-production ZIL-151s). ZIL 6×6 trucks were used throughout Eastern Europe and also in several other countries, e.g. Cuba, Egypt, Israel, etc. In addition to conventional cargo/prime mover trucks, the ZIL 6×6 also appeared with numerous types of special bodies, some of which are listed above. Moreover, the chassis were used for amphibious trucks (resembling the wartime American GMC 'Duck') and armoured personnel carriers (BTR, the bodywork of which featured characteristics of both the American and German half-track APCs of WWII). About 1962 the third generation truck in this class was launched. Designated ZIL-131, this much modernized model went into quantity production in 1967. An interesting development of the ZIL-131 was the 10×10 ZIL-137, consisting of a modified ZIL-131V tractor unit with a tandem-bogie semi-trailer the four wheels of which were driven hydraulically.

Vehicle shown (typical): Truck, 2½-ton, 6×6, Tractor, w/Winch (ZIL-157B, ZIL-157V)

Technical Data:
Engine: ZIL-157 6-cylinder, I-L-W-F, 5550 cc, 109 bhp @ 2800 rpm.
Transmission: 5F1R × 2 (OD top).
Brakes: air.
Tyres: 12.00–18.
Wheelbase: 4.22 m. BC 1.12 m.
Overall dimensions: 6.90 × 2.30 × 2.36 m.
Weight: 5600 kg approx.
Note: Winch (optional) capacity 4½ tons. Tyre pressure adjustable from driver's seat. Used for towing various types of semi-trailers, incl. missile carriers.

Truck, 2½-ton, 6 × 6, Cargo (ZIS-151) 6-cyl., 95 bhp, 5F1R × 2 (OD top), wb 4.22 (BC 1.12) m, 6.95 × 2.31 × 2.35 (cab) m. This was a prototype, produced in 1946. Note civilian type front wings, absence of headlamp protection grilles and single rear tyres. Wooden cargo body.

Truck, 2½-ton, 6 × 6, Shop Van (ZIL-151) 6-cyl., 95 bhp, 5F1R × 2 (OD top), wb 4.22 (BC 1.12) m, 6.93 × 2.40 m. Tyres 8.25–20. 5550-cc (101.6 × 114.3 mm) L-head engine. One of various types of shop vans (used for workshop, signals and other roles) mounted on this 1947–58 chassis.

Truck, 2½-ton, 6 × 6, Cargo, w/Winch (ZIL-157) 6-cyl., 104 bhp, 5F1R × 2 (OD top), wb 4.22 (BC 1.12) m, 6.96 × 2.35 × 2.36 (cab) m, 5800 kg. Note external pipes for tyre-pressure adjusting system. This was later incorporated in the wheel hubs. Payload on roads 4½ tons.

Truck, 2½-ton, 6 × 6, Shop Van, w/Winch (ZIL-157K) 6-cyl., 109 bhp, 5F1R × 2 (OD top), wb 4.22 (BC 1.12) m, 6.95 × 2.40 m approx. Shop van, used as mobile workshop. A-frame crane (carried on roof) could be fitted on front bumper for hoisting engines out of vehicles, etc. Late type front end.

Truck, 2½-ton, 6 × 6, Bridge Laying, w/Winch (ZIL-157-KMM) 6-cyl., 109 bhp, 5F1R × 2 (OD top), wb 4.22 (BC 1.12) m. One of various bridge-laying versions on standard ZIL-151 and -157 chassis/cab. Bridge dimensions: 7.50 × 3.40, load capacity 50 tons. Also carried on AT-L full-track tractor.

Truck, 2½-ton, 6 × 6, Cargo (ZIL-157, modified) 6-cyl., 104 bhp, 5F1R × 2 (OD top). Experimental modification of ZIL-157 cargo truck, c. 1960. Axles almost equally spaced and all mounted on conventional semi-elliptic springs. Tyres 12.00–18 all round.

Truck, 2½-ton, 6 × 6, Amphibious, BAV (ZIL-485) 6-cyl., 95 bhp, 5F1R × 2 (OD top), wb 4.22 (BC 1.12) m, 9.54 × 2.49 × 2.66 m, 7400 kg. Introduced in 1952 on ZIS-151 chassis. Later on ZIL-157 (BAV-A; ZIL-485A). Similar to US GMC DUKW-353 but longer cargo compartment and tailgate.

Truck, 3½-ton, 6 × 6, Cargo, w/Winch (ZIL-131) V-8-cyl., 150 (later 170) bhp, 5F1R × 2, wb 3.97 (BC 1.25) m, 7.04 × 2.50 × 2.97 (2.48) m, 6700 kg. 6-litre engine. Tyres 12.00–20. Payload on roads 5 tons. 4½-ton winch (optional). Commercially available. Derived from ZIL-130 in 1967.

TRUCKS, 4½- to 25-TON
6 × 4 and 6 × 6

Makes and Models: *Note:* JAAZ may be found spelled as JaAZ or YaAZ, KRAZ as KrAZ. JAAZ-210, -210A (12-ton, 6 × 4, 1951; variants: tractor truck (JAAZ-210D), dump trucks (JAAZ-210E, -218), crane truck (K-104), etc.). JAAZ-210G (heavy prime mover, 6 × 4, 1948). KRAZ-214*, -214B (7-ton, 6 × 6, from 1959; variants: tractor truck, rocket launcher, bridging truck, crane, crane shovel, etc.). KRAZ-219* (12-ton, 6 × 4, 1959; variants: tractor truck (KRAZ-221), dump truck (KRAZ-222), crane truck (K-104, etc.). KRAZ-250 (14-ton, 6 × 4, 1966; variants: dump truck (KRAZ-251), COE tractor truck (KRAZ-252), etc.). KRAZ-255(B) (7½-ton, 6 × 6, 1966). KRAZ-257 (12-ton, 6 × 4, 1966; variants: tractor truck (KRAZ-258), dump trucks (KRAZ-254, -256), etc.). MAZ-500 (7½-ton, COE, 6 × 4, 1966; variants: dump truck (MAZ-503), tractor truck (MAZ-504), etc.). NAMI-076 'Yermak' (25-ton COE, 6 × 6, 1965). URAL-375, -375A, -375D, -375T (4½-ton, 6 × 6, from 1961; variants: tractor truck (URAL-375S), rocket launcher (BM-21), crane truck, etc.). URAL-377, -377M (8-ton, 6 × 4, 1967: variants: tractor truck (URAL-377S), dump truck (URAL-377V), etc.). ZIL-133 (8-ton, 6 × 4, 1966; variants: tractor truck (ZIL-133V), dump trucks (ZIL-133B, -133D), etc.). ZIL-E167 (5-ton, 6 × 6, 1967).

General Data: Not mentioned in the above list are several ultra-heavy dump trucks which were used mainly for heavy construction work. Of the models listed, the KRAZ-214 6 × 6 trucks were probably the most widely used. They were made with various types of bodywork and until the introduction of the large 8 × 8 vehicles (see following section) these used to be the largest Soviet all-wheel drive military trucks. It was originally built at Yaroslavl but in 1959 production was transferred to Kremenchug and the name changed. This also applied to the related KRAZ-219 6 × 4 range, which was preceded by the JAAZ-210 series. The latter had a rounded radiator grille, unprotected headlights and a cab similar to that of the old MAZ-200. The URAL-375 series also saw service in large numbers, notably in Russia and DDR.

* formerly (1956–59) produced at Yaroslavl and known as JAAZ (YaAZ).

Vehicle shown (typical): Truck, 4½-ton, 6 × 6, Cargo, w/Winch (URAL-375D)

Technical Data:
Engine: ZIL-375 V-8-cylinder, V-I-W-F, 6960 cc, 200 bhp @ 3000 rpm (earlier models: 180 @ 3200).
Transmission: 5F1R × 2 (OD top).
Brakes: air-hydraulic.
Tyres: 14.00–20.
Wheelbase: 4.20 m. BC 1.40 m.
Overall l × w × h: 7.35 × 2.69 × 2.98 (cab 2.68) m.
Weight: 8400 kg. GVW: 13,300 kg.
Note: Closed or soft-top cab. Payload on made roads 10 tons. Starting heater enabled starting up in 30 min. in arctic weather at −65°C. Various body options, including 'house type' van (mobile workshop, etc.).

Truck, 4½-ton, 6×6, Cargo, w/Winch (URAL-375T) ZIL-375 V-8-cyl., 180 bhp, 5F1R×2 (OD top), wb 4.20 (BC 1.40) m, 7.35×2.69×2.98 (cab 2.68) m, 8400 kg. Tyre pressures adjustable from cab. Also as tractor truck and SP mount for 40-round rocket launcher. Soft-top cab shown.

Truck, 8-ton, 6×4, Cargo (URAL-377M) ZIL-375 JA4 V-8-cyl., 180 bhp, 5F1R×2 (OD top), wb 4.62 (BC 1.40) m, 7.98×2.53×2.49 (cab) m, 6635 kg. Tyres 11.00×400–533. Max. speed 88 km/h. Derived from URAL-375(D) 6×6. Both were commercially available.

Truck, 7-ton, 6×6, Cargo, w/Winch (KRAZ-214) JAAZ-M-206B 6-cyl. 2-stroke diesel, 205 bhp, 5F1R×2 (OD top), wb 5.30 (BC 1.40) m, 8.53×2.70×3.18 (2.88) m, 12,300 kg. Tyres 15.00–20. Air brakes. 12-ton winch. Pre-1959 designation: JAAZ-214. KRAZ-255B (1966) was improved V-8-engined model.

Truck, 7-ton, 6×6, Bridge Laying, TMM (KRAZ-214) Like several other special purpose vehicles based on standard KRAZ-214 chassis/cab. Dimensions in transport position 9.30×3.20×3.15 m, weight incl. bridge 19 tons. Hyd. operated scissors-type bridge with 40-m span for loads of up to 60 tons. Used by most Eastern bloc countries.

Truck, 12-ton, 6×4, Tractor (JAAZ-221) 6-cyl. 2-stroke diesel, 180 bhp, 5F1R×2 (OD top), wb 4.78 (BC 1.40) m, 7.37×2.64×2.62 m, 9300 kg. One of several 6×4 versions of JAAZ/KRAZ-214. Lockable diff. in transfer case. Superseded by KRAZ-258 with 215-bhp JAMZ-238 V-8 4-stroke diesel.

Truck, 8-ton, 6×4, Prime Mover, w/Winch (JAAZ-210 G) 6-cyl. 2-stroke diesel, 200 bhp, 5F1R×2 (OD top), wb 4.78 (BC 1.40) m, 7.37×2.65×2.57 m, 12,360 kg. Replaced 1948 model (165 bhp, different rear body) in 1951. Used with 40-ton tank transporter trailers, etc. 12-ton winch behind cab.

Truck, 10-ton, 6×4, Dump (JAAZ-210 E) 6-cyl. 2-stroke diesel, 165 bhp, 5F1R×2 (OD top), wb 5.48 (BC 1.40) m, 8.19×2.65×2.72 m, 12,000 kg. Rear-dumper, produced from 1951 to 1957, superseded by KRAZ-222 (1959). The latter had the same front end and cab as the KRAZ-214, etc.

Truck, 6×6, Cross-country (ZIL-167 E) Twin V-8-cyl., 180 bhp (each), hydro-mech. trans., wb 3.15+3.15 m, 9.27×3.13×3.06 m, GVW 12,000 kg. Exp. 6×6 version of ZIL-135 8×8, with front and rear wheels steering and each engine driving wheels on one side. Tyres 21.00–28. Torsion bar suspension.

TRUCKS and TRACTORS
8 × 8

Heavy 8 × 8 vehicles of various types have been in use by the Soviet and satellite armed forces in increasing numbers since about 1964. The most common types were the products of MAZ (-535 and -543 series) and ZIL (-135 series). The former steered on the two front axles, whereas the ZIL models had an unsprung centre bogie and steerable front and rear axles. The MAZ-543 had twin 'split' cabs; all other models had a full-width cab. About 1966 the Soviet institute for motor vehicle and engine research produced a smaller 8 × 8 truck, the NAMI-058 'Osminog' (Octopus). The basic MAZ and ZIL models were also used for pipe-laying and other similar civilian purposes. The civilian MAZ was designated 'Pletjewos-481'. The ZIL models (-135 Series) were also referred to as BAZ.

Truck, 10-ton, 8 × 8, Tractor, w/Winch (MAZ-537) D-12-A-375 V-12-cyl. diesel, 375 bhp (de-rated 525-bhp 38.8-litre tank engine), hydro-mech. trans., wb (overall) 6.05 m, 9.00 × 2.88 m approx., 21.6 tons. Tyres 15.00–23.5 or 18.00–24. Air-hyd. brakes. MAZ-535A was cargo/prime mover version.

Truck, 10-ton, 8 × 8, Cargo/Prime Mover (ZIL-135L4) Twin ZIL-375 V-8-cyl., 180 bhp each, hydro-mech. trans., wb 2.41 + 1.50 + 2.14 m, 9.27 × 2.80 × 2.53 m, 10.5 tons. Tyres 16.00–20. 7-litre (108 × 95 mm) engines, each driving wheels on one side. Air brakes. Speed 70 km/h.

Truck, 10-ton, 8 × 8, Missile Launcher (ZIL-135L4) Twin ZIL-375 V-8-cyl., 180 bhp each, hydro-mech. trans., wb 2.41 + 1.50 + 2.41 m, 10.75 × 2.80 × 3.66 m, 20 tons. Chassis also known as ZIL-135L4, equipment as FROG-7. Speed 65 km/h. Rocket: length 9.10 m, range 60 km. Also known as BAZ-135.

Truck, 15-ton, 8 × 8, Cargo and Prime Mover (MAZ-543)
V-12-cyl. diesel, 525 bhp, hydro-mech. trans., wb 2.20 + 3.30 + 2.20 m, 11.70 × 3.05 × 2.65 m, 17½ tons. Tyres 15.00-23.5. This chassis was used for various military and civilian applications. Tank engine, probably down-rated to 375 bhp.

Truck, 15-ton, 8 × 8, Missile Launcher (MAZ-543)
Short-range surface-to-surface guided missile, known as 'SCUD B', mounted on a specially modified version of the MAZ-543. Public debut in November 1965. Same weapon also on tracked vehicle, derived from JS type heavy tank.

Truck, 15-ton, 8 × 8, Missile Launcher (MAZ-543)
Medium-range surface-to-surface guided missile, taken into service in 1967. Missile was carried in special container and vehicle acted as transporter, erector and launcher. Crew consisted of commander and four men, incl. driver.

Truck, 8-ton, 8 × 8, Cargo (Kirovski-TDT) Experimental vehicle, resembling American FWD 'Teracruzer', produced about 1962/63 by the Kirovski Tractor Plant 'Red Star' in Leningrad. Known as 'Uragan-8', it weighed about 9 tons, had turntable steering and reached 60 km/h.

ARMOURED VEHICLES
WHEELED

During WWII the Soviet Army used only a few types of wheeled armoured vehicles of their own design, the others being of American and British origin ('Lend-Lease', incl. US half-tracks). The only Soviet type developed during that period was the BA-64 armoured car, introduced in 1943 on the GAZ-67B 4×4 chassis. This model continued in production and use after 1945 and was popularly known as 'Bobby'. Two APCs appeared shortly after the war, based on the contemporary GAZ-63A 4×4 and ZIS-151 6×6 trucks. These were known as BTR-40 and BTR-152 resp. During their production runs they were frequently modified and modernized. About 1960 a new generation of amphibious types was developed, the BTR-40P (4×4) and BTR-60P (8×8), both with several variants.

Carrier, Armoured, Personnel, 4×4, BTR-40 GAZ-40 6-cyl., 80 bhp, 4F1R×2, wb 2.70 m, 5.00×1.90×1.75 m, 5300 kg. Designed in 1948 on GAZ-63A chassis. Tyres 9.75–18. 4½-ton winch. Also armoured top and twin-MG AA versions. Used by most Communist countries.

Scout Car, Armoured, Amphibious, 4×4, BTR-40P/ BRDM GAZ-40P 6-cyl., 90 bhp, 4F1R×2, wb 2.80 m, 5.70× 2.25×1.90 m, 5100 kg. Tyres 12.00–18. Central tyre pressure control. Small adjustable belly wheels (2 each side). Hydrojet for propulsion in water. Several variants, incl. missile carriers.

Scout Car, Armoured, Amphibious, 4×4, BTR-40P-2/ BRDM-2 Twin M-21 4-cyl. 70-bhp engines at rear, wb 3.00 m, 5.50×2.18×2.15 m, 7000 kg. Superseded BTR-40P in mid-1960s. Speed 110 km/h (10 in water). Similar to Hungarian FUG-65 but single hydrojet and small turret with two MGs.

Carrier, Armoured, Personnel, 6×6, BTR-152 ZIL-123 6-cyl., 110 bhp, 5F1R×2 (OD top), wb 3.84 (BC 1.13) m, 6.70×2.32×2.05 m, 6600 kg. Introduced in 1946 on ZIS-151 chassis with up-rated engine. Employed also as towing vehicle for AT guns, mortars, etc. Hull had features of both American and German WWII half-track APCs.

Carrier, Armoured, Personnel, w/Winch, 6×6, BTR-152V3 ZIL-123 6-cyl., 110 bhp, 5F1R×2 (OD top), wb 3.84 (BC 1.13) m, 6.70×2.35×2.70 m, 6700 kg. Tyres 12.00–18. BTR-152V1 had external air lines to wheel hubs. BTR-152K had overhead armour. BTR-152U was high-top command post variant. APC crew: 2+17.

Carrier, Armoured, Personnel, Amphibious, 8×8, BTR-60P Twin GAZ-40P 6-cyl., 90 bhp (each), wb 1.35+1.52+1.35 m, 7.50×3.00×2.00 m, 10,000 kg approx. Tyres 12.00–18 with central pressure control. Hydrojet water propulsion unit. Used in various Warsaw Pact countries. Similar: Czech/Polish OT-64.

Carrier, Armoured, Personnel, Amphibious, 8×8, BTR-60PB Developed from BTR-60P and -60PK. The latter had overhead armour but not the small turret which distinguishes the BTR-60PB. This turret, similar to that of the 4×4 BTR-40P-2, mounted one 7.62- and one 14.5-mm MG. Engines at rear.

MISCELLANEOUS
VEHICLES, TRACKED

In this section some examples are shown of the wide variety of full-track vehicles used by the Soviet Union since WWII. In recent years many tracked vehicles have been superseded by large 8 × 8 wheeled types in both towing and load-carrying roles. This change-over applied particularly to missile carriers and launchers (high-mobility wheeled vehicles have a longer range of action, are faster, especially on roads, quieter in operation and easier to maintain). Prime mover trucks like the URAL-375 and KRAZ-214 are also used increasingly to tow artillery pieces which used to be towed by tracked tractors. Turretted AFVs and SPs are not included here, although the chassis of some of them form the basis for tracked tractors and special purpose vehicles.

Tractor, Artillery, Full-Track, Light, M2 6-cyl. diesel, 105 bhp, 4.89 × 2.40 × 2.20 m, 8000 kg. Replaced JA (Ya)-12 and -13 shortly after the war. The M2, which was, in turn, superseded by the AT-L, could carry 2700 kg and was employed to tow artillery and heavy mortars.

Tractor, Artillery, Full-Track, Light, AT-L JAAZ-M-204 4-cyl. 2-stroke diesel, 130 bhp, 5.12 × 2.20 × 2.18 m, 8300 kg (laden). Introduced in 1953. Modified in 1956 (five large road wheels, no track support rollers). Several body variants, incl. **shop vans.** Towed load 6 tons. Widened ZIL truck cab.

Tractor, Artillery, Full-Track, Medium, AT-S V-54-T. V-12-cyl. diesel, 250 bhp, 5.87 × 2.57 × 2.53 m, 12 tons. Introduced in 1954. 425-mm tracks, driven by rear sprockets. Also basis for rocket launcher and other applications, incl. bulldozer (OST). Towed load 16 tons.

Carrier, Amphibious, Full-Track, Medium, GT-S GAZ-47 6-cyl., 85 bhp (early models: GAZ-61, 74 bhp), 4.90 × 2.43 × 1.96 m, 4650 kg (laden). 300-mm tracks provided propulsion when in water. Used as cargo carrier and prime mover. Towed load 2 tons.

Carrier, Amphibious, Full-Track, Heavy, GT-T 13-6 6-cyl. diesel, 200 bhp, 10,200 kg (laden). Unarmoured cargo and personnel carrier with low ground pressure (0.24 kg/cm²), suitable for snow and marshy ground. Used in Soviet Far East and arctic areas. Note sloping body panels. Towed load 4 tons.

Tractor, Artillery, Armoured, Full-Track, AT-P ZIL-123F 6-cyl., 110 bhp, 4.05 × 2.33 × 1.71 m, 7200 kg (laden). Early models did not have cover over rear compartment and boxes on sides. Late models had rotating commander's cupola. Speed 50 km/h. Towed load 3.7 tons.

Tractor, Artillery, Full-Track, Medium, ATS-59 A-650 V-12-cyl. diesel, 300 bhp, 6.30 × 2.80 × 2.50 m, 16,000 kg (laden). Engine behind cab. Crew 2 + 14. Payload 3 tons. Towed load 14 tons. Speed 40 km/h. Superseded AT-S in 1959 (different track bogies, lower silhouette, etc.).

Tractor, Heavy, Full-Track, Bulldozer, BAT A-401 V-12-cyl. diesel, 415 bhp, 8.90 × 4.78 (3.80) × 3.00 m, 25,300 kg. Basic vehicle: heavy artillery tractor AT-T (M-50) (6.99 × 3.17 × 3.00 m, 19,800 kg), introduced in 1950 as largest Soviet vehicle of its type. Later used for special purpose vehicles.

Tractor, Heavy, Full-Track, Ditching, BTM Another special engineer vehicle based on the AT-T. Others included BAT/M (bulldozer w/o cargo body), MDK-2M (trench digger/bulldozer) and mobile crane. Piston stroke of the 38.8-litre V-12 engine was 180 mm for the left bank, 186.7 mm for the right.

Truck, 3-ton, Full-Track, Cargo, 'Vitjas' ZIL-130 V-8-cyl., 150 bhp, 6.71 × 3.17 × 2.65 m, 4200 kg. ZIL-130 truck chassis with eight conventional truck wheels (8.25–15 tyres) and 920-mm wide tracks of synthetic material. Used in snow and swamp areas. Undercarriage configuration similar to certain Canadian designs (*qv*).

Carrier, Amphibious, Full-Track, K-61/GBT JAAZ-M204 4-cyl. 2-stroke diesel, 135 bhp, 9.15 × 3.15 × 2.15 m, 9550 kg. Payload, land/water: 3000/5000 kg. Used by several Warsaw Pact forces, from 1950, to transport cargo, personnel, vehicles (such as ZIL-151 truck), etc. in amphibious operations. Large tailgate.

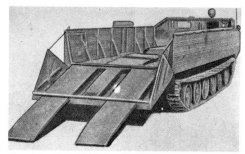

Carrier, Amphibious, Full-Track, PTS-M 6-cyl. diesel, 180 bhp, 11.50 × 3.30 × 2.65 (cab) m, 17,700 kg. Superseded K-61 in the late 1960s. Payload 5 tons (10 in water) or 70 men. Speed 40 km/h (15 in water). Crew 2, in closed cab. Twin propellers. Various modification kits.

Carrier, Amphibious, Armoured, Full-Track, BTR-50PK V-6-cyl. diesel, 240 bhp, 6.90 × 3.18 × 1.97 m, 14,000 kg approx. APC, produced from 1958 on chassis of PT-76 amphibious tank. Several variants, incl. Czech (OT-62) and Polish-built versions with detail differences. Some were open-topped.

Carrier, Rocket Launcher, Full-Track, FROG-5 V-6-cyl. diesel, 240 bhp, 10.55 × 3.18 × 3.05 m, 14,200 kg. Launcher for unguided rockets, mounted on modified PT-76 tank chassis. FROG-3 and -4 similar. FROG-1 and -2 were mounted on heavier carriages. Comparable to US 'Honest John'.

Carrier, Rocket Launcher, Full-Track, SA-4 The SA-4 or 'Ganef' surface-to-air guided missiles were transported in pairs on special armoured fully tracked carriage which also acted as launch vehicle. There were two types of carriages, the other type having sloped sides.

MISCELLANEOUS VEHICLES

In addition to the selection of vehicles shown in the preceding sections, the Soviet industry has produced, and produces, many other special purpose and special equipment vehicles, some of which are shown here. The great variety of vehicles produced in the Soviet Union today may be explained in at least two different ways. Firstly, the Soviet motor industry has developed into a comprehensive and increasingly sophisticated organization which is no longer dependent on foreign assistance to the extent that existed prior to 1945. Secondly, in order to be competitive in foreign export markets and to cater for vastly different climatic and other circumstances in their own country, they have developed vehicles suitable for most, if not all, types of applications under a wide range of temperatures and soil conditions.

Grader, Motorized, 6×4, Medium, D-265 One of several types of Soviet motor graders. The D-265 (1958) measured 7.75×2.46×2.65 m and weighed 8500 kg. Speed up to 32 km/h. Blade 3.00×0.50 m. Cutting angle 28°–70°. Tyre size 12.00–20. Track, F/R: 1.80/1.85 m.

Truck, 0.6-ton, Half-Track, Cargo (UAZ-451S) 4-cyl., 70 bhp, 4F1R. Over-snow vehicle, modification of conventional UAZ-451 4×2 truck. Weight 1800 kg. Speed 47 km/h approx. Driven rear wheels replaced by track bogies, front tyres by skids. Produced experimentally, c. 1968.

Carrier, Over-Snow/Amphibious (LFM-RVD-GPI-66) 6-cyl., 74 bhp. Basically a GT-S (GAZ-47) amphibious carrier (qv) but tracks replaced by cylindrical screw-pontoons, which, filled with plastic foam, provided floating ability and propulsion in water and over snow, by means of spiral blades. Similar to US 'Marsh-screw'.

OTHER COUNTRIES

Included in this section is a number of countries which with regard to military vehicles depend largely (if not fully) on imports from manufacturing countries. Obviously such supplies depend on the contemporary political climate between the countries involved. The US has supplied large quantities of vehicles to 'friendly nations', either commercially (administrative and pseudo-military types) or through MAP (Mil. Assistance Program; 'austere' tactical types). Most notable of the US pseudo-military (all-wheel drive commercial) types were the Jeep 'Universal' and the Dodge 'Power Wagon'. WWII-surplus 'Jeeps', 'Beeps', GMCs, Macks, etc. remained in service with many governments for many years. Great Britain furnished large numbers of WWII-surplus vehicles to many countries, followed by post-war Bedford RL trucks, Land-Rovers, etc., as well as Alvis and Daimler wheeled AFVs. The Soviet Union supplied its allies and several other countries with various types of trucks (mainly GAZ and ZIL) and wheeled AFVs such as the BTR-40 and BTR-152 APCs. The listings are not necessarily complete or up to date and certain vehicles are no longer operational. Full-track types (tractors, AFVs) are not included.

ALBANIA: Mainly Soviet vehicles, incl. GAZ-69A and GAZ-63A 4 × 4, ZIL-151 and ZIL-157 6 × 6 trucks, BTR-40 4 × 4 APCs, etc. Chinese equipment is also in service.

ALGERIA: Since independence from France in 1962 the Army is equipped mainly with Soviet trucks, APCs (BTR-40, -152), etc. Also in service are, or were, British Land-Rovers, Egyptian Walid APCs and vehicles which were abandoned by the French, incl. WWII US A/Cs (M8) and half-track APCs. New Berliet GBC tactical trucks were acquired during 1970/71.

ARGENTINA: Industrias Kaiser Argentina SA (IKA) has produced Jeep vehicles of various types since 1954. Several other large manufacturers also have plants in Argentina, incl. the American 'Big Three' and some European firms. Most military vehicles are imported or produced under licence and have

Argentina: Shortly after WWII the Argentinian Army acquired a fleet of military versions of commercial Volvo trucks of various types, including 5-ton 4 × 2 LV290 Series (shown) and TLV 142 3-ton 4 × 4 (see Swedish section).

Congo Republic: Among the wide variety of vehicles used were the US Kaiser-Jeep CJ3B (military version) and International Harvester 4 × 4 platform stake cargo truck, both seen here during a parade in 1966.

411

included Volvo trucks (4 × 2 and 4 × 4), Mercedes-Benz 'Unimog' S, Thornycroft 'Nubian' 4 × 4 crash tenders and 'Trusty' 4 × 2 tractors with refueller semi-trailers (Air Force), Land-Rovers (Navy), etc. Many WWII US vehicles were also in service, incl. half-tracks.

BOLIVIA: Mainly US trucks, e.g. Kaiser Jeep ¼-ton 4 × 4, M606, Dodge ¾-ton 4 × 4, M37, etc.

BULGARIA: Armed forces equipped with Soviet 4 × 2, 4 × 4 and 6 × 6 trucks of various types, wheeled APCs (BTR-40 and -152), etc.

BURMA: British Land-Rovers, Daimler 'Ferret' A/Cs, Thornycroft 'Mighty Antar' tractors, US 'M Series' 2½-ton 6 × 6 trucks, etc. WWII Humber A/Cs remained in service for many years.

CAMBODIA: Mainly US equipment (incl. WWII M3A1 scout cars and M8 A/Cs), but also British Land-Rovers, Soviet BTR-152 APCs, etc.

CEYLON: British Land-Rover, Ford 'Thames' (1-ton, 4 × 4), Thornycroft 'Nubian' crash tender, Alvis and Daimler wheeled AFVs, etc.

CHAD: French ALM TF4-10R and Citroën FOM 4 × 4 trucks, etc.

CHILE: British and US vehicles, incl. Land-Rovers (Army, Navy, Air Force), White M3A1 scout cars, etc.

CONGO REPUBLIC: Land-Rover and Jeep CJ3B and CJ6 utility trucks, Chevrolet and Dodge 4 × 2 trucks, International 4 × 4 trucks, Daimler 'Ferret' and US WWII M8 A/Cs and White M3A1 scout cars, Swedish SKPF APCs, and many others. New Berliet GBA 6 × 6 trucks were purchased about 1970.

CUBA: Mainly Soviet equipment but also WWII-surplus American 'Staghound' A/Cs, half-track APCs, etc., as well as post-war ¼-ton 4 × 4 Jeep, Land-Rover, etc.

GAMBIA: British Land-Rover, Daimler 'Ferret', etc.

Ghana: AEC 'Militant' 10-ton 6 × 6 recovery vehicle with Mann Egerton 10-ton power-driven turntable crane, Darlington 15,675-lb winch at rear and Marshall cab. Engine: AEC 11.3-litre diesel. Four supplied in 1963.

Ireland (Eire): Most current trucks of the Irish armed forces are of British Rover (Land-Rover) and Vauxhall (Bedford) manufacture. Shown is a Bedford RSC 4 × 4 chassis/cab with wireless van body. 1965.

GHANA: Mostly British equipment, including Land-Rovers, Alvis 'Saladin' A/Cs, Daimler 'Ferret' scout cars, AEC 'Militant' 6 × 6 trucks, etc.

GREECE: Very large assortment of vehicles of various origins, viz.

WWII surplus, Canada: Chevrolet and Ford CMP vehicles, Chevrolet and Dodge modified conventional trucks.

WWII surplus, US: motorcycles, solo (Harley-Davidson WLA), field ambulances (Dodge ¾-ton), trucks, ¼-ton, 4 × 4 (Ford, Willys), ½-ton, 4 × 2 (Ford), ¾-ton, 4 × 4 (Dodge), 1½-ton, 6 × 6 (Dodge), 2½-ton, 4 × 2 (International), 2½-ton, 6 × 4 (GMC, International), 2½-ton, 6 × 6 (GMC), 4-ton, 6 × 6 (Diamond T), 4–5-ton, 4 × 4 (Autocar), 6-ton, 6 × 6 (Brockway, Corbitt, Mack, White), 10-ton, 6 × 4 (White), 12-ton, 6 × 4 (Diamond T), scout cars and half-tracks (White), etc.

Postwar, US: ¼-ton, 4 × 4 (AM M422, Jeep CJ3B, M38, M38A1, M170, International 'Scout'), ¾-ton, 4 × 4 (Dodge M37, M43), 1-ton, 4 × 4 (Dodge M601, M615), 2½-ton, 6 × 6 (GMC, Reo, etc.), 5-ton, 6 × 6 (International, etc.), crash trucks, 6 × 6 (American LaFrance), administrative pass. cars (Chevrolet, Ford), buses (Superior, Wayne) and trucks (4 × 2, cargo, dump, tanker, tractor, etc., made by Chevrolet, Dodge, Ford, International), commercial Autocar, Diamond T and White 4 × 4 and 6 × 4 dump trucks, etc.

Post-war, British: Land-Rover '88' (¼-ton, 4 × 4) and Bedford RL (3-ton, 4 × 4); these were ex-Cyprian/ex-British Army; the following were purchased commercially: Triumph 'Thunderbolt' (motorcycle), Commer 2500 (4 × 2, minibus), Dodge-Kew K160 (4 × 2, minibus) and 500 Series (4 × 2, truck).

Post-war, Czech: Praga S5T and Skoda 706RT 4 × 2, dump trucks.

Post-war, German: Borgward Lkw 0,75 t (4 × 4, truck and 'Kübel'), Ford-Köln G398 SAM (4 × 4, truck and personnel carrier), Kaelble KDV322 (6 × 4, tractor), Magirus-Deutz 'Uranus' (6 × 4, tractor), Mercedes-Benz 'Unimog' S404B (4 × 4, ambulance) and LG315/46 (4 × 4, wrecker); these were ex-German Government; the following were purchased commercially: Magirus-Deutz 'Merkur' (4 × 2, dump), MAN 415 (4 × 2, dump), Mercedes-Benz 220SE and 250SE (pass. cars),

O302 and O320H (buses) and L1113 (4 × 2, truck), Volkswagen 'Transporter' (minibus).

In addition there were French Simca 1301 cars, Italian Fiat 238 minibuses, etc.

INDONESIA: At first ex-Dutch equipment, consisting of WWII surplus Australian, British, Canadian and US vehicles as well as early post-war US commercial types, later supplemented and superseded by more modern vehicles from Austria ('Haflinger'), Britain (Land-Rover, Ford 'Thames Trader'/AWD, Daimler 'Ferret' scout car, Alvis 'Saracen' APC and 'Saladin' A/C), Germany (Auto Union 'Munga'), Soviet Union (GAZ-69 light truck, BTR-152 APC), etc.

IRAN: British Land-Rovers, Commer/AWD 3-ton 4 × 4 trucks and ambulances, Daimler 'Ferret' scout cars, German trucks including Mercedes-Benz L332, Soviet trucks (incl. GAZ-66 4 × 4 and MAZ-537 8 × 8) and wheeled AFVs including BTR-152 (APC), US Jeep vehicles (produced by Sherkate Sahami Jeep in Teheran), 'M-Series' 6 × 6 trucks, WWII surplus M8 and M20 A/Cs, etc.

IRAQ: WWII-surplus Canadian CMP vehicles (Chevrolet, Ford) and US trucks (incl. Corbitt/White 6-ton 6 × 6), supplemented by postwar US Jeeps (CJ3A) and Dodges ('Power Wagon'); British Land-Rovers and Daimler 'Ferrets', etc.

IRELAND (EIRE): Various WWII-surplus trucks and artillery tractors, including AEC 'Matador', Morris 'Quad', Chevrolet, Ford and Diamond T, supplemented by post-war Austin 1-ton 4 × 4 (K9), Land-Rover ¼- and ¾-ton 4 × 4 (SWB and LWB) and various types of Bedford 1- and 3-ton 4 × 2 and 3-ton 4 × 4 trucks. Wheeled AFVs included pre-war Ford 4 × 2 and Swedish Landsverk 180 six-wheeled armoured cars (some with Leyland mechanical components), WWII Standard 'Beaverettes' and post-war French Panhard AML-245s. Irish UN contingents used Daimler 'Ferret' scout cars.

IVORY COAST: French Citroën FOM, US Jeep, Dodge 'Power Wagon', Dodge 1½-ton 6 × 6 (WWII), Ford M8 A/C (WWII), etc.

Jordan: British Commer 10-ton 6 × 4 HD cargo truck with Rootes 3D215 135-bhp diesel engine, Unipower tandem drive rear bogie (with Eaton 2-speed axles and 3rd diff. lock) and Always bodywork. 100 supplied in 1969.

Jordan: To supplement a fleet of 'Constructor' 6 × 6 prime movers with Crane 60-ton S-Ts, acquired in 1961, Jordan ordered Scammell 'Contractor' 6 × 4 units with Cummins engines and with 60-ton Crane Fruehauf S-Ts in 1971.

Libya: One of three British Austin 5K Series III 5-ton LWB petrol-engined mobile workshops with bodywork by G. C. Smith (Coachwork) of Loughboroug¹. Equipment included diesel-engined generating set, lathe, welding kit, etc. 1955.

Libya: Commer 355 'Superpoise' 155-in wb chassis/cab with GS cargo body by Autolifts, one of a fleet supplied in 1954. The Rootes Group (now Chrysler UK Ltd) supplied military versions of commercial Commers to several African and Asian nations.

Malaysia: Commercial-type Bedford trucks are in military service in many countries. Seen here is a TK Series 4 × 2 tractor truck with Taskers 5-ton 'Queen Mary' aircraft transporter S-T, supplied to the Malay Air Force in 1964.

Mexico: Ramirez 'Rural 750' had Warner trans., Spicer axles, 113.8-in wb. 1966–71 model (shown) had Perkins 4.203 diesel engine. From 1971 GM or Automex 6-cyl. petrol or Perkins diesel. 173 × 69 × 71 (cab) in.

JORDAN: Originally a multiplicity of WWII vehicles was in service, including Canadian and Indian trucks and armoured cars. Later these were supplemented by British commercial trucks, incl. Ford 'Thames' and Commer 'Superpoise' 4 × 2, Commer/ Unipower 6 × 4 10-tonners, Land-Rovers, Scammell 'Constructor' 6 × 6 and 'Contractor' 6 × 4 tank-transporter prime movers with S-Ts, and US Ford 4 × 2 trucks of various types. German Mercedes-Benz 'Unimog' S and Japanese Toyota 'Land Cruiser' vehicles were also acquired. Postwar tactical vehicles were supplied mainly by Great Britain (Alvis 'Saladin' and 'Saracen', Daimler 'Ferret') and the US ($\frac{1}{4}$-ton 4 × 4 M38A1 and M151 series, etc.).

KENYA: British Land-Rover, Alvis 'Saracen', Daimler 'Ferret', etc.

KUWAIT: British Land-Rover, Alvis 'Saladin' and 'Saracen', Daimler 'Ferret', US Dodge 'Power Wagon', etc.

LAOS: French Hotchkiss M201 (Jeep), Simca 4 × 4 trucks, etc.

LEBANON: Variety of mainly British and US transport vehicles including Land-Rover and commercial 4 × 4 Chevrolet and Dodge trucks. Wheeled AFVs included WWII British AEC Mk III and US Chevrolet 'Staghound' A/Cs. More recently the US Cadillac V100 'Commando' has made its appearance. In 1960 25 Willème W8DT 6 × 4 tractors with tank-transporter S-Ts were bought from France.

LIBYA: Many British vehicles were used, incl. Land-Rover, Austin, Commer and Morris 3- to 5-ton 4 × 2 trucks, etc. Among Libyan AFVs were the British Alvis 'Saladin' and 'Saracen', the Daimler 'Ferret' and the 'Shorland' armoured patrol car based on the Land-Rover.

LUXEMBOURG: Vehicles used by Luxembourg's small Army were notably American and British WWII-surplus trucks (incl. 'Jeep', Dodge, GMC), supplemented by Ford/Marmon-Herrington 4 × 4 trucks assembled after the war by Ford in Belgium.

MALAYSIA: Mainly British vehicles, incl. Land-Rover, Bedford RL, Bedford TK (tractors with Taskers 'Queen Mary' S-Ts), Daimler 'Ferret' scout car, etc.

MEXICO: Largely US equipment, incl. ¼-ton 4 × 4 Jeep, 6 × 6 'M-Series', Dodge 4 × 2 'W' (administrative truck), WWII-surplus M3A1 scout car, M8 A/C and half-track APC. Italian Fiat ¼-ton 4 × 4 'Campagnola' and 4-ton 4 × 4 trucks were used also. A Mexican firm (Trailers de Monterrey SA, Monterrey) introduced a light 4 × 4 pickup truck, in 1966. It had a British Perkins diesel engine and was designated Ramirez 'Rural 750'. In 1971 it was modified and powered by a GM 6-cyl. petrol engine (Perkins diesel optional). They were supplied for commercial and military use, mainly in Mexico and Peru.

MOROCCO: Wide variety of vehicles, incl. British Land-Rovers, Czech OT-64 ('Skot') 8 × 8 APCs, French Berliet trucks (incl. GBC 8KT) and Panhard A/Cs (AML and EBR), US Jeep and Dodge M37 trucks, M8 A/Cs and half-track APCs, etc.

MUSCAT and OMAN: British Land-Rovers, Bedford RLs (heavy duty modifications by Reynolds Boughton), Daimler 'Ferret' and US Cadillac Gage 'Commando' A/Cs, etc.

NEW ZEALAND: Traditionally mainly British vehicles, manufactured in the UK or Australia or assembled in New Zealand. During the late 1960s these were supplemented by American vehicles. Cars included standard models from British Leyland, Ford (UK), Rootes, Vauxhall and Holden of Australia. Trucks included Land-Rover and Bedford (both of various types and configurations), Scammell (wreckers), etc. Daimler 'Ferret' scout cars were also acquired. The Trekka field car/utility truck (based on Skoda mechanical components) was introduced in 1966 but sold only to civilian customers.

NICARAGUA: British Land-Rover, US ¼-ton 4 × 4 Jeep and M151, 2½- and 5-ton 6 × 6 'M Series', Chevrolet and Dodge 4 × 2 cargo trucks, WWII surplus half-track APCs, etc.

New Zealand: Land-Rover '109' Series II ¾-ton 4 × 4. Hard-top with additional door window units in sides. Many '88' and '109' models were assembled at the NZ Motor Bodies plant at Auckland, incorporating various local-made parts.

New Zealand: Four Scammell 'Explorer' 6 × 6 recovery vehicles were supplied in 1959. They differed from the British std. type (FV11301) mainly in having a diesel engine (Meadows), front bumper, different cab and front wings.

North Korea: Basically the Soviet GAZ-69A four-door 4 × 4 field car but produced in North Korea with restyled front end featuring built-in headlights. A 6-ton 6-wheeled truck, known as Synri 1010, was also made.

Pakistan: Part of an order for 21 Thornycroft 6 × 4 'Mighty Antar' Mk 3 prime movers. They supplemented a number of Mk I units delivered during the 1950s. They were used for towing tank-transporter trailers and had ballast bodies.

NIGERIA: British Land-Rovers, Bedford RL trucks, Alvis 'Saladin' A/Cs, Daimler 'Ferret' scout cars, French Panhard AML A/Cs, etc.

NORTH KOREA: Soviet trucks (GAZ, ZIL, etc.) and wheeled AFVs (GAZ BA-64 'Bobby', BTR-40 and -152 APCs). Two locally-produced vehicles were a four-door field car resembling the Soviet GAZ-69A but with restyled front end and a six-wheeled 6-ton truck called Synri 1010 with a cab resembling that of the Soviet GAZ-51 and -63, also with a distinctive front end incorporating built-in headlamps.

NORTH VIETNAM: The North Vietnamese Army employs trucks from various communist countries, e.g. Chinese CA-10 'Liberation' 4 × 2, Czech Tatra T111 6 × 6, East German Robur LO-1800A 4 × 4 and S4000 4 × 2, Polish Star 66 6 × 6, Soviet GAZ-63 4 × 4, ZIL-130 4 × 2, ZIL-157 6 × 6, etc. Wheeled APCs such as the Soviet BTR-40 were also acquired.

NORWAY: Many WWII-surplus US vehicles, incl. 'Jeep', Dodge, GMC, White M3A1 scout cars, Ford M8 and M20 A/Cs, half-track APCs, full-track 'Weasel' over-snow carriers, etc. Post-war US vehicles such as the 'M-Series' 2½-ton 6 × 6 were later added. Also in service were Czech Skoda 4S artillery tractors (see 'Czechoslovakia'), Canadian wartime GM C15TA APCs, British Land-Rovers and relatively large quantities of the Swedish Volvo 'Laplander' and BM BV202 'Bandvagn'.

PAKISTAN: Large variety of vehicles, including British Bedford, Commer 'Superpoise' and Ford 4 × 2, Thornycroft 'Nubian' 6 × 6 crash tender and 'Mighty Antar' 6 × 4 prime mover; Japanese Toyota 'Land Cruiser'; US Jeep CJ5/M38A1, Dodge M37, 1-ton 'Power Wagon' and heavier 4 × 2 and 4 × 4 trucks, 'M-Series' 2½- and 5-ton 6 × 6 (various models) etc. Also German Tempo 3-wheelers, Italian Fiat trucks and some East European types. In 1970 a commercial field car/utility truck named Skopak was introduced, which, like the New Zealand Trekka, was based on the Czech Skoda 1200 4 × 2 chassis.

PERU: British Land-Rover, US Jeep (incl. M606), Dodge M37, Mexican Ramirez 'Rural 750' etc. Also WWII-surplus vehicles, incl. the White M3A1 scout car.

PHILIPPINES: Japanese and US ¼-ton and ¾-ton 4 × 4 and 2½-ton 6 × 6 trucks of various types. Also some Australian-built vehicles and WWII-surplus US trucks and half-tracks, etc.

QATAR: British Land-Rover, Alvis 'Saladin' and 'Saracen', Daimler 'Ferret', etc.

RHODESIA: British Land-Rover, Bedford (various types), Daimler 'Ferret' scout car, etc. Also a variety of WWII-surplus British and Canadian trucks, US 'Staghound' A/Cs, etc.

SAUDI ARABIA: British cars, buses and trucks, incl. Land-Rover, Bedford, Wolseley; French Panhard AML-245 and WWII-surplus US 'Staghound' M6 and 'Greyhound' M8 A/Cs, etc.

SIERRA LEONE: British Land-Rover, Daimler 'Ferret', etc.

SOMALIA: British Commer/AWD and Italian Fiat 639N2 4 × 4 trucks, Daimler 'Ferret' scout cars, Soviet BTR-152 APCs, US 'Commando' A/Cs, etc.

SOUTH KOREA: US wartime and post-war trucks and AFVs, incl. M8 A/Cs. Also post-war Japanese tactical trucks (¼-, ¾- and 2½-ton) and WWII British types incl. Bedford MW and QL (some modified to 4 × 2 drive).

SOUTH VIETNAM: US trucks (Jeep M606, Dodge 'Power Wagon' M601), WWII surplus M3A1 scout cars, M8 A/Cs and half-track APCs, post-war Cadillac 'Commando' A/Cs, Canadian WWII GM C15A APCs, Japanese Mitsubishi Jeep (CJ3B-J4B and J4C), Toyota (¾-ton, 4 × 4, 2FQ15 and 2½-ton, 6 × 6, 2DW15), etc.

SUDAN: British Alvis 'Saladin' and 'Saracen', Daimler 'Ferret',

Philippines: Sixty US ¼-ton 4 × 4 M606 Jeep trucks, supplied through the Military Assistance Program, were fitted with armour plating and .30-cal. MGs by the AFP research and development division in 1970. Used by Philippine Constabulary.

Rhodesia: Commercial Bedford TA Series 3-ton 4 × 2 (1954 A3 model) truck with military type GS body. Lighter A2 model with pickup body and WWII-surplus Bedfords were also in service with the Federal Army.

Sudan: Commer 'Superpoise' Mk V, Model B1512, 1½-ton 4 × 2 truck, specially adapted for military service in Sudan. Note oversize tyres, radiator brush guard and open cab with folding deflector windscreens.

Tunisia: Chrysler Corporation's 'Power Wagon' (available under DeSoto, Dodge and Fargo name) was post-war commercial edition of wartime Dodge 'Beep'. Available with open or closed cab it was bought by many Governments.

Land-Rover, Commer 'Superpoise', German Auto Union 'Munga', US Cadillac 'Commando', etc.

SYRIA: Vehicles of various origins, incl. British Land-Rovers, Japanese Toyota 'Land-Cruisers', Soviet BTR-152 APCs, US (ex-French) Dodge 4 × 2 armoured trucks, etc.

TAIWAN (Formosa): Japanese and US vehicles of various types, incl. ¼-ton 4 × 4, ¾-ton 4 × 4, 2½-ton 6 × 6, etc. were used by the forces of what is also known as Nationalist China.

TANZANIA: British vehicles incl. Land-Rover, Soviet APCs (BTR-40 and -152), etc.

THAILAND: British Austin, Commer, Land-Rover, etc. US M3A1 scout cars, M8 A/Cs, half-track APCs, etc.

TUNISIA: British Austin 'Gipsy', Land-Rover and Alvis 'Saladin', French Panhard A/Cs, German Magirus-Deutz 4 × 4 trucks, US 'Jeep', Chevrolet 4 × 2, Dodge 4 × 4 'Power Wagon' and 5-ton 6 × 6 'M-Series' trucks, M8 A/Cs, etc.

TURKEY: In recent years several types of locally assembled commercial trucks have appeared. Many of these have simplified body sheet metal, e.g. certain types of American Chrysler (DeSoto, Dodge, Fargo), Jeep and International, British Leyland (Austin, Morris) and German MAN. Others are more or less identical to the original designs (British Bedford and Ford, Czech Skoda (pickup), German MAN (415), Italian Fiat (642 tractor), Soviet UAZ-451, etc.). Some of these types were used by the armed forces. Military pattern vehicles are of various origins. Many WWII types remained in service until the 1970s, including US ¼-ton 'Jeep' (incl. amph.), ½- and ¾-ton Dodge, 2½-ton GMC, 4-ton Diamond T, 4–5-ton Federal, 5–6-ton Autocar, M1A1 wrecker, M25 Pacific/Fruehauf tank transporter, M3A1 White scout car, M2/M3 half-tracks, M4/M5 high-speed full-track tractors, etc. Canadian CMP trucks were also used, as were Czech Praga artillery tractors.

Post-war tactical trucks were mainly US 'M-Series', supplied under the Military Assistance Program (MAP). They included

Willys/Kaiser Jeep CJ3B and M606 ¼-ton 4×4, Dodge M37 ¾-ton 4×4, Dodge M601 'Power Wagon' and Kaiser Jeep 'Gladiator' 1-ton 4×4, Reo/White M602 2½-ton 6×6, International/Kaiser/Mack 5-ton 6×6 (various models), Mack M123/125 10-ton 6×6, etc. Some of the types in the ¼-, 1- and 2½-ton class were assembled in Turkey and incorporated varying amounts of locally made components. In 1959, for example, 1600 Willys CJ3B ¼-tonners were shipped CKD for assembly by Türk Willys-Overland Fabrikalari A.S. at Tuzla (near Istanbul) and in 1965 938 2½-ton 6×6 trucks, made by White (Reo) were furnished for local assembly. Military vehicles supplied by other countries have included British Thornycroft 'Mighty Antar' Mk I heavy prime movers, German Büssing 6000A 6-ton 4×4, Faun 8–12-ton 6×6, Ford 3-ton 4×4, Magirus-Deutz A6500 6½-ton 4×4, Mercedes-Benz 'Unimog' 4×4, Italian Lancia 'Superjolly' 4×2 light trucks, etc.

UGANDA: British Land-Rover, Daimler 'Ferret', Alvis 'Saladin', etc.

URUGUAY: Mainly US equipment.

VENEZUELA: Mainly US equipment. Also British Rover 'Shorland' armoured patrol cars and Italian Fiat trucks.

YUGOSLAVIA: This country's armed forces use Soviet as well as US automotive equipment, the latter consisting mainly of WWII surplus trucks (notably GMC) and AFVs (incl. M8 A/Cs and M3 half-track APCs). Wartime German and Italian military trucks were also in service for many years. Of locally-produced vehicles the Zastava AR-51 and the TAM-4500 are the most important. The former is essentially the Italian Fiat 'Campagnola', produced under licence at Kragujevac in Serbia, the TAM (Tovarna Avtomobilov in Motorjev) was produced in Maribor, Slovenia, under licence from the German Klöckner-Humboldt-Deutz concern. Swiss Saurer 4×4 trucks were at one time produced in Priboj, under the marque name FAP. Imported Soviet vehicles included the GAZ-69, ZIL-157, JAAZ/KRAZ-214, etc.

ZAMBIA: British Land-Rover, Bedford RL, Daimler 'Ferret', etc.

Turkey: One of several locally produced Jeep vehicles: 1-ton 4×4 'Gladiator', 1968. 6 cyl., 140 bhp, 3F1R×2, wb 126 in. Most mechanical components were imported from the USA. Also 1½-ton version with dual rear tyres.

Yugoslavia: Built under Fiat-licence by the *'Crvena Zastava'* (Red Flag) plant at Kragujevac was the Zastava AR-51. Payload 500 kg or 6 persons. 63-bhp engine. 6.50–15 tyres. Also other body styles, incl. ambulance.

INDEX

Note: US 'M-Series' 6 × 6 trucks are listed collectively under Reo (2½-ton types) and International (5-ton types), WWII half-tracks (all makes) under *US half-tracks.*

ACF-Brill 320, 327, 364, 369
ACMA 76, 79
AEC 11, 25, 72, 158, 159, 167, 195, 197–199, 207, 208, 217, 221, 271, 274, 288, 412, 413, 415
Agrip 105
Ahlman 155
ALBANIA 411
Albion 158, 159, 192–194, 197, 199, 207, 265
Alfa Romeo 233, 235, 236, 239, 240
ALGERIA 411
Allis-Chalmers 14, 159, 214, 278, 288, 320, 381, 382
ALM 74, 83, 85, 412
Alvis 6, 14, 23, 25, 46, 95, 154, 159, 192, 193, 209, 210, 215, 217, 220, 287, 302, 411–413, 415, 416, 418–420
Ambassador 324
AMC (American Motors) 320, 324, 330, 333, 344, 348, 349, 368, 413
American LaFrance 321, 364, 366, 413
Ardie 125
ARGENTINA 411
Ariel 26, 160
Armstrong-Siddeley 161
ARO 285
Ashok Leyland 227, 228, 230
Atkinson 219
Austin 7, 9, 26, 31, 33, 50, 66, 76, 80, 158, 159, 161–166, 169–172, 175–177, 179, 180, 182–184, 189, 207, 263, 265, 271, 284, 291, 413–415, 419
AUSTRALIA 6

AUSTRIA 14
Autobianchi 233, 235, 238–240
Autocar 11, 13, 33, 89, 271, 321, 341, 355, 413, 419
Autocars 232
Auto Union 38, 76, 114, 123–127, 171, 262, 263, 413, 419
Avia 51, 54, 58, 59
AWD 186, 190, 207, 208, 211, 287

Baifield 334
Barber-Greene 377
Barkas 114, 117
Barnes & Reinecke 354
Barreiros 284, 288, 289, 291–293
Batignolles-Chatillon 79
Bay City 321, 363
BAZ 387, 402
Bedford 6, 9, 10, 25, 31, 33–35, 65–68, 82, 86, 158, 159, 165–168, 177, 178, 182–189, 191, 192, 195, 196, 209, 212, 216, 221, 228, 268, 271, 284, 287, 291, 312, 327, 411–413
Beech 373
BELAZ 387, 392
BELGIUM 25
Berliet 14, 23, 33, 50, 74, 75, 81, 86, 88, 89, 91, 94–97, 99–104, 107, 108, 110–112, 284, 312, 411, 412, 416
Berna 308, 312, 313
Bernard 99
Bianchi (*see* Autobianchi)
BMW 15, 16, 76, 114, 124–126, 128, 129, 169, 170, 263, 288, 289, 388

Bolinder-Munktell 71, 219, 294, 306, 417
BOLIVIA 412
Bombardier 41, 48
Borgward 66, 123, 124, 126, 129–132, 134, 135, 140, 143, 182, 413
Borg-Warner (*see* Ingersoll Kalamazoo)
Borsuk 281
Bray 159, 212
BRAZIL 38
British Hoist & Crane 213
Brockway 99, 274, 302, 321, 355, 413
Brossel 25, 33, 34
Browning 363
Brunswick 334
BSA 7, 26, 66, 76, 159, 160, 170, 263
BTR(APCs) 62, 69, 70, 121, 223, 232, 285, 396, 404, 405, 409, 411–413, 417–419
Bucegi 285, 286
Bührer 308, 318
Buick 321, 324, 382
BULGARIA 412
BURMA 412
Büssing 74, 123, 124, 126, 129–131, 140, 143, 186, 420

Cadillac 321, 324, 326, 380, 384
Cadillac Gage 41, 321, 380, 415, 416, 418
CAMBODIA 412
CANADA 41
Canadair 41, 48
Cardox 364, 365
Carpati 285, 286

Caterpillar 14, 107, 159, 218, 278, 317, 321, 352, 353, 376, 377, 381, 385
CEYLON 412
CHAD 412
Chausson 74, 75, 81
Chance Vought (*see* LTV)
Checker 321, 327
Chevrolet (Brazilian types) 38, 39
Chevrolet (Canadian types) 31, 33, 66, 67, 82, 83, 89, 265, 268, 271, 287, 413
Chevrolet (US types) 25, 26, 31, 33, 65, 83, 263, 265, 271, 278, 289, 297, 309, 321, 324, 325, 327–329, 333, 334, 337–342, 412, 413, 415, 416, 418, 419
CHILE 412
CHINA (People's Republic) 50
CHINA (Nationalist) 419
Chrysler 7, 41, 44, 152, 169, 288, 297, 308, 321, 324, 334, 336, 344, 347, 360, 361, 370, 372, 374, 380, 414, 419
Citroën 74, 76, 79–83, 86, 87, 89, 91, 93, 107, 165, 232, 263, 268, 309, 412, 413
Clark 212, 214, 321, 341, 343, 352, 372, 375, 376
Coleman 107, 321, 362
Coles 11, 159, 207, 208, 230, 274
Combiquick 114, 122
Commer 33, 86, 159, 165, 167, 177, 178, 182–184, 186, 190, 228, 229, 265, 268, 413–415, 417–419
Condec, Consolidated 319, 321, 338, 339, 355–357, 362, 369, 370, 373, 375
Condor 308–310

CONGO REPUBLIC 412
Continental 74, 105, 108
Corbitt 14, 23, 67, 99, 274, 302, 321, 341, 342, 355, 357, 363, 413
Cournil 74
Crane Shovel 363
Creusot (SFAC) 75, 79
Crofton 327, 330
Crossley 33, 207, 271
Csepel 50, 223–226
CUBA 412
Curtiss Wright 344
Cushman 26, 76, 321, 323
Cuthbertson 222
CZECHOSLOVAKIA 51

DAF 95, 262–266, 268–280, 288, 291, 293, 303, 312, 344
Daimler 6, 41, 70, 111, 159, 161, 162, 215, 216, 278, 284, 287, 411–413, 415, 417, 419, 420
Daimler-Benz (see Mercedes-Benz)
Daiyo 246
Darley 362
Datsun 245, 248
David Brown 159, 206, 278
DDR (EAST GERMANY) 114
Delahaye 74, 76, 77
Demag 306
DENMARK 65
Dennis 33, 159, 167, 206, 208
DeSoto 336, 419
Detroit Arsenal 344, 347, 357, 359, 360
Deutz 124, 157
Diamond T, Diamond Reo 11, 13, 33, 46, 65, 67, 95, 102, 202, 204, 211, 232, 274, 277, 315, 321, 341, 342, 348, 355, 413, 419
DKW (see also Auto Union) 114, 125
Dodge (Australian types) 6–10
Dodge (Brazilian types) 38–40
Dodge (British types) 186, 230, 413
Dodge (Canadian types) 31, 33, 41, 44, 45, 82, 86, 265, 268
Dodge (Indian types) 227–230
Dodge (US types) 14, 15, 19, 21, 25, 31, 32, 33, 65–67, 69, 74, 76, 80, 83, 84, 95, 215, 223, 232, 249, 263, 265, 266, 274, 281, 288, 289, 295, 297, 309, 311, 315, 321, 324–328, 334–338, 340–342, 344, 346, 355, 364, 411–413, 415–420
Douglas 159, 192, 206, 211
Duplex 274, 321, 363, 367

Ebro 288
EGYPT 69
Eidal 361
Eimco 321, 381
EKA 303
EMW 114–116
Engesa 38–40
Ernst Grube 114, 117–121
Euclid 321, 352, 355, 362
EWK 107, 124, 154

Fageol 327
Fahr (see Farmobil)
Famé 89, 91
FAP 420
Fargo 31, 32, 227, 228, 230, 295, 297, 336, 344, 419
Farmobil 126, 169, 170
Faun 33, 89, 91, 123, 124, 126, 128, 130, 140, 144, 146–148, 150–153, 155, 157, 197, 274, 315, 341, 348, 355, 360, 420
FBW 308, 312, 314
Federal 11, 33, 89, 271, 341, 362, 419
Ferguson (see Massey-Ferguson)
Fiat 74, 86, 233–237, 239–244, 274, 288, 413, 416–420

FINLAND 70
Fletcher Flair 330, 333
Flextrac-Nodwell 41, 107
FMC 49, 321, 370, 383, 384
FN 25–28, 31–34, 37
Foden 33, 159, 197, 199
Ford (Australian types) 6–10
Ford (Brazilian types) 38, 39
Ford (British types; incl. Fordson) 26, 31, 33, 66, 67, 69, 71, 82, 89, 136, 158, 159, 161, 166, 167, 184–186, 191–193, 206, 263, 265, 268, 270, 271, 274, 278, 287, 291, 312, 327, 412, 413, 415–417, 419
Ford (Canadian types) 31, 33, 41–44, 82, 83, 89, 265, 268, 271, 278, 287, 312, 313, 413
Ford (French types) 74 75, 83, 86, 87, 89, 90, 263, 268
Ford (German types) 25, 26, 28, 33, 35, 42, 86, 186, 123–125, 130–132, 135, 136, 137, 140, 167, 232, 263, 265, 271, 273, 324, 327, 338, 341, 413, 420
Ford (US types) 14, 15, 25, 29, 31–34, 36, 37, 42, 65–67, 76, 83, 154, 211, 232, 243, 263, 265, 267, 268, 270, 271, 273, 278, 281, 288, 309, 318, 321, 324, 326–331, 333, 334, 337, 338, 341–343, 348, 351, 355, 356, 411–413, 415–420
Fowler 159, 218
Framo 114, 117
FRANCE 74
Frisch 157
Fruehauf 330, 360, 361, 368, 369, 413, 419
FSO 281
FTF 274
FUG (see Rába)
FWD 33, 35, 41, 44, 46, 47, 67, 69, 89, 211, 259, 271, 274, 278, 279, 321, 341, 348, 350, 357, 359, 362–364, 366, 367, 373, 375, 403

Galion 107
GAMBIA 412
Gar Wood 343, 355, 363, 377
GAZ 50, 52, 56, 69, 71, 115, 117, 224, 228, 232, 281, 285, 386–390, 392, 394, 395, 404, 407, 410, 411, 413, 417, 420
Georges Irat 76
GERMANY, DEMOCRATIC REPUBLIC 114
GERMANY, FEDERAL REPUBLIC 123
GHANA 413
Gilera 234
Gillet 25, 26, 28
Gillois 107
GKN Sankey 220
Glas 74, 123, 126, 128
GM (General Motors) 337–339, 344, 347
GMC (Canadian types) 25, 41, 44, 46, 47, 65–67, 274, 278, 284, 417, 418
GMC (US types) 11, 14, 23, 33, 38, 39, 41, 46, 58, 67, 68, 74, 75, 81, 95, 98, 130, 140, 146, 192, 232, 253, 272, 274, 281, 288, 291, 302, 315, 321, 326–328, 333, 338, 341, 344–346, 348, 351, 355, 356, 368, 398, 411, 413, 415, 417, 419, 420
Gnome et Rhône 76
Goliath 123, 124, 126, 127
Gräf & Stift 14, 19, 22–24
GREAT BRITAIN 158
GREECE 413
Griffet 75, 110
Guy 66, 67
Guzzi 233, 234
GZA 387

Hägglünds 299, 304, 307
Hanomag 33, 105, 124, 126, 129–132, 134, 146, 151, 154, 157, 265, 288
Hanson 374

Harley-Davidson 26, 76, 160, 263, 321, 323, 413
Hatra 155
Hendrickson 321, 346, 363, 377
Henschel 81, 86, 89, 124, 130, 140, 144, 146, 148, 152, 154, 156, 157, 312, 315, 316, 318
Hercules 125
Herwaythorn 83, 89, 95
Hillman 26, 159, 161, 163, 165, 170, 263
Hindustan 227, 228
Hino 245, 249, 251, 255–257, 259, 261
Hispano-Suiza 108, 113, 157, 288
Holden 6–8, 414
Horch 114, 117, 118
Hotchkiss 74, 76, 78, 83, 84, 89, 92, 154, 157, 287, 413
Hough 317, 362
Hovercraft 222
Howe 364
Humber 7, 8, 25, 26, 31, 65, 66, 111, 161, 177, 178, 216, 263, 278, 284, 412
HUNGARY 223
Hunting Percival 169, 170
Hürlimann 308, 318
Husqvarna 295

IFA 50, 114, 116–118
IHC (see International)
Ikarus 224
INDIA 227
Indian 26, 76, 263, 323
INDONESIA 413
Ingersoll Kalamazoo (Borg-Warner) 369–372, 384
International (Australian types) 6, 7, 9–13
International (Canadian types) 41, 44
International (US types) 33, 46, 67, 86, 95, 107, 146, 192, 218, 222, 239, 265, 267, 268, 270, 271, 274, 288, 291, 293, 312,

321, 325–330, 333, 334, 336, 338, 341, 343, 348–350, 352, 354–357, 360, 361, 381, 382, 385, 393, 396, 411–413, 419
IRAN 413
IRAQ 413
IRELAND (Eire) 413
Isobloc 75, 80
ISRAEL 232
Isuzu 245, 246, 249, 251–254
ITALY 233
IVORY COAST 413

JA 404
JAAZ 386, 387, 393, 399–401, 406, 408, 420
Jaguar 159, 161, 162, 216, 220
James 160
JAPAN 245
Jawa 51, 52
Jay-Fong 50
Jeep (incl. Willys and Kaiser Jeep) 6, 7, 15, 25, 29–31, 38, 41–43, 50, 52, 66, 69, 74, 76, 78, 171, 227–229, 232, 246, 247, 262–264, 279, 284, 287–290, 295, 297, 298, 308–310, 321, 324–326, 330–332, 334–336, 338–340, 344–346, 348, 349, 388, 411–413, 415–420
Jelcz 51, 282, 283
JORDAN 415

Kaelble 99, 101, 124, 146, 157, 186, 363, 413
Kaiser (see Kaiser Jeep)
Kalmar 304
Karrier 33, 67, 95, 159, 184
Kässbohrer 124
KAVZ 387
KAZ 387, 392
Kenworth 33, 67, 99, 274, 302, 315, 321, 352, 354, 357–361
KENYA 415
Kirovski 387, 403

Klöckner-Humboldt-Deutz (see Magirus-Deutz)
KMZ 387
Kochler 330
Kramer 314
Krauss-Maffei 64, 154
KRAZ 69, 119, 285, 386, 387, 399–401, 406, 420
Kromhout 268, 269
Kronenburg 271, 274, 279
Krupp 36, 124, 140, 144, 152, 153, 288, 312, 360
KUWAIT 415

Labourier 75, 105, 106
Lancer 213
Lancia 31, 74, 233, 235, 238, 239, 241, 244, 420
Land-Rover 6–8, 29–31, 50, 66, 71, 126, 128, 158, 159, 161, 164, 171, 173–177, 180–183, 209, 215, 222, 228, 232, 263, 284, 287–290, 308–310, 411–413, 415–420
Landsverk 294, 413
Lanz 105
LAOS 415
Latil 75–76, 83, 84, 89, 94, 95, 98, 99, 101, 105, 106
LAZ 385
LEBANON 415
LeTourneau (-Westinghouse) 9, 11, 321, 352–354, 362, 369, 375, 376, 378, 379
Leyland 9, 11, 33, 71, 157–159, 167, 186, 189, 192, 195, 197, 200, 202, 203, 207, 214, 232, 262, 287, 288, 355, 413, 416
LIAZ (CS) 51, 54
LIAZ (USSR) 387
Liberation 50, 417
LIBYA 415
Lincoln 324
Link Belt 363
Linn 326
Lockheed 321, 371, 378, 380

Lomount/Rotinoff 197, 202, **315**, 316
Lorraine 112
LTV 321, 371, 372
Lublin 281
LUXEMBOURG 415
Lycoming 370

Mack 14, 23, 33, 35, 46, 74, 89, 99, 202, 207, 274, 321, 342, 348, 353, 355, 357, 358, 360, 411, 413, 420
Madsen 327
Magirus-Deutz 25, 33, 37, 67–69, 71, 89, 123, 124, 130, 136, 138, 140, 145, 146, 149–151, 186, 197, 211, 228, 231, 268, 279, 299, 312, 315, 316, 327, 355, 367, 413, 419, 420
Maico 124, 125
MALAYSIA 416
MAN 33, 34, 76, 123, 124, 128, 136–138, 140, 141, 224, 227, 228, 231, 312, 413, 419
Marmon-Bocquet 75, 83, 89, 92, 108, 109, 112
Marmon-Herrington 31–34, 36, 37, 75, 83, 84, 89, 90, 95, 98, 112, 211, 265, 273, 321, 338, 341, 366, 373, 415
Marshall 214
Massey-Ferguson 159, 206, 306
Matchless 26, 160, 263
Matenin 75, 109
MAZ 50, 119, 285, 386, 387, 402, 403
Mazur 283
MBB 129
Mercedes-Benz 19, 26, 31, 33, 38, 40, 66–69, 71, 76, 81, 83, 86, 89, 105, 123–125, 130–133, 136, 139, 140, 142, 146, 148, 154, 156, 161, 166, 182, 186, 195, 209, 227, 228, 231, 263, 265, 284, 287, 308, 309, 312, 327, 338, 412, 413, 415, **420**

Mercury 66, 263, 324, 326
MEXICO 416
Michigan 159, 212, 214, 317
Mid-America Research Corp. 330, 333
Miesse 25, 33, 34
Minerva 25, 29, 30
Mini 161, 165, 287
Minnesota 362
Mitsubishi 245–247, 249, 255, 257–259, 261, 330, 418
MOAZ 387
Monark 297
Morris, Morris-Commercial 25, 26, 31, 66, 67, 82, 158, 159, 161, 163, 165–167, 169, 171, 177, 179, 184, 185, 228, 284, 413, 415, 419
MOROCCO 416
Moskvitch 115, 387–389
Moto Gilera (see Gilera)
Motor Guzzi (see Guzzi)
Motosacoche 308
Mowag 156, 308–309, 311, 317, 318
MV Agusta 233–235
MUSCAT and OMAN 416
MZ 114, 115

NAMI 402
NEKAF 262, 263
NETHERLANDS 262
NEW ZEALAND 416
NICARAGUA 416
NIGERIA 417
Nimbus 65, 66
Nissan 227, 228, 245–251, 260, 261
Nodwell 41, 48, 49
Nordverk 306
NORTH KOREA 417
NORTH VIETNAM 417
Norton 26, 76, 160, 263
NORWAY 417
Nuffield 171, 172
Nysa 281

ÖAF 14, 19, 312
Oldsmobile 263
OM 31, 233, 235, 237–239, 241, 242, 244, 274
Opel 25, 26, 66, 76, 80–82, 123–125, 130, 132, 133, 161, 263, 324
Oshkosh 44, 321, 341, 357, 364, 367

P2 (M, S), P3 115, 116
Pacific 14, 23, 33, 46, 102, 239, 321, 360, 369, 372, 383, 419
Packard 324, 326
PAKISTAN 417
Panhard 74, 75, 86, 95, 111, 112, 284, 287, 413, 417, 418, 419
PAZ 387
PCF (see Pacific)
Pegaso 288, 291, 293
PERU 418
Peugeot 75–77, 80, 82, 263, 265
Phänomen 114, 117, 118, 288
PHILIPPINES 418
Plymouth 76, 324
Pobieda 281, 387–389
POLAND 281
Pontiac 263, 321, 324, 326, 383
Porsche 123, 124, 126, 127, 155, 333
PORTUGAL 284
Praga 14, 23, 51, 54–56, 58, 59, 63, 69, 232, 413, 419
Puch 14–16

QATAR 418

Rába 223, 224
RAF 387
Rambler 324
Ramirez 415–418
Ratrac 317
Renault 25, 31, 51, 74, 75, 76, 78–83, 85–86, 88, 89, 92, 93, 105, 107, 263, 265, 267, 324
Reo 11, 14, 23, 33, 41, 67, 146, 192, 232, 274, 288, 291, 321, 327, 344–346, 348, 350, 351, 355, 357, 360, 365, 413, 416–420
Rheinmetall 155
RHODESIA 418
Robur 114, 117, 118, 121, 224, 285, 417
Rochet-Schneider 86, 99, 100, 104
Rootes 177, 178, 414, 416
Rotinoff (see Lomount)
Rover (see also Land-Rover) 159, 161, 164, 171
Royal Enfield 26, 76, 160
RRAD (Red River Army Depot) 331
RUMANIA 285

Saab-Scania 40, 294, 295, 297–302, 304–307
Sachsenring 114, 115
Santana 288–290
Sarolea 25, 26, 28
SAUDI ARABIA 418
Saurer (Austrian types) 14, 19, 21, 22, 317
Saurer (French types) 75, 86, 89, 94
Saurer (Swiss types) 308, 312–317
Saviem 51, 74, 75, 80–86, 88, 89, 91–93, 106, 108
SAZ 387
Scammell 11, 33, 67, 69, 158, 159, 196, 197, 201–203, 232, 274, 414–416
Scania-Vabis (see Saab-Scania)
Seagrave 44
SEAT 288, 289
Seddon 262, 268
Sentinel 206
SFAC (Creusot) 75, 79

Shaktiman 228, 231
Shangai 50
Shelvoke & Drewry 9
Shorland 215, 415, 420
Sicard 41, 45, 46, 367
SIERRA LEONE 418
Simca 31, 75, 83, 84, 86, 87, 89, 90, 92, 95, 98, 112, 263, 324, 413, 415
Sinpar 75, 76, 78, 83, 85, 105, 107
Sisu 70–73
Skoda 51–57, 281, 282, 305, 413, 416, 417, 419
Smith 213
SOMALIA 418
SOUTH AFRICA 287
SOUTH KOREA 418
SOUTH VIETNAM 418
Southern Coach 327
SPAIN 288
SR (Steagul Rosu) 285
Standard 161, 163, 165, 169, 227, 265, 413
Star 281–283, 288, 417
Steels 207, 211
Sterling 357–359
Steyr, Steyr-Puch 7, 14–21, 23, 24, 66, 169, 224, 295, 308, 309, 311–313, 315, 413
Still 124, 130
Straussler 26, 128, 292
Studebaker 11, 33, 228, 265, 344–346, 394, 417
SUDAN 418–419
Südwerke (see Krupp)
Suzuki 246
SWEDEN 294
SWITZERLAND 308
Synri 417
SYRIA 419

TAIWAN (Formosa) 419
TAM 420
TANZANIA 419
Tata/Mercedes-Benz 227, 228, 231

Tatra 15, 51–64, 69, 119, 227, 232, 283, 285, 315, 417
Taylor 213
Tempo 31, 124, 126, 128, 130, 165, 265, 295, 417
Terrot 76
THAILAND 419
Thew Lorain 321, 361
Thornycroft 11, 33, 36, 69, 152, 158, 159, 186, 191, 192, 194, 197, 198, 201, 202, 204, 205, 209, 210, 228, 231, 268, 270, 271, 274, 280, 287, 412, 417, 420
Tokyu 260
Toyota 7, 38, 245–250, 252, 253, 334, 344, 415, 417, 419
Trabant 114–116
Trekka 416, 417
Triangel 65
Triumph 159, 169
Triumph (M/C) 26, 42, 160, 263, 264, 413
TUNISIA 419
TURKEY 419
Turner 182
TV 285

Twin Coach 321, 326, 327

UAZ 56, 69, 115, 117, 223, 228, 232, 285, 386–391, 410, 419
UGANDA 420
UMM 52, 285
Unic 75, 83, 89, 90, 92
Unicum 278
Unimog (see Mercedes-Benz)
Unit 363, 377
URAL 119, 224, 387, 392, 399, 400, 406
USA 319
US half-tracks 14, 25, 65, 70, 71, 111, 154, 232, 243, 259, 278, 284, 288, 404, 411–413, 416–420
USS 344, 346
USSR 386

Valmet 70, 71, 73
Vanaja 70–72
Vauxhall 159, 161, 162, 192, 194, 263, 309, 416
Velocette 160

VENEZUELA 420
Verheul 262, 268, 269
Vespa 76, 79, 160, 309
Vevey 308, 318
VIASA 288–290
Vickers 218, 227
Volga 115, 387, 388
Volkswagen 6, 7, 14–16, 19, 26, 31, 38, 44, 66, 81, 82, 123–126, 128, 129, 161, 262, 263, 265, 295, 309, 311, 324, 413
Volvo 33, 65, 66, 67, 71, 197, 219, 294–300, 302, 303, 305–307, 411, 412, 417

WABCO 321
Walid 69, 232, 411
Walter 44, 321, 362, 365, 367
Ward 325
Ward LaFrance 33, 67, 75, 99, 274, 291, 302, 315, 321, 362, 364, 365, 419
Warszawa 281
Wartburg 114–116
Wayne 321, 325, 361, 413
White 11, 14, 23, 25, 33, 67, 74, 99, 232, 243, 271, 274, 278, 288, 291, 302, 321, 341, 344, 348, 351, 355, 412, 413, 416, 418, 419
Willème 75, 86, 88, 89, 94, 99, 101–103, 109, 110, 415
Willys (see Jeep)
WNRE 321, 383
Wolga (see Volga)
Wolseley 171, 172, 418

YerAZ 387
YUGOSLAVIA 420
Yumbo 109

ZAMBIA 420
Zastava 420
ZAZ 387, 388, 391
ZIS/ZIL 50, 58, 69, 71, 119, 224, 226, 232, 285, 386, 387, 392, 393, 396–402, 404, 405, 407, 408, 411, 417, 420
ZIM 387
ZU 126, 128
Zubr 282
Zuk 281

425